Ancient Dynasties

Ancient Dynasties

The Families that Ruled the Classical World, circa 1000 BC to AD 750

John D Grainger

Pen & Sword
MILITARY

First published in Great Britain in 2019 by
Pen & Sword Military
An imprint of
Pen & Sword Books Ltd
Yorkshire – Philadelphia

ISBN 978 1 52674 675 7

Printed and bound in the UK by TJ International Ltd,
Padstow, Cornwall.

Pen & Sword Books Limited incorporates the imprints of Atlas,
Archaeology, Aviation, Discovery, Family History, Fiction, History,
Maritime, Military, Military Classics, Politics, Select, Transport,
True Crime, Air World, Frontline Publishing, Leo Cooper, Remember
When, Seaforth Publishing, The Praetorian Press, Wharncliffe
Local History, Wharncliffe Transport, Wharncliffe True Crime
and White Owl.

For a complete list of Pen & Sword titles please contact

PEN & SWORD BOOKS LIMITED
47 Church Street, Barnsley, South Yorkshire, S70 2AS, England
E-mail: enquiries@pen-and-sword.co.uk
Website: www.pen-and-sword.co.uk

Or

PEN AND SWORD BOOKS
1950 Lawrence Rd, Havertown, PA 19083, USA
E-mail: Uspen-and-sword@casematepublishers.com
Website: www.penandswordbooks.com

Contents

Part I

Dynastic Studies

Introduction

A 'dynasty' is a family of rulers, holding power over a region of the earth. It can be displayed in table form, as in the second part of this study, where the links between the several rulers indicate the descent of authority from one man (it is almost always a man) to the next, usually a relative. The word itself is originally Greek, meaning the wielding of power, and so its origin is still precise and relevant. Dynasties were therefore families of rulers who wielded power over a period of time as well as over a territory.

Any dynasty always owes its existence to the curious reverence of people for a family ruling their territory. Once established in power such a family could count on that reverence as one of its major supports, and it took a great deal of waste, bad behaviour, and political oppression to bring their subjects to rid themselves of any dynasty. In fact, of course, it was extremely rare that a dynasty's subjects should ever do such a thing: usually expulsion or elimination came from much nearer home, either from treachery within the dynastic house or from men of the court who normally owed their position to the dynasts themselves; occasionally extinctions came from without, but not often.

This survey is therefore one of a human institution that is universal, for dynasties have existed from the earliest time when any sort of record survives, and in every part of the world. They have now been reinvented in the present, through, of all things, family succession amongst Communist Party chiefs – as bizarre a turn up as can be imagined. For practical reasons as much as anything else – size, accurate records, relationship – this survey is confined to a period that we may call the Iron Age and it is therefore limited both geographically and temporally.

Limits of the Survey

The geographical range of this study includes all the lands from the western coast of Europe to the Hindu Kush, and from the steppes of Russia to the Sudan. The chronological range is from the beginning of the Iron Age in the Middle East to the end of the great Muslim conquests – and so from roughly 1000 BC to about AD 750. Neither of these limits, geographical or chronological, is set in stone, though it is only the temporal that is breached. In that time and region, the majority of states and the majority of peoples lived under the rule of monarchies of diverse types and descriptions. Most historiographical attention has, by contrast with the monarchic ubiquity, been directed at the republics – notably the Greek and Italian city-states – but these existed for only a comparatively brief time and in two geographically very restricted regions. The main exception to this is Republican Rome.

Rome, however, was a republic for less than five centuries; it had been a monarchy earlier (supposedly for two and a half centuries), and was then an empire for another five, with an extension as the Byzantine Empire. Its longevity as a republic, and the power it wielded in that condition, require it to be considered separately. In a study of dynasties Republican Rome takes its place as a republic that was ruled by a fairly restricted set of aristocratic families – there are ninety-five of them noted here – and these can be tabulated and studied just as can other dynasties that ruled autonomously.

And, on examination, even in the apparently republican times and regions, notably in Greece and its colonies, monarchies existed. Sparta, one of the most studied of the city-states, was a monarchy for virtually all of its independent existence. Other places that are taken to be republics were in fact monarchies at times, when they were ruled by dynasties of 'tyrants' – Syracuse, Corinth, Sicyon and others, and including Athens for a time. These tyrannies are regarded as exceptions, but in fact it was the republics themselves that were the exception to the rule by monarchies. In Sicily, for example, between 500 and 200 BC monarchies – tyrants – ruled for about half that time, suggesting that monarchy might well be the default condition for the region, rather than independent city republicans.

In many areas and times many states were never anything but monarchies. Further, by the end of the last millennium BC, republics had all but disappeared so that monarchy was the rule everywhere, as it had been until about 600 BC, and as it was in some areas at all times.

Monarchies can be ruled by elected kings – often now called presidents – but none of these exist in the ancient world (unless the Visigoths were developing such a method; there are suggestions of this also in Anglo–Saxon England). To be a monarch was necessarily to be a member of a dynastic family – unless you were the founder of that dynasty; even then you were probably following an earlier dynasty that had been replaced or had died out.

It is those dynasties that are the subject of this study. About 200 of them can be distinguished, some of them ruling for a long time, while the time of others was only brief (the range is from two years to almost 500). Given their ubiquity and frequent longevity, and the obvious effect they had on the lives of their subjects – and on those not their subjects – these dynasties are clearly a suitable subject for collective study.

The first necessity is to define the terms. As already noted, the time boundaries are 1000 BC and AD 750, though naturally these are somewhat elastic; dynasties originating before or continuing after those dates are not necessarily to be excluded. These are in fact very few, for both dates are points at which a series of particularly significant dynasties expire or begin. In France, the Carolingians replaced the Merovingians in 751; in Britain most of the early 'Dark Age' dynasties died out in the half-century or so around 750; in Spain the Visigoths ended in 711–714, and no independent Muslim monarchy took their place until 756; at Constantinople the Isaurians failed with the Empress Irene in 802: in the Middle East the Umayyads were eliminated in 750. There are exceptions: in Ireland, several dynasties extend across this artificial boundary, as do some in the Caucasus region. Yet within the great extent of territory between the Irish Sea and Central Asia, only the Isaurians in Constantinople lasted for half a century beyond 750. It would seem that it was the collapse of the ancient empires – the Roman and the Sassanid – that was responsible for this state of affairs. The dynasties that replaced them, those that had seized the chance to rule part of the old imperial territories, were now expiring, and being replaced by dynasties most of whom were much more durable, and that bore history on into Medieval Europe and the Islamic Middle East. It is this coincidence across time and space that has persuaded me to adopt these boundaries.

At the other end of the period, only two dynasties, one in Egypt and one in Assyria, began significantly before 1000 BC, though by contrast half a dozen new dynasties began in the half-century after that date. This was the period during which the new Iron Age dynastic states in the Middle East settled down after the turbulence of the end of the Bronze Age, but before the Assyrian conquests began. In temporal terms, therefore, the period used here is almost as well defined as it is in geographical terms, even if it is somewhat fuzzy at the edges. These few pre-existing dynasties are important, however, for they provided some continuity from the preceding Bronze Age, and so were the inspiration and template for the newly established dynasties – note especially the influence of the preceding Hittite kingdom on the dynasties in its former region in Anatolia and northern Syria, and, of course, the obvious continuity of the Egyptian dynasties. In the same way it was the Roman Imperial model that applied in mediaeval Europe, sometimes, as with the Franks, quite explicitly. It was the Iranian model, derived ultimately from the Akhaimenid dynasty, that affected the later Arab and Turkish dynasties.

I have put a lower limit of three rulers or three generations on the definition of a dynasty, for one can hardly count just one or two rulers as a dynasty; there is, of course, no upper limit either on the number of generations or on the number of rulers. Three successive generations in power does imply a certain stability in the polity they ruled, and will provide some figures – numbers of generations, numbers of kings, a distinct length of time – from which it is possible to draw some conclusions (see Chapter 4, 'Dynastic Durations'). It will be seen, however, that the variety is considerable, and the length of time a dynasty rules, even with three members, can be as low as two years.

Source Limits

If worthwhile information is to be derived, it is necessary that the dynasties are reasonably well-recorded in terms of members, dates, and relationships. The required data includes the sequence and relationships of the rulers (though their names are not wholly necessary), their parentage, and their dates of accession and rule, or at least the dates of the inception and the end of the dynasty, if individual dates are not available. This is the minimum information needed, but this requirement does exclude a number of dynasties that are known to have existed, but where full information is not available. A number of dynasties are problematic in that they are known only in part, with some rulers being unknown or attested only poorly. The Greek Cypriot dynasties in their early manifestations are examples, as are those of early Syria, and the earliest Spartan and Macedonian dynasties; the Hebrew dynasty of Judah is a particular problem here also. The names of the kings of the Meroe and Napata kingdoms in the Sudan are known, and most of their dates, except where some of them took power in Egypt, we have no information about their dynastic relationships. The Baktrian Greek kings are both poorly dated and their relationships are unclear. There are numerous Arabian pre-Muslim dynasties known in list form, but whose dates are vague or have been calculated by a dubious system, and some of the dynasties are probably much longer, but their relationships are unclear or unknown. This applies also to the early Iron Age Syrian dynasties. In both cases the dynasties have to be reconstructed from epigraphic evidence, which can be difficult to interpret. Where possible, however, even with incomplete data, such dynasties have been included. The quantity of data, even with the exclusions, is considerable, and over 200 dynasties meet the above criteria.

Dynastic Members

In considering the people who constitute the dynasties I have counted and included only those who actually rule by reign. This allows all the dynasties to be reduced to their essential personnel. These names may have to be supplemented by other individuals whose inclusion is necessary to make clear the familial descent of the rulers, but if these did not actually rule they are not to be counted as such, except in terms of generations. Sons and daughters not in the direct line, who died before their fathers, are usually omitted. So, also, are wives. Regents, however, who ruled, if they are members of the family, are included.

These are, of course, to some degree arbitrary decisions, which have to be varied at times. In some dynasties there may be more than one ruler with authority simultaneously; the joint rule of some Roman emperors is an example, such as that of Marcus Aurelius and Lucius Verus, or Marcus Aurelius and his son Commodus. All three of these emperors are counted as separate rulers, but Commodus is counted as ruling only from the time of his father's death in 180, not from his promotion to joint emperor in 176. This is, obviously, a disputable judgement, but it is clear that Verus had an authority independent of Marcus, whereas, before 180, Commodus equally clearly did not. (Non-rulers necessarily included in the tables are printed in lower case; actual rulers are in capitals; in some cases the non-rulers are indicated only by letters, usually an 'X', to avoid cluttering up the tables with too many irrelevancies.)

The omission of collateral members of dynasties is not the usual pattern in such tables, but the genealogical tables normally seen in books are usually published so as to make clear the relationship of any of the people to one another who are named in a written text; here, the object is to consider only those who actually ruled. A comparison of my chart of the Julio-Claudian Roman Imperial dynasty with that in any book of the Roman Empire will make the point clear. I may add that in many dynasties it is in fact only the names of the rulers who are known, and the names of the related members often are not, which means that the better documented families are more easily comparable with the rest.

It was, and is normal for dynasties to emphasize, or at times to exaggerate, the length of their ancestry, often by connecting the ruling family with others in the past; in other cases it is clear that the more distant ancestry of rulers is invented, or is so distorted as to be wholly inaccurate (see Chapter 2, 'The Mists of Time'). Egyptian dynasties had a tendency to claim a connection with the preceding dynasty, either by inventing one, or by marrying a surviving female; the Roman Severans adopted themselves retroactively into the preceding Antonine dynasty – and so on. It is necessary to be clear on this, and to take a sceptical view of such claims. The Parthian dynasty of the Arsakids, for example, can be made to seem to have a continuous succession throughout the whole history of that kingdom, but on examination it is clear that there were distinct breaks in the succession in the first century AD, and so the kings are here distinguished as two separate dynasties. It has to be admitted that, given the inadequate state of the Parthian records, this may be wrong – the early kings have only recently been sorted out; there may well be a direct dynastic connection between these several families, but this connection cannot be discerned now, and it would be wrong to make any assumptions about relationships without good evidence. Several dynasties' distant ancestries have been ignored due to lack of corroboration – the Welsh, Spartan, Macedonian, and Judahite dynasties are cases.

Defining a dynasty is not always straightforward. It is particularly difficult when the direct line of succession dies out and a collateral line inherits. In that case a rough rule of thumb is that if the new ruler is a close relative of his predecessor, they are both to be reckoned as the same dynasty; if the two are not more directly related the new man is to be reckoned the founder of a new dynasty. This vague formulation, of course, leaves much unclear. It is intended to. Each case must be judged on its own merits. An example may help. In the case of Wessex, the direct Cerdinga line ended with Coenwalh in 673. He was briefly succeeded by his widow, so she can be included. His next replacement, however, was descended via a junior line, which had not produced a king for four generations; and he was followed by the brother of Coenwalh. In turn, the succession then went to an even more distant relation, and then again to one who was even more remote. All these kings were actually members of the royal family, if one looks at its widest extent, but the actual Cerdinga dynasty ended with Coenwalh's brother; the more distant inheritors cannot be counted.

Amongst the dynasties of the Roman Republic, the practice of adoption to continue a family became a dynastic tool in the second century BC, but this must be taken as a dynastic break. The original family had clearly died out, and the adoptions began a new line, even if the names and the inheritance seemed to continue. They are here treated as distinct dynasties.

Territories

The attachment of a particular dynasty to one country or region is normal, but it is not always firm. The Deinomenid dynasty of tyrants in Sicily in the fifth century BC originated in two separate cities, then spread themselves over several other cities as well, though all within Sicily. This dynasty is also an example of several rulers holding office simultaneously (see Chapter 8, 'Mergers'). The Antigonids eventually settled into the kingship of Macedon, but only after Antigonos I had ruled for thirty and more years in Anatolia and further east; the Mithradatids originated in Pontos, spread for a short time into Cappadocia, but Mithradates VI was eventually expelled from Asia Minor, and by this time he had also taken over the kingdom of the Cimmerian Bosporos, and his family then provided a long-lasting dynasty for that territory. Here again a judgement has to be made as to whether to emphasize the family or the country. In these three cases the decision on tabulating them has been different: I have put the Deinomenids and Antigonids into a single dynasty each, but have separated the Mithradatids into two, in this last case with considerable misgivings. The Parthian dynasty provided families of kings to other regions, and for a time the kings transferred from one kingdom to another; eventually some kings set up their own dynastic lines (in Armenia and Albania), at which point they are treated as separate dynasties. It will be noted that no distinction is made between kings, emperors, tyrants, pharaohs, Great Kings, or other titles; the only qualifications are monarchy, a relationship, three rulers or generations of rule, and, of course, a discernible record.

Rome

One case, the Roman Republic, must be considered separately. There are several moments, scattered through the Roman Republican history, when Roman magistrates demanded and got equality of treatment with kings; perhaps the most notorious case is that of Sulla, the future dictator, when, with no higher office than that of quaestor, he insisted on being treated as an equal by an envoy of the Parthian king. Other examples can be found, but Sulla makes the point clearly enough, that Rome's Republican families were in fact dynasties, and considered themselves virtually royal. These families controlled the city and empire of Rome for five centuries, during which time it developed from a small city in the middle of Italy to a Mediterranean-wide empire. These families formed a group of clear and distinct dynasties – and if any families disposed of power these did – so dynasty is a precise term for them.

I have therefore tabulated in Part II of the Catalogue section the dynasties of Romans who held public office during the republic; 'public office' being defined as holding certain magistracies the holders of which disposed of political power. (For the details see the Introduction to that section.) The result has been to isolate ninety-five dynasties who exercised power in the city between the inauguration of the republic in 509 BC and its extinction in 42 BC. The city appears also, of course, as a monarchy in the 'Cities' section, and as an empire with a series of imperial dynasties.

I looked also for other republican examples, or perhaps of a ruling aristocracy, for example at Athens, or among Egyptian priests, but two considerations prevented further inclusions: failure of the sources to be explicit (or, indeed, in many cases, to exist), and the fact that none of these potential dynasties were in fact treated as, or behaved as, equals of kings. There is no doubt that such dynasties did exist, in such cities as Athens and Corinth, but tabulating them proved to be difficult if not impossible. (An odd case is the appearance in one source of a Corinthian merchant as an ancestor of Roman kings; another is the claimed foundation of the Macedonian kingship by a trio of Argive brothers.) It may be possible to sort out dynasties of priests in Egyptian temples, or the families of the 'Seven' who joined Darius I in seizing power in the Persian Empire in 521, but ensuring a clear dynastic line for any of them is more than difficult. The Roman Republican dynasties may perhaps stand as representatives of these less well-sourced dynasties. These subordinate dynasties, however, unlike the Roman, did not rule, and even if they pretended to rulership or wielded executive power, it was only by permission of an overlord.

The People Included

One of the elements that affected dynastic definitions concerns the descent through the female line. Quite often this is as phoney a descent as the Parthian retrospective claims of all kings to be Arsakids – descendants of the first king, Arsakes I – or of Hellenistic kings' claims to be descended from Alexander the Great. Usurpers not infrequently attached themselves to a previous dynasty by appropriating a daughter of the previous ruler – the Egyptian dynasties already mentioned, or Herod's marriages to more than one female member of the preceding Hasmonean dynasty, are examples; the frequent demand of the kings of various Germanic states for an imperial bride from the fifth century AD was another legitimizing tactic. The marriage usually only took place after the usurper had come to power; it is therefore not to be accepted as a continuation of the previous dynasty, though the usurper may succeed in establishing a new royal family. On the other hand, a judgement needs to be made in individual cases, so that this rule does not become too constrictive. It is also necessary not to exclude women who ruled in their own right, or as regents. If they did so they must be counted: Salome Alexandra of the Hasmoneans is counted, as is the Empress Irene of the Byzantine Isaurians, though one was a regent and the other ruled alone (see Chapter 7, 'Women').

These various conditions and limitations have produced a fairly large and unusual collection of royal families. Most are straightforward, but many of the Roman Imperial dynasties are distinctly odd, as were the dynasties of the pre-Republican Regal period. There are several Anglo–Saxon dynasties, along with Egyptian, Syrian and Iranian; the Irish dynasties are strange (see Chapter 6, 'Modes of Succession'). The Arabians are often only fragments of dynasties, and are dated unreliably. There is a surprising number of Greek dynasties, given the historiographical emphasis on the republican states. There are Christian, pre-Christian and Muslim dynasties, and one consideration must be whether the adoption of Christianity made a difference – for this is one of the adduced reasons for the apparently greater dynastic stability that can be seen in Christian mediaeval Europe (see Chapter 12, 'The New Religions').

Arrangements and Practical Matters

It is not always easy to decide on a dynasty's name or title. Some are known by their geographical territory (Cappadocia, Baktrian, Parthia), others by the name of their founder (Arsakids, Antigonids, Cerdingas), others by their city (Athens, Syracuse, Damascus), or by the people they ruled (Visigoths, Vandals, West Saxons). No hard and fast rule has been imposed, but where necessary several of these names have been included.

Three major divisions have been imposed (apart from segregating the Roman Republican dynasties as a separate set). Several dynasties stand out as imperial, while others were civic. These have been brought into separate parts of the Catalogue; the remainder are regarded as 'regional' states, though this is hardly a very satisfactory word. So the arrangement in Part II is into City dynasties, Roman Republican, regional, and imperial dynasties.

One of the major purposes of this investigation is thus to compare the various dynasties, both as contemporaries and across time and space, and this is implied in every chapter. I shall look at their longevity, or lack of it (see

Chapter 4, 'Dynastic Durations'), at the numbers of their generations and of their rulers, and the length of their generations and of the reigns (see Chapter 5, 'Generations and Reigns'), at the origins of the families and their extinction as rulers (see Chapter 1, 'Beginnings', Chapter 2, 'The Mists of Time', and Chapter 10, 'Terminations'), and the effects on the dynasties of the mode of death of their individual members (see Chapter 9, 'Violent Deaths and Depositions', and Chapter 10, 'Breakdowns'). Averages can at times be used to detect unusual cases, and in all cases explanations must be sought. The interventions of usurpers, of women rulers, of inheritance by children, and the methods of selecting heirs are all topics to be considered, as is the effect of sibling inheritance.

Above all, one of the objects of this study is to highlight the sheer number, extent and ubiquity of ruling dynasties in the ancient world. This has to be seen as the normal method of ruling states of the time, for the republican states are clearly anomalous, and all felt the monarchic rule in the end. The period of the experiment with republics is relatively brief; from the beginning of the first millennium AD none with any power remained, and the rule of dynasties of kings, emperors, *shahanshahs*, and so on, was universal, and remained so until the emergence of early republics in Italy in the Middle Ages.

Chapter 1

Beginnings

There is a wide variety of methods by which a dynasty could become established. I shall here try to distinguish as many as possible, giving examples in each case, in the full knowledge that in many cases single origins are not the only ones that operated. The last section of this chapter, therefore, 'Complications', will look at the case for multiple origins of dynasties.

It will be useful, as a preliminary, to point out that dynasties may be classified as those that created the state they ruled, and those that came to rule an existing state. There are large numbers of both. The Anglo–Saxon kingdoms were all the creations of the dynasties that ruled them, usually emerging during the sixth century AD – or perhaps the kingdoms and the dynasties emerged in tandem. Of the second type, perhaps Egypt is the best example, geographically contained and subject to the rule of a long succession of dynasties. In political terms, the first type may well find a greater loyalty from their peoples, at least at first, than could be directed towards a dynasty that was just the latest in a long sequence.

Once a dynasty had brought a state into existence, of course, it became subject to replacement, and the state it had created was liable to be governed by a succession of several dynasties. There are also certain territories that are particularly fertile in dynasties (Syria, Greece, Anglo–Saxon England, are examples). The role of the earliest dynasty, if it is known, may thus be crucial in defining the state. In English terms, the kingdom of Northumbria would appear to be one such, created with some difficulty by the union of two dynasties and continuing substantially unaltered as a kingdom through several later dynasties. Similarly, the Mercian kingdom was formed by the dynasty descended from Pybba, which brought a group of lesser states into one. Both states were broken up by the Viking conquest, but the fragments tended to come back together in the subsequent period. It took the combined political and military weight of the King of Scots and William the Conqueror to finally divide and subdue Northumbria. Such states were often more durable than the dynasties to which they owed their inception.

The way a dynasty begins is a crucial element for its continuance and may well determine its history and longevity. Warfare is perhaps the most common element in the origins of many dynasties, but not in all, and one must not confuse the everyday work of the kings as warriors with the origins of their families' power. It is a fact that warfare was, in a violent and unstable time, the main preoccupation of most rulers, but was not by any means the only one: even if it is a fact that most dynasties originated in violent events, 'warfare' is too wide and general a term to be wholly satisfactory as an explanation for their origins. A closer look is required to distinguish the different types of violence involved, for these varieties have a long effect on the conduct of the dynastic members who succeeded the founder.

Invaders

Invasion and conquest might be thought to be especially productive of new dynasties, by the establishment of a victorious conqueror in a new land, but relatively few of the ancient dynasties originated in that way, and then only in particular and distinct conditions. Perhaps the most obvious cases were the Germanic war bands that invaded the Roman Empire – the Vandals, Ostrogoths, Visigoths, Franks, Anglo-Saxons, and so on. But not all of these fit the invasion and conquest notion. The Visigothic kingdom, for example, rarely succumbed to dynastic rule for very long, at least once the original dynasty had expired – though that did last for over a century – and the normal method of choosing a king was by election in one way or another. Only the first Visigothic dynasty owed its position to leading the Visigoths in conquest; but these kings were also kings by inheritance and kinship.

The success of the Vandals and the Ostrogoths in establishing kingdoms in their new homelands clearly enhanced the prestige of the leading families who formed their ruling dynasties. These lasted almost as long as the kingdoms' rule was confined to those particular families, but the elective system could also be resorted to, as by the Ostrogoths in the extremity of their defeat by the Byzantine armies. The second Ostrogothic dynasty, therefore, largely owed its existence to the need to defend the kingdom against attackers, the reverse of the origin of the first dynasty.

These early 'invading barbarian' dynasties did not in fact usually last for very long, and one of the briefest was the most violent: the Hun dynasty only lasted for five decades, and in its last two decades it was only a local power in a corner of the Hungarian plain. The Vandals and the first Visigothic dynasty did last a little over a century, but the Burgundians and Ostrogoths expired much earlier. Clearly a common explanation for the early demise will need to be searched for (see Chapter 11, 'Terminations').

Those 'invading barbarian' dynasties that were founded rather later than the first arrivals tended to fare somewhat better, as though the preceding Roman polity had to decay properly before it could be successfully replaced. The Frankish Merovingians are a prime example of the establishment of a dynasty by conquest; they expanded relatively slowly, conquering Gaul piece by piece, while still maintaining control over their original homeland.

The early post-Roman dynasties in Britain might also seem to have been based on conquest, the Kentish and Wessex dynasties supposedly originating with men who actually led the original invasions, yet, while Cerdic of the West Saxons seems historical, and is said to have 'landed' and acquired his kingdom from there, 'Hengist and Horsa' of Kent cannot be accepted as historical figures. The Kentish dynasty, for example, was called the Oiscingas, indicating that its origin is with Oisc, located in the traditional genealogy as the son of Hengist, whereas the earliest king who can be historically attested is Oisc's 'son', Eormanric, who ruled in the mid sixth century, leaving a gap of a century in which only mythical names are recorded. Hengist and Horsa in fact appear to have been invented to account for the twofold Jutish settlement of Kent, where the eastern and the western parts of the country, centred respectively at Canterbury and Rochester, were often treated as distinct kingdoms. They may stand, in fact, for the original mercenaries hired in the fifth century – traditionally in the 440s – to garrison the area and defend it against the enemies of the oligarchy that presumably ruled Kent at the time. Cerdic is just as problematic a founder and has to be dated sometime later than the earliest of the Saxon settlements. He also has a Celtic name and was possibly the leader of a mixed band of invaders and locals. These earliest kings do not seem therefore to have been conquerors but were perhaps the organizers of the settlements sometime after the original arrivals; perhaps they were defenders of the settlers. Certainly they achieved something notable to have been recorded as founders of dynasties.

In Northumbria, on the other hand, it seems that the two dynasties that joined to form the kingdom's first dynasty, emerged from the Anglians only some time after they had settled – this being very like the Kentish experience. This is all the more so in Mercia, where the ruling dynasty descended from Pybba was formed by the union of a whole collection of small Anglian groups; the dynasty did not emerge until several decades after the settlement of the Angles in the Midlands, and appears to have coalesced in the face of aggression out of East Anglia. These unification processes certainly involved violence and conquest.

In Italy the Lombard conquest was slow and piecemeal, like that of the Franks in Gaul. But it remained both incomplete and fragmented, even though it was in its way a successful process. It did require the re-establishment of the ruling dynasty in 584, after a decade-long gap with no kings, to make it secure in the face of continued enmity from the Byzantine powers in the peninsula. This is reminiscent of the Visigothic development once the first (conquest) dynasty had expired. The Lombard dynasty clearly had little of the dynastic drive required for permanence until it was called on to defend the original conquest against revolt and Byzantine revanche. The dynasties of the kingdom, and of the Beneventan duchy, lasted for two centuries; the Merovingians for three. In the east, gradual conquest was the method also of the Parthians in Iran, and their kingdom lasted for centuries rather than the decades of the Ostrogoths and Vandals who had been more spectacularly instantly successful.

The Western 'invading-barbarian' dynasties profited from the crumbling of the Roman Empire and this was also the situation that allowed the Parthian dynasty to become established in the province from which it was named, formerly a satrapy of the Seleukid Empire, having invaded from the steppes to the north. The dynasty expanded by taking over successive sections of that empire, until it occupied almost the same geographical space as its predecessor/enemy. The weakness of the state in eighth century BC Egypt permitted a successful invasion by Nubians from the south, whose leaders formed a new ruling dynasty ('XXV'), though, again, this one did not last very long, at least as rulers in Egypt. It did continue, however, for some uncertain period in its Nubian homeland after being expelled from Egypt. The only other clear case of a dynasty established by invasion and conquest is the Battiad dynasty of Cyrene. This originated with the leader of a group of Greek colonists, settled on the mainland of North Africa, which had been organized and dispatched from the island of Thera. It seems clear that the original Battos, the first of the dynasty, became the leader because he seized the moment when the original settlement group was dithering over how to proceed, and that his leadership over a long period – the traditional length is 'forty years' – was decisive in establishing a viable settlement and later a state; he certainly founded a dynasty that became kings, though it was probably only after a generation or so that their power was so open and hereditary.

Much the same may be said of Gusi, the man for whom the Iron Age north Syrian state of 'Bit-Agusi' ('House of Gusi') was named. He was the leader of an Aramaean group that had settled or had perhaps merely moved into a part of north Syria centred on the existing city of Arpad (near modern Aleppo), and it was the conquest of this city – or possibly the takeover – that established the Gusi dynasty as ruling a kingdom. It may be that this was also the origin of several other of the Syrian dynasties about that same time, but the sources fail us. It certainly seems that the various Syrian states that can be classified as Aramaean – Damascus, particularly, which was later often referred to as 'Aram' – originated in the conquest of fertile lands by invaders from the desert, but only in the case of Gusi and Bit-Agusi can a direct link be made between the leader of the infiltrators and the subsequent state. And yet Gusi may well not have arrived from any distance: he may have originated from the immediate locality, rather than leading a band of raiders from the desert.

The story of similar events that is preserved in the Bible, detailing the supposed invasion by the Hebrews is cautionary in this respect, a story that seems now to be invented, or perhaps distorted and romanticized, but that perhaps describes the sort of methods of infiltration used by the Aramaeans generally, all along the edge of the Syrian Desert. The original Hebrew invasion was said to have been led by a whole variety of leaders – 'judges' in the English translation of the Bible – and was probably spread over several centuries. The subsequent population of the Hebrew kingdoms was descended from an amalgam of invaders and original inhabitants. The first known kings at Damascus and Samal, both Aramaean states, may or may not also have been the invasion leaders: without a clear statement of some sort in the sources it is impossible to be sure.

It will have been noticed that all the dynasties that have been founded during the process of invasion and conquest have in common the fact that they were leading barbarian groups into collapsing civilized states. The one exception is the Battiad dynasty in Cyrenaica. But even Battos commanded only a small group of Theran settlers at first, and no doubt they were regarded as barbarians by the aboriginal Libyan inhabitants. These invasions could only succeed by establishing a coincidence of interests between the invaders and the natives: that is, the commander, the first king, had to conciliate his new, conquered, subjects, and thus tap into their skills and numbers, before a viable state could be produced. The various Syrian states are prime examples of this integration process, as is the Parthian, which employed former Seleukid subjects to run their new empire, and the Frankish Merovingians, where the integration of Gallo-Romans and Franks was slow and difficult, taking a century and more to be completed. The Anglo-Saxon kingdoms were also, it is now assumed, populated by mixtures of invaders and in the genes. The invaders becoming the rulers – they were the warriors, after all – it was their language that prevailed.

The other element that the more successful conquest dynasties had in common was their piecemeal acquisition of the territory they came to rule. Swift conquest was superficial, and such conquests soon dissolved – Alexander's is a good example, as is that of Attila – where a slow and gradual conquest was more likely to be permanent and also to establish the conquering dynasty firmly in power. The Merovingians, Lombards, and Parthians are good examples, though the most successful would be the Romans. Each of these lasted for centuries, not just years or a few decades, and when they ceased to rule it was not because their conquest evaporated.

Foreign Installations

A variation on the invasion and conquest theme is the installation of a dynasty by an invader, who might thereby form a state, or take over an existing one. Mithradates VI the Great of Pontos did this twice, in the first case by installing his son as king of Cappadocia. This new king, Ariarathes IX, was not a success and was soon expelled by a rebellion, but his sister's husband, Ariobarzanes, a native Cappadocian lord, did establish himself as king, partly in opposition to Ariarathes, and partly with his father-in-law's support. Clearly it was only by catching the loyalty of the new subjects that this ploy could succeed. Ariobarzanes was a Cappadocian, unlike Ariarathes, who only had a Cappadocian name, and this may be thought to be a more important element in Ariobarzanes' success than the eventual support he received from Mithradates.

Mithradates did successfully install another new dynasty by taking over control of the kingdom of the Cimmerian Bosporos on the north side of the Black Sea. The Spartokid dynasty there had effectively expired by the time he took over the kingdom, and by ruling the land himself for nearly forty years, and installing two of his sons as his deputies over lengthy periods, he enabled his second son Pharnakes to continue to rule alone after he died. By the time Pharnakes himself died, his family had already ruled the Bosporan kingdom for over sixty years. The subsequent dynasty is one of the most long-lived here studied, lasting for four and a half centuries.

The installation of Garibald I as duke of the Bavarians by the Merovingian king in 589 was another successful exploit of the same sort. That is, it was successful in establishing Garibald as duke, and the Bavarian duchy so established continued to exist for the next millennium and a half, as a duchy, as a kingdom, and today as a German province. The exploit was less successful in having Garibald remain a Merovingian puppet, or in producing a lengthy dynasty. Garibald's heirs were his nephew and that nephew's son, but he also married his daughter to successive Lombard kings of Italy, and the Lombards were long-time enemies of the Merovingians. As a result of Garibald's policies, which might be thought ungrateful, he managed to detach himself and his duchy from direct Merovingian control. But the Merovingian exploit was inevitably doomed to be unsuccessful in the long term: if they had chosen a docile puppet, he could not have maintained his local position in Bavaria, and repeated expeditions would have been needed to reassert Merovingian control; if he was not docile, he would inevitably make moves to enhance his independence, as Garibald actually did. In the end the dynasty was suppressed by the Merovingians' successors, the Carolingians, but Bavaria as a distinct country remained, and remains.

Another example of installation by a foreign power may well be the case at the city of Edessa in Syria, though the process is less clear in this instance. A kingdom had emerged into independence by the 130s BC, out of the collapse of the Seleukid Empire, perhaps initially in the nearby countryside, but probably by 132 the kings had gained control of the city of Edessa itself (a process very like the Aramaean and Hebrew infiltrations mentioned earlier). The first two kings appear to have been unrelated either to each other or to any of the later kings, which might indicate that they were competitors, or that they were bits of some outside authority. Another new king, the third in ten years, appears about 120 BC, and again he was unrelated to his predecessors. By his name, Fradhasht, however, he seems to have been an Iranian, whereas the two earlier kings appear to have had Arab names. (The Edessene population was partly Arab or Aramaean, and partly descended from Macedonian colonists.) Fradhasht ruled for five years and passed his power on to his son and then to his grandson. Thus, the family became established, becoming called, from the name given to, or taken by many of the kings, the Abgarids (using Arab or Aramaic names).

The area and the time was one of conflict between the surviving Seleukids, now based in northern Syria, and the Parthians, whose advance from the east in their usual slow and absorbing way had reached Mesopotamia, while the Romans also intruded later from the north and west. The Iranian Fradhasht might thus have been installed by the Parthians as an advance man, ready for their later exploitation, though this is only a theory. It is equally possible that Fradhasht was unconnected with the Parthian state, despite his Iranian name, and had seized power for himself independently, though during the next century the Parthians were able to intervene in force in Syria on several occasions, suggesting they had controlling power in the Edessene region. It is clear that the political situation in Edessa was highly volatile at the time and later. Either way, it would seem that the new dynasty rapidly gathered local loyalty. Its power and tenure of the kingship was repeatedly interrupted, but, as is often the case, revived, lasting into the 240s AD.

The most successful example, however, of this sort of dynasty-making, is that of the Arsakid dynasty of Parthia. Originally reaching imperial status in the late second century BC by the conquest of Iran and Babylonia, its expansion was stopped in the west by Rome, and in the east by the Kushans of Central Asia. But the dynasty put out two branches that lived on after the extinction of the main line. One was into Armenia, originally by agreement with Rome; the other was into Iberia, a kingdom in the Caucasus. The main imperial Parthian family was eliminated by the Sassanid conquest of Iran in the 220s AD, but the Armenian branch lasted until 428, and the Iberian until 284.

Promoted Governors

A variation on the theme of invader appointees is the group of dynasties that existed in the shadow of the great empires. These dynasties were usually raised up to power by initial imperial appointment, and usually ended by being suppressed by their sponsors. Two rival Arab dynasties on either side of the northern Arabian Desert in the Romano-Sassanid period are examples. The Lakhmid dynasty, based at al-Hira in Babylonia, was sponsored by the Sassanids from the third century, performing the functions of first defence against Arab tribes from out of the desert, and as auxiliary in more formal warfare with the Romans. The sponsors periodically intruded a non-Lakhmid as king, presumably to demonstrate their ultimate control; the Sassanids actually abolished the kingdom not long before the Muslim invasions; had the Lakhmid state existed it might have acted as a shield for the empire – or, of course, as a Trojan horse. In reply the Romans sponsored the Ghassanids in their part of the Syrian Desert from the early sixth century; two earlier Roman-sponsored Arab groups in the same area were the Salih and the Tanukh, whose dynastic lines are not clear, and that did not last long. (In other words the Romans were as anxious to maintain control over their side as were the Sassanids on the east.) Both Lakhmids and Ghassanids were eventually suppressed by their overlords, the former soon after 600, the latter twenty years before. In the Ghassanids' case this was because they proved to be all but uncontrollable by the sponsoring Romans.

Several centuries earlier, in various parts of Syria, the dynasty of Herod had held power in a variety of places for a century and more, always at the whim and bidding of the reigning Roman emperor; members of the family were in fact used by the emperors to rule several areas with which they were barely, or not at all, connected. After the death of Herod himself, in 4 BC, none of the family showed any signs of independent action.

Three centuries earlier, in Anatolia, the Hekatomnid dynasty, whose most notable member was Mausollos (he of the grandiose tomb), was descended from an appointed governor of the Akhaimenid province of Karia; the virtual independence of the dynasty was more the result of Akhaimenid negligence than of any active sponsorship, and it was suppressed in the end by the Akhaimenids' successor, Alexander, if it did not simply die out. This development is clearly a possibility in the times of the decay of older empires, and there are hints in fifth century Europe of similar brief dynasties, though their documentation is as sparse as their lives were short. One that is known is that of the Rugians in Noricum, suppressed by King Odoacar of Italy. In later times the Abbasid dynasty of Islam produced a series of similar successor dynasties, descended from the governors of dissident provinces.

The most persistent example of this process in the ancient world is Armenia, where no less than three successive dynasties all originated as appointees by imperial overlords. The first example is Orontes, who had been satrap of the area for the Akhaimenids, and who returned to his post after the great Akhaimenid defeat at the Battle of Gaugamela, presumably on the instructions of King Darius, with the intention of harassing the Macedonian army's communications. His son succeeded him, and defied the intervention of another Macedonian general who had pretensions to govern that satrapy; his successful defence thus persuaded him to adopt the royal title. This dynasty was eventually displaced by the Seleukid Antiochos III, whose daughter was married to, and then murdered Xerxes, the last king of the Orontid dynasty. Antiochos appointed the replacement governors, Artaxias and Zariadris, but they then detached themselves into independence and royalty when Antiochos was preoccupied elsewhere. This formed another dynasty, the Artaxiads, which was eventually suppressed by Rome, having lasted almost two centuries. Meanwhile the survivors of the Orontid dynasty had retreated northwards and continued to rule part of the land. By an odd partnership, Rome and Parthia between them then installed yet another new Armenian dynasty, a branch of the Arsakid dynasty of Parthia (mentioned above as an example of an installed dynasty). The first of this dynasty owed his appointment to an elaborate coronation ceremony carried out at Rome, but he and his successors succeeded in developing a real independence of both sponsors.

This sequence, of course, was not a peculiarity of the Armenians, though the fact that the Orontids were descended from an appointee certainly provided Antiochos III with a workable excuse for suppressing the dynasty; and once this had happened, it could be repeated by the Seleukids' successor, Rome. The whole situation was really a function of the political geography of the region whereby Armenia was on the margin of every great empire, from Assyria to the Ottomans, and was at the same time, in its mountains, extremely difficult of access. The loyalty developed by the Armenians towards each of the successive dynasties is remarkable, as is the Edessene attachment to the Abgarids; this cannot be detected with the Herodians, by contrast, even in Judaea, and still less in other areas where members of the family were made kings by Rome (that included part of Armenia for the period between dynasties). Like the Bavarian dynasty, these Middle Eastern dynasties rapidly shed any feeling of obligation towards their sponsors; no doubt complete independence was part of their own particular purpose from the start.

Inheritors

The case of Orontes in Armenia, whereby he had resumed his original post as an Akhaimenid satrap to defend it against the Macedonians, is replicated in several other parts of that former empire. Atropates in northern Iran was favoured by Alexander and appointed as his satrap of Media, but set himself up as an independent king when Alexander's empire dissolved into civil war, though he, like the Armenian kings, had to be content in the end with ruling only the mountainous part of his inheritance. Ptolemy in Egypt assumed independence about the same time (though he was technically only satrap for two decades). In Pontos the first Mithradates seems to have had some Akhaimenid past on which to build his independent kingdom, and similarly the first of the Ariarathids in Cappadocia. In a sense the Visigoths began as a dependent government in Aquitaine, becoming an independent state when the Roman Empire vanished from around them. For a time the governor installed by Alexander in Baktria was effectively independent, until suppressed by Seleukos I. In the same region, in the 250s, the Seleukid governor Diodotos I found himself cut off by the advance of the invaders of Parthia, and assumed a degree of independence in the absence of any royal authority, or perhaps of any royal instructions; he stayed in office twenty years, and his son, also Diodotos (II), inherited the post and took the royal title. As the Seleukid power ebbed from Iran, several local dynasties emerged, one in Elymais, one in Persis, though they appear to have been home-grown rather than claiming any legitimacy from the declining empire; but they were accepted as subordinates by the advancing Parthians. In southern Babylonia satrap of Characene, Hyspaosines, organized his territory into a kingdom and founded a dynasty, or at least a kingdom, which lasted three centuries. Edessa was another case, as were its neighbours Adiabene and Kommagene. These kingdoms tended to be small and fragile and easily conquered, unless they were in areas difficult to reach and/or had strong local roots to support them.

Defenders

The reverse of an invader is a defender, and there is a considerable group of dynastic founders whose origin was in leading the defence of their communities against attack from outside. The classic example might be the case of Leo III the Isaurian (or Syrian), the Byzantine emperor who led the defence of Constantinople in the face of the great Muslim attack in 717. The successful defence of the city, and thus of the whole empire, established his family as emperors for almost a century. The preceding dynasty, descended from the Emperor Heraklios, similarly owed its position to the success of Heraklios in recovering territories captured by the Sassanids. On a much smaller scale, the dynasty that ruled the Mesopotamian city of Hatra emerged from among a group of 'lords' as a result of one member, Nasru, leading the successful defence of the city against an attack by the Roman army of the Emperor Trajan; eighty years later another family member defended the city against another emperor, Septimius Severus. It was presumably such expertise that brought the family out of the crowd of 'lords' – four men of different families who seem to have ruled the city with that title in the first half of the second century. The expertise was not, however, hereditary, for the last king of Hatra, Sanatruq II, was unsuccessful in defending the city against attack by the Sassanid King Ardashir, and the end result was the destruction of both the city and the dynasty.

No less than four Anatolian dynasties originated in similar defensive circumstances: Gyges of Lydia fought the Cimmerian invaders in the seventh century BC, after the Cimmerians had already destroyed the preceding Phrygian kingdom. Gyges' victory established his Mermnad dynasty as kings of Lydia in western Asia Minor for several generations; in the aftermath of

Alexander's conquest, the dynasties of Bithynia, Cappadocia, and Pontos all originated with men who successfully defended their lands against attack by Macedonian generals, in the same way as the Orontids in Armenia established their credentials, which thus reinforced their original authority as Akhaimenid satraps. In Iran where a contemporary of Gyges was the first Median king, Phraortes, whose prestige as the defender of his land against Assyrian attack helped to found his dynasty, which went on to take the lead in the destruction of the Assyrian Empire. The fact that the two new kingdoms, Lydia and the Medes, later fought each other is perhaps one of the consequences of putting one's faith too much in military means.

The rise to power of Dionysios I at Syracuse is as classic an example of a successful defender fastening his power on the land he defended as that of the Byzantine Emperor Leo III the Isaurian. Dionysios' carefully limited war of conquest and revenge against Carthaginian power in Sicily was also a classically cynical acknowledgement that, while he was accepted as a successful defender of the Greek part of the island against Carthaginian invasion, he was also essentially unwelcome as a ruler: by carefully leaving the Carthaginian enemy in possession of a foothold in Sicily as a standing threat to Syracuse he claimed to be able to justify his continuation in power. This might also well be the origin of the Judahite dynasty, where the emergence of an aggressive monarchy in Samaria that formed the kingdom of Israel, was a standing menace to the Judahite lands; the earliest king of Judah who is likely to have existed is Jehoshaphat – the earliest men (Saul, David, Solomon and so on) seem to have been invented for the purpose of glorifying Judah by antedating and glorifying the ruling dynasty. The fact that Israel's kingship was deeply unstable and subject to repeated violent military *coups d'état*, as a result of which warriors seized the kingship, may be seen as the basis for the implied comparison.

One of the few documents and well-dated events among the Indo–Baktrian kingdoms is the attack on Euthydemos I by the Seleukid King Antiochos III. Euthydemos had seized the throne from his predecessor Diodotos II, and may thus have been without any legitimate right to rule in the eyes of many of his subjects. (Diodotos was himself the son of the former Seleukid governor who had taken advantage of the kingdom's troubles in Syria to shift himself into independence.) By successfully defending his stolen kingdom against attack by Antiochos, who was perceived as the enemy of both Euthydemos and his subjects, Euthydemos may be seen to have established his family as a ruling dynasty, a position his descendants then held for another century or more.

Rebellions

Movements from within a polity can displace a dynasty, as Euthydemos did. These are perhaps the commonest reasons for new dynasties to come into existence. These movements can be of three types: rebellion, usurpation, or a *coup d'état*. (For the latter two, see the next sections.) Egypt was a prolific source of rebellions that removed ruling dynasties in favour of successors. This circumstance is largely due to the relative frequency of successful invaders, whose rule never failed to produce a native Egyptian reaction, which in time drove out the intruding rulers. The Nubians, the Assyrians, the Persians, and the Macedonians all conquered the land, and in the first three cases sufficient resistance was evoked to make successful dynasties out of the leaders of the successful rebellions. Rebellions against the Macedonian Ptolemies were successful only briefly, and partially; Ptolemy I had been careful to conciliate the Egyptians from the start, and the Macedonian conquest had been perceived as rescuing the Egyptians from the Persian oppression. The Egyptians were also disarmed for a century and more as a further precaution; once a substantial number had gained military training and weapons, rebellions began. These rebellions emerged with the greatest force after a little over a century of Ptolemaic rule, and, in classic style, the rebel leader proclaimed himself pharaoh; his state lasted over twenty years.

At least two of the successful rebellions were led by provincial governors who had been installed by the invaders – by Necho against the Nubians, and by Nektanebo against the original Persian conquest – and rebellions by governors are one of the sources of dynasties. Indeed such rebellions were of relatively frequent occurrence, though few governors actually succeeded in founding dynasties. In the Roman Empire the Flavians and the Severans succeeded in such attempts – both Vespasian and Septimius Severus were prominent governors commanding large armies for a wastrel or dissolute emperor and conduct and character provided a sufficient excuse for their rebellion. In the Byzantine Empire the governor of Africa, Heraklios, was the only provincial rebel governor to produce a dynasty, though many more made the attempt but reached the throne only briefly. Heraklios succeeded in part because he ruled a province that was distant from the capital, but mainly because the emperor who he rebelled against was notably brutal and unpopular. In both the Roman and Byzantine Empires it was the mastery of the capital city and of the army that counted above all, and a province was not usually a sufficiently large political base from which the whole empire could be acquired. In Heraklios' case large areas had been lost by Phokas, his desperately unpopular predecessor. The Roman Republic fell before a rebellion by Julius Caesar, who was a governor and conqueror of provinces at the time, and his success was the preliminary to the establishment of the Julio-Claudians as a ruling dynasty; his example was the ultimate source of the successes of Vespasian, Severus, Heraklios, and many more.

Other rebellions, like those in Egypt, were more likely to succeed by being based within the home territory. The dynasty established by Nabopolassar in Babylon originated in a successful local rebellion in southern Babylonia ('Sealand') against the Assyrians; the Maccabees, rebelling against the Seleukids, succeeded also in their home territory. These rebellious governors succeeded by separating their homelands from the empire against which they contended, but they also bequeathed to their dynastic successors a need to go on fighting to maintain that independence. Their success was thus in part due to their limited rebellious area, but also to their successful defence of their detached territories.

The duchies of Spoleto and Benevento in Lombard Italy became independent when the Lombard kings who were their theoretical overlords were preoccupied elsewhere. Occasional Lombard kings did exert their authority in the south, and they did in the end succeed in bringing Spoleto back into the kingdom and in suppressing its independent dukes; Benevento, however, was effectively abandoned into independence.

Usurpations

It is not always easy to separate rebellions from palace coups, or both from usurpations. Usurpation might be defined as the elimination of one ruler by another in a process that involves violence only to the displaced man, usually by assassination, whereas the rebellion involves much more widespread violence. The rebellion of Heraklios in the Byzantine Empire in 610, therefore, was not a usurpation in that sense, but a rebellion.

The original dynasty of Assyria, which could count its ancestry back over many generations and over many victories and conquests, was displaced by King Sargon II in 721, whose militaristic dynasty lasted another century. It is not wholly clear just what happened to his predecessor, Shalmaneser V, though Sargon's genetic relationship to him and to the earlier dynasty seems to have been non-existent.

Sargon's, and Assyria's great enemy to the north, Urartu, was ruled by a dynasty that originated in the same way, or so it seems, for there appears to be no family connection between the founder of the kingdom, Arame, and his immediate successor, Sarduri I, whose dynasty ruled for almost two centuries. Usurpation may be assumed, though it is not proved.

In the Syrian Iron Age the kingship of Damascus was a byword for succession by usurpation, by Rezon in about 900, and by Hazael about 842, but each man established a dynasty of no more than three kings. At Kition in Cyprus the same occurred, where the Baalmelek dynasty was displaced about 400 BC by Baalram; there were no more than three kings in this new dynasty, which was threatened at least once by a briefly successful usurpation by a man called Demonikos.

Coups d'état

A *coup d'état* may be defined as the displacement of one governing group by another, a process that usually involved violence, sometimes a lot of violence; it is usually concentrated in a small social and/or geographical area, normally the capital city. In this study the new ruling group was a dynasty, which displaced the preceding but different governing system, usually an aristocracy or an oligarchy. (If the displaced regime was that of a single ruler, the procedure must be termed a usurpation.) In Greek history these monarchies are termed tyrannies, though they are better thought of simply as monarchies. The classic examples are those of Corinth and Sikyon, each of which lasted for several decades – a hundred years in the traditional account of Sikyon. The dynasty that ruled at Samos was about as long-lasting, while the dynasties that ruled in Sicily – the Deinomenids, the monarchy of Dionysios, and that of Hiero later – lasted somewhat less; the tyranny of Peisistratos in Athens was one of the shortest; Peisistratos had to make two attempts to seize power, being accompanied by only about fifty men as his supporters when he succeeded (and a statuesque maiden dressed as Athene and riding in a chariot to fool the credulous Athenians).

Why these monarchies should be called tyrannies and yet the monarchy of the Spartokids in the Crimea, which similarly originated in a coup that displaced an aristocracy, should not be so called is only a matter of terminology, though the durability of the Spartokid dynasty – over three centuries – is remarkable and perhaps that is the explanation; established long enough it seems that 'monarchy' becomes the preferred term. Generally, a century is the maximum for such tyrant-dynasties, and to last for half that is generally good going. At Salamis in Cyprus, the family of Evagoras, based in a city with a long monarchical tradition, but having seized power in a coup, lasted a century; in Syria one of the Israelite dynasties, that of Jehu, nearly reached a century, though the only other dynasty that the Israelites achieved, that of Omri, lasted less than five decades. The Umayyad dynasty, whose founder Muawiya seized the throne by a coup, and which was overthrown by a rebellion, scored ninety years. The problem for dynasties that seized power by usurpation or coup, was, of course, that they were open to overthrow by similar means – and this was what happened to most of them. They had, of course, shown their successor-displacers the method.

These brief monarchies, having displaced the ruling aristocracy or oligarchy, were themselves overthrown and replaced often by a democracy. That is, having removed an unpopular system – or else why was it not supported? – it became itself unpopular by holding on to power, and usually becoming oppressive. (The high reputation of Timoleon, the Corinthian who led the Sicilians to the overthrow of the Dionysiad dynasty, and then retired to private life, is due to that conduct, so at variance with the usual.) Violent change of this sort could itself all too easily become an institution, and many places that had overthrown tyrannies found themselves subject to further tyrannies later – Athens is a good example, the democracy that replaced the Peisistratid tyranny was itself overthrown by a coup a century later, and then by another under Demetrios of Phaleron after another century.

The governmental system of the Roman Empire might be considered to have become, by the very origin of its monarchical system, an institutionalized form of *coup d'état*. Augustus had been the victor in a civil war, but the imperial succession never became clear, in part because he pretended to restore the old republican system after his victory. It did not help that neither he nor any of his four successors had sons who survived; the complexity of the situation this produced almost encouraged *coups d'état* – three of the four emperors who succeeded Augustus in the Julio-Claudian 'dynasty' died violently by a *coup d'état* in favour of the next emperor.

The Antonine dynasty, whether one begins it with Nerva or Trajan, originated in a coup that began with the murder of Domitian and the instant installation of Nerva (who was waiting for the good news in the palace even as Domitian was butchered), while Trajan's succession was engineered by his military colleagues, to whose *force majeure* Nerva necessarily submitted – they commanded between them a good half of the Roman army. Hadrian seized power on Trajan's death in a process very like a *coup d'état*, and in which it would seem he was assisted by Trajan's widow.

The later dynasties of the Tetrarchs and the joint houses of Valentinian and Theodosios similarly each began with a military putsch against the preceding emperor, and similarly found they had instant problems in keeping a grip on their usurped authority. During the third century problems, emperors came and went with horrifying frequency, each attempting to found a dynasty, but each family – the Gordians, Messians, Licinians, Aurelians, and there are many others who failed to found a dynasty – managed only a few years each. This process was inherent in the constitutional situation of Rome from the time of Julius Caesar; the third century only saw the normal process speed up.

The very reverse was the case with the second Akhaimenid dynasty. The replacement of Cambyses II and Bardia-Smerdis by Darius I began as a usurpation (against Cambyses by Bardiya-Smerdis) which was then confirmed by a victory in the civil war (by Darius over Bardiya-Smerdis). Darius' dynasty then survived for nearly two centuries, expiring in 336 with the enthronement of Darius III, who was even more distantly related to his predecessor than Darius I had been to Cambyses. But Darius III only became Great King after his two predecessors had been murdered by their leading minister Bagoas, in successive internal coups, who then selected Darius as his next would-be puppet. Darius was also, as a result of the successive massacres of potential competitors by previous kings – that is, other members of their families – the nearest male relative to the last king. The longevity of the dynasty of Darius I is notable among imperial rulers. This is a dynastic success by any measure, but it is the measure by which one must judge the success of other usurping of putschist dynasties.

It is worth noting that the other Iranian dynasties, the Parthians and Sassanids, also achieved a long existence; none of these dynasties, of course, faced the complex constitutional problems of Augustus and his successors; they were absolute rulers from the start, and were accepted as such.

'Restorations'

Darius I claimed by his rebellion to be reclaiming his rightful inheritance, reckoning his descent from way back in the family history – which may or may not be true – and he argued that it was Bardiya-Smerdis who was in fact the interloper. This, more acceptably, is what certain other dynasties did; it was a normal post-coup justification. The Abgarids of Edessa appear to have been restored to power in their city at least twice, but any direct continuance between the earlier and later groups of rulers cannot now be traced, and may have been unknown even at the time; the three sets of rulers have to be treated as three separate dynasties. A little more usual was the revival of a moribund dynasty, which had not actually vanished, but had just faded until its chiefs had little or no power. The old Assyrian dynasty of the Bronze Age was revived by the late eleventh century kings, beginning with Shamshi-Adad IV; the later kings would later claim descent from those of the old kingdom, but the actual genealogical links are now somewhat dubious.

Election

There are several examples of royal dynasties established by the election of their founder. This was the normal pattern that became established for the Visigothic kingship, after the end of the original dynasty, with the result that when a dynasty did become established in that kingdom it did so against the grain of Visigothic constitutional practice, and soon expired. The replacement king was chosen by a group of Visigothic lords; with or without violence. Other examples come essentially from the late Roman and Byzantine polities. In a sense Valentinian I and Valens, the joint founders of the double dynasty of Valentinian/Theodosios, were chosen in that way by the army commanders after the deaths of Julian and Jovian, but more convincing are the Byzantine dynasties of Leo I and Justinian, though the electoral process was, by modern standards, rough and ready, and not really very far removed from being *coups d'état*. The constituency that elected the Visigothic kings was actually very similar in composition to that which chose these Roman emperors, the Visigothic nobility being the effective equivalent of the officers of the Roman army.

In the Roman Republic, of course, election was supposedly the origin of all the aristocratic dynasties, and this is certainly true of those who emerged during the republic's history. On the other hand, it looks very much as though the earliest families – the Horatii, Lucretii, Papirii, Postumii, Valerii, Verginii – whose members held office in the first years of the republic, may well have owed their continuing power originally to usurpation, depending on how the preceding kings of Rome were removed from power. The usually accepted interpretation is that it was an internal coup that aimed to displace the oppressive Tarquinius Superbus, and then was followed by the defeat of his attempted return by the civic forces. Those who participated in the uprising and those who were forward in the subsequent defence became the early consuls, holding power to maintain their usurped authority. That is, the process was similar to the overthrow of Greek tyrants, except that the replacement was by an oligarchy, not the institution of democracy.

At the other end of the republic, usurpation was certainly the origin of the power of the first emperor, Octavian/Augustus, who seized the consulship at the illegally early age of only eighteen years. Earlier, his grand-uncle Julius Caesar had rebelled to maintain his personal authority and to escape prosecution, though he was rebelling against the Senate's champion, Pompeius Magnus, who had forced himself on the republic a generation earlier at the head of an army loyal mainly to him personally. All of these may thus be counted as usurpations of the republic's normal political procedures. Neither Pompey nor Caesar were the first of their families to be republican magistrates, but Octavian was (though his father had reached a rank of praetor), and he was following their examples. Another case of, once a usurpation or a *coup d'état* has been successful, it will almost certainly be followed by imitations. For most of its history, the republic had maintained a strong tradition of election as the basis of public authority, but both at the beginning and the end it was control of military power by an ambitious general that was decisive.

Chieftains

The final type of the origins of a dynasty is the most numerous and often the most durable. It is one that originated with a single capable chieftain who expanded his power, territory, and authority, and succeeded in founding a state, a step forward from the tribal system out of which he had emerged, and then handed all this on to a capable son. The basic requirements are charismatic ability in the founder, followed by ruling capability in more than one succeeding generation, a solid and loyal base, and preferably a long-lived founder. The dynasty that produced Pyrrhos of Epeiros began as a line of chiefs of the Molossi tribe. These men were sometimes called kings, sometimes not, but they had a long pedigree stretching back deep into Greek prehistory. (In this they are, of course, similar to their Macedonian and Spartan contemporaries, and to the royal houses of the cities of Greek Cyprus, and they were just as liable to enhancement in numbers, duration, and prowess as these families.) The Molossi were joined by other tribes to form a confederation, the kingdom of the Epeirotes, whose leader was the Molossian chief as king, a position that was hereditary in the Molossian royal house. As a dynasty it therefore fell into two parts – a characteristic of this type – a preliminary period that is largely invisible to us, which was the tribal chief phase, and whose history was very liable to adjustment and enhancement in later times, then an historic period when the dynasty was grander, more powerful, and, from our point of view, much more visible. Only the second phase can be taken into account here, but the first is vital in providing a geographical, political – and mythical – base for the later grander phase.

The most successful examples of this type of dynasty, at least in terms of geography and longevity, were the two Iranian ones, the first Akhaimenid dynasty and that of the Sassanids, who were both originally based in the province of Fars (also called Persis). After several generations of rule in their homeland, they spread their power first over Iran, and from that base over the neighbouring lands as well. From the same area, but from a smaller base, was a dynasty of Elam, which began in the eighth century BC with Humban-Tahrah; the original kingdom seems to have been very small and it collided with the Assyrian Empire in its most brutal and cunning phase. The Arabian and Syrian deserts produced at least three more such dynasties, in which a chieftain expanded his power over neighbouring territory from a central base: the Nabataeans and Emesan dynasties in Syria, and that of al-Kinda in interior Arabia.

One of the Egyptian dynasties, based at Sais in the Delta, may be regarded as of like origin; although the kings were recognized as governors by their predecessors, they were also tribal chieftains in their own right, and that was clearly their origin. In North Africa Masinissa was originally a local chieftain who seized the opportunity presented by the Second Punic War to establish himself and his dynasty, shouldering aside an earlier king whom he had served. In pre-Roman Britain the only dynasty we know of, that of the Catuvellauni beginning with Cassivellaunus, perhaps began in the same way, as a line of chieftains who preceded Cassivellaunus; he established a considerable kingdom during the next century, which was then threatened as much by divided inheritance as by its ultimate nemesis, the Roman Empire.

In Thrace there were three successive dynasties, which were probably related to each other, at least to judge by the repetition of the same names through all three (though the exact connections between them cannot now be traced); each dynasty had to establish itself anew in power. The first dynasty, in the fifth and fourth centuries BC, had a tendency to disintegrate because of a distributive inheritance system and because of the opportunity thereby given to cadet members to detach themselves into independence when they had been placed in control of subsections, cities, or provinces; the second dynasty is poorly attested, having emerged after a century of Macedonian and Celtic domination in Thrace. It was perhaps only local, rather than controlling all Thrace as the others did. The third dynasty was perhaps the most successful of the three, until it was swallowed by the Roman Empire, as so many other dynasties were. There are clear chronological gaps between all three dynasties, during which Thrace was dominated by outsiders. In each case, whether or not they were all related to one another, these native Thracian dynasties all had a local basis, relied on their control of a portion of Thrace, and used it to expand their authority over the whole of the area.

The many dynasties of Ireland were all local, and all developed out of local roots. They become visible – that is, we have evidence of their existence – from the fifth century AD onwards. The early notices refer in particular to the dynasty of the High Kings that began with Niall Niogiallach ('Niall of the

Nine Hostages'). Many of the later dynasties of the several Irish kingdoms claimed to be connected to the Ui Neill, but they were all essentially of local origin and depended on their control of local territories. The connections to the High Kings may well have been invented later, as were several connections with St Patrick, but they were of little importance except as myths. Power was local in Ireland and the various dynasties were all local as well.

It may be assumed also that the Pictish and Scottish kings originated similarly. The Anglo-Saxon kings, however, might have originated as mercenary commanders at the start, though this was a relatively short phase in their history; later kings, as in Mercia or Wessex, appeared to have begun as chieftains.

These local chieftain dynasties always remained more or less local. Only the Akhaimenids and the Sassanids founded great empires, and the original Akhaimenid dynasty lasted only two generations as an imperial power before succumbing to civil war and the more capable Darius I. The Sassanid Empire was a rearticulation of the preceding Parthian state; it was large enough to be termed an empire, but was essentially an expanded local national state on the same pattern as that of Egypt or Thrace.

Complications

It does not take much consideration for the inadequacy of the analysis that has been made so far to become obvious. On the one hand, the classification of the types of origin is reasonably accurate, and I doubt that more can be discovered; on the other hand, it is a rather simplistic analysis, and is acceptable only as the starting point for a better examination. To ascribe the origin of a dynasty to a single cause, particularly where the dynasty maintained itself in power successfully over several centuries, is clearly insufficient. Further, to imply, as the preceding study of origins might seem to, that a dynasty's origin was subsequently all-important is also misleading. To some extent it was useful, as is shown by the development of such myths to explain those origins; such stories were usually designed, at least in part, to obscure the original, probably less palatable, truth. Yet political systems, dynasties or any other sort, need to be constantly refurbished if they are to continue in power, and in the process they change and adapt and will obviously outgrow their origins. Dynasties need to be constantly aware of the need to reassert their worth, and to recollect the process by which the founder began would be quite unconvincing and irrelevant to their subjects in a fairly short period of time if their rule became oppressive and inefficient. The failure of the Julio-Claudian dynasty of Rome is a perfect example; and the theory of the divine right of kings to rule did not stop his subjects from chopping off Charles I's head, nor did it save Louis XVI, nor prevent the Dutch defying Philip II, or the American colonies from expelling George III's authority. To use another modern analogy, the present British monarchy is clearly alert to the inadequacy of looking always to the past: no one, at least in public, recalls that, as one novelist has put it, the present queen is a 'Woden-born Cerdinga', referring to her supposed distant ancestor Cerdic, the founder of the Saxon kingdom of Wessex. An origin by descent from the most powerful god of the Saxon pantheon may have been useful as a legitimizer in the early Saxon period, but the adoption of Christianity only half a century after Cerdic's arrival would instantly devalue it. At the same time, the pageantry of the modern monarchy is a substitute, linking it with the past, in the same way that every Roman emperor, no matter how obscurely born, took the name Caesar.

However, I am not here concerned so much with the continuation and power of the dynasties under study, as with how they originated. Just as more than the single fact of their origin is needed in order to account for their longevity, or otherwise, so a deeper investigation into their origins than the identification of a single originating event is needed. To take one of my earlier examples, Leo the Isaurian's dynasty may have earned its early support by Leo's successful defence of Constantinople against the Muslim attack in 717, but a closer investigation shows that he was in fact already emperor before that attack took place. Before he became emperor he had gained a great reputation as a defender of the empire on the Saracen frontier; in the process of reaching the throne he gained the support of the only army commander capable of being his imperial rival, he defeated the army of the current emperor, the hopelessly inadequate Theodosios III, who was only too happy to cede his imperial position, he gained the support of both the Patriarch of Constantinople and the Imperial Senate, and he was welcomed into the city by cheering crowds. Only when all this had taken place did Leo take the position of emperor, and only then did he begin preparations for the defence of the city and the empire against the coming Muslim attack.

Sorting out a single cause from all this is clearly impossible: there were many more than one. It seems likely that Leo would have seized power even if no Muslim attack was imminent, and that his obvious ability when compared with the alternatives might well have kept him and his dynasty in power for some decades. So, to ascribe the dynasty's origin solely to his success in defending the city and the empire in the face of the Arab attack is only partly correct. His method of gaining power in fact combined several elements: it was in formal terms a rebellion, in that he fought and beat the current emperor's forces. It also had strong elements of an election about it, since there seems no doubt that, had an election actually taken place he would have won it; the support of the Patriarch, Senate, the citizens, and his army, and even of the defeated Emperor Theodosios, was a clear endorsement of his action and was perhaps the nearest the Byzantine Empire ever got to a real electoral process; yet at the same time the process also had elements of a military putsch to it. His career on the Saracen frontier also makes him into a sort of local chieftain, and the epithet 'Isaurian' also implies that – Isauria being a notoriously primitive region.

All these elements are thus to be taken into account in detecting the origins of Leo's dynasty. Yet one comes back again to the success of his command of the defence of the city in the great siege of 717, a success based on his earlier military experience on the frontier. The attack was surely coming, and the whole empire knew it. Leo, the man in the empire with the most experience of war with the Muslims, was also the most obvious man to command the defence, and he could only do that properly and adequately if he held the position of emperor. Then, by taking command, by his feats of organization and inspiration, by his military and diplomatic expertise, Leo was the soul of the defence, and the memory of that achievement cast a glow over him and his family for the next decades. So, whereas there were several elements involved in Leo's acquisition of the imperial power, it was the attack, its imminence, and the defence against it, which predominated in the continuation of the dynasty after him. It was the success of that defence that ensured Leo continued as emperor: it was thus, in truth, and despite all the other factors involved, the real foundation of his dynasty's power and authority.

We must therefore look more carefully at the origins of the various dynasties. In many cases, like that of the Isaurian dynasty of Byzantium, there were several contributory factors, but in all of them there is thus just one that predominated. The easiest to deal with is the last group distinguished in the previous section: the local chieftains who originated in many cases in small territories from Persia to Ireland. Here I suggest there are two elements. One is the ability of the dynasty's founder, Cyrus II of the Akhaimenids, Ardashir of the Sassanids, Samsigeramos of Emesa, Masinissa of the Numidians, Cassivellaunus in Britain, Niall Niogiallach perhaps, and so on. It was these men whose ability, often military, but necessarily also more broadly political and administrative, and organizational and diplomatic as well – that is, they were outstanding statesman – which brought their small tribe or nation from obscurity to power; they were nation-builders, enlarging their patrimony and binding other groups to it. But behind this also was the generations-long background of their inheritance as local chieftains; the loyalty of their people to the chief as the heir of his ancestors, a factor not to be ignored. Cyrus II looked back on at least four generations of his family as 'Lords of Anshan'; Ardashir's dynasty may be called Sassanid from his grandfather, but he was heir to perhaps ten generations of local rulers in the Parthian province of Fars, or so it was claimed. Alketas I was the successor, no doubt, of as many Molossian chiefs before he enlarged his inheritance by bringing in other Epeirote tribes to form his kingdom of Epeiros. And so on.

The earlier parts of many of these dynasties cannot now be traced in detail but all of them exhibit the same symptoms, a powerful and enduring local loyalty even in adversity; the Roman invasion of Britain soon displaced Cassivellaunus' dynasty, but Caratacus, Cassivellaunus' great-grandson, was able to command a group of resisters for nearly ten more years after the conquest of his ancestral kingdom; Masinissa's family also collided with the power of the Roman Republic more than once, and sometimes it behaved in loyalty-sapping ways, but his successors did continue to command the loyalty of the Numidians for two centuries and more; the Elamite dynasty had an appalling record of defeats at the hands of both Assyrians and Babylonians, but the last of the kings was still fighting in the mountains with a loyal following when he was captured, and the Assyrian invaders so appreciated the strength of this local loyalty that they used members of the dynasty as their own cat's paws and puppets, usually without much success. The Irish dynasties that traced their origins to Niall Niogiallach had to be progressively destroyed in the Viking invasions over a period of two centuries before a High King not of his family, Brian Boru, proved to be acceptable to the Irish as a resistance leader – but he was in fact little more than a war leader. He proved unable, despite his success in combating Viking invasions, to establish his dynasty as permanent king of all Ireland. It took more than success in war to be a dynastic founder. In all these cases, and others of this type, it is both the outstanding abilities of the founders and the power of local loyalty that must be taken into account in discussing the dynasty's origins.

The origins of dynasties is a complicated matter, in which it is fairly easy to detect the main types of origins – local chiefs, conquest, defenders, invaders, usurpers, rebels, victors in a coup, and so on – but in which a more prolonged investigation shows that single origins are unconvincing, and several elements clearly go into their beginnings. It is a political organism, after all, and nothing about politics is simple.

Chapter 2

The Mists of Time

It was the claim of a number of dynasties that their ancestry lay back in a misty, uncertain period in the past, and, in the centuries before monotheistic religions took hold, this ancestry often began with a god or goddess. It was normal, for example, for Anglo-Saxon dynasties to claim descent from Woden, and the *Anglo-Saxon Chronicle* goes out of its way to describe such a descent for the dynasties of Wessex, Kent, Northumbria, Mercia, and Essex. The form was always the same: the time between their divine ancestor and the first historically attested ruler was filled with a sequence of names that may or may not have been of actual people; the names are all short, one syllable words, and the list was clearly easily memorable. The descent was so embedded in dynastic necessity that it was repeated in the ninth century on behalf of the father of Alfred the Great; in that last there was the addition of a biblical ancestry back to Adam, but Woden was still included about halfway along.

The Sassanid dynasty of Iran claimed that there were ten generations of rulers of Fars before the eponymous Sassan, an ancestry that would have taken the origins of the dynasty back to about the time of Christ or earlier; yet the dynasty also claimed to be the true heirs of the Akhaimenids, harking back therefore for still another three or four centuries, which would require at least ten more generations. Ten, of course, is a nice round, easily remembered number, clearly chosen for such a purpose (just as the short Anglo-Saxon ancestry names could be easily memorized). The discrepancy between the number of generations and the supposed connection with the Akhaimenids demonstrates clearly enough that the whole thing – both the ten generations and the connection – was an invention.

In a similar way, Julius Caesar claimed, with how much of his tongue in his cheek we do not know, to be descended from the goddess Venus, and he lavished money on the construction of a temple of Venus Genetrix in the middle of Rome in commemoration of that 'fact'. Alexander the Great's dynasty claimed to be descended from Achilles, a myth that had considerable influence on Alexander's own behaviour; so did the dynasty of Pyrrhos of Epeiros.

In post-Roman Europe, the Gothic rulers claim descent from the eponymous Gaut, father of the Goths, who in Scandinavia was later more or less equated with Odin (that is, the Anglo-Saxon Woden). The Ostrogoths claimed descent from Kamal, in an extended genealogy that is certainly spurious. The Frankish kings were descended from Merovech, the grandfather of their first Great King, Clovis. Only three generations was a very restrained claim of these kings, but this was elaborated to give Merovech a divine father in the form of a monster of Neptune's who impregnated Merovech's mother while she was bathing in the sea; to such an extent that new kings manufacture an extraordinary ancestry. It is clear that the distinguished ancestry was regarded as useful, if not actually essential, to many dynasties' legitimacy. These various claims can be regarded as good entertainment and are dismissed by sceptics as pure propaganda, but it is perhaps also necessary to point out that such gods and goddesses did not actually exist, since it is customary for some modern historians to repeat these claims with a straight face.

Sparta

There are, however, some examples that are not really so different, and that have been taken seriously by historians; this has resulted, in a few cases, in major historiographical consequences. The Spartan dynasty lists, when considered objectively, are highly unlikely to be correct. The high number of generations back to the originator Herakles – a typical divine origin myth – cannot be accepted as cases of direct descent from father to son, such as is claimed in both genealogies. It is necessary here to go rather farther than that, and to state that such a lineage cannot have actually existed in fact (and did not); by contrast it is more than probable that the whole matter was no more than a Spartan patriotic invention or, as it is quaintly termed in some more recent studies, ideology.

The Spartan kings' origin with Herakles is a clear case of the invention of a divine ancestry, similar to Caesar's claim to be descended from Venus, the Saxon claims to be Woden-born, or the Frankish Neptunian sea-monster, and it was designed to legitimize Spartan rule in much of their conquered lands by utilizing such stories as the 'return of the Heraklidae' – another invention, in all probability. Dismiss the Herakles element, and one is left with a list of names for which there is not a single item of corroborative evidence. (One Spartan king's name, Latychidas, does occur in a poem of about 600 BC, but this is not a legitimation of the whole list, only of the existence of one king.) The list is preserved in Herodotos (of the fifth century BC), with an alternative and slightly different list in Pausanias (of the second century AD); the fact that the two do not agree is an indication that both were invented; there were obviously varying traditions. Only if a clear and independent contemporary witness turns up to verify these hearsay lists in detail can the Spartan lineages be authenticated; given that the early years of the claimed Spartan genealogy were a period of illiteracy throughout Greece, this is highly unlikely.

The detail of the connection with Herakles may in fact be linked with the establishment of the Menelaion sanctuary in Sparta city in the eighth century BC. This would thus perhaps be the time when the whole ideological structure was first developed, to be elaborated during the long war that the Spartans waged in their conquest of Messene, as a way of justifying that conquest; but, again, this is not any sort of evidence for the long prehistory of the two dynasties.

The purpose of this invention I have ascribed to Spartan patriotism. Sparta was different, in almost every political and social aspect, from the rest of Greece: it had kings in a republican age, a primitive legislative system, based on shouting assent and dissent to decisions, where other cities' assemblies had been formalized and had developed sophisticated mechanisms; it had a militaristic ethos in an increasingly civilianized land; it had an assertive womanhood where most 'respectable' women lived in virtual purdah; men lived in barracks even after they were married; then there was even the notorious black soup, and so on, and so on. Almost every aspect of its society diverged from what other Greeks considered to be normal. (Arnold Toynbee, in his *Study of History*, was so impressed by the differences that he separated Sparta off as a distinct civilization – an impressive reaction for such a deep-dyed classicist.) Most unpleasant of all for right-thinking democrats, Sparta had conquered its neighbour Messene and enslaved its people, at least those who survived or did not go into exile.

Explanations for these phenomena had to be found by the Spartans, since the other Greeks considered them so odd. Harking back to an explanation based on inheritance from the Dark Age was something other Greeks could accept – Athens had its stories about Theseus and Attikan unification in those very same Dark Ages. An origin for peculiar customs in the far distant and essentially unknown past is always acceptable. So, if Sparta had two kings, the explanation must lie deep in the past - obviously a correct assumption – and it was only one step further to choose a Dark Age hero, and to fill the resulting historical and dynastic gap with a series of royal names. This is not history, however, but myth and invention. And as ideology is a human invention that uses history for its own purposes, it inevitably and always distorts it in the process.

Cyprus

Many of the Cypriot dynasties looked back similarly to an origin in the Dark Age, to the blank period after the collapse of the Mycenaean kingdoms, when Greek-speakers fled Greece, or perhaps simply emigrated, to take refuge in the island. They did not have a Herodotos to preserve a king list, with the result that no more evidence than the claim itself now exists, and perhaps never did exist; the earliest known Cypriot kings are recorded mainly in Assyrian records in the eighth century BC. It is significant that the dynasty of the kings of the city of Paphos claimed to have been founded by two alternative Dark Age ancestral heroes, Kinyras and Agapenor, just as the Spartans claimed to have kings descended from Herakles into two contemporary dynastic lines. In each case the existence of alternatives suggests the manufacture of the origin claim later, for some unknown immediate purposes. In addition, archaeological evidence for the early Greek settlements in the area suggests that they were a fairly small and impoverished group, certainly coming from Greece, if they were not simply Cypriot natives who had acquired possessions that were imported; they were hardly numerous or wealthy enough to form a kingdom for some considerable time. The evidence actually suggests little more than the home of a family – royalty does not seem likely, except retrospectively. No kings' names at Paphos can be discerned before the seventh century, and out of the seventeen kings known by name, mainly from their coins, no dynastic line of any certainty at any time can be derived. The same must be said of the other Cypriot dynasties; the ancient origin of their dynasties in the Dark Ages, unless they can be independently verified, are to be rejected.

Other Examples

Note, in this regard, the parallel with the Irish High King Niall of the Nine Hostages, whose exploits are, at the very least, legendary, and to whom almost all later Irish dynasties claimed to be genetically connected. Niall's term of office as High King can be given a plausible date – but then so can those of the early Spartan kings and others. There is also the case of Iberia in the Caucasus region. The first of the dynasty descends from Samara, a lord of the city (as it became) of Mtskheta. He may or may not have existed; but his three successors, in direct descent, of course, are supposed to have occupied the throne for a total of 190 years – successively for sixty-five, seventy-five, and fifty years. Then suddenly, at the fourth generation from Samara, there are reigns of nineteen and twelve years, and a descent through the female line, cutting out one legitimate line, a much more convincing genealogical situation. In Wales the dynasty of Cunedda claimed descent from Magnus Maximus, a rebel Roman general of the late fourth century AD, and to have been moved from southern Scotland to North Wales; the effect is to detach the dynasty from any local Welsh connection, and by claiming that the community and its king had moved in order to help the Welsh resist the Saxons, it provided a justification for their seizing power (even if this was long before the Saxon settlement began, and on the 'wrong' side of the country, where no Saxon settlements took place).

Judah

The practice of claiming distorted and invented royal ancestry is thus clearly a widespread practice, and one that has to be denoted in genealogies and in king lists. (The kings of Rome are another example of a royalty whose existence is clearly doubtful or invented or both: attempting to make seven kings occupy the throne for two and a half centuries should make the fictional basis clear; only the final dynasty of the Tarquins looks acceptable.)

It is, however, the claim of the dynasty of Judah that has had the strangest and most dire historiographical – and political – consequences, even more so than the near reverence accorded to the Spartans in some quarters. The actual reverence accorded to the contents of the Bible has for far too long hidden its grave defects as an historical source. This can be ascribed overwhelmingly to the insistence of biblical scholars on citing confirmatory references only from the Bible itself, without examining non-biblical evidence – unless they can claim that it supports their case, of course, in which case it is welcomed as 'proof'. Far too much work in this area is merely selecting non-biblical items to help illustrate the biblical narrative. By taking a whole view, however, the historical books of the Old Testament in particular can now be seen to have been constructed long after the events they purport to describe, perhaps in the sixth century BC, perhaps later, and probably as an ideological support for the community of exiled Jews in Babylon – and therefore far from any possible written sources in Palestine, if such material actually ever existed. This was done with a clear ideological purpose, and one of its effects was to insist on the long history and venerableness of the 'House of David'.

It now appears that much of the story of the early Judahite monarchy has to be regarded as an invention, or at least as a concoction based on folk tales and possibly some fragments of actual history. The whole drama of the emergence of the monarchy of Saul, David, and Solomon is at serious odds with the social condition of the Judaean highlands as revealed by archaeology, and with the history of the whole region of the Near East as it is understood from other sources, archaeological and epigraphic. (In this it is similar to the case of Sparta, and of Paphos in Cyprus.) The well populated Palestinian lowlands are supposed to have been conquered by invaders from the thinly populated Judaean highlands – the story of David and Goliath is a myth developed to illustrate that conquest – and the subsequent kingdom is claimed to have been treated as an equal by Pharaonic Egypt, and to have ruled an 'empire' that stretched from the Red Sea to the Euphrates (an ideological claim that has had appalling consequences for the population of Palestine and Syria in the twentieth and twenty-first centuries AD). But the density of settlement and population in the highland areas of Palestine and Syria in the early Iron Age was simply not great enough to act as a demographic basis for these adventures. It was hardly great enough to support a royal family, in fact, and probably never did.

Once again what is needed is corroborative evidence, non-biblical, which might back up the biblical narrative. In fact, there is no reference in any other ancient source to any of the early kings of either Judah or Israel before the ninth century BC, and there is no indication anywhere that any other state or society noticed the existence of David's and Solomon's supposed 'empire', a truly astonishing omission if it had really existed. The earliest non-biblical references are to the dynasty of Omri, referred to in the Assyrian documents, in the person of King Ahab, in 859 BC. There is no earlier reference to either kingdom in any of the Egyptian sources, a much closer neighbour than Assyria. The fact that the Assyrians used the name 'Bit-Humri – 'House of Omri' – for Israel is a strong indication that Omri (who commenced reigning in about 885 BC) was the first king of Israel to cut an international dash. This would thus imply that the earlier kings of Israel claimed by the Bible, from Jeroboam onwards, were either of no account, or did not exist. And if Israel, always larger and richer and more populous and more powerful than Judah could ever hope to be, was insignificant before 885, the date of Omri's accession, then Judah as a state probably did not exist, or was at the very least wholly insignificant, perhaps only a chieftainship. The earliest Judahite king for which there is independent evidence is Ahaz, who was an ally (against Israel) of the Assyrian King Tiglath-Pileser III in 734; this is the first occasion, therefore, that the kingdom of Judah came to international notice; until then it had been wholly unimportant. Its dynasty cannot have been in power earlier than about 880, and may well not have existed before 800 or even later; I would suggest, in fact, that Jehoshaphat was the first of the dynasty to wield any power that was noticed by Judah's neighbours.

This, of course, means that the eleventh and tenth century kings of Judah – Saul, David, Solomon, Rehoboam and his successors – and the Israelite kings from Jeroboam to Omri's supposed predecessors from Baasha to Zimri, cannot be included in any calculations concerning the length of dynasties – the Israelite kings before Omri did not form a dynasty anyway, of course. The invention of the story of the early history of Judah and Israel is to be connected with the hostility between the two states – evidenced in 734 by Judah's alliance with Assyria against Israel – and the self-interest of the Judahite priestly class in gaining political power. The constant refrain in the Judahite story is the need for kings to follow Yahweh's way, which, of course, was that charted by the priests primarily for their own comfort and well-being. The fate of Israel, a sister kingdom with a similar worship of a similar god – the same god who was worshipped under different names throughout Syria – was taken as an awful example of what not to be. (Its fate was sealed, of course, in part by being attacked from behind by Judah when it fell into war with Assyria.)

The historical novelist who created the story of the early kings even used Israelite material transposed into a Judahite context, as in the story of Queen Athaliah, an obvious adaptation of the authentic Jezebel story from Israel. But it is the archaeological evidence that has sapped the foundations of the whole story. The early dynasties in the Syrian and Palestinian region in the early Iron Age before 900 BC were those seated in the former Bronze Age cities such as Tyre, Carchemish, and Damascus, where a surviving urban population provided a sound demographic and economic basis upon which the monarchical regimes could be erected. This applies also to the Philistine cities of the Palestinian coast, and to the other Phoenician cities – Sidon, Arados, and so on – known to be monarchies, but whose dynasties are not fully recorded, except that at Tyre. Such cities did not exist in the poorer and less populated highlands, and Omri's kingdom was based, like some of the other kingdoms in the area, in a wealthy agricultural region, and on his newly founded city of Samaria. (The Assyrian term Bit-Humri strongly implies that Omri was the effective organizer and perhaps originator of the kingdom.) Outside these areas the new city dynasties all appeared at or later than 900 BC: at Samal and Bit-Agusi in the north around 900 BC, in Israel in the 880s, beyond the Jordan in Moab in the time of Omri, the 870s and 880s.

In fact, the emergence, east of the Jordan River, of Moab as a kingdom of some size and power was as a direct result of attacks launched upon it by Omri, which were resisted by the first Moabite king, Mesha; his achievements were carefully recorded on an inscribed stone. No doubt the emergence of a united Judah was a result of the same sort of pressure, probably from the same king, whose ambition compelled the consolidation of the area of Judaea as a kingdom, which became the origin of the story of Saul and David making a kingdom to resist the Philistines. One reason for Omri to have suddenly emerged as a powerful king is the alliance he made with Tyre, a well-established and wealthy city with which he and his son had mutually advantageous commercial relations – exchanging Israelite agricultural products for Tyrian trade goods and manufactures. Judah's resistance to this postulated pressure and the well-attested enmity between Judah and Israel eventually inspired the myth of evil-doing Israelite kings, contrasted with the more reformable kings of Judah. This was allied to the myth of the pure royal descent of the Judahite dynasty, contrasted with the murderous and unstable monarchy of Israel. In the process, that Judahite kingship and the 'House of David' were extended back in time to predate every other Syrian dynasty, and given an empire to rule, which later Judahite kings were expected to aspire to restore.

There is no reason to believe that the dynasty of Judah was any different in all this than its contemporaries in Sparta and Cyprus or other dynasties in the same sort of situation in Anglo-Saxon England, Ireland, Rome, Iberia, or elsewhere. In all such places their kings clearly encouraged an exaggeration of the importance of their ancestry so as to benefit from the resulting inherited glory. The only difference is that the Judahite monarchy's history was annexed in its exaggerations by the priestly novelist. David's career is not seriously different from that of Herakles, and no more convincing in its glorification of the individual and the enhancement of the importance of both his doings and his kingdom; the term 'House of David' gave the Judahite dynasty the same sort of ancestry as the 'Woden-born Cerdingas', or the descendants of the sea-monster of Neptune, or David's contemporary Herakles. Nor is the existence of his immediate descendants to be taken any more seriously. The mists of time prevent any clear view of Spartan, Macedonian, Jutish, and Saxon origins; they similarly obscure and distort those of Judah, despite the apparent precision of the biblical account, which is quite unacceptable as history. Just as the earliest Kentish ancestors, Hengist and Horsa and the first sixteen or seventeen kings of the Spartan dynasties all have to be rejected as non-historical for the purposes of this study, so have the early kings of Judah also to be rejected.

(The discovery of a reference to the Judahite King Ahaziah as a member of the 'House of David' on an inscription from Zinjirli in north Syria, dating to 841, is not proof of Judah's kings' earlier existence, or of a dynasty of kings. It is only proof that the term 'House of David' was in use at the time, and that the kings of Judah claimed a long ancestry for themselves.)

At the same time, one can see why these states and descents were concocted and exaggerated. In some cases, as with Judah and Sparta, there were good political and ideological benefits to be garnered; in others, the perception of a dynasty descended from a god or a great hero was clearly perceived as an advantage, and in a community of kingdoms such as Anglo-Saxon England, once one king's dynasty claimed such a descent, the rest would feel the need to do so as well; the descent of the Macedonian and the Epeirote dynasties from Achilles is a similar case. It was thus no doubt partly a matter of keeping up with the neighbours, but, perhaps more important, it was a necessary reinforcement to kings whose thrones and powers were founded on sand. It is significant that once the immediate descendants of the Anglo-Saxon founders – Oisc, Pybba, Cerdic, and so on – had died out in the eighth century, the Anglo-Saxon kingdoms abandoned dynastic kingship – as had the Visigoths earlier – only for it to be revived under the impact of the Viking attacks, when the annexation of Christianity to the dynastic tables of descent provided a different ideological reinforcement for unsteady thrones.

Conclusion

It follows from all this that these extended early dynastic lists and genealogies cannot be accepted in this study. The dynasty where such claims are made must therefore be 'begun' with the first of the kings who can be reliably attested. It may be necessary to include the mythical kings in the individual lists in the Catalogue but only in order to recall their unacceptability. The sign of this will be an absence of dates for these kings – which cannot be known anyway – and the numbering of the generations will omit them, to begin with the first of the attested kings.

Chapter 3

Legitimacy

In Christian Europe a king who succeeds to the throne will soon be subjected to a coronation ceremony, more or less elaborate, which will have strong religious elements included within it. This is a process of legitimization. The object of the ceremony therefore becomes, as a result, the legitimate sovereign. It is an example of the co-option of religion to the service of the monarchy. For monarchs there was a further useful element; the ceremony, being religious, made him or her a sacred person, whose life was thus consecrated to God, and who therefore was regarded as under divine protection; to kill such a person was therefore sacrilege, the most useful attribute. Such a straightforward method was not available in the preceding period; indeed, there were a number of other ways by which a monarch could be legitimized.

Legitimization by Acclamation

The ancient world did not have an equivalent ceremony of sacralization (though the Christian ceremony was in fact copied, and developed, from one described in the book of Samuel in the Bible). The nearest equivalent ceremony seems to have been the acclamation of the new monarch by a particular group of his subjects. In the Macedonian kingdoms – Macedon and its Near Eastern successors – this group was the army. This originally, in Macedon, was the full armed might of the kingdom, gathered in assembly, and it is recorded as operating in this way to propel Philip II from the regency for the infant Amyntas to the kingship in his own right in 359 or 358 BC. Later, the successor kingdoms of the Seleukids and Ptolemies were much larger, and no such meeting of the whole army could be convened, but still an armed group, usually of guards and courtiers, performed a simulacrum of this task. This development, of course, put the choice of king into a very small group, thus encouraging *coups d'état* and usurpations. In the Ptolemaic kingdom in 222 BC the successor of Ptolemy III was a child, and those who proclaimed him king went on to eliminate his mother, his sister, and his brothers, and presented this as an accomplished fact – giving out specious reasons for their deaths, of course. This was one way to block any competitor.

Legitimization by Ancestry

In pursuit of some stability it became the custom of a king to designate a successor, usually his eldest son, and in some cases he would associate that successor with him as joint king for the last years of his life. This was a clear process of legitimizing the succession. The snag, of course, was that the chosen successor might well anticipate his accession to sole rule by his own *coup d'état*, which would certainly require the killing of the ruling king, but in so acting the perpetrator would not be altering the legitimacy of his own accession, which rested as much on his membership of the royal family, and as the eldest son of the king, as on the latter's designation of him as his chosen successor.

For the main source of legitimacy was the very existence of the dynasty. Any number of dynasties broke down into internecine violence without suffering the indignity of being driven out by their subjects. The Sassanids broke down in such a way at least twice, but recovered, the Seleukids also. Of course, given the restriction on owning and carrying arms among the general population it was a foolhardy exercise for the citizenry to attempt to rebel, but the popular overthrow of a king was very rare (Demetrios I of Macedon is a case in point, and a man without any legitimacy as king in Macedon by descent), and the destruction of a dynasty by popular rage is not known at all.

Legitimacy as king, therefore, existed largely because the ruler was the son of an earlier ruler. And in a circular way, being a member of the dynasty conferred legitimacy; the longer a dynasty lasted the greater legitimacy it could assume. Even when the Seleukid dynasty had fragmented between half a dozen kings in the 90s BC, all of them claiming the legitimacy of being members of the dynasty, only one case is known of one of the kings being killed because of his incapacity, when Antiochos VIII was murdered by his general, Herakleon; the assassin attempted to make himself king, but not being part of the dynasty, he failed; in a second case a new king, Seleukos VI, attempted to impose increased taxes, whereupon the mob in Tarsos burned the palace down, with Seleukos inside it; but a brother took over in his place, for it was not rage at the dynasty that had motivated the mob. There had been a number of usurpers interrupting the dynasty during the second century BC; only one of them made no pretence at being part of the dynasty, and he claimed a different legitimacy as a Macedonian; the rest all fabricated a descent from an earlier king.

Legitimization by Warfare

It is a notorious consideration in studying the great Macedonian or Roman dynasties of the Hellenistic and Imperial periods that each new king or emperor seems to have felt obliged to prove himself on the battlefield, or at least in war, almost as soon as he succeeded; this was one result of the way each of the dynasties began. In the case of the Julio-Claudians, the first Roman Imperial dynasty, the family came to rule by the victory of C. Julius Caesar in the civil war against Cn. Pompeius Magnus and the Senate, which was then reinforced by other victories in more civil wars by his heir and grand-nephew Octavian, who transformed himself later into Augustus. The political positions of both Caesar and Augustus were based on the command-in-chief of a victorious and numerous army, more than on any constitutional office or position they held, though they made sure to hold such positions as well. More generally, this emphasis on militarism-as-legitimation was a result of the similar emphasis within the Roman Republican political system, where consuls had long been expected to conduct a military campaign during their year in office. From the foundation of the imperial system, it was expected that any new emperor would wage war and collect military glory, though if he had already collected such glory before succeeding he was, in effect, excused that exercise. If any emperor did not do so, his support at home tended to decline. It was this expectation that led the utterly unmilitary Emperor Claudius to conduct a campaign for the conquest of Britain and to do so in person, and the next emperor – Nero – was overthrown in part because he had not done so – though he had sent generals to conduct campaigns in his name. The military glory provided by Augustus, and his stepson Tiberius, had been enough to support the next three emperors, militarily incompetent though they were. In the succeeding Flavian dynasty the founder Vespasian was already a successful warrior, leading a campaign in Palestine to suppress the Jewish rebellion, and his eldest son Titus finished off that war. These, therefore, already had the correct military credentials. But Titus' successor, Domitian (Vespasian's younger son), had been too young for that war, and spent most of his reign deliberately organizing new wars – in Dacia, Germany, and Britain – in part as a compensation for missing the earlier campaign, and as a legitimization of his rule.

In the case of the origins of the Hellenistic dynasties, because the contenders were heirs of Alexander the Great, and were fighting to control part of his conquests in a series of Macedonian civil wars, the kings tended also to emphasize their military prowess, and every member of the Ptolemaic and Seleukid dynasties, at least for the first century of their rule, seems to have felt obliged to initiate a war within a year of taking office, usually against each other. This was more distantly the result of the fact that warfare was one of the great necessary preoccupations of the original Macedonian dynasty in Macedonia itself, where it was directly related to the needs of national defence rather than to dynastic expectations. This necessity to make war had an appalling effect on the lives of the Seleukid kings in particular (see Chapter 9, 'Violent Deaths and Depositions').

Even the later Roman dynasties were required to be warlike: Nerva, for example, was clearly vulnerable as an emperor because of his total lack of military experience and expertise (as well, of course, because of his method of taking power, profiting from the murder of his predecessor, in which he was complicit). Claudius and Nero, profoundly unmilitary figures, had been similarly vulnerable, and the wholly unmilitary Antoninus Pius, who scarcely moved more than a hundred miles from Rome during his twenty-three year reign, organized a victory and in advance of the imperial frontier in Britain as soon as he acceded to the throne. The real founder of the Antonine dynasty, Trajan, had, however, piled up quite enough victories in warfare for his successors to live on for some time: Hadrian, however, was apparently determined not to conquer anyone, and as emperor he withdrew from some of Trajan's conquests, nevertheless he deliberately spent much of his reign with the army, supervising its training and inspecting legions in the auxiliaries. Eventually the practice of war became the single most important element in the selection of emperors, with the result that the third century emperors were almost all army men and nothing else.

Legitimization by Victory

The expiry of the Macedonian Argead dynasty in the generation after Alexander's death in 323 provided a situation in which several new dynasties emerged. The Seleukids, Ptolemies, and Antigonids all established themselves as more or less legitimate heirs of Alexander, and the Antipatrids almost did so, though they died out within a single generation of claiming the kingship. To these may be added the Attalids, whose origin was as heir to another failed dynasty, that of Lysimachos. In all cases the founder established his power and then, after a military victory, took the title of king, a title that had previously been reserved to the former royal family, but that now became hereditary in the several new royal families. The pattern thus established became one that several other men and families attempted to emulate in the next two centuries – in Baktria, in Asia Minor, in Cyrene – though only the Baktrians lasted long enough or are well enough known to be included here. It was this process that was essentially adopted at Rome, where the end of the republic and its civil wars produced substantially the same situation – the absence of the old mark of legitimacy – as that produced by the extinction of the old Macedonian dynasty.

It is not clear that such specific means of legitimating a man's title and rule was required in other lands. The Akhaimenids and Sassanids seem not to have conducted wars at their accession, and so were presumably secure on the throne from the start, while the Parthians found themselves so often under attack, or involved in civil warfare, that they found that wars came to them. Egyptian dynasties, and other families who may be said to have ruled 'national' states, such as Pontos and Cappadocia and Bithynia, probably did not need such legitimization, since it was their automatic inheritance to be the kings of their people. On the other hand, it is quite certain that new kings generally needed the support of being victorious, and there are elements of this in the post-Roman Western European dynasties of the early Middle Ages.

Legitimization through Divinity

A further aspect of claiming a legitimacy to rule because of the descent of the kings from earlier kings is the issue of the mythical divine ancestry claimed by a number of dynasties. This has already been discussed in the previous chapter ('The Mists of Time'), but it is worth being reminded of it in this context. Here it may suffice to note that this was one of the legitimizing tactics employed by dynasties whose origin lay far back in the past, in a period when few or no records existed. That is to say, it was generally an invention. However, it was also in many ways very effective.

Such a claim is also a species of that employed or stated by the religious installation of a Christian coronation, suggesting a touch of the divine because of the existence of a god way back in the family tree. Later dynasties in the Hellenistic and Roman kingdoms fabricated a version of this by a process of deification. The Ptolemies regularly proclaimed deceased kings and their wives as gods, and placed them in sarcophagi close to that of Alexander to partake of his divinity and reputation. So also, once Julius Caesar was deified by a Senate composed of men of his party, Octavian, his adopted son, could claim a divine ancestry – 'son of the deified Julius'. It was, of course, no more convincing than that an Anglo-Saxon king was described descended from Woden, and such claims to direct or even to pretended deification scarcely protected men such as Caligula and Ptolemy V from assassination. But the fact that they claimed such protection does suggest that they felt they needed it.

Chapter 4

Dynastic Durations

This chapter is based in many of its aspects on the statistics that are appended to each of the tables in the Catalogue. These are displayed in collective and graphic form in Tables A, B and C as follows.

Table A: Duration of Dynasties.

```
                              Number of Dynasties
                Cities         Regional                       Imperial
Years       1   5   10  15   1   5   10  15  20  25  30  35  40    1   5   10  15
1  -  50    ▯              ⌐========⌐                            ⌐====⌐
51 -  100   ⌐==========⌐   ⌐==================================⌐  ⌐====⌐
101 - 150   ⌐===⌐          ⌐==============================⌐      ⌐=====⌐
151 - 200   ⌐=⌐            ⌐================⌐                     |
201 - 250                  ⌐=============⌐                       ▯
251 - 300   |              ⌐=======⌐                             |
301 - 350   |              ⌐======⌐
351 - 400
401 - 450                  ▯                                     |
451 - 500                  ▯                                     |
```

Table B: Length of Activity of Roman Republican Dynasties.

```
                    Number of Dynasties
                1   5   10  15  20  25  30  35  40
Years
1  -  50        ⌐=======⌐
51 -  100       ⌐=========⌐
101 - 150       ⌐=======================⌐
151 - 200       ⌐=======⌐
201 - 250       ⌐======⌐
251 - 300       ⌐====⌐
301 - 350       ⌐===⌐
351 - 400       ▯
401 - 450       ⌐==⌐
451 - 500       ⌐==⌐
```

Table C: Numbers of Rulers in each Dynasty.

	Cities			Regional								Imperial		
	1	5	10	1	5	10	15	20	25	30	35	1	5	10
1														
2				□										
3	▭			▭▭▭▭								▭		
4	▭			▭▭										
5	▭			▭▭▭								▭		
6	▯			▭▭▭								▭		
7	▭			▭▭								▯		
8	I			▭▭								I		
9	I			▭▭								I		
10	I			▭								I		
11				▭										
12				□										
13	I			▭								▭		
14												I		
15				▭										
16				▯										
17	I			I										
18				I										
19				▭										
20				□								I		
21														
22				▭										
23														
24				I								I		
25				I								I		
26														
27														
28												I		
29												I		
30														
31														
32														
33				I										
34														
35				I										

Some Numerical Comparisons

Having imposed a minimum of three rulers or three generations of kings, or three men holding public office at Rome, on the dynasties I am considering, it is perhaps a little surprising that there are over thirty royal dynasties lasting less than fifty years, including one that lasted only two years (the Roman Imperial Decian dynasty): one might have expected three rulers to have lasted longer than that. At the other extreme there are four dynasties that lasted for more than four centuries (First Assyrian, Mithradatids in the Cimmerian Bosporos, Sassanids and Strathclyde/Alt Clut). Neither of these sets is particularly significant, of course, beside the fact that, of the 196 dynasties whose length can be discerned, half of them – ninety-two – lasted a century or less.

This is not a very good record, though the other side of these figures is that a quarter of the dynasties (fifty-two) lasted more than 150 years, and in fact twenty lasted longer than a quarter of a millennium. Yet even here it must be recalled that the period under investigation is roughly 1,800 years (from before 1000 BC to after AD 750), and that only two of the dynasties lasted even a quarter of that time. Every dynasty of the ancient world was no more than temporary phenomena on the political scene – less temporary than most Republican regimes, perhaps, but short-lived nevertheless. And this is from a human institution whose members would claim, if they ever thought about it, that their dynasty was permanent and never-ending.

In the Roman Republic the record is somewhat different. There were only eight of the families who lasted for less than half a century, and seven that lasted more than four centuries (the maximum possible in this case being about 470 years – 509 to 42 BC). The republican dynasties thus tended to last longer than the royals, though the conditions under which the two operated were considerably different. The Roman politicians held office for only brief periods, and most were not subject to assassination or murder, though they were likely to be killed in battle, given the bellicosity of the Roman state.

There were also some curious correspondences as well. The great majority (138 out of 196) of the royal dynasties lasted less than a century and a half, and this was the duration of just about half of the Romans (fifty-four out of ninety-five). After 150 years the frequency of duration drops off, sharply in the case of the royals, and less so but still decisively in the case of the Romans. It would seem, therefore, that most dynasties could expect at their inception only to rule for about a century and a half; any of them that passed that point were already unusual, and any that passed double that were quite exceptional – thirteen Roman and eighteen royals did so.

Actual years is, however, only one measure of their durations, though it is clearly the simplest and the most obvious one. It is also possible to measure both types of dynasty by the numbers of rulers they each counted – those who reigned in royal families, those who held major offices in Rome – and by the numbers of generations the dynasty lived through and during which they produced rulers or elected officials. Here again, hardly surprisingly, those that were the shortest in years were also the briefest in generations – 93 out of 196 royal dynasties lasted four generations or less; in numbers of rulers eighty-two had only five rulers or less. At the other extreme, however, there stretched a long list of dynasties with high numbers in both generations and rulers. The first Assyrian dynasty (that began well before the beginning of the Iron Age) counted nineteen generations, the descendants of Mithradates of Pontos in the Cimmerian Bosporan kingdom seventeen, and the Sassanid imperial family sixteen; not surprisingly, these also count some of the largest numbers of individual rulers – twenty-nine, thirty-one, and twenty-eight respectively. They are not, however, the highest on this count: the Merovingians, with their particular succession system and curious political organization, whereby power shifted to the Mayors of the Palaces, who sequestered the kings into monasteries whenever one showed any initiative or intention to exercise power, had thirty-three rulers, and the Seleukids, whose kings almost all died in battle or by murder, thus forcing rapid succession, had twenty-five.

The Roman Republican dynasties had a similar range, given the restrictions of the length of the republic's history: forty-six out of the ninety-five dynasties that can be tabulated lasted four generations or less; at the other extreme one family, the Manlii, lasted eighteen generations, and two reached sixteen (the Aemilii and the Sulpicii). Again, there is a certain discrepancy between these high numbers in the number of offices held, the three with high generation counts took fifty-seven, ninety-two and sixty-one offices respectively, but other families did better – the Fabii counted 105 and the Valerii 118. There is also further contrast between the republican dynasties and those that ruled in the subsequent empire – none of the latter lasted much beyond a century, and the number of rulers and generations were both low. Here is another decisive difference between the two polities.

Imperial Dynasties

All these are fairly crude measures, of course, so it is necessary to classify the dynasties in ways other than the length of their existence, or whether by years, rulers, offices, or generation. By classifying royal dynasties into the geographical extent of each dynasty's power and authority, that is as city, regional, or imperial dynasties, some useful comparisons can be attempted. The most prominent are, of course, the imperial dynasties, ruling the Assyrian, Arab, Hun, Roman, Persian or Hellenistic empires. At the other extreme are the dynasties that ruled single cities only, which are mainly located in Syria and Greece. In between are other dynasties that ruled territories too big to be thought of as city-states, but too small to be called empires, and these I have called regional, or sometimes 'national', states.

The imperial dynasties tended to last a relatively short time. Of the twenty-six dynasties that ruled empires, more than half (fifteen) lasted less than a century, and only five more than 200 years. In particular it is very noteworthy, as noted above, that none of the Roman or Byzantine dynasties lasted very long. Thirteen of these can be distinguished, from the Julio-Claudians to the Heraklian and the Isaurian; only three, the Julio-Claudians, the joint Valentinian-Theodosian, and the Heraklid dynasties lasted over a century, if only just, and the first two are very dispersed dynasties indeed. The Julio-Claudian succession process, if such a term exists, was erratic, to say the least, and I have included Julius Caesar in it, so beginning its life in 48 BC, where it might be more widely agreed that the victory at Actium in 31 BC would be a better starting point. (And yet Octavian was a Roman ruler, at first along with Anthony and Lepidus, from 42 onwards, and this is the date at which I have taken the republic to have ended.) Also the rule of the Valentinian-Theodosian family might be better seen as two separate dynasties – though they were extensively intermarried – and the whole is lengthened by the inclusion of the brief emperors Anthemius and Olybrius in 467–472; without them the dynasty would register only 101 years; it was in fact rather less complex than either the Julio-Claudian or the Antonine dynasties. Of the other, non-Roman, imperial dynasties, the Huns, and the two Muslim dynasties, the First Caliphs and the Umayyads also lasted less than a century, though all three are as erratic and complex as the worst of the Roman dynasties. So even the longest of the Roman dynasties are perhaps to be reduced in length, from 116–98 for the Julio-Claudians, and from 108–93 for the Valentinian-Theodosians to end in 457. This would mean that the longest Roman Imperial dynasty was that of Heraklios, whose family ruled for 101 years.

This says a good deal about the Roman Imperial polity and its instability, and if a century was the longest duration for Roman Imperial dynasties, then the rest are much shorter. Instability was extreme in the third century, but scarcely better before or after. None of these Roman Imperial dynasties would ever assume external power was assured. Note also that of the other, non-

Roman, imperial dynasties, the Huns and the two Muslims also lasted less than a century. This shortness is a curiosity that will need to be addressed in the chapter on succession (Chapter 6, 'Modes of Succession') which is where the seat of the problem appears to lie.

The longer-lived imperial dynasties are thus all based in the Middle East. The Iranian Sassanid dynasty, indeed, was one of the longest of the whole ancient world, at 427 years; and the first Assyrian dynasty lasted even longer; the Arsakids and the Seleukids, competitors, each lasted well over two centuries; the second Akhaimenid and the second Assyrian were somewhat shorter, but their durations were still over a century and a half, and so comfortably longer than the Roman maximum. The only imperial rulers of the Middle East who lasted less than a century were the two Muslim dynasties, the First Caliphs and the Umayyads.

Cities

At the other geographical and geopolitical extreme, the dynasties that ruled in city-states had generally even shorter lives: of the twenty-eight dynasties in this group – a slightly smaller number than there were imperial dynasties – only three lasted over two centuries, one of them for just over three, but fourteen lasted a century or less. The longest-lived were the two Spartan dynasties, the Agiads and the Eurypontids.

Two of the three exceptions in fact probably had much longer lives than I have here accepted. The origins of the Spartan dynasties were in the early Iron Age, the Greek Dark Ages, and the evidence for their existence before about 520 BC is secondary and based on myth. The names of the early Spartan kings are known, or at least lists of their names are known, but there is no indication apart from guesswork as to the length of time the dynasty existed – not even if there was a continuous dynastic line; the guesses vary widely, and all are wholly unreliable. I have therefore restricted the reckonable time for these dynasties to what can be more or less certainly accepted. The Argead dynasty of Macedon is in much the same position: seven undated kings precede the documented kings, which would extend the history of the dynasty for up to another century and a half. It is possible that the dynasty of Judah lasted for longer than the 148 years I have allowed it, but independent proof of its early rulers is not available, any more than it is for the early Spartan kings: indeed, the Judahite dynasty may also be considerably shorter. The claimed early Spartan kings cannot be accepted, therefore, and neither can those of Judah or Israel, or Macedon. (The Welsh dynasties are in the same case, and are omitted.)

It is worth also looking at imperial and city dynasties in terms of the number of generations they extended through. The city dynasties fared slightly worse than the imperial, nineteen out of twenty-eight city dynasties lasting four generations or less, but thirteen out of twenty-eight imperials expired at four or less. No doubt the city rulers' vulnerability, living close to their subjects, may provide an explanation for their dynasties' comparatively rapid destruction. By contrast looking at the regional dynasties, a little less than half succumbed in four generations or less (61 out of 136), but as a group they had a significantly longer life than either the imperials or the city dynasties.

These examples do emphasize an important point with regard to the dynasties that were located in city-states, and one that may also apply to those in regional states as well: that their claimed origins in the distant misty, mystical, mythical past may have been one of the major factors in their longevity. Yet other dynasties with similarly misty origins – in Ireland and England – did not last very long. Generalization in this area is exceedingly difficult.

The expectation of life for a city dynasty was thus normally relatively brief. Without the ability to call on the mysticism of an age-old succession, city dynasties were very vulnerable to overthrow, their main enemies being their own subjects. Their power base was small and narrow, both in relation to potential enemies from outside, and to their internal opponents as well. By defending themselves against both threats they rapidly acquired unpopularity by taxing the people to pay for that defence and by appearing to threaten their neighbours and internal enemies by building up their armed forces and employing squads of bodyguards, both expensive luxuries. The fact that most of these dynasties originated in *coups d'état* made them liable to be overthrown by a similar move by their internal opponents, of whom they always had plenty, particularly among those they had deprived of power. Their origins always cast a shadow over their existence, depriving them of the apparent legitimacy conferred by a distant ancestry, or by election – though legitimacy could be acquired if any dynasty lasted long enough. The shortness of the lives of most of the city dynasties was thus a function of the fact that they ruled in cities rather than that they were Greek or Syrian, which is where the great majority were located. Their lack of legitimacy in the eyes of many of their subjects, and probably of their neighbours, was also a source of vulnerability. This is all in direct contrast with the short imperial dynasties, but the fact that so many of the shortest of those ruled the Roman Empire was the decisive factor in their collective brevity.

Regional Dynasties

The third group of dynasties, the regional monarchies, ruling territories greater than a city-state but less than an empire, were very likely to last longer than most of the city or imperial dynasties, and six of them lasted for over three centuries. These longest are a significant group: three Irish dynasties, two in the Cimmerian Bosporos, and one in Caucasian Iberia. What these had in common, of course, was that they existed at the very margins of the ancient world. They were marginal in both the temporal and the geographical senses. In temporal terms all but the Crimean dynasties existed in the period after the fall of the Roman Empire – the Iberian Chosroids overlapped that fall – and in geographical terms they were all remote from the great events in the empires that extinguished so many other dynasties. It is noticeable, however that both the Bosporan and Iberian kingdoms were suppressed eventually by imperial regimes – Roman and Byzantine – when it suited them. It demonstrates that longevity among the regional dynasties was in large part due to the failure of the imperial regimes to reach them; other potentially lengthy dynasties were clearly cut off early because of imperial political convenience, notably those in the Middle East, where Assyria and Rome were responsible for extinguishing many dynasties, particularly in Syria.

A further comment is worth making also on the two Mithradatic dynasties. Mithradates VI, the founder of the second dynasty of the Cimmerian Bosporos was, of course, already king of his ancestral kingdom of Pontos. It may be argued that the two parts of the dynasty, that which ruled Pontos before him and that which ruled Bosporos after him, ought to be put together and considered as a single dynasty, as I have done with the Herodian family, but not with the three Parthian dynasties. Certainly they were both parts of the same family, and to do so would be to recognize a dynasty that lasted for 754 years, counting thirty-seven rulers in twenty-three generations (a reign length average of twenty years, and a generation length average of thirty-three years). This would be a most impressive record indeed. Yet the two elements of the dynasty were really quite separate, except in the person of Mithradates himself. The two kingdoms had little or no connection with each other, except during his and his son's reign. For Mithradates himself only seems to have been in his Bosporan kingdom briefly at the end of his life, and he had ruled it by posting a son there to deputize for him. So the effective connection between the two was his son Pharnakes, installed by Mithradates, but who never ruled in Pontos; before him the dynasty was Pontic, after him it was not. It seems best to keep the two parts separate. This conclusion applies all the stronger to the Irish dynasties, who all claimed a connection with the original dynasty of the High Kings. This may or may not have been correct, but the essential fact is that these were separate dynasties, and ruled separate kingdoms: their claimed origin was little more than a pious fiction.

This decision also applies, perhaps even more vehemently than in Ireland, to the other example of the dynasty divided between states, the Arsakids who ruled in Parthia, Armenia, and Iberia. In all cases these were clearly distinct and separate ruling dynasties who ruled distinct and separate kingdoms. They are therefore all treated, like the Mithradatids, as distinct.

This issue also arises in Republican Rome. There, a number of families produced separate branches, notably, for example, the Cornelii, which had no less than five. Some of these have to be treated as separate because no link can be detected connecting them, as with the Furii, the Iulii, the Minucii, the Claudii, and others, even though they may well be originally of the same descent. (The break almost always occurs in the fourth century BC, where sources are poor.) The fact that there was a break in the descent (if that is what happened) means that those that can be reconstituted must be seen as separate dynasties. The Cornelii and the Fulvii had sub-families that ran in parallel and contemporaneously, and these cannot be treated as the same family. These sub-families operated independently of each other, so far as can be seen. They are thus counted and treated as distinct and separate dynasties.

Of the rest of the regional dynasties, only 17 lasted for less than half a century, and 46 for between 50 and 100 years, but in general they tended to last longer than either the city or imperial dynasties – 49 lasted between 100 and 200 years, and another 20 between 2–300 years, a reversal of the proportion seen among both the city and the imperial dynasties. And the same considerations apply in these long-lived dynasties as with those that lasted even longer; many of them were located away from the great imperial war zones in Greece or Syria, or flourished after the collapse of the Roman Empire, though some were maintained in existence, especially the Middle East, and for a relatively brief period, by Roman permission and support.

It was thus clearly advantageous for a dynasty, if they aimed, as they all surely did, to last as long as possible – aiming surely at immortality, if they ever considered their longevity – to rule over a territory larger than a city-state but smaller than an empire, and its territory should also be somewhat remote from the centre of great and violent events, and in particular well away from the routes of expansion of the great empires. No doubt having a reasonably large territory in which to move about conduced to a king's personal safety, but it is also the case that many of these dynasties also had particularly strong local roots in their territories: in many cases they were as close to being national states as the ancient world can show. The Urartian, Bithynian, Pontic, Cappadocian, and Nabataean states had dynasties, like those of Sparta and Judah, which were home-grown, not imposed from outside, and not imposing themselves on unwilling subjects; so also did the various Irish dynasties. The successive Armenian dynasties, all originating from outside that country, and imposed on the land by imperial neighbours, evidently identified strongly from the first of their kings with their adopted kingdom. The safety of these dynasties lay as much, or more, in the traditional loyalty of the people as in a specific size or area or location of the kingdom, but popular loyalty was clearly more effective in these local states than in the city-states; the imperial dynasties were perhaps too remote and grand to require or indeed attract real loyalty, though they did attract forms of worship, as might be directed at any impersonal natural force. In all this of course these regional dynasties resemble the surviving modern European dynasties, who exist as much by contented local loyalty as by any real political power or need.

This overlaps with the other classification that it is possible to make: by geographical location and ethnic origin. Frequently these two are the same – Cappadocia, Macedon, Numidia, for example, were countries inhabited by Cappadocians, Macedonians and Numidians, distinct peoples with distinct territories, traditions, and languages, and that were governed by men who were native to the countries. But there are other instances that are best thought of as either an area or as a people, without a direct connection between the two. For example, the post-Roman barbarian invaders frequently ended their wanderings as controllers of regional kingdoms, but it is easiest to think of their dynasties as ruling those wandering peoples rather than the territories they acquired during some part of their movements. They were Visigoths, Burgundians, Ostrogoths, Vandals, and Lombards, rather than kings of Spain or Italy or Africa. This distinction is all the easier since they all tended to maintain themselves quite deliberately as a separate people, remaining as distinct as possible from the populations they had conquered, adopting different religions, or maintaining their own languages.

The supposed integrationist policy of the Franks marked them out as different from the start, and as a much more stable polity. These all therefore fall into two groups: the barbarian groups who settled in the former Roman lands close to the Mediterranean and that had fairly short dynastic existences – the Vandal dynasty lasted only a little over a century, the first Ostrogothic half that, while the Visigothic kingdom's longevity contrasted glaringly with the inability of any dynasty to maintain itself for any length of time after the extinction of the original founding dynasty that had lasted only a little over a century; the second Ostrogothic and the Burgundian dynasties vanished even more quickly. These had generally become the target of greater and/ or imperial powers, being thus cut short in the same way as many other dynasties by being the object of imperial expansion. The surviving Roman Empire in Constantinople, for example, accounted for the Vandals and the two Ostrogothic dynasties; their destruction was in large part due to the policy of the ruling peoples remaining separate from the preceding and subjugated Roman inhabitants, so becoming easier targets than if they could rely on support generally; there was little reason for the (native Roman) populations to support the Vandals or the Ostrogoths.

The other group of these barbarian dynasties is composed of those in the north-west, in Gaul and the British Isles, all of whose dynasties (the Merovingians, the Anglo-Saxons, Dalriada, the Picts, the Britons, the Irish) had above-average longevities, though the Dalriadan dynasties were ruling contemporaneously, and they and many of the Irish dynasties only intermittently produced rulers. The difference between the two groups is partly that those around the Mediterranean were vulnerable to the revival of the East Roman Empire under Justinian, though it was not the Romans who eliminated the Burgundians or the Rugians or the Sueves, and the Visigoths had a particular and peculiar antipathy to the establishment of any dynastic succession. The Merovingians' process of division and partible inheritance was the very reverse of the Visigothic preference, and perhaps it was this that allowed the dynasty to last so long – for there was always a member of the dynasty somewhere to inherit. Similarly the Anglo-Saxon dynasties had some preference for direct primogeniture inheritance, but this tended to alter into succession by the eldest royal male later in the dynastic life until they all simply died out. The test, in a way, lies with the later dynasties of Italy: the Lombards in Italy and Benevento established relatively long-lived dynasties where the Ostrogoths had failed, precisely because they were not subjected to an overwhelming attack by the temporarily revived Roman Empire. By the time the Lombards were a serious threat the empire was fully preoccupied with the Sassanid and Islamic threats from the east. Once again it seems that it was distance from a rampaging imperial regime that helped to ensure a dynasty's longevity.

In all this it seems that in longevity the Roman Republican dynasties were more closely similar to the regional dynasties than to those of the cities. (Rome is generally described as a city-state, but it was always large in territory and it was soon clear that it was originally a state, then an empire, even while it was a republic. Most of the Roman aristocrat dynasties were also very much longer-lived than their Imperial Roman successors, who had such distressingly short lives. It is obvious, however, that the conditions under which the Roman Republican dynasties operated were very different from those of the royal dynasties, and still more those of any empire. The Romans in the republic were operating in a much less violent political environment, at least until its last century. They also permitted succession to spread much more widely through the various members of the family than a royal family could afford to do. The strain on the magistrates at Rome, ruling as they did collectively rather than singly, and holding office for only a year or two at a time, was clearly less than that on a single king, at least if he was conscientious, and not least if he had to go to war regularly.

And yet, despite these advantages, it remains the fact that half the Roman dynasties exercised power in the republic's hire offices for less than a century and a half (fifty-four out of ninety-five), and over half lasted five generations or less (fifty-eight out of ninety-five); by comparison the regional royal dynasties did slightly better, with over half lasting both longer than 150 years (97 of 140) and five generations (seventy-eight). The numbers in both, however, are substantially better than those of both imperial and city dynasties. It is clear that the Roman dynasties were, as for much of their existence they will surely have insisted, comparable to royalty, at least in their longevity, just as, for much of its existence, the Roman Republic was more than a city-state and yet less than an empire.

Returning to the 'invading-barbarian' dynasties in the western parts of the defunct Roman Empire, they are part of a wider group of dynasties of similar origin. It is clear that potentially these were dynasties of some longevity, if they could keep clear of the dying blows of an empire whose former territory they were squatting on. Other examples show that same pattern. The Arsakids of Parthia survived the repeated attacks of the Seleukids for a century after they first seized part of that empire. Their survival strategy was to retire into the desert from which they had emerged when an attack came. They did survive, despite until very late in their progress being much the weaker of the contestants. The Battiads colonized the territory, Cyrenaica, which was without a political organization higher than the tribe when they took control; their more efficient political organization, as well as better weaponry, was surely one of the main elements in their survival. On the other hand, the Nubian invaders of Egypt were driven out by the revived native Egyptian dynasty after only two or three generations. The pattern holds: an invader must keep clear of the surviving imperial power. And any that does keep clear has a good chance of a reasonably long existence.

Certain territories were particularly fertile in dynasty production. Asia Minor was one, including in that area Armenia and the Caucasus, in the periods after the collapse of the Bronze Age empires, and before and after the Akhaimenid Empire and before the Roman conquest. Note also the long sequence of Egyptian dynasties. Greek dynasties were relatively few, being mainly located in the colonized areas – Sicily, Cyrenaica, the Bosporos – but the Macedonian dynasties, in Macedon itself and in the east, and the Spartan, had lengthy existences; those located within Greece itself were generally brief – Corinth, Sikyon, Samos, Thessaly – always with the exception of the Spartans. The British Isles in the period after the end of the Roman rule were also prolific in producing dynasties, though they did tend to rule only small territories; later they generally fell victim to the expansionist policies of imperialist neighbours, though these neighbours were usually, at least until the Viking invasion, other Anglo-Saxons.

Reasons

There is, as I have noted briefly, a distinction to be drawn between the three types of dynasty; imperial, regional and civic, in terms of their longevity, or lack of it. The regional dynasties were much more likely to enjoy a reasonably long life than either the dynasties that ruled empires or those confined to cities. The distance from, or proximity to, an expansionist or revengeful empire has been suggested to be one of the decisive factors in a dynasty's longevity, but there are other reasons, particularly in respect of the origins of these dynasties. A dynasty ruling a regional state originated in all likelihood at the same time as the kingdom itself, indeed it may well have formed the kingdom by the conquest of one or two of its early parts, often based on a local place, and often drawing on the loyalties of the local population by its more or less benevolent rule; in other words, they ruled what was as close to a national state as the ancient world could find: Sparta, Macedon, Pontos, Cappadocia, Egypt, are examples. Some of the post-Roman barbarian states had a similar condition, but those that lasted longest were those that integrated their post-Roman populations with their own invading peoples most successfully – contrast the Lombards and the Ostrogoths, the Franks and the Burgundians – or subjugated them utterly (which is another form of a simulation), as seems to have been the case in the Anglo-Saxon kingdoms.

The origins of city and imperial dynasties, on the other hand, were almost always the result of usurpation or violence, or both. By definition an empire was formed by the conquest or enclosure into its territory of the lands of a series of preceding states, a circumstance to which the people of the conquered lands might well take continued exception, and of which their peoples were liable to be reminded by the continued existence of the old kingdom as an imperial province and even of the old royal family as local lords. Even more destabilizing, the first conquest of an imperial dynasty, even if it was that family's own homeland, was usually by force, or by other means, which could be considered to be questionable or illegitimate. Resentment of this could be very long-lasting. Then, in part connected with this inconvenient fact, in none of the great empires was the imperial founding dynasty the one that went on to rule the empire afterwards. The Julio-Claudians overthrew the Roman senatorial republic to form their empire, and during their century of rule the former Roman Republican dynasties almost entirely died out, and one of the results was that the dynasty's original supporters ceased to be able or willing to do so; it fell from power very easily in the chaos of the revolution of AD 69. The founders of the Akhaimenid Empire were displaced by Darius I's collateral dynasty; the Arsakids and Sassanids emerged from Iranian provinces to rule the whole land in place of their predecessors; the Seleukids carved out their empire from the ruins of the Akhaimenid Empire that had been brought down by Alexander's conquest, in the process replacing the first of Alexander's successors, the kingdom of Antigonos. Seleukos I conquered his empire slowly, section by section, over a period of over thirty years. The Assyrian Empire was formed by an increasingly brutal process of conquest and destruction. The original Muslim emperors, the immediate successors of Muhammad, gave way to the dynasty of Muawiya of the Umayyads. Once these empires had been formed their politics ceased to be matters of foreign policy and became an internal contest in which eternal vigilance was the price of imperium: most imperial dynasties were overthrown by an internal revolution, and when that had been accomplished once it could be repeated relatively easily. That is to say, no ruling imperial dynasty could claim the legitimacy that was conferred on an original regional dynasty by its home-grown quality. It is noticeable that several of the great imperial founders – Julius Caesar, Darius I, Seleukos I, Ardashir, Attila, the First Caliphs – were outsiders or dissidents or rebels to the empires they controlled.

The brevity of the city dynasties derived from a similar source. Those that were long-lived – the two Spartans – were rooted in their cities from, in effect, time immemorial, and derived much of their authority and power from that fact. The short-lived dynasties had all too often been founded by a man who had seized power in a *coup d'état* at the expense of an earlier regime, many of whose members survived, either at home or as exiles. This was the origin of all the Greek tyrants, none of whose dynasties lasted beyond a century. The early Syrian city dynasties of the Iron Age were similarly brief: only one of them may have lasted a century and a half (Bit-Agusi, assuming Judah's history is invented); two later Syrian dynasties that lasted well, Kommagene and Emesa, did so in part because of Roman support. Having seized power themselves, these usurping rulers only showed how easy it was to do so. Living, as they had to, close to their subjects, there were also personally vulnerable – hence the necessity of tyrants to begin their tyranny by acquiring a personal bodyguard, a deed that inevitably enhanced local resentment, and that also put armed men in close proximity to that ruler. The Greek tyrants were commonly eventually removed, and a republican regime was then resorted to, not always successfully over the long term, as Sicily's lamentable instability showed; and this instability developed in several of the Syrian states also, though the Assyrian wars of the ninth and eighth centuries BC could delay that process by requiring a constant state of armed vigilance in the Syrian states – or by rulers who accepted Assyrian suzerainty – and that put a premium on army command by the kings, and so enhanced their internal authority. The one really successful tyranny-replacement regime was, of course, the Roman Republic, lasting something over four centuries, though it went through several crises and alterations in that time, any of which threatened to overthrow it – as did in fact happen in the end.

We therefore have the curious circumstance that the dynasties ruling the largest states, the great empires, were most closely similar in their characteristics to those ruling the smallest, the cities; whereas the dynasties that ruled within one city, the Roman Republic, were most closely similar in the same way to the royal kingdoms.

The duration of a dynasty thus depended in large part on the way it grew to power. Other factors, which cannot now be estimated, clearly entered into the equation in individual cases: genetic inheritance is evidently one. The apparent revival of the Ptolemaic dynasty with the marriage of Ptolemy V with the vigorous Seleukid princess Kleopatra Syra, is a clear case; the Seleukids themselves suffered such a sequence of violent deaths (only one of their kings died in his bed) that the dynasty's survival must in part be put down to its genetic inheritance and its prolific rate of reproduction. The consistent failure of the Julio-Claudians to reproduce was a major factor in their failure politically. Later dynasties, until the time of Constantine, were no more prolific; and in the only cases where inheritance went to the sons of emperors in the first three centuries of the empire, only one was not murdered; that was Titus, who ruled for only two years: the rest – Domitian, Commodus, Geta,

Caracalla – were all assassinated. It is clear that the politics of Imperial Rome, unlike that of the preceding republic, was strongly antipathetic towards any sort of genetic succession.

One of the major elements in dynastic succession was the institution of the harem; having several fertile women available clearly meant that the birth of a son was much more likely than in a family condition of monogamy – and this was one reason for the long survival of the Sassanids, the Parthians, and the Akhaimenids. However, being the ruling family of a regional state was the condition most likely to conduce to a dynasty's long life.

Chapter 5

Generations and Reigns

One of the reasons I began this investigation was an irritation at the frequent assumption made by historians and archaeologists concerning the length of a generation of twenty or twenty-five or thirty or thirty-three or thirty-five or even forty years – there is no agreement, even within a single work, on a particular figure, and each worker seems to choose the figure that suits his or her own theory, or perhaps guess. A similar irritation exists over the parallel assumption that a reign is the equivalent of a generation, when a moment's investigation or thought would demonstrate that in most cases this is quite wrong. These dual assumptions lead to a regular over-estimate of the length of the time represented by the reigns of undated or undatable rulers, and since chronology has to be the rock-foundation of all historical study, this means that any historical reconstruction based on such faulty assumptions is automatically wrong as well.

Sparta

The two Spartan and the Macedonian Argead dynasties provide a useful case study on the problem, a study that will illustrate the issues involved. In a peculiar and unique case, Sparta possessed two royal families, the Agiads and the Eurypontids, who reigned in tandem until late in the third century BC. The names of the kings of the two dynasties are well-attested, but both dynasties fall into two parts; from 491 BC to their ends in 227 and 217 BC, the kings, their relationships, their dates of accession and of their deaths (or deposition) are well and clearly known from various sources contemporary with the events. Before 491 BC only the names of the kings are known, and the two sources give slightly different lists. Their dates are not known, though both lines are said to descend in a direct line from father to son in these early generations/reigns. They are said to have originated as twins, which should mean that their originating date was the same.

This early period is crucial for the proper understanding of the Spartan polity, which was as peculiar and unique as its dual monarchy. The origins of its peculiarities are generally assumed to belong to its earliest years, when the dual monarchy was also instituted, though a connection with the difficulties of the war to conquer Messenia in the eighth century seems most likely. It might seem that by assigning an arbitrary period of years to the reign of each of the early kings the approximate originating date of that polity might seem to be detected. To cite only two examples, AHM Jones used a sequence of precise dates, originally used by Eusebios in the fourth century AD, and based on calculations by Eratosthenes in the second century BC and Sosibios in the second century AD – none of these being anywhere near the times of the kings in question. This calculation gave dates for many of the early kings of the undated list (ten of the Agiads, nine of the Europontids), but there were none for the rest (six and five respectively), who separated these early kings from the well-attested and well-dated later kings. This provided a commencing date of 1102 BC for both dynasties, which assumed an average reign length of thirty-five and a half years for the undated Agiad kings, and thirty-eight years for the Europontids, counting back from the first firm date in Spartan dynastic history. This is 491 BC, when King Damaratos was expelled and thus deposed. However, by avoiding giving any dates to the middle kings, this calculation also evaded the precision aspired to – in addition to which the whole scheme was based on a supposed connection to the Trojan War, which itself is undated except by a similar set of unanchored calculation – if, indeed, that war ever actually took place. The whole system depends on a circular argument, which had absolutely no single concrete fact or date within it. In a different calculation LF Fitzhardinge similarly assigned a start date to each dynasty, though this was different for each of them (930 BC for the Agiads, 895 BC for the Europontids), thereby denying the simultaneous origins of the two dynasties. This produces the net result of an Argiad average reign of 29.3 years, and a Europontid reign average of 26.9 years. The rationale for any of these dates is not at all clear.

The issue is not made easier by discrepancies that exist between the lists of the early kings provided by the sources (Herodotus and Pausanias), which are in any case – again – very late by comparison with the putative dates of the earliest kings, not to mention doubts about the reliability of any of the lists in the first place. None of these sources are anything but dubious, either for the names of the kings or for their dates. This is not a problem I can discuss here, as my purpose is mainly to deal with the generation and reign problems. I may say, however, that I do not believe that we can accept that any of the lists are in any way accurate. The only way of checking is by finding other confirmatory sources, and these exist only in occasional details.

The division of the records of the two dynasties at 491 BC does provide, however, a control with which to measure the likelihood of the accuracy of the back-calculations. The period from 491 BC to the end of the two houses contains the reigns of fourteen Agiad kings (over 274 years) and twelve Europontid kings (for 264 years). The average length of the Agiad reigns in that period is thus only 19.6 years and that of the Europontids 22 years. Calculating backwards on these bases the Agiad line should have begun about 824 BC and the Europontid about 865 BC. It will be noted that the differences between Jones' figures and this estimate is two and a half centuries, and between this and Fitzhardinge's lower dates is a century in the Agiad case, but only thirty years in that of the Europontid, which he begins after the Agiad. And yet using these calculations reverses the priority of the Agiads over the Europontids – and again ignores their originating simultaneity.

There is, however, another calculation that can and indeed must be done. The succession of both lines was never distinctly from father to son in the later period, with the attested dates after 491, but it fairly often shifted between brothers or onto cousins, or even skipped from grandfather to grandson. Among the Agiads after 491, there were in fact only six cases of direct succession from father to son, and seven among the Eurypontids, while on seven and four occasions respectively inheritance was not direct. It is therefore necessary to calculate not just the average reign lengths, but also the generational period between the later kings, which provides figures of 30.4 years for the Agiads, and 26.4 years for the Europontids. This calculation thus provides yet another new set of supposed dates for the undated lines. If the earlier succession really was directly from father to son, as is claimed in the late sources, then assuming the generations were the same average length as later, one can calculate that the Agiad line began in 1008 BC and the Europontid in 940 BC.

This works, however, only if the succession among the earlier, undated, kings in both houses really was directly from father to son for all those kings. In each case there were seventeen of these kings – quite an astonishing coincidence of numbers, which was not repeated in the later history of the houses – and the claim of direct succession is made for both of them. Given the later history of the two houses this is so highly unlikely as to be regarded as impossible. If the successions were as erratic and unpredictable in the pre-491 Kings as they were in those after 491, one would expect the seventeen Agiad kings to represent perhaps eleven generations, and that the seventeen Eurypontid kings would represent fourteen generations. This would then provide start dates of the Agiads of 825 BC, and for the Eurypontids of 861 BC.

(It is particularly arresting that this calculation produces dates for both lines within a few years of the reign length calculation made above; not, of course, that this proves anything, but it is worth pointing out.) And so, if the record of the names and numbers of kings is accurate (as it probably is not) these calculations suggest that it is unlikely that the system of the dual Spartan monarchy is earlier than the late ninth century in origin.

There is also a further element involved. The two monarchies are supposed to be descended from twin sons, and before them are said to be five earlier kings, of whom the first was Herakles. Making the same calculations this would provide a whole new set of possible dates for the accession of Herakles as king of Sparta – if indeed he was ever king of Sparta, or, of course, if he ever existed.

By using these methods of calculation, therefore – all equally reasonable, or unreasonable – many different dates for the origin of the Spartan monarchy can be derived, spread over three centuries. Yet the purpose of the exercise is not to cast doubt on the antiquity of the monarchy, nor on that of the political system of which it was an integral part – though it surely does that – but to demonstrate that the methods of calculation using supposed average lengths of reigns or average lengths of generations is extremely hazardous, and that the results are both unreliable and unacceptable; that is, they are not worth doing.

Macedon

The point may be reinforced by a similar calculation that can be made for the Macedonian royal house of the Argeadai. This was supposedly founded by three brothers, originally from Argos, of which the youngest, Perdikkas I, is reckoned to be the first Argead king. Again the undated, unprovenanced kings are said to have descended from father to son, whereas the Macedonian royal house in the well-sourced period is very complicated, with the kingship going to brothers and cousins, and with intervening usurpers. Nevertheless, taking the first six undated generations, and aligning the list with the later seven generations of kings from Alexander I to Alexander IV, the son of Alexander the Great, and taking the latter as the control group, the results can be obtained to show that the origin of the Macedonian Argead dynasty was in or between 571 and 657 BC, as hopeless a result as that with Sparta. And none of these dates can be accepted until the undated kings are verified in the genealogy, and the genealogy itself is also confirmed as accurate. Given the history of the later dated kings, and the violence of Macedonian history in the fifth and fourth century BC, it is highly likely that the lowest possible figure (571 BC) is the nearest to be correct – but its precision is spurious; we do not know, and cannot find out with the present sources, when the dynasty originated.

Another point worth making is to take the actual examples of dynasties with six kings, of which there are twenty-one examples. The averages for the lengths of reign in these cases range from six years to twenty-seven, with the median at seventeen years. But there are only eighteen cases of dynasties of six generations – not just reigns – (assuming the Macedonian succession was from father to son – not impossible by any means), and these have average generation lengths ranging from fourteen years to thirty-six years: the median is at twenty-three years. So the question is: which figure between eight and thirty-six is the one to choose? Only one example falls on the generation median, only one on the reign median. The question therefore answers itself: it is an impossible choice, and any figure that one lights on between eight and thirty-six has only one chance in twenty-five of being right.

The Worth of Calculations

The general point, therefore, is that no single figure for either a 'typical' or an 'average' length of a reign or a generation is attainable. But this conclusion is not simply based on three rather abstruse and theoretical calculations about undated sequences of reigns, whose very existence cannot be verified. It can be demonstrated by contemplating the reigns and generations of the dynasties here under study, that is, those that are known and certain. Taking average lengths of reigns first, the results stretch from one year to thirty-three years. In fact, as one would expect, the extremes might be ignored as either unreliable or atypical. The shortest averages, those of the brief Messian and Aurelian dynasties of the Roman Empire, each with a one-year average, and the Gordian dynasty with two, are odd: these Roman dynasties are clearly anomalous in that they ruled in an exceptionally disturbed period. One might therefore discard them and recalculate. But to begin this way is a slippery proceeding: one quickly finds that almost every dynasty is peculiar or different in some way; this route is thus to be avoided. These low scoring dynasties are well-attested; these low reign length averages must therefore be accepted as quite possible.

At the other extreme, on the other hand, there is a different and more difficult problem. The two dynasties with averages for their reigns of over thirty years are unacceptable for the best of reasons: they are not reliably recorded. The dates of the rulers of the second Thracian dynasty, where three known rulers produce an average reign length of thirty-three years does so only because it is guessed that the dynasty lasted for a century; this is therefore also guesswork. The average for the dynasty of the Medes at thirty-two years is also an estimate as the date of the dynasty's origin is unknown, and there is a possible gap in the sequence of kings, so that there may well be more kings who should be included. On the other hand, the high averages for several dynasties in the upper twenties and at thirty years have to be accepted: Pontos (thirty), and the Second Kition (twenty-nine), the Hieronids of Syracuse and the Bithynian dynasty (both twenty-eight) are fully acceptable, for all these dynasties are well-dated from good sources. Since these well-attested examples produce averages of up to thirty years, the two at thirty-plus may also be accepted, since they are not really outside the bounds of possibility. It therefore seems that an average length of reign of a dynasty may be anywhere between one year and thirty-three years, and that without specific information about the individual king's reigns and dates it is unwise to choose any particular figure in any attempt to calculate the duration of an unknown dynasty. And, since the extreme for known dynasties is thirty-three years, the popular guesses of thirty, thirty-three or thirty-five years are some of the least likely estimates.

There will be others in the Catalogue that exhibit similar uncertainties, but the extremes at one and thirty-three years for average reigns are clear enough to indicate the range of possibilities. An even wider range of possibilities is shown by looking at the reigns of individual rulers. There are many reigns that lasted less than a year, as might be expected. At the other extreme, reigns of over fifty years are by no means uncommon – there are at least twenty-one examples; there are two kings who reigned for seventy-five years; one for seventy, and three for sixty or more.

With such a wide range, both of individual reign lengths, which is only to be expected, and of averages, which is perhaps less looked-for, it is not possible to choose any particular number as representative of the length of reigns as a species, which can be applied as a chronographic insertion to decrease ignorance. As it happens, the average of averages for the length of reigns is 16.6 years, which is perhaps the only figure that could be sensibly used – though it has the disadvantage of a spurious precision. But too much depends on geographical location, numbers of rulers, wars, on internal dynastic disputes and revolutions, and on genetic inheritance, for any average to have any usefulness or meaning.

The Arabian Calculations

This average of averages of 16.6 years has also been arrived at in the only other case of such a calculation I have come across, by KA Kitchen in his work on delimiting ancient Arabian dynasties. He uses as his basis the kings of ancient Egypt, who were numerous enough to provide a good statistical count. However, he then used that figure to ascribe tentative dates to the Arabian kings, a few of whom could be dated by other evidence, though usually to no more than a single year (from, for example, a dated inscription), with the length of their reigns unknown. It is also scarcely necessary to point out that the conditions of life and royal life vary widely between Egypt and Arabia; they are so different that direct comparison is clearly dangerous and must be misleading. The danger of this procedure is that such suggested and tentative dates might be taken seriously. The reign lengths he suggests all hover near the average – and, as I have pointed out above, this is not what occurs in reality. One would expect, given the large number of rulers involved, that their reigns would range from one year (or less) to fifty or sixty years; it attributes these reigns in multiples of five years, five to thirty-five. (I have nonetheless used the suggested dates, unsatisfactory though they are, in the Catalogue of Dynasties.)

Calculations Here

The same general comments can be made in relation to generational lengths. It should perhaps be made clear that a 'generation' in a ruling dynasty is here taken to be the period of time between the death of a ruler and that of the last of his sons or his nephews, or their contemporary cousins, if they were monarchs. In some dynasties, amongst Arabs and Merovingians in particular, but also some of the Anglo-Saxons, the Scots of Dalriada and the Irish, succession went by seniority, so that several members of a single generation, brothers and cousins, could rule successively (but see also on this Chapter 6, 'Modes of Succession'). All these kings will thus count as a single generation. Thus, although the Merovingians had thirty-three kings who ruled (or at least reigned), these were spread over only fourteen generations. (The tables of genealogies in the Catalogue are laid out by generations, which are numbered.)

In considering the results of the calculations, once again the extremes at either end of the list have to be examined with particular care, and this time the extremes will need to be discarded. At the shorter end there are the third century Roman dynasties once again, with an average generation length of one or two years, their reigns were so brief that they cannot be used to provide evidence in this case. They may be discarded. With some reluctance I will include the other Roman third century dynasty, the Licinians, with an average generation length of five years, the Palmyran with six, and the second Ostrogothic with seven. All these are certainly anomalous, and had virtually all their members killed in battle or murdered. But death by violence was perhaps the commonest cause of death of all amongst the ancient dynasties; having all your members die that way was only being even more unfortunate or careless otherwise (see Chapter 9, 'Violent Deaths and Depositions'). I will thus take five years as the lowest average generation length worth including.

At the further extreme there are three poorly dated and very early Irish dynasties of unusual generational length. The highest Irish score, forty years for the dynasty of High Kings of only three generations but eight rulers, each of whom inherited the High Kingship after long intervals – out of the 121 years of their generation spread those eight kings ruled for only fifty-eight years between then. A certain doubt as to the accuracy of all this is surely permissible. The same applies to the other two high-scoring Irish dynasties, and so all three must be discounted. On the other hand, the next two on the list, Numidia and the Artaxiads of Armenia, with thirty-five and thirty-six years respectively, are more convincing, even with a twenty-year gap at one point for the Numidians, and may be taken as authentic, as is the Pontic dynasty at thirty-four years. We may take the Artaxiad average of thirty-six years, therefore, as the maximum generation length that was normally attainable in the ancient world. (It is noticeable that the figure thirty-five is one of the favourite choices for insertion when generational chronologies are being invented; just one year less than the maximum discovered here, and of which there are only two cases. At thirty-four there are also two examples, and at thirty-three, another popular choice, only three. Thirty-five is therefore one of the most unlikely generation lengths, and thirty-three is little better.)

The length of a dynasty's generation may therefore be anything from five years to thirty-six. This is more or less the same range as for average reigns, but the weight of the distribution is markedly higher, with a median of fourteen years, which would, I suppose, if a hypothetical figure is required, be the one to use. And yet there were forty-seven dynasties showing a generation length of ten years and less, and twenty-seven at thirty or more. There were fifty-one dynasties with an average generation length of between thirteen and fifteen years (out of 192), and so there is only a fifteen per cent chance of any generation of rulers landing on the median or within a year of that figure;

there is as big a chance of the length falling below that range, and a slightly smaller chance of it being above that range.

It is not therefore possible to assign any particular length of time to any dynasty by conjuring up some hypothetical average. Any figure that is chosen is likely to have no more than a minor possibility of being correct – that is, it would very probably be wrong, and so, basing any calculations on it would involve ramifying distortions. Only by finding out information about numbers and the relationships of rulers, their precise dates, the particulars of the accession of the first ruler, and the date of the end of the dynasty, is it possible to find any average that applies to any particular dynasty – and, of course, at that point no guess is required. To do the opposite, to derive dates and reign lengths by inventing an average, is simply wrong, and will inevitably result, if the invented figures are used as a basis for other chronological conclusions, in a thorough distortion. It is bad historical practice, a complete waste of time, and as a practice it should be abandoned.

The conclusion must be that to apply any figure at all to try to calculate the length of a dynasty, either by looking at reigns or looking at generations, is to produce a guess – it is no more than that – which has only a one in seven chance of being approximately correct – and it will therefore almost certainly be wrong and will therefore produce a misleading result. No date derived from such calculation can be relied on under any circumstance.

Despite this negative conclusion to one part of this investigation, it is clearly possible to use the results for other, more positive, work. An investigation of reign lengths and generation lengths according to geography and period produces some useful contrasts; of the lowest averages eight are Roman Imperial dynasties, and seven are Irish or Scots. But the greatest number of these very short reign lengths are the result of a mode of succession through siblings and cousins; of those dynasties with average reign lengths of less than ten years – of which there are forty-seven cases – such succession schemes account for at least seventeen of them; sheer brevity of dynastic existence accounts for many of the rest, notably the Roman cases, but also of local dynasties that were battered by conquerors – Elam, the second Ostrogothic, Palmyra.

At the other extreme eighteen dynasties had average reign lengths of twenty-five years or more. Some of these are poorly recorded, so that the estimates of dates may be generous. Many of them were relatively short, with one very long reign increasing the average. The extreme case is the third Syracusan dynasty, where Hiero II held power for fifty-four years out of the fifty-six of the dynasty. Those with higher numbers of rulers, however, tend to approximate the average, for it is in those cases that long reigns are most effectively countered by succeeding short ones. There is, however, a very high incidence of dynasties with direct father-to-son succession and this seems to be the decisive factor: the average reign length is also the average generation length, which is what one would expect.

A different set of factors comes into play with the consideration of generation lengths. Of those dynasties with averages of fifteen years or less – there are thirty of these, eleven existed for thirty years or less, exceptionally briefly, and only four of them lasted for more than fifty years. At this length of existence more than two generations inevitably reduces the average drastically. A short existence usually involved a mature, even elderly, founder with therefore a short reign, and the last ruler being killed young – the paradigm might be the Flavian dynasty of Rome, where Vespasian was in his sixties on his accession, Titus ruled for only two years, and Domitian was murdered. Violent death, indeed, is the basic reason for the brief dynasties: the thirty includes not less than six Roman dynasties; between them the twenty emperors included seventeen who died violently.

At the other extreme, there are also twenty-seven dynasties whose average generation length was thirty years or more. Here the common factor seems to be succession through a series of siblings and cousins, which tended to extend the generation from the death of a father to the death of the youngest son or cousin – though this also tends to reduce the reign length. Additionally it seems that existing in the post-Roman period helped a dynasty to a long life; and it is noticeable that there are no imperial dynasties in this group.

There is a clear contrast within the three group types of dynasty I have used here – imperial, city and regional – and some strange distributions. Amongst the city dynasties only one has a generation length of less than sixteen years, and only three less than twenty. Amongst the imperial dynasties, ignoring the one- and two-year Roman dynasties, there is just one at five years, and otherwise none less than fourteen years. By contrast the regional dynasties show a much more even spread from six years upwards. On the other hand, imperial reign lengths have a tendency to be short, with ten at less than twenty-one years, while among the cities there were only two. It would seem that the city dynasties usually got off to a good start, only to falter later; similarly the imperials began well but none of them had a reign length beyond twenty-one years – they tended to die young, usually, of course, by violence.

Conclusions

It is, as will be very clear by now, impossible to draw too many detailed conclusions from these sets of figures. Broadly, the briefer the life of the dynasty, the shorter its average generation length – yet there are still dynasties with high averages that existed for less than a century. Other factors clearly operate, which it is not always possible to isolate; the incidence of violent death was clearly one of these, and where it can be determined this will be discussed in Chapter 9. The other imponderable is clearly the genetic inheritance of the dynasty's members. The Ptolemaic dynasty is a case in point. The first two kings had reigns of forty-one and thirty-six years, but the average for the first five, including these two, is only twenty-nine years, and the last two of these inherited as children and might be expected to have had long reigns. Ptolemy V – who died at less than thirty years of age – married the Seleukid princess, Kleopatra Syra, rather than one of his sisters, as two of his ancestors had. His successors in the sixth generation, two brothers, lasted sixty-four years, quarrelling constantly. This would clearly imply a sudden genetic refreshment, courtesy of Kleopatra Syra. The dynasty then steadily declined again, by way of sibling marriages – the two brothers both married their sister – assisted by an increase in the practice of dynastic murder. The suggestion is possible because of good information on the dynasty: most other dynasties are simply not well enough known in their central relationships to be investigated in this way.

Roman Republican Dynasties

The Roman Republican dynasties may be studied in the same way so far as generation lengths are concerned, but instead of reigns measured from succession to death, the members of the families held public offices and it is these that must substitute. Once again, the different conditions of accession to power and service will affect the results.

In terms of generation lengths, those of the Roman Republicans are generally appreciably longer than the royals; there is only one less than fifteen years, and only ten less than twenty. Yet the maximum is much the same, at thirty-five – one anomalous one reaches forty-three; and the median is somewhat higher, at twenty-nine. The reason is clearly that there was no possibility of a minority ruler, since only adults could be elected. Children dying before maturity are thus automatically excluded, unlike the practice in royal families. This renders the upper limit of thirty-five years for the length of a generation all the more significant, of course.

In terms of the period of office holding, a calculation was made of the frequency or 'incidence' of offices held by the members of the families. The offices being counted were restricted to those that had some executive power – consul, praetor, pro-magistracies of both, dictator, interrex, military tribunes with consular power, tribunes of the plebs, Pontifex Maximus, and *princeps senatus*. The records are more complete, perhaps more so for patrician families than for plebeians, but this is a fairly minor matter. This produced a calculation showing how often the members of each family held public office, expressed as one office held every so many years. The families with the most frequent appearances in office may be reckoned the most politically active, and they were thus the most powerful families in the city.

All but four of these families held an office between once in three years and once in twenty; two (Caecilius and Pompeius) served once in two years, and four more scored once in twenty (Annius, Duillius, Nautius, Tremelius). Three families with the highest frequency of one in two or three years had the benefit of being active in the early years of the republic, when a much higher number of offices was available with the institution of the military tribunes with consular powers; all three of the families died out in the fourth century, though later branches revived the names. Thirty-five families held an office every four to six years, and three of these included the most famous families – the Fabii, Valerii, Licinii and so on.

There are also some very brief families whose abilities certainly brought them frequent office in a short time – the Flaminii and the Pompeii in particular. And just as with some royal dynasties, the presence of one particularly active man in a family could produce many offices – the Marii, with C Marius, is an example.

The overall figures demonstrate just how closely knit an oligarchy the republic was. Of the ninety-five families whose genealogy can be traced, the median figure for holding office was once every seven years. Of the thirty most active families, it is thus probable that two or three members would be holding an executive office every year. A very small number of men in every generation thus controlled the government of the republic, clearly a very tight-knit oligarchy.

Chapter 6

Modes of Succession

T he great majority of dynasties used the system of succession that is direct from father to eldest son, excluding women (for whom see Chapter 7). Very few dynasties were able to maintain such a system for more than three or four generations, if indeed they themselves lasted so long. If direct succession failed, most adopted a modification by which the ruler was succeeded by another son or, failing that, by another close relative. That is, the dynasty was seen as a family business. However, of course, once this alternative to the basic system was admitted, the way was open to further modifications. There were also other succession systems in use, which were either deliberately chosen from the start, or were adopted as a response to particular circumstances.

There seems to have been no specific statement by any authority on the subject of succession methods; it all has to be deduced from the practices followed in particular dynasties. There were, it seems, three main groups of dynasties according to their succession practices. There were those that were self-evidently, from the reconstruction of their genealogies, clearly using the direct primogeniture system of succession, with its minor variations to cope with failures, premature deaths, genetic factors, and so on. A sub-group of this was one in which the primogeniture system was probably intended to be used, but where it was not actually in use from the start for a variety of reasons. A second group shows a system of succession either through the succession of brothers and between cousins. And a third group consists of dynasties where the succession is difficult to classify.

The first group includes most of the dynasties. However, these are not always as clearly distinguishable from one another as this categorization might suggest. Of those that clearly used the direct male succession system, very few were able to carry it through for very long. Only a few can be seen to have had a direct father-to-son succession for six or more generations; one of these, the Bithynian monarchy, lasted for eight generations, though it was not completely straightforward, on examination, but none exceeded that. Even the Bithynian family had two interruptions, even if primogeniture triumphed over them.

Primogeniture

The dynasties with the longest 'runs' of direct succession are a varied group. All but two are from the Near East, the first Assyrian dynasty ran for ten generations, the first Urartu dynasty, that of Bithynia, and that of the Battiads of Cyrene for seven. The Cappadocian, two Armenian, and two Iberian dynasties, all from eastern Asia Minor, had lines of six generations in direct descent, as did the first Lakhmid, and probably, the Nabataean dynasty and the Ptolemies. (All this is to ignore, of course, the two Spartan dynasties, and that of the Argeads of Macedon, whose early generations were claimed to be direct, but whose record is unreliable.) Ten may thus be taken as the genetic maximum for such an achievement in the ancient world, though in most circumstances five would be much more likely.

This geographical concentration in the Middle East is a little misleading, partly because this is where most dynasties emerged in the first place. The geographical environments of the dynasties varied from desert to high mountains, from coastal kingdoms to deep inland, and this is a further element of variety. Nor is there any obvious chronological conclusion to be drawn, for the dynasties in question were spread throughout the period under consideration. So the only conclusion to be drawn is that it is very difficult for any dynasty, any time or place, to achieve a direct male inheritance for more than six generations and that ten generations would seem to be the maximum possible. The institution of the harem could extend the range, and some Indian, and later Muslim, dynasties did so successfully. This is not true primogeniture, of course, as the harem system generally involves selecting a suitable child, then, often, culling the rest of the male children. The Ottoman dynasty succeeded in maintaining itself under these conditions for several centuries, but others, the Akhaimenids, for example, succumbed to extinction.

The reasons for the ending of a succession by primogeniture vary, from the suppression of the dynasty by an enemy (or a supposed friend), to internal dissension within the family, or even perhaps, dying out. Killing off a king's surplus sons, of course, denied the process, but will often reinforce a family's solidarity. The specific reasons for extinction are not, in fact, very important, since the real result of the enquiry is that some reason or another always intervenes to stop or disrupt the direct descent.

One particular reason, however, is relevant here. Some of the dynasties held to a direct descent for a number of generations, but then underwent a breakdown (as with the Ptolemies) so that the direct succession was replaced by a modification of that descent, whereby brothers or cousins inherited when the direct line failed. There might then result an apparent alteration in the mode of succession for later generations. The Assyrian descent through ten generations was broken in the eighth century when the four sons of Adad-Nirari I succeeded as kings one after the other. It is perhaps no coincidence that the dynasty was then displaced by a new one, where brothers divided the kingdom between them, ruling Assyria and Babylon as joint kingdoms. The brothers were presumably intended to be operating in tandem, though the Assyrian brother was clearly paramount, having command of the main Assyrian army. It did not work well since the intransigent enmity of Babylon could well be assumed by the subordinate brother, leading to a 'rebellion'. (See, on all this, Chapter 10, 'Breakdowns'.)

Once such a breakdown occurred, it proved to be impossible to reassert the original direct line method. The actual result is the eventual destruction of the dynasty, though this may take some time – a century in the case of the second Assyrian dynasty. Without an accepted and enforced family rule of succession, any male member of the family clearly felt entitled to go for the throne. Among the Argeads of Macedon, at one point five different descendants from Alexander I were competing for the kingship. In Babylon the imperial dynasty founded by Nabopolassar, called the Neo-Babylonian, clearly aimed for a direct succession but failed, as a result of a dynastic murder and a popular uprising; one emperor withdrew from the city and lived in the Arabian Desert much of his reign, presumably to escape the fraught atmosphere in the city, perhaps because he was thus out of reach of the conspirators he feared; but he was also out of touch, and was overthrown when he returned.

In the absence of clarity, direct succession could be achieved by force. The later Akhaimenids resorted to sibling murder, whereby the son who inherited the throne (not always the eldest) immediately had his brothers (and therefore his competitors) killed off. The problem here is that this is an almost guaranteed way of bringing the whole dynasty to extinction, for without collateral lines as backup there is no reserve family manpower when the main line fails, as it always does.

Dynasties usually found that, for whatever reason, the direct male succession system had to be modified after several generations. And so it is clear that the dynasties where direct male descent was clearly intended but where it did not develop in the early generations are thus also variations on the male descent theme. The break of system could clearly occur at any point. It is to be noted, however, that in those cases where a clear line of male descent is attested over several generations, a much more stable polity resulted than for those in which the line of descent changed. Compare the Ptolemies, with six generations of clear male descent at first, over a century and a half, with their neighbours and competitors the Seleukids, where an eldest son was executed in the third generation, and there was a civil war between brothers in the fourth. There is a contrast also between the early and late generations of Ptolemies, between a stable and an unstable policy.

A thwarted intention to use the direct line method is clear in a number of cases, where occasional father-to-son inheritance emerges from a welter of confusion. The Agilolfings of Bavaria produced two or three instances of such succession during their two-century history, but this apparent intention was as repeatedly interrupted. The same happened with the Abgarids of Edessa and in the dynasty of Emesa, where the interruptions happened as a result of wars between the Romans and someone else. In these cases the reason was interference by the imperial overlord. In others it is likely that the failure of one son to produce an heir was the real reason; the failure occurring repeatedly in a family line suggests a genetic deficiency rather than anything else – the Attalids are a case in point, where only one case of father-son inheritance happened, though there was a clear and determined pattern of holding the succession within the extended family, to the extent of avoiding intermarriage with other royal families. The first Parthian dynasty also provides a possible case, where it even begins with the succession of a brother in the first generation. In later generations the direct father-son line repeatedly failed, perhaps as much from fraternal rivalry, battle casualties, and assassination as from any genetic problem. The two Spartan dynasties claimed an original father-to-son succession, but where the succession is actually documented from about 500 BC to the end of the dynasties, direct succession occurred only occasionally.

In some cases it is only by the eye of faith that any system is at all visible. The Ostrogothic line founded by Theoderic I, for instance, is so confused that it resembles a Roman Imperial dynastic succession more than anything else, but it may well be that the original aim was succession in the direct male line. Similarly with the Lombards. Where kings had adult sons they inherited, but also often not for very long. And then there is the case of Iberia of the Caucasus, where the succession jumped about (in the first and third dynasties) between rival royal lines; again the intention was clearly male primogeniture; the practice was a good deal more erratic than might be anticipated: there were clearly other influences at work in deciding the successions; those in the Irish and Scottish dynasties were very similarly strange.

These examples may be put together with the more obvious cases of direct succession: it was apparently the aim of most dynasties to produce that method of succession, but events repeatedly disrupted it.

Sibling Succession

Some dynasties, whether deliberately or not, chose a succession method through brothers, that is, sibling succession, by which the succession went from brother to brother by sequence of birth. This system is used in Saudi Arabia at present, and combined with the multiple wife/harem system, it has resulted in the kingship being inherited by increasingly aged and often decrepit men – though it now seems that some common sense has entered the royal minds at last.

Amongst the Attalids of Pergamon this was at first clearly inadvertent, since it happened that neither of the first two kings had sons: the second king was a nephew of the first; the third was his cousin. But this man, Attalos I, had two sons, who inherited successively, even though the elder, Eumenes II, had two sons himself; it seems that the original indirect fraternal succession became the method of choice. The Nubian dynasty that conquered much of Egypt in the eighth century BC seems to have used a similar sibling inheritance system, which was in part designed to have one brother in command in the north, while the other ruled from Thebes in the south; so also did Elam, though here it may have been inadvertent due to the heavy casualties inflicted on the family in the Assyrian wars. In the case of the Hasmoneans it is difficult to decide whether such a succession was intended or not, but it is a fact that only two sons inherited directly from their fathers; all the other kings inherited from a brother or from some other relative. The Indo-Baktrian inheritance system looks to be similar, though the sources for these families are never good enough to be sure; for the Aiakidai of Epeiros, however, this seems certain, though it created a good deal of fighting. This family in the end died out, and the same fate befell the Anglo-Saxon dynasties, which used that system also – Kent, Mercia and Wessex. Two of the tyrant dynasties of Greece, at Samos and Sikyon, show a probable sibling succession method, though the sources are not specific that this was anything but chance. This system, or a variation of it, can also be seen in the first Visigoth dynasty.

How far any of these sibling succession systems was deliberately chosen is very difficult to say. In some cases, the Attalids or Elam, for example, it can be explained as the result of the failure of direct male heirs, though in both cases the succession of siblings seems to have been adopted in the end as normal, the result of the earlier, perhaps accidental, practice. In Elam, because of the heavy casualties inflicted by the Assyrian wars, this meant that an adult king in charge was required. The prime advantage of this system would seem to have been the probability that the succession would go through a series of adults, and succession by a minor would generally be avoided. In these cases, and so perhaps in others where sibling succession appears to be the rule, it may well be that the original intention was direct succession, and sibling succession emerged for any of a variety of reasons, the failure of heirs, or casualties – thus establishing a new custom. What is curious is that it was clearly possible to change the system of succession at need. The system adopted appears to have been chosen for practical not theoretical (still less legal or legislative) reasons.

There is a further element to be taken into account. It was often the practice in a monarchy that the reigning king had an ill-defined right to nominate his successor. This could be done in several ways, the most effective being to make the chosen successor joint king for some time before the older ruler died. When a succession method was uncertain this could be effective. In the Antonine Roman dynasty, it was the apparent choice of Hadrian by Trajan that was decisive (though it was also claimed that Trajan's choice was actually that of his widow). In the last year or two of his life Hadrian, who had no son, sorted through several possibilities for the succession, eliminating some in the most drastic way, and then dictated the succession not only of himself but that of his next successor as well. Marcus Aurelius made his son joint emperor for the last four years of his reign.

This royal choice method is not an alternative to direct inheritance, since in the great majority of cases the ruler chose his own son, thus reinforcing the direct line system, until it became customary. This was certainly the case among the great Hellenistic dynasties. Ptolemy I made his son joint king for the last two years of his life, but this was not his eldest son, who decamped in anger, along with his mother and sisters, when the decision was made. In terms of the stability of the kingdom, it is clear that Ptolemy I's choice was well made; Ptolemy II Philadelphos was a much steadier ruler than Ptolemy Keraunos could ever be. Seleukos I promoted Antiochos I to the same position much earlier, and they ruled jointly for over a decade, though at opposite ends of the kingdom. Antigonos I had himself proclaimed king in 306, and instantly made his son Demetrios I his colleague.

An alternative method, as with Hadrian and Trajan, was to see that the succession went to the dying ruler's nearest male relative. But kings could be capricious, and heirs were often too ambitious, and where the direct line had clearly failed the royal selection was usually decisive. The Attalid succession would seem to be of this type, resulting in the succession of the brother of Eumenes II, and finally of the exclusion of one son of Attalos II in favour of the bequest of the kingdom to the Roman Republic.

This created its own problems, however. The chosen heir might be regarded with jealousy and violence by a son who was passed over – as Ptolemy Keraunos was infuriated at the promotion of Ptolemy II, or when Antiochos Hierax rebelled against the succession of his elder brother Seleukos II. Or the chosen heir might become too impatient to succeed, in which case either he murdered the older king, or he was executed for his presumption. Succession by a line of brothers might produce a series of murders and assassinations rather than a peaceful process. None of these systems of succession were ever foolproof: the prize, after all, was the kingship, something all too many men wanted.

Joint Rule

The dynasties where a direct male line or a sibling succession system cannot be detected show a considerable variety of possible systems of succession. One apparent attitude, however, covers the majority: the assumption that the family is the correct unit to receive the succession. The actual ruler may emerge in a variety of ways. Among the al-Kinda of Arabia, all the sons of the deceased king inherited together. This was also the practice, it seems, in the dynasty of the Catuvellauni in pre-Roman Britain, and the two sons of Peisistratos of Athens ruled jointly and harmoniously. The example of the Nubian dynasty in Egypt has been noted already. In all these cases the practice led to a rapid extinction of the dynasty: in the case of al-Kinda by the disintegration of the kingdom into minor chieftaincies. The Catuvellauni were conquered by Rome, but it does not seem that this had any connection with the joint succession. The Nubians in Egypt did last for some time, but the fraternal system soon changed. The trouble in this case came not with the first inheriting generation, but with the second, by which time each brother was looking to pass on his authority to his son, which would normally lead to the breakup of the kingdom or to civil war, or both.

Joint inheritance might mean that the survivor of the inheriting group would end by eventually ruling alone, as with the Huns, where two pairs of brothers ruled (before Attila), and in each case the death of one left the survivor to rule by himself until his own death. The system worked because the brothers more or less cooperated, and because there were only two of them; but it collapsed when the second successor, Attila, left several sons who decided to divide their inheritance amongst themselves rather than rule jointly: this, as with the al-Kinda, was the end of the polity as well as of the dynasty. The division enabled the subjects to rebel successfully, since the joint fraternal support failed. None of the inheritors retained any size of a kingdom, though a couple did survive for a number of years.

The Numidians in North Africa made their joint inheritance system work, after a fashion. Twice or thrice joint rule ended with the survivor ruling alone, though he survived only by being victorious in the fraternal conflicts. In addition, it was in this case in the interests of the supervising empire, Rome, that the monarchy should continue; at the same time Rome was not unhappy to see the local problems solved locally, and a conflict over the succession conveniently diverted and occupied Numidian attention. The Burgundian inheritance by all the sons of a king seems to have involved a division of the kingdom, which was then gradually reunited as the inheritors died off, usually in battle, so the whole in the end went to the survivor, and this was the system also practised by the Merovingians, modified by the ambitions of the Mayors of the Palace. Ironically it was the Burgundians' divisions that enabled the Merovingians to conquer and annex the Burgundian kingdom. The repeated divisions and redivisions of the Merovingian kingdom itself permitted, for that matter, the growth of the power of their supplanters, the Carolingian Mayors of the Palace, who supplied, for a time, the stability and an empire-wide government and administrative competence that the Merovingians could not provide. The Carolingians then adopted the same inheritance system, to their own eventual ruin. The system of joint succession can thus scarcely be termed successful, though the long history of the Merovingians is certainly impressive. Yet the constant internal conflict, and the constant change their succession system promoted, tended to damage the kingdom, and scarcely promoted the happiness of their subjects – or of the kings, whose deaths in youth were the alternative to being pushed into early monastic retirement.

Another version of this type is that adopted by early Greek tyrants. The Kypselid regime in Corinth extended its control to several Corinthian colonies to the east and west – Kerkyra and Ambrakia to the west and Potidaia in the east. Cadet members of the ruling family were posted to these places as subordinate tyrants. Kypselos' younger brother went to Ambrakia and was succeeded there by his own younger son; others were placed at Kerkyra, and at Potidaia. Ambrakia and Kerkyra were the strategic points along the maritime route to the west, to Italy and Sicily and the metal wealth of Spain; Potidaia was a strategic point for dominating the Chalkidike and the trade of the southern Balkans, the metals and timber of Macedon and Thrace. These sub-tyrants were prefiguring, in a small way, the later Athenian Empire. And the family was able, at least at Ambrakia, to survive the downfall of the parent regime at Corinth.

In Sicily the joint island-wide tyranny of Theron of Akragas and Gelon of Gela and Syracuse also used younger members of the tyrants' families to control other cities in the Greek part of the island. (It is worth noting that Syracuse, the real power base of the monarchy, was originally a Corinthian colony and contact between the two cities was long maintained.) This posting of family members to control cities or regions also seems to have been the method adopted by the first Thracian dynasty in order to control a fairly wide kingdom, whereby younger members were allotted cities or tribes to control on behalf of the whole. In no case were these dynasties successful at holding their states together; instead the detached members tended to remove their territories into independence, or to quarrel with other members; the sight of these disputes then encouraged rebellions – the first Sicilian monarchy, for example, was very brief. The temptation of tyrants to trust their own families regularly came to grief; on the other hand, only by delegating authority to other family members could the states be held together in the first place. The real answer was to develop a competent bureaucracy.

Internal Family Selection

The reverse process was at work in the third Thracian dynasty, and also in Northumbria and with the Lombards. This is the union of two ruling lines, in Thrace in the first century BC, where the Odrysian and Sapean lines joined, and in Northumbria the Deiran and Bernician lines became one dynasty. The union was to be achieved, in theory at least, by intermarriage; in practice it proved impossible to do so peacefully, since union of two into one necessarily meant one branch did not rule. The union only finally arrived when one of the participating lines died out. (See Chapter 8, 'Mergers'.) In the meantime, there was great confusion over the correct inheritances, and the two lines continued in parallel and in competition and conflict for several decades. Among the Lombards the situation was aggravated by the practice of achieving the succession by *coups d'état* from among at least three lines, to which other lines were added, all of them descended from the several dukes who were put in place in different centres during the original conquest as a means of establishing control, and all of them claiming the right to seize the throne.

In Northumbria there are signs of an alternative method, whereby the eldest male of the royal family inherited when the king died, whether or not he was closely related. This is the system that was also in use among the Vandals, and apparently in Mercia and Wessex, and that may well have been adopted in the end in Kent. It was never satisfactory since it required a definition of the acceptable family members – just as with linked families – and a definition of seniority; this process would inevitably exclude some of those who felt that they should be included. Conflict generally ensued, particularly when a distant cousin was preferred over the son of a king. In fact, conflict would occur with or without some definition of acceptability. A variation of this operated amongst the Umayyads, where it is clear that the selection of the next caliph was made from within a group of men who were all apparently considered equally eligible; the succession of Abd al-Malik went to his two eldest sons, then to his nephew, back to two more sons, then to the son of the third of these brothers, to two sons of the eldest brother, and finally to another nephew of Abd al-Malik.

The two Carthaginian dynasties were affected, it seems, by the similar idea that the succession should go the most suitable man of the royal family. The dynasty of the Magonids thus frequently moved to nephews, omitting the sons of kings; the choice seems to have been made by some sort of election, though where presumably the candidates were all necessarily of the royal family, but where the selectors had a choice between a number of adult males. (Alternatively, this may have been a method designed to avoid a direct hereditary succession, perhaps on the assumption that such would lead to a family tyranny.) The other Carthaginian dynasty, the Barkids, became virtually independent of the city in its personal conquest of southern Spain, begun by Hamilcar Barka, but here the test of age and competence also operated: the succession went from Hamilcar, the founder, to his son-in-law Hasdrubal, who was chosen because Hamilcar's sons were too young to command, and when Hasdrubal died, Hamilcar's sons, Hannibal and Hasdrubal, successively ruled, Hasdrubal taking over in Spain when Hannibal went off to invade Italy. Perhaps the oddest system in this category was that of the Hekatomnids, where the sons of Hekatomnos each married a sister, and the whole family, men and women, succeeded in order of birth – Mausollos, his sister/wife, his brother, then his sister/wife, and so on.

Another aspect of this type of dynasty is shown in the history of the Herodians. Beginning with the very first of the family to rule, Herod the Great himself, the male members of this family were used by the Roman government for over a century as a set of men from which rulers could be selected to be put in as kings into a variety of kingdoms in the east. At various times these men were kings in Armenia, Cilicia, Judaea, and various parts of Syria, always at the convenience of Rome; their kingdoms were extinguished at Rome's convenience as well. Here there was no real system of succession at all.

The two strangest systems of inheritance take us to the far distant reaches of any definition of the family as an inheritance device, and, paradoxically, both to the far West and to the great imperial centres. The rulers of the various Irish kingdoms and of the kingdom of Dalriada in western Scotland alternated between branches of the royal family. In Ireland the High Kingship jumped about between the various lines descended from the father of Niall Niogiallach, sometimes lighting on a man whose forebears had not been king for several generations and only on the rarest of occasions passing from father to son (hence the frequent gaps in the genealogical tables as presented in the Catalogue). In Dalriada this process seems to have begun with the two sons of the first king, Domangart I (or at least so later accounts had it; it may be this was just another later rationalization). Separate branches were established as lords in two sections of the kingdom, Cowal and Knapdale. These two branches then alternated in providing kings of the whole kingdom for over a century. The scheme then failed: in the 630s two kings, from the separate lines, were ruling simultaneously for a time, and then the Cowal line died out. It was replaced by a third line, which was then supplemented by a fourth. The situation was, by the 670s, very confused, hardly surprisingly, though the original Knapdale line survived all the rest, not expiring until the 780s. This system had perhaps been imported from Ireland, where a branch of the Dalriada kingdom controlled part of the north-east of the island – or it may have been indigenous to both societies. It was presumably intended to bring the governing power close to the population, and to be fair to the sons of the king. In actual fact, it only led to confusion and disputes, as the candidates at the death of a king were of increasing distances from the origin. In the provincial kingdoms of Ireland, the system that was used in the High Kingship also prevailed, together with interlopers here and there.

The Roman Systems

Rome exhibited a series of modes of succession, which can be roughly equated with the period of the Roman kings (until 509 BC), the republic, and the Empire. It is impossible to prove, but it very much seems that the strange inheritance system attributed to the regal period may well have affected and influenced its successors. In particular, the succession system throughout the Imperial period from the time of Augustus to the fall of the city to the barbarians, is as chaotic and confusing as that of the kings, while the evidence of the republic suggests that several personal systems existed.

To begin, then, at the beginning. The process of regal inheritance among the kings is not believable. Seven kings supposedly occupied the kingship of the city over a period of 244 years. This gives an average reign length of thirty-two years, which is at the highest end of the possibilities. In no case is the inheritance said to have been from father to son, and the descriptions of the activities of the kings, whereby several of them are held to have been responsible for developing or initiating elements of the later Roman constitution, suggest that it is an invented scheme, just as the early Spartan, Argead, and Judahite dynasties were concocted out of folk tales (for ideological purposes).

If this non-system was really a model for the republic the methods of inheritance amongst the Roman rulers were truly an inheritance from the regal past. The legal power of the paterfamilias made it possible for the head of a family to dispose of his property in almost any way he chose. It was necessary for a prominent Roman to be rich in order to participate in politics; a father chose to load one son with the majority of his property, that son would have instant entry into the political contest; if he chose to divide his property equally, this might destroy the political prospects of all his sons at a stroke. Several of the families listed in the Catalogue did disappear, only for men of the name to reappear decades or centuries later, and this might be one of the reasons. No doubt it was great wealth that permitted such families as the Cornelii and the Claudii to separate off into several branches, each of which produced electable magistrates generation after generation. Certainly a family tradition of inheritance directed at the eldest male might account for some families repeatedly producing one office holder every generation.

The whole system was further complicated by the practice of reviving an ailing family by adoption. Legally the adoptee became a member of the family he entered, but in genetic fact he founded a new family, and I have so treated those that appear in the Catalogue. (It was a practice much resorted to later under the empire also.)

The republican succession practices were as one would expect: normally the eldest son succeeded and, if there was wealth enough, other sons took up political affairs as well. The practice was also followed that an ancestor who had held office was sufficient to ensure that a later member of the family could become a member of the Senate, even without having held office. This was therefore a fairly straightforward system, based on recognized custom and practice. There was therefore little or no obvious connection back to the peculiar methods of the kings. And yet the system was biased. Patricians for a century and more monopolized the executive offices, and after that they could still stand for office at a younger age than plebeians. It took a serious upheaval lasting several years to open up most of those offices to plebeians, and even then the intention was that one consulship should be reserved to patricians, despite the much greater number of plebeians who became eligible.

These elements continued into the empire, but the patrician members' numbers had by then seriously declined, so that emperors had to repeatedly transfer plebeians into the patriciate. Within the nobility of the empire the practices as developed under the republic continued, thereby modified by a much more extensive use of adoption.

For the imperial families, however, the succession system resembled the very strange practices of the kings. The very oddest, strangest, and most inefficient succession system devised in the ancient world was that used in the Roman and Byzantine Empires. Almost all the 'dynasties' of the Roman Empire that are included here only enter the Catalogue after careful and diligent examination. The first dynasty, that of Augustus, at least included emperors who had some blood relationship to each other, though it was distant in some cases: Augustus' successor was his stepson Tiberius; he was followed by his grand-nephew Caligula; then came Caligula's uncle, Claudius, followed by Claudius' stepson Nero: they can at least all be fitted into a continuous genealogy. But the Antonine dynasty scarcely deserves the description of 'dynasty'. Trajan was adopted by Nerva, a usurper, under the threat of military rebellion. Hadrian was Trajan's first cousin – a distant blood relationship – but the relationship between Hadrian and Antoninus was only by marriage and very distantly at that – Antoninus was the husband of Hadrian's great-great-grand-niece; Marcus was Antoninus' son-in-law. In this 'dynasty', therefore, the only blood relationship was between the cousins Trajan and Hadrian. Among the dynasty following, the Severans, Elagabalus and Alexander Severus were only distant cousins of Caracalla, and of each other. The third century dynasties were so brief as to be scarcely deserving of the name, though by my definition of three generations and/or three rulers four of them get included. The relationships amongst the emperors of the Tetrarchic dynasty were either non-existent, or as immensely complex and unconvincing as those of the Antonines. And so on. Many of these dynasties tried to resolve the succession problem by the institution of the adoption of adult males, an inheritance device already used among the aristocracy of the Roman Republic, but this became degraded finally when Septimius Severus adopted himself into the preceding Antonine dynasty retrospectively.

It is sometimes suggested that this was a clever scheme to promote the selection of the best men for the job. This might have worked in a few instances, but a system that reverted to hereditary succession when an emperor had a son (the Flavians, Marcus, Severus) and produced such emperors as Caligula, Nero, and Commodus, was not one that evaluated these candidates properly beforehand. In actual fact, the one consistent element running through the imperial succession is that it was subject to military intervention. Not only did Augustus fight his way to sole power at the head of an army, and by fighting several civil wars, but control of the army was fundamental to every later emperor, especially the emperors – Vespasian, Trajan, Hadrian, Severus – who seized the throne by violence at the end of a civil war.

The confusion and trickery involved in the repeated disputes over the imperial succession, together with the strange unwillingness or inability of the imperial families to reproduce themselves, and the all too prevalent practice of killing emperors, is one of the major elements of instability in the Roman and Byzantine Empires. (Only two emperors were succeeded by adult sons in the first two centuries of the imperial system: Vespasian by Titus, and Marcus Aurelius by Commodus; eleven emperors were murdered out of twenty-three rulers from these four first dynasties, and their intervening usurpers.) Eventually it became too easy to murder an emperor and set up a successor, since the dead man all too often had no obvious or designated successor to block the usurper or to take revenge; indeed, extraordinarily few emperors had sons. It is not until the family of Constantine in the fourth century, after the imperial regime had been in place for nearly four centuries, that an imperial family lasted for three generations in a direct line of succession. This pattern of brief dynasties, usually separated by several brief and unrelated emperors, continued on into the Byzantine Empire, where even the semi-divinity that the emperors wrapped themselves in – developed in fact by the anti-Christian Emperor Diocletian – could not save many of them from assassination, or at least deposition; Christian practice provided a new means of deposition by allowing deposed rulers to be pushed into monasteries. No dynasty between the Julio-Claudians and the Isaurians (that is between 48 BC and AD 800) lasted for more than 120 years. The two longest-lasting were the joint Valentinian-Theodosian family, which was extended by more than twenty years by marriages into the family, and the Heraklids, who actually achieved three direct father-to-son successions before the final emperor had to be deposed and was then later murdered.

This is, one might say, no way to run an empire. But the system – or lack of system – was so persistent that it would seem to have been ingrained in Roman social expectations. On the surface it seems that the regal method and the imperial have strong similarities, but that the republic was different. The first two used a method of succession that in its way might have been intended, if any clear intention could be discerned behind the history, to select a suitable man to succeed from any of those who might be considered eligible. This is in effect what Hadrian did in his last years, and in a sense what happened among the Julio-Claudians. In the Antonine dynasty, it has to be said, the system did produce a line of effective rulers, from Trajan to Marcus; among the Julio-Claudians, however, it produced such feckless ninnies as Caligula and Nero.

Asserting that the republican system is different, more 'normal', however, is to ignore what was actually happening inside the republican dynasties. In theory, if there was one, primogeniture was the expectation. In fact, it is generally more complex than that. Political power went with election, and it is common to find sons being brought forward to accept office by their fathers. But it is also common to find a group of brothers all achieving political office within a relatively short time; clearly the younger brothers were assisted by the elder. But this also tended to produce a series of parallel sub-families, each of which had sons who expected, or were expected, to achieve public office. Given that political office was held for only a year or two, this was often a very successful device, since there were plenty of offices to go round, and gradually a ladder of achievement was devised. And, with many lines of descent, if one line failed, another was always available. The restricted nature of the Roman Republican oligarchy meant that if a son of a magistrate existed, he was very likely to be able to gain election, at least to the earliest magistracies.

These families were thus more like collective entities than normal, or Royal, dynasties, though this was more the result of the political system they were part of than by any specific choice. This would seem to be the connecting link between the regal and imperial systems of succession. All three were evidently based not on direct male primogeniture, but on a vaguely defined family grouping that might select one man to go forward into office, or might decide that the family was wealthy enough to promote several men one after the other. The curious succession process among the Tarquin dynasty – from the elder Tarquin to Servius Tullius, a sort of servant-guardian, supposedly promoted and installed at the insistence of Tarquin's widow, and then to Tarquin's son, who might have been expected to succeed directly after his father's death. This curious process may have been part of the collective system of inheritance of the nobility of the regal period, and so had been continued by the patricians who ruled the city for a century and a half, and it then reappears in the imperial system.

The Roman families, despite the peculiarities of quasi-collective action and adoption, were, of course, just as likely to die out by failure of inheritance as the royal families. They had a slightly better chance of a longer life because of their connectivity, and the absence, at least in the republic, of elimination by murder or assassination, at least until the Gracchan revolution, but even so only five families can be followed right through from the fifth to the first centuries BC, and in none of them can a direct line of succession be traced from first to last. Of the ninety-five family dynasties tabulated in the Catalogue, no more than half existed at any one time: families disappeared regularly, and were replaced by new names. Further, it is a notorious fact in Roman studies that almost all of the old families had died out by the end of the first century BC, and that very few lived on into the Imperial period. There had thus been a constant process of extinction all along. But this is not really to be surprised at, for this had been the fate of families all through the republic: the succession of sons had regularly failed.

Conclusion

The methods of inheritance that diverged from the presumed original intention of primogeniture have taken up considerable space, but that should not hide the fact that the most common method of succession was always the basic system of male primogeniture, or a version thereof, and that this operated, with modifications to take in brothers, in all societies with the exception of post-Roman Western Europe, where the English, Scottish, Irish, Frankish, Vandal, Visigoth, Bavarian, and Lombard dynasties were different, as was, of course, all through, Rome. Certain differences also occur in Central Asia, where the Indo–Baktrian dynasties seem to have adopted a local custom, and the Umayyads, whose scheme seems to have been their own invention. Otherwise the clear aim – not always carried out, of course – was that the eldest son should succeed the father. The problem was that there was not always an eldest son to succeed, and there were always the further problems of incompetence, or youth, or ambition stirring in others.

Kings and emperors led a life of constant danger. They were expected to command in battle, which left them open to death in the fighting – the death rate among the fighting kings of the Seleukid dynasty can only be described as appalling (see Chapter 9, 'Violent Deaths and Depositions'). If kings did not command their armies they were held in contempt and were liable to be murdered – thus they were likely to lose either way. War in the ancient world was a young man's activity, so this was inevitably a major factor in the extinction of dynasties, since it was always possible for a king to be killed before he had children. One of the most telling arguments in Macedon against Alexander's expedition into Asia was that he had no son to succeed him: when he died thirteen years later, he still had no legitimate successor and his empire collapsed within a couple of years. The Roman system of adult adoption might be thought to be an answer to this, and to the possibility of incompetence, except that the Roman record scarcely inspired emulation, and when an emperor had a son, he carefully arranged him to succeed. This produced Commodus, Caracalla, and other monsters.

In addition, kings and emperors were expected to be accessible to large numbers of people for much of their lives. They could be accosted by petitioners at almost any time. The same story is told of Demetrios I and Hadrian, that they were very offhand when an old woman presented a petition; she is said to have had a sharp tongue and to have reminded them of their responsibilities, but it is clear that, whether the story is true or not, kings and emperors were easily accessible. Roman emperors held regular gatherings in the palace where they greeted, and were greeted by, their visitors in person. They held more restricted meetings with smaller groups of men who might well contain their bitterest enemies. Kings were the same. These meetings were quite essential for their authority, since recognition by the king or emperor was a form of authority for his guests. But it did leave them open to being killed by their 'Friends', which was, of course, a formal title and not necessarily a description of the relationship. Ptolemy V was murdered by a courtier when he mused aloud that a coming war might be paid for by taxing the wealthy; Domitian was murdered by a servant instructed by his chamberlain, who was put forward to do the deed by a group of Roman aristocrats who had been Domitian's counsellors. Caligula was killed in walking between his palace and the stadium. At least two emperors were murdered in their baths. Life for rulers was dangerous, and they must have been always conscious of that.

For the sake of their subjects, therefore, the rule of male primogeniture was the best way of ensuring a stable state since it made it clear well in advance who the successor was, and gave some assurance that the chosen successor was being trained to follow on. The success of such dynasties as those of Bithynia and Pontos, where the succession was clear and regular, is a pointer. But no system can guarantee stability. What can be said is that the clarity of a monarchical system using primogeniture made it less likely that the dynasty and the country ruled would collapse into conflict than any other comparable system, either monarchic or otherwise.

Chapter 7

Women

T he principal role that women played in ancient dynasties was basic, first of all, that of the biological agent for producing heirs. As wives, they were expected to become pregnant, and to deliver live and healthy babies, preferably sons. Then, second, as daughters, they were at the disposal of their fathers and brothers to be married without protest to men who had been chosen as suitable husbands, usually for political reasons, and usually to men they had never met.

This is well known and well understood, and is no different from the wider practices of Greek and Roman society – and that of every other ancient (and mediaeval) society; it was not a specialty of dynasties. At all other levels of society the reasons for a marriage might be less political and more economic, and perhaps the choice of a husband could be a little freer for the bride, but the position of women of lower social classes was not in reality any different, only harder. At the level of royalty, however, any deviations from these basic patterns and conditions entailed large consequences. Women emerge from the shadows in about twenty of the dynasties listed here in three or four particular guises: as regents, as rulers by right of birth, and, ominously, as clear indications of the end of the dynasty.

Ptolemies

The Ptolemaic dynasty may be taken as that in which women most obviously emerge in all these varied roles; it is in this dynasty that these differing positions and possibilities are best illustrated. As early as the reign of Ptolemy II, the king's sister Arsinoe (II) had had a notable, active, and visible career in Asia and Macedon as the wife of King Lysimachos (presented to him by her father Ptolemy I at the age of about 15), and then as the wife of her own half-brother Ptolemy Keraunos (who murdered two of her children by Lysimachos – the marriage was brief). After the death of the children she returned to Egypt, and soon married Ptolemy II, her full brother, by which time she was about 40 years of age. It is often assumed that in this they were adopting the old Egyptian custom of sibling marriage, but that is no more than a modern assumption – the first Ptolemies always emphasized their Macedonian-ness, not their Egyptian-ness, and in fact there had been no case of pharaohs marrying their sisters in the previous several hundred years. Arsinoe was credited by the malicious as putting backbone into the king, but he was a successful and experienced ruler already.

Arsinoe's final marriage was without children – Ptolemy II had at least four children by a previous marriage – but sibling marriage had thus entered the Ptolemaic political lexicon. It was repeated by Ptolemy IV, who married his full sister, another Arsinoe (III), and their son Ptolemy V succeeded to the throne as a child, at which time their other siblings were killed off to forestall competition; it seems clear that this was Ptolemy's own doing, but his minister Sosibios was also involved. Ptolemy V was married to the Seleukid princess, Kleopatra Syra, in 194 as part of the peace agreement to end the Fifth Syrian War. He was murdered in 180, still no more than 30 years old, and Kleopatra, then in her mid twenties and with three small children, emerged as their guardian and the official regent for her eldest son, the 6-year-old Ptolemy VI. She held this position for four years, dying in 176. Her success may be judged by the mess subsequently made of affairs by later regents, culminating in the total defeat of Ptolemaic forces in a war against Kleopatra's brother, Seleukid King Antiochos IV.

Ptolemy III had married Berenike, the daughter of Magas the king of Cyrenaica. Magas had detached his Cyrenaican kingdom from Ptolemaic rule, in part by marrying another Seleukid princess, Apama. Berenike was betrothed to Ptolemy III, but to actually carry through the marriage she had to murder her mother's choice of a new husband, Demetrios the Fair. When she married Ptolemy she therefore brought with her into the Ptolemaic system the Cyrenaican kingdom. She was the mother of six children in the first seven years of marriage. She was one of those who were murdered after her husband's death; no doubt as an accomplished murderer of one king, she was seen to be far too dangerous to be allowed to live. This was a rather startling example of female assertiveness; it was also an example of male resentment.

The women of the Ptolemaic royal house were valued above all because they were royal, and this is one of the main justifications for the sibling marriages, for any husband who was married to a royal princess might use his royal wife's rank to put himself forward, at least into a position of power, if not actually as king. But it was only one step from that point of view to having a royal woman ruling the kingdom in her own right; Kleopatra Syra thus showed the way. This became not uncommon in and after the seventh generation of the Ptolemaic family, after the death of Kleopatra Syra's younger son Ptolemy

VIII. Kleopatra III, the daughter of Kleopatra Syra, had been married successively to her brothers Ptolemy VI and VIII, but then ruled effectively in her own right after the latter's death, and at least four more women of the royal house then ruled that kingdom either alone or as regents at various times in the next eighty years, until the last and most renowned of them all, Kleopatra VII, who was, in a situation too often ignored, actually acting as regent for a succession of sons.

These Ptolemaic examples illustrate the various circumstances in which women could emerge as rulers in the ancient world – as regents, as ruling queens, as conveyors of a kingdom to their husbands: they were acceptable (to men) as regents and guardians for their infant children, but only as a result of paralysing disputes among other possible (male) candidates for the regency; only the most strong-willed of women could expand that position in the one of actually ruling – the achievement of the first Kleopatra (Syra) in this is thus altogether remarkable. Once this had been achieved by one woman, of course, others could follow, but they were always technically subordinate to a male king, who might be a husband or a son, even an infant son. Royal daughters such as Kleopatra III or Kleopatra VII might claim to rule by right of birth, but they only ever ruled alone in the most unusual circumstances, only generally briefly, and, it was fully understood, only as a temporary measure. There was never any question of a woman entering the line of succession in her own right.

The chronology of the Ptolemaic dynasty shows that women only emerged as real and independent powers in the family in the last century of its rule. The precursor, Kleopatra Syra, was regent in 180–176, Kleopatra III ruled between 116 and 100. In the next sixty years, several other royal women exercised power, usually only briefly and sometimes alone; Kleopatra VII ruled between about 50 BC and 30. There can be no doubt that this female prominence was due above all to the failure of the men of the dynasty to display the vigour expected of a king, particularly in warfare. At the same time it must be pointed out that the scope for royal warfare by the late Ptolemaic kings was strictly limited. And yet Kleopatra III conducted the Eighth Syrian War (103–101) herself, though she was murdered at the end. Stories of kings' voluptuous lifestyles, nicknames such as 'Flute-player', or 'the Fat', suggest a considerable contempt in the general population for the males of the later generations of the family, in some members of which the ruthlessness expected of a royal ruler degenerated into viciousness and capricious cruelty.

Regents

These are the three situations in which royal women emerged as political figures in an ancient world dynasty. Those who were successful regents held their political power only so long as their children were not old enough to rule alone. Kleopatra Syra clearly did so, though by dying early her work remained incomplete; yet the vigour and ability shown by her elder son Ptolemy VI and in a different way also by her younger son Ptolemy VIII and her daughter Kleopatra III, testify to her genetic inheritance and her effective nurture. In this she was the equal of several other women in other dynasties who found themselves in a similar position. The widow of the Assyrian King Shamshi-Adad V, Sammaramat, ruled the Assyrian state for five years until her son Adad-Nirari III came of age; she was so successful (or perhaps so unusual) that she became a legendary figure in the Greek world as Semiramis. In the Battiad dynasty of Cyrene, Pheretime exercised the same sort of power without becoming such a widely known legend.

In the Seleukid dynasty women were occasionally prominent as marriage objects, and at times had some influence on their husbands and sons, but one wife, the Ptolemaic princess, Kleopatra Thea, acted as regent for her children for a decade, and was only too eager to rule alone. She contrived the death of her eldest son Seleukos V, which earned her another four years of power as regent for her next son, Antiochos VIII, but when he also indicated an intention to take power to himself, he managed to deflect her new murderous plot, and contrived Kleopatra's own death. (She features also in the next section of this chapter.)

Among the Hasmoneans, Salome Alexandra ruled for her son Hyrkanos II, having been married successively to two earlier kings, brothers. At Palmyra the widow of Septimius Odainat, the man who had saved the Roman Empire in the east, ruled on behalf of her infant son: she has fascinated men for two millennia as Zenobia, the conqueror and Roman prisoner. In the Roman and Byzantine Empires the position of imperial women was notoriously strong and prominent, but normally only as wives, and so at times as regents. Livia was powerfully influential on her husband Augustus, and on her son the Emperor Tiberius; Plotina the widow of Trajan played a powerful, even decisive, role in the accession of Hadrian; Julia Domna was probably influential on her husband Septimius Severus, but had little influence on her son Caracalla. These are examples that could be multiplied and repeated throughout history of both empires. They were occasional regents also: the last emperor of the dynasty of Justinian, Justin II, was intermittently insane and his wife Sophia ruled for him; once he died, however, she was easily pushed aside.

These examples are not numerous. They may be increased by noting some other cases where women began as regents but then, at least in the eyes of men, usurped the kingship. When men did this it was usually excused as political necessity, at least if they followed up their usurpation with a successful reign. Women did not get such an indulgence. In biblical history, Athaliah of Judah is said to have carried out a wholesale massacre of her male relations in order to rule the kingdom after her husband died; the tale is highly suspect for many reasons, not least because she is said to have missed killing her own grandson, who was hidden away and was then brought out to confound her six years later, but also because she is said to have been a princess from Israel, who thus could be said to have contaminated the pure House of David with Israelite practices – or so the later historian, who had his own agenda, claimed.

A better attested case is that of the Empress Irene of the Isaurian dynasty of Byzantium, who ruled alone after the death of her husband and the murder of her son Constantine IV, which was carried out on her orders when he came of age to rule in his own right. None of these ladies lasted very long – Athaliah (if she existed) for six years, Irene for five – and both were either murdered or deposed in favour of men. The cruelty and violence that they are said, by men, to have practised was no doubt due to the opposition they faced, from men, because they were women rulers. They were thus trapped: dealing with opponents in a firm way produced accusations of cruelty; not dealing with them firmly produced other accusations, of weakness.

Rulers by Right

Several women, like Kleopatra VII, ruled by right of inheritance, but usually only because they were the only children of earlier kings, and, when married, their husbands became kings. They were thus great marriage prizes. The dynasties of the Cimmerian Bosporos show several cases. Early on, Prytanis ruled alone (her husband's name, if she was married, is not known) but presumably only until her nephew and successor grew up. Later in the same dynasty, Kamasarye, daughter of Spartokos IV, was married to Parysades III, who thus by right of this marriage, became king. She survived him, and her son became king as Parysades IV; she is reckoned as a ruler in her own right for some years after her son's accession, because of her descent and presumably because her son required a regent. In the next dynasty, descended from Mithradates of Pontos, the daughter of his son Pharnakes, Dynamis, married three successive husbands, who therefore gained the throne, and she also ruled alone herself twice between husbands; a third husband, Polemon

I, survived her, and had a second wife, Pythodoris, who herself appears to have ruled after him, and the next king's widow, Gepaipyris, is also noted as a ruler for a short time. The explanation for all this confusion is unknown, but the easiest way to account for it is to note the failure of the male line, giving Dynamis and the other women an opening to gain power for themselves. No doubt the Roman overlords had a say in matters as well, as would have the local aristocracy; Pythodoris was later married to Archelaos, the Roman choice as king of Cappadocia, and one of Dynamis' husbands was an unknown Roman called Scribonius. Gaining the throne through marriage to a princess or queen certainly gave the husbands the title of king; it is less clear how much influence the ladies retained within the marriage. An assertive wife under such circumstances might well have the determination, because of her birth, to act as assertively as Kleopatra Syra or Kleopatra Thea; in the case of the Cimmerian Bosporos kingdom, however, it is not at all clear that they did so. Women's place in the society was rarely prominent enough to give them any role models to emulate.

Among the descendants and associates of Herod the Great, several women were prominent. Berenike the daughter of Agrippa II was the mistress of the Emperor Titus for a time. The last kings of Armenia were married to Erato – one was her brother – and she is usually reckoned as one of the kingdom's rulers; her effect on affairs was minimal, however, and her rule was short; with her death the dynasty ended.

In the Lombard dynasty, another case of a marriage hoisting a man to royal power occurs, where the wife of King Authari, Theodelinda, survived him, and took a second husband, Agilulf, who became king himself; their daughter's two husbands also became kings. Clearly there was more involved here than mere royal descent – Theodelinda was only the niece of the king – and we may assume that it was convenient for all involved to regard the ladies as transferring royalty to their husbands along with the marriage vows. Earlier, also in Italy, the daughter of Theoderic I of the Ostrogoths, Amalasuntha, had the same influence, but her contempt for any man not born of a king prevented her from wielding any real power; she was eventually murdered. (Among the last of the Ptolemies Berenike IV married a survivor of the Seleukid family but then had him murdered after a few days, complaining of his smell.)

Among the Byzantine dynasties, women in such a position could be influential, as with the daughter of Leo I, Ariadne, who carefully selected a second husband, after the death of her first and of their infant son, in the full knowledge that her choice would make him emperor; having made the choice, however, she herself then exercised only very limited power thereafter, and probably had no wish to rule personally, though she had taken the responsibility of her situation very seriously. The Hekatomnid dynasty in Karia, of course, regarded women as having the full rights of rulership, but then made them marry their brothers, presumably as a method of keeping power within the family, but this helped ensure the extinction of the dynasty; two of the women, however, ruled alone after the deaths of their husbands/ brothers.

Dynastic Endings

The appearance of women rulers is more than once the signal that the dynasty is about to expire. The Ptolemaic dynasty was clearly weakened by the prevalence of women of the royal family in power in the first century BC, and no matter how able Kleopatra VII might have been, she only ruled alone for a brief period; she was otherwise always a consort, either of her husband/ brother or her son(s), or, eventually, Mark Antony. This was the case also with earlier women rulers of this dynasty. The position of Erato of Armenia and the women of the Hekatomnid dynasty was also a sign of the approaching end of their dynasties.

In the Seleukid dynasty no ruling queens appear, the dynasty being all too prolific in male children. Towards the end, however, one woman in particular became prominent, so much so that she aspired to rule alone. This was a Ptolemaic princess, Kleopatra Thea, and daughter of Ptolemy VI, who was married to a usurper, Alexander I, as a transparent legitimizing tactic, and then, when he failed, to the legitimate Seleukid King Demetrios I – in both cases at the behest of her father; she had no choice in the matter. When Demetrios was captured in war with the Parthians and disappeared into a comfortable captivity (with a new wife provided by the Parthian king from his family), she swiftly married his brother, Antiochos VII, probably even before Demetrios had been captured. This third husband was in turn killed fighting the Parthians, and Demetrios returned, but she would have none of him, however, and is said to have arranged his murder. She had sons by all her husbands, and after Demetrios' death she ruled through two of them. When the eldest, Seleukos V, would not do as he was told, she murdered him; his brother and successor, Antiochos VIII, took due notice and turned the tables and forced her to commit suicide when he was of age to rule himself. Her posthumous revenge was civil war between her sons by two of her husbands, which continued into the following generation; from the beginning of that civil war, the dynasty and the kingdom were never again united. It might be claimed, by men, that she was the cause of the decline of the dynasty, but in truth the kings did it all themselves, though her career of marriages and killings scarcely helped the dynasty to operate successfully.

In the Sassanid dynasty women scarcely figure, except in the great dynastic crisis in the period 628–632, when two royal princesses, Boran and Amarigdukht, were briefly made ruling queens; they were, or rather their promoters were, unable to maintain their positions, and both were murdered; their successor, Yazdgard III, was the last of the dynasty, and was steadily driven eastwards by the Muslim Arab invasion until finally he was murdered. The Orontid dynasty of Armenia died out with Queen Erato, who first ruled as the wife of her husband/brother, and then briefly alone. In the same way the last of the Aiakid dynasty of Epeiros, Deidameia, usually described as a princess rather than a ruling queen, ruled only briefly before being murdered, which was presumably done as a way of removing both the dynasty and the Epeirote kingship itself.

One rather curious case is that of Queen Seaxburh of Wessex, who was the widow of King Coenwalh, and who ruled alone for a year or so after her husband's death; she was then succeeded by a cousin, and then by her brother-in-law, Coenwalh's brother. The only source for all this, the *Anglo-Saxon Chronicle*, gives no reason for her period in power, though Coenwalh had had a very bad time as king in a war with Mercia. It may be that she ruled only until the male successor was located. In other words, she was keeping the throne warm. What is particularly odd is that two successors were clearly available when Coenwalh died, and both they and others had good hereditary claims to the throne: why then, the woman and the delay? We do not know. It looks very much like an emergency measure until a new king could be persuaded to take the throne.

Conclusion

Royal women in the ancient world thus played only a very limited role in political affairs, and only, like Seaxburh, in emergencies – minorities, disputed successions, the failure of a male heir. Given the tenor of society of the time, and the likely short lives of women even of the highest rank, even when they had access to good food, clean air, and the best medical attention, this is no surprise. But men gave themselves away by conceding even such a limited role to women. If they were to be allowed to rule during those emergencies, all the more should women have been able to do so in normal times.

Chapter 8

Mergers

It was not uncommon for one dynasty to replace an earlier one, even peacefully; the replacement of the expired Spartokid dynasty by the Mithradatids in the kingdom of the Cimmerian Bosporos was a notably successful case. The standard method of legitimizing such a takeover was for the new dynasty's first ruler to marry the daughter of the last ruler of the previous dynasty, if there was one; there are examples of that too, as in the Egyptian dynasty 'XXI', where the first king married the daughter of the last of the Ramessides. There are also a few examples of dynasties running side by side for a time. The most glaring example is, of course, Sparta, where the Agiad and Eurypontid dynasties coexisted together during several hundred years. In the end one of them failed. The pairing was so institutionalized by then that a replacement was transferred from the surviving line to restart the expiree, though such was the dire state of the Spartan polity by that time, that the whole system of the dual monarchy was abolished only ten years later, an example of a minor change demonstrating that a cherished institution is, after all, unnecessary and vulnerable.

This parallelism seems also to have been one of the major factors in the Roman oligarchic system, and it contributed to the relative success of several families in maintaining access to power over a long period during the republic. As an example, the Aemilii at one point in the later fourth century BC had six branches of the family in operation (the sixth generation). One branch failed in that generation, and another a little later. A third, the Balbula branch, expired in the late third century, but the Paulli, Lepidi, and Papi lasted another thirty years. By then the Lepidi had subdivided so that for another generation there were still three active branches. Then the Paulli expired (having given away two sons to adoption). The Lepidi continued with two branches until the 60s BC, at which point one died out, but the other again subdivided. Throughout its existence the Aemilius family never had less than two branches that were simultaneously politically active.

Sparta was unique in maintaining, deliberately, the two royal dynasties in parallel, which usually ensured that at least one was adult at any time. The kingship in Dalriada had similarities; in this case two lines were descended from the first king, Domangart I (the apparent first King Fergus was probably a myth, possibly Domangart also) just as the Spartan kings claimed to be descended from the twin sons of Aristodemos. In Dalriada, however, the branches alternated in supplying kings to the kingdom, rather than ruling jointly. This lasted a century or more before one line died out, and then two other lines were brought in as replacements. Transferring the kingship between lines of descent was an Irish institution also, with the result that there the relationship between successive kings became increasingly attenuated.

In the case of Dalriada, the succession system was presumably the basis of the process. In Sparta, however, the dual kingship's origins are more obscure. The claim that twin sons inherited jointly is no explanation, since that did not require that both should be succeeded by sons who became kings; until then the succession had been by primogeniture. Anyway, the whole story is thoroughly unlikely; it has all the signs of a later rationalization, combined with invention, of an existing institution. Rather more likely is the theory that the two lines were originally independent of each other, and that their joint rule was the price paid for the political unification of two minor states. The union was then rationalized in myth as the joint inheritance. But this is still hardly adequate – quite apart from the lack of evidence for it – since the dual kingship was hardly necessary, and in fact might well be seen as perpetuating the division that the union was supposed to remove.

A rather more likely event is that one dynasty would extinguish another, probably its weaker rival. Thus, the Rugian kingdom in Noricum in the fifth century AD was subdued by the Italian King Odoacar, and then removed into Italy. In Spain the minor kingdom of the Sueves was taken over by the Visigoths and its dynasty disappeared; the Burgundian kingship was taken by the Merovingians, and the dynasty ended. These were, of course, conquests, not an uncommon situation, but there were also unifications of two states, usually one large and one small. The Roman Republic was active in such work in the east and North Africa from the second century BC onwards – even before that the Syracusan kingdom had been the first to surrender, carelessly changing sides the wrong way in the Second Punic War, and so earning extinction just as did the Rugians seven centuries later. The Attalid, the Bithynian, and the Cyrenaican kingdoms were all surrendered by their kings, in a process that was in fact the merger of their kingdoms with the Roman Republic. Under the empire the process was somewhat different, in that the imperial government had a tendency to create kingdoms, particularly in Syria and Asia Minor, and then after a time take them over. This had happened also in the Alps where the dynasty of Cottius had been promoted as a means of controlling part of the Alpine area, and was then suppressed and the kingdom united with the empire as a minor province.

There are also three cases where two dynasties merged more or less successfully, if with some difficulty. In all three it was clearly an attempt to unite two neighbouring kingdoms in the interests of increasing their joint power, on the lines that a union would be more effective than two kingdoms operating separately – or perhaps, in union is strength. It was, however, a process that was clearly extremely difficult to bring to completion, in part because by the time the idea developed the two dynasties, or kingdoms, and their own identities, and, in personal terms, the kings were ambitious and disliked each other, which got in the way. Unification is always difficult.

The earliest case – apart from that of Sparta – is that of the two dynasties of tyrants in Greek Sicily. The two originators were Theron, the tyrant of Akragas, and Gelon, the tyrant of Gela and Syracuse. By a complexity of marriages they formed a firm political alliance in which they, their sons, and their brothers were placed as tyrants in several cities as a means of controlling the restless population. The resulting joint power was not so much a single state or kingdom as a sort of tyrants' federation, but as a military power it was the greatest in the Greek world of the time, and performed successfully in 480 in defeating a Carthaginian attack. But it was also a personal creation of the two leaders, Theron and Gelon, and their joint state broke up and their tyranny disappeared only a few years after their deaths. The tyranny of Dionysios, also in Sicily, half a century later, developed in a rather similar way, when Dionysios organized a series of marriages to unite his family with that of Hipparinos, a rival great man in Syracuse, though in this case the union carried power all one way, into Dionysios' hands, rather than sharing it.

The third dynasty of Thrace developed out of two rival Thracian dynasties, the Odrysian and the Sapaean, located north and south respectively of the Hebros River. They existed and ruled separately for some decades until the two dynasties were linked by the marriage of a Sapaean daughter to the Odrysian King Cotys V. The result was a fairly confused situation, not aided for modern students by some uncertain dating for the kings. The confusion was also helped along by some intermarriages and by Roman Imperial interference. In the end, after half a century of confused successions, a single line emerged under Rhoemetalces I, but his family then produced separate lines of successors so that the inheritance went first jointly to his brother and his son, then to the sons of these two, in succession. The joint kingdom was then suppressed after twenty years by a Roman annexation.

The two Anglian kingdoms in northern England, Deira (more or less modern Yorkshire), and Bernicia (modern Durham, Northumberland, and the Lothians) each developed its own dynasty of kings from the mid sixth century. Neither dynasty was secure, though no subordinate or competing lines established themselves, despite the intervention of usurping kings from outside these families. Perhaps in part because of this competitive threat, both dynasties seem to have considered themselves rivals for both kingdoms from the start. There was, for example, only one marriage to link the two before a later and more decisive match between King Oswiu and Princess Eanflaed, so joint inheritance was not the issue. That first marriage, however, between the Bernician King Aethelfrith and the daughter of the Deiran King Aelle, was partly the foundation of Aethelfrith's career of conquest; he was king of both kingdoms for a dozen years, until overthrown by his wife's brother Edwin. Edwin in turn fell before Aethelfrith's eldest son Oswald, whose successor was his second son Oswiu. The second linking marriage jointed Oswiu with Eanflaed, Edwin's daughter; inheritance and marriage made Oswiu king of both kingdoms, by now being called Northumbria. No doubt the intent to unify was in part a product of the attitude of their Anglian subjects, who were in control, at the start anyway, of only relatively small coastal territories, and who faced powerful, if divided, Celtic enemies inland – Cadwallon of North Wales for example campaigned as far north as Hadrian's Wall, in the process killing at least two of the northern kings.

By the time of Oswiu's death in 670 the two kingdoms had been jointly ruled by three kings for a total of forty-six years out of the previous sixty-four. Deira was the reluctant partner, with intermittent local kings, often from the overtaken local dynasty, popping up during all that time. There were thus as powerful internal forces tending towards separation as there were for conjunction. The last of Aelle's Deiran line, Oswine, King of Deira, died in 651, and from then the union become a near certainty, though even then a man of the Bernician line ruled Deira separately for another four years – rather as the Eurypontid Eukleidas was transferred to the Agiad line in Sparta when the latter failed. But from 655 the two kingdoms were united for two centuries or so, until a new invasion, by the Viking Great Army, broke the joint kingdom apart again, on much the same geographical lines.

The difficulty in joining these two kingdoms was thus very great, even though they were little more than half a century old when the uniting process began. In the end it was as much the threat of attacks from Wales, from Mercia, and from Scotland as it was the joining of the rival dynasties, which propelled the two into one.

These examples are obvious cases of unification, but there are also Roman dynasties that were in a somewhat similar condition. The first dynasty of Roman emperors is called 'Julio-Claudian' because it included, in the persons of Augustus ('C. Julius Caesar') and his stepson Tiberius ('Ti. Claudius Nero'), both the Julian and Claudian families; the union came about by the marriage of Augustus to Tiberius' mother Livia, who had been earlier married to a Claudius, the father of Tiberius. The dynasty also brought in, by other marriages, the families of Marcus Antonius and Cn. Domitius Ahenobarbus. It was thus not so much a dynasty as a coalition.

This was, in fact, a continuation of the Roman aristocratic practices of the late republic, where marriages were made and broken off as a part of the political process, and it is in part one of the reasons for the inability of the Roman Imperial system to produce a stable dynastic succession; for many of the other Roman aristocratic families considered themselves to be the equals of the emperor's family, and were thus rivals for imperial power. One of the reasons for the murder of Domitian and the elimination of the Flavian dynasty was that it looked as though it would actually establish a successful continuing dynasty.

The third Roman dynasty, conventionally called Antonine, was another union, by a complex of marriages, of three or four families, and the later dynasties were some similar unions of this type – Severan of two, the Tetrarchy of four, and the Valentinian-Theodosian dynasty of two families. In no case was the process a success in producing a stable dynasty, except in the short term. Success would be shown by the establishment of a dynasty for a lengthy period, with a clear and undisputed line of succession for perhaps at least two centuries – which would be double the length achieved by the longest reigning dynasty of the empire, for none of these Roman dynasties lasted much over a century, and most expired well short of that.

It is a curious echo, in fact, of the regal period at Rome, where the first two kings, Romulus and Titus Tatius, are said to have ruled together. Tatius married his daughter to the next king, Numa Pompilius, and their daughter was married to a Marcius, who fathered the fourth king, Ancus Marcius. The final dynasty was similar: Tarquinius Priscus' successor was his son-in-law Servius Tullius, who was then succeeded by Tarquinius' son, Tarquinius Superbus, who was also Servius' son-in-law. At least this is how the story has reached us: there are many elements that seem thoroughly unlikely, and probably invented, above all that extraordinary sequence of successions. Yet such a weird succession probably had its effect on later Roman attitudes, and several episodes have the appearance of a deliberate political policy of merging several aristocratic lines into a single royal family.

The apparent pairing and joining of lines as early as the kingdom of Rome, may have been replicated in the republic by the double praetorships and double consulships that were chosen to rule the new state. Alternatively, the double magistracies having been instituted, and such pairing was common among other Italian city-states at the time. The curious stories of the preceding regal period were perhaps developed in order to claim an earlier legitimacy for the unusual doubling of offices. (In the same way the Spartans imagined that their double kingship originated with twin sons.) It is a fact that the Roman polity, regal, Republican, Imperial, repeatedly resorted to double rule – Augustus and Tiberius, Vespasian and Titus, the Tetrarchs, Valens and Valentinian, and so on – and it must be said that, even if individual dynasties repeatedly failed in the Imperial period, it cannot be claimed that Rome was an unsuccessful state.

The ambition to unite kingdoms and families by such a comfortable method as marriage was laudable; in fact it proved, all too often, also to be like marriage itself, only too troublesome. A single family to which the succession to the kingship was confined prevented much confusion.

Chapter 9

Violent Deaths and Depositions

T
he causes of the deaths of kings and emperors and others in these dynasties are in large part quite unknown, though by that very fact they are likely to have been mainly natural, on the assumption that any other kind of death – murder, assassination, death in battle, poisoning, and so on – is more likely to have produced a clear record than is a death from old age or illness. And so it is really only these deaths by violence, and the depositions, usually well-noted also, which it is possible to investigate. But again, the sources for many of the dynasties are not adequate even to isolate these more spectacular deaths, though there is enough information for about fifty dynasties to draw some conclusions. Some others have inadequate information, such as the Parthian dynasties, and these can therefore not be considered.

Those dynasties for which records of deaths are absent or inadequate are excluded. Some other limitations may also be mentioned. It is not certain that all the violent deaths – murders, suicides, battle-deaths – are known for those dynasties included in the list; the records are therefore of minimum cases, and no doubt other killings also happened. How representative a sample of the totality of dynasties they are is also less than certain. Certainly many dynasties saw few or no such deaths and depositions, and so it is not possible to claim that the totals can be applied across the board as an indication of the general incidence of death. Even so, it is worth noting that in this group of dynasties – a quarter of the total – violent death or forcible deposition accounted for just about half the rulers.

Some dynasties suffered constant, repeated, death by violence. The Seleukid dynasty had twenty-five kings; of these eleven were murdered or executed, and eleven died in battle; two more, the last two, were deposed; so only one ruling king in this family died a 'natural' death – though with this record, it is clear that the natural way of death in the family was actually by violence. The dynasty of Heraklios that ruled in Byzantium in the seventh century AD had many fewer rulers – only six – but three of them were murdered and one was deposed; only two died naturally. The record of Roman emperors is just as bad: of the fifty emperors noted in the dynasties included in the Catalogue, seventeen were murdered, four died in battle, three committed suicide, and one was deposed – half the total (and this omits the intervening non-dynastic or short-dynasty emperors, many of whom also died violent deaths). Some of these Roman dynasties had worse records than others, of course; four out of the five Severan emperors were murdered, but only one of the Antonines, and one of the Flavian dynasty; all three of the Gordians died violently. But the overall record is obviously very bad. To become Roman emperor was to court a death by violence.

The single murders in the Flavian and Antonine dynasties were in fact the deaths of the last rulers in those dynasties, Domitian and Commodus, and brought about the ends of these dynasties. This is the normal pattern, for dynasties did not retire gracefully from the scene; dynastic abdication is extremely rare. Only one of those fifty Roman emperors actually abdicated – Diocletian – and it is almost unknown anywhere else, except among the Anglo-Saxons and the Merovingians, where the use of forced or voluntary abdication was often in fact deposition. And as the case of Diocletian shows, in any dynasty the abdication of one ruler is always in favour of his own chosen successor; it does not signal the end of the dynasty itself – indeed, abdication and deposition was in fact a means of perpetuating the dynasty, since the departing king may be desperately unpopular and moving out of obvious power would defuse that enmity, while, at the same time, his continuation alive permitted him to intervene when the furore had died down – as Diocletian did more than once. Several of these men did in fact return to power – Justin II, for example. So the only way to remove a dynasty, if that was what was desired, was to kill the last member or members of it, and by killing him or her to ensure its extinction, and this is a fairly common occurrence. Apart from the Flavian and Antonine dynasties, a good dozen of those with good records of causes of death end with the violent death of the last member.

More significant is the fact that, as evidenced by the record of the Seleukid dynasty already mentioned, the long record of the violent deaths of its rulers does not seem to have prevented that dynasty from continuing to rule, unless the last member of the dynasty had no successors of his body, nor any designated successor. Here was the reason for the extinction of both the Flavians and Antonines, and so it was not the murders that ended these dynasties, but the carelessness of those last members in avoiding their genetic duty. (Alexander the Great was essentially in the same situation; he had one possible successor, and his wife was pregnant with another, but this left his people with the choice between an unborn infant and a halfwit. They chose both, but neither survived to rule.)

Death in battle might be seen as a heroic confirmation of the dynasty's worth and could consolidate support. Certainly the deaths of individual kings and emperors were important, and perhaps even prevented vital developments, and in some cases certainly seem to have had important effects, but the dynasty went on. In the case of the Seleukids, the murder of Seleukos IV began a long process of internal dispute, when his brother took the throne from the dead king's son, who later took his own revenge – and both men killed the sons of the man they displaced. This set up a repeating pattern of usurpation and murder that operated for a century until the dynasty broke up into constant warfare, and broke up the kingdom as well. In the end it took the conquest of the final fragments of their territories by Rome, and the forcible deposition of the last two kings – there were other members of the family still alive as well – to eliminate the dynasty's final fragment of political power. That is to say, the dynasty was prolific as well as violent, and never more so than in the last two generations, and this had ensured its survival until the Roman intervention, and would have ensured its continuation had Rome refrained. Similarly with the Ptolemies, who indulged in much mutual killing in the later generations – three deaths in battle, six murders – but even when reduced to rule by Kleopatra VII alone, she had three children who could have succeeded her, if Rome had permitted it.

There is one dynasty, however, where a series of violent deaths, combined with one peculiar and very nasty internal dynastic practice, succeeded in bringing it to extinction. This was the second Akhaimenid dynasty, descended from Darius I. The death of each king brought trouble, from the death of Xerxes I in 464 onwards, which was usually the rebellion of a brother of the chosen successor, or by a man who seized the throne that resulted in the death of one of the contenders. At the death of Artaxerxes II in 359/358, a successor, Artaxerxes III, pre-empted that problem by culling all the relatives who might be thought to pose a challenge to him. Then when he was murdered by his vizir Bagoas in 338, his murderer also saw to the killing of the dead king's sons, except for one, Arses, whom he made king. Only two years later, when it became clear that Arses could not be controlled, the vizir killed that replacement and all his sons. As a result of all this there were no longer any near relatives of any of these kings; the Akhaimenid dynasty had been killed off. There were, however, many possible claimants, thanks to the previous kings' policy of presenting royal princesses to deserving satraps. Before serious trouble could arise, Bagoas found (or had already selected) a distant cousin and made him king as Darius III; he in turn promptly killed the vizir. Darius III was the last of the Akhaimenid Great Kings, and when he in turn was murdered by his subjects after several successive defeats by Alexander the Great's Macedonian/Greek army there was no member of the Akhaimenid family available to rally his former subjects (though there were numerous collateral relations, such as, for example, Orontes who made himself king in Armenia). The provinces then fought their own battles against Alexander, and duly lost.

One would expect Darius III to have had children, for the harem was originally a Persian institution, but only a daughter appears in the sources, and she was annexed by Alexander in a pre-emptive move, as another wife. No sons therefore emerged as later claimants. The aristocrats of the defunct Empire had received Akhaimenid princesses as wives often enough in the past, and it is curious that no claims were made on grounds of descent from these earlier kings. It would appear that the final defeat had also resulted in the disgrace of the imperial family. The potential claimants seem to have seen greater potential and personal profit in seizing power in the provinces – several later dynasties (Pontos, Atropatene, Armenia) were descended from Akhaimenid governors.

So the killing of members of dynasties is only crucial if it is the last living member who is killed, or if it is done so systematically that none of the family survives, as with the Akhaimenids – and even there it was the death of Darius III that was decisive, not the deaths of his distant cousins earlier; or if the last member is prevented from ruling by the exercise of *force majeure*, as with the last of the Attalids, the last Seleukids, and the last Ptolemies, all of whom were suppressed by Rome. Death by violence was clearly a constant hazard that all rulers had to cope with, but only in exceptional circumstances would it bring a dynasty to an end.

The last group of Roman emperors in the west, in the twenty years following the death of Valentinian III in 455, were barely connected with the main dynasty, which was now settled at Constantinople. Only one of these emperors, Majorian, showed any real abilities, and he died fighting. The others, like the last Akhaimenids, were under the control of warlords who elevated and installed them, or removed them as they pleased. There can have been little or no regret felt for the removal of these ineffectual men, and the last, Romulus Augustulus, was a mere teenage boy. When he was deposed and allowed to go into semi-exile in a luxurious villa in Campania, there was no local regret and no demand for an imperial replacement. The final warlord, Odoacar, contemptuously sent the imperial regalia to Constantinople with the ironic message that there was no need for a new emperor in the west, since he would henceforth recognize the authority of the man in Constantinople, which was, in effect, the declaration of independence. Both the Akhaimenid and Western Roman emperors had lost the respect of their subjects by their ineffectuality – the same could be said of the last of the Seleukids, two squabbling cousins who were in effect under the control of local Arab kings, and of Ptolemaic Kleopatra, whose marital antics were less than pleasing to her subjects, as were her extravagances, and the several murders she had contrived.

One of the main duties of rulers, and in some cases one of their main occupations, was warfare. Death in battle was thus not an unlikely fate, since it was the practice of commanders to fight, spear in hand, in the ranks, until battles became so complicated that commanders needed to be outside the ranks to exercise some control. Battles were fought by grown men, usually already married and having begotten children. The objection of the Macedonian lords, voiced to Alexander the Great when he set off to conquer the world, that he should marry and have a son first, was all too prophetic. He did go off, unmarried, and died leaving a pregnant wife, but no other legitimate heir, a striking abnegation of responsibility in a king. The lesson was well learnt by later generations and dynasties. When the Seleukid Antiochos III inherited the kingship in 222 BC, he was the only member of his family left alive. His life was in constant danger for several years. He had several active enemies seeking to replace him, and was guided against them in turn by his vizir Hermeias who was less than trustworthy. At last Antiochos asserted himself to fight the main enemy, the usurper Molon in the east, after Hermeias insisted that since Molon had made himself king, only a king could fight him. It is likely that Hermeias' deeper purpose was to contrive Antiochos' own death; instead, like Darius III, it was Antiochos who arranged for Hermeias' demise; he had to organize a *coup d'état* in his own court to remove the minister.

The incidence of violent death, as noted already, is by no means confined to the great imperial dynasties that I have discussed so far, though they do seem to have been particularly liable. It is notable also that death by murder is the most common of these causes, though in certain dynasties – Elam, Lydia, Northumbria, the Seleukids, the Spartan Agiads – it was death in battle that was the worst cause. It clearly depended on the military or non-military traditions of the dynasty.

But I cannot help drawing attention to three dynasties in particular, all of which have records of violent deaths or depositions approaching one hundred per cent – the Seleukids and the Gordians whom I have already mentioned, but note also the Barkids of Carthage, all of whom died in battle except Hannibal, who was murdered. To be a member of any of these dynasties was in effect to be sentenced to a possibly painful death – but no one ever abdicated.

Chapter 10

Breakdowns

Of the many reasons for dynasties to vanish, the possibility of internecine conflict – that is, conflict within the dynastic family – is one of the most likely to remove public approval. And it is only with public approval and acceptance that any dynasty can continue to rule. The answer to such disapproval, which would be manifested in disobedience, desertion from the forces, riots, failing to pay taxes, and so on, would first of all be to use force; but this would further erode their approval rating. Dynasties may claim a variety of sanctions for continuing in power, divine right, antiquity, inherited glory, durability, competence, but it is only by the acceptance of their power by the potentially powerful individuals and groups in their domains that they can continue. They may maintain themselves by armed force for a time in the absence of public approval, but that disapproval will wear away their power and authority in the end, and relying on armed force alone is exceptionally hazardous, since the armed forces are one of the institutions whose approval is crucial, and which have the power to take action. Even the longest-lived dynasties vanished in the end, removed by one means or another, and many did so because they had forfeited the approval of those of their subjects who had the means of making their disapproval decisive.

It is this that is surely the basic cause of the replacement of the Roman Republic by the imperial system. The republic had been ruled by a relatively large number of dynastic families, whose rate of expiry and creation had held open the possibility of new families joining the ruling group, at least since the fifth century BC, and these had done so fairly regularly for several centuries, and yet large numbers were excluded, so any change was resisted strongly by those with power. Rome's problems were largely externalized for a long time, in the sense that constant aggression against Rome's neighbours provided a powerful outlet for any discontent, and a powerful mechanism for promoting the new families, or, in effect, expelling the unwanted. But the internal discontents did not thereby go away, and by the late second century BC they had begun to focus on the role of the ruling elite, whose acceptance of new families was slowing down, and whose negative attitude was, unprecedentedly for Rome, manifested in murder and assassination – the Gracchi and their followers in particular. Their monopoly of the control of armed force was broken, and the discontents erupted by way of the army, led in most cases by discontented members of the elite – Marius, Sulla, Pompey, Caesar, and others. The approval of the ordinary soldiers had been withdrawn from the ruling families as rulers, their domestic pretensions having become unable to cope with the new situation; they turned to populist generals for relief.

The forfeiture of approval is usually a fairly long-drawn-out matter, as at Rome, particularly if the dynasty has a monopoly of force in a state and is prepared to use it against internal discontent. It is signalled by a high incidence of dynastic civil war, murders, assassinations, and depositions. As an example there is the Julio-Claudian dynasty at Rome, established firmly in power by victories in two civil wars – by Julius Caesar in 48–44 and then by Octavian in the 30s BC – and consolidated by the long, successful, and internally peaceful principates of Augustus and Tiberius. This was fortified by extensive external conquests and for a long time the dynasty's power and authority was overshadowed by the memories of the civil war that no one wish to repeat. All these were major factors in legitimizing the dynasty and ensuring its continuation.

By the time Tiberius died, however, in AD 37, after nearly seven decades of rule by Augustus and Tiberius, there were no men of power alive to recall those old evil days; indeed, Tiberius himself, born in 42 BC, must have been one of the last men with any such memories. After Tiberius, the emperors of the dynasty became erratic and uncertain, personally obnoxious, and were despised and feared. Two, Caligula and Claudius, were murdered, and Nero was effectively deposed and driven to commit suicide, while none of these three evoked any real respect as a person or as a ruler. The original legitimacy acquired by the first two rulers was thus forfeited by the last three.

There is also another element to watch for. Tiberius was clearly marked out by Augustus as his successor for several years, even decades, before his death; he was also Augustus' stepson who had been married to Augustus' only child, and was adopted by Augustus as his son. Given that Augustus had no son of his body, Tiberius became emperor as much by hereditary right as by the choice of, and adoption by, Augustus. But the later emperors of the dynasty could not claim that hereditary right, and the succession jumped about: Caligula was Tiberius' grand-nephew, Claudius was Caligula's uncle, Nero was Claudius' stepson, and owed his rule as sole emperor only to the murder of Claudius' own son Britannicus. And by the end of the dynasty, when Nero died, there were no members of the family left to claim any real relationship with any of the preceding emperors. Nero may well have had technical command of the armies of the Roman state, though he had never seen any of the legions, but the withdrawal of public approval of him, by the senators, by the army commanders, by the Roman populace, left him alone at the end, and the option of using force to continue his rule was no longer possible. In the history of the Julio-Claudian dynasty, therefore, there were two phases; the long period of public acceptance under Augustus and Tiberius, and the subsequent much shorter phase of progressively increasing public disapproval under the three final rulers.

This second phase, from AD 37 to 68, is an example of the process of dynastic breakdown. It is one that can be seen to occur in a good thirty or more other dynasties. The causes in individual dynastic detail are many and varied, but in general they can be summed up as the result of personal ambitions among those outside the dynasty, combined with an attitude amongst those in power that implied that the dynasty was a permanent political institution and that no amount of misbehaviour by the ruler would cause it political harm – dynastic arrogance, in essence. This is an attitude all too likely to be proved mistaken. It is also clearly evident among the Roman Republican dynasties during the Roman revolution of the first century BC, and even after, among the few surviving republican dynasties. As late as the end of the first century AD, a Calpurnius, a member of one of the very few republican families still existing, plotted against the Emperor Nerva, believing that his own high birth entitled him to be emperor, and that this was quite sufficient to ensure success without requiring any effort on his own part. The display in Nerva's hand of an unsheathed sword – and no doubt the presence of the emperor's guard – sufficed to deter him. And this was Nerva! The emperor who, as Sir Ronald Syme put it, had 'never seen a province or an army'. A generation earlier the last of the Sulpicii had become emperor, in part due to his exalted birth, but Galba lasted only a few months, being a poor politician. High birth is never enough; ability is required very much more. The crisis was resolved by a civil war; one of the nastier ways by which ability wins out.

In a dynastic genealogy the characteristic signs of a dynastic breakdown are civil wars, disputed successions, and those murders and depositions that disfigured the Julio-Claudian line, together with a rapid series of short reigns. The appearance of women in ruling positions is another sign of dynastic breakdown (see Chapter 7, 'Women'). This combination of factors leads to evermore remote and distant members of the dynasty achieving power, with the overall result that the wider support for the dynasty, which is usually based on a perception of legitimate descent, wears away. In Wessex, for example, the succession was reasonably straightforward from the 530s, when the first of the dynasty, Cerdic, emerged as king in the area of Hampshire and Wiltshire, until 672, with the death of Coenwalh, the seventh king, a sequence of rulers only one of which ruled for less than a decade, and all of whom were within a recognizable line of succession from Cerdic. The succession to the kingship then went first to Coenwalh's widow, to his brother, to a distant cousin, to a distant cousin in a different line, and finally to yet another distant cousin in yet a third line of descent, and all within sixteen years. Of those ephemeral rulers, one was a woman (unprecedented until then in Anglo-Saxon England), one king was deposed, and one was assassinated. By the end of that process any loyalty to the original dynasty as such had vanished, for it had demonstrated the incompetence of its members; it was now up to each king to attract anew the necessary loyalty; direct dynastic succession in Wessex was in effect abandoned for the next century. It only resumed with the family descended from Egbert, who in fact came from a Kentish family, ruled for forty years, was victorious, extended his kingdom, and left several sons – that is, was a second founder of the kingdom and was powerful enough to change the succession system back to primogeniture.

The end of the second Akhaimenid dynasty was somewhat similar, and has been touched on already. Within three years (338–336) two kings were murdered, apparently by their vizir Bagoas, and then the succession went to a distant cousin who killed Bagoas; he was then attacked and defeated by the Macedonian invasion led by Alexander; he was finally murdered by his own people. Without the destabilizing influence of Bagoas and the resulting rapid succession of ephemeral kings, it seems likely that the Macedonian attack would have been much less successful – if Alexander had faced Artaxerxes II, for example, a successful king who had ruled for twenty years, and an accomplished warrior, he would have met a distinctly tougher and wilier opponent than Darius III.

The joint dynasties numbering 'XXII' and 'XXIII' in Egypt (ruling from 945 to 715 BC) exhibit the same sort of conditions as with the later Akhaimenids, but over a longer period. The dynasty was originally a single family, though one branch of it was installed at Thebes while the main seat of the kings was in the north, at Memphis or in the Delta. The Theban branch based its power on holding the position of chief priest of Amun in the great temple in that city, and had been installed there deliberately by the northern pharaoh precisely because it was a powerful and influential post, able to deploy great wealth (and would therefore pose a major threat to the king in the north). A member of the dynastic family was needed there to control that wealth and potential power, but above all the kings needed to prevent others gaining the use of it. This branch had no military power or resources, so the northern pharaoh had little difficulty in slapping the Thebans down when it became necessary in his view. Then in 818 a more serious division developed, when the dynasty's northern branch split into two separate ruling branches based at Tanis and Leontopolis, both in the Delta (and so even more distant from Thebes), though there seems to have been no real hostility between these two (who are referred to as dynasties 'XXII' and 'XXIII' respectively). Nevertheless this division clearly reduced the capability of the northern kings for controlling the south – and they even lost control of parts of the Delta, much closer to home. Soon a new and foreign dynasty, out of Nubia to the south of Thebes, was able to invade Egypt with impunity, conquering Thebes without difficulty. King Piankhy of the Nubian dynasty installed his sister at Thebes as the 'Divine Adoratrice' in place of the earlier representatives from the Egyptian dynasty. From there, having in the same way as the earlier dynasty secured control of Thebes, the temple, and its wealth, he went on to reduce the divided north to subservience as well. All three branches of dynasties 'XXII/XXIII' had vanished by 715. In this case the reason was simply and solely the dynastic division that rendered the dynasty weak, and so made it vulnerable to foreign conquest, thus it lost public approval: murder and assassination were not in this case required.

The practice of sibling inheritance could be profoundly destabilizing, even when it was the accepted practice of the dynasty. Consider the case of the family of the Muslim caliphs of the Umayyad dynasty. This was, in effect, two successive dynasties: that founded by Muawiya, the first of the dynasty, who reigned for nineteen years, and his son and grandson then ruled for only three years altogether. The dynasty was then rescued by a cousin, Marwan, whose own early death brought the caliphate to the third founder, Abd al-Malik, the fourth caliph in as many years. He held the throne for a reign that lasted for twenty years. He was followed by his four sons, only one of whom, Hisham, ruled for any length of time (nineteen years). He in turn was succeeded by four caliphs within a year, one of whom was murdered, and one deposed. Thus, the dynasty consisted of three men who each ruled for about twenty years, and eleven other men who ruled for less than twenty years between them. The whole sequence was obviously profoundly unsettling – quite apart from a series of religious disputes in which they were all also involved – and the incidence of good government amongst these men was depressingly low. The very fact that they could claim a religious sanction for their position made their luxury-loving and unpleasant behaviour all the more difficult for their subjects to bear. Nevertheless, it was only with the intrusion of personal violence into the internal affairs of the family that the real breakdown of the dynasty came. The last of the family was oppressive, which, combined with the final sequence of brief and incompetent reigns, brought a classic forfeit of public approval and support.

Another, earlier, Arab dynasty, that of al-Kinda, had practised sibling inheritance, with the result that the inevitable internal fighting between inheritors, and/or the division of the inheritance, brought the dynasty to a state of political dissolution within a few years after the death of the first king, al-Harith, in 528. He was succeeded by four sons, who ruled simultaneously. At least two were dead within a year; one of the survivors was then followed by his three sons. The result was five simultaneous kings, and the effective end of the dynasty's pretensions to any serious political power.

The Merovingian dynasty of the Franks, contemporary with both al-Kinda and the Umayyads, had a succession system that involved simultaneous sibling and cousin kings who could be assigned to a variety of territories, each a fragment of the whole, in a system of inheritance and government that needs a map and a genealogy to follow. The result was a generalized Frankish attachment to the dynasty, but not to any individual members, the development of a political and administrative system that effectively ignored the kings, and the detachment of parts of the kingdom into effective independence under their own rulers, particularly Aquitaine and Bavaria. The central political figures of the whole kingdom became the Mayors of the Palace for each of the major provinces, for the several sections of the whole kingdom each had one. Between 676 and 679 three kings, Childeric II, Clovis III, and Dagobert II, were successively murdered as they each made a serious attempt to assert themselves against the Mayors. They all failed, and after 679 the Mayors clearly had the upper hand, and were able to impose their own kings as they chose, or to leave the throne empty for some years. Possible inheritors were frequently confined to monasteries, where they could be left to languish, or could be plucked out again at need to occupy the throne as symbols. The inevitable result was that the Merovingian dynasty was ultimately reduced to a single man, and similarly the Mayors of the several provinces were reduced to a single man for the whole kingdom; he eventually usurped the kingship, and established a new royal dynasty, the Carolingian, in 751. It turned out that the Merovingians were not essential after all.

The Umayyad dynasty lasted about ninety years; the Merovingians about three centuries; the second Akhaimenid and the Wessex dynasty each lasted less than two centuries; the Julio-Claudians ruled for about one century. That is to say, the breakdown of a dynasty can occur at any stage or age of the dynasty, and length of time is not relevant. In the Antipatrid dynasty that ruled in Macedon after Alexander the Great, the breakdown came in the third generation, but the dynasty as a whole lasted less than three decades; the breakdown came in the reigns of disputing brothers and resulted in their murders.

The Spartan dynasties, having ruled perhaps six or seven centuries, so it was claimed, broke down more or less simultaneously in the face of intractable social pressures and military defeat, and facing political manifestations that they could not control. One of the lines, the Eurypontid, failed and was renewed only by the appointment of an Agiad, Eukleidas, as joint king by a sort of dynastic transfer; further murders and depositions at the hands of rebels and revolutionaries and plotters eliminated both lines by 217. The whole process of the breakdown took place over perhaps fifty years. Despite Sparta's frequent wars, violent deaths among the kings had been fairly rare until the last years; but there were four depositions and two murders in the last two decades; a clear sign that affairs had gone wrong. This is as clear an example of progressive dynastic breakdown as with the Julio-Claudians.

The Arsakid dynasty of Parthia eventually disintegrated during the first century BC to such a degree that it is possible now to reconstruct a continuous family tree only by leaving several kings to one side. After a period of confusion, a new line of kings, probably, but not certainly Arsakid in ancestry, fastened a firm grip on the state, and maintained a clear line of succession – very different from the earlier dynasty – until the end. This was another case of dynastic recovery, and the new regime lasted until two successive brothers fought their joint enemy, the insurrectionary Sassanids, until both were killed. Needless to say, the longer a dynasty lasted the more likely it was to break down. Short-lived dynasties were usually short-lived for other reasons.

It was also possible for dynasties to recover from a breakdown, just as empires and kingdoms could recover from a civil war. The Roman Empire repeatedly broke down into civil wars over who should rule – in 68–69, almost in 96, in 192–197, and more widely in the third century, when Roman Imperial history was a continual sequence of coups, wars, usurpers, and invaders. It was obviously easier for a territorial state to recover than for a dynasty. The Sassanids recovered from several breakdowns, and even when in the 620s the fourth or fifth breakdown was succeeded by the Muslim invasions, the recovery forced the invaders to fight for thirty years; the dynasty still had much power and could command considerable loyalty until the very end.

It was therefore possible for a dynasty to recover from a breakdown, but that depended on the weight of the pressures upon it, and on its capacity for continued reproduction. The Parthian recovery has already been mentioned.

Alternatively, like the 'XXII/XXIII' dynasties in Egypt, the agony of the breakdown might simply extend itself over an apparently ever lengthening period. The Merovingian dynasty's power had effectively ended by about 680, but the kings continued in office, if not in power, for another seventy years, maintained in office by the Mayors, until the latter shrugged off the last king.

The Ptolemaic dynasty shows a long period of successive breakdowns. The two sons of Ptolemy V and Kleopatra Syra repeatedly disputed the throne, and they were followed by disputes between the survivor, Ptolemy VIII, and his sister, and then between that sister Kleopatra III, and her children, and then the attempted joint rule of the brothers Ptolemy IX and X and their cousin Kleopatra III continued the quarrel and was unsuccessful. Of the three, one died in battle, one (Kleopatra) was murdered, and one was deposed but then returned to power. The next generation saw three murders and one deposition. It had become necessary that, for a ruler to hold on to power, he or she had to kill off those of his or her generation who competed, which was the situation that had also brought the second Akhaimenid dynasty to its knees. The eventual result was a single ruler, Kleopatra VII, as a child and young woman. The prominence of women rulers in the later part of this dynasty is an indication of the disintegration of the dynasty's power and authority – not because women rulers were incompetent – Kleopatra VII clearly was an effective ruler – but because if the succession fell to a woman it meant that the male members of the dynasty had been already eliminated.

Nevertheless, despite these dynastic disputes, the Ptolemies staged several recoveries. After the breakdown during the infancy of Ptolemy VI and VIII (175–163), Ptolemy VI's rule for twenty years was a time of suppressing rebellion and firm rule; his brother then succeeded him, and ruled competently for ten years or so. But from then on the recoveries were shorter, and the breakdowns lasted longer. Kleopatra VII's reign, despite her apparent success as a ruler, was a time of internal conflict and external invasion. The Roman rule that followed may well have been a relief.

Examples of recovery after a breakdown come in the Epeirote dynasty of the Aiakidai and the Seleukid dynasty. Among the Aiakidai of Epeiros there were three occasions when the ruling king was deposed and subsequently returned to office; first with Arybas, deposed in 343 in favour of Alexander I; Arybas returned briefly in 323–322, and his son succeeded him; however, Alexander's son Neoptolemus II maintained his position, and the feud extended into the next generation of Arybas' family. In effect, the Epeirote kingship was in dispute between the rival royal lines for about fifty years. The final beneficiary was Arybas' grandson, Pyrrhos, who established a firm grip on the state and seemed to halt the process of breakdown. But his grandchildren failed to reproduce and when the last one – a woman, the Princess Deidameia – was murdered in 231, the monarchy was abolished, and a Republican regime put in its place. This coincided with the decline of Epeiros into impotence and unimportance.

Among the Seleukids, breakdowns were even more frequent than with their Ptolemaic contemporaries and rivals, and occurred earlier in the dynasty's history. Two potential crises were evaded even in the first half-century: when Seleukos I surrendered his wife Stratonike to his son and sent them off to govern Central Asia, a solution to a problem that combined political finesse and the good of the empire. The second came when Antiochos' first son Seleukos was executed; his offence is not known, but it can hardly have been less than an attempt to seize the kingship from his father. This was clearly a major political crisis solved in the most drastic manner. There had thus been a dynastic crisis in each of the first two generations of the dynasty. They do not seem to have had wider effects, but they are indicative of a possible dynastic problem. Sure enough, the sons of Antiochos II waged a dynastic war for nearly two decades. Then in the fourth generation the dynasty was reduced to a single unmarried teenaged king, Antiochos III, who in his first years faced defeat in war, several rebellions, and more than one court conspiracy. There were dynastic disputes and murders in every succeeding generation, in 175, 164, 162, 150 and so on, so much so that breakdown seems an inadequate term for the dynasty's condition.

The dynasty itself was a permanent crisis; every king except three (out of twenty-five) died a violent death, and two of those three were deposed by the Romans. Each generation therefore saw a breakdown followed by dynastic recovery, but each generation's breakdown was more serious than the one before. After the dynastic war of 241–227, the next really serious dynastic crisis came in 164–162, which was only resolved when Demetrios I ordered the murder of his cousin Antiochos V; this was followed from 152–138 by a new condition of civil war, involving one king killed in battle, one captured by the Parthians, two usurpers, and invasions by the Parthians and the Ptolemies. The dynastic civil war was resumed as a permanent condition of affairs from 115 onwards, through three generations, and resulted in the division of the kingdom between the surviving candidates, and each of these generations saw the territory subject to the dynasty reduced.

On the other hand, it is inaccurate to describe such a condition as one of continuous breakdown. Like Pyrrhos of Epeiros, Antiochos III was able to institute a recovery that re-established the dynasty for over half a century, above all by ruling for three decades, and by annual military campaigns turning the attention of the empire outwards. The appalling record of violent deaths in the family was not in itself and by itself a sign of dynastic breakdown, for that only came when a series of other conditions came into play, in particular disputed successions, together with the intervention of non-Seleukid usurpers and, later, the civil warfare that was theoretically aimed at solving such disputes. Even then the reigns of Demetrios II and Antiochos VII (150–126) eventually produced another recovery. Only with the succession dispute between the sons of these two kings – Antiochos XII and XIII – from 115 onwards did the breakdown become irretrievable. One of the problems within a long dispute was the intervention of the wives of two of the conflicting kings, both Ptolemaic women, those murders exacerbated the issue; a version of the sign of breakdown that saw women ruling.

The most remarkable example of repeated breakdown and recovery is perhaps that of the Sassanids of Iran. Of course, this was an extremely long-enduring dynasty, but its ability to recover after every internal breakdown is unique in the dynasties of the ancient world. There were four occasions of serious breakdown, in AD 383–389, 484–498, 590–591, and 628–632. In each case, except the last, recovery came by way of a long reign that succeeded the breakdowns, and which was then followed by a period of settled succession. The first three breakdowns, it will be noticed, came at roughly century intervals, though the last, and the most serious, came only one generation after the third. Also, the last two breakdowns saw the intervention of non-Sassanid usurpers who succeeded, if only briefly, in seizing the throne. The last breakdown, in the early seventh century, also coincided with the invasion of the homeland by the resurgent Byzantine Empire under the Emperor Heraklios and the approach of the newly united Muslim invaders out of Arabia. The similarity with the Seleukids is striking; it is also similar, in a less extreme way, to the Roman experience, if one substitutes a state breakdown for a dynastic.

The last Sassanid breakdown saw the deposition of a very long-ruling king, Khusrau II, the death of his son and successor within a few months, the murder of that king's son, the intervention and deaths of two usurpers, the seizure of the throne by two royal women, who were then murdered, and the accession of a cousin, all within four years. It was a compendium of the symptoms of breakdown. But that latest king, Yazdgard III, reunited the dynasty, eliminated rivals, and was accepted as king by legitimate descent. He also fought valiantly for nearly thirty years to combat the Muslim invasion, before being finally murdered by his exasperated subjects. That is, the dynasty in effect had recovered once more, yet it is also obvious that the preceding dynastic breakdown can only have encouraged the invaders, and had weakened the Sassanid response. The murder of the last king by his subjects was thus due to the dynasty's failure to combat the invasions; it had become less onerous to submit to the invaders than to go on fighting. The similarity with the fate of the Seleukids thus extends to the *coup de grâce* being administered by an invader and their subjects together, though it took two invading enemies to kill off the Seleukid state (Parthia and Rome), while only one dealt with the Sassanids.

Dynastic breakdowns were clearly a hazard that ruling families had to face; the cause was the attraction of political power for other men (usually) who were often already close to the source of power, and in these disputes usurpers and invaders were automatically attacked to exploit the problem; the consequence in most cases was the eventual elimination of the dynasty's power. Any recovery required a great deal of effort, and the need to expend that effort was liable to weaken the afflicted dynasty permanently. Yet the process of decline could be long-drawn-out and agonizing, as if a series of strokes was progressively debilitating the patient. But it was not just the dynasty that suffered; the subjects had an even worse time. The civil wars were self-indulgent on the part of the dynasty's members, and their subjects saw that all too clearly.

Chapter 11

Terminations

D ynasties came to their ends as a result of one or more of several causes. The breakdowns leading to extinction or recovery have been discussed in the last chapter. A substantial number of dynasties succumbed to the conquest of their lands by an enemy, and others were suppressed, usually rather less violently, by their overlords. Rather fewer were removed by an internal rebellion or a coup or a usurpation, and were then replaced by another regime, either monarchic or, in some cases, by a republic. A fairly substantial number of dynasties simply died out, and this was the normal conclusion for the Roman Republican dynasties as well. These less than startling conclusions hide some intriguing variations on the basic themes.

Suppression

Conquest and suppression tended to go together. When the Emperor Claudius invaded Britain, the first target of his army was to conquer the kingdom of the Catuvellauni, which had grown to dominate the south-eastern quarter of the island in the previous hundred years; this required the elimination of the current representatives of the dynasty that had constructed that kingdom, and the job could not be thought complete until the last member of that dynasty, Caratacus, who escaped the conquest of his homeland and continued the fight from the western lands, was captured and removed from Britannia to be sequestrated in Italy, several years after the initial conquest of the kingdom. Only now was the suppression of the Catuvellauni dynasty complete.

Rome was not, and never had been, particular about the type of regime with which it associated. Alliances had been made with monarchies or republics whenever they were met and wherever an alliance was required. Two of the allies of Claudius in the invasion of Britain were the kings of the Iceni in modern Norfolk, and the Regni in Sussex, both of whom were feeling under pressure from the expanding Catuvellauni. The monarchy of Hiero in Syracuse and eastern Sicily was a Roman ally for most of its existence, but, when Hiero's grandson, Hieronymos, attempted to escape this political embrace, his kingdom was conquered, and the dynasty and the kingdom suppressed without any sentimental qualms about the previous friendship. The same sequence can be seen in operation in the case of Assyria and Israel: Israel was assisted to acquire control of the Vale of Jezreel by Assyria, but when a different king wanted to break the Assyrian alliance he and his kingdom were conquered, the Assyrian ally in this case being Judah.

The majority of conquered dynasties fell to these two empires: Assyria and Rome. The Assyrians were particularly brutal in their conquests, by which they removed dynasties from states on all their borders, from Elam in Iran round to Egypt. Rome was also fairly ruthless, but in the late republic and early empire, particularly in the Middle East, it became the Roman practice to enfold the local kingdoms into the Roman Empire whole and entire, leaving the dynasties in office, and then finally, after some decades, pluck the ruling dynasty out, annex the kingdom, and then convert the kingdom into a province, or part of one, and make the members of the old dynasty into Roman nobles, equipped quite often with consulships at Rome and rich estates – the Kommagenean, Emesan, Herodian, Thracian, and Cottian dynasties all went through this early approval and later suppression process.

There is, of course, a sort of progression involved in this. The Roman Republic's response to enmity was normally military, so conquest was the inevitable fate of the dynasty of Hiero at Syracuse and of the Antigonid dynasty in Macedon, but as Rome became evermore overwhelmingly powerful, resistance to its demands became all the more obviously futile. The last king of Bithynia and the last of the Attalids tried to solve the problem by bequeathing their kingdoms to Rome, but this did not stop Roman magistrates from using extensive violence in their takeover, and sequestrated large quantities of loot to their own use – indeed the impression exists that the violence was provoked in order that the looting could then take place. This, in a way, was a transitional phase; under the later republic and the early Empire, neither conquest nor a bequest became necessary. A simple decision at Rome could snuff out a kingdom and dethrone the dynasty: the Numidian kingdom was annexed for two decades, restored, and then suppressed again, and its inoffensive last king was executed by the whim of the Emperor Caligula. Resistance to such annexations tended to come not so much from the kings themselves, who could see the odds more clearly, as from their subjects, who could see the looming disadvantages of the Roman takeover. Aristonikos in Asia Minor had widespread local support in his claim to the Attalid kingdom after the bequest to Rome by his brother. The Jews of Palestine resisted the Roman conquest in 63 and 37 BC, and in AD 67 it was the Herodian King Agrippa II who tried to persuade the inhabitants of Jerusalem that Rome was too powerful to be resisted. It was no consolation to either side, but he was right.

Widespread annexations in Syria by Vespasian followed the Jewish War, not just in Palestine but throughout Syria. It became clear to him during his command against the Jews that these kingdoms could muster a sizeable force; had they chosen to join the Jews, all Syria at least could have been instantly lost to Rome, and the war would have been much greater and more difficult. Annexation both suppressed the kings, who might lead such a war, and gathered in their armies to reinforce the Roman army, and help replace its casualties – which had been extensive in the Jewish fighting. Only the Kommageneans put up a serious resistance to the annexation. For the rulers, suicide was sometimes the last dynastic gesture available, as with the last of the Ptolemies, Kleopatra VII, but most rulers made their accommodation with Rome quite comfortably, as Caratacus eventually did, and as the Herodians, Emesans, Kommageneans, Thracians, and many other kings did.

The Assyrians used much the same variety of methods, though rather more brutally. Some neighbouring rulers were loyal and when they were dethroned they were pensioned-off to live in luxury in Nineveh; this was the fate of the last king of Samal, for example. Some were killed, and their kingdoms annexed, and the population was probably transported to a foreign land or perhaps, if skilled, to help build one or other of the Assyrian capital cities. Resisters were executed if they survived the fighting, and their kingdoms were then despoiled and annexed. In the same way, the Ptolemaic annexation of the Cypriot kingdoms involved all these methods, including murdering several kings and permitting one to commit ritual family suicide; just one of the island's kings – Eunostos of Soloi survived to reign until his (natural) death, but this was only because he was married to a daughter of Ptolemy I, the annexer.

Between conquest and suppression, Rome accounted for almost forty dynasties; and the successor Byzantine Empire for several more. Assyria eliminated a dozen at least. Otherwise only the Ptolemies dealt with more than one or two, and those were all in Cyprus. It is curious that the greatest of all empires, the Islamic Arab under the Umayyads, only suppressed two dynasties, the Sassanids and the Sindhu dynasty in the Indus Valley, though perhaps the last of the Visigothic dynasties should also be included. The Visigoths themselves suppressed the Suevic dynasty; the Merovingian Franks suppressed the Burgundian dynasty; and the Carolingians, having suppressed the Merovingians, later suppressed the Bavarian dynasty, and still later conquered the Lombards, whose dynastic system had by then already failed.

The Bavarian case highlights another aspect. The Agilolfing dynasty had been installed by the Merovingians two centuries before it was suppressed by the Carolingians; they had chosen a local lord to be their puppet duke. This process was usually a preliminary step towards annexation, but the Merovingians did not take that next step. Rome had done this with the Herodians, and in Thrace, and in the Cottian Alps; the second Abgarid dynasty at Edessa was installed by the Parthian Empire (and so perhaps was the first), and the third was emplaced by a Roman decision, as was the last of the Kommagenean kings, only for him to be deposed three decades later. Armenia was repeatedly treated in this way, by the Seleukids, the Romans, and the Parthians, but usually foiled their intentions – if annexation was ultimately intended – by adopting the imposed dynasties as their own. Having been installed by an imperial power, of course, it was difficult for such dynasties to resist eventual suppression, and they were almost always unsuccessful in attempting it.

The replacement of dynasties from within the polity they had ruled was the second most likely cause of dynastic demise, and, as with their origins, the three methods were rebellion, *coups d'état*, and usurpation. It is not always easy to separate these, particularly the last two. Was the removal of the Empress Irene from power in Constantinople in 802 a usurpation or a coup? The normal method of ending a Roman or Byzantine dynasty was by a coup, either at Rome or in an army camp, normally involving the murder of the last of the expiring dynasty. Domitian and Commodus were murdered at Rome, Gordian III and Julian in the army's camp while on campaign, Alexander Severus at Cologne; the last members of the dynasties of Justin and Heraklios fell at Constantinople. In the circumstances Irene's removal was quite within the normal Roman tradition.

Rebellion was a relatively infrequent method of eliminating a dynasty. It was one that was attempted often enough, but only rarely with success. It took much effort to produce a worthwhile rebel army, and meanwhile the regular army was more likely to support the dynasty that would and could reward it, rather than join the rebels. Oddly enough, four of the few successful rebellions occurred in the great empires. The relatively mild risings against the Emperor Nero in Gaul in AD 68 pushed him to commit suicide, but the cause of the end of his dynasty was ultimately the rebellion of Galba in Spain. The first Akhaimenid dynasty succumbed to a rebellion led by Darius I against the prospect of Smerdis/Bardia inheriting his brother's throne. In the same territory the Abbasid rebellion against the Umayyad caliphs was similarly successful. In all cases, of course, the rebellion came with a great deal of tacit support from within the elites and from the masses – Nero's suicide came when he finally realized that both the Roman Senate and the populace were against him, and that he would get no support from the army.

A spectacular example of successful rebellion was the almost instant collapse of the Hun Empire in central Europe on the death of Attila, during a series of rebellions by the many subject peoples provoked by the prospect of continued Hun rule. Attila had been an effective, if brutal, ruler, but the division of the empire between his numerous sons had begun the process of collapse. The rebellion of the subject peoples was energized by their quarrels and disputes. Similarly, the collapse of the dynasty of Dionysios in Sicily, when the small force led by Timoleon landed in the island on its mission of liberation, demonstrated that the foundations of the dynasty's power in Sicily were shallower than many had thought; how far this can be classed as a rebellion is problematic, but Timoleon did soon gather plenty of local support. In some cases a rebellion looks very like a usurpation, as in the gory endings of the two Israelite dynasties of Omri and Jehu at the hands of disaffected, ambitious army commanders.

The replacement for the Dionysiad dynasty in Sicily was not another monarchy, or at least not immediately; instead the subject cities all regained their independence – which they managed to keep for all of two decades before falling before the revived monarchy of Agathokles, or a Carthaginian invasion. This replacement of monarchy by a republic was a possible outcome that some other Greek communities essayed. Corinth and Sikyon removed their hereditary tyrants, as did Athens, though in the larger histories of those cities it is the tyrannies that in the long run were anomalous, not the republics, whereas in Sicily it was monarchy that had become the norm. For Epeiros in 231, Sparta in 217, and the Battiad kingdom in Cyrenaica in *c.*440, however, the Republican regimes were new. In several cases, Epeiros and Sparta particularly, the replacement of the dynasty tended to be a new type of one-man rule – in Epeiros by Charops, in Sparta by Nabis – which earlier Greeks would have termed tyrannies. In Carthage the republic that followed the end of the Magonid dynasty was soon replaced by a new monarchy but only briefly, and an oligarchic republic was finally established in 306. The Barkid dynasty was expelled with Hannibal a century later, perhaps on the assumption that he was using his renown to develop a tyranny, but the city remained plagued by altogether too many powerful individuals until its destruction.

In addition to these examples, of course, the Roman monarchy was replaced by a republic in 509 BC. It is worth noting that this revolution took place at much the same time that Corinth, Sikyon, and Athens overthrew their own monarchies, and only a generation before Syracuse did the same. Also worth noting is that the troubles the Roman Republican regime had in establishing itself are paralleled in these other cities – and Rome, Syracuse, and Athens soon set about conquering their neighbours and establishing minor empires. So Rome was quite in the fashion with its republican revolution.

Normally, however, one dynasty's demise was another dynasty's opportunity, though not necessarily always at once. The Israelite monarchy lurched from institutionalized coups to brief dynasties more than once in its lifetime of less than two centuries, and this was probably the pattern of many of the cities in contemporary Syria – Tyre certainly, also Damascus and perhaps Samal as well seem to have gone through the same sequence. By definition usurpations only lead to a continuation of the monarchy in different hands, but repeated usurpations tended to degrade the whole monarchic institution.

End of Empires

The decay of great empires provided opportunities for local dynasties to become established. In the case of the end of the Roman Empire these were frequently 'invading-barbarian' groups, though some indigenous dynasties did appear, as with the Byzantine remnant that maintained the fiction that it was the Roman Empire continuing. Most of these new states generally had very shallow roots and proved to be exceedingly vulnerable to either the revival of the decrepit empire, or to their fellow invaders. Of the ten barbarian peoples who invaded the Roman Empire in the fifth and sixth centuries, only three; the Visigoths, the Franks, and the tardy Lombards established kingdoms that lasted longer than half a century, and of these three the Lombards fell to the Franks and the Visigoths to the Muslims.

The Angles and Saxons and Jutes who moved into the future England were successful, and their dynasties survived and prospered, but it is questionable whether they had invaded the Roman Empire. Some at least, the mercenaries, were invited in, and any arrivals after AD 410 were not invading the empire, but an independent succession state, or states. Since the dynasties were established and survived it would seem that the best practice was to wait until Roman power had receded, then move in – that is, of course, what the Franks and Lombards also did. As in other forms of warfare, the earliest attackers – Vandals, Ostrogoths, Rugians, Sueves and so on – suffered heavy casualties and soon expired.

The progressive failure of the Seleukid Empire was partly caused by the local rebellions of such groups as the Greco-Baktrians and the Palestinian

Jews, followed by the quiet detachment – rebellion is too strong a word for the process – of other cities and regions such as Edessa, Emesa, and Kommagene in the last decades, while the several kings fought each other. The dynasties who came to take the place of the Seleukids in these regions scarcely had to rebel against these kings, for the authority of the Seleukid king in effect simply vanished from the territories they came to control.

A surprisingly large number of dynasties simply died out. This process was at times assisted by the violent death of the last member, but to reach that stage, where a dynasty could be extinguished by one death, it had to be reduced to a single ruler's life, with no heirs, and its end was clearly approaching, however the last man died. It is, however, not always possible to discern that condition. The Ptolemaic dynasty, for instance, ended with Kleopatra VII in 30 BC, but she had at least three children, who were not permitted to inherit in Egypt. It cannot therefore really be said that the dynasty had died out with Kleopatra, but no one could be in any doubt, even before the fact, that it was Kleopatra's own life on which that of the dynasty itself depended. The murder of the last of the Aiakidai of Epeiros, Deidameia, in 231 BC did bring that dynasty to an end, and it seems highly likely that she was murdered – in a particularly brutal and sacrilegious way – precisely because she was the last of the line, in order to extinguish both it and the kingdom. This was certainly the case with the murder of Alexander IV, the son of Alexander the Great, the last of the Macedonian Argeadai, when he reached adulthood. His existence had, by that fact, become wholly inconvenient to all of the usurping Macedonian generals who had carved up the empire of his father, Alexander the Great, between them. Just to make sure, Kleopatra, the sister of Alexander the Great, and Herakles, his son by a concubine, were also killed in the next year or so. This finally extinguished the dynasty. It was a collective action by the usurpers.

It is a curious fact that all the dynasties of which we have detailed knowledge in Britain in AD 700 died out within the next hundred years; the Kentish Oiscings in 762, the second Mercian dynasty by 796 (the first had ended in 716), that of Wessex in 726 or perhaps earlier, depending on how wide the definition of the dynasty is cast, the first Northumbrian dynasty in 729, and its replacement in 788, the first East Saxon dynasty in 746, that of the East Angles in 749, and the Dalriadan dynasty by *c.*780. This was, of course, a fairly violent time and competing kings died in battle and were murdered, but the incidence of such violence is not really any greater in the eighth century than in other centuries. That all these dynasties should die out in a relatively short time seems to be rather too coincidental. A contributory factor was a brief fashion for kings to abdicate to the monasteries, but this only usually occurred when they had ruled for some time, and after they had produced heirs. In fact the Mercian and Wessex dynasties had almost expired once already, as had the first Northumbrian. They and the Kentish Oiscing dynasty all lasted about two centuries. They were all replaced by kings who were apparently chosen to rule for life rather than succeeding by hereditary right – as with the Visigoths in Spain – but a continuing dynasty was only established in Wessex at the beginning of the ninth century.

It is quite possible that these cases were the beginning of a process by which the dynastic principle was falling out of use in Western Europe, or at least that of succession by primogeniture. The Irish and Dalriadan dynasties had rarely practised a pure form of dynastic succession, and their kings apparently succeeded as the eldest male of the extended family, which resulted in many short reigns, disagreements as to the successor, and general governmental inefficiency. The Anglo-Saxon dynasties that died out were replaced by kings who were apparently chosen by the nobles of the kingdom from amongst themselves, a method that had been used by the Visigoths since the sixth century. As the Visigothic experience has shown, this was a process that works against the establishment of any dynasty of kings, since it was clearly in the interest of participating nobles to keep the succession option open, which would not be the case if hereditary succession was accepted. At the same time any king chosen in that way would automatically attempt to secure the succession for his sons but there was a constant tension over the succession; not only the person of the successor, but the method of choosing him. This might be no bad thing, and could be used to eliminate unsuitable candidates; but it could, and did, produce dynastic wars. The succession to the expiring Mercian dynasty oscillated between three aristocratic families, none of which was able to establish itself for more than two kings in succession. In Frankish Gaul the kings of the Merovingian dynasty were hardly ornaments of the royal profession by the eighth century; in Italy direct dynastic succession amongst the Lombards was as unpopular a method as it was amongst the Visigoths, and the Bavarian dynasty, related to the Lombards, could not show a clear line of succession either.

In 751 the last of the Merovings was replaced by the first of the Carolings. This successor regime then soon suppressed both the Lombard and the Bavarian dynasties. Earlier, the Visigothic state, briefly being ruled by another new dynasty at the time, had gone down before a relatively small Arab-Berber army. These various events throughout the region seem to have been the beginning of a reversal of the trend that had seemed likely to see the institution of quasi-elective monarchy in many of the Western European countries. But, of course, the electors – always local nobles – were scarcely denying the whole dynastic principle, only as it applied to the monarchy. The prospect was, perhaps, of a new polity of the same sort as the old Roman Republic, a dynastic oligarchy. In the Anglo-Saxon kingdoms in the early ninth century, only that of Wessex maintained a clear dynastic succession, and that only since the succession of Egbert in 802; in the other kingdoms a choice between different families seems to have been the norm. In Scotland the old Dalriadic ruling families failed by 780; among the Picts no clear dynastic succession appears ever to have been practised. Had the Carolingians failed it seems quite possible that an elective form of monarchy – that is, in effect an oligarchy – would have become established. Perhaps, following the Roman model, monarchy itself would have vanished from the European political scene a thousand years earlier than it did.

Instead, the succession of Charlemagne in the Frankish kingdom, and of Egbert in Wessex, produced two kings who were long-lived, very capable and successful, and who had capable sons to inherit after them. If there ever had been a moment when the European aristocracy might have inherited power, it was gone. And the ninth century was also the century of the Vikings, the Saracens, and the Magyars. In England the only dynasty that survived the Viking assault, that of Wessex, proved itself to be the rallying point for resistance to the attackers and invaders and went on to conquer the rest of England. In Scotland similarly, a member of the Scottish royal house rallied the joint Scots-Pictish kingdom, forming a new and united kingdom of the two former states. Among the Franks the family of the Carolingians eventually failed in this task, but local kings in Germany and France, and in France in the subsequent counties and duchies, performed the same service; in Spain the family of Pelayo in the Cantabrian Mountains led the resistance and later the Reconquista. It would therefore seem that the dynastic principle was re-established anew in the royal families by the attacks of Europe's enemies.

It is hardly surprising that the longer-enduring dynasties were more likely to die out naturally than the shorter ones. In fact, only two dynasties that lasted less than a century can be classified as 'naturally expiring', and both of them are unusual. The dynasty of Leo I of Byzantium finished with the successive marriages of his daughter Ariadne to Zeno and then Athanasios, neither of these men being young and had no children, either by Ariadne or by any earlier marriages. The other case is that of the Hekatomnids of Karia, whose succession method was extremely involved, not to say both curious and unique, and which concluded with the succession of Ada II, a childless widow and the last of her line. The family practised repeated sibling marriages, and no doubt this was to the detriment of their reproducibility.

At the other duration extreme, twelve of the dynasties that lasted longer than two centuries died out naturally, as did five more that lasted between 150 and 200 years. Yet at the same time these figures are less than half of all the dynasties in those categories. It is clear that even the longest-lived dynasties could have continued longer if they had not suffered violence – the pained Sassanids were conquered by the Arabs after ruling (as an imperial dynasty) for over four centuries, and the last emperor went down fighting; the Ptolemaic and Seleukid dynasties were removed by Rome after almost three and over two and a half centuries of rule respectively, and in both cases there were male heirs of the last rulers who could have made a serious effort to recover power: the Mithradatid dynasty in the Cimmerian Bosporos was suppressed after four and a half centuries, and had shown no signs of expiring until Rome suppressed it.

The duration range of the naturally expiring cases, from the sixty-one years of the dynasty of Leo I to the 327 years of the Spartokid dynasty, shows that no limit may be placed on the life expectancy of any dynasty, but it also emphasizes that dynasties in the ancient world came to an end mainly by some sort of enemy action, either from outside or from within their kingdom, but that the most lethal contingency was to be a neighbour to, or a client of, an expanding empire.

Chapter 12

The New Religions

In the Middle Ages one of the major elements in settling successions and enforcing (and increasing) royal power was the alliance between royalty and Christianity. The sacral ceremony of coronation by a Christian cleric, and the anointing with holy oil, transferred at least some of the aura of holiness to the kings, a practice effectively originated by Charlemagne in Western Europe for his revived Roman Empire, but also attested elsewhere earlier in a less decisive form. Charlemagne and his father, who was the first of the family to seize the throne, were no doubt in part animated by the need to reinforce their authority by as many props as possible, for theirs was, after all, a usurping dynasty. This was also in fact the westernization of the practices of the Byzantine monarchy, and this in turn was an inheritance from the practices of the later Roman Empire, in part based on the attempt by third century emperors to preserve their lives in that rebellious age (and based on Old Testament accounts of the coronation of Judahite kings). Further east the new dynasty of the Umayyads combined both secular and religious power in their persons as caliphs, successors to the Prophet Muhammad. Muhammad had been compelled to secure secular authority in order that his religious message should be heard. These developments were obvious, but at first only potential enhancements of the royal power, that had been, in all conscience, powerful enough before. It is worth asking if these new religions had any noticeable effect on the survivability of the dynasties that adopted them.

For it has to be emphasized that it was always a political decision to convert to one of these religions, and to adopt it as the sole preferred religion of the state. The choice was usually made for good political reasons, notably for the enhanced power and alliance with Christianity or Islam, in any of their various versions could bring to the king or emperor. (It was not, in most cases, the result of the conversion of the ruler to the new religion's beliefs.) One of those political reasons was dynastic, by which the sacramentation by the religion would help perpetuate the convert's family in power.

It has to be said that there is little evidence that such an effect occurred. The fate of the Umayyad dynasty is salutary in this respect. The caliph was the direct successor of the Prophet, and could and did claim full religious authority within Islam, and indeed beyond it, both as his chosen successor and as a member of the Prophet's family, yet that dynasty lasted only ninety years and four generations, with the last three caliphs either deposed or murdered. Even among the immediate successors of Muhammad, the 'First Caliphs', murders took place. All this implies that their assumed sacredness was not much protection. The result of the destruction of the Umayyad dynasty (in battle and murder) was the replacement of that family by the Abbasid dynasty, which made the same claim to the same religious authority, but also claimed to be more devout and orthodox than the Umayyads. This reveals a new danger for any professedly religious dynasty, that the compromises inherent in the exercise of political power opened the way to effective criticism from those who had a narrower and more vehement view of affairs. Needless to say, the claim to greater devotion might be maintained, but practice soon fell before the constraints, demands, and opportunities of supreme secular power.

The Umayyads lasted rather less well than many of the other Arab dynasties of the ancient world – at least than those who we can date with some precision. The Lakhmids and the Ghassanids both lasted longer, both in terms of years and generations, though both were interrupted and finally suppressed by their imperial patrons. The al-Kinda dynasty had a similar history to that of the Umayyads, lasting ninety years or so and five generations, and, again like the Umayyads, it disintegrated in the end in a disputed succession, partly as a result of the system of sibling succession it adopted. There were many other Arab dynasties, particularly those in the south of the peninsula, in modern Yemen, and several can be traced through six or seven generations, though precise dates are very scarce, and the records are probably incomplete.

It would seem that the caliphate in Umayyad hands exposed the dynasty to the new danger of being accused of infidelity or apostasy, but without any compensating increase in dynastic longevity; nor did its internal dynastic quarrels help in extending the dynasty's life. It is noticeable that later Muslim dynasties tended to separate the caliphate from the exercise of similar power, thereby to some extent imitating (perhaps not consciously) Christian practice. The caliphal Abbasid dynasty yielded to the power of army commanders who took control of the governing system as vizirs, leaving the caliph in impotent state in Baghdad. In effect the vizirs became the kings; it was these who set about campaigning and governing. But the original example of combined secular and religious authority proved to be highly attractive: one result was the multiplication of caliphs from Morocco to India; the last case (so far) was that of the Ottoman sultans, whose caliphal authority was largely nominal – they were always referred to as sultans, after all. (They also claimed authority as successors of the Roman Empire, thus collecting a whole series of claims to legitimacy; none were effective in the final result.)

The Christianized dynasties of Europe, in the period here under study, fared no better than those of Islam. The Byzantine emperors from Constantine the Great onwards were always Christian (except for the brief Emperor Julian), but no dynasty lasted a century, which was no improvement on the earlier Roman dynasties (the Heraklids lasted 106 years, but actually held office and power for only 91). The several Christian dynasties suffered almost as badly from usurpations and rebellions, and counted as many of their members as victims of murder, as their non-Christian predecessors (or their Muslim rivals): out of eighteen emperors in the four dynasties from the Leonids to the Isaurians, Christians all, three were murdered and four deposed, much the same proportion as amongst their non-Christian imperial predecessors. And this was despite the elaborate distancing they adopted from courtiers and the populace and the sacralizing ceremonial they all went through.

For the other Christian dynasties in the Mediterranean area – the 'invading-barbarian' dynasties – the problem was that they generally chose to adopt the Arian version of Christianity as a deliberate means of distancing themselves and their people from their new Roman subjects, and from their Byzantine enemies, in an attempt to preserve their ethnic purity. Like the Umayyads they thereupon exposed themselves to opposition in the name of religion as well as events in politics. For those dynasties that eschewed Arianism in favour of Catholicism a different dynastic hazard appeared. In each of the early Wessex and Mercian dynasties two kings abdicated in order to enter a monastery, or to go to Rome on pilgrimage, and not long after both of these dynasties died out. It was a new problem, since a king who considered such a move essential for his soul's well-being was probably a good man to have as king in some respects – after all, few enough kings ever allowed their consciences to interfere in their realpolitik. Yet by abdicating, the king was deserting his post. Amongst the Merovingians it was also a practice used by the Mayors of the Palace to control the kings by immuring them in monasteries if they became too assertive; this was also a useful device for keeping spare candidates available in case the current one died or had to be replaced. It was perhaps an advance on murder or assassination, but just as politically unsettling.

It may also be a factor in the ongoing issue of dynastic continuation that monogamy was a normal Christian marriage practice. Of course, kings and emperors always tended to ignore such inconvenient sexual restrictions, but the Church would only recognize the offspring of a religious marriage as 'legitimate' and so capable of inheriting the throne; this clearly restricted the chances of biological reproduction – another dynastic hazard. This applied as much to Christian rulers as anyone else. The Emperor Heraklios, for example, insisted on marrying his niece Martina, despite clerical disapproval, but was eventually able to get such disapproval waived.

The Muslim dynasties, on the other hand, adopted, or continued, the institution of the harem. Muhammad himself had eleven wives and at least two concubines, and his early successors also had many marital partners. One result for a dynasty was a much longer dynastic succession – the Abbasids maintained a clear succession through five centuries at Baghdad, and there was also available a family member after the Mongol sack of the city and the murder of the current caliph for his family to revive the (powerless) dynasty of caliphs in Egypt later. This was clearly a result of the harem system where reproduction was much easier to achieve. Monogamy could restrict and disrupt dynastic succession by marrying two people who were genetically incompatible.

The Arian dynasties fared a good deal worse than any of the others. The Ostrogoths succumbed to the Byzantine recovery, in part because of their continued Arian-ness, which alienated them from their Catholic subjects in Italy, who in effect stood aside in the fight, or took the Byzantine side. The Visigothic kingdom did last for three centuries, but its dynasties were never firmly established: indeed the first dynasty suffered very badly from violent deaths – four kings were murdered, two died in battle, and one was deposed, out of a total of nine kings altogether. Late in the sixth century the Visigoths shifted to Catholicism with some difficulty, and this defused some of the internal tensions in the kingdom. The Vandals escaped much of that fate, but they lasted in North Africa little more than a century before succumbing to the Byzantine recovery; again their Catholic subjects stood aside; they may not have liked the Vandal rulers, but they were just as unwelcoming to the Byzantine system of taxation and bureaucracy. Christianization for these dynasties was of no assistance whatsoever.

These Western European barbarian dynasties all adopted Christianity by choice. In at least two cases, the Franks and the Mercians, the decision was taken explicitly for political motives; in the Mercian case to help the previously aggressively pagan dynasty's recovery from defeat and rebellion and apparent destruction. In the Frankish case the choice was made of the Roman version of Christianity rather than the Arian, partly to distinguish the dynasty from the others of its ilk, such as their enemies, the Visigoths and Ostrogoths (both Arian), but also as a way of gaining support from the former Roman subjects or their Catholic descendants whom the kings were bringing under their control.

And it worked to some extent: both dynasties flourished for the next century and more. But at the same time they and others did not explicitly disavow their pagan origins. The old claim to be Woden-born was maintained by all Anglo-Saxon dynasties even after conversion. The Merovingian descent from a Neptunian monster was still claimed, and the talisman of long hair for the kings – scarcely a Christian symbol – was being persisted in.

The adoption of Christianity may not have been very comfortable in personal terms, but it did provide the newly converted kings with another means of extending their power. In England the Kentish King Aethelberht used his new religion to try to compel his neighbours to adopt it – notably the East Saxon and East Anglian kings, with the clear aim of extending his authority over them. When the Mercian kings persisted in paganism it was the East Anglian king, now Christian, who could use his religion as a helpful weapon in their wars. The process of converting was never smooth, and Northumbria in particular went through much upheaval as a result, not only in converting to the new religion, but in deciding which version, Roman or Celtic, to adhere to. The decision was made on political grounds, not religious. The effect of Christianity on the dynasties was, in the immediate term, too often destructive – and their subjects were liable to suffer badly also.

The longevity and safety of these converted dynasties was thus not enhanced in any significant way by their adoption of Islam or Christianity, of any version. Pre-monotheistic dynasties had always claimed religious sanction as well, with as little effect. Either all religions were equally ineffective – but the Zoroastrian Sassanids lasted a very long time – or, more likely, religion was irrelevant to the dynasties' prospects.

Chapter 13

Comparisons

The Singularity of Rome

A ll dynasties, whether of rulers or republican aristocrats, aim to exist for eternity. It is part of their reason for existence. They do not succeed, of course, but one result of such an attitude and aim is that they fight to retain their positions and privileges, against competitors or usurpers, or treacherous members of their families, or rival aristocrats. Hence, in part, the high casualty rates. And some have longer runs than others.

In separating the recorded ancient dynasties into four groups – city dynasties, Roman Republican families, regional powers, and empires – it is possible to detect some comparisons and contrasts between them, and since this is essentially a matter of numbers, it has been possible to produce some simple graphs to illustrate the matter. These are produced as Table A, to show the durations of the royal dynasties, Table B for the length of existence of republican families, and Table C as a comparison of the numbers of rulers of the royal dynasties. (These are located in Chapter 4, 'Dynastic Durations'.)

The first thing to notice about the two groups showing durations is that the numbers of Roman families and of the regional powers are both much greater and so liable to last much longer than those of the city or imperial dynasties. The graphs of royal and Roman dynasties are in fact very similar, with heavy concentrations in both in the first three categories, up to 150 years' duration: this, of course, is repeated in the city and imperial graphs, but at that point both the Roman and regional graphs continue, with slowly diminishing numbers down to a little over 450 years, whereas the city and imperials virtually stop at about 150 years' duration, except for a few longer cases. This pattern is repeated, of course, in the graphs of numbers of rulers, in which the cut-off point is seven rulers, after which the regional dynasties go on in the graph with reasonably substantial numbers down to twenty-two members, whereas the city dynasties effectively stop at seven, and the imperials last only a little longer.

Therefore it seems that the dynasties ruling the smallest and the largest polities have the shortest lives with the fewest numbers. The reasons are fairly obvious, and have been examined in more than one place in these studies; both groups of dynasties are vulnerable in different ways. City rulers – tyrants to the Greeks – lived very much among their subjects, from whom they had publicly removed both their liberty by subjecting them to whatever restrictions the tyrants imposed, and their wealth by taking taxes from them, usually to pay for a bodyguard to protect themselves from those annoyed subjects; the imperial rulers were rich and powerful, and yet often found it necessary to conduct war in person, so that they were liable to be assassinated by jealous relatives and rivals, to die in battle, or to succumb to a military conspiracy. These conditions are rather less likely to apply in regional powers, whose lack of military strength could inhibit warfare, and whose more assiduous attention to their subjects' needs, combined with a certain distance from the people, left them more likely to live on.

But it is also worth considering the graph in a different way: by taking the Roman Republic as a city and so comparing its dynastic families with other city dynasties. In that case it presents a very strong contrast with those other cities. The Roman state for much of the republican period may have been geopolitically a large and growing regional power, but it was still operating as a single city-state for several centuries. And in this comparison the city of Rome stands out as wholly anomalous.

In particular, in the first place, by replacing its overthrown monarchy with an aristocratic republic rather than, as was commonly done in other cities, with the democracy; then for four centuries Rome fell into a condition that those other cities might have seen as one of arrested development. Even if a city's eventual replacement for the kings or tyrants was an aristocracy or oligarchy, these relatively quickly slid into a democracy. In Rome this did not ever happen, though in the last republican century some movement towards a democracy took place, only for this to be overtaken by what the Greeks would have called tyranny, under Augustus. It was in the long-continued regime of the aristocratic republic that Rome was principally anomalous, as well as in its conquests – and these two effects were clearly linked. It was aristocratic competition within the city that drove the acquisition of the empire.

Then again, in considering the imperial dynasties, the brevity of the Roman Imperial dynasties stands in strong contrast to those of several of the other empires. Only two dynasties in the Roman Empire lasted over a century, and both of them expired before they reached 110 years; and yet the empire lasted five centuries, and continued for as long again in its Byzantine guise – with dynasties once more limited in duration to about a century or less. So the majority of other imperial dynasties were longer in duration; or rather the

Roman dynasties were almost universally shorter in duration than those of other empires; the Assyrians, the Sassanids, the Seleukids, the Parthians, all maintained their dynastic continuity for three or four times as long as the longest Roman dynasty, despite suffering as badly from violent deaths: once again Rome stands out as thoroughly anomalous.

The Roman Empire was therefore unusual in its succession of ruling dynasties. Others were empires of the ruling family, which were usually the creation of the first of the dynasty, hence the personal names – Seleukids, Sassanids, and so on. But the Roman Imperial regime took over the existing republican empire as a going concern. So where the Seleukid Empire could only exist while the Seleukid kings ruled, the Roman Empire could go on under a succession of dynasties – nor did it much matter that some rulers were incompetent, because the structure of the empire was strong enough to survive. It is doubtful, for instance, if any other ancient empire could have survived the frequent regime changes and collapses of the third century as Rome did.

It is therefore clear, if there were ever any doubt, that the dynasties of the Roman Republic and Empire (and the royal dynasties also) were of a different type from all the rest. That is, from its very origins Rome was politically, socially, and constitutionally at variance with other equivalent cities, republics, and empires. The point has been made that the kings of Rome of the pre-Republican period, in so far as the evidence for them can be accepted, were just as different from their fellow kings and dynasties as the Roman Imperial dynasties, and as the Roman Republican system from their contemporaries, and that the kings' dynastic history appears to be more similar to those of the succeeding Roman Republicans and the later imperials than to any other royal dynasty, either in the ancient or modern world. (In fact, the best comparison of the republican dynastic system may well be the English aristocracy from the fifteenth to the nineteenth centuries, with its domination of the parliamentary system.)

Now, the fact that Rome was different is scarcely a surprise; after all no other city grew in such a way and ended ruling an empire whose memory has scarcely faded at any time since its fall. To become imperial was the aim of many succeeding royal dynasties; 'Roman' occurred in the titulature of the Byzantine, Ottoman, Carolingian, and Teutonic dynasties, even that of Tsarist Russia, kaiser and emperor are Roman-derived titles. It makes such powers out as aspirants to universal rule, though none of them ruled in Rome itself for more than two decades or, in the Ottoman and Russian cases, not at all. Even the founding Treaty of the European Union was, quite deliberately, signed in the city of Rome; the popes have maintained their aspiration to universal ecclesiastical authority since they emerged as politically important and effective in the last years of the empire's existence. No other ancient state, not even Athens or Sparta, has had such an influence or left such a memory. Rome was certainly different.

But it is curious, and perhaps significant, that this difference, by which Rome can be seen to be unlike other states, and that was clearly one of the marks of Rome's success in conquest and expansion, seems to date right back to the period of the kings. It is a truism that Rome was a city-state, and was even claimed as an Hellenic city, and expelled its kings in the same period as the Greeks were doing the same to their tyrants, so Roman political development was running in parallel with that of Greece until then. This, and the fact that other city-states, in Latium and Etruria, in Greece and in North Africa, and in Syria, were originally also ruled by kings, has tended to mask the fact of Rome's singularity. But a polity consists of the people who inhabit it, and the curious composition of the royal families of Rome who are said to have ruled the city in the early years would seem to have had an effect that ramified through its later history. For the kings' mode of succession is inexplicable except as a means of bringing a fairly wide range of aristocratic families into contact with the centre of power, presumably as a means of supporting the kingly authority.

This is exactly what was done in the empire, when the Julio-Claudian dynasty was a coalition of at least four republican families, and where the Antonine 'dynasty' also included at least four, while others were linked. Indeed, one can interpret the republic as a (sometimes disputatious) coalition of aristocratic families; and certainly the prominent political families took care to sponsor other groups and families as potential allies and supporters. The name of the regime might change from royal to republic to empire, but the political behaviour of those in power remained much the same.

It is theorized that the various elements in Roman society that were understood to be important by the men of the republic, or at least by the historians, have been attached retrospectively to several of the kings – the city's founding to Romulus, the religious practices to Numa Pompilius, while Tullus Hostilius and Ancus Marcius were conquerors of nearby territory, and the first Tarquin was a constitutional organizer. All of these changes and developments clearly happened, but it is naive to credit such developments to individual kings. It also marks as the real continuity, the continuing aristocratic nexus.

The names of the kings – Hostilius, Marcius, Pompilius – and of the assorted aristocrats are those of many of the aristocratic families who were prominent in the early republic. Several of them were linked to the kings by marriages, and this, of course, is a common practice in monarchies and aristocracies, where eligible royal daughters can be married into aristocratic families, and where royal sons can select wives from those same families. In Rome the practice went further and extended to formal adoption, and to the inheritance of the throne by men only distantly connected by blood with the kings. Then, once the kings had been expelled – by, among others, several of those very families – a similarly fairly restricted set of families monopolized political power in the city for the first half-century of the republic. The 'fairly wide range' of families attached to the royal power is much the same as the 'restricted set of families' in the republic – it is a matter of perspective only.

In the circumstances it is clear that the legacy of the kings was decisive in several areas of Rome's politics and society. The republican aristocracy worked in a collective way from the start, and its internal disputes rarely became lethal. Its relative openness to the acceptance of new families into the ruling group continued into being open to other aristocracies from other cities – Ancus Marcius was said to be a Sabine, and the Claudius family arrived from that same region in the first decade of the republic. They were welcomed as immigrants and as participants in power. The Roman aristocracy also eventually displayed a relative openness to originally non-noble Roman families who were rising to wealth and power. The republic went through a series of crises, some of them prolonged, but which were often resolved by some sort of compromise, at least until the republic's last century. (One of the reasons for the relative longevity of Roman Republican dynasties was clearly the absence of violent deaths within Roman political society, apart from on the field of battle, by comparison with royal dynasties.) In this it is evident that the reaction to the last Tarquin, and his exclusion from the city, was another aspect that had its later effect in Roman behaviour – for Tarquin was excluded, not assassinated or executed, a trait the Romans upheld for the next four centuries.

The royal methods had included legal adoption (as with King Servius Tullius), another peculiarly Roman practice that continued through the Roman Republic into the Imperial period, to be apparently abandoned when the empire became Christian. Even the very constitution of the regal families, whereby kings appeared from different branches of the collective family tree, is replicated in a sense in the aristocratic families of the republic, where the branches of several extended families were active at the same time.

Rome was as different from other societies in many other respects – in its warfare, its size, its political methods, its openness to outside influences, its wealth, and its fertility of political invention – but above all these it was different in the constitution of its aristocracy from other polities, monarchies, Republican, or Imperial. No other ancient state, monarchy or republic, city, region, or empire, had that collection of distinctive qualities. And it was that set of qualities that was the main ingredient in the development of the city to position a world power. And primary amongst these qualities, though they were actually only variations on the overall themes detectable in other societies, particularly city-states, and eventually empires. It was that set of distinctive qualities that was the main ingredient in the development of the city to a position of world power. And primary amongst those qualities was the aristocracy, hydra-headed, intensely competitive, but which accepted clear social restraints on behaviour and conduct, inured to the city's political ways from youth, its men wholly determined to succeed in the city. It brought the city to empire, was the source of the republic's wealth and power, but also in the end, when the old methods began to seem too restrictive, they brought the republic to destruction. They were then the real human foundation of the empire, but the century of civil conflict before the establishment of the imperial system had introduced assassination into the political system and it was never expunged – though an imperial regime, with its closed court society, was much more liable to internal violence than an open society such as the republic. The characteristics of that aristocracy are, however, clearly in part inherited from the old royalty, and were passed on into the imperial system. But how it was that the kings developed as they did is not at all clear. It would seem that Rome's singularity originated in its very foundation.

Comparisons beyond the Classical World

I have deliberately restricted my survey of dynasties to a definite historical period and area, in part because 'ancient world' dynasties are not studied in themselves as a set. It is, however, worth also looking briefly at other times and places to see if the results of an 'ancient world' investigation are replicated elsewhere and elsewhen, and if they are in fact 'typical' in that the same overall results can apply to dynasties in those other times and places; alternatively, any differences might also be of some significance.

Geographical areas that produced a large number of dynasties include the most ancient Babylonia and Egypt, mediaeval and modern Europe, China and Japan, India, South East Asia, the Muslim Middle East, West Africa, and to a degree, Central and South America. Any of these might produce a set of statistics that could be large enough to be used in comparison with those of the ancient world. Here I shall restrict my comparisons to those of Europe in the mediaeval and modern period, and China and Japan. Without exhaustively collecting data on all possible dynasties, it is nevertheless possible to suggest that the European dynasties diverged from those of the ancient world in their statistical results, while those of the Far East largely conform to those of the ancient world.

Just over fifty dynasties in Europe can be counted – in Britain, France, the Netherlands, Italy, Germany, Scandinavia, Eastern Europe, and Russia – and there have been almost thirty in China and Japan. There are a mixture of national and provincial dynasties in Europe, but no imperial dynasties – the Carolingians and the Habsburgs were never more than local rulers with an imperial title; the Chinese dynasties were partly imperial and partly those of the regional states into which the empire repeatedly split between imperial regimes, and in Japan there were both imperial and regency dynasties. There is thus largely the same mixture of imperial and regional dynasties in the Far East as in the ancient world, with the exception of the city dynasties, and in Europe the dynasties studied would in the ancient world all be classified as regional. (European city-states, in Germany and Italy, were rarely monarchies, and if they did produce a monarchy this quickly expanded its power to regional size.) Italy did produce a number of such dynasties in the later mediaeval period and after, though they were relatively few, and were large enough to be counted as regional powers.

The first point of difference that appears is that European dynasties tended to last longer than in the ancient world. The median duration for the European dynasties is 236 years, that compares with the median of the ancient dynasties' duration of no more than a century. The Far East median is also a little over a century. (The apparent predominance of China as an imperial state is largely an illusion in terms of dynasties – Chinese dynasties proved to be as vulnerable to destruction, murder and deposition as all others.)

With this higher dynastic duration the European dynasties also, of course, had a higher number both of generations and of rulers, but it is the averages for both which are more instructive. For the Europeans the median figure for the average length of generations is twenty-eight years; for the Far Eastern dynasties it is only twenty years. In terms of the lengths of reigns the median of averages for Europeans is nineteen years; for the Far East it is as low as twelve years. (These figures reinforce the conclusion arrived at earlier: no particular figure can be used to estimate reign or generation length, or the chronology of any dynasty.) Allowance must be made in the case of the Far Eastern dynasties for the prevalence of abdication in the Japanese imperial dynasty and in some of the Chinese dynasties, but this does not seriously affect the length of generations. It has to be concluded, at least tentatively, that the European dynasties lasted longer, that the generations of rulers were longer, and that those rulers individually ruled for longer than those either in the ancient world or in the Far East. The political and social effect of this was to enhance the stability of the states ruled, since a change of ruler was always a dangerous and destabilizing moment; and it may be noted that the geopolitical arrangement of powers in Western and Northern Europe has been very stable since the mediaeval period, despite the frequency of their warfare.

(Some Islamic, Indian, African, and American dynasties' details that are easily accessible were investigated, giving a total of twenty more dynasties. Generation and reign length averages were all uniformly lower than the European figures but slightly above the Far East, but the number of dynasties is not large enough to be significant – and the differences are hardly great enough to be significant. One African dynasty, however, that of imperial Ethiopia, lasted over five centuries, and the Malagasy dynasty registered a generation average of thirty-nine years, equal to the highest European score; the frequency of women rulers was presumably relevant here.)

However, the longest-lived dynasty, longer than any other by nearly five centuries, is that of the Japanese imperial dynasty, which is still reigning. (Still reigning dynasties have been counted only to the accession of the current reign – so the British Hanoverian house – now 'Mountbatten-Windsor' – has been included only until 1952, and the Japanese to 1989.) The imperial Japanese dynasty has a credible genealogy reaching back to AD 510, with a brief and unconnected dynasty preceding it. (By contrast no Chinese dynasty lasted as long as three centuries; the longest was the Tang, at 289 years, but it was largely powerless during its last half-century.) That Japanese dynasty is exceptional in every way, though not just in its duration; its longevity is due to a combination of two factors: powerlessness since the eleventh century, and it veneration as a sacred emblem of Japan. The other Japanese dynasties, the several regency regimes that have ruled for the emperors during the past millennium or so, all fit into the same pattern as the Chinese dynasties, with durations of less than three centuries in all cases. In addition there are a considerable number of Chinese dynasties that lasted only decades rather than centuries. This is all very similar to the patterns detected in the study of the ancient world dynasties.

No European dynasty can match the Japanese imperial for longevity, but there are no less than nine European dynasties that lasted longer than the longest dynasty of the ancient world. (For comparison three times as many ancient world dynasties were tabulated as European, an index of their comparative brevity, of course.) These Europeans are a mixture of provincial dynasties – Lorraine, Savoy, Brunswick – and dynasties ruling larger kingdoms – the Capetians of France, the Habsburgs, Spanish kings, kings of Denmark, Prussia, Poland, England, Scotland, and so on. The longest in duration is the dynasty of Spain (originally just Castile: 982 years, but with twentieth century interruption) and Savoy (later Italy: 831 years). It is noticeable that the three provincial dynasties with exceptionally long lives eventually became rulers of larger kingdoms: the Savoyard dynasty became kings of Italy, the Lorrainers married into the Habsburgs, the Brunswickers became kings of England; and all three thereby eventually lost control of their home territories, Lorraine by exchange with Tuscany and then the Holy Roman Empire, Savoy by cession to France in 1859, and Brunswick by conquest by the Hohenzollerns in 1866; of these only the Brunswicker dynasty is still reigning, in Britain, but the Castilian dynasty has been revived.

On all counts, therefore, the dynasties of mediaeval and modern Europe stand out from the general collection of dynasties in the world since 1000 BC, lasting longer on average, having a higher generation length, and having a substantially longer average length of reign. Why this is so, is not immediately clear but several reasons may be suggested. The wider respect awarded dynastic rule by an alliance of royalty with the Church may be part of it, though this alliance broke down as often as it was honoured, and when it broke down the result was usually a defeat for the Church. Partly it is the practice of dynastic intermarriage that allowed branches to flourish where the main stem died out – Brunswick/Hanover/Britain, for example, or the Piast dynasty of Poland, which lasted over 700 years, but in a variety of guises – a comparison with several of the segmented Roman Republican dynasties seems reasonable here. But there are plenty of examples of countries where dynasties were discarded or died out at frequent intervals. Britain and Sweden in particular are examples, where eight dynasties have followed each other in each country since the early Middle Ages, all technically connected genealogically, but sometimes very tenuously. Also note that the casualty rate of dynastic extermination has steadily increased since the end of the Habsburg dynasty of Spain in 1700, as better educated and more politically aware populations became increasingly annoyed at dynastic pretensions, notably their general incompetence involving Europe in the Great War of

1914–1918, and their continuing incompetence in waging it. So the reason for their collective longevity is the widespread acceptance of two things in the mediaeval period: the 'rightness' of dynastic rule – symbolized by the eventual theory of the 'divine right of kings', embraced by several dynasties, though generally scorned by their peoples – and the general legal applicability of rules of inheritance, especially that of succession by male primogeniture. This combination established a condition that largely precluded sibling rebellion and usurpation, at least until the curious concept of the divine right of kings finally exasperated several dynasties' subjects beyond endurance. A further element is clearly the end of the practice of kings to command in battle, which reduced their casualties – though this was also the practice elsewhere, and so may not be too significant, except in comparison with the ancient dynasties, whose rulers, from the Assyrians to the Emperor Leo at the siege of Constantinople in 717, were expected to be warriors.

The salvation of the surviving dynasties of the twentieth century has been their self-effacement. This was not something available to any dynasty in the ancient world, or in the Far East – with the telling exception of the Japanese imperial family, which was effectively finally stripped of power by the twelfth century, and thereby sanctified into a necessarily continually powerless existence. So one of the main reasons why the European dynasties survived for so long was by surrendering much of their power – including their practice of command in war. The divine right of kings turned out to be a recipe for arrogance and a highway to disaster – and was usually a desperate throw by dynasties who felt themselves threatened. Thus the invention of consultative parliaments by which non-royal politicians could be blamed for political disasters paradoxically tended to save the dynasties that worked with and through them. By extension, the ancient world dynasties had such relatively short existences because they did not surrender their power; instead they went down fighting.

Part II

Catalogue of Dynasties

Introduction

The intention here is to present the raw material on which the studies in Part I have been based. The dynasties are presented in four sets. Section 1 has dynasties that ruled in cities; Section 2 contains the dynasties of Roman Republican officials; Section 3 has the dynasties of regional kingdoms – that is, territories larger than that of a city-state, but less than an empire; Section 4 lists the dynasties of imperial states. They are presented in stripped-down form, omitting non-rulers except where these are needed to make clear the links between the actual rulers. Each table is accompanied by a commentary in which the most pertinent elements are mentioned – including any doubts that exist about dates and names and relationships. In each case also the statistics on reigns and generations are presented. Finally, a selection of sources from which the material collected is given: in Section 2, on the Roman Republican dynasties, this is not needed, for the sources are few and so they are listed instead in the introduction to that section.

As the commentaries also often have to make clear, there are doubts about the facts in all too many cases, and the tables, the dates, and therefore the calculations, have to be accepted with some scepticism. The disputes are not always all that profound, and the calculations that result from alternatives will vary by only one or two years or numbers from my own; taking the whole set of dynasties as a group, therefore, the variations are clearly damped out. One might, I contend, generally rely on the overall picture. In some cases, however, we have information about only a part of a dynasty, particularly the Arabian families; these are flagged as 'fragmentary', in the headings.

Arrangement

In Sections 1 and 3 of the Catalogue the city and regional dynasties are listed alphabetically. This listing creates difficulties, since some dynasties are known by a dynastic name (e.g. Attalids), some by the place they ruled (e.g. Macedon), and some by the people they ruled (e.g. Burgundians). If necessary they are given a location, as well as either a dynastic name or the people they ruled – or all three if it helps and/or seems necessary.

The Roman Republican dynasties listed in Section 2 are easily classified by the names of the families, that is, alphabetically, but there are also some families with subsections (such as the several Cornelii).

The imperial dynasties, those that spread so widely that they cannot be classified in a particular territory, are listed chronologically.

Questions marks (?) indicate either uncertainty or lack of knowledge or information.

Conventions

- Names in CAPITALS are the names of rulers.
- Names in lower case are the names of non-rulers, included for connecting or explicatory reasons.
- Single letters (usually 'X') indicate unknown or omitted or unnamed persons.
- Vertical links indicate parentage; horizontal links indicate siblings.
- Equals signs (=) indicate a marriage or another sexual link.
- Numbers in brackets and linked by dashes (–) are dates of reigns or periods in power; those linked by slashes (/) are the earliest or latest dates in power; single dates are the only known or the approximate ('*c.*') dates in power.
- Generations are numbered down the left side of the page, beginning with the first attested ruler of the family, who is not always the first in the table.
- Names unconnected by links are rulers who are probably known, but with uncertain familial links and/or dates. These are usually omitted in the calculations of reign and generational lengths.

Abbreviations

A – abdicated	)
B – killed in battle	) only indicated
D – deposed	) where certainty
M – murdered	) exists.
S – suicide	)
X – executed	
d – daughter	
s – son	
x – name or gender unknown	
w – wife.	

Section I

Cities' Dynasties

Athens, Greece, 561–510 BC

```
1              PEISISTRATOS (561-556, 546-527)
         _____ | _____
         |                                  |
2     HIPPARCHOS                         HIPPIAS
      (527-514)                         (527-510)
```

Statistics
Duration: 51 years, reigning for 41; 2 generations, average length, $51/2 =$ 25 years; 3 reigns, average length of reign, $41/3 = 14$ years.

Commentary
The brief Athenian tyranny was established by a foreign invasion of Athens (led by Peisistratos), and removed by another, by the Spartans. Peisistratos had made two or three previous but unsuccessful attempts to foist his personal rule on the city before 561, and was ousted once after his initial success, but when in place from 546, he was reasonably secure. His sons inherited without trouble and ruled jointly and quite harmoniously. However, when Hipparchos was killed in a private quarrel, Hippias became nervous and apprehensive, and his new oppressiveness lost him much of his internal support. He was removed by an internal revolution assisted by the Spartan intervention. After his deposition he continued to rule a small city at the Hellespont and was available for restoration during the Persian invasions that he encouraged and accompanied. As a dynasty, therefore, this is brief and inglorious, without much interest for this study.

References
A Andrewes, *The Greek Tyrants* (London, 1956).
AR Burn, *Persia and the Greeks*, 2nd Ed (London, 1984).

Beroia, Syria, 96–64 BC

```
1                        HERAKLEION  (96-)
           _____|_____
           |                               |
2       STRATO                         DIONYSIOS
        (      )                         (-64)
```

Statistics
Duration: 32 years; 2 generations, average length $32/2 = 2$; 16 years; 3 rulers, average length of reign $32/3 = 11$ years.

Commentary
Herakleion was a Seleukid commander who attempted to impose rigid discipline on his soldiers during the dynastic war between Antiochos VIII and Antiochos IX. The soldiers voiced the usual complaints, and the complainants were supported by the king, whose weakness in this is possibly one reason why the war had already lasted for nearly two decades. Herakleion murdered the king in a rage, then, having failed to secure the kingship for himself – he had no connections to the dynasty – he withdrew to the city of Beroia (modern Aleppo) and in effect seceded from the kingdom; he gained control of two other local towns in addition. His second son was still ruling when the Roman conqueror Pompey arrived and probably removed him. The dates for Strato are not known.

References
Strabo 14.2.7; Josephos, *Antiquities of the Jews*, 13.14.3.
JD Grainger, *The Seleukid Cities of Syria* (Oxford, 1990).

Bit-Agusi, Syria, *c.*870–*c.*750 BC (fragmentary)

```
1                       GUSI (c.870)
                          |
2                       HADRAM (c.860-c.830)
                          |
3                       ATTAR-SHUMKI I (c.830-800)
                          |
4                       BIR-HADAD (c.800-)
                          |
5                       ATTAR-SHUMKI II
                          |
6                       MAL'ILU (-c.750)
```

Statistics
Duration: about 120 years; 6 generations, average length, 120/6 = 20 years;
6 rulers, average length of reign, 120/6 = 20 years.

Commentary
Gusi was the founder both of the dynasty and of the state, which occupied part
of the north Syrian plain centred on the old city of Arpad; it was his capture
of the city that marked the emergence of the dynasty. The state was named
from the dynasty (i.e. 'House of Gusi'), in Assyrian records; we do not know
what they called themselves. It was one of several city-states that emerged in
the early Iron Age in Syria, centred often on existing, if faded, Bronze Age
cities. The sources for this dynasty are poor, being mainly in the records of its
enemies, and the dates are all estimates. One assumption has been that each
of the kings ruled for about forty years, which seemed highly unlikely, and a
more conservative estimate would suggest an average reign length of about
twenty years. The ending of the dynasty was the result of conquest by the
Assyrians, and is thus approximately dated. There is no guarantee that the
record of the dynasty is complete.

References
T Bryce, *The World of the Neo-Hittite Kingdoms* (Oxford, 2012).
K Klengel, *Syria 3000–300 BC* (Berlin, 1992).
HS Sader, *Les états araméens de Syrie: depuis leur fondation jusqu'à leur
    transformation en provinces assyriennes* (Beirut, 1987).

Carchemish, Syria

A. *Suhanid Dynasty, c.970-c.870 (fragmentary).*

```
1                       SUHAS I (c.970)
                             |
2                       ASTUWATAMANZA
                             |
3                        SUHAS II
                             |
4                       KATUWAS (-c.870)
```

Statistics

Duration: about 100 years; 4 generations, average length 100/4 = 25 years; 4 rulers, average length of reign, 100/4 = 25 years.

Commentary

The names of the dynasty of kings of Carchemish in the late Bronze Age are known, but there is a break in the sequence after the mid eleventh century. By about 970 BC a new dynasty (presumably) was ruling, that of Suhas, three of whose ruling descendants are known. A new king, Sangara, not apparently related to the previous dynasty, was king by about 870, so Suhas' line had lasted about a century. At least two kings between the former dynasty and Suhas I are known, so Suhas' accession may well be earlier than 970. The dates of the start and end of the dynasty are, however, little more than guesses.

None of Sangara's immediate successors, of whom four are known by name, can be connected genealogically with him or with his predecessors. The dynasty was succeeded, or replaced, by another, headed by Astiruwa.

B. *Astiruwan Dynasty, c.800-717 BC.*

```
        ASTIRUWA (c.800-)
             |                    YARIRI (Regent)
          KAMANI


                              SASTURA (Vizir)
                                   |
                              PISIRI (c.732-717)
```

Statistics

Duration: about 80 years; 4 generations, average length 80/4 = 20 years; 5 rulers, average length of reign 80/5 = 16 years.

Commentary

This may or may not be an actual dynasty. Yariri operated as regent for
Astiruwa, who was either sickly or a child, and in either case was presumably
a member of a ruling dynasty – a child could not have succeeded without such
legitimation. Kamani succeeded as a child, and Sastura operated as his vizir,
but then he engineered the succession of his own son, Pisiri. Pisiri was the
last king of independent, or nearly independent, Carchemish, but operated
under Assyrian suzerainty. When he was detected intriguing with an enemy
of Assyria he was deported to Nineveh with his whole family. The fate of
Kamani is not known, but it may be that, like his father, he died young.

References

T Bryce, *The World of the Neo-Hittite Kingdoms* (Oxford, 2012).

D Hawkins, 'Karkamish', *Reallexikon der Assyrologie und Vorderasiatischen
Archaologie*, 5–6 (1960) pp. 432–445.

K Klengel, *Syria 3000–300 BC* (Berlin, 1992).

HS Sader, *Les états araméens de Syrie: depuis leur fondation jusqu'à leur
transformation en provinces assyriennes* (Beirut, 1987).

D Ussishkin, 'Some Monuments from Carchemish', *Journal of Near Eastern
Studies*, 26 (1967) pp. 85–97.

Corinth, Greece (Kypselids), 658–565 BC

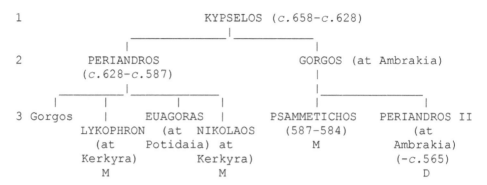

```
1                          KYPSELOS (c.658-c.628)
                   _____|_____
           |                          |
2       PERIANDROS                  GORGOS (at Ambrakia)
        (c.628-c.587)                  |
      _____|_____               |_____
     |     |      |      |           |           |
3 Gorgos  |   EUAGORAS  |        PSAMMETICHOS  PERIANDROS II
       LYKOPHRON  (at   NIKOLAOS    (587-584)      (at
        (at    Potidaia) at             M        Ambrakia)
       Kerkyra)         Kerkyra)                  (-c.565)
          M                M                         D
```

Statistics
Duration: 93 years; 3 generations, average length 93/3 = 31 years; 8 rulers, average length of reign, 93/8 = 12 years.

Commentary
The tyranny of Kypselos at Corinth is the archetype of Greek tyrannies, from the more or less peaceful seizure of power from an oppressive aristocracy with great popular support, through the acquisition of a bodyguard by the rulers – paid for out of increased taxation – to the oppression by, and overthrow of, his fearful and paranoid grandson, Psammetichos. It was, however, of rather wider contemporary significance than simply for the city of Corinth, and the family did not end with Psammetichos' murder.

Several members of the family were sent to govern other cities outside Corinth – Kerkyra, Ambrakia, Potidaia – which had been founded by, or seized by, Corinthians, so producing a small monarchical imperial state. One member of the family, the second Periandros, continued to rule in Ambrakia for about two decades after the end of the tyranny at Corinth itself. Note also that Periandros II was deposed, whereas his brother in Corinth and two of his cousins at Kerkyra were murdered by their subjects. It would seem unlikely that Ambrakia suffered badly or was too unhappy under the sub-dynasty of Periandros and his father.

The dates of these rulers are all uncertain, and those I have used must be seen as approximate, though they cannot be too far out. The dynasty may best be compared with the first Thracian dynasty and that of the Deinomenids of Sicily, both of whom used members of the dynastic family to control subject cities and areas.

References
A Andrewes, *The Greek Tyrants* (London, 1956).
J Salmon, *Wealthy Corinth* (Oxford, 1984).

Damascus, Syria, *c.*950–732

A   *Rezonid Dynasty,* c.950-844 BC.

1   REZON (mid C10)
                                 |
2   HEZION (late C10)
                                 |
3   TAB-RIMMON (late C10)
                                 |
4   BAR-HADAD I (*c.*910)
                                 |
5   HADADEZER (-844)

Statistics
Duration: about 106 years; 5 generations, average length 106/5 = 21 years;
5 rulers, average length of reign, 106/5 = 21 years.

B.   *Hazaelid Dynasty,* 844-732 BC.

1   HAZAEL (844-803)
                                 |
2   BAR-HADAD II (803-775)
                                 |
3   HADYAN II (775-*c.*750)
                                 |
4   RUSYAN (*c.*750-732)

Statistics
Duration: 112 years; 4 generations, average length, 112/4 = 28 years; 4 rulers,
average length of reign, 112/4 = 28 years.

Commentary
Two successive dynasties can be detected ruling in Iron Age Damascus, though
their names and dates are not always clear or certain. The separation between
them is at 844 BC when Hazael seized power from the last king of the first
dynasty, Hadadezer. The results of the latest investigations are summarized
here. It is by no means final or wholly accepted.

   The origin of the first dynasty is with the takeover by an Aramaean group
of the ancient Bronze Age city, control of which also meant control of the
Ghuta, the fertile oasis in which Damascus sits. This, and the city's strategic
position, automatically makes the ruler of the city a local Syrian great power;
the geographical position of the city in Syria gives the ruler the ability to
expand in all directions. The evidence for the first three kings of the first

dynasty is purely biblical and may not be correct. They are, however, included here. The founder of the dynasty seems to have been Rezon, of whom little is known, but who may be dated to the mid tenth century. His successors became powerful enough to resist Assyrian attacks successfully for a time.

Hazael, described in the Bible, with ineffable snobbishness, as the 'son of a nobody', carried through a successful coup in 844 and emerged as even more powerful than the family he had displaced. Hazael's dynasty, however, failed in the third and fourth genrations in the face of repeated and more powerful Assyrian attacks, and Rusyan only survived for a few years as an Assyrian vassal. When he was removed, the city became an Assyrian province. The dating of the second dynasty is reasonably firm, though that of the first is not – and both depend ultimately on biblical chronology, which is not necessarily reliable.

References
T Bryce, *The World of the Neo-Hittite Kings* (Oxford, 2012).
Ross Burns, *Damascus, a History* (London, 2005).
WT Pitard, *Ancient Damascus: a Historical Study of the Syrian city-state from Earliest Times until its fall to the Assyrians in 732 BCE* (Winona Lake, 1987).
HS Sader, *Le etats Arameens de Syrie, depuis leur fondation jusqu'a leur transformation en provinces Assyriennes* (Wiesbaden, 1987).

Emesa, Syria, *c.*90 BC–AD 73

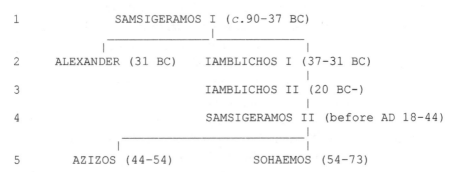

```
1                 SAMSIGERAMOS I (c.90-37 BC)
           _____|_____
          |                                         |
2     ALEXANDER (31 BC)      IAMBLICHOS I (37-31 BC)
                                          |
3                             IAMBLICHOS II (20 BC-)
                                          |
4                             SAMSIGERAMOS II (before AD 18-44)
           _____|
          |                                |
5     AZIZOS (44-54)            SOHAEMOS (54-73)
```

Statistics
Duration: about 163 years, reigning for 152; 5 generations, average length, $163/5 = 33$ years; 7 rulers, average length of reign, $152/7 = 22$ years.

Commentary
This was a dynasty, regarded as Arab, which emerged with Samsigeramos I during the collapse of the Seleukid dynasty. Essentially it controlled just the city of Emesa (modern Homs) and the land round about, though it was in a useful position from which to control trade routes between the coastal Phoenician ports and Palmyra and points east. The two sons of Samsigeramos became mixed in with both sides in the final Roman civil war in 31–30 BC, and each was executed by one of the two contenders. Augustus restored the dynasty in the person of Iamblichos II in 20 BC. Vespasian suppressed it finally, along with several other Syrian dynasties, in 73, following the Jewish War, when a substantial Emesan force had assisted the Romans. The family may be genetically connected with the Severan dynasty of Rome, which emerged in this region, but all attempts to establish a genealogical link have so far failed.

References
CJ Chad, *Les Dynastes d'Emese* (Beirut, 1972).
H Seyrig, 'Characteres de l'Histoire d'Emese', *Syria*, 36 (1959) pp. 184–192.
RD Sullivan, 'The Dynasty of Emesa', *Aufsteig und Niedergang des Romischen Welt II*, 8 (1977) pp. 198–219.

Gurgum, Syria, *c.*1000–*c.*800 BC

```
1        ASTUWARAMUNZA (late C11)
         |
2        MUWATALLI I (late C11-early C10)
         |
3        LARAMA I (-c.970)
         |
4        MUWIZI (late C10)
         |
5        HALPARUNTIYA I (early C9)
         |
6        MUWATALLI II (in 898)
         |
7        HALPARUNTIYA II (in 853)
         |
8        LARAMA II (late C9)
         |
9        HALPARUNTIYA III (in 805-800)
```

Statistics
Duration: at least 200 years and perhaps 20 more; 9 generations, average length 220/9 = 24 years; 9 rulers, average length of reign, 220/9 = 24 years.

Commentary
Gurgum was a small kingdom in north-west Syria, one of many Syrian city-states that existed in the Iron Age, until conquered and destroyed by the Assyrians. This genealogy is well-attested by inscriptions. The last king here, Halparuntiya III, was succeeded by a gap in the list of kings. Two more kings, father and son, are known before the kingdom was annexed by Assyria in 711; the last two may or may not be connected to the main dynastic line. Perhaps a certain scepticism as to the direct line of descent from father to son over nine generations may be admitted.

References
T Bryce, *The World of the Neo-Hittite Kingdoms* (Oxford, 2012).

HS Sader, *Les états araméens de Syrie: depuis leur fondation jusqu'à leur transformation en provinces assyriennes* (Beirut, 1987).

Hamath, Syria, *c.*880–810 BC (fragmentary)

```
1                    PARITA (c.880-c.860)
                        |
2                    URHILINA (c.860-c.830 - in 853-845)
                        |
3                    URATAMI (in c.830)
```

Statistics

Duration: about 50 years; 3 generations, average length 50/3 = 16 years;
3 rulers, average length of reign 50/3 = 16 years.

Commentary

Hamath (modern Hama) was one of the many city kingdoms of early Iron Age Syria, and was one of the more powerful. Its dynasty is barely known, and the dates of these three kings are partly guesswork. Their names would suggest that the family was perhaps Hittite or Hurrian in origin, and so the kings may have been able to trace their ancestry back into the Bronze Age; this would mean that we have only a small fragment of the dynasty. The dynasty certainly expired by *c.*800, when the king of a different dynasty is known to be ruling; this makes the end of this dynasty some years before that.

References

T Bryce, *The World of the Neo-Hittite Kingdoms* (Oxford, 2012).

HS Sader, *Les états araméens de Syrie: depuis leur fondation jusqu'à leur transformation en provinces assyriennes* (Beirut, 1987).

Hatra, Mesopotamia, AD 158–241

```
1   Worod, `Lord'   Nasru `Lord',   NSRYHB `Lord'  Ma'anu `Lord'
    (105-115)       (115-135)       (135-145)      (145-154)
                        |_____
                |                               |
2           SANATRUQ                           WLKS
        `Lord' (166-167)                   `Lord' (155-158)
         King (167-190)                     King (158-166)
             |
3           ABDSIMYA (190-200)
             |
4           SANATRUQ II (200-240/1)
```

Statistics
Duration: 125 years; 4 generations, average length $125/4 = 31$ years; 5 rulers, average length of reign, $125/5 = 25$ years.

Commentary
Hatra was a trading city on the desert edge on the border of Mesopotamia and Babylonia, originally under the control of an oligarchy (the four 'Lords' of the first generation), out of which there emerged a family that took the title of king after leading a successful defence against a Roman attack under the Emperor Trajan. The original title of 'Lord' for the head of the state was changed to 'King' with 'WLKS', though the dynasty actually begins with his father Nasru, one of the four 'lords' of the city in the previous fifty years. (The sources for all this are usually inscriptions, not all of which can be readily transliterated, hence the difficulty in naming some of the dynasty.) The city was at the interface of Rome and Parthia, and suffered from the hostile attentions of both powers; like Palmyra, it became wealthy out of long-distance trade, and this made it a target. In the end, in 233 Sanatruq II allowed a Roman occupation without resistance; in reply the Sassanids destroyed the city and annexed it.

References
Malcolm AR Colledge, *Parthian Art* (London, 1977).
JT Milik, *Dédicaces faites par des dieux* (Paris, 1972).
F Safar and MA Mustapha, *Hatra, the City of the Sun God* (Baghdad, 1974).

Herakleia Pontike, Asia Minor, 364-284 BC

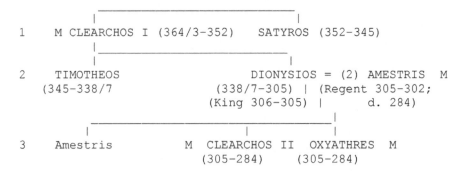

```
            |                                   |
1     M CLEARCHOS I (364/3-352)     SATYROS (352-345)
            |_____
            |                                   |
2     TIMOTHEOS                      DIONYSIOS = (2) AMESTRIS   M
      (345-338/7                     (338/7-305) | (Regent 305-302;
                                     (King 306-305) |      d. 284)
            _____|
            |                         |          |
3     Amestris            M  CLEARCHOS II  OXYATHRES  M
                             (305-284)     (305-284)
```

Statistics

Duration: 80 years; 3 generations, average length 80/3 = 27 years; 7 rulers, average length of reign 80/7 = 11 years.

Commentary

The first Clearchos made himself tyrant of Herakleia Pontike ('on the Black Sea') in the traditional manner of a *coup d'état* against an oppressive oligarchy, but was able to enlarge his city's range of action when in power. He was succeeded by his brother and then his sons. Dionysios married a daughter of the Akhaimenid king, who had been discarded in a friendly fashion by the Macedonian warlord Krateros. After Dionysios' death she became regent for her sons, and then married briefly another Macedonian warlord, Lysimachos. These marriages meant that she and the dynasty succeeded in surviving the wars of Alexander's successors. She continued to act as regent for her sons, who appear to have ruled in tandem. They were all murdered in a revolution in 284.

References

S Burstein, *Outpost of Hellenism: the Emergence of Herakleia on the Black Sea* (Berkeley and Los Angeles, 1976).

Kition, Cyprus (495–312 BC)

```
A   The First Dynasty, 495-400 BC.

1                     BAALMELEK I (c.495-475)
                               |
2                        AZBAAL (475-425)
                               |
3                     BAALMELEK II (425-400)
```

Statistics
Duration: 95 years, 3 generations, average length, 95/3 = 32 years; 3 rulers,
average length of reign, 95/3 = 32 years.

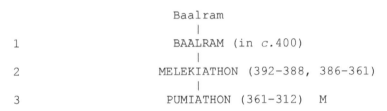

```
B.   The Second Dynasty, 400-312 BC.

                         Baalram
                            |
1                      BAALRAM (in c.400)
                            |
2              MELEKIATHON (392-388, 386-361)
                            |
3                  PUMIATHON (361-312)   M
```

Statistics
Duration: 88 years, reigning for 86; 3 generations, average length, 88/3 =
29 years; 3 rulers, average length of reign, 86/3 = 29 years.

Commentary
Kition, called Qart-Hadasht ('New City') by the Phoenicians who founded the
city, was an independent kingdom at least from 707 BC, though the names of
the earliest kings are not known. A new dynasty was installed by the Persians
after the failure of the great Cypriot revolt in 499. Baalmelek I was appointed
about 495 or so, and founded a dynasty that lasted at least three generations
and that extended Kition's domination throughout south-east Cyprus, with
Persian assistance.

About 400 a king called Baalram succeeded. He is known to have been the
son of another Baalram, and so he may either be the founder of a new dynasty,
or possibly the son of a younger branch of the old dynasty; the evidence does
not permit a decision, so he is treated here as the founder of a new dynasty.
The shortness of his reign might imply either alternative – he was probably
already of a good age when he became king. His son was briefly evicted
by the victory of Evagoras I of Salamis in 388, who installed an Athenian,
Demonikos, as king, but Melekiathon was soon reinstated with Persian help.

The last ruler of the dynasty, Pumiathon, carefully maintained himself for two decades amid the storms of Alexander's conquests and the subsequent warfare – a considerable achievement in view of the long association of the Kition dynasties with Persia. Once Cyprus fell to a single ruler, however, in the person of Ptolemy I, all the kings in the island were eliminated, and Pumiathon was killed.

The long reigns of the kings of both dynasties are noteworthy, suggesting a peaceful disposition.

References
Sir George Hill, *A History of Cyprus*, vol. 1 (Cambridge, 1940).
K Nicolaou, *The Historical Topography of Kition* (Goteborg, 1976).
PJ Stylianou, *The Age of the Kingdoms, the Political History of Cyprus in the Archaic and Classical Periods* (Nicosia, 1989).

Malatya, Asia Minor (fragmentary)

A   *The First Dynasty.*

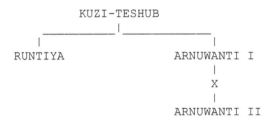

```
                    KUZI-TESHUB
         _____|_____
        |                       |
     RUNTIYA              ARNUWANTI I
                               |
                               X
                               |
                         ARNUWANTI II
```

B   *The Second Dynasty.*

```
                ?TARAS
                  |
             WASURUNTIYA
                  |
             HASPASULUPI
```

Statistics
No dates other than a vague attribution to a century are known of any of these kings.

Commentary
Malatya (ancient Melitene) is on the Euphrates in southern Anatolia, which puts it within the territory of the defunct Hittite Empire; of the kings who are known, all bear Hittite names. Twenty kings are known of altogether, though not all their actual names – hence the X in the list. Out of these, two dynasties can be discerned but their dates are unknown – the first dynasty was probably in the eleventh century BC, the second in the tenth. Kings continued to reign until the seventh century, but the relationships of the later kings are generally unknown.

References
T Bryce, *The World of the Neo-Hittite Kingdoms* (Oxford, 2012).

Masuwari (Til Barsip), Syria, *c*.10/9 BC

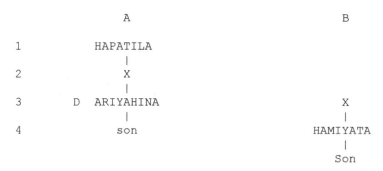

	A		B
1	HAPATILA		
2	X		
3	D ARIYAHINA		X
4	son		HAMIYATA
			Son

Statistics

No calculations are possible in the absence of reliable dates.

Commentary

Masuwari was a small kingdom on the Euphrates south of Carchemish; it was also called Til Barsip later, perhaps in an indication of ethnic shifts in the rulers of the city. There was certainly dynastic conflict. The two known dynasties run in parallel, dynasty A ruled until the father of Hamiyata usurped the throne, but it seems that the son of Ariyahina usurped it back again. Dating is too vague to support more than an approximation, but the whole sequence seems to begin in the late tenth century and end in the mid ninth.

References

T Bryce, *The World of the Neo-Hittite Kingdoms* (Oxford, 2012).

HS Sader, *Les états araméens de Syrie: depuis leur fondation jusqu'à leur transformation en provinces assyriennes* (Beirut, 1987).

Patin, Syria, *c.*870–831 BC (a fragment only)

```
1              LUBARNA I  (c.870-858)    B?
               |
2          SUPPILULIUMA  (-858/7)        B?
               |
3          HALPARUNTIYA  (858/7-c.853)
               |
4             LUBARNA II  (c.853-831)    M
```

Statistics
Duration: 39 years, 4 generations, average length 39/4 = 10 years; 4 rulers, average length of reign, 39/4–10 years.

Commentary
Patin was an important Iron Age Syrian kingdom, whose known kings all had Hittite names. It was situated in the wealthy and productive Amuq plain (where Antioch was later founded). It was an independent kingdom until conquered and annexed by Assyria in 738, but of the eight kings only four can be reconstituted as a dynastic line, mainly from Assyrian sources. Lubarna I and Suppiluliuma were both defeated by Assyrian invasions, and possibly killed in battle; Lubarna II was killed in an internal revolt against subordination to Assyrian tributary demands.

References
T Bryce, *The World of the Neo-Hittite Kingdoms* (Oxford, 2012).
HS Sader, *Les états araméens de Syrie: depuis leur fondation jusqu'à leur transformation en provinces assyriennes* (Beirut, 1987).

Rome, Italy, *c.*625–509 BC

A   *The First 'Dynasty'.*

```
                    |                              |
1               ROMULUS = Hersilia          Hostilius
                                                   |
2                                          Hostus Hostilius
                                                   |
3                                          TULLUS HOSTILIUS
```

B.   *The Second 'Dynasty'.*

```
1                      Pompilius Pompus   TITUS TATIUS
                            |                   |
2     Marcius          NUMA POMPILIUS   =  Tatia
      |_____                       |
                     |                        |
3            Numa Marcius    =   Pompilia
                             |
4                      ANCUS MARCIUS
```

C.   *The Third (Tarquin) Dynasty.*

```
1                       TARQUINIUS PRISCUS
        _____|_____
        |                                      |
2   TARQUINIUS SUPERBUS              d = SERVIUS TULLIUS
       (-509)
```

Commentary

The Roman royal dynasties that preceded the establishment of the republic in 509 BC are much disputed as to status, date, and relationships. It seems necessary, however, to include some account of them if only to point out the implausibilities and difficulties in understanding them. There were in fact three distinct dynasties and there were no discernible relationships between them. It is also highly doubtful that the first and second 'dynasties' were ever really royal, and maybe they never even existed.

Only the third dynasty can be dated in any vague way. Tarquinius Superbus was driven out of the city in 509 BC, and given that the dynasty existed for just two generations, it is unlikely that Tarquinius Priscus became king much earlier than 560 or 550 BC. The whole set of seven kings can hardly have occupied more than a century or a century and a quarter; the traditional dates, which dated the 'kingship' of Romulus to the foundation of the city in

753 BC, may be discarded. It is highly unlikely that the first dynasty were really kings of any sort. Romulus' name is clearly a construct based on the name of the city, and the way later generations distributed the social development of the community among the several early kings and their achievements, rather suggests that this was a much later rationalization of little known events that existed only in folklore. One point that may be made, however, is that these dynasties are constructed in the same complex way that one normally finds in many dynasties of the ancient world, with marriages, inheritances by attached branches and interventions from outside. In that, the dynastic constructions mirrored the practices of these other dynasties (and many of the later Republican and Imperial Roman families). Their brief existences were also typical of such dynasties. The whole regal period therefore looks very like a deliberate invention of later rationalizing historians. The Tarquin dynasty, however, has the appearance of a typical Greek tyranny, seizing power in a *coup d'état*, beginning well, but then rapidly becoming oppressive until it was overthrown. Note that the end of the kingship comes just at the same period that Greek tyrannies – Corinth, Syracuse, Athens – were disappearing.

References
TJ Cornell, *The Beginning of Rome* (London, 1995).
J Huergon, *The Rise of Rome to 264 BC* (London, 1973).
K Lomas, *The Rise of Rome from the Iron Age to the Punic Wars* (London, 2017).

Salamis, Cyprus *c.*560–312 BC

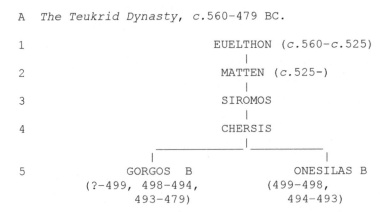

A   *The Teukrid Dynasty,   c.560-479 BC.*

1		EUELTHON (c.560-c.525)
2		MATTEN (c.525-)
3		SIROMOS
4		CHERSIS
5	GORGOS B (?-499, 498-494, 493-479)	ONESILAS B (499-498, 494-493)

Statistics

Duration: 81 years; 5 generations, average length 81/5 = 16 years; 6 rulers, average length of reign, 81/6 = 14 years.

Commentary

Two dynasties are known from the city of Salamis in Cyprus, though there were many more kings earlier. The earlier dynasty is claimed to be descended from the Dark Age hero Teukros, but the first known king of a clear and connected dynasty is Euelthon, who died in a vain revolt against Persian control. The connection between Matten and Siromos is not attested, but it seems probable that they were son and father. The dates of the reigns of Siromos and Chersis are not known, though since coins were issued in their names, they certainly appear to have been kings. The Ionian revolt caused a split between the brothers Gorgos and Onesilas: the latter seized power, was displaced by Gorgos with Persian help, recovered briefly, and was finally defeated. Gorgos took part in the great invasion of Greece in 480 on the Persian side, but perhaps perished in the defeat. Both the originating and terminating dates of this dynasty are thus uncertain, as is the genealogical descent, and the table must be seen as tentative only. All kings, however, claimed descent from the supposed founder Teukros.

B. *The Evagorid Dynasty*, 411-312 BC.

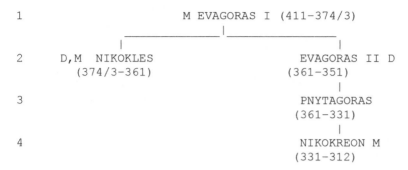

```
1                        M EVAGORAS I (411-374/3)
                  _____|_____
         |                                          |
2    D,M  NIKOKLES                          EVAGORAS II D
       (374/3-361)                            (361-351)
                                                 |
3                                           PNYTAGORAS
                                             (361-331)
                                                 |
4                                           NIKOKREON M
                                             (331-312)
```

Statistics

Duration: 99 years; 4 generations, average length 99/4 = 25 years; 5 rulers, average length of reign, 99/5 = 20 years.

Commentary

The city remained a monarchy through the fifth century, and there are several kings known in the period following the presumed death of Gorgos and before the accession of Evagoras, but any genealogical connections between them, or with the two dynasties here presented, are unknown; two of the kings at least were of Phoenician origin, judging by their names. The line of descent was thus probably broken with the death of Gorgos, and the fifth century kings were probably Persian appointees, a situation in which direct inheritance was discouraged.

The seizure of power by Evagoras in 411 displaced the current Phoenician king, and Evagoras and his family ruled Salamis until the Ptolemaic takeover in 312. Evagoras bade fair for a time to bring the whole of the island of Cyprus under his rule, but the opposition of Cypriots, both Greeks and Phoenicians, and of Persia, forced his failure; he was, however, able to retain his own city throne until his murder (in a private quarrel). His two surviving sons, who succeeded in sequence, were evicted after each became involved in a Persian war, which the Persians termed a rebellion: Nikokles by the Persians, Evagoras II by the pro-Persian party in the city. The last king, Nikokreon, fell to Ptolemy I.

The relationships of the five kings are not altogether certain: Evagoras II may have been the son rather than the brother of Nikokles, and Pnytagoras may have been the son of another brother who was killed with Evagoras. But the number of kings, their dates, and the total number of generations are certain enough.

Clearly Salamis was a city where monarchy was the governing institution of choice. There are no signs of any attempt at replacing it by a Republican regime, despite the several upheavals, foreign interventions, and coups. At the same time, the overwhelming presence of the Persian Empire, which had systematically conquered the cities of Cyprus, ensured that the kings, even Evagoras I, were only intermittently independent. Dynastic inheritance in such circumstances depended on the will of the Persian Great King.

References
Sir George Hill, *A History of Cyprus*, vol. 1 (Cambridge, 1940).
PJ Stylianou, *The Age of the Kingdoms, the Political History of Cyprus in the Archaic and Classical Periods* (Nicosia, 1989).

Samal, Syria, *c*.900–713/711

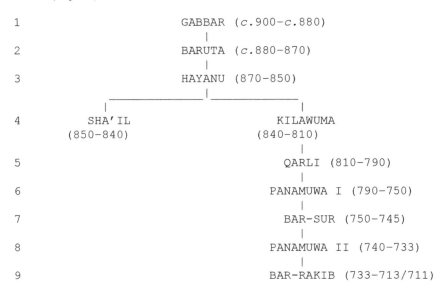

```
1                      GABBAR  (c.900-c.880)
                           |
2                      BARUTA  (c.880-870)
                           |
3                      HAYANU  (870-850)
        _____|_____
        |                                      |
4     SHA'IL                              KILAWUMA
     (850-840)                            (840-810)
                                              |
5                                 QARLI  (810-790)
                                              |
6                                 PANAMUWA I  (790-750)
                                              |
7                                 BAR-SUR  (750-745)
                                              |
8                                 PANAMUWA II  (740-733)
                                              |
9                                 BAR-RAKIB  (733-713/711)
```

Statistics

Duration: 187 years, reigning for 182; 9 generations, average length, 187/9 = 21 years; 10 rulers, average length of reign, 182/10 = 18 years.

Commentary

Samal was a city-state centred at the site now called Zincirli, in southern Turkey, near the border with Syria. As with other local states in ancient Syria (Hamath, Arpad, Damascus, Israel, and others), the sources for those who ruled the city are essentially Assyrian, supplemented by some local inscriptions. The earliest known king of the city, Gabbar, was apparently the founder of the dynasty, and recent research has sorted out an unusually long dynastic succession for the region, though the dates are only approximate. (A usurper interrupted the sequence between Bar-Sur and Panamuwa II.) The dynasty was very largely loyal to Assyria – Panamuwa II was killed as an Assyrian ally at the attack on Damascus – and prospered as a result: it was annexed as an Assyrian province on the death of Bar-Rakib.

References

T Bryce, *The World of the Neo-Hittite Kingdoms* (Oxford, 2012).

HS Sader, *Les états araméens de Syrie: depuis leur fondation jusqu'à leur transformation en provinces assyriennes* (Beirut, 1987).

Samos, Greece, *c.*590–480 BC

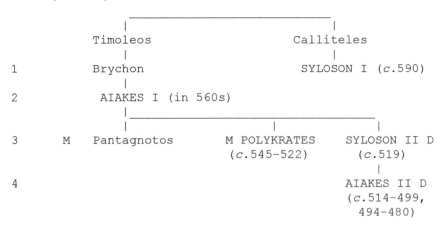

```
              |                                |
          Timoleos                        Calliteles
              |                                |
1         Brychon                      SYLOSON I  (c.590)
              |
2         AIAKES I  (in 560s)
              |_____
              |                    |                   |
3    M    Pantagnotos        M POLYKRATES        SYLOSON II D
                              (c.545-522)           (c.519)
                                                       |
4                                               AIAKES II D
                                                (c.514-499,
                                                   494-480)
```

Statistics
Duration: 110 years, reigning for 97; 4 generations, average length $110/4 =$ 27 years; 5 rulers, average length of reign, $97/5 = 19$ years.

Commentary
The early years of the Samian tyranny are poorly recorded, but power does seem to have descended through the members of a single family, beginning with Syloson I, who was tyrant in the city about 590. Assuming he held power for a generation and passed his position to his cousin Aiakes I, who is known to have been tyrant in the 560s, we certainly have a dynasty that lasted for a century or so, which will be about average for the Greek tyrant dynasties of the period.

The greatest name in the family was Polykrates, whose power was widely respected or, perhaps, feared. His successors, however, were not. Syloson II was removed by an internal revolution; Aiakes II returned the family to power after a few years, but then became involved in the Ionian revolt against the Persian Empire, and so also in the great Persian Wars; his periods of power in Samos coincided with Persian control and his expulsions with Greek victories. Like many tyrants at the time, he chose the wrong side.

The dating of the various rulers is clearly difficult. It may be that there were other members of the family ruling in the early years, and the intervals of expulsion in the later period are uncertain.

References
G Shipley, *A History of Samos, 800–186 BC* (Oxford, 1987).

Sikyon, Greece, *c.*650-*c.*550 BC

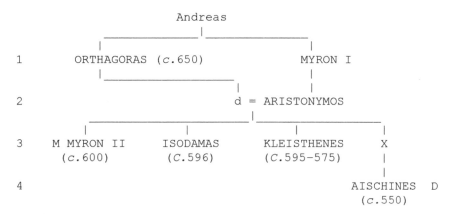

```
                         Andreas
              _____|_____
              |                               |
1        ORTHAGORAS (c.650)              MYRON I
              |_____           |
                                   |           |
2                                  d   =   ARISTONYMOS
              _____|_____
              |             |             |                    |
3       M MYRON II      ISODAMAS      KLEISTHENES              X
          (c.600)        (C.596)     (C.595-575)              |
                                                              |
4                                                         AISCHINES  D
                                                            (c.550)
```

Statistics

Duration: 100 years (traditionally), 4 generations, average length 100/4 = 25 years; 7 rulers, average length of reign, 100/7 = 14 years.

Commentary

The dates of the rulers of the Orthagorid tyrants of Sikyon are so unclear that only the most approximate dates of the start and end of their rule can be stated. The dates in the table are therefore those when members of the dynasty are attested in office. The dynasty conventionally lasted a century, but how accurate that estimate was is not known. However, the relationships between the various rulers are probably correct.

Orthagoras seized power in a coup. Within a generation the family was exhibiting characteristic dynastic behaviour: marriage within the family, and violent family disputes leading to murder. The end came with the deposition of the last, and barely competent, member.

References

A Griffin, *Sikyon* (Oxford, 1982).

Soloi, Cyprus, *c.*360–*c.*300 BC (fragmentary)

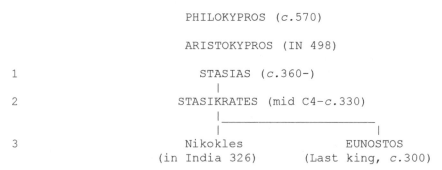

```
                         PHILOKYPROS (c.570)

                         ARISTOKYPROS (IN 498)

1                            STASIAS (c.360-)
                                 |
2                        STASIKRATES (mid C4-c.330)
                                 |_____
                                 |                       |
3                            Nikokles              EUNOSTOS
                         (in India 326)      (Last king, c.300)
```

Statistics
Duration, 60 years; 3 generations, average length, 60/3 = 20 years; 3 rulers,
average length of reign, 60/3 = 20 years.

Commentary
Not enough is known of the Soloi dynasty to be able to complete the
genealogical table except for the last members of the (presumed) family.
Aristokypros and Philokypros are probably too far apart in date to be son
and father, and what the connection was between Aristokypros and Stasias
is unknown. However, all were apparently members of the same family, and
certainly claimed to be so. The family apparently took the Macedonian side
in Alexander's war, and Nikokles is recorded as commanding in India under
Alexander. His brother Eunostos was unique amongst Cypriot kings in
surviving the Ptolemaic conquest of the island in 312 – he was married to a
daughter of Ptolemy I – but the dynasty was extinguished on his death all the
same. The dates of Stasias' and Stastikrates' rule are unknown: I have guessed
the former began in about 360. Nikokles was one of Alexander the Great's
commanders; he and Eunostos clearly played their cards well, thus protecting
the dynasty for a time.

References
PJ Stylianou, *The Age of the Kingdoms, the Political History of Cyprus in the Archaic
    and Classical Periods* (Nicosia, 1989).

Sparta, Greece

A   *Agiad Dynasty*, 520–217 BC.

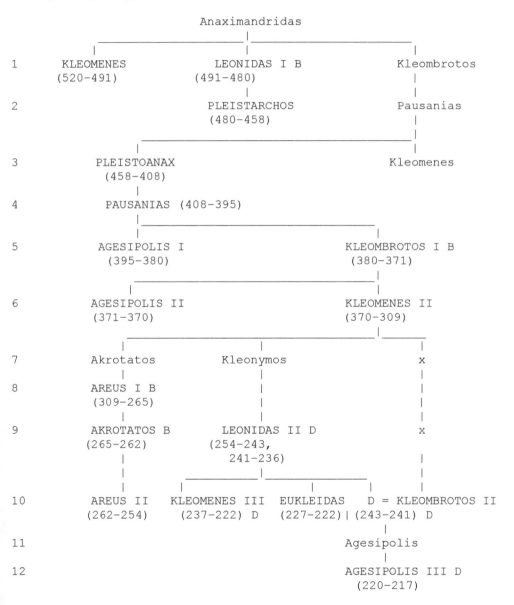

```
                            Anaximandridas
          _____|_____
         |                        |                                |
1    KLEOMENES               LEONIDAS I B                    Kleombrotos
     (520-491)               (491-480)                           |
                                 |                               |
2                            PLEISTARCHOS                    Pausanias
                             (480-458)                           |
          _____           |
         |                                            |          |
3    PLEISTOANAX                                  Kleomenes
     (458-408)
         |
4    PAUSANIAS  (408-395)
         |_____
         |                                                |
5    AGESIPOLIS I                              KLEOMBROTOS I B
     (395-380)                                 (380-371)
          _____|
         |                                              |
6    AGESIPOLIS II                             KLEOMENES II
     (371-370)                                 (370-309)
          _____|_____
         |                     |                            |
7    Akrotatos             Kleonymos                         x
         |                     |                             |
8    AREUS I B                 |                             |
     (309-265)                 |                             |
         |                     |                             |
9    AKROTATOS B           LEONIDAS II D                      x
     (265-262)             (254-243,
         |                  241-236)                          |
         |          _____|_____             |
         |         |                    |        |           |
10   AREUS II  KLEOMENES III    EUKLEIDAS    D = KLEOMBROTOS II
     (262-254) (237-222) D      (227-222)|  (243-241) D
                                          |
11                               Agesipolis
                                          |
12                               AGESIPOLIS III D
                                 (220-217)
```

Statistics

Duration: 303 years; 12 generations, average length $303/12 = 25$ years;
17 rulers, average length of reign, $303/17 = 18$ years.

B.   *Eurypontid Dynasty*, 515-227 BC.

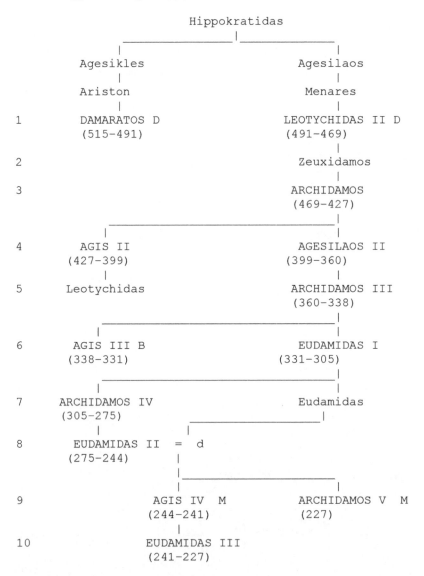

```
                          Hippokratidas
        _____|_____
       |                                                 |
    Agesikles                                         Agesilaos
       |                                                 |
    Ariston                                           Menares
       |                                                 |
1   DAMARATOS D                                   LEOTYCHIDAS II D
    (515-491)                                       (491-469)
                                                         |
2                                                    Zeuxidamos
                                                         |
3                                                    ARCHIDAMOS
                                                     (469-427)
        _____|
       |                                                 |
4    AGIS II                                          AGESILAOS II
    (427-399)                                         (399-360)
       |                                                 |
5   Leotychidas                                      ARCHIDAMOS III
                                                      (360-338)
        _____|
       |                                                 |
6    AGIS III B                                       EUDAMIDAS I
    (338-331)                                         (331-305)
        _____|
       |                                                 |
7   ARCHIDAMOS IV                                     Eudamidas
    (305-275)                  _____|
       |                      |
8   EUDAMIDAS II    =   d
    (275-244)             |
                          |
                          |_____
                          |                                 |
9                      AGIS IV   M                   ARCHIDAMOS V   M
                      (244-241)                         (227)
                          |
10                    EUDAMIDAS III
                      (241-227)
```

Statistics
Duration: 288 years; 10 generations, average length 288/10 = 29 years;
13 rulers, average length of reign, 288/13 = 29 years.

Commentary
The dual monarchy of Sparta in which two dynasties of kings coexisted and
ruled together in apparent harmony, or nearly so, for centuries, is distinctly

curious and difficult to explain: perhaps a compromise in the distant past, as a result of the political union of two territories. Both dynasties claimed to have originated with the hero Herakles, and to have separated when twin sons jointly inherited the kingship, but in each case the early kings, claiming a constant inheritance from father to son over many generations, cannot be accepted as accurate. Nor can their claimed early dates of origin, calculated in the second century AD with reference to the (undated and undatable) Trojan War. Only the second halves of the two dynasties from about 520 BC onwards are accurately known and dated, and so only these later parts can be taken into consideration here; calculations therefore have to begin with the Agiad Kleomenes I and the Eurypontid Damaratos, as the earliest kings to be more or less securely dated.

As is only to be expected with kings whose primary function was as war leaders, casualties by violence were fairly frequent, but there were as many depositions – that is, removals as the result of internal disputes – as there were deaths in battle (six depositions, six deaths in battle, also two executions). The frequency of depositions and violent deaths in the last century is a clear sign that the dynasties were heading for destruction, as is the erratic succession at the end. This also throws into high relief the claim that the earlier kings succeeded one another from father to son for so long (hence my disbelief). The fact that both dynasties came to an end at more or less the same time is a clear indication that the problem was not so much dynastic as societal. (In fact, one Agiad king, Eukleidas, was adopted across into the Eurypontid line, as a way of continuing that line of kings, but even such a desperate measure did not succeed in holding the old system together for more than a few years.) There were in fact also three later kings, who were claimed to be part of the royal lines, but their precise relationships are unclear.

References
Herodotos 7.204; 8.131; 10.10.
Pausanias 7.2–10.
P Cartledge, *Sparta and Laconia* (London, 1979).
WG Forrest, *A History of Sparta, 950–193 bc* (London, 1968).
AHM Jones, *Sparta* (Oxford, 1967).

Tuwana, Asia Minor (fragmentary)

```
1                    MUWAHARANI I (-C.740)
                          |
2                    WARPALAWA II (740-705)
                          |
3                    MUWAHARANI II (705-)
```

Statistics
The lack of reliable dating evidence makes calculations impossible.

Commentary
Tuwana was one of the kingdoms of Tabal in central Anatolia, part of the defunct Hittite kingdom. Only three kings are known, and only from the early eighth century BC, but these three can be linked into a dynasty. All three kings were Assyrian sub-kings by this time, and the kingdom was probably converted into a province about 700 BC.

References
T Bryce, *The World of the Neo-Hittite Kingdoms* (Oxford, 2012).

Tyre, Syria, *c.*990–774 BC (fragmentary)

A   *The First Dynasty, c.990-910 BC.*

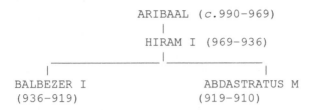

```
                      ARIBAAL (c.990-969)
                              |
                      HIRAM I (969-936)
          _____|_____
          |                               |
   BALBEZER I                        ABDASTRATUS M
   (936-919)                         (919-910)
```

Statistics

Duration: 80 years; 3 generations, average length 80/3 = 26 years; 4 rulers, average length of reign, 80/4 = 20 years.

B.   *The Second Dynasty, 910-888 BC.*

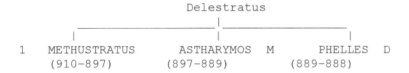

```
                      Delestratus
                              |
      _____|_____
      |                       |                        |
1  METHUSTRATUS         ASTHARYMOS  M            PHELLES  D
   (910-897)            (897-889)               (889-888)
```

Statistics

Duration: 22 years; 1 generation, 22 years; 3 rulers, average length of reign, 22/3 = 7 years.

C.   *The Third Dynasty, 887-774 BC.*

```
1                          ETHBAAL I (887-856)
                                   |
2                          BAAL-AZOR (856-821)
*                                  |
3                          MATTAN I (829-821)
                                   |
4                          PUMIATHON (821-774)
```

Statistics

Duration: 113 years; 4 generations, average length 113/4 = 28 years; 4 rulers, average length of reign 113/4 = 28 years.

Commentary

Tyre, the great and wealthy city of the Phoenician coast, was a monarchy for most of the period from 1000 BC to the Akhaimenid conquest. Over twenty kings are known by name, but only half of these are capable of being tabulated into dynasties. This is only in part due to the source problem; the political history of the city shows a good deal of instability as well, partly internal, and partly due to interference from outside.

The first known dynasty, descended from Abibaal, was displaced by a coup by the sons of the last king's nurse, who murdered Abdastratus; the three brothers (the second dynasty here) ruled in succession until the third murdered the second, at which the last of them was removed by a coup by the high priest Ethbaal, who founded the third dynasty. The last king of that dynasty, Pumiathon (also known as Pygmalion by the Greeks) may or may not have been followed by other members of his family – the same royal names recur throughout the city's history – but the evidence to connect them fails us.

It is noticeable that all three dynasties maintained a high average generation length – though the initial date for Abibaal is only presumed, and the reign average for the second dynasty is inevitably low. In each case, however, these high numbers are in part the result of one king in each dynasty (Hiram and Pumiathon) having a particularly long reign; this is a sign, of course, of the instability in the city, for it would seem that only firm rule kept a king in power, and a weaker ruler was fairly easily overthrown. Pumiathon's reign was also disturbed by the expulsion (or flight) of his daughter, who led a refugee group of Tyrians to found Carthage.

References

ME Aubet, *The Phoenicians in the West, Politics, Colonies, and Trade*, 2nd ed. (Cambridge, 2001).

HJ Katzenstein, *A History of Tyre from the Beginning of the second millennium BCE until the fall of the Neo-Babylonian Empire in 538 bCE* (Jerusalem, 1973).

Section II

Roman Republican Dynasties

Introduction

The arrangement here is the same as for the royal dynasties in other sections, with the exception that references are not included for each dynasty. There are relatively few of these, and all are generally required for each dynasty. They are listed below.

The arrangement is alphabetical by the family name, the nomen.

The dates are those of an individual's occupation of a restricted selection of public offices. This was usually for a single year. There is thus no means of estimating reign length, or in this case length of time active in politics, since this clearly began before the first office held and continued after as a member of the Senate. Instead the number of public offices is counted. The offices used here are consul, praetor, censor, and tribune of the plebs, together with any proconsular and propraetorial extensions of their imperium; in addition dictator, interrex, magister equitum, and the early institution of military tribunes with consular powers are counted; the posts of Pontifex Maximus and *princeps senatus* are counted once only, at first appointment. This is, of course, an inaccurate proceeding, partly because the earlier offices of tribune and aedile and quaestor are omitted – they are often scarcely known – and partly because the record is extremely erratic. But it is erratic for everyone; the conditions and omissions are the same for all.

It will be seen that in several tables the genealogical connections are not included. In these cases I have made the assumption that the men listed were part of the same family based on their names alone. They are laid out in the tables as though in a genetic relationship, but without the connections for which evidence does not exist.

Abbreviations

Offices:
Cens – censor
Cos – consul
Dec – decemvir
Dict – dictator
Int – interrex
Meq – magister equitum
Pc – Proconsul
Pont Max – Pontifex Maximus
Pp – Propraetor
Pr – Praetor
Pr Sen – Princeps Senatus
MT – Military Tribune with consular powers.
TO – Tribune of the Plebs

Praenomina:

A – Aulus
Agr – Agrippa
Ap – Appius
C – Caius
Cn – Cnaeus
D – Decimus
K – Kaeso
L – Lucius
M – Marcus
M'– Manius
Mam – Mamilius
N – Numerius
P – Publius
Post – Postumus
Proc – Proculus
Q – Quintus
Ser – Servius
Sex – Sextus
T – Titus
Ti – Tiberius
Vol – Volusus
Occasionally other private nomina are spelt out in full.

The basic source of this work is Livy, despite the gaps that exist, and the difficulties in interpretation. The only work in which the sort of material is examined in detail is that of Frederick Munzer, *Roman Aristocratic Parties and Families*, published in 1920, translated into English by Therese Ridley, and published by Johns Hopkins University Press in 1999. It contains a great deal of subtle interpretation, and a set of genealogical tables, but most of these are only fragments of the larger and longer families. Here I have attempted to produce tables as complete for all the families as possible – inaccurate or not – who held recorded office in the Roman Republic. This has meant relying perhaps too greatly on the text of Livy (but there is really no alternative). The basic source therefore for this work is Livy, until 167.

Two substantial works list the holders of offices: TRS Broughton's *The Magistrates of the Roman Republic*, 3 vols. (New York, 1951–1960) and T Corey Brennan's *The Praetorship in the Roman Republic*, 2 vols. (Oxford, 2000). None of these concentrate on the families of the Roman Republican rulers. Useful also has been Christian Settipani, *Continuité gentilice et continuité familiale dans les familles sénatoriales romaines à l'époque impérial, mythe et réalité*, (Oxford, 2000), which casts its net rather wider than the title suggests.

Certain basic practices in constructing the genealogical tables need to be pointed out. The repetitions of nomen and cognomen are taken to be the basic elements in constituting a family tree, and they will be referred to repeatedly. But the paucity of Roman praenomina creates difficulties for identifications that can only be overcome by making assumptions, particularly in the early republic, where Livy's sources are unclear and where the record, either in his sources or in Livy's text, may well have been altered by time and family emotion and exaggeration.

The omission of records of the lower offices – quaestors, aediles, and so on – is a limitation, though since it is to be assumed that all the holders of the higher offices will have held those earlier in their careers, omitting them will not have made a great deal of difference.

It may be emphasized that the records are of offices held by individuals. It is not possible to describe the total length of the political career of any individual (though it might be assumed that he might have held his earliest office at about the age of 18 or 20). Therefore the duration of a family's active political work is clearly longer than that which each table displays. So instead of guessing how long each man operated, I have simply listed the offices held (subject to the limitations mentioned above), and used this as the basis for an index of the family's political activity.

The attempt has therefore been made here to portray the ruling families of the Roman Republic in genealogical form. Certain limits have been imposed, however, as with the royal dynasties, of which the main one is a lower limit of three generations or three men holding office. There are some families where the records are incomplete, or whose political careers have been very short. Where possible these have been included if it can be seen that they appear to form a clear family, even if connections between generations cannot be verified. In addition there are the major problems that much of the fourth century BC account of Roman history in Livy is missing, and that his history effectively ceases at 167. In several cases this has meant that a long-lived family is not recorded in those decades and the only way of dealing with this is to present the two sections of the family, before and after the break, in separate genealogical tables. This is unfortunate, but looking at the results of research into the families it is quite astonishing how much has survived, and how many families can be reconstructed covering several centuries.

In numerous cases certain men who appear from their names to be part of some families cannot be fitted convincingly into the tables; these have been listed at the end of the entry, together with their offices, but have not been included in the calculations.

Acilius (plebeian), 201–66 BC

```
                    L. Acilius
                        |
            C. Acilius Glabrio            K. Acilius
                    |                         |
1           M'. Acilius Glabrio       L. Acilius Balbus
            (TP 201; Pr 196;             (Pr 197)
             Cos 191; Pc 190)                |
                    |                         |
2           M'. Acilius Glabrio       L. Acilius Balbus
            (Pr c.157; Cos 154)       (Pr c.153; Cos 150)
                    |                         |
3           M'. Acilius Glabrio       M'. Acilius Balbus
                 (TP 122)             (Pr c.117; Cos 114
                    |
4           M'. Acilius Glabrio
          (Pr 70; Cos 67; Pc 66)
```

Statistics

Duration: 135 years; 4 generations, average length $135/4 = 34$ years;
15 magistracies, incidence of office, $135/15 =$ once in 9 years.

Commentary

The repetition of the praenomen Manius (M'.) in both sequences suggests that the Glabrio and Balbus lines were related, as does their simultaneous appearance on the political scene, products of the Second Punic War, and apparently sponsored by Scipio Africanus, who certainly did so for M'. Glabrio (Cos 191). The link between the families may be that Gaius and Kaeso were brothers, or it was perhaps a generation earlier, though no evidence exists on this. The first M'. Glabrio, consul in 191, was certainly a novus homo, a man, that is, who had no senatorial ancestors; he performed with skill in Asia Minor in the aftermath of the Battle of Magnesia, and established the Roman position in the area quite firmly. The family were notably philhellenic, had interests in Greece, and may have originated in southern Italy.

The record of the family is highly successful. The only member not to reach the consulship, the son of the consul of 154, did in fact become tribune of the plebs in that most awkward year of 122, but reached no higher, presumably dying young. There are several other family members on record in minor magistracies – tribunes, quaestors, monetary officials – which might suggest a careful and deliberate family plan to concentrate all the family's ambitions on a single member in each generation. This family, in fact, is the ancestor, by adoption, of a very long-lived imperial family that is traceable through to the fifth century AD.

Aebutius (patrician), 499–435 BC

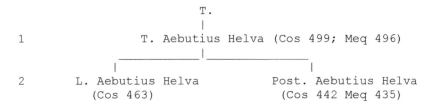

```
                            T.
                            |
1                 T. Aebutius Helva  (Cos 499; Meq 496)
            _____|_____
            |                               |
2     L. Aebutius Helva          Post. Aebutius Helva
         (Cos 463)                 (Cos 442 Meq 435)
```

Statistics
Duration: 64 years; 2 generations, average length, 64/2 = 32 years;
5 magistracies, incidence of office, 64/5 = 1 in 13 years

Also: T. Aebutius Parrus (Pr 178)
         M. Aebutius Helva (Pr 168)

Commentary
An example of a family that was clearly of some prominence in the early years
of the republic, but whose members did not achieve, or possibly did not
seek, office thereafter for the next two centuries. The recovery in the second
century was clearly brief and perhaps unsuccessful, but the repetition of the
cognomen Helva implies that the family had continued all through.

Aelius (plebeian), 337–167 BC

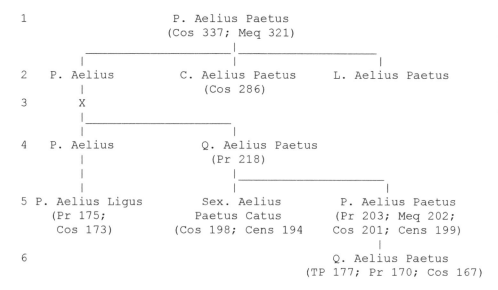

```
1                                P. Aelius Paetus
                                 (Cos 337; Meq 321)
                  _____|_____
                 |                       |                        |
2       P. Aelius            C. Aelius Paetus         L. Aelius Paetus
                 |                 (Cos 286)
3                X
                 |
                 |_____
                 |                       |
4       P. Aelius                Q. Aelius Paetus
                 |                  (Pr 218)
                 |                       |
                 |                       |_____
                 |                       |                        |
5  P. Aelius Ligus          Sex. Aelius            P. Aelius Paetus
       (Pr 175;             Paetus Catus           (Pr 203; Meq 202;
        Cos 173)         (Cos 198; Cens 194         Cos 201; Cens 199)
                                                          |
6                                               Q. Aelius Paetus
                                        (TP 177; Pr 170; Cos 167)
```

Statistics
Duration: 170 years; 6 generations, average length 170/6 = 28 years;
18 magistracies, incidence of office: 170/18 = once in 9 years.

Also: C. Aelius Tubero (Pr c.218)
        P. Aelius Tubero (Pr 201; II 177)
        L. Aelius Tubero (Pr 49)

Commentary
A family of distinction for only two brief periods. An ancestor is known to
have been quaestor in 409 BC, but achievement then skipped a generation
to the consul of 337, two of whose sons also reached elective office (Lucius
became aedile). Again a period of little achievement followed (though a
Q. Aelius Paetus was a pontifex until 216). The gap between the consul of 286
and the praetor of 218 may have included members of the family in office,
but this is the time of deficient records. The brothers who were consuls in
201 and 198 and the cousins in 172 and 167, however, ended the family's real
achievements. Minor offices were held by later members, but essentially the
family's time of power ended with the two last consuls. It may be assumed
that the Tubero branch was part of the family, though their precise link with
the main part of the family is not recorded, nor is the link between those three
men.

Aemilius (patrician), 484–42 BC

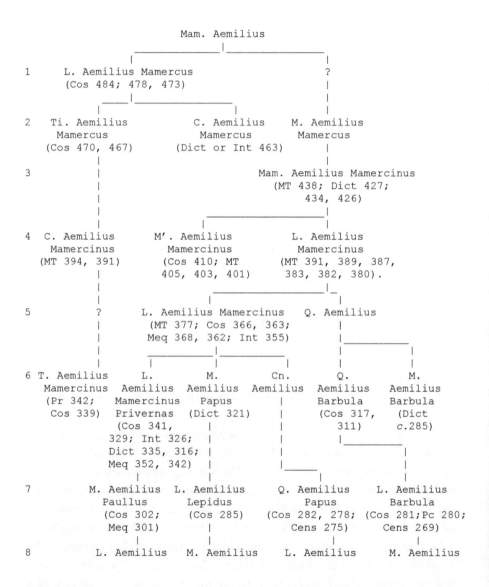

```
                              Mam. Aemilius
              _____|_____
             |                                       |
   1      L. Aemilius Mamercus                        ?
          (Cos 484; 478, 473)                         |
         ____|_____                      |
        |                       |                     |
   2  Ti. Aemilius         C. Aemilius          M. Aemilius
       Mamercus             Mamercus             Mamercus
      (Cos 470, 467)    (Dict or Int 463)            |
             |                                        |
   3         |                             Mam. Aemilius Mamercinus
             |                               (MT 438; Dict 427;
             |                                     434, 426)
             |                       _____|
             |                      |                 |
   4  C. Aemilius          M'. Aemilius          L. Aemilius
       Mamercinus           Mamercinus            Mamercinus
      (MT 394, 391)        (Cos 410; MT        (MT 391, 389, 387,
             |              405, 403, 401)      383, 382, 380).
             |                      _____|_
             |                     |                  |
   5         ?         L. Aemilius Mamercinus    Q. Aemilius
             |           (MT 377; Cos 366, 363;       |
             |           Meq 368, 362; Int 355)       |_____
             |             _____|_____        |          |
             |            |                   |       |          |
   6 T. Aemilius       L.          M.       Cn.      Q.         M.
     Mamercinus     Aemilius   Aemilius   Aemilius Aemilius   Aemilius
     (Pr 342;       Mamercinus  Papus        |     Barbula    Barbula
      Cos 339)      Privernas  (Dict 321)    |    (Cos 317,    (Dict
                    (Cos 341,      |         |      311)       c.285)
                    329; Int 326;  |         |       |_____
                    Dict 335, 316; |         |                 |
                    Meq 352, 342)  |         |_____             |
                         |         |               |           |
   7         M. Aemilius    L. Aemilius    Q. Aemilius    L. Aemilius
              Paullus        Lepidus         Papus          Barbula
             (Cos 302;      (Cos 285)    (Cos 282, 278; (Cos 281;Pc 280;
              Meq 301)          |          Cens 275)      Cens 269)
                 |             |               |            |
   8        L. Aemilius   M. Aemilius     L. Aemilius   M. Aemilius
```

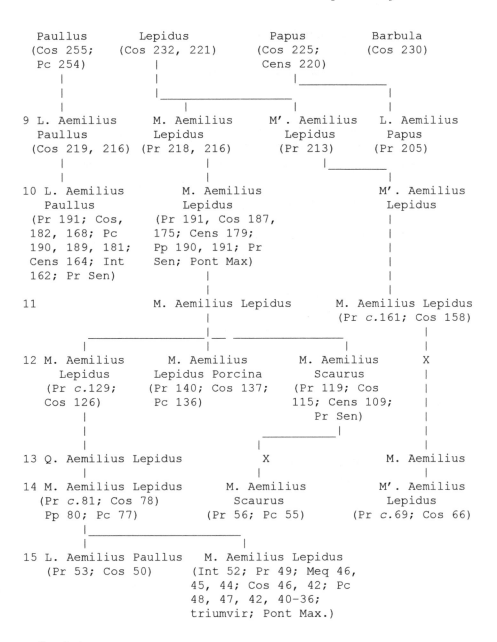

```
Paullus          Lepidus              Papus            Barbula
(Cos 255;    (Cos 232, 221)       (Cos 225;        (Cos 230)
 Pc 254)         |                  Cens 220)
   |             |                      |
   |             |_____   |_____
   |             |                   |  |             |
9 L. Aemilius    M. Aemilius      M'. Aemilius    L. Aemilius
   Paullus          Lepidus          Lepidus          Papus
(Cos 219, 216) (Pr 218, 216)     (Pr 213)        (Pr 205)
   |             |                  |_____
   |             |                  |         |
10 L. Aemilius       M. Aemilius                M'. Aemilius
   Paullus              Lepidus                    Lepidus
(Pr 191; Cos,    (Pr 191, Cos 187,                  |
182, 168; Pc     175; Cens 179;                     |
190, 189, 181;   Pp 190, 191; Pr                    |
Cens 164; Int    Sen; Pont Max)                     |
162; Pr Sen)         |                              |
11               M. Aemilius Lepidus       M. Aemilius Lepidus
                     |                      (Pr c.161; Cos 158)
       _____|__ _____           |
       |                |              |            |
12 M. Aemilius    M. Aemilius      M. Aemilius      X
   Lepidus        Lepidus Porcina    Scaurus        |
   (Pr c.129;     (Pr 140; Cos 137; (Pr 119; Cos    |
   Cos 126)       Pc 136)           115; Cens 109;  |
       |                            Pr Sen)         |
       |                 _____|              |
       |                 |                          |
13 Q. Aemilius Lepidus   X                     M. Aemilius
       |                 |                          |
14 M. Aemilius Lepidus   M. Aemilius           M'. Aemilius
   (Pr c.81; Cos 78)        Scaurus                Lepidus
   Pp 80; Pc 77)         (Pr 56; Pc 55)        (Pr c.69; Cos 66)
       |_____
       |                        |
15 L. Aemilius Paullus   M. Aemilius Lepidus
   (Pr 53; Cos 50)       (Int 52; Pr 49; Meq 46,
                         45, 44; Cos 46, 42; Pc
                         48, 47, 42, 40-36;
                         triumvir; Pont Max.)
```

Statistics

Duration: 442 years (ignoring offices held after 42); 15 generations, average length, 442/15 = 29 years; 111 magistracies, incidence of office: 442/111 = 1 in 4 years.

Also: M. Aemilius Regillus (Pr 217)
         L. Aemilius Regillus (P 190)
         Mam. Aemilius Mam. f. Lepidus Luvienses (Pr 90)

Commentary

The Aemilii was one of the few patrician families that survived all through the republican period, regularly holding office. Dynastically the reason was clearly the ability to produce multiple offspring, and to promote several family lines so that if one failed – as the elder, Mamercinus, line did after the consul of 339 – another line was available. Thus there were four separate lines, all potentially active, from the late fourth and right through the third centuries – Paullus, Lepidus, Papus, Barbula, and later Scaurus. (The Regillius branch emerged briefly in the second century, but their connection to the main family cannot be discovered.)

One method of continuing a failing family was to adopt a man from another family. The two sons of Paullus (consul in 168) were adopted into other families, but then his two other sons died before him, so ending the Paullus line.

There came another break after the consuls of 137 and 126 (filled in part by the Scaurus line) after which recovery began with the counter-revolution of Sulla, which brought the consul of 78 to that office. The final triumph, and end, of the dynasty came with the triumvir of the civil war, whose multiple offices did not stop him being easily outmanoeuvred politically by Octavian; he served on as Pontifex Maximus until 12 BC. The family's prestige counted for little under the empire; two more generations finished it off.

Annius (plebeian), 156–55 BC

```
                    T. Annius Luscus
              _____|_____
              |                              |
1    T. Annius                    T. Annius Luscus (Pr 156; Cos 153)
                                                |
2                                 T. Annius Rufus (Pr 131; Cos 128)
                                                |
3                                 C. Annius Luscus (Pr 81; Pp 81)
                                                |
4                                 T. Annius Libo Luscianus (Pr 55)
```

Statistics
Duration: 101 years; 4 generations, average length $101/4 = 25$ years;
4 magistracies, incidence of office, $101/4 = 1$ in 25 years.

Also: L. Annius (TP 110).

Commentary
A family of no great distinction, occupying only two consulships, and clearly
declining in effectiveness in its last two generations. It may be connected with
the Annius family of the Flavian and Antonine period in the empire, who used
the cognomen Libo occasionally, but after the praetor of 55 the family became
submerged for at least a century.

Antistius (plebeian), 103–56 BC

```
         Ti. Antistius (TP 422)      L. Antistius (TP 420)

                 L. Antistius (MT 370)

                 M. Antistius (TP 319)


1                L. Antistius Reginus (TP 103)

2                P. Antistius (TP 88)

3                C. Antistius Vetus (Pr 70; Pp 69, 68)

4        L. Antistius (TP 56)   Antistius Vetus (TP 56)
```

Statistics
Duration: 47 years; 4 generations, average length 47/4 = 12 years;
7 magistracies, incidence of office, 47/7 = 1 in 7 years.

Commentary
The earliest members of the family, in the early republic (in office in 422 to
319), could be reconstituted as a three-generation unit, though the length of
the generations would be unacceptably long. I have limited the calculations
therefore to the first century family, which again might well be displayed as
a connected unit, but the evidence does not exist for displaying parentages
and familial connections. This was a family that had emerged (or re-emerged)
amid the difficulties of the first century BC, and that in fact flourished in a
minor way into the first century of the empire, finally disappearing at AD 100.

Antonius (plebeian), 167–42 BC

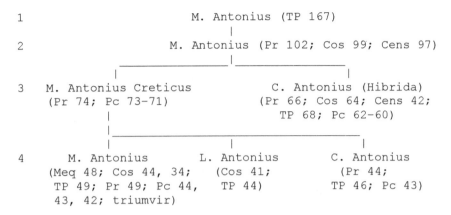

```
1                         M. Antonius (TP 167)
                               |
2                    M. Antonius (Pr 102; Cos 99; Cens 97)
          _____|_____
         |                                   |
3   M. Antonius Creticus            C. Antonius (Hibrida)
    (Pr 74; Pc 73-71)               (Pr 66; Cos 64; Cens 42;
         |                              TP 68; Pc 62-60)
         |
         |_____
         |                    |                  |
4     M. Antonius       L. Antonius        C. Antonius
    (Meq 48; Cos 44, 34;  (Cos 41;           (Pr 44;
     TP 49; Pr 49; Pc 44,  TP 44)           TP 46; Pc 43)
     43, 42; triumvir)
```

Statistics

Duration: 125 years; 4 generations, average length 125/4 = 31 years;
28 magistracies (omitting cos 34), incidence of office 125/28 = 1 in 4 years)
Also: Q. Antonius Balbus (Pr 82).

Commentary

The first Antonius to achieve office was as magister equitum in 334, but no others of the family are recorded in any office until one was elected tribune of the plebs in 167. The consul of 99, his grandson, gained office above all by his oratorical abilities, and produced a family of brief but substantial achievements. The family survived the troubles of the revolution, in which the praetor of 74 failed in several campaigns against the Cretan pirates, while the consul of 63 incurred the enmity of Julius Caesar. The triumvir ('Mark Antony') was a Caesarean of sufficient power and ability to divide the empire with Octavian and Lepidus, and dominated the politics of the last decade of the republican empire. The advantage of having multiple dynastic resources is clearly evident.

The triumvir's sons (he was married four times) were enclosed within the imperial Julio-Claudian family, or quietly faded away, with honorary offices. One line, the children of his wife Octavia (Augustus' sister), produced the emperors Claudius and Nero; in effect, therefore, Mark Antony was the dominant genetic ancestor of the second part of the Julio-Claudian family of emperors.

Appuleius (plebeian), 166–43 BC

1   L Appuleius Saturninus (Pr 166)

2   L. Appuleius Saturninus   C. Appuleius Decianus
           (TP 103, 100, 99)   (TP 98)

3   L. Appuleius Saturninus (Pr 59; Pc 58)

4   P. Appuleius (TP 43)

Statistics

Duration 123 years; 4 generations, average length $123/4 = 31$ years;
8 magistracies, incidence of office $123/8 = 1$ in 15 years.

Commentary

In all probability, the repetition of the cognomen Saturninus guarantees
that the five men here listed are a single family, though an extra generation
between the praetor of 166 and the tribunes of 103–98 would make it
more comfortable. The tribune of 103 attempted to revive elements of the
democratic programme of the Gracchi, but used violence to achieve these
aims; in the result he suffered the same violence he had meted out to his
opponents, thereby replicating the fate of the Gracchi. One notes, however,
that neither his (apparent) brother Decianus nor his probable son, the praetor
of 59, suffered in any way a denial of office.

Aquillius (plebeian), 259–43 BC

```
1                  C. Aquillius Florus (Cos 259; Pc 258)

2        M'. Aquillius              P. Aquillius (TP 211)
             |
3        M'. Aquillius              L. Aquillius Gallus (Pr 176)
             |
4        M'. Aquillius (Pr 132;
         Cos 129; Pc 128-126)
             |
5        M'. Aquillius (Pr 104;
         Cos 101; Pc 100, 99)

6                        P. Aquillius Gallus   C. Aquillius Gallus
                             (TP 55)               (Pr 66)

7        M' Aquillius Crassus
               (Pr 43)
```

Statistics

Duration: 216 years; 7 generations, average length to 216/7 = 31 years;
16 magistracies, incidence of office 216/16 = 1 in 13 years.

Commentary

The main member of the family is the consul of 129, who campaigned
successfully in Asia Minor to suppress the 'rebellion' of the former Attalid
subjects against annexation by Rome. It was certainly a family of some
longevity, but it must be noted that most of the members did not reach the
consulship, though they did so as supporters of Octavian/Augustus later.
Though the genetic connections are not recorded at the beginning and in the
first century BC, it seems reasonable to assume that the 'unconnected' men
listed here really were part of the main family.

Atilius (plebeian), 444–106 BC

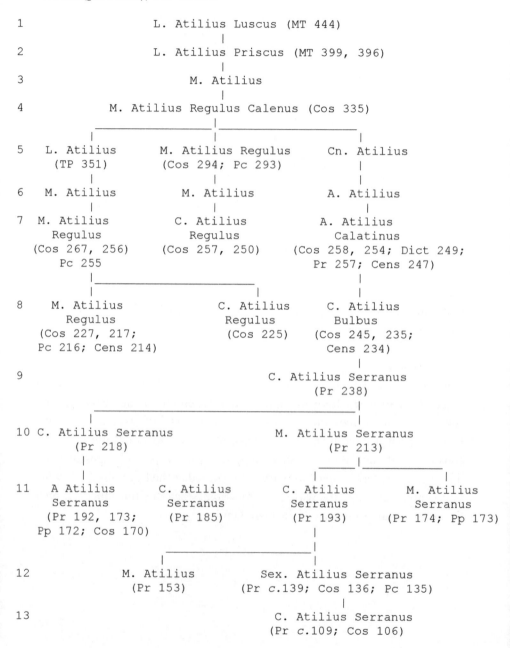

```
1                    L. Atilius Luscus (MT 444)
                                 |
2                    L. Atilius Priscus (MT 399, 396)
                                 |
3                         M. Atilius
                                 |
4              M. Atilius Regulus Calenus (Cos 335)
         _____|_____
        |                        |                        |
5   L. Atilius          M. Atilius Regulus          Cn. Atilius
     (TP 351)           (Cos 294; Pc 293)                |
        |                        |                        |
6   M. Atilius              M. Atilius                A. Atilius
        |                        |                        |
7   M. Atilius              C. Atilius                A. Atilius
     Regulus                 Regulus                  Calatinus
   (Cos 267, 256)          (Cos 257, 250)         (Cos 258, 254; Dict 249;
      Pc 255                                         Pr 257; Cens 247)
        |_____                         |
        |                       |                         |
8    M. Atilius            C. Atilius                C. Atilius
      Regulus               Regulus                   Bulbus
   (Cos 227, 217;          (Cos 225)              (Cos 245, 235;
   Pc 216; Cens 214)                                 Cens 234)
                                                         |
9                                              C. Atilius Serranus
                                                    (Pr 238)
            _____|
           |                                              |
10 C. Atilius Serranus                         M. Atilius Serranus
        (Pr 218)                                    (Pr 213)
           |                                    _____|_____
           |                                   |                     |
11   A Atilius          C. Atilius        C. Atilius           M. Atilius
      Serranus           Serranus          Serranus             Serranus
   (Pr 192, 173;        (Pr 185)          (Pr 193)         (Pr 174; Pp 173)
   Pp 172; Cos 170)                           |
                                  _____|
                                 |            |
12          M. Atilius              Sex. Atilius Serranus
             (Pr 153)           (Pr c.139; Cos 136; Pc 135)
                                             |
13                                 C. Atilius Serranus
                                   (Pr c.109; Cos 106)
```

Statistics

Duration: 338 years; 13 generations, average length 338/13 = 26 years;
45 magistracies, incidence of office, 338/45 = 1 in 8 years.

Commentary

An unusually successful plebeian family, which produced men who were in the governing circle as early as the mid fifth century. However, the family only really got going when the potential for office holding by plebeians opened out in the later fourth century, after which every generation saw consuls until the end of the second century BC, in this case strongly assisted by allies and by sponsorship from the Fabian family. Such relationships could protect where cowardice was suspected (as with the fall of Calatinus (Cos 258), or even a greater failure, as with the disastrous war of the consul of 256 who invaded Africa and was defeated. But the years after the First Punic War saw a failure of any of the family to rise above praetor, no doubt connected with that military failure, until Serranus' consulship in 170. Paradoxically for a plebeian family, there are very few tribunes of the plebs amongst the office holders, and the anti-aristocratic temper of Roman politics after 120 appears to have finished the family off. A few Atilii held minor offices in the first century BC, but it seems that the family died out, certainly politically, if not biologically.

Atinius (plebeian), 195–121 BC

1	C. Atinius Labeo (TP 195; Pr 195)	C. Atinius Labeo (Pr 190)	C. Atinius (Pr 188)
2		Atinius (TP 149)	
3		C. Atinius Labeo Macedo (TP 131; Pr 121)	

Statistics
Duration: 74 years; 3 generations, average length 74/3 = 25 years;
7 magistracies, incidence of office 74/7 = 1 in 10 years.

Commentary
The lack of detail makes it impossible to reconstruct a proper family genealogy, but it seems fairly clear from the names and the dating of the five men involved that the first three were brothers, or perhaps more likely first cousins, and the next two generations could be son and grandson. The tribune of 149 was notoriously awkward, even proposing in the Senate at one point to throw the censor off the Tarpeian Rock for blocking a law he wished to pass. One would not call this, in the end, a successful family, despite its accumulation of offices.

Aurelius, 252–49 BC

A *Aurelius Cotta* (plebeian), 252–49 BC.

```
                          C. Aurelius
                              |
                          L. Aurelius
                              |
1                         C. Aurelius Cotta
                  (Cos 252, 248; Cens 241; Meq 231)
          _____|_____
          |                                        |
2    C. Aurelius Cotta                      M. Aurelius Cotta
          |_____
          |                      |                     |
3    C. Aurelius Cotta    L. Aurelius Cotta    M. Aurelius Cotta
     (Pr 218, 202; Cos           |
     200; Pp 201)                |
4                         L. Aurelius Cotta
                     (TP 154; Pr 147; Cos 144)
            _____|__
            |                   |
5    L. Aurelius Cotta    M. Aurelius Cotta
        (Pr 122; Cos 119)        |
            |              _____|_____
            |             |             |                  |
6    L. Aurelius    C. Aurelius    M. Aurelius       L. Aurelius
        Cotta          Cotta          Cotta             Cotta
     (TP 103; Pr c.95)(Pr 78; Cos 75; (Pr 77; Pc 73   (Pr 70; Cos
                        Pc 74)        - 70; Cos 74)  65; Cens 64)
                                           |
7                                   M. Aurelius Cotta
                                    (Pr 50; Pp 49)
```

Statistics
Duration: 203 years; 7 generations, average length 203/7 = 29 years;
29 magistracies, incidence of office, 203/29 = 1 in 7 years.

B *Aurelius Orestes* (plebeian), 160–103 BC.

```
                          L. Aurelius
                              |
                          L. Aurelius
                              |
1                         L. Aurelius Orestes
                      (Pr c.160, Cos 157)
                              |
2                         L. Aurelius Orestes
                  (Pr c.129; Cos 126; Pc 125–122)
                              |
3                         L. Aurelius Orestes
                       (Pr c.106; Cos 103)
```

Statistics

Duration: 57 years; 3 generations, average length $57/3 = 19$ years;
10 magistracies, incidence in office, $57/10 = 1$ in 6 years.

Also: C. Aurelius Scaurus (Pr 186)
         M. Aurelius Scaurus (Pr 111; Cos 108)

Commentary

The two lines of this family – three perhaps with the Scauri, who were probably grandfather and grandson – may not be connected; if they are, the link lies back in the third century, perhaps in the second generation, where L. Aurelius might be seen as the third son of C. Cotta. When the Orestes line emerged to public office, in 160, it was effectively a separate family. The Cotta line had a splendid start with the first of the family to reach the consulship, but the next generation failed to reach even the quaestorship, so far as we know; they may have been casualties in the great war with Hannibal.

From 200 BC onwards, however, a Cotta consul came along every generation, and the family successfully negotiated the eventful politics of the revolution on the Sullan, aristocratic, side. The last on the table, the praetor of 50, had no sons, but one of his daughters was the grandmother of an unfortunate wife of Emperor Caligula; the daughter of the consul of 119 was the mother of Julius Caesar. Such connections usually doomed any family eventually.

The Orestes line appears to have died out; the daughter of the consul of 103 was married to P. Plautius Hypseaus, and had no children.

The discrepancy between the two lines in the dating of generations is worth noting: the first of the Orestai was little more than a decade in front of his Cotta contemporary; two generations later the difference was more than half a century.

Baebius (plebeian), 218–168 BC

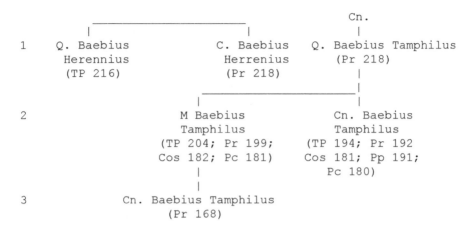

```
                                                           Cn.
            |_____|                      |
1    Q. Baebius              C. Baebius       Q. Baebius Tamphilus
     Herennius               Herrenius            (Pr 218)
     (TP 216)                (Pr 218)                 |
                                                      |
                       |_____|
                       |                            |
2                 M Baebius                    Cn. Baebius
                  Tamphilus                    Tamphilus
              (TP 204; Pr 199;             (TP 194; Pr 192
               Cos 182; Pc 181)            Cos 181; Pp 191;
                      |                        Pc 180)
                      |
3         Cn. Baebius Tamphilus
                (Pr 168)
```

Statistics

Duration: 50 years; 3 generations, average length 50/3 = 17 years;
13 magistracies, incidence of office 50/13 = 1 in 4 years.

Also: Q. Baebius (TP 200)
       L. Baebius Dives (Pr 189)
       Q. Baebius Sulca (Pr 175)
       C. Baebius (TP 111)

Commentary

A family with considerable achievements in the short period during which it
was active. This would be even more impressive, and longer, if the four Baebii
who cannot be linked directly could be included as part of the family. The
family did continue until the end of the second century BC, but its members
did not reach as high as the praetorship ever again.

Caecilius (plebeian), 284–46 BC

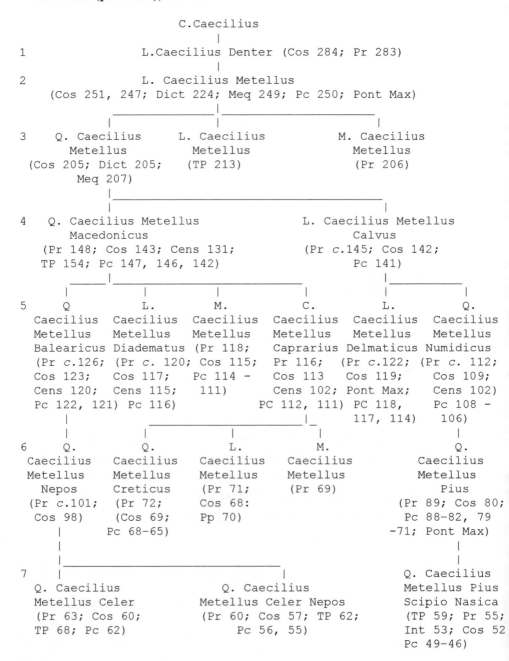

```
                        C.Caecilius
                            |
1                   L.Caecilius Denter (Cos 284; Pr 283)
                            |
2                   L. Caecilius Metellus
        (Cos 251, 247; Dict 224; Meq 249; Pc 250; Pont Max)
                            |
        _____|_____
        |                   |                    |
3   Q. Caecilius       L. Caecilius        M. Caecilius
      Metellus           Metellus            Metellus
  (Cos 205; Dict 205;   (TP 213)            (Pr 206)
      Meq 207)
        |
        |_____
        |                                           |
4   Q. Caecilius Metellus            L. Caecilius Metellus
       Macedonicus                          Calvus
    (Pr 148; Cos 143; Cens 131;     (Pr c.145; Cos 142;
     TP 154; Pc 147, 146, 142)            Pc 141)
     _____|_____    _____|_____
     |       |        |           |           |          |         |
5    Q       L.       M.          C.          L.         Q.
  Caecilius Caecilius Caecilius Caecilius  Caecilius  Caecilius
  Metellus  Metellus  Metellus  Metellus   Metellus   Metellus
  Balearicus Diadematus (Pr 118; Caprarius Delmaticus Numidicus
  (Pr c.126; (Pr c. 120; Cos 115; Pr 116;  (Pr c.122; (Pr c. 112;
   Cos 123;   Cos 117;  Pc 114 -  Cos 113   Cos 119;   Cos 109;
   Cens 120;  Cens 115;  111)     Cens 102; Pont Max;  Cens 102)
   Pc 122, 121) Pc 116)          PC 112, 111) PC 118,  Pc 108 -
     |                                         117, 114)  106)
     |        _____|_
     |        |            |              |                |
6    Q.       Q.           L.             M.               Q.
  Caecilius Caecilius  Caecilius      Caecilius        Caecilius
  Metellus  Metellus   Metellus       Metellus         Metellus
   Nepos     Creticus   (Pr 71;       (Pr 69)            Pius
  (Pr c.101; (Pr 72;    Cos 68:                        (Pr 89; Cos 80;
   Cos 98)   (Cos 69;   Pp 70)                          Pc 88-82, 79
     |        Pc 68-65)                                 -71; Pont Max)
     |                                                      |
     |_____         |
7    |                                           |     Q. Caecilius
   Q. Caecilius              Q. Caecilius              Metellus Pius
   Metellus Celer            Metellus Celer Nepos      Scipio Nasica
   (Pr 63; Cos 60;           (Pr 60; Cos 57; TP 62;    (TP 59; Pr 55;
    TP 68; Pc 62)                 Pc 56, 55)            Int 53; Cos 52
                                                        Pc 49-46)
```

Statistics

Duration: 238 years; 7 generations, average length of 238/7 = 34 years; 103 magistracies; incidence in office, 238/103 = 1 in 2 years.

Also: Q. Caecilius (TP 439)
         L. Caecilius Denter (Pr 182)
         M. Caecilius Cornutus (Pr 91)
         C. Caecilius Cornutus (Pr 90)
         Q. Caecilius Metellus Celer (TP 90)
         C. Caecilius Cornutus (TP 61; Pr 57; Pp 56)
         L. Caecilius L.f. Rufus (Pr 57)
         C. Caecilius Cornutus (Pr 57)

Commentary

The Caecilii benefited, in their quest for power and prestige, from a biological fertility that produced several sons in each generation. A member of the gens is recorded in a minor office in the fifth century, but none in the fourth, probably due to the absence of Livy's text for that time; its emergence to power came with the ending of the Italian Wars, with the first consul, Denter; there then followed men holding regular offices until the end of the republic, which also saw the end of the gens. Quite abruptly and curiously this happened in the 50s BC, only half a century after it had all but monopolized the consulship in the last two decades of the second century. For a previously prolific family, its expiry is quite surprising, for even in the 60s they had held four consulships. The family vanished into the imperial aristocracy through the marriages of daughters and by way of adoptions.

There are a disturbing number of unallocated men of the family – their names indicate quite clearly their membership, and the Cornuti clearly should be considered a separate line, but the connections and sequence are wholly unclear. And there is a long generation gap between generations 3 and 4. I have reluctantly avoided including the praetor of 182 in that gap, but the temptation was strong.

Calpurnius (plebeian), 211–50 BC

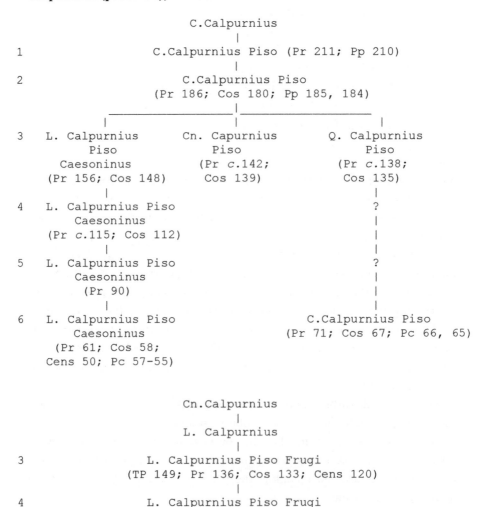

```
                        C.Calpurnius
                            |
1              C.Calpurnius Piso (Pr 211; Pp 210)
                            |
2                   C.Calpurnius Piso
                 (Pr 186; Cos 180; Pp 185, 184)
         _____|_____
         |                      |                       |
3   L. Calpurnius        Cn. Capurnius         Q. Calpurnius
        Piso                  Piso                   Piso
     Caesoninus            (Pr c.142;             (Pr c.138;
   (Pr 156; Cos 148)        Cos 139)               Cos 135)
         |                                            |
4   L. Calpurnius Piso                                ?
        Caesoninus                                    |
     (Pr c.115; Cos 112)                              |
         |                                            |
5   L. Calpurnius Piso                                ?
        Caesoninus                                    |
         (Pr 90)                                      |
         |                                            |
6   L. Calpurnius Piso                    C.Calpurnius Piso
        Caesoninus               (Pr 71; Cos 67; Pc 66, 65)
      (Pr 61; Cos 58;
    Cens 50; Pc 57-55)



                        Cn.Calpurnius
                            |
                        L. Calpurnius
                            |
3                   L. Calpurnius Piso Frugi
              (TP 149; Pr 136; Cos 133; Cens 120)
                            |
4                   L. Calpurnius Piso Frugi
                         (Pr 111)
                            |
5                   L. Calpurnius Piso Frugi
                       (TP 89; Pr 74)
```

Statistics
Duration: 161 years; 6 generations, average length 161/6 = 27 years;
31 magistracies, incidence of office, 161/31 = 1 in 5 years.

Also: L. Calpurnius Bestia (TP 121; Pr 114; Cos 111)
         M. Calpurnius C.f. Bibulus (Pr 62; Cos 59; Pc 51, 50)
         L. Calpurnius Bestia (TP 62)

Commentary

The Calpurnii emerged in the Second Punic War, with a praetor whose son reached the consulship (during which he died). This man appears to have had four sons, three of whom also reached the rank of consul. A parallel branch of the family, descended from a Cnaeus who is known to have fought in the Hannibalic War, must be connected to the main line in some way: perhaps he was a brother of the praetor of 211; this branch uses the same cognomen of Piso, with the addition of Frugi, a good indication of its connection to the main line, but just how this worked is not discernible. The sources again fail us for the ancestry of the consul of 67, who was the grandson of one of the consuls of the 130s, but the names of the intervening man or men is not known. There are several Calpurnii in minor magistracies who cannot be linked decisively to either branch.

The family survived into the Imperial period, producing consuls every generation into the early third century AD, with members regularly becoming victims of emperors, whose position they felt should be theirs, though they usually simply assumed that it would come to them by right of birth. The nearest they came was when one member of the family was selected by the Emperor Galba as his heir, but he was soon murdered along with the emperor.

Carvilius (plebeian), 293–212 BC

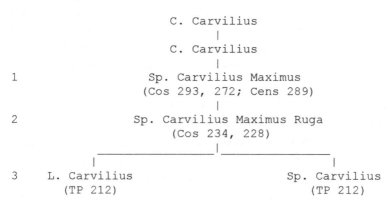

```
                        C. Carvilius
                             |
                        C. Carvilius
                             |
1                      Sp. Carvilius Maximus
                       (Cos 293, 272; Cens 289)
                             |
2                  Sp. Carvilius Maximus Ruga
                          (Cos 234, 228)
            _____|_____
            |                                  |
3    L. Carvilius                        Sp. Carvilius
       (TP 212)                             (TP 212)
```

Statistics

Duration: 81 years; 3 generations, average length 81/3 = 27 years;
7 magistracies, incidence of office, 81/7 = 1 in 12 years.

Commentary

A family in which just two generations reached the highest offices. Ironically their use of the cognomen Maximus seems to have ended as their activity declined. The family appears to have faded away during the Hannibalic War. Two more men are known during the second century, but only as senators, a position to which they were entitled as descendants of earlier senators, and so one that they did not need to have earned.

Cassius (plebeian), 174–42 BC

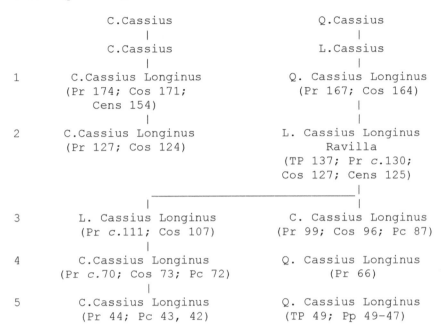

```
                C.Cassius                    Q.Cassius
                    |                            |
                C.Cassius                    L.Cassius
                    |                            |
1       C.Cassius Longinus           Q. Cassius Longinus
        (Pr 174; Cos 171;              (Pr 167; Cos 164)
           Cens 154)                         |
               |                             |
2       C.Cassius Longinus           L. Cassius Longinus
        (Pr 127; Cos 124)                  Ravilla
                                     (TP 137; Pr c.130;
                                     Cos 127; Cens 125)
                                             |
            _____|
            |                            |
3       L. Cassius Longinus          C. Cassius Longinus
        (Pr c.111; Cos 107)          (Pr 99; Cos 96; Pc 87)
               |
4       C.Cassius Longinus           Q. Cassius Longinus
        (Pr c.70; Cos 73; Pc 72)          (Pr 66)
               |
5       C.Cassius Longinus           Q. Cassius Longinus
        (Pr 44; Pc 43, 42)           (TP 49; Pp 49-47)
```

Statistics

Duration: 132 years; 5 generations, average length $132/5 = 26$ years; 27 magistracies, incidence in office $130/27 = 1$ in 5 years.

Also: L. Cassius Longinus (TP 104)
      C. Cassius (Pr 90; Pc 89, 88)
      L. Cassius (TP 89)
      M. Cassius M.f.P.n (Pr 73)
      L. Cassius Longinus (Pr 66)
      L. Cassius Longinus (Pr 44; Pc 48)
      Cassius (TP 56)

Commentary

The use of the same cognomen means that these two lines have a common ancestor, but he cannot be located in the recorded names; he must have lived in the early third century at the latest. It has to be said that these tables are somewhat speculative, since the affiliations of the consuls after the first generation are not recorded, though these men are clearly all of one family. The last man here, the praetor of 44, was one of the assassins of Julius Caesar. Despite this, his descendants survived in high positions until the mid first century AD. There are an uncomfortable number of men who were clearly of the family, but cannot be directly linked to it.

Claudius (patrician) 495–47 BC

A   *Claudius Inregillensis/Caecus/Pulcher*, 495–48 BC.

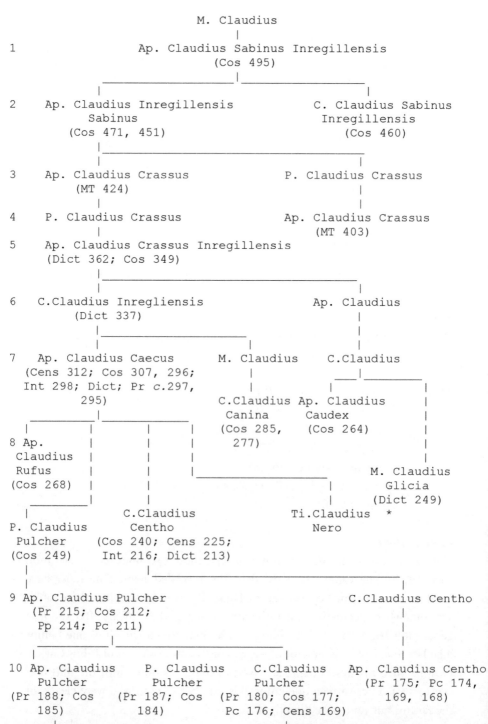

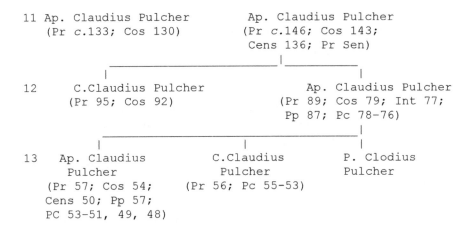

11 Ap. Claudius Pulcher   Ap. Claudius Pulcher
     (Pr *c*.133; Cos 130)   (Pr *c*.146; Cos 143;
                             Cens 136; Pr Sen)

12   C.Claudius Pulcher   Ap. Claudius Pulcher
        (Pr 95; Cos 92)   (Pr 89; Cos 79; Int 77;
                             Pp 87; Pc 78-76)

13   Ap. Claudius   C.Claudius   P. Clodius
      Pulcher   Pulcher   Pulcher
    (Pr 57; Cos 54;   (Pr 56; Pc 55-53)
    Cens 50; Pp 57;
    PC 53-51, 49, 48)

Statistics

Duration: 447 years; 14 generations, average length 447/14 = 32 years;
69 magistracies, incidence of office, 447/69 = 1 in 6 years.

B   *Claudius Nero*, 212-67 BC.

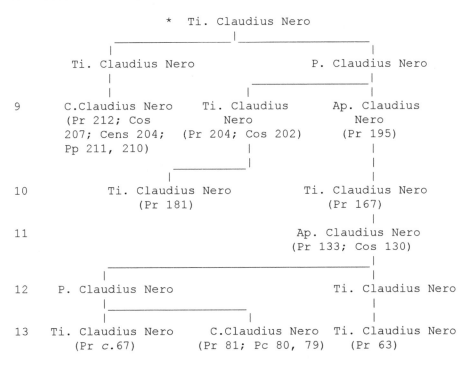

                         *   Ti. Claudius Nero

        Ti. Claudius Nero   P. Claudius Nero

9   C.Claudius Nero   Ti. Claudius   Ap. Claudius
       (Pr 212; Cos   Nero   Nero
       207; Cens 204;   (Pr 204; Cos 202)   (Pr 195)
       Pp 211, 210)

10   Ti. Claudius Nero   Ti. Claudius Nero
          (Pr 181)   (Pr 167)

11   Ap. Claudius Nero
                          (Pr 133; Cos 130)

12   P. Claudius Nero   Ti. Claudius Nero

13   Ti. Claudius Nero   C.Claudius Nero   Ti. Claudius Nero
      (Pr *c*.67)   (Pr 81; Pc 80, 79)   (Pr 63)

Statistics

Duration: 145 years; 5 generations, average length 145/5 = 29 years;
17 magistracies, incidence of office, 145/17 = 1 in 8 years.

Commentary

The Claudii were a most persistent and distinguished patrician family, prolific
enough to show office holders in every generation from the overthrow of the
kings to the installation of the emperors. It was a family that is said to have
originated outside the city and to have immigrated from the Sabine region
at the beginning of the republic. The family continued into the first century
of the empire, with one branch producing emperors (Tiberius, Claudius,
Caligula, Nero), a practice that ensured their extinction. The Pulchri died
out sooner. The subdivision of the family into numerous sections, particularly
in the mid third century, and again at the end of that century, resulted in
the great accumulation of magistracies in the family. It was also adaptable
even to the extent of some members changing the spelling to Clodius as a
way of bidding for popular electoral support. The line descended from Ti.
Claudius Nero has been separated off since it appears to have been effectively
independent from the time of the general who defeated Hasdrubal in 207.

Claudius (plebeian, 331–50 BC)

```
                        C.Claudius
                            |
                        C.Claudius
                            |
1              M. Claudius Marcellus (Cos 331; Dict 327)
                            |
2              M. Claudius Marcellus (Cos 287)
                            |
3                 M. Claudius Marcellus
                            |
4                 M. Claudius Marcellus
         (Pr c.224, 218, 216; Cos 222, 215, 214, 210,
          208; Pc 215, 213-211, 209)
                _____|_____
                |                         |
5      M. Claudius               M. Claudius
         Marcellus                 Marcellus
      (TP 204; Pr 198;          (Pr 188; Cos 183;
      Clos 186; Cens 189)        Pc 182, 181)
            |
6    M. Claudius Marcellus
     (TP 171; Pr 169; Cos 166,
      155, 152; Pc 168, 151)
            |
7    M. Claudius Marcellus
            (Pr 137)
            |
8    M. Claudius Marcellus
           (Pr 90)
            |_____
            |                                       |
9    M. Claudius Marcellus           C.Claudius Marcellus
         (Pr c.75)                       (Pr 80; Pc 79)
            |_____      |
            |                         |      |
10  M. Claudius              C.Claudius    C.Claudius
      Marcellus               Marcellus     Marcellus
     (Pr c.54;               (Pr c.52;      (Pr c.53;
      Cos 51)                 Cos 49)        Cos 50)
```

Statistics
Duration: 281 years; 10 generations, average length, $281/10 = 28$ years; 43 magistracies, incidence of office, $281/43 = 1$ in 6 years.

Commentary
The lamentable uninventiveness of Roman Republican personal names is particularly well displayed in this family, with its continual repetition of the same name in every generation.

The prestige gathered by the Marcellus of the fourth generation, who was so successful during the war with Hannibal, was so great that Marcus became the obvious name for all males of the family from then on. The decline of the family after the three times consular of 166–152 is noticeable, with the next two generations only reaching the praetorship during the troubled years when the aristocracy was under serious attack. The recovery of authority by the last generation (three consuls in three years, 51–49) was deceptive. One of the family married Augustus' sister, a marriage that produced another Marcellus, who then married his daughter Julia. The line thereupon died out in the male line.

Cornelius (patrician) 485–44 BC

A *Cornelius Maluginensis/Cossus*, 485–322 BC.

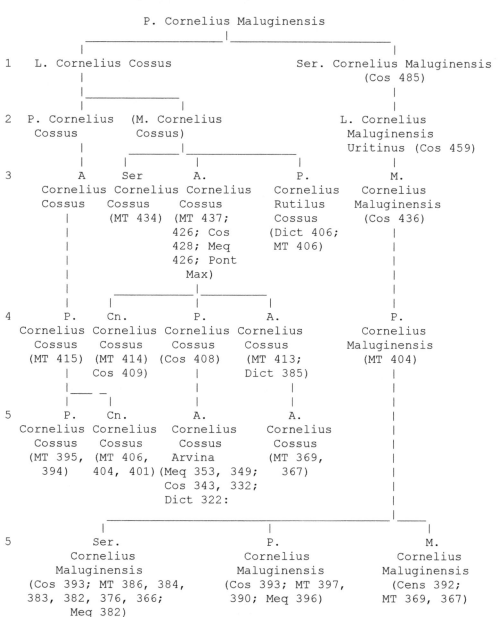

P. Cornelius Maluginensis

1 L. Cornelius Cossus   Ser. Cornelius Maluginensis
                                                    (Cos 485)

2 P. Cornelius   (M. Cornelius   L. Cornelius
   Cossus   Cossus)   Maluginensis
                                         Uritinus (Cos 459)

3   A   Ser   A.   P.   M.
  Cornelius Cornelius Cornelius Cornelius   Cornelius
   Cossus   Cossus   Cossus   Rutilus   Maluginensis
          (MT 434) (MT 437;   Cossus   (Cos 436)
                    426; Cos   (Dict 406;
                    428; Meq   MT 406)
                    426; Pont
                    Max)

4   P.   Cn.   P.   A.   P.
  Cornelius Cornelius Cornelius Cornelius   Cornelius
   Cossus   Cossus   Cossus   Cossus   Maluginensis
  (MT 415) (MT 414) (Cos 408) (MT 413;   (MT 404)
           Cos 409)   Dict 385)

5   P.   Cn.   A.   A.
  Cornelius Cornelius Cornelius Cornelius
   Cossus   Cossus   Cossus   Cossus
  (MT 395, (MT 406, Arvina   (MT 369,
   394)   404, 401)(Meq 353, 349; 367)
                     Cos 343, 332;
                     Dict 322:

5   Ser.   P.   M.
        Cornelius   Cornelius   Cornelius
        Maluginensis   Maluginensis   Maluginensis
  (Cos 393; MT 386, 384, (Cos 393; MT 397,   (Cens 392;
  383, 382, 376, 366;   390; Meq 396)   MT 369, 367)
        Meq 382)

Statistics

Duration: 163 years; 5 generations, average length 163/5 = 32 years;
44 magistracies, incidence of office, 163/44 = 1 in 4 years.

```
B    Cornelius Scipio (patrician), 395-52 BC.

1                          P. Cornelius Scipio

                      (MT 395, 394; Int 391, 389)
         _____|_____
        |                                             |
2    P. Cornelius Scipio              L. Cornelius Scipio
        (Meq 350)                    (Cos 350; Int 352; Cens
        |                                             |
3    P. Cornelius Scipio              Cn. Cornelius Scipio
       Barbatus                       Barbatus (Pont Max)
     (Cos 328; Dict 306)                              |
4                                      L. Cornelius Scipio
                                         Barbatus
                                       (Pr 295; Cos 298;
                                       Cens 280; Pont Max)
         _____|
        |                                           |
5    Cn. Cornelius Scipio Asina       L. Cornelius Scipio
       (Pr 253; Cos 260, 254)         (Cos 259; Cens 258)
              |                  _____|
              |                 |                     |
6      P. Cornelius    Cn. Cornelius          P. Cornelius
       Scipio Asina    Scipio Calvus            Scipio
     (Cos 221; Int 216) (Cos 222; Pc         (Cos 218; Pc
                          217 - 211)           217-211)
         _____|            _____|___
        |                  |           |               |
7    Cn. Cornelius   P. Cornelius  P. Cornelius  L.Cornelius
       Scipio          Scipio        Scipio        Scipio
      Hispallus         Nasica       Africanus    Asiaticus
     (Pr 179; Cos 176) (Pr 194;    (Cos 205, 194) (Pr 193;
              |         Cos 191;    Pc 210-206;    Cos 190;
              |        Pc 193, 190) 204-201        Pc 189)
              !              |       Cens 199;         |
              |              |       Pr Sen)           |
              |              |          |              |
8    Cn. Cornelius   P. Cornelius  L. Cornelius  L. Cornelius
       Scipio          Scipio        Scipio        Scipio
      Hispanus          Nasica      (Pr 174)         |
      (Pr 139)         Corculum                      |
              |     (Pr 165; Cos 162, 155;           |
              |      Cens 159; Pont Max;             |
              |        Pr Sen)                        |
              |           |                           |
```

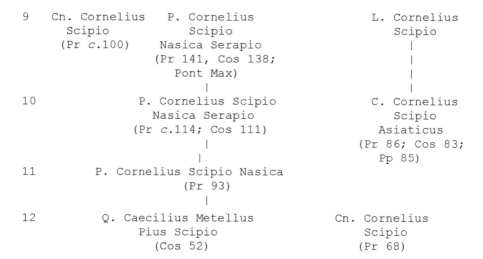

```
9   Cn. Cornelius    P. Cornelius                    L. Cornelius
       Scipio            Scipio                         Scipio
      (Pr c.100)      Nasica Serapio                      |
                      (Pr 141, Cos 138;                   |
                        Pont Max)                         |
                           |                              |
10                  P. Cornelius Scipio             C. Cornelius
                      Nasica Serapio                   Scipio
                    (Pr c.114; Cos 111)              Asiaticus
                                                   (Pr 86; Cos 83;
                           |                          Pp 85)
11          P. Cornelius Scipio Nasica
                     (Pr 93)
                        |
12        Q. Caecilius Metellus          Cn. Cornelius
              Pius Scipio                    Scipio
               (Cos 52)                     (Pr 68)
```

Statistics

Duration: 343 years; 12 generations, average length 343/12 = 29 years;
80 magistracies, incidence of office 343/80 = 1 in 4 years.

C   *Cornelius Lentulus* (patrician), 327–49 BC.

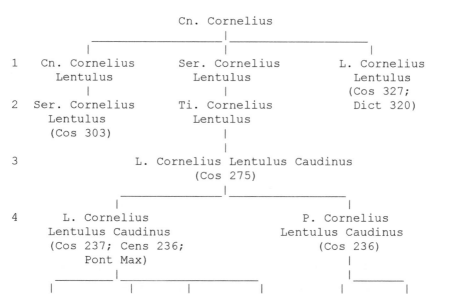

```
                          Cn. Cornelius
            _____|_____
           |                       |                       |
1    Cn. Cornelius           Ser. Cornelius          L. Cornelius
        Lentulus                Lentulus                Lentulus
           |                       |                   (Cos 327;
2    Ser. Cornelius          Ti. Cornelius             Dict 320)
        Lentulus                Lentulus
        (Cos 303)                  |
                                   |
3               L. Cornelius Lentulus Caudinus
                         (Cos 275)
               _____|_____
              |                                             |
4       L. Cornelius                          P. Cornelius
     Lentulus Caudinus                     Lentulus Caudinus
     (Cos 237; Cens 236;                        (Cos 236)
         Pont Max)                                  |
      _____|_____            _____|_____
     |         |          |         |         |            |
```

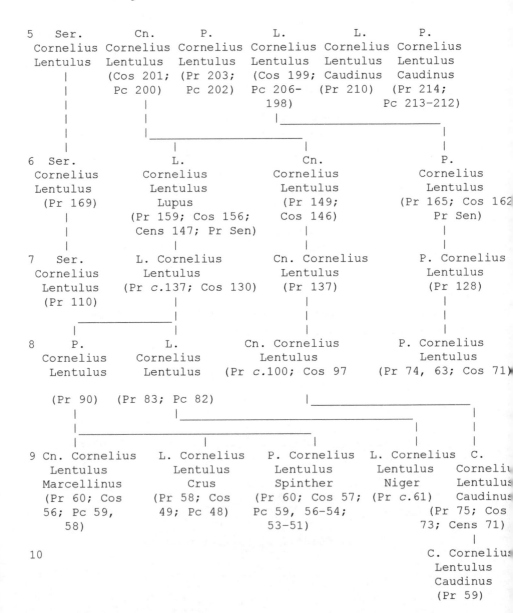

```
5   Ser.        Cn.         P.          L.          L.          P.
 Cornelius  Cornelius   Cornelius   Cornelius   Cornelius   Cornelius
 Lentulus   Lentulus    Lentulus    Lentulus    Lentulus    Lentulus
    |       (Cos 201;   (Pr 203;    (Cos 199;   Caudinus    Caudinus
    |        Pc 200)     Pc 202)     Pc 206-     (Pr 210)    (Pr 214;
    |           |                    198)                    Pc 213-212)
    |           |                     |                         |
    |           |_____                       |
    |                   |            |             |            |
6   Ser.               L.           Cn.                P.
 Cornelius          Cornelius     Cornelius         Cornelius
 Lentulus           Lentulus      Lentulus          Lentulus
   (Pr 169)          Lupus         (Pr 149;         (Pr 165; Cos 162
    |              (Pr 159; Cos 156;  Cos 146)         Pr Sen)
    |              Cens 147; Pr Sen)    |                |
    |                  |                |                |
7   Ser.          L. Cornelius    Cn. Cornelius      P. Cornelius
 Cornelius          Lentulus        Lentulus          Lentulus
 Lentulus         (Pr c.137; Cos 130)  (Pr 137)        (Pr 128)
   (Pr 110)           |                |                |
    _____|               |                |
    |                  |               |                |
8      P.             L.         Cn. Cornelius      P. Cornelius
 Cornelius         Cornelius      Lentulus           Lentulus
 Lentulus          Lentulus      (Pr c.100; Cos 97  (Pr 74, 63; Cos 71)

   (Pr 90)      (Pr 83; Pc 82)                |
     |              |_____
     |              |                                  |           |
     |_____          |           |
     |               |            |         |          |           |
9 Cn. Cornelius  L. Cornelius  P. Cornelius  L. Cornelius  C.
   Lentulus        Lentulus      Lentulus      Lentulus   Corneliu
   Marcellinus      Crus         Spinther      Niger      Lentulus
   (Pr 60; Cos   (Pr 58; Cos   (Pr 60; Cos 57; (Pr c.61)  Caudinus
   56; Pc 59,    49; Pc 48)    Pc 59, 56-54;             (Pr 75; Cos
   58)                         53-51)                     73; Cens 71)
                                                            |
10                                                    C. Cornelius
                                                      Lentulus
                                                      Caudinus
                                                      (Pr 59)
```

Statistics

Duration: 278 years; 10 generations, average length, 278/10 = 28 years;
70 magistracies, incidence of office: 278/70 = 1 in 4 years.

D *Cornelius Dolabella* (patrician), 283–44 BC.

```
1                              P. Cornelius (Cos 283)
                                     |
2                                    ?
                                     |
3                              Cn. Cornelius
              _____|_____
             |                               |
4      L. Cornelius              Cn. Cornelius Dolabella
             |                          (Cos 159)
             |                               |
5      P. Cornelius                          |
             |                               |
             |_____               |
             |               |               |
6      L. Cornelius   Cn. Cornelius   Cn. Cornelius   Cn. Cornelius
       (Pr 99; Pc        Dolabella       Dolabella       Dolabella
        99-98)        (Pr 81; Pc   (Pr 84; Cos 81;     (Pr 100)
                        80-79)       Pc 80-77)


7                    P. Cornelius Dolabella
                        (Pr 69; Pc 68)


8                    P. Cornelius Dolabella
                  (TP 47; Cos 44; Pc 44 - 43)
```

Statistics

Duration: 239 years; 8 generations, average length, 239/8 = 30 years;
21 magistracies, incidence of office, 239/21 = 1 in 11 years.

E *Cornelius Cethegus* (patrician), 211–83 BC.

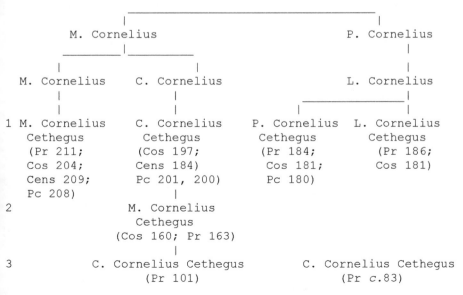

```
              _____
             |                                           |
       M. Cornelius                              P. Cornelius
       _____|_____                             |
      |                     |                            |
 M. Cornelius        C. Cornelius                  L. Cornelius
      |                     |                      _____|
      |                     |                     |           |
1 M. Cornelius        C. Cornelius        P. Cornelius   L. Cornelius
   Cethegus             Cethegus            Cethegus        Cethegus
   (Pr 211;             (Cos 197;           (Pr 184;        (Pr 186;
   Cos 204;             Cens 184)           Cos 181;        Cos 181)
   Cens 209;            Pc 201, 200)        Pc 180)
   Pc 208)                  |
2                     M. Cornelius
                        Cethegus
                   (Cos 160; Pr 163)
                           |
3           C. Cornelius Cethegus          C. Cornelius Cethegus
                 (Pr 101)                       (Pr c.83)
```

Statistics
Duration: 128 years; 3 generations, average length 128/3 = 43 years;
17 magistracies, incidence of office: 128/17 = 1 in 7 years.

Commentary
The enormous Cornelian gens showed a tendency to subdivide as early as the mid fifth century, by when the Cossus and Maluginensis lines had become visibly distinct. By the end of that century the Scipio line was also distinct, and in another half-century so was the Lentulus line. The Cethegus and Dolabella lines continued the process and there were also smaller Blasio and Balbus branches. This is a process not visible in all other gentes, certainly not to the same extent, though the Domitii and Aemilii indulged in it. The cause is presumably the combined wealth and fertility of the family, which permitted branches from the main trunk to flourish. In this case there are so many branches that it has been necessary to plot them on separate tables.

These subsections also had a tendency to die out. The Maluginensis line expired in the fourth century, as did the associated Cossus line. The Cethegus line lasted less than half a century. The Lentulus and Scipio lines, however, continued vigorously into the period of the revolution. They even survived in high positions into the first century of the empire, before expiring.

It has been impossible to locate the connections between the Maluginenses and the Cossi, on the one hand, and the Scipiones and Lentuli on the other, nor the precise connections to the main family of the lesser and later branches. Thus they have been treated as separate dynasties, with this single commentary as the main indication that the whole gens was really one.

There are several other men whose names indicate that they were part of this gens, but whose precise affiliation is not known, but there are not more than two or three in each subsection of the whole family. In the Cethegi, however, the line of the consul of 181 is only speculatively attached to the main group. In the Dolabella line it is also difficult to be certain of the full relationships, but the distinctive cognomen puts the whole group into a single family.

Cosconius (plebeian), 135–54 BC

```
                         C. Cosconius
                             |
1                        M. Cosconius (Pr 135; Pc 134-132)

2                           C. Cosconius (Pr 89, 79; Pc 78-76)
                              _____|_____
                             |                            |
3        C. Cosconius Calidianus          C. Cosconius
              (Pr 63; Pc 62)           (TP 59; Pr 54; Pc 53, 52))
```

Statistics

Duration: 81 years; 3 generations, average length 81/3 = 27 years;
15 magistracies, incidence of office, 81/15 = 1 in 5 years.

Commentary

A family that emerged in the late second century, but only to the level of praetor and tribune of the plebs, and yet it held a comparatively large number of offices at those levels. On the other hand, had it appeared a century earlier no doubt its members would have risen higher; the first century BC was a dangerous time for ambitious men. The distinctive nomen implies that the praetor of 135 and that of 89 were related, and the time distance between them would suggest there might have been an intervening generation.

Decius (plebeian), 340–265 BC

```
                          Q. Decius
                             |
1                    P. Decius Mus  (Cos 340)
                             |
2                        Q. Decius Mus              M. Decius
                   (Cos 312, 308, 297, 295;         (TP 311)
                      Cens 304; Meq 306)
                             |
3                    P. Decius Mus  (Cos 279, 265)
```

Statistics

Duration: 75 years; 3 generations, average length, 75/3 = 25 years;
10 magistracies, incidence of office, 75/10 = 1 in 8 years.

Also: L. Decius (TP 415)
        M. Decius (TP 491)
        P. Decius Subula (TP 120; Pr 115)
        P. Decius (TP *c.*52)

Commentary

A brief but doomed family, counting seven consulships in little more than
half a century. After 279 there are only a few later Decii known in the second
century, one of whom reached the praetorship in 115; these men may or may
not be of the same family. The consuls were warriors of a particularly violent
type; they also had suicidal tendencies that ensured that the family would not
last long. The consuls of 340 and 295 'devoted' themselves in battle to ensure
Roman victories – that is, they committed ritual suicide. The consul of 279 is
reputed to have done the same, but this is clearly a much later family legend,
for he is known to have become consul again later. The ending of the Italian
Wars after 272, in a sense, removed the family's justification. The tribune of
311 may well be a son of the consul of 340, but evidence does not exist.

Domitius, 194–46 BC

A *Domitius Ahenobarbus* (plebeian), 194–48 BC.

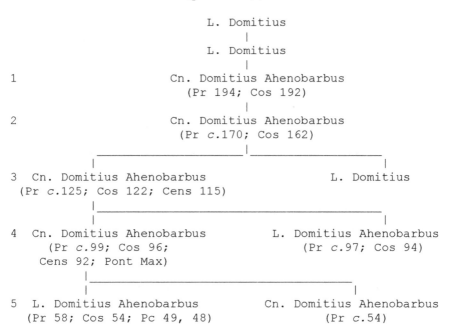

```
                        L. Domitius
                            |
                        L. Domitius
                            |
1                  Cn. Domitius Ahenobarbus
                       (Pr 194; Cos 192)
                            |
2                  Cn. Domitius Ahenobarbus
                       (Pr c.170; Cos 162)
              _____|_____
             |                                 |
3  Cn. Domitius Ahenobarbus              L. Domitius
   (Pr c.125; Cos 122; Cens 115)
         |_____
         |                                 |
4  Cn. Domitius Ahenobarbus        L. Domitius Ahenobarbus
      (Pr c.99; Cos 96;               (Pr c.97; Cos 94)
      Cens 92; Pont Max)
         |_____
         |                                 |
5  L. Domitius Ahenobarbus         Cn. Domitius Ahenobarbus
   (Pr 58; Cos 54; Pc 49, 48)           (Pr c.54)
```

Statistics

Duration: 146 years; 5 generations, average length 146/5 = 29 years;
18 magistracies, incidence of office, 146/18 = 1 in 8 years.

Commentary

A new family that emerged from the fighting against Hannibal, with a highly distinctive cognomen. The regular appearance of consuls from the family in every generation was interrupted by the revolution after the 90s, though the youth of the males of the fifth generation probably saved the family from having to make serious choices until the 50s, when they sided first with Pompey, and then with Mark Antony. For all that, the family reconciled itself quickly enough to the rule of Augustus and married into the ruling family. The eventual result was the Emperor Nero.

A collateral branch was the following; it is not possible to connect the two branches, but it would seem probable that they were one and the same family.

```
B   Domitius Calvinus (plebeian), 80-46 BC

                       P. Domitius
                           |
                       M. Domitius
                           |
1                  M. Domitius Calvinus (Pr 80; Pc 79)
                           |
2                    Cn. Domitius Calvinus
                 (TP 59; Pr 56; Cos 53; Pc 48-46)
```

Statistics
Duration: 34 years; 2 generations, average length 34/2 = 17 years;
8 magistracies, incidence of office, 34/8 = 1 in 4 years

Also: Cn. Domitius Calvinus (Cos 332)
         Cn. Domitius Calvinus Maximus (Cos 283; Dict 280; Cens 280)

Commentary
A family that was only very briefly in office, if one disregards the much earlier
magistrates, who were clearly ancestors but who cannot be directly linked to
the later members who gained election. The first century BC members held a
commendably large number of offices in their brief career.

Duillius (plebeian), 470–231 BC

```
1               K. Duillius     M. Duillius (TP 470, 449)
                     |
2               K. Duillius
                     |
3               K. Duillius Longus (MT 399)
                     |
4               M. Duillius (TP 357)
                     |
5               K. Duillius (Cos 336)


            M. Duillius
                 |
            M. Duillius
                 |
7           C. Duillius (Cos 260; Cens 258; Dict 231)
```

Statistics
Duration: 239 years; 7 generations, average length 239/7 = 34 years;
8 offices, incidence of office, 239/8 = 1 in 30 years.

Commentary
A family that is not well-recorded except for the final office holder. The first in office, the tribune of the plebs of 470, can only be connected to the rest by assumption from the name; similarly the last, the consul of 260, but the distinctive name does seem sufficient. The consul of 260 played a notable part in the naval warfare in the First Punic War.

Fabius (patrician), 485–45 BC

A   *Fabius Vibulanus/Ambustus/Maximus*, 485-45 BC.

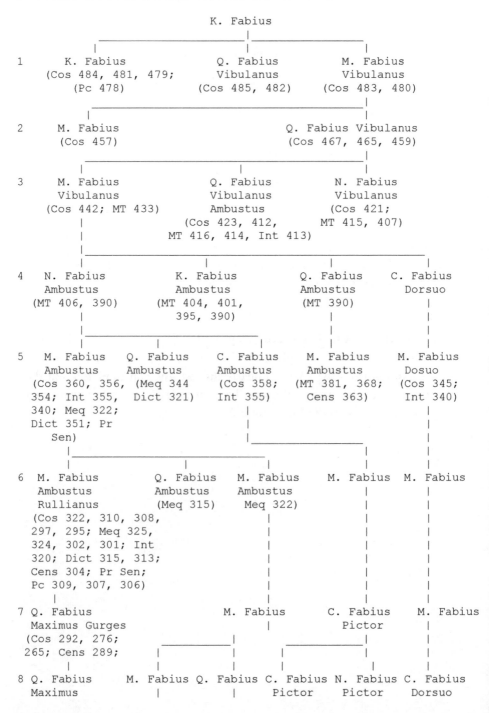

```
                              K. Fabius
                                  |
        _____|_____
        |                         |                         |
1       K. Fabius            Q. Fabius              M. Fabius
   (Cos 484, 481, 479;       Vibulanus              Vibulanus
        (Pc 478)          (Cos 485, 482)         (Cos 483, 480)
                                                          |
        _____
        |                                                 |
2     M. Fabius                              Q. Fabius Vibulanus
      (Cos 457)                              (Cos 467, 465, 459)
                                                          |
        _____
        |                         |                       |
3     M. Fabius            Q. Fabius              N. Fabius
      Vibulanus            Vibulanus              Vibulanus
   (Cos 442; MT 433)       Ambustus             (Cos 421;
        |                (Cos 423, 412,         MT 415, 407)
        |             MT 416, 414, Int 413)
        |
        |_____
        |                    |                     |               |
4    N. Fabius          K. Fabius            Q. Fabius      C. Fabius
     Ambustus           Ambustus             Ambustus       Dorsuo
   (MT 406, 390)     (MT 404, 401,          (MT 390)          |
        |              395, 390)                |             |
        |_____             |             |
        |              |          |            |             |
5    M. Fabius    Q. Fabius   C. Fabius   M. Fabius      M. Fabius
     Ambustus     Ambustus    Ambustus    Ambustus       Dosuo
   (Cos 360, 356, (Meq 344    (Cos 358;   (MT 381, 368;  (Cos 345;
   354; Int 355,  Dict 321)   Int 355)    Cens 363)      Int 340)
   340; Meq 322;                 |                          |
   Dict 351; Pr                  |                          |
     Sen)                        |_____          |
        |                        |               |          |
        |_____               |          |
        |              |          |              |          |
6    M. Fabius    Q. Fabius   M. Fabius     M. Fabius  M. Fabius
     Ambustus     Ambustus    Ambustus         |          |
     Rullianus    (Meq 315)   Meq 322)         |          |
   (Cos 322, 310, 308,           |             |          |
   297, 295; Meq 325,            |             |          |
   324, 302, 301; Int            |             |          |
   320; Dict 315, 313;           |             |          |
   Cens 304; Pr Sen;             |             |          |
   Pc 309, 307, 306)             |             |          |
        |                        |             |          |
7 Q. Fabius              M. Fabius       C. Fabius    M. Fabius
   Maximus Gurges            |           Pictor           |
   (Cos 292, 276;       _____       _____       |
   265; Cens 289;       |        |       |        |       |
        |               |        |       |        |       |
8 Q. Fabius      M. Fabius Q. Fabius C. Fabius N. Fabius C. Fabius
   Maximus           |        |      Pictor    Pictor    Dorsuo
```

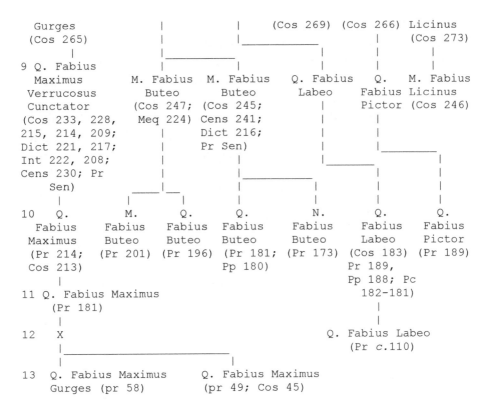

```
Gurges              |           |      (Cos 269) (Cos 266) Licinus
(Cos 265)           |           |_____          |      (Cos 273)
   |                |           |           |        |        |
9 Q. Fabius         |           |           |        |        |
   Maximus      M. Fabius  M. Fabius    Q. Fabius   Q.    M. Fabius
   Verrucosus      Buteo      Buteo        Labeo   Fabius  Licinus
   Cunctator   (Cos 247;  (Cos 245;        |      Pictor (Cos 246)
(Cos 233, 228,  Meq 224) Cens 241;         |        |
215, 214, 209;     |     Dict 216;         |        |
Dict 221, 217;     |     Pr Sen)           |        |
Int 222, 208;      |        |              |        |_____
Cens 230; Pr       |        |              |_____|         |
    Sen)           |        |_____    |        |         |
    |         ___|__    |           |       |        |         |
    |        |      |   |           |       |        |         |
10   Q.      M.     Q.  Q.          N.      Q.        Q.
   Fabius  Fabius Fabius Fabius    Fabius  Fabius   Fabius
   Maximus Buteo  Buteo  Buteo     Buteo   Labeo    Pictor
  (Pr 214; (Pr 201)(Pr 196)(Pr 181;(Pr 173)(Cos 183)(Pr 189)
   Cos 213)              Pp 180)           Pr 189,
    |                                      Pp 188; Pc
11 Q. Fabius Maximus                        182-181)
    (Pr 181)                                  |
    |                                         |
12   X                                Q. Fabius Labeo
    |                                    (Pr c.110)
    |_____
    |                               |
13 Q. Fabius Maximus          Q. Fabius Maximus
   Gurges (pr 58)             (pr 49; Cos 45)
```

Statistics

Duration: 440 years; 13 generations, average length, 440/13 = 34 years; 109 magistracies, incidence in office, 440/109 = 1 in 4 years.

B   *Fabius Aemilianus* (patrician), 149–45 BC.

```
1                  Q. Fabius Maximus Aemilianus
                   (Pr 149; Cos 145; Pc 144, 143)
                                |
2                  Q. Fabius Maximus Allobrogicus
                (Pr 123; Cos 121; Pp 123; Pc 120-117)
                                |
3                      Q. Fabius Maximus
                          (Pr 91)
                                |
4                      Q. Fabius Maximus
                          (Cos 45)
```

Statistics

Duration: 104 years; 4 generations, average length 104/4 = 26 years; 13 magistracies, incidence of office, 104/13 = 1 in 8 years.

Also: C. Fabius Hadrianus (Pr 58; Pc 57)
          C. Fabius Hadrianus (Pr 84; Pp 83, 82)

Commentary

The Fabian family emerged very soon to a dominating position in the early republic, notoriously indulging at one point in its own foreign policy and fighting a private war with Veii. Rarely did more than a decade pass without a Fabius featuring as one of the ruling magistrates until the 80s BC.

The family subdivided in the usual way, but branches also regularly died out, or at least ceased to produce office holders. The Maximus line expired in the 180s, and was only revived by adopting grown men from two other families: this line, which is not genetically connected to the original, is therefore separated off into a different table as the Aemilianus line. In the same decade was the last of the Pictor line. The one continuing bloodline was that of Labeo, and that itself ceased with the praetor of 110.

The adoptive lines were less than successful substitutes. Two grown men were adopted into the family, from the Servilii and from the Aemilii. The Servilian line lasted only two generations (consuls in 146 and 116), without accumulating enough offices to justify inclusion here. The Aemilian line did better, with four republican generations, and living on into Tiberius' reign, but then it also expired.

There was a period, when Fabius Cunctator (generation 9) was at the height of his power, when the family was pre-eminent to a dangerous extent. It may be the memory of this dominance that led to the reduction in the family's influence in the following generation, but its effective extinction is still remarkable.

Fannius (plebeian), 184–48 BC

```
1                         C. Fannius (TP 184)
                 _____|_____
          |                                       |
2      C. Fannius Strabo                      M. Fannius
       (Pr 164; Cos 161)                          |
          |                                       |
3        C. Fannius                          C. Fannius
       (Pr pre-118)                   (TP 142; Pr 126; Cos 122)


4                         M. Fannius
                            (Pr 80)


5                         C. Fannius
                  (TP 58; Pr 54; Pp 49, 48)
```

Statistics

Duration: 136 years; 5 generations, average length $136/5 = 27$ years;
12 magistracies, incidence of office, $136/12 = 1$ in 11 years.

Commentary

A family of moderate success, though only producing two consuls in over a
century. The precise connection of the last two of the family in generations 4
and 5 cannot be discerned but their names and their dates in office are clear
indications of their family and generation.

Flaminius (plebeian), 232–187 BC

```
1                          C. Flaminius
                (TP 232; Pr 227; Cos 223, 217;
                    Meq 221; Cens 220)
                              |
2                          C. Flaminius
                (Pr 193; Cos 187; Pp 192-190)
```

Statistics
Duration: 45 years; 2 generations, average length $45/2 = 22$ years;
11 magistracies, incidence of office, $45/11 = 1$ in 4 years.

Commentary
Only two members of this family reached the required offices to be included
here, though there were members of the family holding minor offices for the
rest of the republic, including one who stood for election as tribune of the plebs
as late as 44 BC. The family's renown, of course, rested upon the achievements
of C. Flaminius, the consul of 223 and 217 (defeated by Hannibal), and this
no doubt assisted his son to office.

Fonteius (plebeian), 178–54 BC

```
                     |
         |                     |
1    T. Fonteius        P. Fonteius        P. Fonteius       M. Fonteius
        Capito             Capito             Balbus           (Pr 166)
       (Pr 178;          (Pr 169;           (Pr 168)
      Pc 177, 176)      Pp 168, 167)


3             M. Fonteius           M. Fonteius
                 (Pr 77)        (Pr 75; Pp 74-72)


4                      C.? Fonteius
                         (Pr 54)
```

Statistics
Duration: 124 years; 4 generations, average length, 124/4 = 31 years;
14 magistracies, incidence of office, 124/14 = 1 in 9 years.

Commentary
This was a family that was clearly politically busy; in addition to those in the
table, several other members also held minor offices throughout this period.
I have postulated a missing generation between the first and third, but the
precise continuing connections are not clear. One would suppose that the four
men of the first generation could well be brothers or possibly two pairs of
brothers. The sources do not exist to decide.

Fulvius (plebeian), 322–125 BC

A   *Fulvius Curvus/Nobilior*, 322-136 BC.

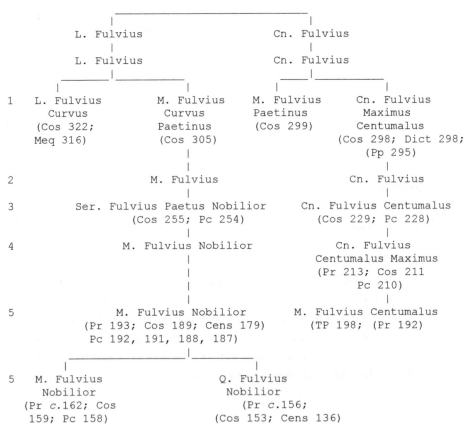

```
                    |                        |
          L. Fulvius                 Cn. Fulvius
                    |                        |
          L. Fulvius                 Cn. Fulvius
           _____|_____        _____|_____
          |                  |       |                 |
1    L. Fulvius       M. Fulvius   M. Fulvius    Cn. Fulvius
      Curvus           Curvus       Paetinus       Maximus
     (Cos 322;        Paetinus     (Cos 299)     Centumalus
     Meq 316)         (Cos 305)               (Cos 298; Dict 298;
                          |                         (Pp 295)
                          |                            |
2                    M. Fulvius                 Cn. Fulvius
                          |                            |
3        Ser. Fulvius Paetus Nobilior       Cn. Fulvius Centumalus
              (Cos 255; Pc 254)                (Cos 229; Pc 228)
                          |                            |
4            M. Fulvius Nobilior               Cn. Fulvius
                          |                   Centumalus Maximus
                          |                   (Pr 213; Cos 211
                          |                          Pc 210)
                          |                            |
5            M. Fulvius Nobilior         M. Fulvius Centumalus
        (Pr 193; Cos 189; Cens 179)       (TP 198; (Pr 192)
           Pc 192, 191, 188, 187)
              _____|_____
             |                              |
5     M. Fulvius                   Q. Fulvius
        Nobilior                     Nobilior
     (Pr c.162; Cos               (Pr c.156;
      159; Pc 158)             (Cos 153; Cens 136)
```

Statistics

Duration: 186 years; 6 generations, average length 186/6 = 31 years;
29 magistracies, incidence of office 186/29 = 1 in 6 years.

B   *Fulvius Flaccus* (plebeian) 264-125 BC.

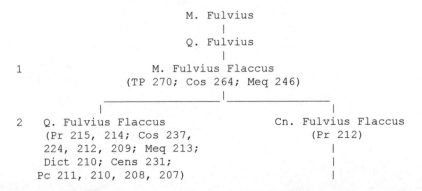

```
                        M. Fulvius
                            |
                        Q. Fulvius
                            |
1               M. Fulvius Flaccus
           (TP 270; Cos 264; Meq 246)
          _____|_____
         |                                            |
2   Q. Fulvius Flaccus                       Cn. Fulvius Flaccus
    (Pr 215, 214; Cos 237,                        (Pr 212)
     224, 212, 209; Meq 213;                          |
     Dict 210; Cens 231;                              |
     Pc 211, 210, 208, 207)                           |
```

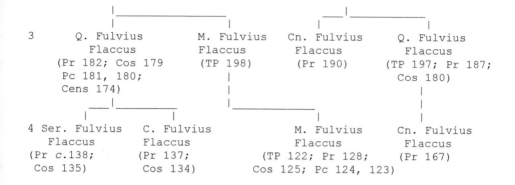

3   Q. Fulvius   M. Fulvius   Cn. Fulvius   Q. Fulvius
       Flaccus   Flaccus   Flaccus   Flaccus
   (Pr 182; Cos 179   (TP 198)   (Pr 190)   (TP 197; Pr 187;
    Pc 181, 180;   Cos 180)
    Cens 174)

4 Ser. Fulvius   C. Fulvius   M. Fulvius   Cn. Fulvius
    Flaccus   Flaccus   Flaccus   Flaccus
  (Pr c.138;   (Pr 137;   (TP 122; Pr 128;   (Pr 167)
   Cos 135)   Cos 134)   Cos 125; Pc 124, 123)

Statistics

Duration: 139 years; 4 generations, average length $139/4 = 35$ years; 37 magistracies, incidence of office, $139/37 = 1$ in 4 years.

Also: Q. Fulvius (Pr 200)
        Q. Fulvius Gillo (TP 197)

Commentary

The Fulvii emerged to hold offices in the late fourth century and split into three major sections, the Flacci, the Curvi, and the Centumali; the fourth section, the Nobiliores, split off from the Curvi later. The link between the Curvus and Flaccus families, however, cannot be detected, and so the latter is treated as a distinct dynasty. All four lines expired during the second century, more or less simultaneously. There is an interesting contrast between the Flaccus family and the other three, considered as a group. The Flacci lasted the longest, and had the most intense record of achievement, with double the rate of office holding to the others. This is clearly due to greater fertility. Yet only one member of the whole family collected an unusually large number of offices – Q. Flaccus in the second generation.

Furius (patrician), 488–115 BC

```
        |                |              |              |              |
1  Sex.            Sp.              P.            L.            Sp.
   Furius          Furius           Furius        Furius        Furius
   (Cos 488)       Fusus            Medulinus     Medulinus     Medulinus
        |          (Cos 481;        Fusus         Fusus         (Cos 464;
        |          Pc 478)          (Cos 472)     (Cos 474)     453)
        |                |_____            |
2 Sex.          Agr. Furius     C. Furius      Q. Furius     L. Furius
  Furius             Fusus         Pacilis        Pacilis       Medulinus
        |          (Cos 446)       Fusus        (Pont Max)     (MT 432,
        |                |        (Cos 441; MT                  425, 420)
        |                |         426, Cens 435)                    |
        |                |              |        _____|____
        |                |              |       |          |             |
3 Agr.          M. Furius     C. Furius     M.          L.           Sp.
  Furius            Fusus         Pacilis     Furius *    Furius *     Furius
  Fusus          (MT 403;       (Cos 412)   Camillus   Medulinus    Medulinus
        |         Cos 389;           |        (Cens 403) (Cos 413;   (MT 400)
        |         Cens 389)          |                    409)            |
        |                |_____|     ____|_____                    |
        |                |              |              |                   |
4 Agr. Furius   C. Furius      L. Furius     Sp. Furius    L. Furius
  Fusus             Pacilis        Camillus      Camillus      Medulinus
  (MT 391)         (Cos 351)     (Cos 350, 349;  (Pr 366)     MT 381, 370;
        |                         Dict 345)          |         Cens 383)
        |_____        |
        |                       |         |
5 M. Furius       Sp. Furius     L. Furius Camillus
  (MT 389)        (MT 378)       (Cos 338, 325)
                                        |
6                         L. Furius Camillus (Pr 318)
                                        |
7                              M. Furius
                                        |
8                             Sp. Furius
                                        |
   _____|_____
  |                             |                               |
9   C. Furius           P. Furius Philus                  Sp. Furius
        |              (Pr 224, 218, 216; Cos 223;              |
        |                     Cens 214)                         |
        |              _____|_____                    |
        |             |                     |                   |
10  M. Furius    P. Furius            L. Furius        L. Furius
    Cassipes        Philus               Philus           Purpureo
    (Pr 187, 173)  (Pr 174)            (Pr 171)      (Pr 200, Cos 196)
        |                                   |
11 L. Furius Cassipes            L. Furius Philus
        |                        (Pr c.139; Cos 136)
        |
12 L. Furius Cassipes
     (Pr c.115)
```

* Omitted offices: M. Camillus: MT 401, 398, 396, 394, 386, 384, 381; Dict 396, 390, 389, 368, 367; Int 396, 391, 389.
L. Medullinus: MT 407, 405, 398, 397, 394, 391.

Statistics

Duration: 373 years, 12 generations, average length $373/12 = 31$ years; 72 magistracies, incidence of office, $373/72 = 1$ in 5 years.

Also: L. Furius Crassipes (Pr 49)

L. Furius (TP 308)

L. Furius (Pr 75)

P. Furius (TP 99)

L. Furius Bibaculus (Pr pre-219)

(For a different reconstruction of this family see Settipani, *Continuité gentilice*, p. 66).

Commentary

The patrician gens of the Furii got off to a good start with five consular brothers in the first half-century of the republic, and then maintained this good going with frequent appearances in the office of military tribunes with consular power. The abilities of the two Camillus brothers in the third generation are well reflected in their offices, thirteen of which they held between them. There was, however, a distinct falling off during the fourth century.

No member of the family held an office between 318 and 224, possibly an effect of the poor sources. The precise evidence to connect the praetor of 318 with the consul of 223 does not exist, but the consul's father's and grandfather's lifetimes neatly fill the time gap between them, as I have assumed that M. Furius is the son of the praetor of 318.

The family recovered in the late third century, with the consul of 223, but the achievement of later generations was clearly limited – only two consulships, though six men did reach the praetorship. This is the same pattern as is seen in the period after the great Camillus, but this time there was no revival.

Geganius (patrician), 492–367 BC

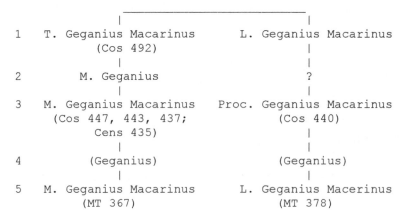

```
                  |            _____|_____
                  |           |                                 |
1   T. Geganius Macarinus         L. Geganius Macarinus
           (Cos 492)                         |
                  |                           |
2          M. Geganius                        ?
                  |                           |
3   M. Geganius Macarinus      Proc. Geganius Macarinus
       (Cos 447, 443, 437;             (Cos 440)
             Cens 435)                        |
                  |                           |
4          (Geganius)                    (Geganius)
                  |                           |
5   M. Geganius Macarinus         L. Geganius Macerinus
           (MT 367)                      (MT 378)
```

Statistics

Duration: 125 years; 5 generations, average length 125/5 = 25 years; 8 magistracies, incidence of office, 125/8 = 1 in 16 years.

Commentary

The Geganii was a patrician gens that was powerful in the first years of the republic. However, only one of the men on this table collected more than one magistracy, and there were two generations with none at all. (The table is thus to a degree speculative, the assumption being that the fourth generation did not take office.) Even with the numerous posts of military tribunes with consular powers that were available in the late fifth and early fourth centuries, the family failed to capitalize on its early strength until the very end. This was not a family with a powerful urge to power; it appears to have faded away after 367.

Genucius (plebeian), 451–193 BC

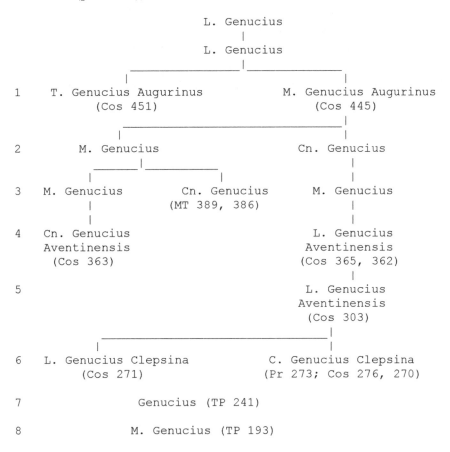

```
                          L. Genucius
                               |
                          L. Genucius
                  _____|_____
                 |                           |
1     T. Genucius Augurinus        M. Genucius Augurinus
            (Cos 451)                    (Cos 445)
                                             |
           _____|
          |                                   |
2      M. Genucius                       Cn. Genucius
       _____|_____                          |
      |             |                          |
3  M. Genucius   Cn. Genucius            M. Genucius
      |          (MT 389, 386)                 |
      |                                        |
4  Cn. Genucius                          L. Genucius
   Aventinensis                          Aventinensis
    (Cos 363)                            (Cos 365, 362)
                                              |
5                                        L. Genucius
                                         Aventinensis
                                          (Cos 303)
                                              |
          _____|
         |                                     |
6  L. Genucius Clepsina            C. Genucius Clepsina
      (Cos 271)                    (Pr 273; Cos 276, 270)

7                 Genucius (TP 241)

8              M. Genucius (TP 193)
```

Statistics

Duration: 258 years; 8 generations, average length $258/8 = 32$ years; 14 magistracies, incidence in office, $258/14 = 1$ in 16 years.

Also: T. Genucius (TP 476)
        Cn. Genucius (TP 473)
        L. Genucius (TP 342)

Commentary

The Genucii only emerged to political power slowly after the establishment of the republic, and they never were very prominent at any time. A slow rate of reproduction may be part of the reason. It is noticeable, however, that tenures of office are clustered – in the 360s and the 270s. This was, of course, one of the characteristics of Roman Republican politics, where one member of a family assisted another to power, and alliances between clans helped each other into office. The Genucii do not seem to have been avid for power – an unusually large number of men did not hold any office. I have somewhat tentatively included the last two items (generations 7 and 8), to extend the family to 193; the family did continue to hold minor offices for sometime longer, and a senator of the name is known in the late second century, but its period of power really ended in 270.

Horatius (patrician), 509–378 BC

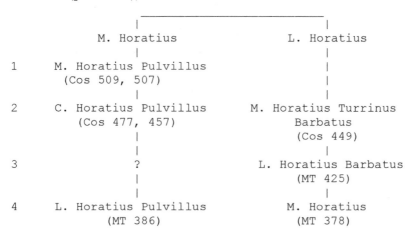

```
                    |                              |
              M. Horatius                    L. Horatius
                    |                              |
1       M. Horatius Pulvillus                      |
            (Cos 509, 507)                         |
                    |                              |
2       C. Horatius Pulvillus          M. Horatius Turrinus
            (Cos 477, 457)                   Barbatus
                    |                        (Cos 449)
                    |                              |
3                   ?                  L. Horatius Barbatus
                    |                        (MT 425)
                    |                              |
4       L. Horatius Pulvillus            M. Horatius
             (MT 386)                     (MT 378)
```

Statistics

Duration: 131 years; 4 generations, average length $131/4 = 32$ years; 8 magistracies, incidence of office, $131/8 = 1$ in 16 years.

Commentary

The Horatii were a prominent family under the monarchy and one of them was consul twice in the first years of the republic – the consul of 509 was presumably he of the battle at the bridge. The consuls of 477 and 449 I have assumed were cousins in the same family, though evidence of the connection is lacking. The urge to power, or perhaps the resources to support ambition, clearly failed in the early fourth century. No further Horatii are in any office until the first century BC.

Hortensius (plebeian), 170–42 BC

```
1                              L. Hortensius (Pr 170)

3                              L. Hortensius (Pr c.111; Cos 108)
                                    |_____
                                                   |
4            L. Hortensius                Q. Hortensius Hortalus
             (Pr 87)                         (Pr 72; Cos 69)
                                                   |
5                                         Q. Hortensius
                                          (Pr 45; Pc 44-42)
```

Statistics

Duration: 128 years; 5(?) generations, average length $128/5 = 25$ years;
10 magistracies, incidence of office $128/10 = 1$ in 13 years.

Also: L. Hortensius (TP 422)
         Q. Hortensius (Dict 287)

Commentary

A family that could count two magistrates in the distant past, but which only
secured access to power in the second century. The precise connections of
these later members are not clear, still less are any back to the early members; I
assume that the names of the unattached men can guarantee their membership
of the family.

Hostilius (plebeian), 180–145 BC

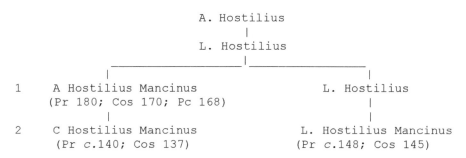

```
                          A. Hostilius
                               |
                          L. Hostilius
        _____|_____
        |                          |                  |
1       A Hostilius Mancinus                L. Hostilius
        (Pr 180; Cos 170; Pc 168)                |
              |                                  |
2       C Hostilius Mancinus              L. Hostilius Mancinus
        (Pr c.140; Cos 137)              (Pr c.148; Cos 145)
```

Statistics

Duration: 35 years; 2 generations, average length of 35/2 = 18 years;
7 magistracies, incidence in office, 35/7 = 1 in 5 years.

Also: A. Hostilius Cato (Pr 207)
       C. Hostilius Cato (Pr 207)
       C. Hostilius Tubulus (Pr 209, Pp 208, 206–204)
       L. Hostilius Tubulus (Pr 142)
       L. Hostilius Dasienus (TP 68)
       C. Hostilius Saserna (TP 44)
       Tullus Hostilius (TP 42)

Commentary

A brief dynasty that came to grief with the consul of 137, who failed in
Spanish warfare (as his father had also failed in warfare in Greece). During
the war with Hannibal, other Hostilii had emerged at praetorian rank (the
Cato and Tubulus families), but if they were related to the Mancini there is
no evidence. A helping hand from such a relative might explain the success of
the consul of 170, whose election is on the surface surprising after the long
interval since his praetorship. It is a good example of the fact that simple
influence – the consul of 170 was related to the Fulvii – when unaccompanied
by real ability was not sufficient.

Iulius (patrician), 489–379, 267–44 BC

A   *Iulius Iullus*, 489–379 BC.

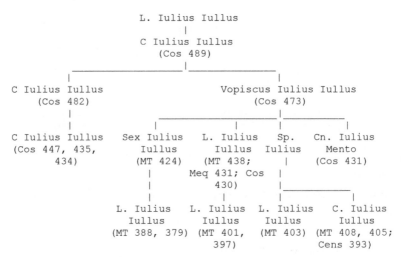

```
                              L. Iulius Iullus
                                     |
                              C Iulius Iullus
                                 (Cos 489)
       _____|_____
      |                                                          |
  C Iulius Iullus                           Vopiscus Iulius Iullus
    (Cos 482)                                     (Cos 473)
      |                            _____|_____
      |                           |          |          |          |
  C Iulius Iullus    Sex Iulius   L. Iulius  Sp.   Cn. Iulius
  (Cos 447, 435,       Iullus      Iullus  Iulius    Mento
      434)           (MT 424)    (MT 438;    |     (Cos 431)
                        |         Meq 431; Cos |
                        |            430)      |_____
                        |            |       |          |
                   L. Iulius    L. Iulius  L. Iulius   C. Iulius
                     Iullus       Iullus     Iullus     Iullus
                  (MT 388, 379) (MT 401,   (MT 403)  (MT 408, 405;
                                  397)                 Cens 393)
```

Statistics

Duration: 110 years; 4 generations, average length 110/4 = 28 years;
20 magistracies, incidence of office, 110/20 = 1 in 5 years.

B   *Iulius Caesar*, 267–44 BC.

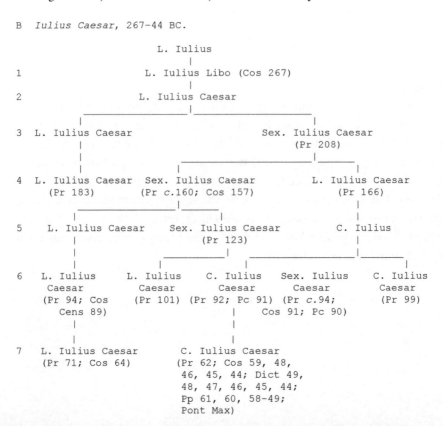

```
                         L. Iulius
                              |
1                 L. Iulius Libo (Cos 267)
                              |
2                 L. Iulius Caesar
        _____|_____
       |                                                 |
3  L. Iulius Caesar                      Sex. Iulius Caesar
       |                                        (Pr 208)
       |                        _____|_____
       |                       |          |               |
4  L. Iulius Caesar  Sex. Iulius Caesar      L. Iulius Caesar
     (Pr 183)        (Pr c.160; Cos 157)        (Pr 166)
       |_____|_____                    |
       |                      |                     |
5   L. Iulius Caesar    Sex. Iulius Caesar      C. Iulius
       |                    (Pr 123)                |
       |                 _____|_____|_____
       |                |          |              |          |
6   L. Iulius     L. Iulius  C. Iulius   Sex. Iulius  C. Iulius
    Caesar         Caesar     Caesar       Caesar       Caesar
    (Pr 94; Cos   (Pr 101) (Pr 92; Pc 91) (Pr c.94;    (Pr 99)
      Cens 89)                |            Cos 91; Pc 90)
       |                      |
       |                      |
7   L. Iulius Caesar     C. Iulius Caesar
    (Pr 71; Cos 64)      (Pr 62; Cos 59, 48,
                         46, 45, 44; Dict 49,
                         48, 47, 46, 45, 44;
                         Pp 61, 60, 58-49;
                         Pont Max)
```

Statistics
Duration: 223 years; 7 generations, average length 223/7 = 32 years;
35 magistracies, incidence in office, 233/35 = 1 in 7 years.

Commentary
The patrician Iulian gens, like several others, was successful during the early aristocratic republic, in the fifth century, but clearly failed to maintain itself during the fourth century (unless this is an effect of poor sources). The Caesar line, being patrician, was clearly descended from the Iulli, but the precise links during the fourth century are not known. The revival of the family came with the consul of 267, but even then only one man of the family reached the consulship during the next century and a half (in 157); otherwise the family was effectively of praetorian rank until the 90s, and then only occasionally, hardly a great success. The revolution of the Social War and its aftermath thus raised the family once more into power, with four consulships between 91 and 59. However, it is noticeable that, of the thirty-five offices held by members of the second dynasty, the great majority (twenty-five) were held by the dictator. Thus the family cannot be said to have been powerful or prominent until his time, and, since he had no son, he would be the last of his line.

Iunius (plebeian), 325–45 BC

A   *Iunius Brutus*, 325–45 BC.

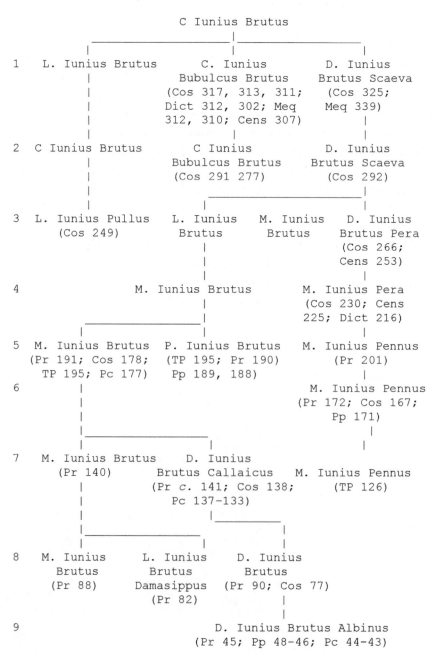

```
                          C Iunius Brutus
         _____|_____
        |                   |                   |
1   L. Iunius Brutus     C. Iunius          D. Iunius
        |                Bubulcus Brutus     Brutus Scaeva
        |                (Cos 317, 313, 311; (Cos 325;
        |                Dict 312, 302; Meq  Meq 339)
        |                312, 310; Cens 307)      |
        |                     |                   |
2   C Iunius Brutus        C Iunius            D. Iunius
        |                Bubulcus Brutus      Brutus Scaeva
        |                (Cos 291 277)        (Cos 292)
        |                                          |
        |                 _____|
        |                |        |               |
3   L. Iunius Pullus   L. Iunius  M. Iunius   D. Iunius
    (Cos 249)          Brutus     Brutus      Brutus Pera
                           |                  (Cos 266;
                           |                  Cens 253)
                           |                       |
4                M. Iunius Brutus          M. Iunius Pera
                           |               (Cos 230; Cens
              _____|               225; Dict 216)
             |             |                       |
5   M. Iunius Brutus   P. Iunius Brutus   M. Iunius Pennus
    (Pr 191; Cos 178;  (TP 195; Pr 190)   (Pr 201)
    TP 195; Pc 177)    Pp 189, 188)            |
6       |                                 M. Iunius Pennus
        |                                 (Pr 172; Cos 167;
        |                                    Pp 171)
        |                                      |
        |_____                     |
        |                 |                     |
7   M. Iunius Brutus   D. Iunius               |
    (Pr 140)           Brutus Callaicus   M. Iunius Pennus
        |              (Pr c. 141; Cos 138;    (TP 126)
        |              Pc 137-133)
        |                     |_____
        |_____     |         |
        |                |    |         |
8   M. Iunius      L. Iunius   D. Iunius
    Brutus         Brutus      Brutus
    (Pr 88)        Damasippus  (Pr 90; Cos 77)
                   (Pr 82)          |
                                    |
9                         D. Iunius Brutus Albinus
                          (Pr 45; Pp 48-46; Pc 44-43)
```

Statistics
Duration: 280 years; 9 generations, average length 280/9 = 31 years;
47 magistracies, incidence of office, 280/47 = 1 in 6 years.

B   *Iunius Silanus*, 212–76 BC.

```
1                          M. Iunius Silanus
                         (Pr 212; Pp 211-206)

2                             D. Iunius
                                  |
3                       D. Iunius Silanus Manlianus
                                (Pr 141)
          _____|_____
         |                                                    |
4   M. Iunius Silanus                          L. Iunius Silanus
      (TP 123; Pr c.112;                              |
       Cos 109; Pc 108)                               |
          |_____                    |
         |                        |                    |
5  D. Iunius Silanus    M. Iunius Silanus    D. Iunius Silanus
     (Pr c.67; Cos 62)    (Pr 77; Pp 76)
```

Statistics
Duration: 146 years; 5 generations, average length, 146/5 = 29 years;
16 magistracies, incidence of office, 146/16 = 1 in 9 years.

Also: L. Iunius Brutus (Cos 509)
       L. Iunius Brutus (TP 493)
       Q. Iunius (TP 439)
       C. Iunius (TP 423)
       T. Iunius L.f. (Pr 90)
       M. Iunius (Pr 67)
       M. Iunius Iuncus (Pr 76)

Commentary
The Iunii emerged during the Italian Wars with two successful military
brothers; members of the family then succeeded in reaching the consulship
in every subsequent generation until the end of the republic, though it was
clearly difficult in the last years, and the family disappeared after the praetor
of 45 (the tyrannicide).

The second dynasty, the Silani, was presumably a branch of the main
family, but the connection cannot be made. It had to refresh itself by adoption
from the Manlii Torquati, with the praetor of 141, who in effect began a new
dynasty. It was not especially successful, but revived under Augustus, and
became a prominent family under the principate.

Iuventius (plebeian), 194–148 BC.

```
            T. Iuventius
               |
1         T. Iuventius Thalna (Pr 194)
               |
2         M'. Iuventius Thalna (TP 170; Pr 167; Cos 163)
               |
3         P. Iuventius Thalna (Pr 149; Pp 148)
```

Statistics

Duration: 46 years; 3 generations, average length 46/3 = 15 years;
6 magistracies, incidence in office, 46/6 = 1 in 8 years.

Commentary

A family that was doing well until the third generation, but after the praetor
of 149 failed in a minor war in Macedon the family declined. Successors held
a few minor offices over the next century, including one praetorship in 51, but
essentially the family had ended in 148.

Licinius (plebeian), 256–53 BC

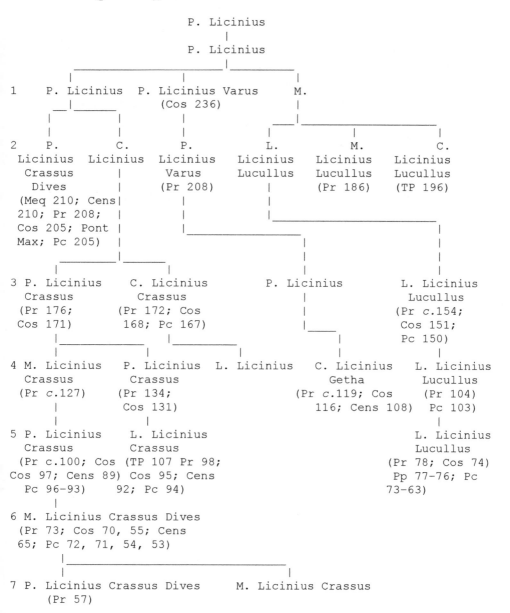

```
                          P. Licinius
                              |
                          P. Licinius
          _____|_____
         |                 |                     |
1     P. Licinius    P. Licinius Varus        M.
      __|_____          (Cos 236)            |
     |        |              |             ___|_____
     |        |              |            |           |            |
2     P.       C.        P.            L.         M.           C.
   Licinius Licinius   Licinius     Licinius   Licinius     Licinius
   Crassus    |        Varus       Lucullus   Lucullus     Lucullus
   Dives      |        (Pr 208)       |       (Pr 186)     (TP 196)
   (Meq 210; Cens|         |          |
   210; Pr 208; |          |          |
   Cos 205; Pont|          |          |_____
   Max; Pc 205) |          |                                          |
     _____|_____    |                                          |
    |                 |    |_____                  |
    |                 |                            |                  |
3 P. Licinius   C. Licinius          P. Licinius       L. Licinius
   Crassus        Crassus               |              Lucullus
   (Pr 176;      (Pr 172; Cos           |             (Pr c.154;
   Cos 171)      168; Pc 167)           |____          Cos 151;
     |_____  |_____            |          Pc 150)
    |               |          |             |            |
4 M. Licinius   P. Licinius  L. Licinius  C. Licinius   L. Licinius
   Crassus       Crassus                   Getha        Lucullus
   (Pr c.127)    (Pr 134;              (Pr c.119; Cos   (Pr 104)
     |           Cos 131)              116; Cens 108)   Pc 103)
     |             |                                      |
5 P. Licinius   L. Licinius                            L. Licinius
   Crassus        Crassus                              Lucullus
   (Pr c.100; Cos (TP 107 Pr 98;                       (Pr 78; Cos 74)
   Cos 97; Cens 89) Cos 95; Cens                       Pp 77-76; Pc
   Pc 96-93)      92; Pc 94)                            73-63)
     |
6 M. Licinius Crassus Dives
   (Pr 73; Cos 70, 55; Cens
   65; Pc 72, 71, 54, 53)
     |_____
     |                                    |
7 P. Licinius Crassus Dives      M. Licinius Crassus
   (Pr 57)
```

Statistics

Duration: 203 years; 7 generations, average length 203/7 = 29 years;
62 magistracies, incidence of office, 199/62 = 1 in 3 years.

Commentary

The Licinii had occasional magistrates, including a consul, in the early years of the republic, but only with the consul of 236 did the family begin a consistent run. (There were also other lines, notably the Licinii Murenae, who cannot be fitted into the table.) A byword for wealth (the consul of 210 was already 'Dives') the family culminated with a triumvir in the consul of 70 and 55 – again immensely wealthy – but his death in war against the Parthians in 53 effectively ended the family. His grandson reached the consulship in 30 by favour of Octavian (of all years), but he had to adopt to ensure that the family name continued.

The Lucullus branch saw the same predilection for accumulating wealth and the same pattern of alternating consular with praetorian rank with the generations. It also died out during the revolutionary period.

Livius (plebeian), 268–50 BC

```
1                    M. Livius Drusus (Pr 268)

2                      M. Livius Salinator
                   (Cos 219, 207; Dict 207;
                    Pp 206-204; Cens 204
                               |
3                       C Livius Salinator
                   (Pr 202; 191; Pp 190; Cos 188)


4                C Livius M. Aemiliani f.M Drusus
                       (Pr 150; Cos 147)
                               |
5                M. Livius C.f.M. Aemiliani Drusus
         (TP 122; Pr 115; Cos 112. Pp 111, 110; Cens 109)
                               |
6                   M. Livius Drusus (TP 91)
                               |
7                M. Livius Drusus Claudianus
                          (Pr 50)
```

Statistics

Duration: 218 years; 7 generations, average length $218/7 = 31$ years;
22 magistracies, incidence in office $218/22 = 1$ in 10 years

Also: Livius (TP 146)

Commentary

The family's succession was interrupted in the mid second century by the adoption from the Aemilius family. It is here treated as a single succession, but with a gap to indicate the adoption. Generally speaking, it was a successful family, collecting numerous offices until about the end of the second century after which it clearly faded away.

Lucretius (patrician), 509–381 BC

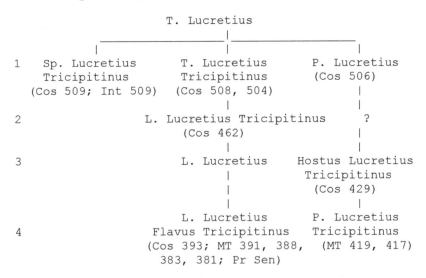

```
                            T. Lucretius
              _____|_____
             |                       |                       |
1      Sp. Lucretius            T. Lucretius            P. Lucretius
       Tricipitinus            Tricipitinus              (Cos 506)
       (Cos 509; Int 509)      (Cos 508, 504)                |
                                       |                      |
2                        L. Lucretius Tricipitinus            ?
                              (Cos 462)                       |
                                       |                      |
3                             L. Lucretius        Hostus Lucretius
                                   |                 Tricipitinus
                                   |                   (Cos 429)
                                   |                      |
                              L. Lucretius          P. Lucretius
4                       Flavus Tricipitinus         Tricipitinus
                        (Cos 393; MT 391, 388,      (MT 419, 417)
                         383, 381; Pr Sen)
```

Statistics
Duration: 128 years; 4 generations, average length 128/4 = 32 years;
15 magistracies, incidence of office, 128/15 = 1 in 8 years.

Commentary
The connection of the Lucretii with the former royal house, and their involvement in its overthrow, ensured the family's prominence in the early republic, but it also helped to reduce its power later. The record is thin throughout most of the fifth century, and only the consul of 393 exhibits any real appetite for power and office. The family apparently then died out.

Lucretius (plebeian), 210–82 BC

```
1     M. Lucretius            Sp. Lucretius
        (TP 210)           (Pr 205; Pp 204-202)

2     M. Lucretius            Sp. Lucretius          Q. Lucretius
        (TP 172)           (Pr 172; Pc 171)            Gallus
                                                      (Pr 171)

4                      Q. Lucretius Ofella
                            (Pr 82)
```

Statistics

Duration: 122 years; 4 generations, average length $122/4 = 31$ years; 10 magistracies, incidence of office, $122/10 = 1$ in 12 years.

Commentary

The fact that these men were of a plebeian family might not indicate a connection with the preceding patrician Lucretian family, which appears to have died out a century earlier. It is impossible given the condition of the sources to link up the various men in a coherent genealogical connection, but the names, dates, and offices do suggest that they formed a single family. It remained throughout at only praetorian rank, never achieving the consulship.

Lutatius (plebeian), 242–65 BC

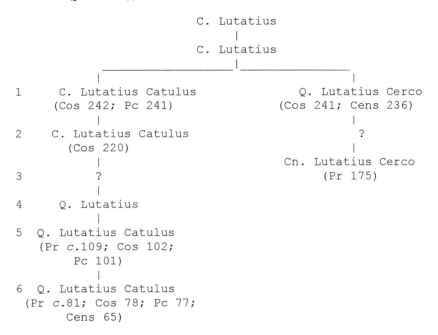

```
                        C. Lutatius
                            |
                        C. Lutatius
          _____|_____
          |                                      |
1     C. Lutatius Catulus              Q. Lutatius Cerco
      (Cos 242; Pc 241)                (Cos 241; Cens 236)
          |                                      |
2     C. Lutatius Catulus                        ?
      (Cos 220)                                  |
          |                            Cn. Lutatius Cerco
3         ?                                 (Pr 175)
          |
4     Q. Lutatius
          |
5   Q. Lutatius Catulus
    (Pr c.109; Cos 102;
        Pc 101)
          |
6   Q. Lutatius Catulus
   (Pr c.81; Cos 78; Pc 77;
        Cens 65)
```

Statistics

Duration: 177 years; 6 generations, average length $177/6 = 30$ years;
13 magistracies, incidence of office $177/13 = 1$ in 13 years.

Commentary

The repetition of the two cognomina Catulus and Cerco ensures that all these men are of the same overall family, though the precise connections are not always clear, and the number of generations is not guaranteed. After a good start at the end of the First Punic War – the two consuls arranged the peace treaty to finish off the war – the family rather languished during the second century, revived in the fifth and sixth generations, but then vanished again after the consul of 78.

Mamilius (plebeian), 265–206 BC

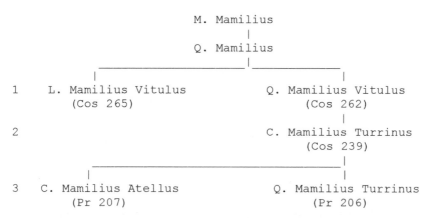

```
                          M. Mamilius
                               |
                          Q. Mamilius
        _____|_____
       |                                             |
1   L. Mamilius Vitulus                        Q. Mamilius Vitulus
        (Cos 265)                                   (Cos 262)
                                                        |
2                                              C. Mamilius Turrinus
                                                    (Cos 239)
                         _____|
       |                                             |
3   C. Mamilius Atellus                        Q. Mamilius Turrinus
        (Pr 207)                                    (Pr 206)
```

Statistics

Duration: 59 years; 3 generations, average length, 59/3 = 19 years;
5 magistracies, incidence of office, 59/5 = 1 in 12 years.

Commentary

The Mamilii emerged during the warfare of the First Punic War, but clearly did not maintain their political authority in peacetime, or in the later wars. The consul of the second generation could expect that office by virtue of his parentage, but the lack of distinction of the third generation (in another war) is clear. A few later members occupied minor offices during the second century.

Manilius (plebeian), 157–52 BC

```
                    P. Manilius
                         |
                    P. Manilius
                         |
1                   M'. Manilius (Pr 157; Cos 154; Pc 148)

2                   P. Manilius (Pr 123; Cos 120)

3                      Manilius (Pr c.88)

4                   Q. Manilius Cumanus (TP 52)
```

Statistics

Duration: 105 years; 4 generations, average length, 105/4 = 26 years;
7 magistracies, incidence of office, 105/7 = 1 in 15 years.

Commentary

The eye of faith can reconstruct the four office holders into a family spread
over four generations, but this might not be taken as the final word. On the
other hand, these men clearly do form a family of sorts, even though the
vertical connection, genealogically speaking, cannot be proved.

Manlius (plebeian), 480–45 BC

A *Manlius Vulso/Captolinus/Torquatus*, 480–45 BC.

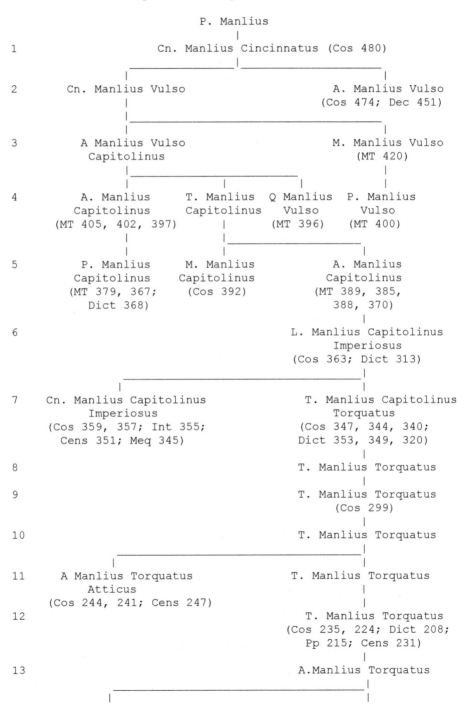

```
                              P. Manlius
                                  |
1                    Cn. Manlius Cincinnatus (Cos 480)
                   _____|_____
                   |                               |
2         Cn. Manlius Vulso                  A. Manlius Vulso
                   |                          (Cos 474; Dec 451)
                   |
                   |_____
                   |                                   |
3            A Manlius Vulso                    M. Manlius Vulso
               Capitolinus                          (MT 420)
                   |_____        |
                   |            |            |          |
4          A. Manlius     T. Manlius   Q Manlius   P. Manlius
            Capitolinus   Capitolinus    Vulso        Vulso
          (MT 405, 402, 397)    |       (MT 396)     (MT 400)
                   |            |_____
                   |            |                    |
5          P. Manlius      M. Manlius          A. Manlius
            Capitolinus    Capitolinus         Capitolinus
          (MT 379, 367;    (Cos 392)          (MT 389, 385,
            Dict 368)                           388, 370)
                                                     |
6                                          L. Manlius Capitolinus
                                               Imperiosus
                                            (Cos 363; Dict 313)
                                                     |
          _____|
          |                                         |
7   Cn. Manlius Capitolinus                 T. Manlius Capitolinus
          Imperiosus                              Torquatus
    (Cos 359, 357; Int 355;                 (Cos 347, 344, 340;
     Cens 351; Meq 345)                     Dict 353, 349, 320)
                                                     |
8                                           T. Manlius Torquatus
                                                     |
9                                           T. Manlius Torquatus
                                                 (Cos 299)
                                                     |
10                                          T. Manlius Torquatus
          _____|
          |                                           |
11  A Manlius Torquatus                      T. Manlius Torquatus
          Atticus                                     |
    (Cos 244, 241; Cens 247)                          |
12                                          T. Manlius Torquatus
                                            (Cos 235, 224; Dict 208;
                                             Pp 215; Cens 231)
                                                     |
13                                          A.Manlius Torquatus
          _____|
          |                                           |
```

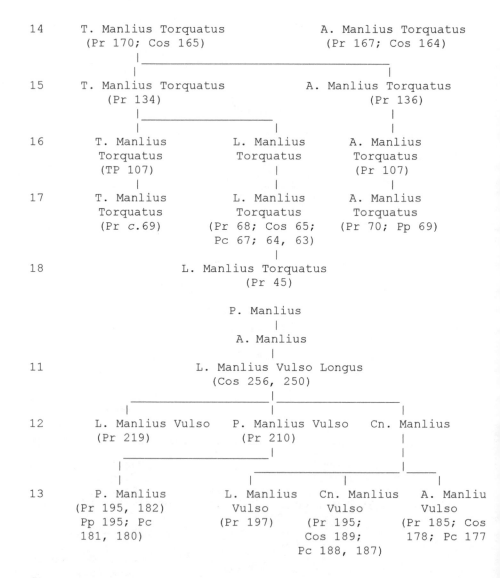

14   T. Manlius Torquatus   A. Manlius Torquatus
         (Pr 170; Cos 165)   (Pr 167; Cos 164)

15   T. Manlius Torquatus   A. Manlius Torquatus
            (Pr 134)   (Pr 136)

16   T. Manlius   L. Manlius   A. Manlius
         Torquatus   Torquatus   Torquatus
         (TP 107)   (Pr 107)

17   T. Manlius   L. Manlius   A. Manlius
         Torquatus   Torquatus   Torquatus
         (Pr c.69)   (Pr 68; Cos 65;   (Pr 70; Pp 69)
                           Pc 67; 64, 63)

18   L. Manlius Torquatus
                            (Pr 45)

                         P. Manlius

                         A. Manlius

11   L. Manlius Vulso Longus
                        (Cos 256, 250)

12   L. Manlius Vulso   P. Manlius Vulso   Cn. Manlius
           (Pr 219)   (Pr 210)

13   P. Manlius   L. Manlius   Cn. Manlius   A. Manliu
       (Pr 195, 182)   Vulso   Vulso   Vulso
        Pp 195; Pc   (Pr 197)   (Pr 195;   (Pr 185; Cos
         181, 180)   Cos 189;   178; Pc 177
                                         Pc 188, 187)

Statistics
Duration: 435 years; 18 generations, average length, 435/18 = 24 years;
73 magistracies, incidence of office 435/73 = 1 in 6 years.

Also: Cn. Manlius (Pr 72)
        L. Manlius (Pr 79, Pc 78)
        Q Manlius (TB 69)
        L. Manlius L.f. Acidinus (Pr 210; Pp 207; Pc 206–199)
        L. Manlius L.f.L Acidinus Fulvius (Pr 188, Pc 187–186; Cos 179)
        L. Manlius L.f. (PR 126)

Commentary

This major gens was prominent and active from the republic's inauguration to its ending, but with some significant gaps in the record. As with similarly long-lasting gentes the secret of survival lay in having multiple branches, so that when one line expired, another could be promoted. So the Capitolinus line died out, but the line of the Torquati went on, though with less determination as the failure of both the father and the son of the consul of 299 to achieve high office suggests. The parallel Vulso line (which has to be placed separately, there being no room on the main table for it) cannot be linked directly with the main trunk, but its patrician status and the use of the cognomen are decisive links. When the Torquatus line faltered, the Vulsones took up the family torch. But in the later second century both were failing. Indeed, but for the consul of 65, it would be difficult to justify including the last four generations.

The dynasty may have lasted and held office during the time of the republic, but in detail there are times when no members were in power. They had only one military tribune with consular power, for example, between 451 and 405, only one consul between the dictator of 320 and the consul of 256; between the consuls of 250 and 189, the family only achieved praetorships; and of course they had only one praetorship between 164 and 70. The achievement was thus very erratic. The family died out with two sons of the praetor of 70.

Marcius (plebeian), 390–42 BC

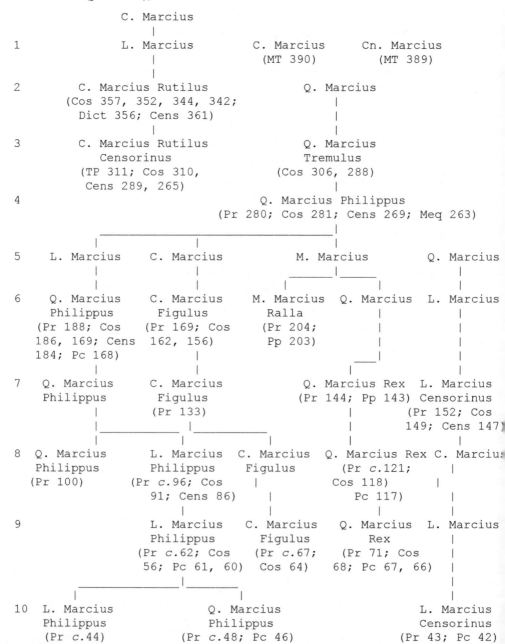

```
                    C. Marcius
                        |
1           L. Marcius          C. Marcius        Cn. Marcius
                 |              (MT 390)            (MT 389)
                 |
2        C. Marcius Rutilus              Q. Marcius
         (Cos 357, 352, 344, 342;           |
          Dict 356; Cens 361)               |
                 |                          |
3        C. Marcius Rutilus            Q. Marcius
             Censorinus                  Tremulus
           (TP 311; Cos 310,          (Cos 306, 288)
            Cens 289, 265)                  |
4                                 Q. Marcius Philippus
                         (Pr 280; Cos 281; Cens 269; Meq 263)

         _____|
         |              |                         |
5    L. Marcius    C. Marcius          M. Marcius           Q. Marcius
         |              |            _____|_____             |
         |              |            |            |             |
6    Q. Marcius    C. Marcius    M. Marcius  Q. Marcius  L. Marcius
      Philippus     Figulus       Ralla         |           |
     (Pr 188; Cos  (Pr 169; Cos  (Pr 204;       |           |
     186, 169; Cens 162, 156)    Pp 203)        |           |
     184; Pc 168)      |                      __|           |
         |             |                      |             |
7    Q. Marcius    C. Marcius         Q. Marcius Rex  L. Marcius
      Philippus     Figulus           (Pr 144; Pp 143) Censorinus
         |         (Pr 133)                 |           (Pr 152; Cos
         |_____|_____           |          149; Cens 147)
         |             |         |           |             |
8    Q. Marcius    L. Marcius  C. Marcius  Q. Marcius Rex  C. Marcius
      Philippus     Philippus   Figulus     (Pr c.121;       |
     (Pr 100)     (Pr c.96; Cos    |        Cos 118)         |
                   91; Cens 86)    |         Pc 117)         |
                        |          |           |             |
9                   L. Marcius  C. Marcius  Q. Marcius   L. Marcius
                     Philippus   Figulus      Rex            |
                    (Pr c.62; Cos (Pr c.67;  (Pr 71; Cos     |
                    56; Pc 61, 60) Cos 64)   68; Pc 67, 66)  |
                    _____|_____                    |
                    |                   |                    |
10   L. Marcius          Q. Marcius              L. Marcius
      Philippus           Philippus              Censorinus
     (Pr c.44)         (Pr c.48; Pc 46)        (Pr 43; Pc 42)
```

Statistics

Duration: 348 years; 10 generations, average length $348/10 = 35$ years; 57 magistracies, incidence of office, $348/57 = 1$ in 6 years.

Also: Q. Marcius (TP 68)
        Cn. Marcius Censorinus (TP 122)
        Q. Marcius Crispus (Pr 46, Pc 45–43)
        Q. Marcius Scilla (Pr 172)
        M. Marcius Sermo (Pr172)

Commentary

A family that emerged during the fourth century, a little hesitantly at first, but with regular consular rank from 357 onwards for a century. (The two military tribunes with consular power in the first generation are presumably members of this family, perhaps brothers, and perhaps brothers of the Lucius attested as the father of the consul of 357, but they cannot be definitely connected.) The fifth generation, of which Marcus was Rex Sacrorum, seems not to have reached even praetorian rank, but from the next generation consulships were regularly achieved for the next century and a half. The family shows several branches, not all of which were politically active all the time. The Censorinus branch with the consul of 149 would seem to be descended from the consul of 310, but the intervening names are not known. It was a family that on the whole successfully negotiated the revolution, and were Caesarians all through – one member had tried to shield Julius Caesar on the Ides of March, and the consul of 56 was the second husband of Augustus' mother. The Philippus line died out, but the Censorinus line and that of Rex lived on into the early empire.

Marius (plebeian), 119–62 BC

```
        C.Marius
          |
        C.Marius
          |
1          C. Marius           M. Marius       M. Marius
      (Tp 119; Pr 115; Pp 114;  (Pr 102, Pp 101) (Pr 99)
      Cos 107, 104, 103, 102,
      101, 100, 86; Pc 106,
      105, 90, 88, 87)
          |
2          C. Marius                M. Marius Gaditanus
        (Cos 82)                      (Pr 85, 82)

3                                   M. Marius (TP 62)
```

Statistics

Duration: 57 years; 3 generations, average length 57/3 = 19 years;
22 magistracies, incidence of office 57/22 = 1 in 3 years.

Commentary

The family of the warrior Marius, conqueror of Jugurtha and of the invading Cimbri, is difficult to tabulate. I have assumed that the men listed above are in fact all one family, though the sources to demonstrate this are not extant. What is particularly noticeable is that the family essentially consisted of one man and his achievements – fifteen magistracies out of the family's twenty-two were his responsibility.

Menenius (patrician), 503–356 BC

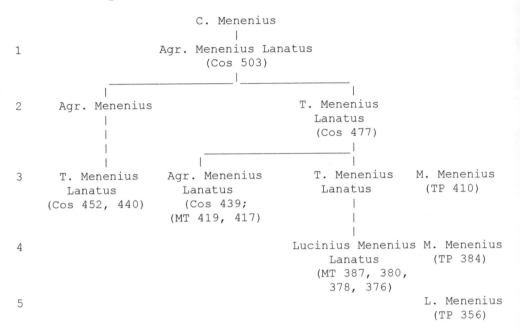

```
                        C. Menenius
                            |
1                   Agr. Menenius Lanatus
                         (Cos 503)
         _____|_____
         |                                      |
2    Agr. Menenius                          T. Menenius
         |                                     Lanatus
         |                                    (Cos 477)
         |                                        |
         |                        _____|
         |                        |               |
3    T. Menenius         Agr. Menenius     T. Menenius    M. Menenius
       Lanatus               Lanatus         Lanatus       (TP 410)
   (Cos 452, 440)          (Cos 439;            |
                           (MT 419, 417)        |
                                                |
4                                       Lucinius Menenius M. Menenius
                                             Lanatus        (TP 384)
                                          (MT 387, 380,
                                             378, 376)
5                                                        L. Menenius
                                                           (TP 356)
```

Statistics
Duration: 147 years; 5 generations, average length 147/5 = 29 years;
14 magistracies, incidence of office, 147/14 = 1 in 10 years.

Commentary
A family with access to positions of power in the early years of the republic
but which appears to have died out in the early fourth century. The third and
fourth generations were clearly active and successful politically, which would
normally mean at least one more generation would achieve high office. The
three disconnected Menenii who were tribunes of the plebs between 410 and
356 cannot be linked genealogically, but it seems reasonable to count them
as family. The absence of office holders after the events the 360s BC strongly
implies the extinction of the family after the tribune of 356.

Minucius, 497–439, 505–49 BC

A   *Minucius Augurinus* (patrician), 497-439 BC.

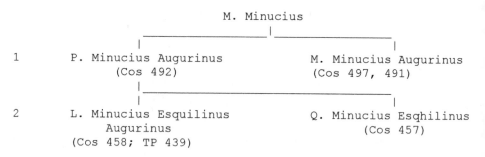

```
                              M. Minucius
          _____|_____
          |                                             |
1    P. Minucius Augurinus              M. Minucius Augurinus
         (Cos 492)                         (Cos 497, 491)
          |
          |_____
          |                                           |
2    L. Minucius Esquilinus              Q. Minucius Esqhilinus
         Augurinus                          (Cos 457)
      (Cos 458; TP 439)
```

Statistics

Duration: 58 years; 2 generations, average length 58/2 = 29 years;
6 magistracies, incidence of office, 58/6 = 1 in 10 years.

B   *Minucius Rufus/Thermus* (plebeian), 305-49 BC.

```
1                           Ti. Minucius Augurinus (Cos 305)
                                         |
2                                 C. Minucius
                                         |
3                                 C. Minucius               L. Minucius
            _____|                      |
            |                            |                      |
4      C. Minucius              M. Minucius Rufus         Q. Minucius
            |                   (Cos 221; Meq 217;             |
            |                        Dict 217)                 |
5      Q. Minucius Rufus                                Q. Minucius Thermus
       (Pr 200; Cos 197)                               (TP 201; Pr 196; Cos 1
            |                                            (Pp 195; 192-190)
            |                                        _____|___
            |                                        |              |
6      Q. Minucius                              L. Minucius    Q. Minuciu
            |_____                Thermus     Thermus
            |                       |                             (Pr 164)
7 M. Minucius Rufus       Q. Minucius
  (TP 121; Pr c.113;        (Pr 110)
  Cos 110; Pc 109-106)         |
                               |
8                     M. Minucius Thermus
                        (Pr 81; Pp 80)
                               |
9                     Q. Minucius Thermus
                  (TP 62; Pr 58; Pp 52-49)
```

Statistics

Duration: 256 years; 9 generations, average length 256/9 = 28 years;
30 magistracies, incidence in office, 256/30 = 1 in 9 years.

Also: M. Minucius (TP 401)
        M. Minucius (TP 216)
        C. Minucius Augurinus (TP 184)
        Ti. Minucius Molliculus (Pr 180)
        M. Minucius Rufus (Pr 177)
        Minucius (TP 133)
        Minucius (TP c.91)
        A. Minucius Thermus (Pr 67)
        Q. Minucius Thermos (Pr 51)
        L. Minucius Basilis (Pr 45)
        Minucius (Pr 43)

Commentary

Two distinct dynasties, separated in time and by status (one patrician, one
plebeian) but linked by the cognomen Augurinus, which also appears in the
names of several monetary officials and tribunes of the plebs during the second
and first centuries BC. Either one branch slid over to plebeian status in the
fourth century, or another Minucian family adopted the honorific cognomen.

The patrician family did not last very long, though there may be other
members, such as Sp. Minucius, who is poorly recorded as Pontifex Maximus
in 420 and M. Minucius the tribune of the plebs of 401. They, and a
distressingly large number of later possible members, cannot be fitted into the
table. The plebeian family had a rather longer existence than the patrician, but
its occupation of elective offices is somewhat intermittent, despite there being
several branches of the family in operation.

Mucius (plebeian), 220–95 BC

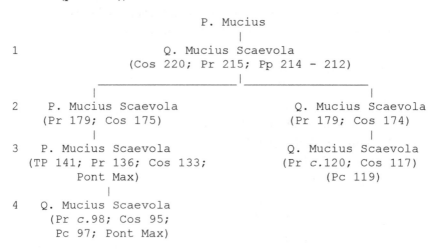

```
                              P. Mucius
                                  |
1                        Q. Mucius Scaevola
                     (Cos 220; Pr 215; Pp 214 - 212)
                                  |
          |_____|_____
          |                                               |
2    P. Mucius Scaevola                      Q. Mucius Scaevola
     (Pr 179; Cos 175)                       (Pr 179; Cos 174)
          |                                               |
3    P. Mucius Scaevola                       Q. Mucius Scaevola
   (TP 141; Pr 136; Cos 133;                 (Pr c.120; Cos 117)
        Pont Max)                                 (Pc 119)
          |
4    Q. Mucius Scaevola
     (Pr c.98; Cos 95;
      Pc 97; Pont Max)
```

Statistics

Duration: 125 years; 4 generations, average length 125/4 = 31 years;
20 magistracies, incidence of office, 125/20 = 1 in 6 years.

Also: Q Mucius Orestinus (TP 64)
         P Mucius Scaevola (TP 54)

Commentary

It seemed that the consul of 220 either abdicated or was elected in a faulty way, and so he may perhaps not be correctly reckoned as consul (though his colleagues apparently did so). His sons, however, were more successful, and his grandsons also, adding the prestigious post of Pontifex Maximus to their other offices. There are Mucii recorded during the next generation, but the family failed to maintain its occupation of the higher offices into the Imperial period. In effect, the members failed to be elected to the most important offices once the revolution got under way.

Mummius (plebeian), 187–70 BC

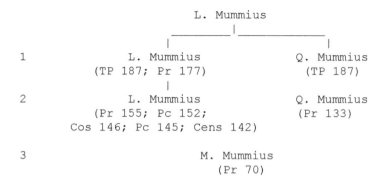

```
                        L. Mummius
                  _____|_____
                 |                          |
1            L. Mummius              Q. Mummius
          (TP 187; Pr 177)            (TP 187)
                 |
2            L. Mummius              Q. Mummius
          (Pr 155; Pc 152;           (Pr 133)
       Cos 146; Pc 145; Cens 142)

3                          M. Mummius
                            (Pr 70)
```

Statistics
Duration: 117 years; 3 generations, average length 117/3 = 29 years;
10 magistracies, incidence of office, 117/10 = 1 in 12 years.

Commentary
The consul of 146 was the victor in the war against the Achaian League, and
the destroyer of Corinth. It is reputed that he became very wealthy from
the loot he collected. But it is clear that this did not translate into a family
history of power. It is, so to say, a one-man family, like that of Marius. The
connections of the praetors of 133 and 70 with the rest of the family, assuming
there were some, are not known.

Nautius (patrician), 488–287 BC

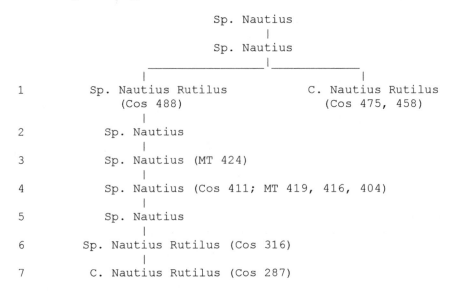

```
                              Sp. Nautius
                                   |
                              Sp. Nautius
              _____|_____
             |                                    |
1       Sp. Nautius Rutilus              C. Nautius Rutilus
           (Cos 488)                        (Cos 475, 458)
             |
2         Sp. Nautius
             |
3         Sp. Nautius (MT 424)
             |
4         Sp. Nautius (Cos 411; MT 419, 416, 404)
             |
5         Sp. Nautius
             |
6     Sp. Nautius Rutilus (Cos 316)
             |
7      C. Nautius Rutilus (Cos 287)
```

Statistics

Duration: 201 years; 7 generations, average length, 201/7 = 29 years;
10 magistracies, incidence in office 201/10 = 1 in 20 years.

Commentary

A family that produced a consul, or equivalent, in most of the early republican generations, but one not apparently very fertile in extra sons. The succession as shown in the table is not fully attested by evidence, but the family certainly produced office holders regularly. There were two generations (2 and 5) without officials, and it seems likely that the family simply died out. (It might be better to insert another generation between the fifth and sixth.)

Octavius (plebeian), 205–74 BC

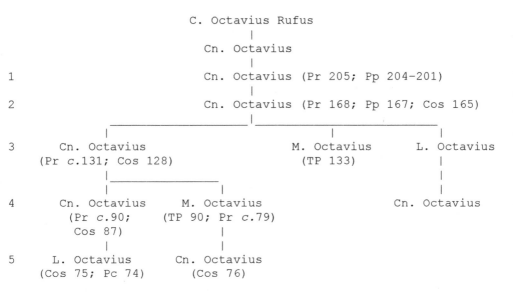

```
                      C. Octavius Rufus
                             |
                       Cn. Octavius
                             |
1                      Cn. Octavius (Pr 205; Pp 204-201)
                             |
2                      Cn. Octavius (Pr 168; Pp 167; Cos 165)
          _____|_____
          |                        |              |
3     Cn. Octavius            M. Octavius      L. Octavius
      (Pr c.131; Cos 128)       (TP 133)          |
          |_____                     |
          |                 |                      |
4     Cn. Octavius      M. Octavius          Cn. Octavius
       (Pr c.90;       (TP 90; Pr c.79)
        Cos 87)              |
          |                  |
5     L. Octavius       Cn. Octavius
      (Cos 75; Pc 74)    (Cos 76)
```

Statistics
Duration: 131 years; 5 generations, average length 131/5 = 26 years;
18 magistracies, incidence in office 131/18 = 1 in 7 years.

Also: Cn. Octavius Q.f. Ruso (Pr 90)
        C. Octavius (Pr 61)

Commentary
A family (not apparently related to that of Augustus) that climbed very
satisfactorily to a notable series of offices between 168 and 75, despite the
consul of 165 allowing his arrogance to leave him open to assassination while
on a Syrian diplomatic mission. The family then faded out, probably as a
result of the revolution and its casualties, in the first century BC.

See also, L. Pietala-Castren, 'The Ancestry and Career of Cn. Octavius',
Arctos 18, (1984) pp. 75–92.

Otacilius (plebeian), 263–211 BC

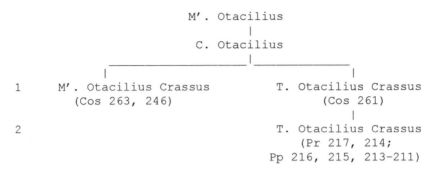

```
                        M' . Otacilius
                             |
                        C. Otacilius
        _____|_____
        |                                      |
1    M' . Otacilius Crassus          T. Otacilius Crassus
       (Cos 263, 246)                    (Cos 261)
                                             |
2                                    T. Otacilius Crassus
                                        (Pr 217, 214;
                                     Pp 216, 215, 213-211)
```

Statistics
Duration: 52 years; 2 generations, average length 52/2 = 26 years;
10 magistracies, incidence of office 52/10 = 1 in 5 years.

Commentary
A brief dynasty, holding offices for only half a century, during which its
members were involved heavily in the fighting in the First and Second Punic
Wars, always, in fact, in Sicily; the praetor of the second generation died in
those wars. It seems likely that this was above all a military family. Descendants
appear in the first century, but never above the rank of legate, fighting on the
republican side in the various civil wars.

Papirius (patrician), 509–62 BC

A *Papirius Crassus* (patrician), 509–176 BC.

```
1                         C. Papirius (Pont Max)
               _____|_____
              |                               |
              ?                               ?
          ___|_____                    _____|_____
         |          |                    |          |          |
2 M. Papirius  L. Papirius  M. Papirius  L. Papirius  C Papirius
   Crassus      Mugillanus   Atratinus    Crassus      Crassus
   (Pont Max)  (Cos 444;    (Cos 441)    (Cos 436;    (Cos 430)
                Cens 443)                  430)          |
           _____|___          _____|          |
          |             |      |      |                     ____|____
3 L. Papirius   M. Papirius   L. Papirius    |          ?   Sp. Papirius
   Mugillanus    Mugillanus        |         |              (MT 382)   |
   (Cos 427; Int (MT 418, 416;     |         |                      |     *
   420; MT 422;   Cos 411)         |         |                      |     |
   Cens 418)    _____|      _____|__           |     |
      |        |          |        |      |         |  |        |     |
      |        |          |        |      |         | Ti.       |     |
     L.       L.         M.       C.      |       Papirius      |
4 Papirius Papirius  Papirius  Papirius   |       Crassus   L.
  Mugillanus Crassus  Crassus  Crassus   Sp.               Papirius
  (MT 382,  (MT 382)     |     (MT 384) Papirius (MT       Crassus
  376, 380;     |        |             Crassus  380)     (MT 368)
  Cens 389)     |        |             (MT 377)
      |         |        |_____
      |         |_____            |
      |        |              |         |            |
5 M. Papirius  L. Papirius   M. Papirius  L. Papirius
      |         Crassus        Crassus     Crassus
      |        (Cos 336, 330;  (Dict 332)     |
      |       Dict 340; Pr 340, 332)          |
      |                                       |
6 L. Papirius                             L. Papirius
      |                                      Crassus
      |                                (Pr 322; Cens 318)
      |
7 L. Papirius
  Praetextatus
   (Cens 272)


4                      * L. Papirius Cursor
                       (Cens 393; MT 387, 385)
                                 |
5                        L. Papirius Cursor
                           (MT 382, 380)
                                 |
6                          Sp. Papirius
                                 |
7                        L. Papirius Cursor
```

```
                    (Cos 326, 320, 319, 315, 313;
          Meq 340, 320; Pr 332; Dict 325, 324, 310)
                                  |
8                        L. Papirius Cursor
                        (Cos 293, 272; Pr 292)
                                  |
9                           C. Papirius
                                  |
10                       C. Papirius Maso
                            (Cos 231)
                                  |
11                        L. Papirius
                                  |
12                       C. Papirius Maso
                            (Pr 176)
```

Statistics

Duration: 333 years; 12 generations, average length, 333/12 = 28 years;
55 magistracies, incidence in office 333/55 = 1 in 6 years.

B   *Papirius Carbo* (plebeian), 168–62 BC.

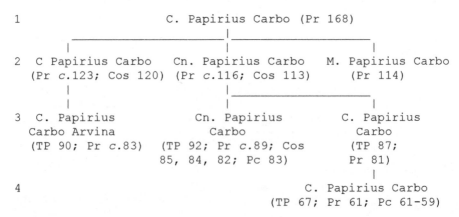

```
1                    C. Papirius Carbo (Pr 168)
                                 |
   _____
   |                          |                          |
2  C Papirius Carbo    Cn. Papirius Carbo    M. Papirius Carbo
   (Pr c.123; Cos 120) (Pr c.116; Cos 113)      (Pr 114)
         |                    |
         |                    |_____
3  C. Papirius          Cn. Papirius          C. Papirius
   Carbo Arvina            Carbo                 Carbo
   (TP 90; Pr c.83)    (TP 92; Pr c.89; Cos    (TP 87;
                        85, 84, 82; Pc 83)      Pr 81)
                                                    |
4                                           C. Papirius Carbo
                                        (TP 67; Pr 61; Pc 61–59)
```

Statistics

Duration: 106 years; 4 generations, average length 106/4 = 27 years;
21 magistracies, incidence of office, 106/21 = 1 in 5 years.

Also: C. Papirius L.f. Maso (Pr 218)
         Q. Papirius (TP *c.*154)

Commentary

The patrician Papirii were assigned some of the sacerdotal elements of the defunct kingship in 509, and moved into political affairs half a century later, with great success, a success in part attributable to their prolific production of sons. The Cursor/Maso branch, also patrician, will be part of the same family. The first Cursor, active in the 390s and 380s, may have been the son of any of the previous generation with the praenomen Lucius; the grandfather of the Maso consul of 231 is presumably the Cursor consul of 293 and 272. (This branch could not be fitted onto the main table, but the generation numbers indicate where they should fit.)

The patrician family ceased to reach office after 176, and presumably died out, its earlier fertility having clearly declined. A plebeian family with the same name and the cognomen Carbo gained office for a century from 168, no doubt helped by the name, but independently. They fell foul of the revolution. The triple consul of 85–82 took the Marian side in the 80s, suffered in the defeat, and only praetorships were available afterwards.

Perperna (plebeian), 133–83 BC

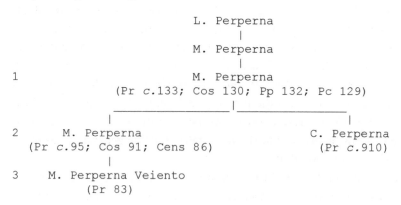

```
                              L. Perperna
                                   |
                              M. Perperna
                                   |
1                             M. Perperna
                     (Pr c.133; Cos 130; Pp 132; Pc 129)
                     _____|_____
                    |                                |
2        M. Perperna                            C. Perperna
    (Pr c.95; Cos 91; Cens 86)                   (Pr c.910)
            |
3     M. Perperna Veiento
          (Pr 83)
```

Statistics

Duration: 50 years; 3 generations, average length, 50/3 = 17 years;
9 magistracies, incidence of office, 50/9 = 1 in 6 years.

Commentary

A brief dynasty, originally out of Etruria, which began with the father of
the consul of 130 acting as an envoy in the 160s (and thus probably holding
at some point a minor magistracy). The males of the family tended to long
lives (the consul of 92 lived on until 49 BC), but no further members can be
detected in office after 82.

Plautius (plebeian), 358–312, 189–55 BC.

A *Plautius Venox, 358-312 BC.*

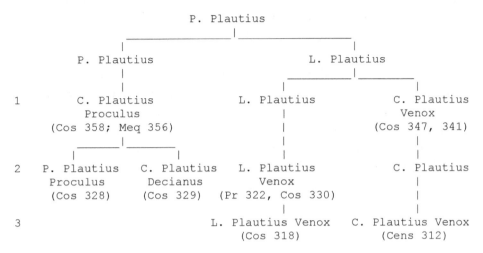

```
                              P. Plautius
                   _____|_____
                   |                                   |
           P. Plautius                           L. Plautius
                   |                         _____|_____
                   |                         |                 |
1          C. Plautius              L. Plautius         C. Plautius
             Proculus                     |               Venox
           (Cos 358; Meq 356)             |             (Cos 347, 341)
           _____|_____              |                   |
           |               |              |                   |
2   P. Plautius    C. Plautius    L. Plautius         C. Plautius
      Proculus       Decianus         Venox                   |
     (Cos 328)      (Cos 329)    (Pr 322, Cos 330)            |
                                          |                   |
3                             L. Plautius Venox    C. Plautius Venox
                                   (Cos 318)           (Cens 312)
```

Statistics
Duration: 46 years; 3 generations, average length $46/3 = 15$ years;
10 magistracies, incidence of office, $46/10 = 1$ in 5 years.

B *Plautius Hypsaeus (plebeian), 189-55 BC.*

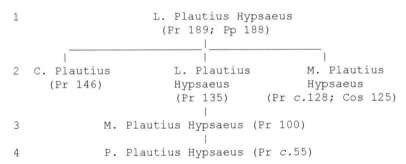

```
1                      L. Plautius Hypsaeus
                          (Pr 189; Pp 188)
        _____|_____
        |                  |                  |
2  C. Plautius      L. Plautius       M. Plautius
     (Pr 146)        Hypsaeus          Hypsaeus
                     (Pr 135)      (Pr c.128; Cos 125)
                                          |
3                 M. Plautius Hypsaeus (Pr 100)
                                          |
4                 P. Plautius Hypsaeus (Pr c.55)
```

Statistics
Duration: 134 years; 4 generations, average length $134/4 = 33$ years;
8 magistracies, incidence of office, $134/8 = 1$ in 17 years.

Also: M. Plautius Silvanus (TP 87)
        A. Plautius (Pr 51)

Commentary

There may be a genetic link between these two families, but no Plautius is on record in any office at any point in the third century BC, so it is best to assume that they are separate dynasties, though a link was later claimed by a Plautian moneyer. The first family was short-lived, the second longer but with fewer magistracies to show for it. The successive offices of the sons of the praetor of 189 suggest helping hands by the three brothers, but the whole second family was distinctly of the second rank, with only one consul in four generations. The first family, however, was clearly successful in its brief career – seven consulships in less than half a century – but appears to have died out.

There was another Plautius family, which was prominent in the early empire (including the commander of the invasion of Britain in AD 43), but it was not connected with either of these earlier families.

Poetilius (plebeian), 360–313 BC

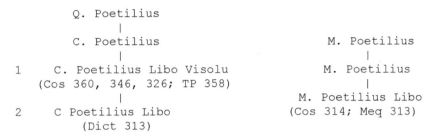

```
        Q. Poetilius
             |
        C. Poetilius                        M. Poetilius
             |                                   |
1     C. Poetilius Libo Visolu             M. Poetilius
      (Cos 360, 346, 326; TP 358)               |
             |                           M. Poetilius Libo
2     C Poetilius Libo                   (Cos 314; Meq 313)
           (Dict 313)
```

Statistics

Duration: 47 years; 2 generations, average length 47/2 = 24 years;
7 magistracies, incidence of office, 47/7 = 1 in 7 years.

Commentary

A family that only just squeezes into this Catalogue. The name is sufficiently unusual to persuade me that, by the repetition of the cognomen Libo, both lines were of one family, though the link between the C. and M. branches must lie deep in the fifth century. Just one more member of the family is known of in later years in a minor office.

Pompeius (plebeian), 141–42 BC

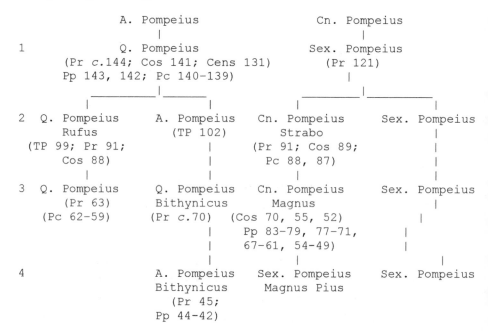

```
                A. Pompeius                      Cn. Pompeius
                    |                                 |
1               Q. Pompeius                      Sex. Pompeius
        (Pr c.144; Cos 141; Cens 131)              (Pr 121)
        Pp 143, 142; Pc 140-139)                      |
                    |                        _____|_____
          _____|_____       _____|                    |
          |                |      |                               |
2  Q. Pompeius      A. Pompeius  Cn. Pompeius          Sex. Pompeius
      Rufus          (TP 102)      Strabo                    |
   (TP 99; Pr 91;        |      (Pr 91; Cos 89;              |
      Cos 88)           |          Pc 88, 87)               |
          |             |             |                     |
3  Q. Pompeius      Q. Pompeius  Cn. Pompeius          Sex. Pompeius
      (Pr 63)       Bithynicus     Magnus                    |
   (Pc 62-59)       (Pr c.70)  (Cos 70, 55, 52)              |
                       |        Pp 83-79, 77-71,    |
                       |        67-61, 54-49)       |
                       |             |              |
4                 A. Pompeius   Sex. Pompeius   Sex. Pompeius
                  Bithynicus    Magnus Pius          |
                   (Pr 45;
                   Pp 44-42)
```

Statistics
Duration: 99 years; 4 generations, average length 99/4 = 26 years;
49 magistracies, incidence of office, 99/49 = 1 in 2 years.

Commentary
The two Pompeian families were certainly related, though they were scarcely
on the best of terms (Strabo the consul of 89 may well have organized the
murder of his consular successor Rufus). The family came from Picentum on
the Adriatic coast. Strabo and Magnus as much as any men were responsible
for initiating the destruction of the republic, with their complete lack of
scruple in the pursuit of their personal ambitions. Neither family could have
expected to succeed otherwise. The family of Rufus slid into praetorian rank;
after Magnus, only his cousin Sextus reached the consulship. (His son, also
Sextus, was eliminated by Octavian before he could take up the consulship he
had bullied his way towards in 35.)

Pomponius (plebeian), 233–161 BC

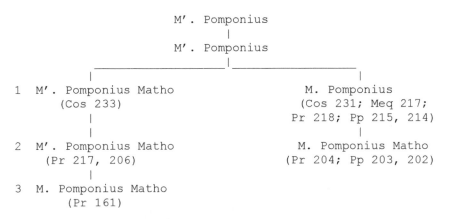

```
                          M' . Pomponius
                                |
                          M' . Pomponius
                                |
        _____|_____
       |                          |                          |
1  M' . Pomponius Matho                           M. Pomponius
       (Cos 233)                                  (Cos 231; Meq 217;
          |                                        Pr 218; Pp 215, 214)
          |                                           |
2  M' . Pomponius Matho                           M. Pomponius Matho
       (Pr 217, 206)                              (Pr 204; Pp 203, 202)
          |
3  M. Pomponius Matho
       (Pr 161)
```

Statistics
Duration: 72 years; 3 generations, average length 72/3 = 24 years;
12 magistracies, incidence of office, 72/12 = 1 in 6 years.

Also: M. Pomponius (TP 449)
        M Pomponius Rufus (MT 399)
        Q. Pomponius (TP 395, 394)
        M. Pomponius (TP 362)
        Cn. Pomponius (TP 90)
        Pomponius (TP 45)

Commentary
The earlier Pomponii between 449 and 362 BC cannot be directly linked to
the family as displayed in the table, but it seems probable they were actually
all one; if so, there was a long gap between 362 and 233, rather too long to be
ascribed to the lack of third century sources. I conclude that the family went
into temporary eclipse.

The revival began with brothers who both reached the consulship in
the 230s, and who showed their public spirit in the war with Hannibal by
taking on several offices. The Pomponius of 161 is not for certain the son
of the man suggested here but may be the son of the praetor of 204. There
are several Pomponii in minor offices in the last decades of the republic, but
effectively the family had faded out (once more) after 161. The members of
the family used the names Manius and Marcus almost exclusively, and in their
abbreviated form their names are easily confused, so the family's history is not
always clear.

Popilius (plebeian), 359–316, 176–68 BC

A   *Popilius Laenas (First)*, 359–316 BC.

```
                    C. Popilius
                        |
                    M. Popilius
                        |
1                M. Popilius Laenas
             (Cos 359, 356, 354, 348)
                        |
2                M. Popilius Laenas
                    (Cos 316)
```

Statistics
Duration: 43 years; 2 generations, average length 43/2 = 22 years;
5 magistracies, incidence of office, 43/5 = 1 in 9 years.

B   *Popilius Laenas (Second)*, 176–68 BC.

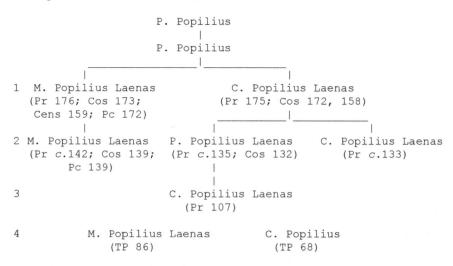

```
                        P. Popilius
                            |
                        P. Popilius
       _____|_____
      |                                      |
1  M. Popilius Laenas            C. Popilius Laenas
   (Pr 176; Cos 173;             (Pr 175; Cos 172, 158)
   Cens 159; Pc 172)               _____|_____
      |                           |                       |
2 M. Popilius Laenas    P. Popilius Laenas    C. Popilius Laenas
  (Pr c.142; Cos 139;   (Pr c.135; Cos 132)     (Pr c.133)
       Pc 139)                   |
                                 |
3                        C. Popilius Laenas
                            (Pr 107)

4           M. Popilius Laenas          C. Popilius
                (TP 86)                   (TP 68)
```

Statistics
Duration: 108 years; 4 generations, average length, 108/4 = 27 years;
16 magistracies, incidence of office, 108/16 = 1 in 7 years.

Commentary
The repetition of the cognomen Laenas guarantees that these are two
parts of the same family, but the connections during the third century have
disappeared; the first known Popilius in the second century could well be
the grandson of the consul of 316. The extraordinary coincidence of the
generation lengths and office holding of the two parts is curious. The large
number of consulships each part accumulated was clearly no guarantee that
their descendants would rise to similar positions.

Porcius (plebeian), 207–54 BC

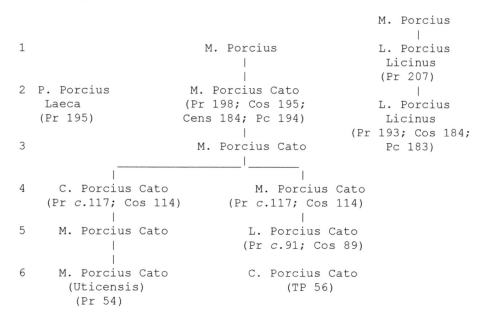

```
                                                        M. Porcius
                                                            |
1                          M. Porcius                   L. Porcius
                               |                          Licinus
                               |                          (Pr 207)
2  P. Porcius            M. Porcius Cato                    |
     Laeca              (Pr 198; Cos 195;                L. Porcius
    (Pr 195)            Cens 184; Pc 194)                 Licinus
                               |                    (Pr 193; Cos 184;
3                        M. Porcius Cato                  Pc 183)
                  _____|_____
                 |                    |
4      C. Porcius Cato           M. Porcius Cato
      (Pr c.117; Cos 114)       (Pr c.117; Cos 114)
              |                         |
5      M. Porcius Cato           L. Porcius Cato
              |                 (Pr c.91; Cos 89)
              |
6      M. Porcius Cato           C. Porcius Cato
        (Uticensis)                 (TP 56)
         (Pr 54)
```

Statistics

Duration: 153 years; 6 generations, average length 153/6 = 26 years;
17 magistracies, incidence of office, 153/17 = 1 in 9 years.

Commentary

Three men called Porcius emerged simultaneously in the latter years of the
war with Hannibal and reached public office in or shortly after that war. It
is highly likely that they were related, and that they assisted each other in
achieving office, but the links are not visible in our sources. The Licinus
line soon died out, and the Cato line was the only one that became fully
established, and that was because a second marriage replaced the eldest son of
Cato, the censor of 184, with a second late-born son. There is thus the curious
circumstance that the son was a contemporary of his nephew (consuls of 118
and 114). The praetor of 54 was the effective end of the family for his son died
in battle in the civil war, as did the father.

Postumius (patrician), 505–54 BC

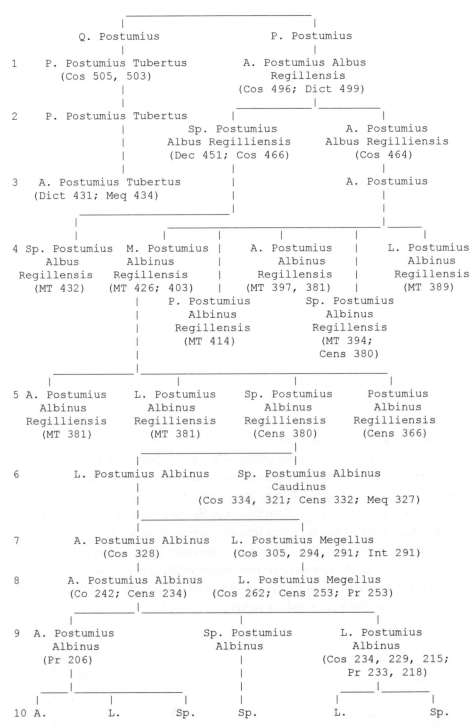

```
                    |                              |
            Q. Postumius                    P. Postumius
                    |                              |
1      P. Postumius Tubertus          A. Postumius Albus
         (Cos 505, 503)                   Regillensis
                    |                  (Cos 496; Dict 499)
                    |
2      P. Postumius Tubertus     |_____|_____
                    |         Sp. Postumius         A. Postumius
                    |       Albus Regilliensis    Albus Regilliensis
                    |        (Dec 451; Cos 466)       (Cos 464)
                    |                 |                    |
3   A. Postumius Tubertus            |           A. Postumius
       (Dict 431; Meq 434)           |                    |
                    |                |                    |
      _____|_____      |                    |
      |                 _____|_____|____
      |               |      |       |       |       |        |
4 Sp. Postumius  M. Postumius |  A. Postumius  |  L. Postumius
     Albus         Albinus    |    Albinus     |    Albinus
   Regillensis   Regillensis  |  Regillensis   |  Regillensis
   (MT 432)      (MT 426; 403) | (MT 397, 381)  |   (MT 389)
                          |  P. Postumius   Sp. Postumius
                          |    Albinus        Albinus
                          |  Regillensis    Regillensis
                          |   (MT 414)       (MT 394;
                          |                  Cens 380)
      _____|_____
      |                 |                |                |
5 A. Postumius    L. Postumius    Sp. Postumius      Postumius
     Albinus         Albinus         Albinus         Albinus
   Regilliensis   Regilliensis    Regilliensis     Regilliensis
    (MT 381)        (MT 381)       (Cens 380)       (Cens 366)
                       _____|
                      |                      |
6         L. Postumius Albinus      Sp. Postumius Albinus
                      |                  Caudinus
                      |        (Cos 334, 321; Cens 332; Meq 327)
                      |_____
                      |                        |
7      A. Postumius Albinus    L. Postumius Megellus
            (Cos 328)       (Cos 305, 294, 291; Int 291)
                      |                        |
8      A. Postumius Albinus    L. Postumius Megellus
     (Co 242; Cens 234)    (Cos 262; Cens 253; Pr 253)
           _____|_____
           |                      |                |
9  A. Postumius        Sp. Postumius        L. Postumius
      Albinus             Albinus              Albinus
    (Pr 206)                 |           (Cos 234, 229, 215;
        |                    |             Pr 233, 218)
     ___|_____    |            ___|_____
     |      |        |       |           |          |
10 A.     L.      Sp.      Sp.         L.        Sp.
```

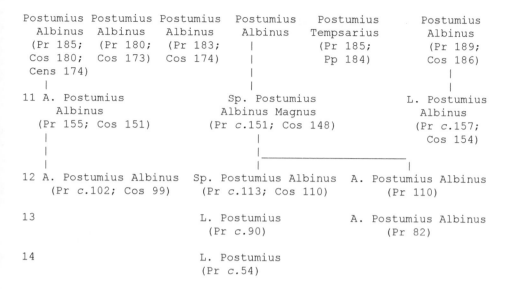

```
Postumius  Postumius  Postumius   Postumius    Postumius           Postumius
 Albinus    Albinus    Albinus     Albinus     Tempsarius           Albinus
(Pr 185;   (Pr 180;   (Pr 183;        |        (Pr 185;            (Pr 189;
Cos 180;   Cos 173)   Cos 174)        |         Pp 184)            Cos 186)
Cens 174)                             |                                |
    |                                 |                                 |
11 A. Postumius              Sp. Postumius              L. Postumius
     Albinus                 Albinus Magnus                Albinus
   (Pr 155; Cos 151)        (Pr c.151; Cos 148)         (Pr c.157;
    |                               |                     Cos 154)
    |                               |_____       |
    |                               |                    |      |
12 A. Postumius Albinus   Sp. Postumius Albinus   A. Postumius Albinus
   (Pr c.102; Cos 99)       (Pr c.113; Cos 110)        (Pr 110)

13                         L. Postumius              A. Postumius Albinus
                           (Pr c.90)                      (Pr 82)

14                         L. Postumius
                           (Pr c.54)
```

Statistics

Duration: 451 years; 14 generations, average length, 451/14 = 32 years;
67 magistracies, incidence of office, 451/67 = 1 in 7 years.

Also: L. Postumius (Cos 457)

Commentary

A remarkably consistently successful family, with members in office throughout
the republic's history, without missing a single generation; a family, moreover,
with direct succession throughout, only in the second century splitting into
subsections. Yet in the end they fade from sight during the revolution. The
praetor of 90 was killed in the Social War, and the praetor of about 54 is
only vaguely recorded; further, neither of these can be connected to the main
genealogical line; a few other men held other offices, but the family apparently
then expired.

Publilius (plebeian), 472–315 BC

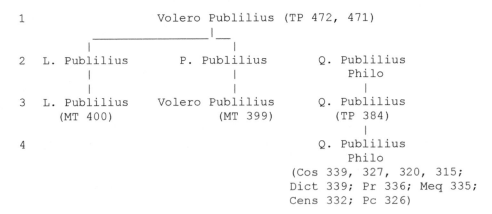

```
1                       Volero Publilius (TP 472, 471)
                _____|__
          |                  |
2   L. Publilius      P. Publilius          Q. Publilius
          |                  |                 Philo
          |                  |                   |
3   L. Publilius      Volero Publilius       Q. Publilius
      (MT 400)            (MT 399)            (TP 384)
                                                 |
4                                            Q. Publilius
                                                Philo
                                       (Cos 339, 327, 320, 315;
                                       Dict 339; Pr 336; Meq 335;
                                       Cens 332; Pc 326)
```

Statistics

Duration 157 years; 4 generations, average length, 157/4 = 34 years;
14 magistracies, incidence of office, 157/14 = 1 in 11 years.

Commentary

The progenitor Volero was a tribune of the plebs early in the fifth century;
his grandsons reached the position of military tribunes with consular power.
The four-time consul was of the same family, judging by the cognomen Philo;
his grandfather would be of the same generation as the tribunes. His four
consulships are two thirds of the total for the family, and there are no others
who can be included. The family faded out; in effect it had been another one-
man family.

Quinctius (patrician), 471–74 BC

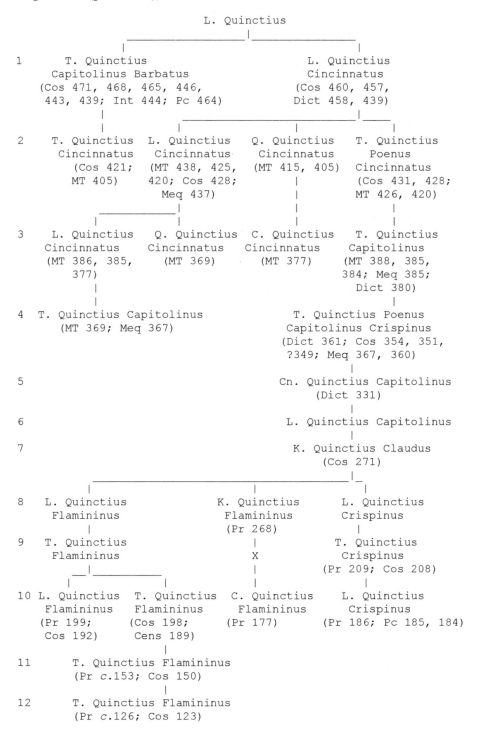

```
                          L. Quinctius
        _____|_____
       |                                        |
1    T. Quinctius                           L. Quinctius
     Capitolinus Barbatus                   Cincinnatus
     (Cos 471, 468, 465, 446,               (Cos 460, 457,
      443, 439; Int 444; Pc 464)             Dict 458, 439)
           |                    _____|____
           |                   |                 |           |
2    T. Quinctius      L. Quinctius      Q. Quinctius    T. Quinctius
     Cincinnatus       Cincinnatus       Cincinnatus      Poenus
      (Cos 421;        (MT 438, 425,     (MT 415, 405)   Cincinnatus
       MT 405)         420; Cos 428;         |           (Cos 431, 428;
                        Meq 437)             |            MT 426, 420)
          _____|                      |                |
         |            |                      |                |
3    L. Quinctius   Q. Quinctius      C. Quinctius     T. Quinctius
     Cincinnatus    Cincinnatus       Cincinnatus      Capitolinus
     (MT 386, 385,   (MT 369)          (MT 377)        (MT 388, 385,
      377)                                              384; Meq 385;
        |                                                Dict 380)
        |                                                   |
4    T. Quinctius Capitolinus              T. Quinctius Poenus
        (MT 369; Meq 367)                  Capitolinus Crispinus
                                           (Dict 361; Cos 354, 351,
                                            ?349; Meq 367, 360)
                                                     |
5                                          Cn. Quinctius Capitolinus
                                                (Dict 331)
                                                     |
6                                          L. Quinctius Capitolinus
                                                     |
7                                          K. Quinctius Claudus
                                                (Cos 271)
        _____|_
       |                             |                   |
8    L. Quinctius            K. Quinctius         L. Quinctius
     Flamininus              Flamininus           Crispinus
        |                    (Pr 268)                |
9    T. Quinctius               |                 T. Quinctius
     Flamininus                 X                 Crispinus
        __|_____          |                 (Pr 209; Cos 208)
       |             |          |                    |
10 L. Quinctius   T. Quinctius  C. Quinctius    L. Quinctius
   Flamininus     Flamininus    Flamininus      Crispinus
   (Pr 199;       (Cos 198;     (Pr 177)        (Pr 186; Pc 185, 184)
    Cos 192)       Cens 189)
                      |
11      T. Quinctius Flamininus
           (Pr c.153; Cos 150)
                      |
12      T. Quinctius Flamininus
           (Pr c.126; Cos 123)
```

Statistics

Duration: 397 years; 13 generations, average length 397/13 = 31 years;
62 magistracies (omitting cos 349), incidence of office 397/62 = 1 in 6 years.

Also: K. Quinctius Flaminius (Pr 218)
         Quinctius (?Pr 143)

Commentary

The long-lived and successful Quinctius family migrated to Rome from
Tusculum (like Cato later) and only appeared in the magistrate lists in the
second generation of the republic. It lasted through to the beginning of the
breakdown of the aristocratic republican system in the late second century,
with just one praetor during the confusion – he cannot be linked genealogically
with the rest of the family, but his name rather guarantees a connection.
The family maintained a very good rate of reaching office until 123, though
with gaps in the third century (when records, to be sure, are poor). In the
second century, however, both lines either died out or simply faded away. The
family did survive into Augustus' reign, when they were awarded a couple of
consulships, but then the family had to adopt sons to continue the name.

Rutilius (plebeian), 169–49 BC.

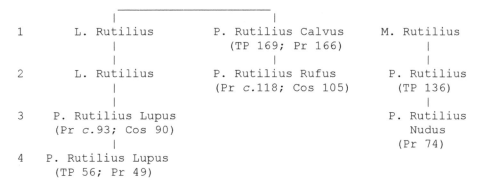

1	L. Rutilius	P. Rutilius Calvus (TP 169; Pr 166)	M. Rutilius
2	L. Rutilius	P. Rutilius Rufus (Pr *c.*118; Cos 105)	P. Rutilius (TP 136)
3	P. Rutilius Lupus (Pr *c.*93; Cos 90)		P. Rutilius Nudus (Pr 74)
4	P. Rutilius Lupus (TP 56; Pr 49)		

Statistics

Duration: 120 years; 4 generations, average length 120/4 = 30 years; 10 magistracies, incidence of office, 120/10 = 1 in 12 years.

Commentary

A family that may have had a third branch (a P. Rutilius, son of Marcus, was a tribune in 136). The connection between the two in the table cannot be documented, but it is clearly probable. The earliest magistrate, the praetor of 166, came up through the ranks of tribunes; his son reached the praetorship but had to wait a long time for his consulship. The third generation seems to have succeeded more easily, but the consul of 90 was killed in battle in the Social War; his son then chose the Pompeian side in 48; the family did not survive the last civil wars.

Scribonius (plebeian), 216–49 BC.

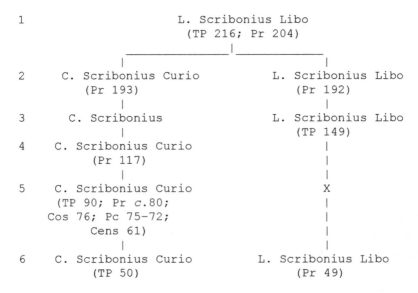

```
1                      L. Scribonius Libo
                        (TP 216; Pr 204)
                               |
        _____|_____
        |                                   |
2    C. Scribonius Curio          L. Scribonius Libo
        (Pr 193)                       (Pr 192)
           |                               |
3    C. Scribonius                L. Scribonius Libo
           |                          (TP 149)
4    C. Scribonius Curio                   |
        (Pr 117)                           |
           |                               |
5    C. Scribonius Curio                   X
     (TP 90; Pr c.80;                      |
     Cos 76; Pc 75-72;                     |
        Cens 61)                           |
           |                               |
6    C. Scribonius Curio          L. Scribonius Libo
        (TP 50)                        (Pr 49)
```

Statistics

Duration: 167 years; 6 generations, average length 167/6 = 28 years; 16 magistracies, incidence of office, 167/16 = 1 in 10 years.

Commentary

A family that was essentially of praetorian rank, with only one member reaching the consulship. Emerging originally in the stress of the Hannibalic War, only the consul of 76 – significant date – had more to show for his political career than a single office. Members of the family, however, did go on to hold offices until the end of the republic.

Sempronius, 497 – 122 BC.

A   *Sempronius Atratinus* (patrician), 497–380 BC.

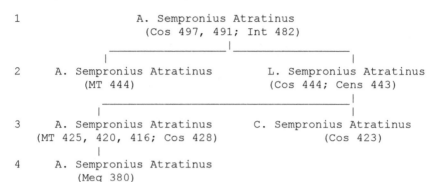

```
1                      A. Sempronius Atratinus
                         (Cos 497, 491; Int 482)
        _____|_____
        |                                               |
2   A. Sempronius Atratinus              L. Sempronius Atratinus
        (MT 444)                            (Cos 444; Cens 443)
             _____|
             |                                      |
3   A. Sempronius Atratinus          C. Sempronius Atratinus
    (MT 425, 420, 416; Cos 428)              (Cos 423)
             |
4   A. Sempronius Atratinus
        (Meq 380)
```

Statistics

Duration: 117 years; 4 generations, average length 117/4 = 29 years;
12 magistracies, incidence of office, 117/12 = 1 in 10 years.

B   *Sempronius Sophus/Gracchus* (plebeian), 304–122 BC.

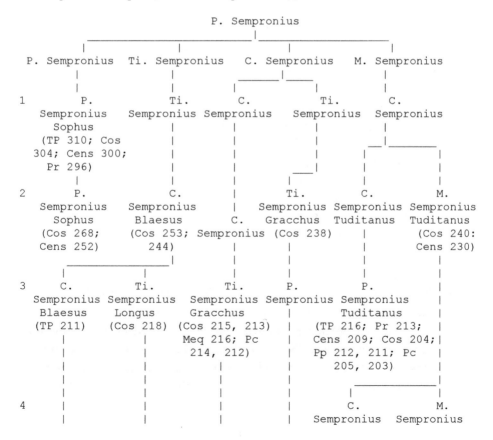

```
                          P. Sempronius
        _____|_____
        |             |              |              |
P. Sempronius  Ti. Sempronius  C. Sempronius   M. Sempronius
        |             |         _____|____         |
        |             |         |       |          |
1       P.           Ti.        C.     Ti.         C.
    Sempronius   Sempronius Sempronius Sempronius Sempronius
     Sophus          |         |         |          |
   (TP 310; Cos      |         |         |       __|_____
   304; Cens 300;    |         |         |       |       |
    Pr 296)          |         |       __|       |       |
        |            |         |       |         |       |
2       P.           C.        |      Ti.        C.      M.
    Sempronius   Sempronius    |  Sempronius Sempronius Sempronius
     Sophus       Blaesus      C.   Gracchus  Tuditanus Tuditanus
    (Cos 268;    (Cos 253; Sempronius (Cos 238)   |    (Cos 240:
    Cens 252)      244)       |         |          |    Cens 230)
      _____|          |         |          |       |
      |            |          |         |          |       |
3     C.          Ti.        Ti.        P.         P.       |
  Sempronius  Sempronius Sempronius Sempronius Sempronius   |
   Blaesus      Longus    Gracchus      |     Tuditanus     |
   (TP 211)   (Cos 218) (Cos 215, 213)  |   (TP 216; Pr 213; |
      |           |       Meq 216; Pc   |   Cens 209; Cos 204;|
      |           |        214, 212)    |   Pp 212, 211; Pc  |
      |           |            |        |     205, 203)      |
      |           |            |        |                    |
      |           |            |        |        _____|
      |           |            |        |        |           |
4     |           |            |        |        C.          M.
      |           |            |        |    Sempronius  Sempronius
```

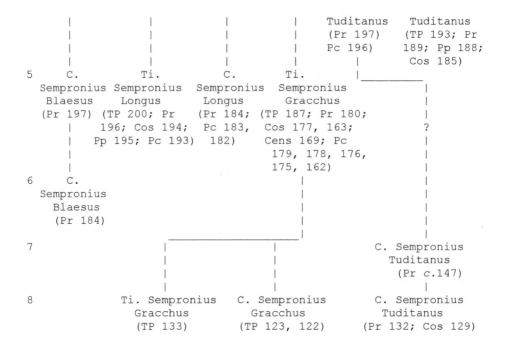

Statistics
Duration: 182 years; 8 generations, average length 182/8 = 30 years;
58 magistracies, incidence in office, 182/58 = 1 in 4 years.

Also: P. Sempronius Blaesus (TP 191)
        P. Sempronius Gracchus (TP 189)
        C. Sempronius Rutilus (TP 189)
        Ti. Sempronius (TP 167)
        L. Sempronius Asellio (Pr 93)
        C. Sempronius Longus (Pr 94)
        A. Sempronius Asellio (Pr 89)
        C. Sempronius Rufus (Pr 44)

Commentary
The Sempronius dynasties are probably different families, since the first was
patrician and the second plebeian – though movement from the former to
the latter was not unknown. The patrician family lasted in power only for
the period of the exclusively aristocratic republic. The plebeian family –
separated from the patrician by only seventy years, but with a very different
set of praenomina and cognomina – lasted rather longer, and had a very

distinguished set of achievements. But the whole family went down to ruin with the two reforming tribunes of 133 and 123/122, who are important enough to be included here, though they did not reach the praetorship. The generational correspondence between the various branches became skewed in the second century.

Sergius (patrician), 437–380 BC.

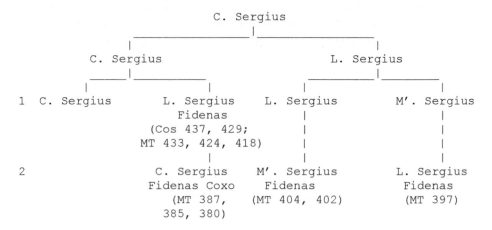

Statistics

Duration: 57 years; 2 generations, average length 57/2 = 29 years;
11 magistracies, incidence in office, 57/11 = 1 in 5 years.

Also: C. Sergius Plautus (Pr 200)
          M. Sergius Silva (Pr 197)
          M. Sergius M.f. (Pr 115)
          L. Sergius Catilina (Pr 68)

Commentary

A brief patrician dynasty that did not achieve political prominence until the
republic was well established and even then, did not last very long. Most of
the offices held by the family were in the time of the military tribunes with
consular power, but the family did continue, and it surfaced again in the
second century with several praetors, including, later, the notorious Catilina;
the connections of these later members, and between themselves and with the
original family, are not in evidence.

Servilius (patrician), 495–44 BC.

A *Servilius Ahala*, 495–351 BC.

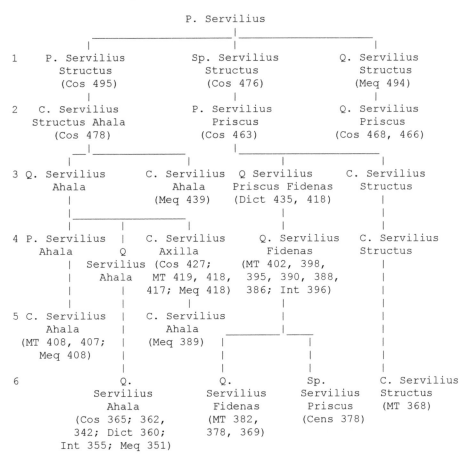

Statistics
Duration: 144 years; 6 generations, average length 144/6 = 24 years;
37 magistracies, incidence of office, 144/37 = 1 in 4 years.

B *Servilius Geminus/Caepio*, (patrician) 284–44 BC.

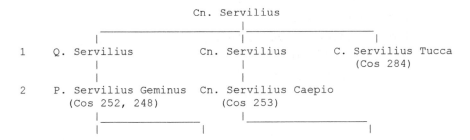

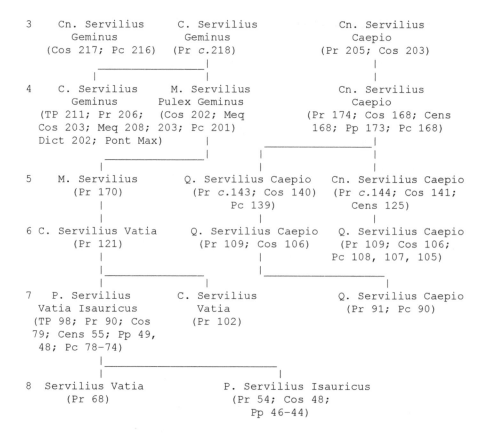

3   Cn. Servilius   C. Servilius   Cn. Servilius
         Geminus   Geminus   Caepio
      (Cos 217; Pc 216)   (Pr *c.*218)   (Pr 205; Cos 203)

4   C. Servilius   M. Servilius   Cn. Servilius
         Geminus   Pulex Geminus   Caepio
      (TP 211; Pr 206;   (Cos 202; Meq   (Pr 174; Cos 168; Cens
       Cos 203; Meq 208; 203; Pc 201)   168; Pp 173; Pc 168)
       Dict 202; Pont Max)

5   M. Servilius   Q. Servilius Caepio   Cn. Servilius Caepio
         (Pr 170)   (Pr *c.*143; Cos 140) (Pr *c.*144; Cos 141;
                              Pc 139)   Cens 125)

6 C. Servilius Vatia   Q. Servilius Caepio   Q. Servilius Caepio
       (Pr 121)   (Pr 109; Cos 106)   (Pr 109; Cos 106;
                                               Pc 108, 107, 105)

7   P. Servilius   C. Servilius   Q. Servilius Caepio
      Vatia Isauricus   Vatia   (Pr 91; Pc 90)
      (TP 98; Pr 90; Cos   (Pr 102)
       79; Cens 55; Pp 49,
       48; Pc 78-74)

8   Servilius Vatia   P. Servilius Isauricus
        (Pr 68)   (Pr 54; Cos 48;
                                    Pp 46-44)

Statistics

Duration: 240 years; 8 generations, average length 240/8 = 30 years;
58 magistracies, incidence of office, 240/58 = 1 in 5 years.

Also: C. Servilius Casca (TP 212)
        C. Servilius Cn.f.(Pr *c.*126)
        C. Servilius Glacia (TP 101; Pr 100)
        Servilius (Pr 88)
        M. Servilius C.f. (Pr 87)
        P. Servilius Globulus (TP 67; Pr 64; Pp 63)
        P. Servilius M.f. Rullus (TP 63)
        C. Servilius Casca (TP 44
        P. Servilius Casca Longus (TP 43)
        M. Servilius (TP 43)

Commentary

A patrician gens of major achievement, with the exception of a break in the fourth century, where no direct connection can be traced between the military tribunes with consular power of the 360s and the father of the consul of 284 – which is exactly the period of the Italian Wars. Cn. Servilius, the first of the second table, is said to be a descendant of C. Servilius Asella in the fourth generation of the first table, but this is rather too vague to be accepted. The second dynasty is also patrician, so there was certainly a genetic connection between the two sets. The first dynasty shows a commendable diligence in acquiring office frequently and with great regularity. The second dynasty was almost as diligent, with occasional gaps in the later third and early first century. Both branches were still active in the time of the first century revolutions, but faded away and went extinct during Augustus' time.

Sextius (plebeian), 202–42 BC

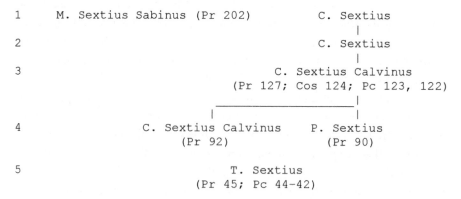

```
1      M. Sextius Sabinus (Pr 202)              C. Sextius
                                                    |
2                                               C. Sextius
                                                    |
3                                          C. Sextius Calvinus
                                      (Pr 127; Cos 124; Pc 123, 122)
                                                                 |
                              _____
                              |                            |
4                 C. Sextius Calvinus           P. Sextius
                       (Pr 92)                    (Pr 90)

5                            T. Sextius
                         (Pr 45; Pc 44-42)
```

Statistics

Duration: 160 years; 5 generations, average length $160/5 = 32$ years;
11 magistracies, incidence of office, $160/11 = 1$ in 14 years.

Also: M. Sextius (TP 414)
         L. Sextius Sex. f. N. Sextinus Lateranus (TP 376, 367, Cos 366)

Commentary

The two unconnected members of the early republic were probably the
ancestors of the men appearing in the table, but no connection over the
intervening century and a half is visible. Generally it was a family able to
reach praetorian rank, but only one member went on to the consulship.

Sulpicius (patrician), 500–42 BC

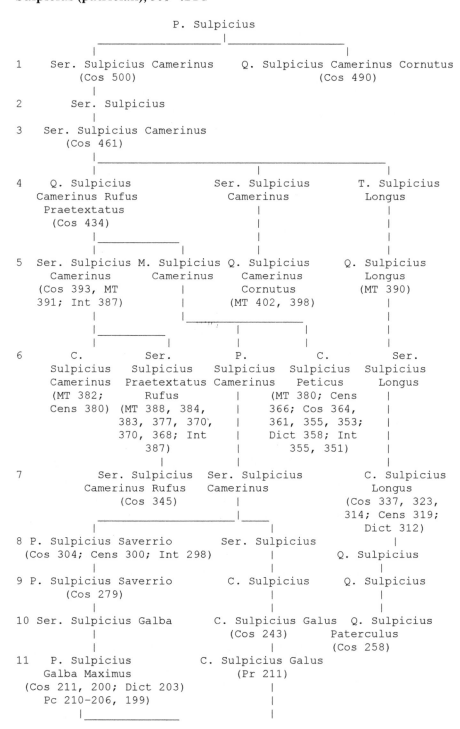

```
                          P. Sulpicius
              _____|_____
              |                                    |
1    Ser. Sulpicius Camerinus      Q. Sulpicius Camerinus Cornutus
           (Cos 500)                        (Cos 490)
              |
2       Ser. Sulpicius
              |
3    Ser. Sulpicius Camerinus
         (Cos 461)
              |_____
              |                      |                        |
4     Q. Sulpicius          Ser. Sulpicius           T. Sulpicius
      Camerinus Rufus          Camerinus                Longus
      Praetextatus                 |                       |
        (Cos 434)                  |                       |
            |_____           |                       |
            |          |           |                       |
5    Ser. Sulpicius M. Sulpicius Q. Sulpicius       Q. Sulpicius
      Camerinus    Camerinus    Camerinus             Longus
      (Cos 393, MT     |        Cornutus             (MT 390)
      391; Int 387)    |        (MT 402, 398)            |
            |          |                                 |
            |_____   |_____                   |
            |      |          |       |                   |
6     C.        Ser.      P.         C.                Ser.
    Sulpicius Sulpicius Sulpicius Sulpicius          Sulpicius
    Camerinus Praetextatus Camerinus Peticus          Longus
    (MT 382;   Rufus        |     (MT 380; Cens         |
    Cens 380) (MT 388, 384, |     366; Cos 364,         |
              383, 377, 370,|     361, 355, 353;        |
              370, 368; Int |     Dict 358; Int         |
                 387)       |        355, 351)          |
                   |        |                           |
7         Ser. Sulpicius Ser. Sulpicius       C. Sulpicius
          Camerinus Rufus  Camerinus             Longus
            (Cos 345)         |               (Cos 337, 323,
          _____|____              314; Cens 319;
          |                   |                  Dict 312)
8 P. Sulpicius Saverrio    Ser. Sulpicius          |
  (Cos 304; Cens 300; Int 298)     |            Q. Sulpicius
          |                        |                 |
9 P. Sulpicius Saverrio     C. Sulpicius      Q. Sulpicius
      (Cos 279)                  |                 |
          |                      |                 |
10 Ser. Sulpicius Galba    C. Sulpicius Galus Q. Sulpicius
          |                  (Cos 243)       Paterculus
          |                      |            (Cos 258)
11   P. Sulpicius          C. Sulpicius Galus
     Galba Maximus           (Pr 211)
   (Cos 211, 200; Dict 203)      |
     Pc 210-206, 199)            |
          |_____        |
```

```
      |                    |                   |
12 Ser. Sulpicius    C. Sulpicius    C. Sulpicius Galus
     Galba               Galba       (Pr 169; Cos 166)
    (Pr 187)            (Pr 171)
      |
13 Ser. Sulpicius Galba
   (Pr 151; Cos 144)
         |_____
         |                              |
14 C. Sulpicius Galba      Ser. Sulpicius Galba
      (Pr 110)             (Pr c.111; Cos 108)
         |            _____|__
         |           |               |
15 Ser. Sulpicius Ser. Sulpicius P. Sulpicius  P. Sulpicius Q.
Sulpicius
      Galba        Galba        Galba      Rufus        Rufus
     (Pr c.91)    (Pr 54)      (Pr 66)    (TP 88)          |
      Pc 90)                   _____|            |
         |                    |                            |
16 C. Sulpicius Galba  P. Sulpicius Rufus        Ser. Sulpicius Rufus
      (Pr c.63)        (Pr 48; Cens 42;            (Pr 65; Int 52;
                        Pc 46,  45)              Cos 51; Pc 46,  45)
```

Statistics

Duration: 458 years; 16 generations, average length, $458/16 = 29$ years; 74 magistracies, incidence of office, $458/74 = 1$ in 6 years.

Commentary

A very successful patrician clan, in office in every generation except one during the lifetime of the republic. There was a lengthy gap in the late third century, after 243, but the family's fortunes then recovered in masterly fashion with the double consul of 211 and 200. A certain falling off is visible in the last republican generation in the main Galba branch, but the Rufus branch (which, like the Paterculus branch to which it may be connected, cannot be certainly linked to the main family) produced two consuls and a censor in the last years. The family survived into the Imperial period, helped by Augustus' policy of restoring and using the old families. The praetor of 45 was the great-grandfather of the emperor, Galba, with whom the whole family expired.

Terentius (plebeian), 218–43 BC

```
1                C. Terentius Varro          Q. Terentius
                 (Pr 218; Cos 216;           (Pr 218)
               Pc 215-213, 208, 207)

2     A. Terentius      L. Terentius      Q. Terentius   C. Terentius
         Varro          Massiliota           Culleo         Istra
      (Pr 184; Pc       (Pr 182)         (TP 189;       (Pr 182)
       183, 182)                          Pr 187)

3           Terentius              M. Terentius Varro
             Varro                      Lucullus
          (Pr 78; Pp 77)        (Pr 76; Cos 73; Pc 72, 71)

4     M. Terentius          Terentius          Q. Terentius
         Varro              (TP 54)               Culleo
       (Pr 67)                                  (Pr 58)

5      M. Terentius Varro Galba
              (Pr 43)
```

Statistics
Duration: 175 years; 5 generations, average length, 175/5 = 33 years;
25 magistracies, incidence of office, 175/25 = 1 in 7 years.

Commentary
The Terentius family suffered the disaster of having the consul of 216 fight
and lose but survive the Battle of Cannae, and though he was employed often
enough in the next ten years, one cannot help feeling that the family's fortunes
lay under that black cloud ever after. Certainly they could be elected as
praetors, but in the rest of the family's history only one more member reached
the consulship. The lack of any parental indications in any of these men's
names makes it impossible to link the various members in a true genealogical
table, but the recurrence of the cognomen Varro is an adequate indication of
relationships. I have arranged them in a probable generational pattern.

Tremelius (plebeian), 202–51 BC

1	Cn. Tremelius Flaccus (Pr 202)
2	Cn. Tremelius (Pr 159)
3	L. Tremelius Scrofa (Pr 135)
4	Tremelius Scrofa (Pr 105)
5	Cn. Tremelius Scrofa (Pr 75)
6	Cn. Tremelius Scrofa (Pr 51)

Statistics
Duration: 151 years; 6 generations, average length $151/6 = 25$ years;
6 magistracies, incidents of office, $151/6 = 1$ in 25 years.

Commentary
The single attested genealogical link between two men in this list is reinforced
by the recurrence of the praenomen Cnaeus and the cognomen Scrofa. The
family was one of those that never reached the highest offices, but consistently
over its history operated successfully as praetors.

Valerius (patrician), 509–53 BC

```
                        Volusus Valerius
         _____|_____
        |                        |                          |
1  P. Valerius Poplicola     M. Valerius              M'. Valerius
   (Cos 509, 508, 507,       (Cos 505)                Maximus   *
       506, 504)                 |
        |                        |_____
        |                        |                |
2  P. Valerius Poplicola     L. Valerius       Vol Valerius
   (Cos 475, 460; Int 462)    Potitus           Potitus
        |                    (Cos 483, 470)          |
        |                                            |
3 L. Valerius Poplicola Potitus        L. Valerius Potitus
        (Cos 449)                               |
        |                                       |
4 L. Valerius Poplicola Potitus      C. Valerius Potitus Volusus
   (MT 414, 406, 403, 401, 398;        (MT 415, 407, 404;
      Cos 393, 392; Meq 390;                Cos 410)
      Int 396, 391, 367)
        |_____
        |                        |                      |
5 L. Valerius Poplicola    P. Valerius Potitus    C. Valerius
   (MT 394, 389, 387,       (MT 386, 384, 380,       Potitus
   383, 380; Meq 390)        377, 370, 367)         (MT 370)
        |_____
        |                        |               |
6 M. Valerius Poplicola    C. Valerius       L. Valerius
   (Cos 355, 353; Meq 358)  Potitus           Poplicola
                           (Cos 331;      (Cos 352; Pr 350; Dict
                           Meq 331)        344; Meq 332)
                                |
7                          L. Valerius Flamma


                   Volusus Valerius (From above)
                                |
1                   *  M'. Valerius Maximus
                      (Dict 501, 484; Pr Sen)
                                |
2                   M. Valerius Maximus Lactuca
                           (Cos 456)
                                |
3                   M. Valerius Lactuca Maximus
                           (MT 437)
                                |
4                   M. Valerius Lactucinus Maximus
                           (MT 398, 395)
                                |
5                     M. Valerius Maximus
                                |
6                       M. Valerius Corvus
      (Cos 348, 346, 343, 335, 300, 299; Dict 342, 302;
       Int 340, 332, 320; Pr 347, 308; Cens 307)
                                |
```

```
7                M. Valerius Maximus Corvinus        **
                       (Cos 312, 289, 286)
                               |
8            M'. Valerius Maximus Messala        ***
                     (Cos 263; Cens 252)
                               |
9                   M. Valerius Messala
                        (Cos 226)
                               |
10                  M. Valerius Messala
                    (Pr 193; Cos 188)
                               |
11                  M. Valerius Messala
                (Pr c.164; Cos 161; Cens 154)
            _____|_____
           |                                   |
12 M'. Valerius Messala              M. Valerius Messala
        (Pr 120)                             |
           |                                 |
13 M'. Valerius Messala              M. Valerius Messala
        (Pr 90)                              |
           |                                 |
14 M. Valerius Messala Rufus     M. Valerius Messala Niger
   (Pr 62; Cos 53)               (Pr c.64; Cos 61; Int 55,
                                     53, 52; Cens 55)


7                   L. Valerius Flaccus   **
                        (Meq 321)
                            |
8                  M. Valerius Flaccus
                            |
9                  L. Valerius Flaccus
                        (Cos 261)
                            |
10                 P. Valerius Flaccus
                        (Cos 227)
            _____|_____
           |                          |
11 C. Valerius Flaccus        L. Valerius Flaccus
        (Pr 183)              (Pr 199; Cos 195; Cens 184;
                                 Pc 199; Pr Sen)
                                      |
            _____|
           |                              |
12 C. Valerius Flaccus          L. Valerius Flaccus
           |                    (Pr 155; Cos 152)
           |                           |
13         X                    L. Valerius Flaccus
           |                        (Pr 134; Cos 131;
           |                     Int 82; Meq 82; Cens 97)
           |_____            |
           |                |           |
14  C. Valerius       L. Valerius   L. Valerius
      Flaccus           Flaccus       Flaccus
  (Pr 96; Cos 93;  (Pr c.90; Cos 86; (Pr 103; Cos 100;
   Pc 92, 85-81)     Pc 92, 91)     Int 82; Meq 82;
```

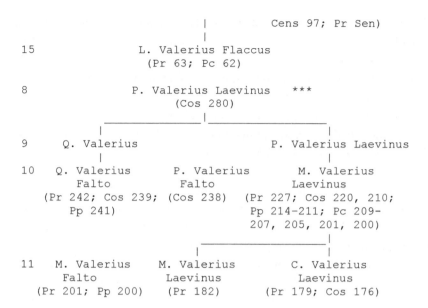

```
                         |            Cens 97; Pr Sen)
                         |
 15              L. Valerius Flaccus
                     (Pr 63; Pc 62)


 8           P. Valerius Laevinus    ***
                    (Cos 280)
             _____|_____
             |                                     |
 9      Q. Valerius                      P. Valerius Laevinus
             |                                     |
 10    Q. Valerius        P. Valerius         M. Valerius
          Falto             Falto              Laevinus
      (Pr 242; Cos 239;   (Cos 238)      (Pr 227; Cos 220, 210;
          Pp 241)                         Pp 214-211; Pc 209-
                                          207, 205, 201, 200)
                                         _____|
                                         |                   |
 11    M. Valerius    M. Valerius         C. Valerius
          Falto          Laevinus           Laevinus
      (Pr 201; Pp 200)  (Pr 182)       (Pr 179; Cos 176)
```

Statistics

Duration: 456 years; 15 generations, average length, 456/15 = 30 years; 151 magistracies, incidence of office, 456/151 = 1 in 3 years.

Also: M. Valerius Triarius (Pr 227)
         L. Valerius Tappo (TP 195; Pr 192; Pp 191)
         C. Valerius Tappo (TP 188)
         Q. Valerius Soranus (TP 82)
         L. Valerius Triarius (Pr 78; Pp 77)
         C. Valerius Triarius (Pr 74)
         P. Valerius (Pr 73)
         M. Valerius (TP 68)
         Q. Valerius Orca (Pr 57, Pc 56)

Commentary

Perhaps the most consistently successful patrician clan in the republic, the Valerii began with six consulships in the first six years after the expulsion of the kings and ended with two consulships in the last years before the Battle of Actium; in between, members of the family acquired a major office every four years.

The family rapidly split into two main branches one of which, the Maximus/ Messala line, showed a remarkable record of direct father-to-son succession throughout the five centuries of the family's republican history. Two further branches developed in the fourth century, the Flaccus line descended from Valerius Potitus ('**'), and that which began with the Laevinus/Falto line, which probably descended from M. Valerius Maximus Corvinus ('***'); these are tabulated separately for space reasons, not because they separated off. All these branches, being patrician, were clearly related to the main original family, though the precise connections in the beginning cannot always be discerned. In a typical way the whole family was periodically and repeatedly refreshed.

At the end of the republic, however, the family was reduced to the Messala and Flaccus lines. The latter faded out, possibly producing descendants but without any political achievements during the empire. The former, however, became involved with the imperial family in the early empire, producing most notoriously the Messalina who was the wife of the emperor, Claudius. There were male members of the family holding consulships until his reign, but this branch also died out. Apart from the Cornelii, the Valerians were the longest-lived of the republican families.

Verginius (patrician), 502–389 BC

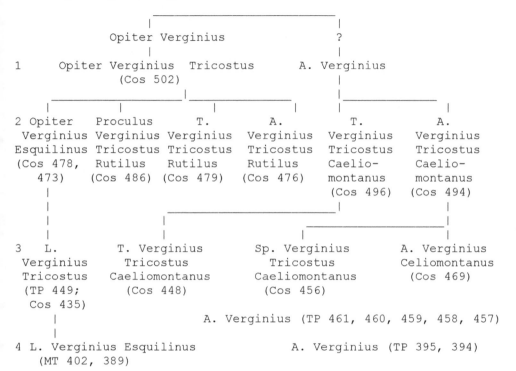

Opiter Verginius	?

1   Opiter Verginius Tricostus   A. Verginius
              (Cos 502)

2 Opiter   Proculus   T.   A.   T.   A.
Verginius Verginius Verginius Verginius Verginius Verginius
Esquilinus Tricostus Tricostus Tricostus Tricostus Tricostus
(Cos 478, Rutilus   Rutilus   Rutilus   Caelio-   Caelio-
  473)   (Cos 486) (Cos 479) (Cos 476) montanus   montanus
                                            (Cos 496) (Cos 494)

3   L.   T. Verginius   Sp. Verginius   A. Verginius
Verginius   Tricostus   Tricostus   Celiomontanus
Tricostus   Caeliomontanus   Caeliomontanus   (Cos 469)
(TP 449;   (Cos 448)   (Cos 456)
 Cos 435)
                        A. Verginius (TP 461, 460, 459, 458, 457)

4 L. Verginius Esquilinus   A. Verginius (TP 395, 394)
    (MT 402, 389)

Statistics

Duration: 113 years; 4 generations, average length 113/4 = 28 years;
22 magistracies, incidence of office, 113/22 = 1 in 5 years.

Commentary

This was a patrician clan that made a good start, but one that would seem
to have deliberately shared out the available offices amongst its members –
seven consulships to the seven members between 502 and 476. If so, this is
a sign of the strict control that the small group of patricians exercised on
the early republic, and a good reason why they lost their control. The family
barely lasted a century and seems to have ceased political activity in the face
of the changes of the late fifth century. Two unconnected members cannot be
directly linked, but their names and offices strongly imply that they were part
of the family.

Veturius (patrician), 499–205 BC

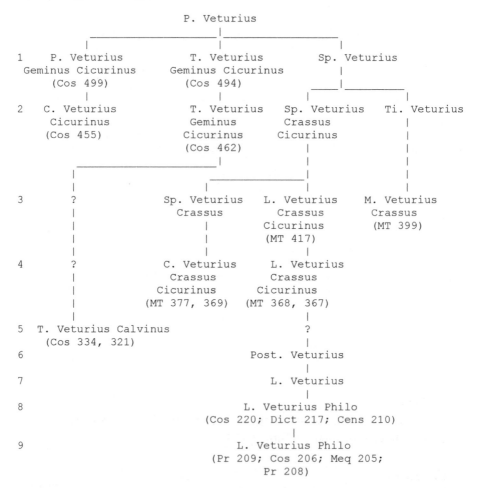

```
                             P. Veturius
          _____|_____
         |                           |                       |
1     P. Veturius               T. Veturius          Sp. Veturius
   Geminus Cicurinus         Geminus Cicurinus              |
      (Cos 499)                 (Cos 494)            _____|_____
         |                           |             |                  |
2     C. Veturius               T. Veturius    Sp. Veturius    Ti. Veturius
       Cicurinus                 Geminus         Crassus              |
      (Cos 455)                  Cicurinus       Cicurinus            |
                                (Cos 462)            |                |
       _____|              |                |
      |                               |       _____|_____          |
      |                               |      |              |         |
3     ?                        Sp. Veturius  L. Veturius  M. Veturius
      |                           Crassus      Crassus      Crassus
      |                              |        Cicurinus     (MT 399)
      |                              |         (MT 417)
      |                              |            |
4     ?                        C. Veturius   L. Veturius
      |                          Crassus       Crassus
      |                         Cicurinus     Cicurinus
      |                       (MT 377, 369)  (MT 368, 367)
      |                                          |
5  T. Veturius Calvinus                          ?
     (Cos 334, 321)                              |
6                                        Post. Veturius
                                                 |
7                                         L. Veturius
                                                 |
8                                      L. Veturius Philo
                              (Cos 220; Dict 217; Cens 210)
                                                 |
9                                      L. Veturius Philo
                                  (Pr 209; Cos 206; Meq 205;
                                          Pr 208)
```

Statistics

Duration: 294 years; 9 generations, average length, 294/9 = 33 years; 19 magistracies, incidence of office, 294/19 = 1 in 15 years.

Commentary

A patrician clan that had a certain success until about 450 BC, but then held only occasional offices until the late fourth century. The consul of 334 was from a branch that expired with him; his precise descent is not known, but his name guarantees his membership. A gap in the fourth century is due to the lack of sources, but the family revived with the two Philones at the end of the third century. This was not sustained, and it is difficult to convincingly connect this group with earlier generations, though since both were patrician and bore the family name and cognomen some connection will have existed. The family is not heard of again after 205.

Section III

Regional Dynasties

Introduction

The following dynasties are distinguished from those of cities and empires by their middling size. Some of them were city based, such as Edessa or Syracuse, but controlled a wider area than was usual for a city-state, while some were large enough almost to be counted as empires, such as the realm of the Ptolemies or the Merovingians. And of course some grew and some dwindled during their lives – the classic example would be Rome, which is included here as a kingdom (for it was always rather more than a single city) and later as an empire in the imperial list, while it is also entitled to its own special section because of the records available of its aristocrats. This regional group constitutes the great majority of the dynasties of the ancient world.

The records of some of these dynasties are often poor, especially in their earliest years. It is evident that in a number of cases the transmitted genealogies cannot be trusted. The practice of constructing a lengthy preliminary genetic inheritance was common in many areas, amongst the Anglo-Saxons a distant descent from the god Woden for example, or amongst the Greeks one of the gods or heroes of the then ancient past (Chapter 2, 'The Mists of Time').

This aspect will be discussed in the individual cases, but it will be worth pointing out that this has meant that some dynasties have had to be excluded altogether because of this practice. It is revealed usually by an insistence on a direct descent over many generations from father to son, whereas any other well-attested genealogy very rarely extends over any more than perhaps four or five generations at the most without the line of descent shifting to a brother or some other relation. The most notable cases of this practice are Macedon, the early Pictish genealogy, Sparta, and Judah.

The most serious casualty in this is the Welsh dynasties. There are lengthy king lists for the main Welsh kingdoms that emerged from the Roman province in the fifth century – Gwynedd, Powys, Dyfed – but they are no more than lists, and, to the modern sceptical eye, they are unconvincing. The names may well be those of kings, but without other evidence that they describe the dynasties accurately, they cannot be accepted. Only two minor Welsh kingdoms, Ergyng and Glywysing, have believable dynastic successions in this early period, and these are derived from charter evidence, not the genealogies.

Adiabene, Mesopotamia, AD *c*.15–116 (fragmentary)

```
1                              IZATES I (?-15/30)
                        _____|_____
                       |              |
2               HELENA    =   MONOBAZOS I (30-36)
              _____|_____
             |                            |
3     IZATES II (36-c.60)      MONOBAZOS II (60-75?)

?5                        MEBERSAPES (-116)   D
```

Statistics
Duration: over 60 years (omitting Mebersapes); 3 generations: average length; $60/3 = 20$ years; 5 rulers: average length of reign: $60/5 = 12$ years.

Commentary
Adiabene was on the borders of Babylonia and Mesopotamia, a former minor province of the Seleukid kingdom, and later a subject kingdom of Parthia, but also a state with its own royal family. It had emerged into brief independence as the Seleukid Empire crumbled but before the Parthian advance resumed. Its dynasty is little known, as the table above shows, except for the five kings, who only impinge on the sources indirectly – Helena may have ruled on behalf of her sons; she is recorded as a convert to Judaism, though this may be a fiction, and Judaism did not become the kingdom's religion. This is no more than a fragment of the dynasty, of little use for any wider study. The last known king, Mebersapes, has a suspiciously Iranian name, and may well be a scion of the Parthian dynasty.

References
MAR Colledge, *Parthian Art* (London, 1977).
J Teixidor, 'The Kingdoms of Adiabene and Hatra', *Berytus*, 46 (1967–1968) pp. 1–11.

Albania, Caucasus, AD *c.*400–510

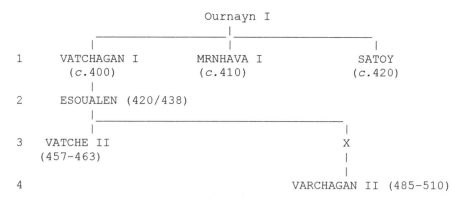

```
                          Ournayn I
             |_____|_____
             |                   |                   |
1      VATCHAGAN I          MRNHAVA I             SATOY
        (c.400)              (c.410)             (c.420)
             |
2      ESOUALEN (420/438)
             |_____
             |                                         |
3    VATCHE II                                         X
     (457-463)                                         |
                                                       |
4                              VARCHAGAN II (485-510)
```

Statistics

Duration: 110 years, reigning for 88; 4 generations, average length 110/4 = 28 years; 6 rulers, average length of reign, 88/6 = 15 years.

Commentary

Albania was a small kingdom in the eastern Caucasus whose kings are known only for a brief period and not accurately. While the dynastic relationships seem well enough established, the dates of the known rulers are largely guesswork, and that of Varchagan II in the fourth generation uncertain. In all probability this was only a section of a much longer dynasty, but more information does not exist. Two generations earlier than Ournayn I are known, but are here omitted from doubts and inaccuracy.

References

D Braund, *Georgia in Antiquity* (Oxford, 1994).
C Tourmanoff, *Studies in Christian Caucasian History* (Georgetown, 1963).

Armenia, 331 BC–AD 428.

A   *Orontids*, 331-202 BC.

```
Darius III*              Hydarnes (satrap c.425-424)
    |               _____|_____
    |              |                 |
Amestris = Terituchmes      Stateira = Artaxerxes III*
          (Satrap)         _____|
                          |
              Rhodogune = Orontes I (satrap (-331)
                          |
1                    ORONTES II (331-330)
                          |
2                    MITHRANES (330-317)
                          |
3                    ORONTES III (317-275)
                          |
4                      SAMOS (275-255)
                          |
5                    ARSAMES (255-228) B
                          |
6                    ABDISARES (228-215) M
                          |
7                    XERXES (215-212) M
```

* Akhaimenid kings

Statistics
Duration: 119 years; 7 generations, average length, 119/7 = 17 years; 7 rulers, average length of reign: 119/7 = 17 years.

Commentary
The first king of this dynasty was Orontes II, who had been satrap of the Akhaimenid province of Armenia in the last years of the Akhaimenid Empire. He was of Akhaimenid royal family descent through his mother, and was appointed as a satrap by the ill-fated Darius III, the last of the Akhaimenid Great Kings, and a distant relative. He took the office in succession to Orontes I, his father. The family thus had strong hereditary local connections in Armenia even before the end of the Persian Empire. Orontes II survived the great Persian defeat at Gaugamela, and then returned to his satrapy, where he maintained himself as the local ruler for a short while. He took the royal title shortly before he died, when he heard of the death of Darius. He passed his ambitions on to his son, who succeeded him and stood off more than one attack by intruding and ambitious Macedonian chiefs after Alexander the Great's death.

The kings moved the political centre of the country northwards, deeper into the tangled Armenian Mountains, to avoid clashing with their powerful Seleukid neighbours. Such clashes could not be wholly avoided, however, and King Xerxes, the last of the dynasty, was compelled to submit to Antiochos III, but was then murdered by his wife, Antiochos' daughter, when she discovered him plotting against her father. Antiochos then set up two new men as joint satraps (see Artaxiad dynasty, next), who defeated and killed Xerxes' son. A branch of the family seems to have survived as local kings in Sophene under Seleukid overlordship, but its connection with the main line is not readily clear.

The dates of the various kings in the table are not wholly reliable, and the relationships can be disputed, but the number of kings and the beginning and end of the dynasty are firm.

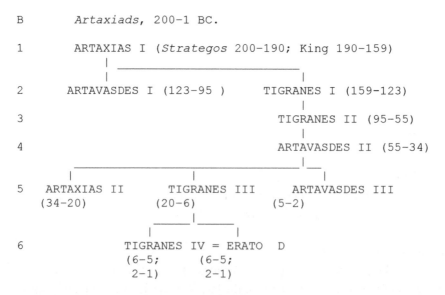

```
B        Artaxiads, 200-1 BC.

1        ARTAXIAS I (Strategos 200-190; King 190-159)
             |
             | _____
             |                                  |
2        ARTAVASDES I (123-95 )      TIGRANES I (159-123)
                                             |
3                                     TIGRANES II (95-55)
                                             |
4                                     ARTAVASDES II (55-34)
        _____|__
        |                    |                 |
5    ARTAXIAS II       TIGRANES III      ARTAVASDES III
     (34-20)           (20-6)            (5-2)
                          |_____
                          |        |
6                TIGRANES IV = ERATO   D
                 (6-5;      (6-5;
                  2-1)       2-1)
```

Statistics
Duration: 199 years; 6 generations, average length, 199/6 = 33 years;
10 rulers, average length of reign: 199/10 = 20 years.

Commentary
The founder, Artaxias I, was appointed as satrap (or *strategos*) by Antiochos III, but, being apparently of local and possibly royal origin, he was able soon to claim the kingship – which Antiochos had earlier suppressed – when Antiochos suffered a catastrophic defeat at Roman hands. (It is claimed that Artaxias was in fact a son of, or at least a descendant of, the Orontid dynasty;

this may be so, but in fact the break indicates that it must be treated as a new dynasty.)

By centring their power deep in the Armenian Mountains, and aided by the slow collapse of the Seleukid dynasty, the Artaxiad kings flourished. Artavasdes I and Tigranes II are not definitely brothers, and on the face of it such a relationship is unlikely: Artaxias I was a mature adult when appointed satrap in 200 so it does not seem very likely that a son of his would be still alive in 95; but Artaxias did live until 159, and it is just possible that Tigranes was a son of his old age. Tigranes II, called 'the Great', briefly became the ruler of a great power in the region, expanding his territory deep into Syria and into Mesopotamia and Iran, but then he bumped up against Rome, and went down to destruction.

The later members of the dynasty found themselves confronting both Rome and Parthia until the family died out with the brother-sister marriage and joint kingship of Tigranes IV and Erato at the end of the first millennium BC. From 1 BC the kingship was in constant dispute, with a rapid sequence of often unrelated kings appointed by the great imperial powers.

```
C    Arsakids, AD 180-428.

1                        VOLOGAESES I (180-191)
                                 |
2                        CHOSROES I (191-216/217)
                                 |
3                        TIRIDATES II (216/7-252)
                    ———————————|———————————
             |                                  |
4     CHOSROES II (279/80-287)    TIRIDATES III (287-298)
             |
5      TIRIDATES IV (298-330)
             |
6      CHOSROES III (330-336, 339)
             |
7      TIGRANES V (339-350)
             |
8       ARSAKES II (350-364) S
             |
9        PAP I (368/9-374)
        ___|_____
        |                    |                 |
10      X                ARSAKES III      VOLOGAESES II
        |                (379-390)        (379-386)
        |
11    VARAZDAT I (374-378)
        |_____
        |                              |
12  CHOSROES IV (384-389)   VRAMSCHAPUH (401-417)
                                       |
13                          ARTAXIAS IV (422-428)
```

Statistics
Duration: 248 years; reigning for 196 years; 13 generations, average length, 248/13 = 19 years; 16 rulers, average length of reign: 196/16 = 12 years.

Commentary
The Armenian branch of the Arsakid Parthian dynasty was installed in AD 66 as a compromise between Rome and Parthia after a major crisis in their relations. The succession for the first century or so is unclear and erratic, and many of the Armenian Arsakids succeeded to the Parthian throne after ruling for a time in Armenia, giving up the lesser to gain the greater. From 180, however, the Armenian branch became locally hereditary and can be reconstructed with some confidence. It survived the destruction of the parent Parthian dynasty in the 220s, but, as can be seen from the table, its tenure of the Armenian throne was always precarious, and subject to the blundering attentions of the great empires that were its neighbours. There were thus interruptions in the dynasty's control in 252–279, in the 330s, the 360s, the 390s and in 417–422. All this makes precision in reconstructing the dynasty very difficult, and this table has to be taken as only approximately correct in all particulars.

References
M Chahin, *The Kingdom of Armenia* (Beckenham, Kent, 1987).
ML Chaumont, 'L'Armenie entre Rome et l'Iran I: De l'avenement d'Auguste a l'avenement de Diocletian', *Aufsteig und Niedergang des Romischen Welt* II, 9.1 (1977) pp. 71–194.
A Grousset, *Histoire de l'Armenie* (Paris, 1947).

Atropatene, Iran, 67 BC–AD 6 (fragmentary)

```
              ATROPATES (in 323 BC)

              ARTAVASDES (in 221 BC)

1             MITHRADATES I (in 67 BC)

2             DARIUS the Mede (in 65 BC)

3             ARIOBARZANES I
                  |
4             ARTAVASDES I (-20 BC)
                  |
5             ARIOBARZANES II (20 BC-AD 4)
                  |
6             ARTAVASDES II (AD 4-6)
```

Statistics
Duration: 73 years; 6 generations, average length, 73/6 = 12 years; 6 rulers, average length of reign, 73/6 = 12 years.

Commentary
Atropatene emerged as a kingdom in the aftermath of the Macedonian conquest, named for the Akhaimenid satrap Atropates, who was reappointed by Alexander. He quietly detached the land from Macedonian rule in the confusion after Alexander's death, and the kingdom maintained an out-of-the-way quasi-independence all through the Hellenistic period. The dynasty was recognized as continuous from Atropates until the first century BC, but the intervening links cannot now be traced, and this continuity may not be correct. The kings are only known from occasional names until the Roman conquest of Syria, and the dates of Mithradates, Darius the Mede and Ariobarzanes I are not accurately known, though it may be presumed that Mithradates had died by 65, when Darius was recorded as king. Nor is the relationship between these three clear; that the dynasty had been reputed to be continuous persuades me to make all these a single family.

This therefore is a mere fragment of a much longer dynasty, which began much earlier than Mithradates and lasted beyond these men and dates. The dynasty, as with others in this area and period, became entangled in the Roman and Parthian advances, and intermarried with the Arsakids; later kings appear to have been Arsakids, the kingdom being used as a sub-state of the Parthian Empire.

References
RD Sullivan, 'Papyri reflecting the Eastern Dynastic Network', *Aufstieg und Niedergan des Romische Welt*, II 8 (1977) pp. 908–937.
RD Sullivan, *Near Eastern Royalty and Rome* (Toronto, 1989).
Ronald Syme, 'The Dynasty of Media Atropatene', *Anatolica*, pp. 308–316.

Attalids, Asia Minor, 281–128 BC.

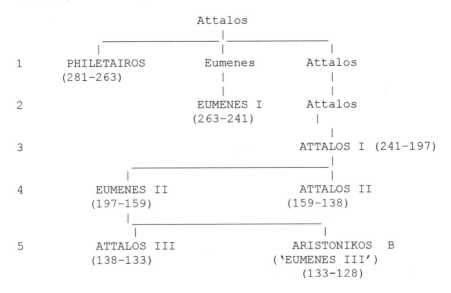

```
                          Attalos
                             |
      _____|_____
      |                       |                        |
1   PHILETAIROS            Eumenes                  Attalos
    (281-263)                 |                        |
                              |                        |
2                          EUMENES I                Attalos
                           (263-241)                   |
                                                       |
3                                            ATTALOS I  (241-197)
                                                       |
                        _____|
                        |                              |
4                   EUMENES II                    ATTALOS II
                    (197-159)                      (159-138)
                        |
                        |_____
                        |                              |
5                   ATTALOS III                   ARISTONIKOS   B
                    (138-133)                     ('EUMENES III')
                                                    (133-128)
```

Statistics
Duration: 153 years; 5 generations, average length 153/5 = 31 years; 7 rulers, average length of reign: 153/7 = 22 years.

Commentary
The first of the family to rule in Pergamon, Philetairos, had been placed there as royal governor and treasurer by King Lysimachos and was not removed by Seleukos I when he defeated Lysimachos and took over his kingdom. When Seleukos himself was murdered less than a year after his victory, Philetairos took advantage of the subsequent confusion to effect his independence, helping himself to the treasure left in his keeping by Lysimachos; by seeing to the funeral ceremonies for Seleukos he gained the gratitude of Antiochos I, and this provided a useful basis for his continuing rule in Pergamon, for the moment as a Seleukid vassal.

Philetairos had no sons (he was said, by his enemies, to be a eunuch), and was succeeded by his nephew, who had no direct successor either, though Eumenes I expanded his territory from a single city to the size of a small province, and took the title of king after defeating the Seleukid Antiochos I, or one of his generals, in a minor battle. The kings also gained a high reputation by staunchly fighting against the invading Galatians, defending not only their own territory but the nearby Greek cities as well.

The family was very close-knit, with no internecine family disputes at all during its history that we know of, until the very end. Attalos III, another childless king, bequeathed the state, by then controlling half of Asia Minor, to the Roman Republic. His half-brother Aristonikos (said to be the son of a concubine) disputed this, and kept the Romans busy for five years before succumbing to their armies. The repeated failure of direct heirs in the family – four of the rulers had no children – implies a genetic deficiency (and so throws some doubt on the story of Philetairos as a eunuch). The one king with several sons, Attalos I (who had four), was also the most vigorous politically and the longest-lived.

References
RE Allen, *The Attalids of Pergamon, a Constitutional History* (Oxford, 1983).
EV Hansen, *The Attalids of Pergamon*, 2nd ed. (Ithaca, 1971).

Ausan, Arabia, *c.*90–*c.*20 BC (a fragment only)

```
1        MA'ADIL I (90-75)
             |
2        YASDAQIL FARI'IM I (75-60)
             |
3        MA'ADIL II SALHA (60-45)
             |
4   YADAQIL FARI'IM SHARABHAT (45-20)
```

Statistics
Duration, about 70 years; 4 generations, average length, 70/4 = 17 years;
4 rulers, average length of reign, 70/4 = 17 years.

Commentary
Ausan was a small kingdom in south Arabia, poorly known now, whose
independence was brief and intermittent. Out of a longer list of kings this
one family of kings in an independent period can be reconstructed, but the
dynasty is dated without any precision.

References
KA Kitchen, *Documentation of Ancient Arabia*, I (Liverpool, 1994).

Babylon, *c.*1003–813 BC

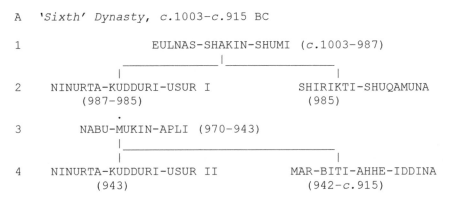

A *'Sixth' Dynasty, c.1003-c.915 BC*

1   EULNAS-SHAKIN-SHUMI (*c*.1003-987)

2   NINURTA-KUDDURI-USUR I   SHIRIKTI-SHUQAMUNA
         (987-985)   (985)

3   NABU-MUKIN-APLI (970-943)

4   NINURTA-KUDDURI-USUR II   MAR-BITI-AHHE-IDDINA
         (943)   (942-*c*.915)

Statistics

Duration: 88 years (reigning for 73); 4 generations, average length, 88/4 = 22 years; 6 rulers, average length of reign, 73/6 = 12 years.

Commentary

The period between about 1000 BC and 626 BC in Babylonia is confused, the chronology of events and kings is unclear, and the relationships of the numerous kings to one another are just as uncertain. The naming of dynasties is, to a degree, arbitrary, and at times misleading. There are two groups of kings whose relationships are known and can be tabulated as dynasties, however, and the first to be included here is called the sixth dynasty.

The line of descent is not wholly certain between the first and second generations, when there was an Elamite invasion and occupation, but the repetition of the name Ninurti-Kudduri-Usur in the first and third generations, where the first is by no means a distinguished ruler, makes the connection likely, and the dating implies that the first was the second's grandfather.

The date at which the last king, Mar-biti-ahhe-Iddina, ceased to reign is not known. It was certainly before 910, but how long before that date is the problem: there is no evidence that even bears on the point. There was only one king between him and the king who came to the throne in about 895, so I have assigned the intermediary king twenty years, and Mar-biti-ahhe-Iddina a death in *c.*915. Given the instability of the period this dynasty turned in quite a creditable history by lasting for nearly a century, but it essentially amounted to a single long reign, with only brief preliminary members and failing successors.

B   *'Eighth'* Dynasty, c.895–813.

1   NABU-SHUMA-UKIN I (*c*.895–*c*.887)
                                    |
2   NABU-APLA-IDDINA (*c*.887–*c*.855)
                                    |
3   MARDUK-ZAKIR-SHUMI (*c*.855–*c*.827)
                                    |
4   MARDUK-BALASSI-IQBI (*c*.827–813)   D

Statistics
Duration: 82 years; 4 generations, average length 82/4 = 21 years; 4 rulers,
average length of reign, 82/4 = 21 years.

Commentary
The dates of the first three kings are approximate only, but they are not out
by more than a few years. The date of the deposition of Marduk-balassi-iqbi
is certain – he was captured by the Assyrians and taken to Assur, and this
is recorded by the meticulously bureaucratic Assyrians. The calculations
are thus fairly reliable, as are the relationships. This dynasty presided over a
cultural revival at Babylon, assisted by friendship and alliance between Nabu-
apli-Iddina and the Assyrian king, Shalmaneser. But Marduk-zakir-shumi
took advantage of a rebellion against the next Assyrian king, and his two
successors, including his son, saw their kingdom destroyed by an Assyrian
attack.

(See also 'Neo-Babylonian' in the imperial list.)

References
EJ Brinkman, *Political History of the Post-Kassite Babylonia* (Rome, 1968).
KA Kitchen, *Documentation for Ancient Arabia*, I (Liverpool, 1994).
JG McLean, *Babylon* (London, 1964).
G Roux, *Ancient Iraq* 2nd ed. (Harmondsworth, 1980).

Baktria, Central Asia, 235–55 BC

A   *Euthydemids*, 235-85 BC.

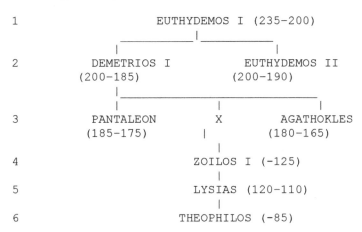

```
1                      EUTHYDEMOS I (235-200)
                 _____|_____
          |                              |
2     DEMETRIOS I                  EUTHYDEMOS II
      (200-185)                    (200-190)
          |
          |_____
          |                    |                 |
3     PANTALEON                 X            AGATHOKLES
      (185-175)                 |            (180-165)
                                |
4                        ZOILOS I (-125)
                                |
5                        LYSIAS (120-110)
                                |
6                      THEOPHILOS (-85)
```

Statistics

Duration: 150 years; 6 generations, average length $150/6 = 25$ years; 8 rulers, average length of reign: $150/8 = 19$ years.

B   *Antimachids*, 190-70 BC.

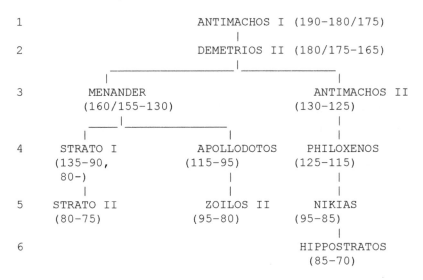

```
1                            ANTIMACHOS I (190-180/175)
                                        |
2                            DEMETRIOS II (180/175-165)
              _____|_____
          |                                           |
3     MENANDER                               ANTIMACHOS II
      (160/155-130)                          (130-125)
       ____|_____                       |
      |                    |                        |
4  STRATO I          APOLLODOTOS              PHILOXENOS
   (135-90,          (115-95)                 (125-115)
    80-)                  |                        |
      |                   |                        |
5  STRATO II          ZOILOS II                 NIKIAS
   (80-75)            (95-80)                   (95-85)
                                                   |
6                                          HIPPOSTRATOS
                                           (85-70)
```

Statistics

Duration: 120 years; 6 generations, average length, $120/6 = 20$ years; 11 rulers, average length of reign: $120/11 = 11$ years.

C   *Eukratidids*, 171-55 BC.

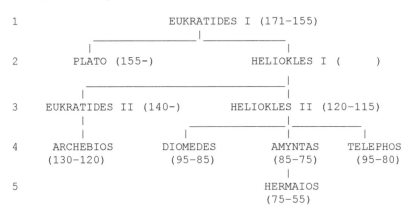

1   EUKRATIDES I (171-155)

2   PLATO (155-)   HELIOKLES I (   )

3   EUKRATIDES II (140-)   HELIOKLES II (120-115)

4   ARCHEBIOS   DIOMEDES   AMYNTAS   TELEPHOS
      (130-120)   (95-85)   (85-75)   (95-80)

5   HERMAIOS
                                         (75-55)

Statistics

Duration: 116 years; 5 generations, average length, 116/5 = 23 years; 10 rulers, average length of reign: 116/10 = 12 years.

Commentary

The evidence for the Baktrian Greek dynasties in the territories east of Iran is exiguous and extremely difficult to interpret, much of it depending on the dating and interpretation of their coins. These three genealogies are based on a few Greek and Indian references, and on a large number of those coins, with a few inscriptions to help out. The relationships and dates are therefore to a large degree conjectural – the round figures of the dates, and the gaps, are a clear indication of their unreliability.

The history of these dynasties is a tale of usurpation and division. Euthydemos I seized the throne from the family of the Seleukid governor of Baktria, who had made himself independent, and Eukratides was also a usurper. The Antimachids' relationship to the Euthydemids is not known, nor are the later histories of the three dynasties, who clearly reigned in parallel, and so in a divided Baktria; they also spread their rule into north-west India. The complete set of kings were suppressed by nomad invaders from the Central Asian steppes, or by being absorbed in India. It may be assumed that violent deaths were common, but only one or two precise cases are known; they are not here included.

References

FM Holt, *Thundering Zeus, the Making of Hellenistic Baktria* (Berkeley and Los Angeles, 1999).

FM Holt, *The Lost World of the Golden King, in Search of Ancient Afghanistan* (Berkeley and Los Angeles, 2012).

RK Narain, *The Indo-Greeks* (Oxford, 1957).

WW Tarn, *The Greeks in Baktria and India*, 3rd ed. (Cambridge, 1951).

Battiads, Cyrenaica, 629–*c*.440 BC

```
1                        BATTOS I  (629-589)
                             |
2                     ARKESILAOS I  (589-583)
                             |
3                        BATTOS II  (583-560)
                     _____|_____
                    |                        |
4      Eryxo = ARKESILAOS II M        LAARCHOS   M
            |  (after 570- )           (c.570)
            |
            |
5        BATTOS III = PHERETIME
         (mid C6)   |   (mid c6)
                    |
6            M  ARKESILAOS III  (pre-525-after 522)
                    |
7               BATTOS IV  (c.515-before 462)
                    |
8         M   ARKESILAOS IV  (pre-462-c.440)
```

Statistics
Duration: 189 years; 8 generations, average length, 189/8 = 24 years;
10 rulers, average length of reign: 189/10 = 19 years.

Commentary
The founder of the Cyrenian monarchy, Battos I, was the leader who emerged from the near disaster of an early colonization project that had been mounted from the island of Thera to what became Cyrenaica. By holding authority for forty years – though this is perhaps a traditional figure merely meaning 'a long time' – Battos was able to pass his position on to his son, and when a third generation continued the line, a monarchy and a dynasty of kings had clearly emerged. This is in a sense also signalled by the relentless repetition of the same 'royal' names in the dynasty.

The fourth generation faced internal unrest, with two kings murdered, and Battos III's wife Pheretime was regent for a time. The lengthy history of the dynasty therefore rather masks its basically insecure position. After 525 the kings were under Persian supervision and probably only maintained their position by means of Persian support. The dynasty fell to internal revolt once that support vanished with the removal of Persian power from Egypt. Note the casualties – four out of the nine kings were murdered.

The dates of all the kings are uncertain, but the overall length of the dynasty is correct to within a couple of years.

References
F Chamoux, *Cyrene sous le monarchie des Battiades* (Paris, 1953).
L Matten, *Kyrene* (Berlin, 1911).

Bavaria, Agilolfing Dynasty, Germany, AD 555–788

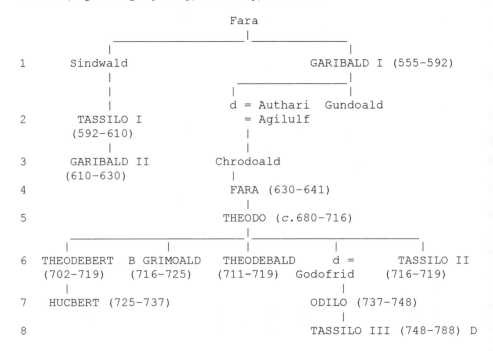

Statistics
Duration: 233 years, reigning for 194; 8 generations, average length 233/8 = 29 years; 12 rulers, average length of reign, 194/12 = 16 years.

Commentary
The first Bavarian ruler (usually regarded as a duke), Garibald I, was put in place by a Merovingian expedition, though he was already a local magnate. He was thus in a difficult position, subject to conflicting pressures from his suzerain and from his subjects. The succession in the family was uncertain for a time, partly, no doubt, because of these awkward pressures. Garibald's daughter married into the Lombard royal family in Italy, but when the Sindwald line failed in 630, Garibald's great-grandson on the Lombard side, Fara, was chosen as duke. By this time the family and the duchy had gained a good deal of local support and independence, mainly as a result of Merovingian weakness, which became steadily worse from the 630s onwards. The succession between Fara and Theodo is uncertain. Theodo's sons divided the kingdom between them, which was reunited under Grimoald, who clashed with his suzerain and died in battle.

As a dynasty the family is thus somewhat disjointed, with their independence always limited by Merovingian interference, or the threat of it, yet their local power also needed Merovingian support. It may in fact be better to see them as two dynasties, the first from Garibald I to Garibald II, and the second from Fara to the end, though they regarded themselves as one. Tassilo III inherited the duchy as a child, and was always dominated by the Carolingians, who replaced the Merovingians in 751, and the independence of the dynasty and the state was eventually suppressed by Charlemagne, despite Tassilo's political manoeuvrings.

References
W Stormer, 'Agilolfinger', *Lexicon des Mittelalters*, 1, pp. 207–208.
I Wood, *The Merovingian Kingdoms 450–751* (London, 1994).

Benevento, Italy, AD 642–758.

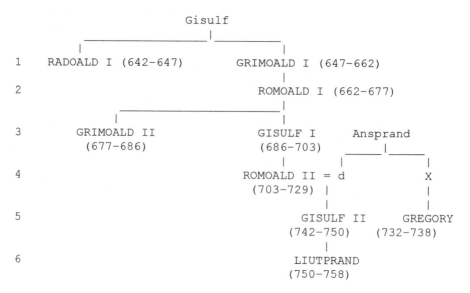

```
                        Gisulf
          _____|_____
          |                         |
1    RADOALD I (642-647)      GRIMOALD I (647-662)
                                    |
2                             ROMOALD I (662-677)
                                    |
          _____
          |                         |
3    GRIMOALD II                GISULF I      Ansprand
     (677-686)                 (686-703)   _____|_____
                                    |      |         |
4                             ROMOALD II = d         X
                              (703-729) |            |
                                        |            |
5                                  GISULF II      GREGORY
                                 (742-750)      (732-738)
                                        |
6                                  LIUTPRAND
                                  (750-758)
```

Statistics

Duration: 116 years, reigning for 109; 6 generations, average length 116/6 = 19 years; 9 rulers, average length of reign, 109/9 = 12 years.

Commentary

The first dukes of Benevento, Lombard invaders in the sixth century and appointed by the Lombard kings, were unrelated to one another. Radoald I was the son of the Lombard Duke Gisulf of Friuli, and he was followed by his brother. The Lombard kings were inimical to the development of sub-dynasties, but Benevento was remote from the centre of royal power, and their authority was faint. Radoald's brother, Grimoald I, succeeded to the Lombard throne, and put his own son in place as his successor at Benevento. Romoald I was thus the real founder of the ducal dynasty, for it was he who planted the family in hereditary power in the south of Italy. Benevento was sufficiently distant from the king's base in Lombardy to be effectively independent most of the time, though there were interruptions to the main line in the 730s: the intrusion of Duke Gregory and of a duke unconnected with the dynasty, was the result of a royal expedition after the main Beneventan line seemed to expire with the death of Romoald II and his brother. Duke Liutprand had no direct heirs, but the duchy continued in independence after his death, when a new duke was appointed by the Lombard king (he was the son of that king – again). That duke took the distinctive local title of prince – a gesture that was a claim to full independence – when the main Lombard kingdom was conquered by the Franks. The first Lombard dynasty thus oversaw the foundation of a long-standing polity, which in a variety of guises lasted until the nineteenth century.

References

PS Barnwell, *Kings, Courtiers, and Imperium: the Barbarian West 565–725* (London, 1997).

N Christie, *The Lombards: the Ancient Lombards* (Oxford, 1995).

C Wickham, *Early Mediaeval Italy* (London, 1981).

Bithynia, Asia Minor, 297-74 BC

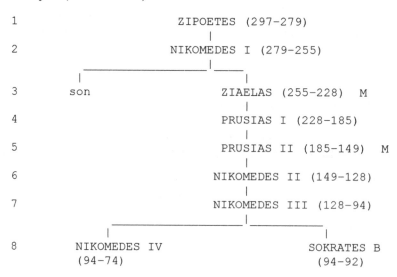

```
1                        ZIPOETES (297-279)
                               |
2                       NIKOMEDES I (279-255)
        _____|____
        |                       |
3      son               ZIAELAS (255-228)   M
                               |
4                        PRUSIAS I (228-185)
                               |
5                        PRUSIAS II (185-149)   M
                               |
6                       NIKOMEDES II (149-128)
                               |
7                       NIKOMEDES III (128-94)
        _____|_____
        |                       |          |
8   NIKOMEDES IV                        SOKRATES B
     (94-74)                             (94-92)
```

Statistics

Duration: 223 years; 8 generations, average length, 223/8 = 28 years; 9 rulers, average length of reign: 223/9 = 25 years.

Commentary

The founder Zipoetes made his name by leading the defence of his people, a tribe that formed a part of the future Bithynian kingdom, against an invasion by a Hellenistic general. As a result of his victory he took the royal title, and I have taken that date as the point of origin of the dynasty, though Zipoetes had in fact been chief of the tribe for some time before that. Zipoetes was also fortunate in that more important matters then distracted every Hellenistic power in his neighbourhood, allowing him to consolidate, expand, and survive. His successor provided further distraction for his more powerful neighbours by arranging for the Galatians to pass through his territory from the Balkans into Asia Minor, where they terrorized and preoccupied everyone for the next generation. It was not unfitting that the third king, Ziaelas, was killed by some of the Galatians his father had employed. But by this time the kingdom was fully established.

Nikomedes I systematically modernized, extended, and fortified his kingdom, importing Greek immigrants and founding cities; the names of the later kings show this Greek influence. Nikomedes I also adopted the late Akhaimenid custom of sibling killing on his accession, with the result that the royal family was in constant turmoil from then on. Ziaelas seized the throne from the designated successor, his elder brother, whom he killed. Nikomedes II murdered his father (who had taken refuge in a temple and was clinging to the altar); Nikomedes IV had to contend with a brother, engagingly named Sokrates, who had been deliberately spared by their father, and who was intent on supplanting his elder brother. Sokrates got his authority recognized in part of the kingdom for a couple of years. The inevitable result of this internal conflict and the regular killing of potential heirs was that the dynasty died out. Nikomedes IV had no children, and his brother had been killed in the fighting. Nikomedes then left his kingdom to Rome, to which he claimed most of its wealth was already owed anyway.

The apparent direct succession of the dynasty is thus somewhat misleading. Despite the fratricidal nature of the internal family history, once they were enthroned most of the kings were comparatively long-lived.

References

D Magie, *Roman Rule in Asia Minor*, 2 Vols (Princeton, 1950).

G Perl, 'Zür Chronologie Des Konigreiche Bithynia, Pontos und Bosporos', *Studien zur geschichte und Philosphie des Altertums*, ed. J. Harmatta (Amsterdam, 1968) pp. 299–330.

G Vitucci, *Il regno di Bitinia* (Rome, 1953).

Bulgaria (Dulo dynasty), AD 584–753

```
1                         KUBRAT (584-642)
                                 |
2                         BEJMER (642-645)
                                 |
3                         ASPARACH (645-701) B
                                 |
4                          TERVEL (701-721)
                                 |
5                         KORMESIY (721-738)
                                 |
6                           SEVAR (738-753) D
```

Statistics

Duration: 169 years; 6 generations, average length, 169/6 = 28 years; 6 rulers, average length of reign, 169/6 = 28 years.

Commentary

In 680 the Bulgars crossed the Danube into the Byzantine Empire. They were led by Asparach, who defeated the Byzantine army and established his people by agreement with the emperor in the wide lands between the Danube and the Balkan Mountains. This was, in fact, only one of several movements of Bulgars into various lands. They had lived on the steppes for several centuries, and others of their people remained there, moving north out of the way of a new nomad invasion from the east. Some moved west, one group into Pannonia, where for a time they became subject to the Avars, and a further small group ended up in southern Italy as part of the Lombard invasion.

Asparach was a member of a family that had been prominent for centuries. He was the leader of the Dulo tribe, which for a time provided rulers to the Transdanubian branch of the people. The other groups were said to have been led by his brothers, which was probably no more than a folk tale; the ancestor of the family was Avitokhol, who is claimed to have ruled for 300 years, rather confirming the elements of folk tale in the story. The first of the family who is independently and reliably attested is Kubrat (or Kirt) who had a long reign of well over half a century and led the first invasion over the Danube. Not surprisingly, his son ruled only briefly, no doubt being old long before acceding. From then on son succeeded father, though Asparach's grandson's name is not known (it may be Kormesiy, and I have assumed it so).

References

R Browning, *Byzantium and Bulgaria* (London, 1975).
S Runciman, *A History of the First Bulgarian Empire* (London, 1930).

Burgundians, AD 413–534.

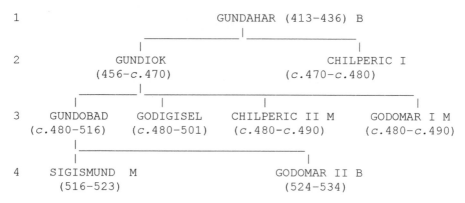

```
1                                        GUNDAHAR (413-436) B
                         |
         |                                          |
2              GUNDIOK                        CHILPERIC I
             (456-c.470)                     (c.470-c.480)
              |
      |             |              |                    |
3  GUNDOBAD     GODIGISEL     CHILPERIC II M        GODOMAR I M
  (c.480-516)  (c.480-501)   (c.480-c.490)        (c.480-c.490)
      |
      |                                    |
4  SIGISMUND  M                        GODOMAR II B
    (516-523)                           (524-534)
```

Statistics

Duration: 121 years, reigning for 101; 4 generations, average length 121/4 = 30 years; 9 rulers, average length of reign, 101/9 = 11 years.

Commentary

The first king named here, Gundahar, is in fact the fourth or fifth in the Burgundian royal line, but the earlier ones are mere names, just as the Burgundians were no more than an incipient German tribe before settling in eastern Gaul. It was Gundahar who settled the people whom he led into a permanent kingdom in what became Burgundy in 413, helped by the wealth and position he had gained in a career as a high Roman officer. He was killed in battle in 436, and there is then a gap in the royal record. The Burgundians suffered severely in the Hunnish wars, and the remnant were settled again in Burgundy by the Roman authorities. The next kings are only known from 456. They were probably the sons of Gundahar (they were certainly siblings, and certainly of the royal line). It would be more convincing if there was another generation between Gundahar and the two brothers – Gundahar had a long career before becoming king – but the father/son relationship is just about acceptable.

The most notable king of the family was Gundobad, who intrigued his way from a quarter share of the kingship to sole rule by betraying and killing two of his brothers. His successors were just as brutal; they suffered the fate of the brutal. The kingdom was too small to survive surrounded by greedy enemies – Romans killed Gundahar, Franks and Goths combined against Sigismund, and brutality is no substitute for subtlety in the survival stakes for small states. The dynasty died with Godomar II, who was defeated and probably killed in the process. The people were incorporated into the Frankish kingdom; the main legacy of the dynasty is that their fate became part of the story of the *Niebelungenlied*, and, of course, a geographical name.

References
H Wolfram, *The Roman Empire and its Germanic Peoples* (Berkeley and Los Angeles, 1997).

Cappadocia, Asia Minor, 280–40 BC.

A *Ariarathids*, 280–97 BC.

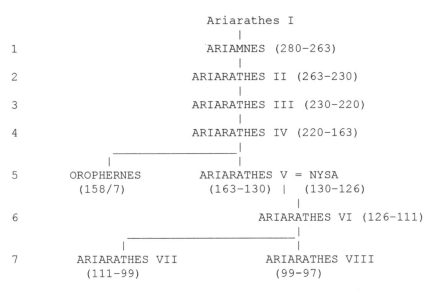

```
                          Ariarathes I
                               |
1                        ARIAMNES (280-263)
                               |
2                      ARIARATHES II (263-230)
                               |
3                     ARIARATHES III (230-220)
                               |
4                      ARIARATHES IV (220-163)
                   _____|
              |                |
5         OROPHERNES      ARIARATHES V = NYSA
           (158/7)        (163-130)  |  (130-126)
                                     |
6                              ARIARATHES VI (126-111)
                   _____|
              |                      |
7      ARIARATHES VII          ARIARATHES VIII
         (111-99)                  (99-97)
```

Statistics

Duration: 183 years; 7 generations, average length, 183/7 = 26 years;
10 rulers, average length of reign, 183/10 = 18 years.

Commentary

The first member of the family to establish himself securely as an independent ruler in Cappadocia was Ariamnes, who emerged in the aftermath of the murder of Seleukos I in 281. He is assumed to have conducted the defence of Cappadocia against the invasion of the Galatians, and was the ruler over a fairly wide area of interior Anatolia. His father had been satrap in Cappadocia in the last years of Akhaimenid rule and had not been removed until 321; whether he survived the removal personally or as a ruler is not known. He was, however, a native of the area, though Cappadocia was not in any way really independent of Macedonian rule until after Seleukos I died, when Ariamnes established himself. Ariamnes ruled independently, though it is clear that he was able to call on substantial local goodwill towards himself as a result of his father's incumbency earlier.

His son Ariarathes II took the royal title in 255, though he also accepted Seleukid suzerainty (his wife was a Seleukid princess). This helped the dynasty to survive until the removal of Seleukid power from Asia Minor to south of the Taurus in 188. A brief dispute between brothers in the 150s was the only break to the succession. The dynasty was eventually suppressed by Mithradates VI of Pontos in 97, who first tried to install his own son as king, but then accepted a local family, the Ariobarzanids, as kings. The basis of Ariarathid authority was clearly widespread local support in a large but thinly populated kingdom.

B   *Ariobarzanids*, 100–40 BC.

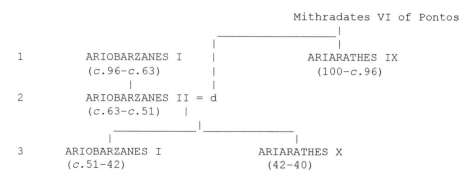

```
                                          Mithradates VI of Pontos
                                                      |
                            _____
                           |                              |
1        ARIOBARZANES I     |              ARIARATHES IX
         (c.96-c.63)        |              (100-c.96)
              |             |
2        ARIOBARZANES II = d
         (c.63-c.51)      |
         _____
        |                              |
3    ARIOBARZANES I              ARIARATHES X
     (c.51-42)                   (42-40)
```

Statistics

Duration: 60 years; 3 generations, average length 60/3 = 20 years; 5 rulers, average length of reign 60/5 = 12 years.

Commentary

The suppression of the Ariarathids by Mithradates VI of Pontos opened the way for the local lord, Ariobarzanes I, to claim the kingship. He had to see off Mithradates' son Ariarathes IX (so named as part of the process of claiming the kingship), which he did mainly by being strictly Cappadocian, and so appealing to local dislike of the Pontians. The solution was essentially to form a marriage alliance, whereby Mithradates' daughter, Ariarathes' sister, married Ariobarzanes' son, so saving Mithradates' face. By balancing themselves between Rome and Pontos the kings of this brief dynasty survived for a time, but they finally succumbed to the contradictory internal and Roman pressures. A balancing act always ends in a tumble. The Romans still felt that Cappadocia was best ruled by a king, and appointed a replacement, Archelaos, a man who was unrelated to the earlier dynasties.

References

N Davis and CM Kraay, *The Hellenistic Kingdoms, Portrait Coins and History* (London, 1973).

BC McGing, *The Foreign Policy of Mithridates VI Eupator, King of Pontus* (Leiden, 1986).

Carthage, North Africa, *c.*550–195 BC.

A   *Magonids, c.550-373 BC.*

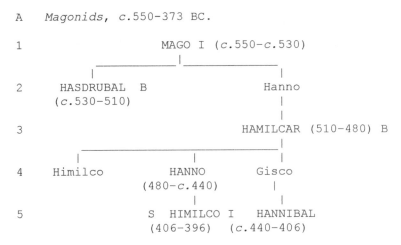

```
1                        MAGO I (c.550-c.530)
                  _____|_____
          |                              |
2     HASDRUBAL  B                      Hanno
      (c.530-510)                         |
                                          |
3                             HAMILCAR (510-480) B
                     _____|
          |                    |          |
4      Himilco              HANNO       Gisco
                          (480-c.440)     |
                               |          |
5                      S  HIMILCO I   HANNIBAL
                         (406-396)   (c.440-406)
```

Statistics
Duration: 177 years; 5 generations, average length, 177/5 = 35 years; 6 rulers, average length of reign: 177/6 = 29 years.

Commentary
The monarchy of Carthage probably dates from the original settlement of the city by Tyrians, who were led by the daughter of the Tyrian king and her husband, the high priest of that city, who no doubt became the first Carthaginian king. However, no royal names are known until about 550 BC, when Mago I is known to have been king, and he is thought to have been the founder of a new dynasty. As a result of his priority the family are called the Magonids.

The succession seems to have been regulated in some way by an electoral process, but the candidates were always drawn from the same family. Hasdrubal, the second king, for example, certainly had adult sons, but they were passed over when Hamilcar was chosen. Similarly Hamilcar's eldest son Himilco was passed over for his second son Hanno, who is credited with expanding the Carthaginian control over parts of North Africa.

The dynasty ended during the wars in Sicily, in which Himilco I failed and committed suicide, after Hannibal had failed but died of age and perhaps illness. The monarchy continued, but without any dynastic connection. Such suicides imply that the kings had sacerdotal functions as well as those of military leadership.

This dynasty is at times ignored by historians, the kings being regarded as no more than military commanders, but it evidently did exist as a sequence of men holding power. In all likelihood the men were in part war leaders, with only limited discretionary domestic power, and perhaps had some religious functions as well. The monarchy appears to have been finally abandoned by 308 – that is, its several functions were distributed among elected magistrates.

```
B   Barkids, 237-195 BC.

1                        B   HAMILCAR (237-228)
    _____|_____
    |              |            |                      |
2   HANNIBAL D  HASDRUBAL II B  d = HASDRUBAL I M     Mago
    (221-195)    (219-206)        (228-221)
```

Statistics
Duration: 42 years; 2 generations, average length, 42/2 = 21 years; 4 rulers, average length of reigns 42/4 = 10 years.

Commentary
A new Carthaginian quasi-monarchy emerged in Spain after 237 when Hamilcar Barka, a successful general in the Roman war (the 'First Punic' War), began the conquest of the south of that country. His son-in-law Hasdrubal I and then two of his sons, Hannibal and Hasdrubal II, successively ruled the conquered territory (as local kings, and were portrayed wearing the diadem, the symbol of royalty). Spain was lost during the Second Punic War, but Hannibal was re-elected as ruler of Carthage ('Suffete') for a time after his final defeat in Africa in that war. He eventually fled when his position became untenable at home, and was murdered when he took refuge in Bithynia, at Roman instigation. The family may be seen as one of the several failed dynasties of the Hellenistic period; its record of violent death and deposition is almost unequalled.

References
F Decret, *Carthage ou l'empire de la Mer* (Paris, 1977).
D Hoyos, *Hannibal's Dynasty* (London, 2003).
R Miles, *Carthage must be Destroyed, the Rise and Fall of an Ancient Civilization* (London, 2010).
GC and L Picard, *Carthage* (London, 1968).
BH Warmington, *Carthage* (London, 1960).

Catuvellauni, England, 55 BC-AD 43

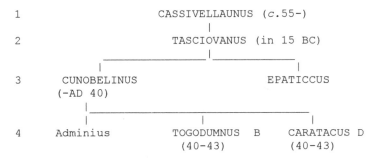

```
1                    CASSIVELLAUNUS (c.55-)
                            |
2                    TASCIOVANUS (in 15 BC)
        _____|_____
        |                               |
3   CUNOBELINUS                      EPATICCUS
    (-AD 40)
        |_____
        |                   |                    |
4   Adminius           TOGODUMNUS   B      CARATACUS  D
                        (40-43)            (40-43)
```

Statistics
Duration: 98 years; 4 generations, average length, 98/4 = 25 years; 6 rulers, average length of reign: 98/6 = 16 years.

Commentary
The only dynasty that can be reconstructed from Iron Age Britain is the most important one, reasonably enough. Cassivellaunus was already leader, perhaps king, of the tribe of the Catuvellauni in the south-east Midlands, when Julius Caesar undertook his expeditions to Britain in 55 and 54 BC. The resistance that he led to this invasion raised him from a tribal leader to the position of power and allowed him to expand his base to a true kingdom, which covered much of the land north of the Thames. And so the origin of the dynasty may be placed at 55 BC, even though he, and presumably his family, had been chiefs earlier. His successor Tasciovanus was in office forty years later, though it is only an assumption that he was Cassivellaunus' son and the father of the third generation. The dates of the later kings remain conjectural, except for the date of Caratacus' capture and deportation to Italy in 51 (though he had been expelled from his kingdom in 43), but the names of the kings are well-attested.

The family seems to have been capable of amicable joint rule, and Cunobelinus and Epaticcus shared power, as did Togodumnus and Caratacus in the brief period between Cunobelinus' death in about AD 40 and the Roman invasion in 43. The sharing was geographical, not simply political, and this clearly had the potential to break up the kingdom and the dynasty. Adminius, for example, was discontented and fled to Rome about the time of his father's death. The power of the family was brought to an end by the invasion launched by Emperor Claudius in 43, though Caratacus continued his fight as a guerrilla leader operating beyond the Roman province until 51.

References
P Salway, *Roman Britain* (Oxford, 1981).
G Webster, *The Roman Invasion of Britain* (London, 1980).

Cimmerian Bosporos, Crimea, 438 BC–AD 342

A   *Spartokids*, 438–109 BC.

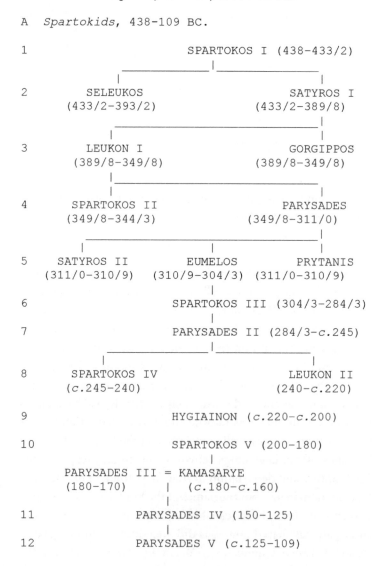

```
1                          SPARTOKOS I (438-433/2)
                   _____|_____
             |                                   |
2         SELEUKOS                            SATYROS I
        (433/2-393/2)                       (433/2-389/8)
             _____|
             |                                   |
3         LEUKON I                            GORGIPPOS
        (389/8-349/8)                       (389/8-349/8)
             _____|
             |                                   |
4       SPARTOKOS II                          PARYSADES
        (349/8-344/3)                       (349/8-311/0)
                                  _____|
             |                    |              |
5      SATYROS II            EUMELOS         PRYTANIS
    (311/0-310/9)      (310/9-304/3)    (311/0-310/9)
                                  |
6                         SPARTOKOS III (304/3-284/3)
                                  |
7                         PARYSADES II (284/3-c.245)
                   _____|_____
             |                                   |
8       SPARTOKOS IV                            LEUKON II
        (c.245-240)                          (240-c.220)

9                         HYGIAINON (c.220-c.200)

10                        SPARTOKOS V (200-180)
                                  |
         PARYSADES III  =  KAMASARYE
        (180-170)        |   (c.180-c.160)
                         |
11                  PARYSADES IV (150-125)
                         |
12                  PARYSADES V (c.125-109)
```

Statistics
Duration: 329 years; 13 generations, average length, 329/13 = 25 years;
20 rulers, average length of reign: 329/20 = 16 years.

Commentary
The dynasty that ruled in the Cimmerian Bosporos (part of the modern
Crimea) for over three centuries came to power as a result of a *coup d'état* in

the city of Pantikapaion, and began as a fairly typical Greek civic tyranny: the first king, Spartokos I, seized power in the city from an aristocratic group that had gathered a large degree of unpopularity. Spartokos was reputed to be part-Greek and part-Scythian, which appears to have given him extra authority, but also marked him as an outsider according to the aristocrats he had displaced. He could to some degree use one group to control the other. The longevity of the dynasty belies its origins as a Greek tyranny, perhaps because of that extra non-city authority. It was soon a regional power, and the authority of the kings was not just confined to the city.

The early pattern of the dynasty was for brothers to share power, the survivor continuing to rule alone; this system continued for four generations. The first pair, particularly Satyros I, extended the kingdom to control several other cities in the region, thus developing the initial city tyranny into a fairly extensive kingdom.

The early pattern of joint succession continued until 310, when it included a sister, Prytanis, as well as her two brothers, but from then on single-person rule became the norm. The reason for the change is not known, perhaps simply an absence of brothers. The history of the dynasty is in fact fairly vague, since its geographical remoteness made Greek chroniclers ignore it. The genealogy and the dates of the rulers are probably fairly accurate, where known.

The dynasty exhibits several characteristics well-known in self-conscious dynasties, including the use of a restricted set of 'royal' names, and marriages within the family. The lack of clarity of the later stages in the late third century is also a characteristic of the sources for minor states in the Hellenistic period. It is not clear if Hygiainon was part of the dynasty, but he was certainly king according to his coins. He is here, with some misgivings, included in the dynasty. It is the coinage that is the main source for the later kings, and so there may have been other rulers in addition, though there are few gaps of any size to accommodate them. The round figures for the late rulers are clearly only approximations.

Note the prominence of royal women, two of whom are reckoned as independent rulers (Prytanis and Kamasarye) and several others were clearly important dynastically. The dates of many of the kings are not certain, but the start and the end of the dynasty are correct. The dynasty appears to have simply died out with Parysades 'the Last'; he was followed by the even longer-lived dynasty of Mithradates.

B   *Mithradatids*, 110 BC–AD 342.

```
1                        MITHRADATES (110–63)   S
                 _____|_____
                 |                          |
2      MACHARES (79–65)            PHARNAKES (63–48)
                                            |
3    ASANDROS (1) SCRIBONIUS (2) = DYNAMIS
       (47–17)      (c.15)        (20–16, = (3) POLEMO =(3) PYTHODORIS
         |                         ?–AD 8)       (14–8)      (9 BC–?)
         |
4    ASPURGOS    =    GEPAIPYRIS
     (AD 10/11–38)|     (38–39)
                 |
                 |_____
                 |                              |
5       MITHRADATES II (39–45)        KOTYS I (45–68)
                                                |
6                                     RHESKUPORIS I (68–92)
                                                |
7                                     SAUROMATES I (93–124)
                                                |
8                                       KOTYS II (124–131)
                                                |
9                                     RHOIMETALKES (131–154)
                     _____|
                     |                        |
10         SAUROMATES II (174–211)    EUPATOR (154–171)
                     |
11         RHESKUPORIS II (211–229)
                     |
                     |_____
                     |                          |
12         SAUROMATES III (229–232)   KOTYS III (227–234)

           RHESKUPORIS III (233–234)   ININTHIMAIOS (235–239)

13         PHASANZAES (254–255)        RHESKUPORIS IV (242–277)

14         SAUROMATES IV       TEIRANES        CHEDOSBIOS
               (276)           (276–279)        (278–286)

15                          THOTHORSES (286–310)

16                          RHADAMSAIDES (310–323)

17                          RHESKUPORIS VI (215–342)
```

Statistics

Duration: 452 years; 17 generations, average length, 452/17 = 27 years;
33 rulers, average length of reigns: 452/33 = 14 years.

Commentary

The acquisition by Mithradates I (VI of Pontos) of the kingdom of the Cimmerian Bosporos set his family on a long career of kingship, as an appendix to his predecessors' rule in his home kingdom. This dynasty is not, in fact, very well-attested after the first three centuries, as the absence of relationship signs in the table for the last six generations suggests. Relationships after Kotys III (died AD 234) are not known; some kings seem to be interlopers, such as Phasanzaes and Chedosbios, and others may well be (Ininthimaios), and at least two kings' names are quite unknown, but most of them seem to be descendants of the original dynasty, at least to judge by the names many of them used.

The kingdom was effectively under Roman domination all through the life of this dynasty, but it was a distinctly distant oversight that largely permitted the dynasty to arrange its own affairs. The early admixture of Roman citizens (such as Scribonius and Pythodoris, a descendant of M. Antonius) was not maintained, no doubt because the emperors were not keen to see Roman citizens becoming semi-independent rulers. Two kings, Eupator and Teiranes, were certainly Roman citizens, and probably all of the rest could claim that distinction. Eupator's full Roman name was C. Iulius Eupator, which implies a grant of citizenship by Augustus. The prevalence of women among the rulers, at least in the early years, is noteworthy, as it was also with the preceding Spartokids.

For all its longevity, this is hardly an important dynasty. Indeed its longevity, given the prevailing Roman suspicion of Eastern dynasties, is probably due in large part to its unimportance, and perhaps to its role in the supervision of the grain trade from the Ukrainian steppe to feed the great cities of the Aegean coastlands.

Sources for the dynasty are generally poor: the incidence of violent death is not known. It may be presumed, however, to be fairly high, considering the discrepancy between the averages for generation length and reign length.

References

VF Gujdakevic, *Die Bosporanische Reich* (Berlin, 1971).
BC McGing, *The Foreign Policy of Mithridates VI Eupator, King of Pontus* (Leiden, 1986).
FH Minns, *Scythians and Greeks* (Cambridge, 1913).
MI Rostovtseff, *Iranians and Greeks in Southern Russia* (Oxford, 1922).
A Werner, 'Die dynastie der Spartokiden', *Historia*, 4 (1955) pp. 412–444.

Kommagene, Syria, 163 BC–AD 72

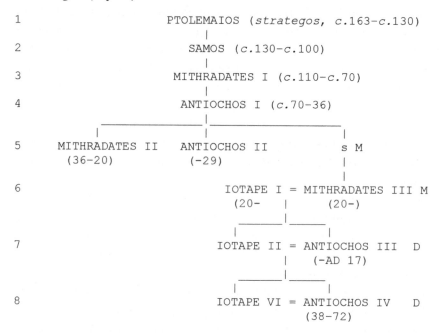

```
1                        PTOLEMAIOS (strategos, c.163-c.130)
                                |
2                            SAMOS (c.130-c.100)
                                |
3                        MITHRADATES I (c.110-c.70)
                                |
4                         ANTIOCHOS I (c.70-36)
         _____|_____
        |                        |                       |
5   MITHRADATES II          ANTIOCHOS II               s M
      (36-20)                  (-29)                     |
                                                         |
6                            IOTAPE I = MITHRADATES III M
                               (20-    |       (20-)
                                       |_____
                                   |           |
7                            IOTAPE II = ANTIOCHOS III   D
                                     |      (-AD 17)
                                  ___|_____
                                 |         |
8                            IOTAPE VI = ANTIOCHOS IV    D
                                          (38-72)
```

Statistics
Duration: 235 years, reigning for 214 years; 8 generations, average length,
235/8 = 29 years; 10 rulers, average length of reign: 214/10 = 21 years.

Commentary
Ptolemaios, the founder of the dynasty, was probably the local governor
(*strategos*) of the minor Seleukid province of Kommagene. Being on the fringe
of the kingdom, he had been able to assert his local power and to claim his
virtual independence by playing off his non-Seleukid northern neighbours
against the Seleukid kings until the effective collapse of the main kingdom
about the time of his death; his son was probably the first to take the royal
title.

The kingdom was at first located in the mountainous area of the Taurus,
along the Euphrates River, centred on the great fortress of Samosata, but was
later able to expand southwards into northern Syria. Ptolemaios' successors
had to defend themselves against encroachment by every neighbour in order
to survive attacks by the various conquerors who marched through the
Near East in the next two centuries. They were successful enough for that
time, though the Roman civil wars accounted for several of the kings, and
the kingdom became a Roman province for two decades under the Emperor
Tiberius.

The family were generally mutually supportive, though Mithradates II apparently found it necessary to execute his (unnamed) brother. The result was the succession of a child, who was quickly married to an adult, Iotape of the Atropatene dynasty, who then acted as regent for some years. The last king, Antiochos IV, had a long reign, but was finally deposed, as his father had been by Tiberius, as part of Vespasian's annexation of several Syrian kingdoms; he spent much of his time and much of his kingdom's wealth, no doubt, in developing a great royal shrine on Nemrut Dagh.

The dynasty always kept a low profile, submitting where necessary to anyone who was too powerful to be resisted, and marrying into every other local dynasty within reach, though the last two generations adopted the dangerous practice of sibling marriage, and Antiochos III and IV exhibited major megalomaniac tendencies. Survival, however, was clearly a hereditary trait, and resulted in a surprisingly long life for a dynasty that ruled a small and strategically important kingdom. Antiochos IV did make a brief fight of it when the Roman annexation finally became certain in 72, but not enough to provoke serious punishment. His children survived to become Roman consuls and provincial governors in the reign of the Emperor Trajan.

References
RD Sullivan, 'The Dynasty of Commagene', *Aufsteig und Niedergang des Romischen Welt*, II, 8, 1 (1977).

RD Sullivan, *Near Eastern Royalty and Rome, 100–30 BC* (Toronto, 1989).

Connacht, Ireland, AD *c.*450–792

A   *Ui Fiachrach, c.450-773.*

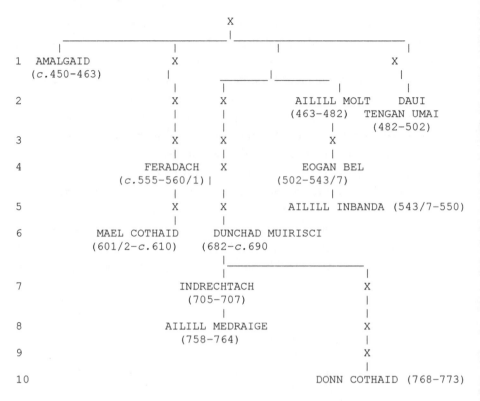

```
                                      X
           _____|_____
          |              |               |                    |
1    AMALGAID            X                                     X
     (c.450-463)         |         _____|_____           |
                         |        |                 |          |
2                        X        X          AILILL MOLT     DAUI
                         |        |          (463-482)    TENGAN UMAI
                         |        |                |       (482-502)
3                        X        X                X
                         |        |                |
4                   FERADACH      X            EOGAN BEL
                  (c.555-560/1)|              (502-543/7)
                         |        |                |
5                        X        X        AILILL INBANDA (543/7-550)
                         |        |
6              MAEL COTHAID     DUNCHAD MUIRISCI
               (601/2-c.610)    (682-c.690
                                     |_____
                                     |                        |
7                              INDRECHTACH                    X
                                (705-707)                     |
                                     |                        |
8                            AILILL MEDRAIGE                  X
                                (758-764)                     |
9                                                             X
                                                              |
10                                          DONN COTHAID (768-773)
```

Statistics
Duration: 323 years, reigning for 137; 10 generations, average length,
323/10 = 32 years; 11 rulers, average length of reign, 137/11 = 12 years.

B   *Second Connacht Dynasty, c.610-696.*

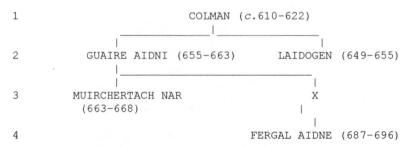

```
1                        COLMAN (c.610-622)
           _____|_____
          |                                 |
2    GUAIRE AIDNI (655-663)         LAIDOGEN (649-655)
          |_____
          |                            |
3    MUIRCHERTACH NAR                  X
       (663-668)                       |
                                       |
4                          FERGAL AIDNE (687-696)
```

Statistics

Duration: 86 years, reigning for 40; 4 generations, average length 86/4 = 22 years; 5 rulers, average length of reign, 40/5 = 8 years.

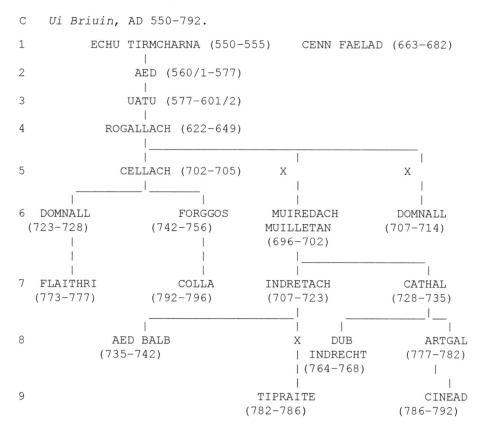

```
C    Ui Briuin, AD 550-792.

1              ECHU TIRMCHARNA (550-555)      CENN FAELAD (663-682)
                        |
2                  AED (560/1-577)
                        |
3                 UATU (577-601/2)
                        |
4             ROGALLACH (622-649)
                        |_____
                        |                    |               |
5              CELLACH (702-705)             X               X
          _____|_____                  |               |
          |              |                    |               |
6   DOMNALL          FORGGOS           MUIREDACH          DOMNALL
   (723-728)        (742-756)          MUILLETAN         (707-714)
        |                |             (696-702)
        |                |                  |_____
        |                |                  |                   |
7   FLAITHRI           COLLA           INDRETACH            CATHAL
   (773-777)        (792-796)          (707-723)           (728-735)
               _____|        _____|__
               |                      |        |                |
8         AED BALB                    X      DUB            ARTGAL
         (735-742)                    | INDRECHT          (777-782)
                                      |(764-768)              |
                                      |                       |
9                                 TIPRAITE               CINEAD
                                 (782-786)              (786-792)
```

Statistics

Duration: 242 years, reigning for 183; 9 generations, average length, 242/9 = 27 years; 19 rulers, average length of reign, 183/19 = 10 years.

(For a commentary on all the Irish dynasties, see the entry on Ireland: High Kings.)

Cottian Dynasty, Italy, 40 BC–AD 63

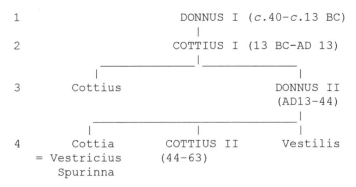

```
1                              DONNUS I (c.40-c.13 BC)
                                   |
2                              COTTIUS I (13 BC-AD 13)
         _____|_____
        |                                          |
3    Cottius                                   DONNUS II
                                               (AD13-44)
                                                   |
         _____
        |                    |                  |
4     Cottia            COTTIUS II         Vestilis
   = Vestricius          (44-63)
      Spurinna
```

Statistics
Duration: 103 years; 4 generations, average length, 103/4 - 26 years; 4 rulers, average length of reign, 103/4 = 26 years.

Commentary
Donnus was an Alpine ruler made king by the Senate as a means of controlling a section of the Alps through which armies and travellers passed on the way to Gaul, which had been recently conquered. His dynasty existed as one in an area that was less than pacified, but only as long as the Roman government found the arrangement convenient. In the process Rome gained a cheap administration, the inhabitants were not subject to direct Roman rule and exploitation, and the Cottian family prestige grew. In the final generation Cottius II's sister married one of the most eminent contemporary Roman senators, considered at times worthy of the imperial throne. On annexation the kingdom was converted into a minor province, Alpes Cottiae, which still gives its name to the Cottian Alps.

References
A Letta, 'La dinastia del Cozii e la Romanizzazione della Alpi Occidentali', *Athenaeum*, 59 (1976) pp. 37–76.

Dacia, AD *c*.50–106

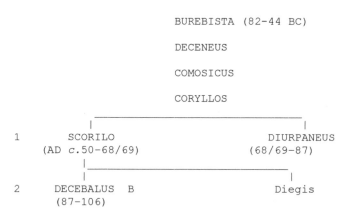

```
                    BUREBISTA (82-44 BC)

                    DECENEUS

                    COMOSICUS

                    CORYLLOS

         |                                    |
1        SCORILO                         DIURPANEUS
      (AD c.50-68/69)                    (68/69-87)
         |
         |                                    |
2     DECEBALUS  B                         Diegis
      (87-106)
```

Statistics
Duration: about 56 years; 2 generations; average length, 56/2 = 28 years; 3 rulers, average length of reign: 56/3 = 19 years.

Commentary
The Dacian kingdom emerged under, or was constructed by, Burebista, and lasted almost two centuries. It broke down for a time in the early first century AD. The connections between the earlier kings are not known, but the last three kings formed a dynasty, though again their precise relationships are not certain. There are, indeed, probably several other kings between Coryllos and Scorilo, but probably they did not rule more than a part of Dacia each. The accession date of Scorilo is only a guess, but he appears to have been the refounder of the united kingdom and so must be allotted at least two decades.

The greatest of these kings were Burebista, the founder of the original united state, based in the Carpathian Mountains of Romania, and Decebalus. Its wealth lay largely in control of substantial mineral resources, particularly gold. Decebalus was a major ruler who withstood two powerful Roman attacks, until finally succumbing to overwhelming forces under the Emperor Trajan. The Roman conquest was hardly necessary, for Romanization was proceeding apace once the kingdom came into existence, but no Roman emperor could permit any rival focus of power to persist.

The succession went from brother to brother and then to the first brother's son. It is not known if this was the normal succession pattern, or if Diurpaneus was acting as regent for Decebalus.

References
J Bennett, *Trajan, Optimus Princeps* (London, 1997).
H Daicoviciu and J Trynkowski, 'Les rois Daces de Burebista a Decebalu', *Dacia*, 14 (1970) pp. 159–166.

Dalriada, Scotland, AD 501–747

A   *First Dynasty*, AD 501–781.

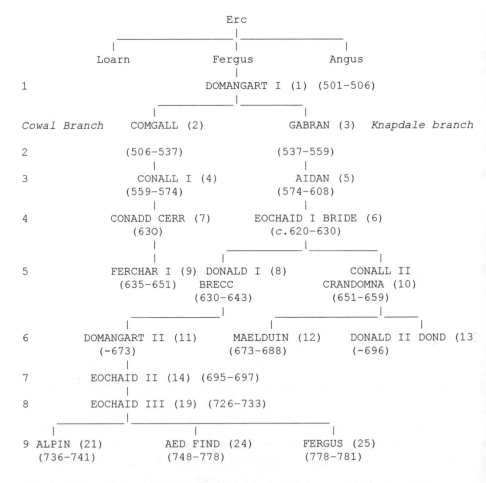

```
                            Erc
           _____|_____
          |                   |                  |
       Loarn              Fergus              Angus
                              |
1                     DOMANGART I (1) (501-506)
                  _____|_____
                 |                        |
Cowal Branch  COMGALL (2)              GABRAN (3)  Knapdale branch

2              (506-537)               (537-559)
                   |                       |
3              CONALL I (4)             AIDAN (5)
               (559-574)               (574-608)
                   |                       |
4           CONADD CERR (7)      EOCHAID I BRIDE (6)
               (630)               (c.620-630)
                   |            _____|_____
                   |          |                   |
5           FERCHAR I (9)  DONALD I (8)        CONALL II
            (635-651)       BRECC           CRANDOMNA (10)
                           (630-643)          (651-659)
              _____|          _____|_____
             |                     |                 |
6      DOMANGART II (11)     MAELDUIN (12)    DONALD II DOND (13)
           (-673)            (673-688)           (-696)
             |
7      EOCHAID II (14) (695-697)
             |
8      EOCHAID III (19) (726-733)
    _____|_____
   |               |                            |
9 ALPIN (21)    AED FIND (24)            FERGUS (25)
  (736-741)     (748-778)               (778-781)
```

Statistics
Duration: 280 years, reigning for 229; 9 generations, average length, 280/9 = 31 years; 18 rulers, average length of reign, 229/18 = 13 years.

B   *Second Dynasty*, AD 651–741.

```
                    Duban
                      |
1              DUNCAN (651-659)
                      |
2                  Ossene
                      |
3            FIANNAMAIL (698-700)
                      |
4            INDRECHLACH (741)
```

C   *Third Dynasty*, AD 677-747.

```
                         Feredach
                            |
1                    FERCHAR II FOTA (677-697)
           _____|_____
           |                           |
2    AINFCELLACH (697-698)       SELBACH (701-723)
           |                           |
3    MUIREDACH (733-736)         DUNGAL (723-726)
           |
4      EOGAN (741-747)
```

Statistics
Duration: 90 years, reigning for 11; 4 generations, average length, 90/4 = 23 years; 3 rulers, average length of reign, 11/3 = 4 years.

Statistics
Duration: 70 years, reigning for 55; 4 generations, average length, 70/4 = 18 years; 6 rulers, average length of reign, 55/6 = 9 years.

Commentary
The kingdom of Dalriada in western Scotland was traditionally said to have been founded by Scots immigrants from Ireland about AD 500, though this has been challenged in favour of an indigenous origin. Domangart I is reckoned the first king, though he and his father and uncles may by mythical. Inheritance was shared by the two branches of the family founded by Domangart's sons (the Cowal and Knapdale lines). When the elder branch died out, the two sons of Eochaid I founded separate lines, and these were later followed by two other families (the 'second' and 'third' dynasties), who occasionally intervened. The result was much confusion and a very low average reign length. Over the whole period, from 501 to 781 (280 years) there were twenty-seven kings, with an average reign length of only ten years (though this is very similar to their contemporaries, the Pictish kings).

The second and third dynasties interrupted the succession in the first, and there were also intrusions from Ireland, from other parts of what became Scotland, and disputes within each branch. The original dynasty can be followed again after these intrusions, when Eochaid III received the kingship in 726, but none of the dynasties can be satisfactorily traced after about 781. They had intermarried with the Pictish kings and eventually a descendant of both Scots and Picts united the two kingdoms. His precise descent from these kings is unclear.

This descent sequence is complicated on paper, but seems to have worked well enough in practice. It is, of course, reminiscent of Irish schemes, but it also has similarities elsewhere in Europe at the time.

References
AO Anderson, *Early Sources of Scottish History*, vol. 1 (Edinburgh, 1922).

MO Anderson, *Kings and Kingship in Early Scotland* (Edinburgh, 1973).

E Campbell, 'Were the Scots Irish?', *Antiquity*, 75 (2001).

JE Fraser, *From Caledonia to Pictland: Scotland to 795* (Edinburgh, 2009).

Dhu Raydan, South Arabia, AD 20–100

A. *First Dynasty*, AD 20-70.

```
1                        YADA'IL WATAR II (20-25)
                                   |
2                     DHARMA'ALAY BAYYIN II (25-45)
                                   |
3                   KARIBIL WATAR YUHAN'IM (45-60)
          _____|_____
          |                                        |
4      Halkamar                    AMDAN BAYYIN YUHAQBID (60-70)
```

Statistics
Duration: 50 years; 4 generations, average length, 50/4 = 12 years; 4 rulers, average length of reign, 50/4 = 12 years.

B. *Second Dynasty*, AD 70-100.

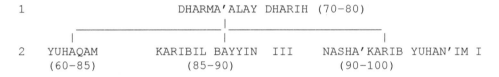

```
1                       DHARMA'ALAY DHARIH (70-80)
          _____|_____
          |                        |                               |
2     YUHAQAM            KARIBIL BAYYIN  III      NASHA'KARIB YUHAN'IM I
      (60-85)                 (85-90)                   (90-100)
```

Statistics
Duration: 30 years; 2 generations, average length 30/2 = 15 years; 4 rulers, average length of reign, 30/4 = 8 years.

Commentary
The Dhu Raydan kingdom took over control of Himyar and Saba in Yemen, forming a united kingdom. Several sequences of kings are known, of which the two dynasties tabulated here can be sorted out. They were succeeded by the empire of Himyar, which united all the various parts of south Arabia into one state. The dates are, as is obvious, no more than estimates, and very few are included with any precision.

References
KA Kitchen, *Documentation for Ancient Arabia*, I (Liverpool, 1994).

East Angles, England, AD *c*.600–749

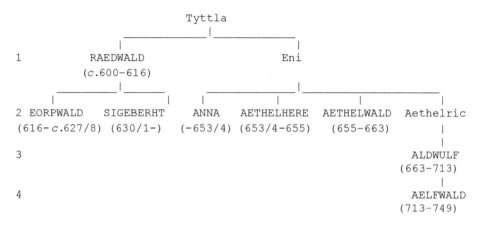

```
                          Tyttla
              _____|_____
             |                       |
1         RAEDWALD                   Eni
         (c.600-616)
         _____|_____    _____|_____
        |                 |   |           |           |         |
2 EORPWALD    SIGEBERHT    ANNA   AETHELHERE  AETHELWALD   Aethelric
(616-c.627/8) (630/1-)  (-653/4) (653/4-655)  (655-663)        |
                                                               |
3                                                          ALDWULF
                                                          (663-713)
                                                               |
4                                                          AELFWALD
                                                          (713-749)
```

Statistics
Duration: 149 years; 4 generations, average length, 149/4 = 35 years; 8 rulers, average length of reign, 149/8 = 20 years.

Commentary
The East Anglian royal house first emerges from the sources in the person of Raedwald, who is thought to be the man buried in the ship burial at Sutton Hoo in Suffolk. Several more of the mounds have been investigated and may be the burial places of other men of this dynasty. Raedwald was such a powerful ruler that one might safely suggest that the kingdom had been already well-organized before his accession, though we do not hear of any earlier kings. Succession went to his sons, then his nephews, and so was well-controlled. Succession clearly went to siblings, though it may be that none of the second generation kings had sons – unlikely though this may be; Anna certainly had three daughters.

After Aelfwald's death in 749 there were another seven kings of East Anglia, but for only two are relationships known. Mercian power intruded in the 780s, but was driven out finally in the 820s. The kings' names are known, but not how they were connected. One king claimed to be descended from Raedwald, but that is a claim one would expect to be made.

References
EB Fryde, *Handbook of British Chronology*, 3rd ed. (London, 1986).
B Yorke, *Kings and Kingdoms of Early Anglo-Saxon England* (London, 1990).
DP Kirby, *The Earliest English Kings*, 2nd ed. (London, 2000).

East Saxons, England, AD *c.*587–*c.*825

A.   *Sledding Dynasty*, AD c.587–c.760.

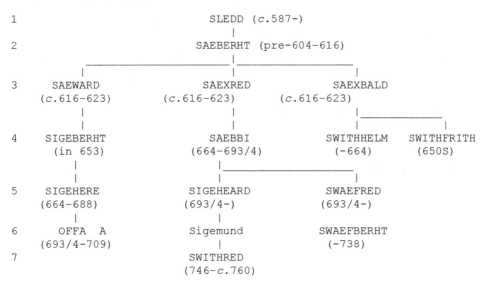

```
1                        SLEDD (c.587-)
                           |
2                        SAEBERHT (pre-604-616)
         _____|_____
        |                    |                    |
3    SAEWARD              SAEXRED             SAEXBALD
    (c.616-623)         (c.616-623)         (c.616-623)
        |                    |                    |_____
        |                    |                    |               |
4    SIGEBERHT             SAEBBI            SWITHHELM        SWITHFRITH
    (in 653)            (664-693/4)          (-664)           (650S)
        |                    |_____
        |                    |                        |
5    SIGEHERE             SIGEHEARD               SWAEFRED
    (664-688)            (693/4-)                (693/4-)
        |                    |
6     OFFA  A             Sigemund               SWAEFBERHT
    (693/4-709)             |                     (-738)
7                        SWITHRED
                        (746-c.760)
```

Statistics
Duration: 173 years, reigning for 165; 7 generations, average length, 173/7 = 25 years; 15 rulers, average length of reign, 165/15 = 11 years.

B.   *Second Dynasty*, 738–c.825.

```
1                        SELERED (738-746)
                           |
2                        SIGERIC I (c.760-798)   A
                           |
3                        SIGERED (798-825)
                           |
                         Sigeric 'II' (-c.835)
```

Statistics
Duration: 87 years, reigning 73; 3 generations, average length, 87/3 = 29 years; 3 rulers, average length of reign, 73/3 = 24 years.

Commentary
The East Saxon dynasty is only known from the late sixth century, with Sledd, who was prominent enough to marry a Kentish princess, the sister of the Great King, Aethelberht. He is thus here taken to be the earliest king of this dynasty, though there may well have been some earlier kings. His son was

succeeded by three sons, apparently ruling collectively, and the succession thereafter is occasionally shared.

The three brothers seem to have ruled jointly, sharing power, but later cases of joint inheritance seem to have involved a physical division of the kingdom. Swaefberht cannot be located precisely within the dynasty, but his name certainly implies that he was a member of the family. Swithfrith is not definitely a son of Saexbald, but again the name does suggest that he was of the family.

The king between Swaefberht and Swithred was Selered, the sixth in descent from Sledd, but by a junior line. In effect, therefore, he began a new dynasty, though Swithred of the first dynasty continued. By this time, and even earlier, the kingdom was in vassalage for most of the time to the Mercians, and the second dynasty gradually declined in importance. Sigered was the last king of the family to be styled king, and by the end of his reign the kingdom had been taken by the West Saxons and made into a sub-kingdom for a son of the king of Wessex. Sigered 'II' was a Mercian nobleman.

References

EB Fryde, *Handbook of British Chronology*, 3rd ed. (London, 1986).
DP Kirby, *The Earliest English Kings*, 2nd ed. (London, 2000).
B Yorke, *Kings and Kingdoms of Early Anglo-Saxon England* (London, 1990).

Edessa, Abgarid Dynasty, Mesopotamia, 120 BC–AD 242

A. *First Dynasty*, 120–26 BC.

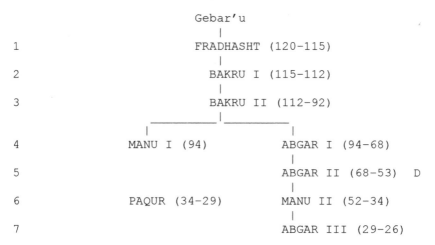

```
                        Gebar'u
                          |
1                     FRADHASHT (120-115)
                          |
2                     BAKRU I (115-112)
                          |
3                     BAKRU II (112-92)
              _____|_____
              |                      |
4        MANU I (94)            ABGAR I (94-68)
                                     |
5                               ABGAR II (68-53)   D
                                     |
6        PAQUR (34-29)           MANU II (52-34)
                                     |
7                               ABGAR III (29-26)
```

Statistics

Duration: 94 years; reigning for 88 years; 7 generations, average length: 94/7 = 13 years; 8 rulers, average length of reign: 88/8 = 11 years

B. *Second Dynasty*, 23 BC–AD 91.

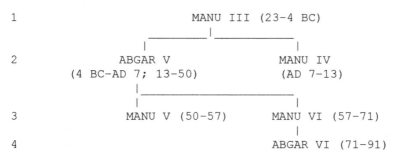

```
1                        MANU III (23-4 BC)
                 _____|_____
                 |                         |
2            ABGAR V                    MANU IV
          (4 BC-AD 7; 13-50)           (AD 7-13)
                 |_____
                 |                           |
3            MANU V (50-57)             MANU VI (57-71)
                                             |
4                                       ABGAR VI (71-91)
```

Statistics

Duration 114 years; 4 generations; average length: 114/4 = 29 years; 6 rulers: average length of reign: 114/6 = 19 years.

C.   *Third Dynasty, 109-242*

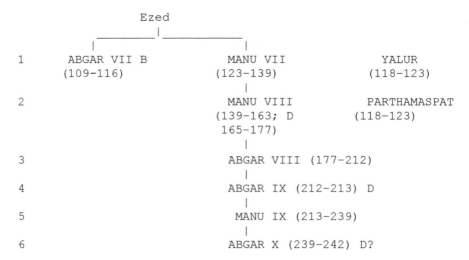

```
                    Ezed
          _____|_____
          |                     |
1    ABGAR VII B          MANU VII              YALUR
     (109-116)            (123-139)             (118-123)
                              |
2                        MANU VIII            PARTHAMASPAT
                         (139-163; D          (118-123)
                         165-177)
                              |
3                        ABGAR VIII  (177-212)
                              |
4                        ABGAR IX  (212-213)  D
                              |
5                        MANU IX  (213-239)
                              |
6                        ABGAR X  (239-242)  D?
```

Statistics

Duration: 133 years, reigning for 124 years; 6 generations, average length: $133/6 = 22$ years; 7 rulers, average length of reign: $124/7 = 18$ years.

Commentary

The city of Edessa (modern Urfa or Sanliurfa) was a Macedonian colony east of the Euphrates in Mesopotamia, and became the seat of an independent or quasi-independent ruler from 132 BC. The kingdom he ruled was a small province of the declining Seleukid kingdom called Osrhoene, of which Edessa was the urban centre. The kingdom maintained its existence, sometimes very precariously, until the mid third century AD, when it was finally annexed to Rome.

The first two kings (not listed on the table) were apparently unrelated either to each other or to the later kings, and had names that suggest Arab origin; they are assumed to be local chieftains. In 124 Fradhasht became king; he had an Iranian name, though his father and his son both had Arab names. It may be conjectured that Fradhasht was installed at Edessa by the Parthians, who had been advancing westwards, gradually taking over the Seleukid kingdom in easily digestible pieces. There were other ex-Seleukid provinces in the region, such as Adiabene or Characene, whose rulers had accepted Parthian suzerainty. On the other hand, he may simply have been the latest in a series of ephemeral local rulers, but one who succeeded in passing on his power to his son.

Whatever was the precise origin and status of Fradhasht, he succeeded in establishing the family as kings of Osrhoene. The king, when the Romans came into contact with the area, was Abgar I, and the dynasty was referred to as Abgarid as a result. Abgar II became involved in the attack by the Roman triumvir P. Licinius Crassus on Parthia, which failed in the spectacular disaster at Carrhai (in Edessan territory) in 53 BC. Abgar was accused of disloyalty by Rome and was deposed in that year. After a year's interregnum a new king took office, who is generally thought to have been Abgar's son Manu II, and it is so assumed here. He was succeeded by Paqur, a man unrelated to the main family, and then by another Abgar (III), who is assumed to be Manu's son. This broken dynastic history is in part a consequence of the Romano-Parthian conflict of the time, but it is also characteristic of a dynasty in the process of failing. The succession sequence as here set out must therefore be regarded as uncertain.

The repetition of the names Manu and Abgar among the kings after this first dynasty may be a sign that the original dynasty had returned to power in 23 BC after a three-year gap; alternatively it may be that this was a new dynasty that simply used these dynastic names to establish its own credentials for ruling the kingdom. This 'second' dynasty was composed of men with only these names, and is separated from Abgar III by two other kings, whose relationships are unknown, and who appear to have ruled simultaneously.

The precise connections of all of these kings between 52 and 23 BC are not known, and it is very likely that the direct succession had been broken. Again, between 91 and 109 there was another interregnum, and the restoration of the kingship in 109 was in the person of Abgar son of Ezed, or Izat. Ezed may well have been a scion of the Adiabenian royal house, installed at Edessa by the Parthians, and it certainly appears that this was a new dynasty, with little or no connection to the two previous ones, though the family took on the names associated with the earlier dynasty/ies. The Parthian ambition to control the kingdom was a long-standing one, dating back to the second century BC, and it resurfaced every now and again afterwards. However by this time the whole of Mesopotamia had been taken over by Rome, so that whatever the origins of the dynasty, the kings now owed their position to Rome.

There are thus probably three separate dynasties at Edessa, all using the same royal names, but all of different origins. It is clear that the kingdom was regularly subject to interference from the great powers to either side of it. In the end, in 242 it was annexed to Rome.

The dynasty was thus frequently interrupted by Roman (or Parthian) interference. It was all too easy for kings to fall foul of an empire, hence the relative frequency of such depositions. It is only surprising that the kingdom lasted in independence or quasi-independence as long as it did.

References
R Duval, *Histoire Politique et Litteraire d'Edesse jusqu'a la premiere Croisade* (Paris, 1892).
SK Ross, *Roman Edessa* (London, 1999).
JB Segal, *Edessa: 'the Blessed City'* (Oxford, 1976).

Egypt, 1080–343 BC.

A. Dynasty 'XXI', 1080-945 BC.

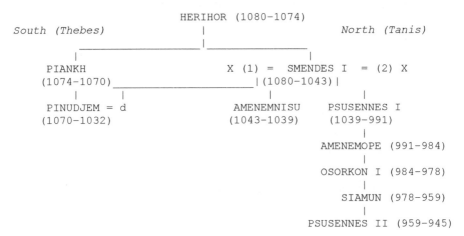

```
                          HERIHOR (1080-1074)
South (Thebes)                 |                        North (Tanis)
        _____|_____
        |                              |
      PIANKH              X (1)  =  SMENDES I  =  (2) X
    (1074-1070)_____|(1080-1043)|
        |       |                       |          |
    PINUDJEM = d                   AMENEMNISU   PSUSENNES I
    (1070-1032)                   (1043-1039)   (1039-991)
                                                    |
                                           AMENEMOPE (991-984)
                                                    |
                                           OSORKON I (984-978)
                                                    |
                                             SIAMUN (978-959)
                                                    |
                                         PSUSENNES II (959-945)
```

Statistics

Duration: 135 years; 7 generations, average length 135/7 = 19 years;
10 rulers, average length of reign, 135 = 14 years.

B. Dynasty 'XXII/XXIII', 945-715 BC.

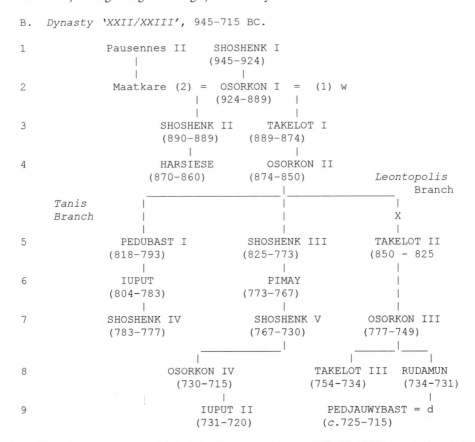

```
1            Pausennes II    SHOSHENK I
                  |          (945-924)
                  |              |
2            Maatkare (2) =  OSORKON I  =  (1) w
                  |          (924-889)  |
                  |              |       |
3                 SHOSHENK II       TAKELOT I
                  (890-889)      (889-874)
                      |              |
4                 HARSIESE        OSORKON II
                  (870-860)      (874-850)             Leontopolis
                                     |                     Branch
         Tanis        |              |              |
         Branch       |              |              X
                      |              |              |
5                PEDUBAST I      SHOSHENK III    TAKELOT II
                 (818-793)       (825-773)       (850 - 825
                      |              |              |
6                  IUPUT           PIMAY           |
                 (804-783)       (773-767)          |
                      |              |              |
7              SHOSHENK IV      SHOSHENK V      OSORKON III
                (783-777)       (767-730)       (777-749)
                          _____|_____        _|___
                          |              |         |     |
8                     OSORKON IV      TAKELOT III  RUDAMUN
                      (730-715)       (754-734)   (734-731)
                          |                            |
9                      IUPUT II       PEDJAUWYBAST = d
                      (731-720)       (c.725-715)
```

Statistics

Duration: 230 years; 9 generations, average length, 230/9 = 24 years;
19 rulers, average length of reign, 230/19 = 12 years.

C. *Dynasty 'XXV' (Nubian), c.780-542.*

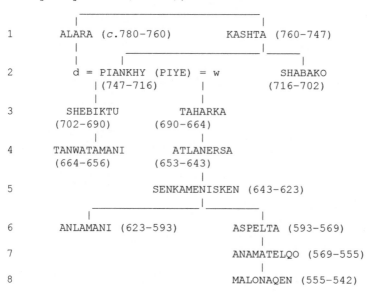

```
                |                          |
1          ALARA (c.780-760)         KASHTA (760-747)
                |          _____|_____
                |         |                       |
2          d = PIANKHY (PIYE) = w            SHABAKO
             |(747-716)        |             (716-702)
             |                 |
3         SHEBIKTU          TAHARKA
         (702-690)         (690-664)
             |                 |
4        TANWATAMANI        ATLANERSA
         (664-656)         (653-643)
                               |
5                  SENKAMENISKEN (643-623)
                  _____|_____
                 |                            |
6       ANLAMANI (623-593)          ASPELTA (593-569)
                                             |
7                                   ANAMATELQO (569-555)
                                             |
8                                   MALONAQEN (555-542)
```

Statistics

Duration: 238 years; 8 generations, average length, 238/8 = 29 years;
13 rulers, average length of reign, 238/13 = 16 years.

D. *Dynasty 'XXVI' (Saite), 672-570 BC.*

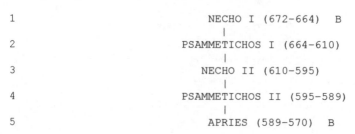

```
1                         NECHO I (672-664)   B
                                 |
2                    PSAMMETICHOS I (664-610)
                                 |
3                         NECHO II (610-595)
                                 |
4                   PSAMMETICHOS II (595-589)
                                 |
5                      APRIES (589-570)   B
```

Statistics

Duration: 102 years; 5 generations, average length, 102/5 = 20 years; 5
rulers, average length of reign, 102/5 = 20 years.

E. *Dynasty 'XXX'*, 380-343 BC.

```
1                    NEKTANEBO I (380-362)
                          |
2                     TACHOS (362-360)   D
                          |
3                     Tjahepimu
                          |
4                    NEKTANEBO II (360-343)
```

Statistics
Duration: 37 years; 4 generations, average length 37/4 = 8 years; 3 rulers, average length of reign, 37/3 = 12 years.

Commentary
The genealogies of Dynasties XXI–XXIII are very complex, subject to much disagreement and rearrangement. Those presented here is only one version, but the sequence of kings is about right, as is the length of the dynasties; some kings are not necessarily part of the family descent.

It was the practice of new Egyptian dynasties to link themselves, if possible, with the previous dynasty. At the demise of dynasty 'XXI', the daughter of Psusennes II, who descended from the preceding dynasty, was married to Osorkon, the son of the new king, Shoshenk I. This connection is, however, not enough to make the two into a single dynasty. Shoshenk had been Psusennes' chief army commander, and Maatkare's high birth ensured that both sons of Osorkon I inherited high positions, Shoshenk II as chief priest of Amun at Thebes in Upper Egypt, and Takelot I as pharaoh, based at Memphis in the north. A previous division of the country was thus renewed for a time, until the pharaoh (Osorkon II in this case) asserted his latent political power to subordinate the chief priest, and united the two branches.

As a result the two dynasties numbered 'XXII' and 'XXIII' have been combined in the table. The numbering of the dynasties was produced by the Hellenistic Egyptian historian Manetho, and is often an obstacle to proper understanding, for it implies a sequence of dynasties, whereas in fact many dynasties were contemporaries, as with these two. Therefore, where possible, I have added a name to the number, and the numbers are in quotation marks to indicate their artificiality. In fact it might be better to divide 'XXII/XXIII' into three dynasties, starting this with Takelot II.

Takelot's younger son Pedubast I seceded from the kingdom ruled by his brother Shoshenk III, setting himself up as king at Leontopolis, while Shoshenk III ruled from Tanis. Thus there might be reckoned a dynasty from Shoshenk I to Osorkon II (945–850, four generations, six kings), one at Tanis from Takelot II to Osorkon IV (850–715, five generations, five kings) and one at Leontopolis from Pedubast I to Iuput II and Pedjauwybast (818–715, six generations, seven kings). However, the whole group were really one family, and very largely seems to have been able to rule more or less collectively without too much infighting. Their internal contests were largely centred on the acquisition of religious positions in the main temples, and so on access to the wealth of the temples, and on the control of a few major garrisons. The division of authority and the kingdom did present opportunities for others, of course, and the kings' authority gradually declined, with a good half of the Delta being outside their control by the end: but the end came from outside.

The collapse of the Egyptian 'XXII/XXIII' dynastic regime opened the way for conquest from the south. A dynasty of kings had been established at Napata in Nubia for the past century or so. These kings encroached on Egypt slowly during the eighth century BC. The first of the kings who held authority in Egypt, Alara, and his brother Kashka, made only minor progress, but Kashka's son Piankhy/Piye was able to campaign as far as the Delta, having gained control of Thebes and Upper Egypt. In the north this apparent threat brought the Delta kings at Tanis and Leontopolis into alliance, but Piankhy beat them. He then confirmed them as governors in the cities they had ruled before his victory – but they did not last long, and all of them had given way to regularly appointed governors by 715. The Nubian dynasty was thoroughly unpopular, and was driven out of Egypt under Tamwatamani, but the family continued to rule in Nubia, perhaps as far as the fourth century AD (see 'Nubia' below). It is possible, even likely, that several more kings will be added to this dynasty by future researchers.

The source of resistance to the Nubian dynasty was one of the Delta cities, Sais, which thus became the seat of the next ruling dynasty ('XXVI', also 'Saite'). The Nubians had been in part driven out by the Assyrians, in alliance with the Saites; in return, Necho I was encouraged to expand his power as an Assyrian vassal. For twenty years he and his son did just that, until in 653 Psammetichos I was strong enough to repudiate Assyrian overlordship. This dynasty ended with a king, Apries, who provoked a civil war, and he was replaced by Amasis, whose two-member dynasty lasted until the conquest of Egypt by the Persians in 525.

The last dynasty of native Egyptian kings, dynasty 'XXX', emerged from the confusion of the near breakdown of the Persian Empire in 404. (Dynasties XXVII–XXIX are either Persian kings or unconnected kings.) The leader of the way into independence, Nepherites I, was the first of six kings in the next quarter century, only three of whom were related; the others are included in

Manetho's dynasty list under the number 'XXIX'. The sixth was Nektanebo, but his dynasty only held power until the Persian King Artaxerxes II made a sustained and determined effort to reunite his empire. After several attempts this was finally accomplished in 343. Twelve years later Egypt fell to the Macedonians, and Alexander the Great was welcomed as a liberator from Persian rule. But Egypt was not to be independent under its own king ever again.

For the succeeding dynasty, see 'Ptolemies'.

References
A Dobson and D Hulton, *The Complete Royal Families of Ancient Egypt* (London, 2004).
N Grimal, *A History of Egypt* (Oxford, 1992).
KA Kitchen, *The Late Intermediate Period in Egypt (1100–650 BC)* (Warminster, 1986).
DA Welsby, *The Kingdom of Kush, the Napatan and Meroitic Empires* (London, 1996).

Elam, Iran, *c.*760–644 BC

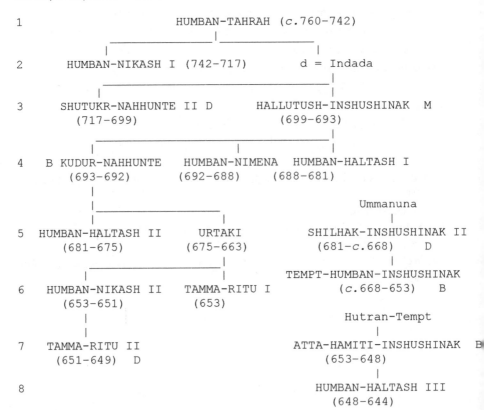

1   HUMBAN-TAHRAH (*c.*760–742)

2   HUMBAN-NIKASH I (742–717)   d = Indada

3   SHUTUKR-NAHHUNTE II D   HALLUTUSH-INSHUSHINAK   M
       (717–699)   (699–693)

4   B KUDUR-NAHHUNTE   HUMBAN-NIMENA   HUMBAN-HALTASH I
     (693–692)   (692–688)   (688–681)

                                    Ummanuna

5 HUMBAN-HALTASH II   URTAKI   SHILHAK-INSHUSHINAK II
    (681–675)   (675–663)   (681–*c.*668)   D

                               TEMPT-HUMBAN-INSHUSHINAK
6 HUMBAN-NIKASH II   TAMMA-RITU I   (*c.*668–653)   B
    (653–651)   (653)

                                Hutran-Tempt

7 TAMMA-RITU II   ATTA-HAMITI-INSHUSHINAK B
    (651–649)   D   (653–648)

8   HUMBAN-HALTASH III
                        (648–644)

Statistics

Duration: 116 years; 8 generations, average length $116/8 = 14$ years; 16 rulers, average length of reign $116/16 = 7$ years.

Commentary

This dynasty is largely known from the records of its enemies, notably the Assyrians, for whom this country was a constant nuisance and irritant on its borders. For a century they found the Elamite kingdom too large, awkward, distant, and resistant to suppress entirely. The ruling dynasty appears to have originated with a successful local chieftain in the hills on Elam's borders; Humban-Tahrah's conquest of the country took place as the Assyrians were concentrating heavily on Syria and the west, and by the third generation the family was in firm control. They had full local support, and harked back to earlier Elamite kingdoms in choosing their royal names. This was in effect a national state, with people and dynasty united in resistance to Assyrian attacks.

The Assyrians became active in the area in the 690s, having subjugated Babylonia. They campaigned repeatedly into the country; one king was removed, one assassinated (Hallutash–Inshushinak), and one died in battle (Kudur-Nahhunte), all within seven years. By 680 another Assyrian ploy was being used, recognizing two kings at once, in the hope of stimulating a debilitating competition, but this does not seem to have been very successful. Several Elamite princes were usually kept in captivity in Babylon for disruptive use in Elam whenever the Assyrians felt threatened. Four depositions or deaths in battle put the number of royal casualties at seven during little more than half a century. The average reign length for this dynasty is appallingly low. The dynasty suffered as badly as the people it ruled over in this warfare.

The records are not always explicit on the relationship of one king to another, but it is stated by their modern historian that all these kings were 'cousins', and so presumably all were of the royal line and descended from the first king. The several breaks in the succession therefore have been marked here by gaps, but are ignored in the calculations, which assume a single family.

The dynasty was eventually extinguished by the Assyrians, the last king being reduced, like the dynasty's founder, to a fugitive life in the hills of their origin. The Assyrian Empire outlasted the kingdom by only a generation. The true successor of the Elamite state was the Akhaimenid Empire, whose base was 'behind' Elam; Elam thus in effect sheltered the incipient Akhaimenid state from Assyrian assault. It was scarcely a consolation.

References
W Hinz, *The Lost World of Elam* (London, 1972).
G Roux, *Ancient Iraq* (Harmondsworth, 1966).

Epeiros, Aiakidai Dynasty, Greece, 385–231 BC

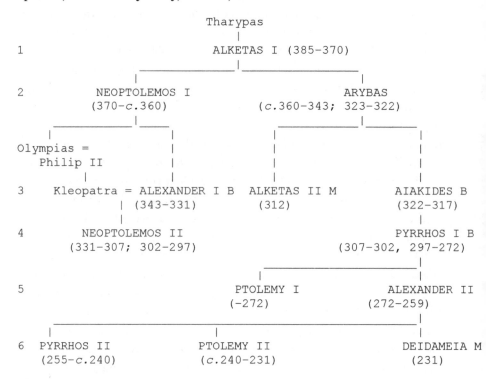

```
                              Tharypas
                                 |
1                        ALKETAS  I  (385-370)
          _____|_____
         |                                               |
2        NEOPTOLEMOS  I                               ARYBAS
            (370-c.360)                        (c.360-343;  323-322)
         _____|_____                     _____|_____
        |                 |                   |                      |
Olympias =                |                   |                      |
   Philip II              |                   |                      |
        |                 |                   |                      |
3    Kleopatra = ALEXANDER I B    ALKETAS II M          AIAKIDES B
           |  (343-331)              (312)              (322-317)
           |                                                 |
4        NEOPTOLEMOS II                              PYRRHOS I B
         (331-307;  302-297)                   (307-302,  297-272)
                                            _____|_____
                                           |                            |
5                              PTOLEMY I              ALEXANDER II
                                 (-272)                 (272-259)
                                                            |
                _____|
               |                 |                          |
6    PYRRHOS II            PTOLEMY II                 DEIDAMEIA M
     (255-c.240)          (c.240-231)                   (231)
```

Statistics

Durations: 154 years, 6 generations, average length 154/6 = 25 years;
13 rulers, average length of reign: 154/13 = 12 years.

Commentary

The kingdom of Epeiros was formed by the federation of several local tribes, of which the most important was the Molossoi, and it was the hereditary kings of the Molossoi who became kings of the Epeirotes. The earlier part of the dynasty, when the family were Molossian chieftains, is only a list of names, inaccurately recorded and manipulated later, and is here ignored, in part because of this, and in part because they only ruled as tribal chiefs and not as kings of fully organized states.

The first king of the united Epeirotes, Alketas I, is therefore taken as the founder of a new dynasty. He was exiled for ten years but returned in about 385 during a war in which all the Epeirote tribes had suffered from hostile invasions: a perfect situation for the unification of the several groups in the face of mutual danger. He thus had a weighty argument to advance.

The dynasty was, however, insecure, in part because of its external enemies, but mainly due to the internal tensions within the federation. So there is a break in the succession in the 320s when the country was subject to Macedonian rule, and the two branches of the royal line disputed the throne in the next two decades – Neoptolemos II's long first reign is largely one of powerlessness. Murder and deposition in the dynasty were common. One of the reasons for the wide-ranging military and conquering career of Pyrrhos I, who fought every neighbour from Macedon to Rome, was to escape these internal tensions. In the end they got the better of the dynasty, when it was reduced to a single, unmarried woman. Deidameia's murder, a brutal and sacrilegious business, removed both her rule and the dynasty, and opened the way for the Republican regime that followed.

The precise descent and dating of individual kings is not always clear, in part because of the internal complications of the dynastic situation, and in part because, except during Pyrrhos I's career, Epeiros was of only peripheral interest to Greeks generally, and to historians in the ancient world. However, there do not seem to be any missing kings, and the start and end of the dynasty are correct to within a year or so, so the calculations are valid. The fate of all the kings is not known for certain, but violence accounted for a considerable number of them.

References
P Garoufalas, *Pyrrhos* (London, 1979).
NGL Hammond, *Epirus* (Oxford, 1967).

Ergyng, Wales, AD *c.*555–*c.*620 (fragmentary)

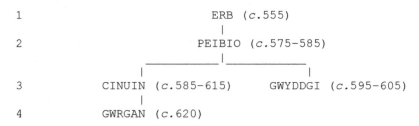

```
1                               ERB  (c.555)
                                 |
2                            PEIBIO (c.575-585)
                    _____|_____
             |                                |
3       CINUIN (c.585-615)        GWYDDGI (c.595-605)
             |
4       GWRGAN (c.620)
```

Statistics
Duration: 65 years; 4 generations, average length, 65/4 = 16 years; 5 rulers, average length of reign, 65/5 = 13 years.

Commentary
Ergyng was a small kingdom on the borders of South Wales and England. The names of these kings are recorded in charters issued by them, although the dating is very uncertain. It is probable that the dynasty lasted a good time longer than shown in the table, but the information simply does not exist. This section would seem to be accurate, however.

References
W Davies, *An Early Welsh Microcosm* (London, 1978).

Galatia, (Deiotarids), Asia Minor, 63–6 BC

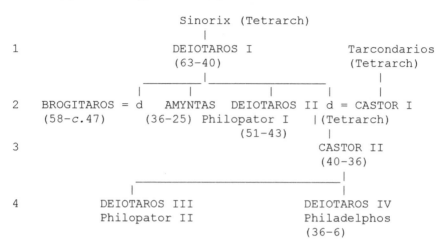

```
                        Sinorix (Tetrarch)
                              |
1                       DEIOTAROS I                Tarcondarios
                          (63-40)                   (Tetrarch)
                _____|_____               |
          |         |           |        |             |
2    BROGITAROS = d  AMYNTAS  DEIOTAROS II d = CASTOR I
     (58-c.47)     (36-25)  Philopator I  |(Tetrarch)
                             (51-43)       |
3                                         CASTOR II
                                          (40-36)
                                             |
          _____|
          |                                   |
4     DEIOTAROS III                     DEIOTAROS IV
      Philopator II                     Philadelphos
                                        (36-6)
```

Statistics
Duration: 57 years; 4 generations, average length, 57/4 = 16 years; 8 rulers, average length of reign, 57/8 = 7 years.

Commentary
Galatia was a section of interior Asia Minor occupied by the invading Gauls in the third century BC, and ruled by the chieftains of the three constituent tribes. By the first century BC disparities of wealth and the pressure of Rome led to the emergence of pre-eminent families in all three tribes, who bore the titles of tetrarch. Rome promoted some to kings, and they were used to control their land, and sometimes other lands (Deiotaros IV Philadelphos was made king of Paphlagonia, for instance). The conversion of Galatia into a Roman province in 25 BC put an end to the dynasty in that country, such as it was. (In the calculations, only kings are included – Deiotaros III Philopator II does not seem to have actually ruled.) The result is, of course, an untidy dynasty, a situation that recurred with other Roman dominated rulers.

References
S Mitchell, *Anatolia, Land, Men and Gods in Asia Minor*, vol. 1 (Oxford, 1993).
RD Sullivan, *Near Eastern Royalty and Rome, 100–30 BC* (Toronto, 1989).

Ghassanids, North Arabia, AD 502–583

```
                        Thalaba
                           |
1                    AL-HARITH I (502-c.518)
                           |
2                    DJABALA (c.518-529)
                           |
3                    AL-HARITH II (529-569)
                           |
4                    AL-MUNDHIR (569-582) D
                           |
5                    AL-NUMAN (582-583) D
```

Statistics

Duration: 81 years; 5 generations, average length $81/5 = 16$ years; 5 rulers, average length of reign, $81/5 = 16$ years.

Commentary

The Byzantine borderland along the Syrian Desert was the scene of several sub-kingdoms sponsored by the Byzantine emperors from the fourth century onwards. Only the Ghassanids are known well enough to be included here. They were organizers of the kingdom under al-Harith I as a counterpoint to a similar kingdom on the Iraqi borderland (the Lakhmids) which had existed for some time under Sassanid suzerainty. It was thus sponsored by the Byzantine Empire, and was never really independent. It was, however, also liable to escape from Byzantine control without constant supervision. After the death of the long-lived al-Harith II, the most powerful and successful of the Ghassanid kings, his two sons were disposed of successively by their sponsors and the tribal kingdom was then broken up. A descendant was still fighting for the Byzantine government at the time of the Islamic invasion, but he was by then only an army officer.

References

PK Hitti, *History of the Arabs* (London, 1961).

KA Kitchen, *Documentation for Ancient Arabia*, I (Liverpool, 1992) pp. 164 and 252.

I Shahid, *Byzantium and the Arabs in the Fourth Century* (Washington DC, 1984).

Glywysing, Wales, AD *c.*620–785

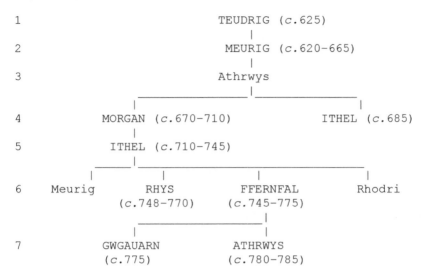

```
1                                    TEUDRIG  (c.625)
                                         |
2                                    MEURIG  (c.620-665)
                                         |
3                                    Athrwys
                     _____|_____
                    |                                         |
4        MORGAN  (c.670-710)                      ITHEL  (c.685)
                    |
5            ITHEL  (c.710-745)
        _____|_____
       |            |                     |                  |
6   Meurig        RHYS                 FFERNFAL           Rhodri
                (c.748-770)          (c.745-775)
                                         |
                          _____|
                         |               |
7                    GWGAUARN         ATHRWYS
                     (c.775)          (c.780-785)
```

Statistics
Duration: 165 years; 7 generations, average length, 165/7 = 24 years; 9 rulers, average length of reign, 165/9 = 18 years.

Commentary
The sources for this dynasty are a series of witness lists attached to charters issued by the kings of Glywysing, which is more or less the modern county of Glamorgan in South Wales. Dating has had to be teased out by long and tedious comparisons of the names on the lists, assisted by occasional outside references to the kings, or to others on the list. It is not certain, therefore, that all kings are included, but the genealogy seems certain enough. Dating is not, however; only one date on the table is firm, since it is known that Ffernfal died in 775. A century later another family can be traced for some time in the kingdom, and this may or may not be connected with this dynasty.

References
W Davies, *An Early Welsh Microcosm* (London, 1978).

Hadramaut, South Arabia, AD 245–post 265 (fragmentary)

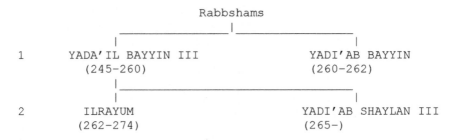

```
                          Rabbshams
         _____|_____
         |                               |
1     YADA'IL BAYYIN III              YADI'AB BAYYIN
         (245-260)                       (260-262)
         |
         |_____
         |                               |
2        ILRAYUM                       YADI'AB SHAYLAN III
         (262-274)                       (265-)
```

Statistics
Duration: 20 years plus; 2 generations, average length 20/2 = 10 years;
4 rulers, average length of reign, 20/4 = 5 years.

Commentary
Hadramaut in southern Arabia has produced evidence of monarchical rule at
several periods in the ancient world, but the relationships between the several
kings whose names are known, and the sections of dynasties are never clear;
the evidence is mainly from inscriptions, and the dates are extremely vague.
No dynasty longer than two generations or two kings can be detected, apart
from the one shown here, and the dates suggested are probably inaccurate; the
dynasty certainly lasted longer than twenty years.

References
KA Kitchen, *Documentation for Ancient Arabia*, I (Liverpool, 1994).

Himyar, South Arabia, AD 140–170 (fragmentary)

```
1                    YASIR YUHASDIQ (140-145)
                              |
2              DHARMA'ALAY YUHABIRR I (145-160)
                              |
3                      THA'RAN (160-170)
```

Statistics
Duration: 30 years; 3 generations, average length of $30/3 = 10$ years;
3 rulers, average length of reign $30/3 = 10$ years.

Commentary
Himyar was a south Arabian state that for a time linked all the sections of the area under its own rule, so much so that it is at times called an empire. The names of over thirty rulers are known, both before and during its imperial period, but only the three here listed can be linked together as a family. It seems probable that most of the named rulers were in fact all one dynasty, but the evidence does not exist to show it.

References
KA Kitchen, *Documentation for Ancient Arabia*, I (Liverpool, 1994).

Hwicce, England, AD *c.*645–*c.*780

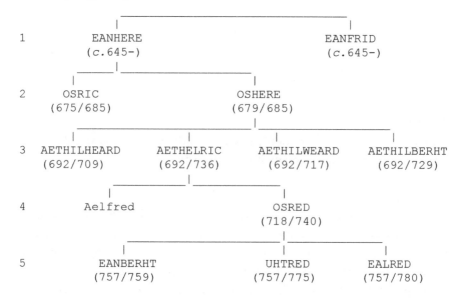

1	EANHERE (*c.*645-)
	EANFRID (*c.*645-)

Statistics
Duration: about 135 years; 5 generations, average length 135/5 = 27 years; 12 rulers, average length of reign 135/12 = 11 years.

Commentary
The Hwicce were people located in modern Gloucestershire, who were created as a principality by King Penda of Mercia after the Battle of Cirencester in 628. The date when he organized the principality is not known, but it must be after 628. I have assumed it was at the same time as the creation of the Magonsaete across the Severn, which cannot seriously have been earlier than 645.

It has been theorized from the names of some of the kings that they originated from Northumbria, exiles from their homes fighting in alliance with Penda. The relationships are certainly accurate, based on charter evidence. It is because of this evidence that the dates are so uncertain; only the earliest and latest records can be relied on. And it is impossible that the principality lasted longer than is suggested here.

The purpose of the principality was as a buffer state against Mercia's enemies in Wales and in Wessex. The rulers were at first referred to as kings, but the last generation were simply called princes; in other words the principality declined in importance in the eyes of those producing the charters, and therefore presumably those ruling Mercia. The construction of Offa's Dyke in the 780s as an agreed boundary between Mercia and Wales probably rendered the Hwicce unnecessary as a state; in the ninth century it was clearly reckoned as part of Mercia without any ruler of its own.

References
HPR Finberg, 'The Princes of the Magonsaete', in *The Early Charters of the West Midlands*, 2nd ed. (Leicester, 1972).

Iberia, Caucasus, 109 BC–AD 580

A. *Pharnabazid Dynasty*, 109 BC–AD 189.

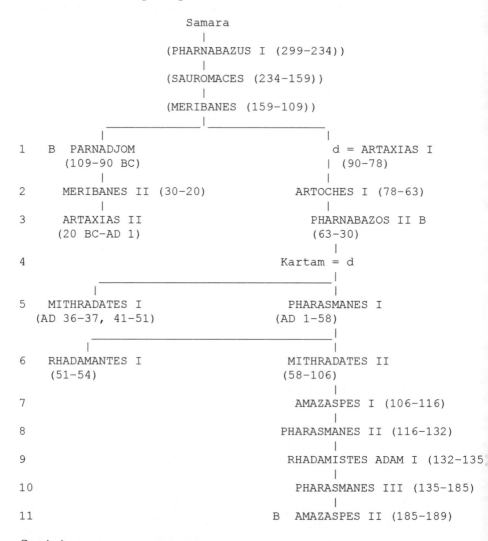

```
                         Samara
                           |
                (PHARNABAZUS I (299-234))
                           |
                (SAUROMACES (234-159))
                           |
                (MERIBANES (159-109))
         _____|_____
         |                                          |
1   B  PARNADJOM                          d = ARTAXIAS I
        (109-90 BC)                       |  (90-78)
           |                                 |
2       MERIBANES II (30-20)            ARTOCHES I (78-63)
           |                                 |
3       ARTAXIAS II                    PHARNABAZOS II B
        (20 BC-AD 1)                    (63-30)
                                             |
4                                       Kartam = d
            _____|
            |                               |
5       MITHRADATES I                   PHARASMANES I
        (AD 36-37, 41-51)               (AD 1-58)
                                             |
            _____|
            |                               |
6       RHADAMANTES I                   MITHRADATES II
        (51-54)                         (58-106)
                                             |
7                                       AMAZASPES I (106-116)
                                             |
8                                       PHARASMANES II (116-132)
                                             |
9                                       RHADAMISTES ADAM I (132-135)
                                             |
10                                      PHARASMANES III (135-185)
                                             |
11                                 B    AMAZASPES II (185-189)
```

Statistics
Duration: 298 years; 11 generations, average length, 298/11 = 27 years;
15 rulers, average length of reign, 298/15 = 20 years.

Commentary
Iberia was a small kingdom in the Caucasus area. Its first known ruler, Samara,
was lord of the city Mtskheta, but he and his next three descendants cannot
be accepted in this dynastic study: three generations covering over 190 years

is clearly the product of myth rather than history. It is quite possible the kings did exist, and in this order, but the correct dates are not known, and perhaps other kings need to be inserted. From Parnadjom I onwards, however, the record is acceptable.

The pattern of inheritance is unusual: Parnadjom I was succeeded by his brother-in-law, whose family ruled for the next sixty years, and then were succeeded by Parnadjom's son, whose own son was then succeeded by another cousin. This pattern points to a process of selecting the king based on a direct hereditary succession, but choosing one male of the family to rule for life. The disputes that are evident in the first century AD may well be the result of the change in this process, for the rest of the dynasty saw a new scheme, of direct father-to-son succession.

The very long claimed reigns at the start of the dynasty are replicated also by those of Pharasmanes I and Mithradates II, and then by Pharasmanes III, but these are in fact separated by several shorter reigns. Three in a row at the beginning averaging, $190/3 = 63$ years per generation, won't do.

```
B.   Arsakid Dynasty, AD 189-284.

                    Vologaeses II of Armenia and Parthia
                            |
1                       REV I (189-216)
                            |
2                       VATCHE I (216-234)
                            |
3                     BACURIUS I (234-249)
                            |
4                   MITHRADATES II (249-265)
                            |
5                   ASPACURAS I (265-284)
```

Statistics
Duration: 95 years; 5 generations, average length $95/5 = 19$ years; 5 rulers, average length of reign, $95/5 = 19$ years.

Commentary
The first Iberian dynasty had been native to the area, so far as can be seen, with a mixture of Iranian and Armenian names for the kings, an indication of the cultural area it inhabited. In 189, however, a branch of the Parthian Arsakid family acceded, descended from a Parthian king who had been king in Armenia before taking over as Great King in Parthia. How Rev I was chosen as king is not clear, perhaps by marriage, perhaps by the previous

dynasty dying out; the last of the dynasty was killed in battle, which is a clear
enough clue.

C.   *Chosroid Dynasty*, AD 284-580.

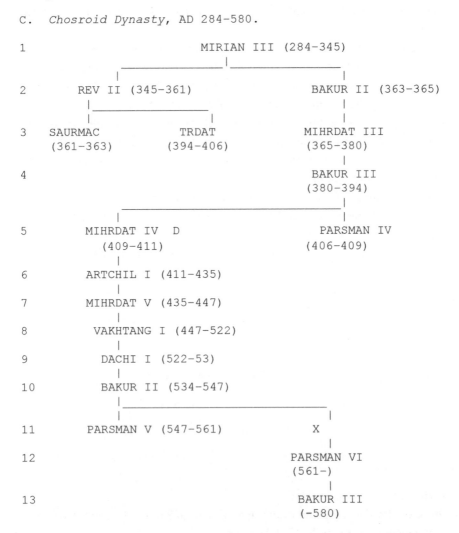

```
1                              MIRIAN III (284-345)
                    _____|_____
                   |                                  |
2          REV II (345-361)                  BAKUR II  (363-365)
             |_____                        |
             |               |                       |
3     SAURMAC            TRDAT             MIHRDAT III
      (361-363)          (394-406)         (365-380)
                                                     |
4                                          BAKUR III
                                           (380-394)
                                                     |
           _____|
          |                                          |
5     MIHRDAT IV  D                         PARSMAN IV
         (409-411)                          (406-409)
            |
6     ARTCHIL I (411-435)
            |
7     MIHRDAT V (435-447)
            |
8      VAKHTANG I (447-522)
            |
9       DACHI I (522-53)
            |
10     BAKUR II (534-547)
            |_____
            |                             |
11    PARSMAN V (547-561)                 X
                                          |
12                                 PARSMAN VI
                                   (561-)
                                          |
13                                 BAKUR III
                                   (-580)
```

Statistics
Duration: 296 years; 13 generations, average length, $296/13 = 23$ years;
17 rulers, average length of reign, $296/17 = 17$ years.

Commentary
The third Iberian dynasty, which replaced the Arsakid line, was local once
more. This dynasty was extremely long-lived, and had a curious method of
inheritance at the start, reminiscent of the method used by the Pharnabazid

dynasty. The dynasty ruling in Iberia lasted until 580, and a subordinate dynasty descended from that one continued to rule in a small principality for some centuries yet.

References
David Braund, *Georgia in Antiquity: a History of Colchis and Trancaucasian Iberia, 550 BC–AD 562* (Oxford, 1994).
C Toumanoff, *Manuel de genealogie et de chronologie de la Caucasus chretienne* (Rome, 1976).

Ireland, High Kings, AD 445–565

The genealogies of the Irish dynasties are broken and divided, because the system of succession skipped about between dynasties as well as between individuals. The only way to display the Irish rulers as dynasties is to isolate the names of the kings, and ignore the gaps. These gaps can appear as chronological spaces, or as absent individuals, entered as X. (See also Connacht, Leinster, Meath, Munster, Ulster.)

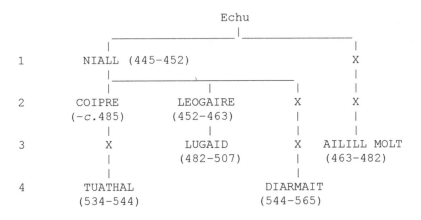

```
                                Echu
                                  |
         _____|_____
         |                                                  |
1     NIALL  (445-452)                                       X
         |                                                   |
         |_____                      |
         |                    \           |           |      |
2     COIPRE           LEOGAIRE           X           X
      (-c.485)         (452-463)          |           |
         |                    |           |           |
3        X               LUGAID           X       AILILL  MOLT
         |               (482-507)        |       (463-482)
         |                    |           |
4     TUATHAL                      DIARMAIT
      (534-544)                    (544-565)
```

Statistics
Duration: 120 years, reigning for 93; 4 generations, average length, 120/4 = 30 years; 7 rulers, average length of reign, 93/7 = 13 years.

Commentary
The early kings in Ireland, of various lines, are seemingly well-recorded, but considerable imagination is also employed in the records. The earliest kings are badly dated, or not at all, all too many of them being linked in some way with the mission effort of St Patrick, and several men seem to migrate from one line to another. As a result the earliest kings must be rejected as too badly recorded to be accepted.

Then there is the problem of the system of succession. This was based in theory on the elevation to the kingship of the eldest male of the extended family; in fact, it was also often a free-for-all. The result of all this is that it has proved to be very difficult to decide which dynasties to include.

The first decision was to exclude all dynasties below the provincial level. This confined the possibilities to half a dozen lines: that of the High Kings, and those of Leinster, Connacht, Meath, and Munster, and the two competing lines in Ulster. The decision to exclude dynasties at the sub-provincial level was all the easier because of the poor, fragmentary, and unreliable records.

A second decision involved the continuations of the dynasties. More than one had descendants into and beyond the eighth or ninth centuries. The Ui Neill High Kings continued beyond several of the lines listed here, though as it happened only one was significant, the descendants of Aed Uaridnach, whose great-grandson Fergal was High King in 710–723 and founded the notable line of the Northern Ui Neill who were kings in Ailech into the eleventh century. Similarly the Dal Fiatach line of the kings of Ulster revived after the death of Matudan in 857 in a new line of kings descended from Eochaid, a line that lasted until 1201. Their rivals of the Cruthin line continued to compete with a line lasting into the late tenth century. The later kings of Leinster descended also into the eleventh century from Faelan (who died in 666) in a large and complex dynasty. In Munster the Eoganacht line revived after the death of Artri in 820 in a line descended from Colcu that lasted into the tenth century, and in a further extension as kings of Desmond into the fourteenth century.

These extensions, however, did not produce new information on dynasties as a group, though they do undermine my argument that the mid eighth century saw a decisive break with the dynasties of the ancient world. Ireland, of course, like Scotland, had scarcely been a part of that ancient world centred on the Mediterranean and the Near East, and so there is no reason to expect it to conform to any pattern that existed in these areas – indeed, the fact that the Irish dynasties were different in so many ways might be thought to confirm the mid eighth century as a decisive break-point of the ancient world proper. Accordingly I have chosen more or less suitable breaks in the Irish dynasties in the eighth and early ninth centuries as cut-off points. The calculations of generation and reign lengths and the pattern of succession did not materially change over the next centuries.

A further decision forced itself on me as I drew out the diagrams. It was clear that simply putting in all the possible names would be misleading, distracting, and confusing. So those who are not actually kings have been marked, in these tables only, simply with an 'X'. This brings out the names of the kings, and emphasizes the extraordinary mode of succession. It also brought out the fact that several of these royal families were in fact made up of distinct dynasties within the whole extended family. In Ulster the two competing families, the Cruthin and the Dal Fiatach, were always distinct, and more or less alternated in providing kings. In effect this pattern also applied in older dynasties. The High Kings of the Ui Neill sub-divided into four distinct dynasties, in Connacht there are three, in Leinster two, and in Ulster the Dal Fiatach can be divided into two also. Only in Munster did the

Eoganacht dynasty remain more or less one, though I was certainly tempted to recognize sub-divisions.

The problem of dates, both the lack of them for the earliest kings, and their probable inaccuracy before the eighth century, forced me to ignore some of the early rulers in the calculations. Also the sub-divisions of the several dynasties I have adopted made it difficult to make sensible calculations: I have therefore distinguished generation and ruler years, the latter being only the number of years the sub-dynasty actually provided kings.

The calculations demonstrate that the mode of succession resulted in a series of brief rulers, largely because so many kings acceded at an advanced age. The wide disparity between generation lengths, which are unusually high, in the upper twenties or higher, and the average reign lengths, often in single figures, is the statistical manifestation of this. This clearly had consequences for royal power, and for the general history of the island. Only kings with a chance of a lengthy reign can achieve serious and long-term political results, and if such a king is succeeded by elderly men with brief reigns, any of his achievements are liable to be undone. The patrilineal succession of the Norman invaders was one of their major secret weapons.

Lastly the detail in these tables is not necessarily accurate; the source material is usually much later than the lives of the kings, and the record has undoubtedly in many cases been manipulated in order to enhance the reputations of families, or to provide a claim to some title or territory, or to denigrate another. This caveat must be constantly borne in mind.

(In several of the tables it is clear that the various branches of the families do not synchronize well. I have not attempted to do more than tabulate them as recorded, with the result that some kings reign long after their theoretical contemporaries. But these dynasties are complicated enough already; fiddling with the intervening generations would make things even worse.)

References
TW Moody, FX Martin, FJ Byrne, *A Hew History of Ireland*, vol. IX (Oxford, 1994).

Israel, Palestine, 885–753 BC

A. *Omrids*, 885–841 BC.

```
1                               OMRI  (885-874)
                                  |
2                  Jezebel  =  AHAB  (874-853)   B
          _____|_____
          |                                     |
3   AHAZIAH  (853-852)             JORAM  (852-841)  M
```

Statistics
Duration: 44 years; 3 generations, average length, $44/3 = 15$ years; 4 rulers, average length of reign, $44/4 = 11$ years.

Commentary
Omri was the effective founder of the kingdom of Israel, above all by his development of the city of Samaria as his central stronghold, and, in recognition of this, the kingdom was called 'bit-Humri' ('House of Omri') by the Assyrians. (Earlier kings, recorded in the Bible, may or may not have existed – but they were not dynastically connected with Omri.) It was, however, an unstable state. Omri, a military man, had to fight a five-year civil war to make good his kingship, which is perhaps an indication of the difficulty of his campaign to form the state, and his dynasty did not last very long. That this short-lived dynasty is seen as successful is a measure of the kingdom's plight.

Ahab was as vigorous a ruler as his father, but was trapped in an international situation he could not dominate. His marriage to Jezebel of Tyre was a result of an alliance with that city, but was not enough to ensure loyalty to the dynasty. Ahab's death in battle was followed by his eldest son's death without issue, and his second son's murder in the next military coup, led by Jehu.

B. *Jehunids*, 841–753 BC.

```
1                        JEHU  (841-814)
                           |
2                   JEHOAHAZ  (814-798)
                           |
3                   JEHOASH  (798-782)
                           |
4                   JEROBOAM II  (782-753)
                           |
5                   ZECHARIAH  (753)   M
```

Statistics

Duration: 88 years; 5 generations, average length 88/5 = 18 years; 5 rulers, average length of reign, 88/5 = 18 years.

Commentary

Jehu seized power in Israel by murdering the previous king and all his family, and thereupon founded the longest-lived dynasty of the kingdom. The bloodthirsty coup ensured his own power for the rest of his life, though his aggressiveness also ensured his and his kingdom's isolation. Only with the third and fourth kings was some sort of internal stability achieved, and that was in part due also to the absence of Assyrian attacks. But even that lengthy period could not remove the canker at the heart of Israel's politics. The last king of the dynasty, Zechariah, was murdered by a man called Shallum, who lasted as king for only a month. From then on Israel continued to exist as a state only on Assyrian sufferance, and this powerfully increased the dynastic instability. Less than a quarter of a century after Zechariah's death, Israel had been destroyed as a kingdom.

References

J Bright, *A History of Israel* (London, 1960).
EW Heaton, *The Hebrew Kingdoms* (Oxford, 1968).
WOE Oesterly and TH Robinson, *A History of Israel*, vol. 1 (Oxford, 1932).

Judaea, Palestine, 166 BC–AD 100

A. *Hasmoneans (or Maccabaeans), 166–35 BC.*

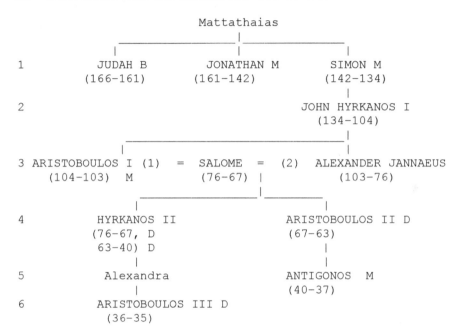

```
                              Mattathaias
                    _____|_____
             |                 |                    |
1         JUDAH B        JONATHAN M            SIMON M
         (166-161)      (161-142)             (142-134)
                                                  |
2                                          JOHN HYRKANOS I
                                              (134-104)
                                                  |
                    _____|
             |                                    |
3 ARISTOBOULOS I (1)    =    SALOME    =    (2)   ALEXANDER JANNAEUS
    (104-103)   M           (76-67)  |              (103-76)
                    _____|_____
             |                              |
4         HYRKANOS II                 ARISTOBOULOS II D
         (76-67, D                    (67-63)
         63-40) D                         |
             |                            |
5         Alexandra                  ANTIGONOS   M
             |                       (40-37)
6      ARISTOBOULOS III D
         (36-35)
```

Statistics

Duration: 131 years; 6 generations, average length 131/6 = 22 years; 11 rulers, average length of reign, 131/11 = 12 years.

Commentary

The Maccabean rebellion against Seleukid rule in Palestine rapidly produced a new state. Ironically this was organized on the same lines as the Seleukid state that was being rejected, and this included a ruling dynasty descended from the leaders of the rebellion. It was an aggressive state, and its internal politics were always turbulent, reflecting its illicit origin. Of the first three rulers, Judah died in battle with the Seleukids, Jonathan was killed by a Seleukid usurper, and Simon was murdered in an internal family-cum-political dispute – this set of deaths being in effect a reflection of the state's problems.

The last generation fell foul of both sides in the Romano-Parthian wars and the Roman civil wars. Most of the kings were deposed by Roman warriors who found Hasmonean independence as unacceptable as had the Seleukid kings. In the end the whole dynasty was eliminated in favour of Herod, who was far more acceptable to Rome, not least because of his obsequious loyalty combined with a ruthless ability to control the Jewish state.

The dynasty is thus a complex business, the kings very liable to violent death or deposition. It was rescued for a time by the widow of Alexander Jannaeus, Salome, but her sons fell to disputing the throne, so leaving the opportunity open for Roman interference. From 63 BC onwards the kings were little more than Roman subordinates.

B.   *Herodians*, 37 BC–AD 100.

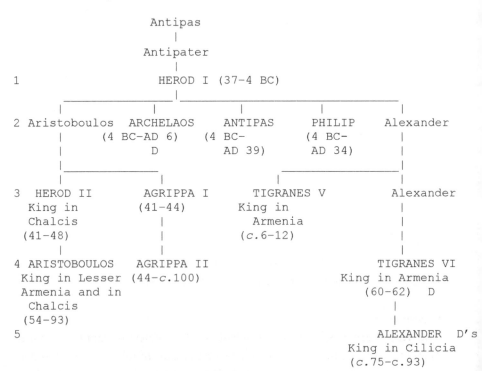

```
                        Antipas
                           |
                        Antipater
                           |
1                       HEROD I (37-4 BC)
        _____|_____
        |               |          |          |           |
2 Aristoboulos    ARCHELAOS     ANTIPAS     PHILIP     Alexander
        |          (4 BC-AD 6)   (4 BC-     (4 BC-         |
        |               D         AD 39)     AD 34)        |
        |                                                  |
        |_____                         _____
        |              |              |          |              |
3  HEROD II       AGRIPPA I       TIGRANES V              Alexander
   King in        (41-44)         King in                     |
   Chalcis           |            Armenia                     |
   (41-48)           |            (c.6-12)                    |
        |            |                                        |
4 ARISTOBOULOS   AGRIPPA II                           TIGRANES VI
  King in Lesser (44-c.100)                         King in Armenia
  Armenia and in                                      (60-62)   D
  Chalcis                                                  |
  (54-93)                                                  |
5                                                   ALEXANDER   D's
                                                    King in Cilicia
                                                    (c.75-c.93)
```

Statistics
Duration: 137 years, reigning for 132; 5 generations, average length, 137/5 = 27 years; 11 rulers, average length of reign 132/11 = 12 years.

Commentary
The full genealogy of the descendants of Herod the Great is made extraordinarily complex by his numerous marriages. It is also further complicated by the use made of the family by the Roman government, which posted various members to rule various kingdoms and territories in the east, ranging from Armenia to Judaea. Eliminating non-rulers and wives

does simplify the basic structure somewhat, but it does not remove all the territorial complications.

Herod himself, in fact, was from Idumaea, a southern province of the Jewish state whose population had been conquered and forcibly converted to Judaism (or massacred, or expelled) by the Hasmoneans. He promoted himself to the Judaean kingship in succession to the last Hasmoneans, who had finally been removed by the Romans for allying with the Parthians (though he married a Hasmonaean princess as a claim to legitimacy). Herod's father Antipater had been a major politician under the last of the Hasmoneans, and Herod grew up in a political atmosphere. His usefulness and obsequiousness to successive Roman governors, triumvirs, and emperors, together with his undoubted ability, ensured both support from Rome and his subjects' hatred. After his death the kingdom was dismantled and his children each inherited sections of the kingdom; Archelaos was eventually deposed and exiled by Augustus for some misdemeanour, in reality for incapacity. Antipas and Philip each ruled their small states well and competently until their deaths.

The next generation saw a further scattering. Herod II ruled Chalcis (he is usually called 'Herod of Chalcis'), a small state north of Judaea in modern Lebanon; Agrippa II reunited all the Judaean fragments for a brief reign of only three years (courtesy of his friend the Emperor Claudius); Tigranes V was appointed to Armenia – hence his name – but only briefly. Agrippa II's success was due almost entirely to friendship with the emperor, whom he had assisted in timely fashion in the crisis of his accession after the murder of Caligula. (Women of the dynasty were also married off into other royal houses in the region, including that of Emesa, Pontos, and Kommagene.) The final generations ruled in Armenia, Chalcis, across the Jordan, and in Cilicia, but never again in Judaea, though they retained influence there, since most of them were practising Jews. The last of the family to rule a kingdom, Alexander in Cilicia, either resigned or was deposed and then moved to Rome where his sons became consuls and provincial governors.

This was a dynasty only lightly rooted in any single territory, as is shown by the variety of kingdoms, and by the frequency of depositions imposed upon them when Rome changed its mind – Herod the Great himself was never regarded as wholly Jewish. So the dynasty only survived as long as the Roman government had a use for it. This does not seem likely to have been the future envisaged for his family by Herod when he fought for the Judaean throne, but it was the future path he set it on by his own behaviour towards Rome.

References

JD Grainger, *The Wars of the Maccabees* (Barnsley, 2012).

M Grant, *Herod the Great* (New York, 1971).

N Kokkinos, *The Herodian Dynasty, Origins, Role in Society, and Eclipse* (Sheffield, 1998).

S Perowne, *The Later Herods, the Political Background to the New Testament* (London, 1958).

P Richardson, *Herod, King of the Jews and Friend of the Romans* (Columbia, SC, 1996).

E Schurer, *The History of the Jewish People in the Age of Jesus Christ*, ed. and rev. by G Vermes, F Millar, and M Black, vol. 1 (Edinburgh, 1973).

RD Sullivan, 'The Dynasty of Judaea in the First Century', *Aufsteig und Niedergang des Romischen Welt* II, 8 (1977) pp. 296–354.

Judah, Palestine, 869–587 BC

A. *House of David*, 869-735 BC.

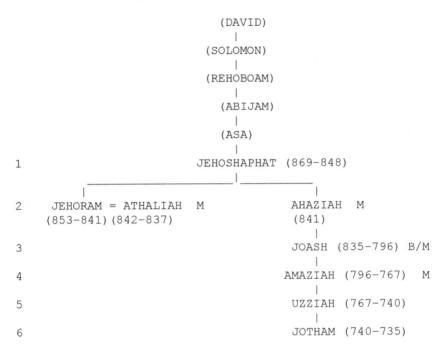

```
                              (DAVID)
                                 |
                             (SOLOMON)
                                 |
                             (REHOBOAM)
                                 |
                              (ABIJAM)
                                 |
                               (ASA)
                                 |
1                       JEHOSHAPHAT  (869-848)
            _____|_____
            |                                     |
2    JEHORAM = ATHALIAH   M              AHAZIAH   M
     (853-841)(842-837)                   (841)
                                             |
3                                        JOASH  (835-796)  B/M
                                             |
4                                       AMAZIAH  (796-767)   M
                                             |
5                                        UZZIAH  (767-740)
                                             |
6                                        JOTHAM  (740-735)
```

Statistics

Duration: 134 years; 6 generations, average length 134/6 = 22 years; 8 rulers, average length of reign 134/8 = 17 years.

B. *Second Dynasty*, 735-587 BC.

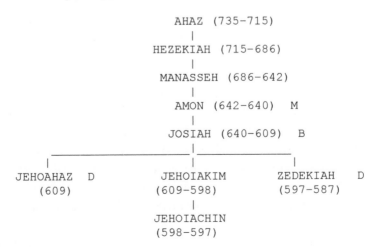

```
                         AHAZ  (735-715)
                              |
                       HEZEKIAH  (715-686)
                              |
                       MANASSEH  (686-642)
                              |
                         AMON  (642-640)   M
                              |
                        JOSIAH  (640-609)   B
            _____|_____
            |                 |                 |
      JEHOAHAZ   D       JEHOIAKIM         ZEDEKIAH   D
        (609)            (609-598)         (597-587)
                              |
                         JEHOIACHIN
                         (598-597)
```

Statistics
Duration: 148 years, 7 generations, average length 148/= 21 years; 9 rulers, average length of reign, 148/9 = 16 years.

Commentary
The dynasty of Judah is called the House of David, from the name its supposed ancestor, but evidence outside the biblical account in the books of *Samuel* and *Kings* (and *Chronicles*) does not exist for the early rulers – these books were actually written in exile in Babylonia, far from the Jews' homeland and far from source material. I have therefore decided to separate off the first generations and to regard them as partly legendary, their careers distorted as propaganda, or perhaps invented. (A recently discovered inscription from north Syria does describe Ahaziah as 'king of the House of David', though this is in connection with an event in 841, and is from north Syria, so there has been plenty of time for the legend of David to become firmly fixed.)

The biblical account insists on a direct royal succession by males for over four centuries and through nineteen generations. No other dynasty in either the ancient or the modern world can even approximate this record. (The attempt by the French dynasty to create such a succession, by means of their conveniently invented Salic Law, produced a constant male succession, as was its aim, but not by a direct line; the best it could do was 341 years of the Capetian dynasty before the succession broke down.) In the circumstances acceptance of the biblical account of the Judahite succession is an act of faith, not something for which there is independent or acceptable evidence. The first man in the list likely to have been a real king seems to be Jehoshaphat, a contemporary of Omri of Israel; the emergence of a strong monarchy in the richer lands of Israel to the north may well thus have stimulated a defensive reaction among his neighbours in Judaea; it certainly did so in Moab, across the Jordan River to the east. On the other hand, the earliest king for whom we have any independent evidence of his existence is Ahaziah in the inscription noted earlier. Ahab is also noted in this inscription.

The episode of Athaliah is a characteristic problem of this dynasty. It is evidently adapted from the events in Israel associated with Queen Jezebel, the wife of King Ahab, a few years before. Athaliah is reported to have murdered all the House of David who had survived an earlier massacre by Jehu of Israel, but she missed the 1-year-old Joash, her grandson – surely an unlikely omission. The deed itself is not that unlikely, and can be paralleled elsewhere. An alternative view is that she did not carry out the massacre, but acted as regent for Joash after Ahaziah's murder. But we now know that Ahaziah died in battle. Yet another alternative would be to suppose that the murders were carried out successfully, and that a substitute Joash was produced (at the age of seven) by the anti-Athaliah opposition, once Athaliah had made herself seriously unpopular. The whole story can only be accepted if its contradictions are ignored – and its implausibility – in the interests of the lurid plot. Joash is said to have been long-lived; whatever may have happened in his childhood (if anything), by the end of his forty-year reign it was in the interests of all to accept the story. The whole sequence of events is thus extremely suspect; independent non-biblical evidence for it is required.

There are other problems with the whole tradition. The book of *Kings* kindly provides the ages of kings from the accession of Jehoshaphat to the end of the dynasty. If they are all accurate it is clear that many of the kings procreated very young – seven were born while their fathers were in their teens, one when his father was aged only eleven. It is also clear that the father-to-son succession was disrupted at least twice, in clear contradiction to the claim: Jehoram was born in 885 and his successor, supposedly his son, was born only two years later – he and Ahaziah were thus no doubt brothers, and they are so treated here (if they existed, of course). And the end of the dynasty saw the second son of Josiah, Jehoahaz, succeed before his elder brother Jehoakim, and the last king, Zedekiah, was the uncle of his predecessor Jehoiachin.

There are two periods of death by violence: the early years and the end of the dynasty. The latter is the only one independently tested, and was associated with the international violence of the collapse of the Assyrian Empire and the establishment of its Babylonian successor.

But the real difficulty is to accept that the kingdom actually existed in the early years between the eleventh and the ninth centuries. The elaborate stories of Saul, David, and Solomon imply that they were all well known; Solomon in particular is said to have had diplomatic and marital relations with Egypt, and David and Solomon are said to have ruled as far north as the Euphrates River. But archaeological evidence in the heartland of their supposed kingdom, the highlands of Judaea, is quite explicit; the land was thinly inhabited by people who were very poor. That is, the demographic and economic basis for a militant and successful conquering dynasty simply did not exist. Together with the absence of any independent evidence for the Judahite dynasty in these early years, it is necessary here to relegate the early generations as far as Ahab towards the realm of myth, and to ignore them as parts of the Judahite dynasty.

References
J Bright, *A History of Israel* (London, 1960).
EW Heaton, *The Hebrew Kingdoms* (Oxford, 1968).

Kaminahu, North Arabia, *c.*530–475 BC (fragmentary)

```
1                    ILSAM'I I (c.530-515)
                           |
2                 NABAT'ALI AMIR (c.515-495)
                           |
3               ILSAM'I NABAT (c.495-475)
```

Statistics

Duration, about 55 years; 3 generations, average length 55/3 = 18 years; 3 rulers, average length of reign 55/3 = 18 years.

Commentary

Kaminahu was a minor north Arabian kingdom, very little known, in which eight rulers are known by name. Since many of them are known to have shared rule, their family relationship is very probable; only these three, however, can be shown to be directly related; the dates are clearly very approximate.

References

KA Kitchen, *Documentation for Ancient Arabia*, I (Liverpool, 1994).

Karia, Asia Minor, *c.*500–336 BC

A. *Lygdamids, c.500-c.450 BC*

```
1                      LYGDAMIS (satrap c.500 BC)
                          |
2                      ARTEMISIA   =   X (satrap pre-480)
                       (satrap in 480)|
                                      |
3                           PISINDELIS
                            (?satrap)
                               |
4                           LYGDAMIS II
                            (satrap c.450)
```

Statistics
Duration: about 50 years; 4 generations, average length 50/4 = 12 years;
5 rulers, average length of reign, 50/5 = 10 years.

B. *Hekatomnids, 392-c.326 BC.*

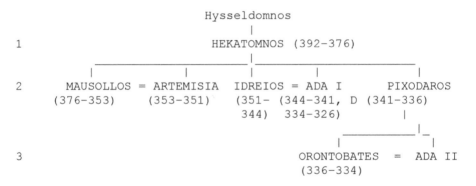

```
                         Hysseldomnos
                              |
1                     HEKATOMNOS (392-376)
                              |
      |          |         |         |            |
2  MAUSOLLOS = ARTEMISIA IDREIOS = ADA I      PIXODAROS
   (376-353)  (353-351)  (351-  (344-341, D (341-336)
                         344)   334-326)         |
                                          _____|_
                                          |       |
3                              ORONTOBATES = ADA II
                               (336-334)
```

Statistics
Duration: 66 years; 3 generations, average length 66/3 = 22 years; 8 rulers,
average length of reign, 66/8 = 8 years

Commentary
Karia in south-western Asia Minor was a satrapy of the Akhaimenid Empire
on the very remote edge of that empire. Twice the satraps emerged into
virtual independence – this was a trait that was repeated in the subsequent
Hellenistic period.

The dynasty of Lygdamis included the notable 'Queen' Artemisia who
contributed five ships to Xerxes' fleet against Greece in 480 and emerged
as a notable commander. Her father, her husband, and her grandson were

all satraps, a position she took over when her husband died, and it is to be presumed that her son was also – technically she was presumably his regent.

The dynasty of Lygdamis appears to have been notably loyal to the Akhaimenids, but in the early fourth century the slackening of central imperial control permitted the satrap Hekatomnos to establish himself and his family in hereditary control and in virtual independence. (His father might have been satrap for a year or so before him.) In this the family were assisted by the considerable political abilities of the founder and his immediate successor Mausollos.

The dynasty, though fairly brief, is curious in its habit of sibling marriage; on two occasions the surviving sister-wives (Artemisia and Ada I) themselves became recognized as satraps after the death of their husbands – it is not clear that Ada II ever ruled independent of her husband, but the women of the family fairly clearly had their own power and authority, so she has been counted as a ruler. Presumably there was a local Karian custom here being followed.

The origin of the dynasty was obviously local, and Hekatomnos was a native Karian. The end of the dynasty is unclear: Ada I was pushed out by her brother Pixadoros, and Orontobates by Alexander's conquest. He brought back Ada I, who had survived, and made her 'Queen' of Karia. She had disappeared by the time Alexander's successors began fighting for the inheritance, and it is only an assumption that she died about 326.

References
'Artemisia of Halicarnassus', *Wikipedia*, accessed 23 January 2018.
S Hornblower, *Mausollos* (Oxford, 1982).

Kent, England, AD *c.*580–762

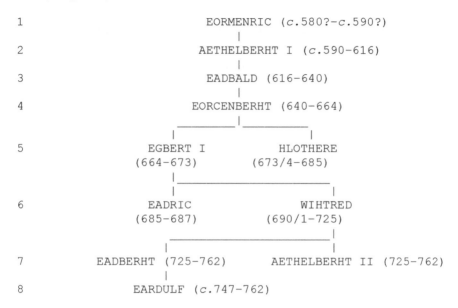

```
1                          EORMENRIC (c.580?-c.590?)
                                    |
2                        AETHELBERHT I (c.590-616)
                                    |
3                          EADBALD (616-640)
                                    |
4                        EORCENBERHT (640-664)
                        _____|_____
                       |                     |
5                  EGBERT I              HLOTHERE
                  (664-673)            (673/4-685)
                       |_____
                       |                      |
6                  EADRIC                  WIHTRED
                  (685-687)             (690/1-725)
                      _____|
                     |                    |
7        EADBERHT (725-762)        AETHELBERHT II (725-762)
                     |
8        EARDULF (c.747-762)
```

Statistics

Duration: 182 years, reigning for 178; 8 generations, average length 182/8 = 23 years; 11 rulers, average length of reign, 178/11 = 16 years.

Commentary

The traditional origin of the Kentish royal house was with the German mercenary leaders Hengist and Horsa, who are now thought to be myths, and the earliest king who can be demonstrated to have ruled in the Kent area is Eormanric, though his dates remain very uncertain. His son Aethelberht I was the most powerful king in England in his time. The family is in fact called after Oisc, said to be the son of Hengist, but he may well be as mythical as his 'father'.

Kent was in fact formed of two kingdoms, East and West Kent, and the kings of the former, centred at Canterbury, were usually able to impose themselves on the latter, whose centre was at Rochester, often by placing a son there as sub-king. This is not invariable, however, and some non-Oiscing kings of West Kent are on record. This situation was clearly a source of weakness for the state as a whole. It seems there was a fairly strict succession system in practice also, though this did not prevent usurpations and civil wars being launched by some of the family who felt excluded. These various elements finally produced the joint rule of Aethelberht II and Eadberht, who in turn also shared with Eardwulf. But from *c.*762 onwards the succession seems to have broken down completely, and for thirty years or so royal relationships are unclear, while at times foreign kings could be imposed, and even the native Kentish kings ruled by permission of the Mercians. From 798 onwards first the Mercians, and later the West Saxons, ruled the kingdom.

References
EB Fryde, *Handbook of British Chronology*, 3rd ed. (London, 1986).
DP Kirby, *The Earliest English Kings*, 2nd ed. (London, 2000).
B Yorke, *Kings and Kingdoms of Early Anglo-Saxon England* (London, 1990).

Al-Kinda, Eastern Arabia, AD *c*.450–*c*.540

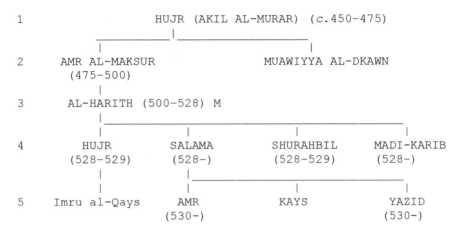

```
1                    HUJR (AKIL AL-MURAR) (c.450-475)
              _____|_____
              |                                |
2      AMR AL-MAKSUR                   MUAWIYYA AL-DKAWN
        (475-500)
           |
3      AL-HARITH (500-528) M
           |_____
           |             |              |                 |
4       HUJR          SALAMA        SHURAHBIL        MADI-KARIB
      (528-529)       (528-)        (528-529)          (528-)
           |             |_____
           |             |              |         |
5    Imru al-Qays       AMR            KAYS      YAZID
                       (530-)                    (530-)
```

Statistics

Duration: 90 years approximately; 5 generations, average length 90/5 = 18 years; 11 rulers, average length of reign 90/11 = 8 years.

Commentary

The Kinda kingdom was a minor state that existed in central and eastern Arabia for a brief period, originally organized by Hujr, also called Akil al-Murar, and his sons. These men established a supremacy over several clans and tribes to form a locally powerful kingdom. Precise dates are all too rare, but the sixth century dates seem to be correct enough. The brevity of the dynasty is partly due to the uncertain social foundations of the kingdom, but more to the practice of joint succession by all the sons. This method is fine, even useful, when the sons agree and work together, as did the second generation, and Al-Maksur and Muawiyya al-Dkawn, who had worked with Hujr in constructing the kingdom, but the fourth generation, the sons of al-Harith, were both short-lived and quarrelsome. The kingdom disintegrated into its tribal components in the fifth generation, if not before, though the dynasty continued as tribal chiefs.

The historical significance of the kingdom is as a precursor to the Muslim unification of Arabia, carried through a century later by Muhammad, indicating a willingness to think in such terms. The inspiration may perhaps have gone from the Lakhmid and Ghassanid kingdoms that had been installed and sponsored for their own purposes by the Sassanid and Byzantine empires. It is worth comparing the structure of this dynasty with that of the first Muslim dynasty, the Umayyads.

References

Encyclopaedia of Islam, sv 'al-Kinda'.

KA Kitchen, *Documentation for Ancient Arabia*, I (Liverpool, 1994).

G Olinder, *The Kings of Kinda* (Lund-Leipzig, 1927).

S Smith, 'Events in Arabia in the Sixth Century AD', *BSOAS* 16 (1954).

Lakhmid Dynasty, Eastern Arabia, AD *c.*265–602

A.   *First Dynasty*, AD *c.*265–502.

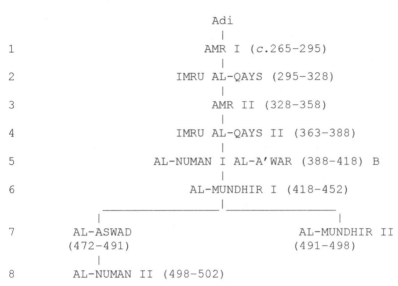

```
                            Adi
                             |
1                       AMR I (c.265-295)
                             |
2                   IMRU AL-QAYS (295-328)
                             |
3                       AMR II (328-358)
                             |
4                   IMRU AL-QAYS II (363-388)
                             |
5               AL-NUMAN I AL-A'WAR (388-418) B
                             |
6                   AL-MUNDHIR I (418-452)
         _____|_____
         |                                               |
7     AL-ASWAD                                      AL-MUNDHIR II
      (472-491)                                     (491-498)
         |
8     AL-NUMAN II (498-502)
```

Statistics
Duration: 237 years, reigning for 212; 8 generations, average length, 237/8 = 30 years; 9 rulers, average length of reign, to 212/9 = 24 years.

B.   *Second Dynasty*, AD 505–602.

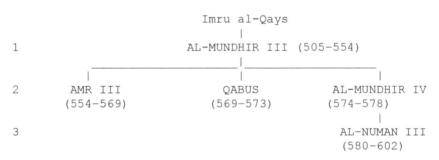

```
                         Imru al-Qays
                              |
1                   AL-MUNDHIR III (505-554)
         _____|_____
         |                    |                     |
2     AMR III              QABUS              AL-MUNDHIR IV
      (554-569)           (569-573)            (574-578)
                                                    |
3                                             AL-NUMAN III
                                              (580-602)
```

Statistics
Duration: 97 years, reigning for 94; 3 generations, average length 97/3 = 32 years; 5 rulers, average length of reign, 94/5 = 19 years.

Commentary

The Lakhmid state was based at Hira in southern Babylonia, and controlled an area of north Arabia. It was a client of the Sassanid Persian Empire, employed partly to act as a shield against Arab raids from deeper in the desert and partly as a source of auxiliary troops to be employed in the various wars against Rome. It was some time before the dynasty was fully established at Hira, and Imru al-Qays, the second king, was actually commemorated at his death by an epitaph in the Roman province of Arabia.

The dates of the early kings are vague, but those of the later ones are well-attested. Despite their military function, few of the kings died violent deaths, in part because in many ways they had more in common with, and were more sympathetic towards, their supposed Arab enemies than to their Persian employers. When Rome developed its own Arab client states, first the Tanukh, then the Ghassanids, and later the Salih, the matter became even more difficult, with Arab feuds sometimes superseding their patrons' grand strategies. Nevertheless the Lakhmids had a good long run, though at times (as in 358 and 452) non-Lakhmid kings were inserted, presumably by the Sassanids, and presumably as a way of emphasizing the overlord's control.

The second dynasty may well be connected to the first, and certainly used the same names, but the actual connection is not known. This dynasty, after another brief interruption in 578–580, was eventually suppressed by the Sassanids in 602. Other kings and governors of the Lakhmid state were appointed until 633, when the state fell to the Muslim Arabs in their first foray outside Arabia. The high generation average is worth notice, due in the case of the second dynasty to the long reign of al-Mundhir III, followed by the succession of his three sons.

References

KA Kitchen, *Documentation for Ancient Arabia*, I (Liverpool, 1994).
G Rothstein, *Die Dynastie des Lakmiden in al-Hira* (Berlin, 1899).
I Shahid, 'Lakhmids', *Encyclopaedia of Islam*, new ed., vol. V (Leiden, 1986).

Leinster, Ireland, AD 495–715

A.   *Ui Dunlainge*, AD 495–666.

```
                   |─────────────────────────|
1              ILLANN (495-527)         AILILL ( 527-)
                                             |
2                                         CORMAC
                                             |
3                                         COIPRE
                                             |
4                                    COLMAN MAR (-c.590)
                                             |
5                                     FAELAN (631-666)
```

Statistics
Duration: 171 years, reigning for 130; 5 generations, average length, 171/5
= 34 years; 6 rulers, average length of reign, 130/6 = 22 years.

B.   *Ui Mail*, AD *c*.590–715.

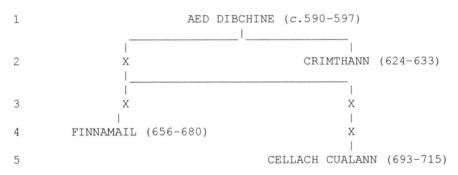

```
1                          AED DIBCHINE (c.590-597)
                   ───────────────|───────────────
                   |                             |
2                  X                    CRIMTHANN (624-633)
                   |─────────────────────────────|
                   |                             |
3                  X                             X
                   |                             |
4         FINNAMAIL (656-680)                    X
                                                 |
5                                   CELLACH CUALANN (693-715)
```

Statistics
Duration: 125 years, reigning for 62; 5 generations, average length 125/5 =
25 years; 4 rulers, average length of reign, 62/4 = 16 years.

   (For a commentary on all the Irish dynasties, see the entry on Ireland:
High Kings.)

Lihyan, South Arabia, 320–190 BC

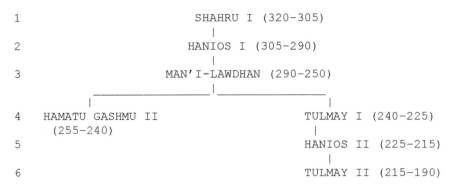

```
1                          SHAHRU I (320-305)
                                  |
2                          HANIOS I (305-290)
                                  |
3                      MAN'I-LAWDHAN (290-250)
            _____|_____
           |                                 |
4    HAMATU GASHMU II                  TULMAY I (240-225)
       (255-240)                              |
5                                      HANIOS II (225-215)
                                              |
6                                      TULMAY II (215-190)
```

Statistics
Duration: 130 years; 6 generations, average length 130/6 = 22 years; 7 rulers, average length of reign 130/7 = 19 years.

Commentary
Lihyan was a south Arabian kingdom, most of whose kings are known both by name and relationship. There was one king before Shahru II (presumably his father) and two more at the end of the kingdom, but their relationships cannot be demonstrated. Dates, however, are not known other than by guesswork, as here, and there may well have been other kings in addition.

References
KA Kitchen, *Documentation for Ancient Arabia* I (Liverpool, 1994).

Lombards, Italy, AD 510–744

A. *First Dynasty*, AD 510–712.

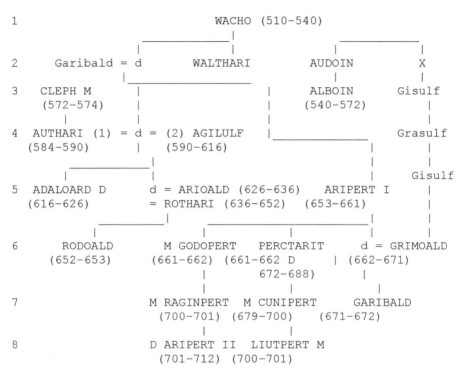

```
1                              WACHO  (510-540)
                                  |
            |          |                   |              |
2      Garibald = d        WALTHARI       AUDOIN          X
               |_____|    |            |
3      CLEPH M            |               |  ALBOIN      Gisulf
       (572-574)          |               |  (540-572)     |
            |             |               |                |
4    AUTHARI (1) = d = (2) AGILULF        |             Grasulf
     (584-590)    |   (590-616)           |                |
            |_____|             |_____   |
            |               |             |            |   |
            |               |             |            | Gisulf
5    ADALOARD D       d = ARIOALD (626-636)  ARIPERT I  |
     (616-626)        = ROTHARI (636-652)  (653-661)    |
            |_____|        |_____|   |
            |             |          |              |       |
6      RODOALD       M GODOPERT   PERCTARIT    d = GRIMOALD
       (652-653)     (661-662)  (661-662 D    |  (662-671)
                           |     672-688)     |
                           |         |        |      |
7               M RAGINPERT   M CUNIPERT    GARIBALD
                (700-701)    (679-700)    (671-672)
                      |            |
8               D ARIPERT II  LIUTPERT M
                (701-712)    (700-701)
```

Statistics

Duration: 202 years, reigning for 192; 8 generations, average length, 202/8 = 25 years; 20 reigns, average length of reign, 192/20 = 10 years.

B. *Second Dynasty*, AD 712–744.

```
1                      ANSPRAND (712)
                            |
            |_____|
            |                            |
2        LIUTPRAND                        X
         (712-744)                        |
3                                    HILDIPRAND
                                      (744)
```

Statistics

Duration: 32 years; 3 generations, average length 32/3 = 11 years; 3 reigns, average length of reign, 32/3 = 11 years.

Commentary

The Lombards, a coalition of various smaller barbarian groups who had survived the Hun Empire, moved into Italy in the aftermath of the reconquest of the peninsula by the Byzantines, in a period when all the combatants, and Italy itself, were exhausted. Their conquest was slow, piecemeal, and never complete. The dynasty's first king in Italy was Alboin, whose father replaced Walthari, who died young, and whose own father Wacho, had ruled in Pannonia and was always regarded as a usurper. Wacho, however, was also the effective founder of the power of the dynasty and the kingdom. The invasion of Italy was accomplished as much by local Lombard forces, who seized on centres of which their leaders became dukes, as by the direction of the kings.

This set the pattern for the dynasty – repeated usurpation by Lombard nobles with strong local roots, and a weak kingship always striving both to expand its territory and its authority. The kingship was even abandoned for a time in 574–584, and some of the dukes, especially in Benevento, were never brought under the control of the kings. A further cause of division was religious, some Lombards holding to their old Arian Christianity, while others became Catholic.

The result was a very unstable kingdom, subject to repeated coups by local dukes, and so the dynasty was marred by violent death, short reigns, and depositions. It is, in fact, only with the eye of faith that a single dynasty can be discerned, though relationships between all the kings, even if distant, did exist. But violence and *coups d'état* finally extinguished the first dynasty in 712. Over the next half-century there were three brief dynasties, only one of which had more than two kings, though King Liutprand was the most effective of all the Lombard kings. The dynastic instability – new dynasties in 712, 744 and 756 – encouraged the Franks, old enemies of the Lombards, to invade and conquer the kingdom in 774; the kingship and the dynasty were thus extinguished.

References

PS Barnwell, *Kings, Courtiers, and Imperium: the Barbarian West 565–725* (London, 1997).

N Christie, *The Lombards: the Ancient Lombards* (Oxford, 1995).

C Wickham, *Early Mediaeval Italy* (London, 1981).

Lydia, Mermnad dynasty, Asia Minor, 687–547 BC

```
1                       GYGES  (687-645)   B
                          |
2                       ARDYS  (645-624)
                          |
3                     SADYATTES  (624-610)
                          |
4                     ALYATTES  (610-560)
                          |
5                     CROISOS  (560-547)   D
```

Statistics

Duration: 140 years; 5 generations, average length $140/5 = 28$ years; 5 rulers, average length of reign $140/5 = 28$ years.

Commentary

Gyges seized the chance to establish his independence from the decaying Phrygian kingdom when it was badly damaged and overthrown by a barbarian invasion; he then justified his political move by defeating those same invaders – though he was later killed in battle himself. His authority seems to have been fully established over much of western Asia Minor during the first quarter of the seventh century, certainly by *c*.675.

The dynasty thus founded appeared to be successful, until the final king, Croisos, of legendary wealth, collided with the expanding Persian Empire of Cyrus the Great. After little more than a single battle, the Lydian kingdom fell under Persian rule and the kingship was extinguished. This rather suggests a less than well-rooted foundation for the dynasty.

References

AR Burn, *Persia and the Greeks*, 2nd ed. (London, 1983).
JG Pedley, *Sardis in the Age of Croesus* (Norman, OK, 1968).

Lykia, Asia Minor, *c.*526–380 BC

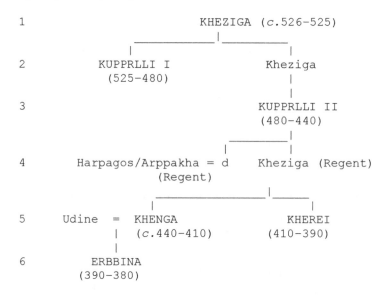

```
1                          KHEZIGA  (c.526-525)
                  _____|_____
                  |                         |
2            KUPPRLLI I                   Kheziga
             (525-480)                      |
                                            |
3                                       KUPPRLLI II
                                        (480-440)
                                            |
                                  _____|
                                  |         |
4        Harpagos/Arppakha = d       Kheziga  (Regent)
                (Regent)
                              _____|_____
                              |                         |
5       Udine  =  KHENGA                           KHEREI
                |  (c.440-410)                     (410-390)
                |
6           ERBBINA
           (390-380)
```

Statistics
Duration: 146 years; 6 generations, average length, 146/6 = 24 years; 9 rulers (including regents), average length of reign 146/9 = 14 years.

Commentary
A minor dynasty promoted by the Akhaimenid imperial administration as a local government in Lykia. The original base for the dynasty was no more than a single valley, but this was enlarged with Persian help until a large area of the south coastal region of Asia Minor was under its authority. Many of the members of the dynasty also had either Greek or Iranian names. It is an example of the Akhaimenid tendency to promote minor local governments under local rulers, rather than undergo the travail of ruling themselves.

References
TR Bryce, *The Lycians in Literary and Epigraphic Sources* (Copenhagen, 1986).
Anthony G Keen, *Dynastic Lycia* (Leiden, 1998).

Macedon, Greece, *c.*520–167 BC

A.　*Argead Dynasty, c.520-309 BC.*

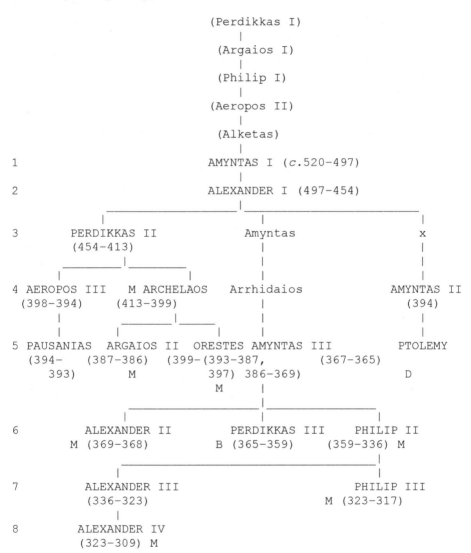

```
                              (Perdikkas I)
                                    |
                              (Argaios I)
                                    |
                              (Philip I)
                                    |
                              (Aeropos II)
                                    |
                              (Alketas)
                                    |
1                             AMYNTAS I (c.520-497)
                                    |
2                             ALEXANDER I (497-454)
        _____|_____
        |                           |                                |
3    PERDIKKAS II                 Amyntas                            x
      (454-413)                     |                                |
     _____|_____            |                                |
     |                 |            |                                |
4 AEROPOS III  M ARCHELAOS     Arrhidaios                        AMYNTAS II
  (398-394)     (413-399)          |                              (394)
     |          _____|_____     |                                |
     |          |            |     |                                |
5 PAUSANIAS ARGAIOS II  ORESTES AMYNTAS III                      PTOLEMY
   (394-    (387-386)  (399-(393-387,                           (367-365)
    393)         M      397) 386-369)                              D
                              M      |
                _____|_____
                |                   |                 |
6           ALEXANDER II       PERDIKKAS III     PHILIP II
        M (369-368)            B (365-359)      (359-336) M
                _____|
                |                                      |
7           ALEXANDER III                         PHILIP III
            (336-323)                          M (323-317)
                |
8           ALEXANDER IV
            (323-309) M
```

Statistics

Duration 211 years, 13 generations, average length, 211/13 = 16 years;
24 rulers, average length of reign, 211/24 = 11 years.

Commentary

The Macedonian dynasty of the Argeadai traced its ancestry back to three brothers who were said to have moved to Macedon from Argos, the third of whom, Perdikkas I, began the formation of the Macedonian kingdom. The sequence, dates, and relationships of the first five generations on this table are all unclear, may well be mythical, and cannot be relied on. From Amyntas I, however, details are more or less reliable. The complexity of the succession after Alexander I makes it necessary to be wholly sceptical of the first five generations, where direct father-to-son succession is claimed. Comparison with the record of the later part of the dynasty demonstrates how unlikely that is. The calculations thus begin with Amyntas I.

After Perdikkas II's death in 413, although the system of succession seems likely to have been intended to be by primogeniture, in fact it became that of the eldest living male of the family. Since this was not ever formulated or accepted, disputes were constant, and in the fourth century reigns were short, with deaths normally by violence. In the last four generations nine kings died by violence, and only one of them died in battle: the rest were murdered. Ironically the most violent of them all, Alexander III, called the Great, died in bed.

The effect of the long sequence of violent deaths can be seen in the contrast between the reign lengths and the generation lengths, of which the average of reigns is less than half that of the latter. In the end, of course, such conduct kills off a dynasty. After Alexander III there was only a halfwit (Philip III) and a child, both murdered: in the circumstances neither could have expected to last long, nor did they.

B.   *Antipatrids*, 334-279 BC.

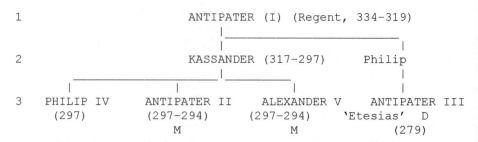

Statistics

Duration: 55 years, reigning for 40; 3 generations, average length 55/3 = 18 years; 6 rulers, average length of reign, 40/6 = 7 years.

Commentary

Antipater (I) was left in Macedon as regent for Alexander the Great while the king was off a-conquering in Asia. After Alexander's death, he became one of the two regents for Alexander's heirs, and then sole regent; since he was in control of the kingdom for all that time he has been counted here as one of its rulers. Within two years of Antipater's death his son Kassander had imposed himself as his successor as ruler of Macedon, and he took the royal title sometime after the death of the last of the preceding royal line. In effect, like his father, he was the ruler from 317.

Kassander passed on his position to his sons, who successively failed to hold on to it. The eldest son died only four months after his father; the two younger sons were supposed to rule jointly but they quarrelled and both were murdered.

The acceptance by the Macedonians of the rule of Kassander and his family was never wholehearted, and the incompetence of his sons finally destroyed their support. Kassander's nephew Antipater Etesias surfaced fifteen years later during a great barbarian invasion, either to claim the kingship or to be put in that place, but he held it only for a brief summer.

C. *Antigonids*, 315-167 BC.

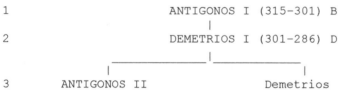

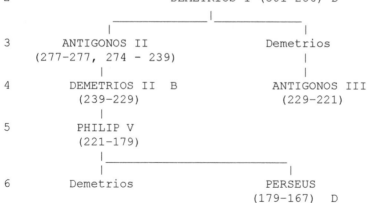

```
1                          ANTIGONOS I (315-301) B
                                    |
2                          DEMETRIOS I (301-286) D
                   _____|_____
                   |                                 |
3          ANTIGONOS II                          Demetrios
         (277-277, 274 - 239)                        |
                   |                                 |
4          DEMETRIOS II  B                      ANTIGONOS III
             (239-229)                           (229-221)
                   |
5          PHILIP V
           (221-179)
                   |_____
                   |                                 |
6          Demetrios                             PERSEUS
                                                (179-167)  D
```

Statistics

Duration 148 years, reigning for 139; 6 generations, average length 148/6 = 25 years; 7 rulers, average length of reign, 139/7 = 20 years.

Commentary

Antigonos I had been a Macedonian noble and was governor of Phrygia in Asia Minor when Alexander the Great died. He intrigued, manoeuvred, and fought his way to effective control of much of the Macedonian Empire by 315, and he and his son took the vacant title of king in 306 (in which action they were quickly followed by several rivals). He went down to defeat in battle in 301, and his son Demetrios, after some years of wandering and fighting, and six years as king in Macedon, a position he usurped from Kassander's sons, followed him to final defeat in 285, though he had been deposed from the kingship in Macedon the year before.

The second Antigonos, seeing all this, became much less ambitious, and succeeded in gaining precarious control of a devastated and exhausted Macedon in 277. He was expelled for a time by an enemy, but regained the kingdom fully and permanently in 274. From then on, the family ruled in Macedon in a traditional 'father of the people' fashion for a century. The family was unusually harmonious during most of that time, and when Demetrios II died young, leaving a child as his heir, Antigonos III Doson acted faithfully as regent for the child, Philip V; the force of Macedonian public opinion was thus a strong check on royal behaviour, though Philip V did have his son Demetrios executed. Perseus, the one king of the family without a Macedonian 'royal' name, was eventually, like his father, attacked and defeated by Rome, lost his kingdom, and died a prisoner in Italy.

The dynasty was exceptionally well-rooted in Macedonian society, being accepted originally as saviours from barbarian invasions. In later generations they were clearly seen as embodying the kingdom, but the loyalty of the people was not sufficient to preserve their throne against the overwhelming power of the Roman Republic.

References

EN Borza, *In the Shadow of Olympus, the Emergence of Macedon* (Princeton, NJ, 1990).

M Errington, *A History of Macedonia* (Berkeley and Los Angeles, 1990).

JD Grainger, *Antipater's Dynasty* (Barnsley, 2018).

NGL Hammond, *The Macedonian State, the Origins, Institutions and History* (Oxford, 1989).

NGL Hammond (ed.), *A History of Macedonia*, 3 vols. (Oxford, 1979–1988).

DA Marsh, 'The Kings of Macedon, 399–369 BC', *Historia*, 44 (1995) pp. 257–282.

WW Tarn, *Antigonos Gonatas* (Cambridge, 1913).

Magonsaete, England, *c.*640–*c.*730

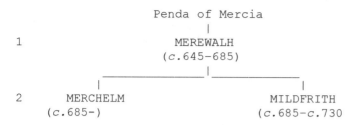

```
                    Penda of Mercia
                          |
1                      MEREWALH
                      (c.645-685)
          _____|_____
          |                                  |
2      MERCHELM                          MILDFRITH
       (c.685-)                        (c.685-c.730
```

Statistics
Duration: about 85 years; two generations, average length 85/2 = 42 years; three reigns, average length of reign, 85/3 = 28 years.

Commentary
The Magonsaete were a people living west of the River Severn, between that river and the Welsh border. Penda of Mercia conquered that area after the Battle of Cirencester in 628. It is not known when he set up the principality of the Magonsaete, but he installed his son Merewalh as king and Merewalh appears to have been born about 625. Merewalh's two sons inherited the kingdom, probably ruling in tandem, but Mildfrith appears to have lived the longest. He is commemorated in a memorial dated in the late 730s, so his date of death *c.*730 is a mere estimate. The purpose of the principality was to act as a buffer state between Mercia proper and the Welsh; it presumably began to suffer badly when the Welsh began serious raiding in the first decade of the eighth century; it is quite possible that the principality was suppressed by the Mercian Kings before then.

References
HPR Finberg, 'The Princes of the Magonsaete', in *The Early Charters of the West Midlands*, 2nd ed. (Leicester, 1972).

Ma'in, North Arabia, *c.***400-210**

A.   *First Dynasty*, 400-350 BC.

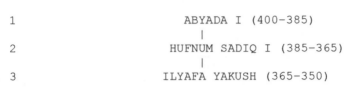

```
1                          ABYADA I (400-385)
                                  |
2                          HUFNUM SADIQ I (385-365)
                                  |
3                          ILYAFA YAKUSH (365-350)
```

Statistics
Duration: about 50 years; 3 generations, average length 50/3 = 17 years;
3 rulers, average length of reign, 50/3 = 17 years.

B.   *Second Dynasty*, 350-300 BC.

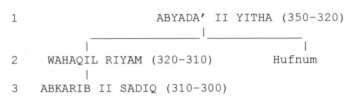

```
1                          ABYADA' II YITHA (350-320)
          _____|_____
          |                                  |
2    WAHAQIL RIYAM (320-310)             Hufnum
          |
3    ABKARIB II SADIQ (310-300)
```

Statistics
Duration: about 50 years; 3 generations, average length 50/3 = 17 years;
3 rulers, average length of reign, 50/3 = 17 years.

C.   *Third Dynasty*, 300-275 BC

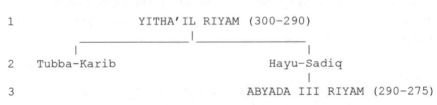

```
1                     YITHA'IL RIYAM (300-290)
          _____|_____
          |                                  |
2    Tubba-Karib                        Hayu-Sadiq
                                             |
3                                       ABYADA III RIYAM (290-275)
```

Statistics
Duration: about 25 years; 3 generations, average length 25/3 = 8 years;
2 rulers, average length of reign, 25/2 = 12 years.

Statistics
Duration: about 75 years; 6 generations, average length 75/6 = 12 years;
6 rulers, average length of reign, 75/6 = 12 years.

```
D.   Fourth Dynasty, 285-210 BC.

1                    ILYAFA' YITHA' (285-270)
                            |
2                    ABYADA IV RIYAM (270-265)
                            |
3                    HALKARIB SADIQ (265-250)
                            |
4                     HUFNUM YITHA' (250-240)
```

Commentary
Ma'in was a kingdom of considerable power and longevity in north Arabia.
Of the twenty-six kings known by name, fourteen can be linked together into
the four dynasties here tabulated. It is probable that the other kings could
also be linked, and the various groups suggest a single overall family, though
the proof fails us. Dating is vague, but the kingdom expired at some time in
the first century BC. It occupied a territory that overlapped in part that of the
slightly later Nabataeans, though what connection there was between the two
is unknown; it is likely that it was suppressed by the Nabataeans.

References
KA Kitchen, *Documentation for Ancient Arabia* I (Liverpool, 1994).

Meath, Sil nAede Slaine, Ireland, AD 598–728

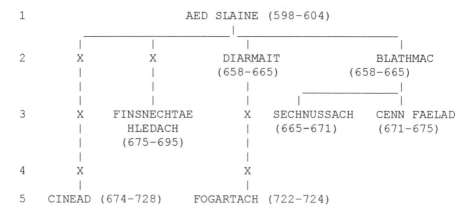

```
1                       AED SLAINE (598-604)
                               |
         _____|_____
        |            |           |                        |
2       X            X        DIARMAIT              BLATHMAC
        |            |        (658-665)            (658-665)
        |            |           |                        |
        |            |           |        _____|
        |            |           |       |                |
3       X        FINSNECHTAE     X    SECHNUSSACH    CENN FAELAD
        |         HLEDACH        |    (665-671)      (671-675)
        |         (675-695)      |
        |                        |
4       X                        X
        |                        |
5   CINEAD (674-728)      FOGARTACH (722-724)
```

Statistics

Duration: 130 years, reigning for 49; 5 generations, average length 130/5 = 26 years; 8 rulers, average length of reign, 49/8 = 6 years.

(For a commentary on all the Irish dynasties, see the entry on Ireland: High Kings.)

Medes, Iran, *c.*674–549 BC

```
1                    PHRAORTES (c.647-624)
                         |
2                    CYAXARES (624-585)
                         |
3                    ASTYAGES (585-549)   D
```

Statistics
Duration: 98 years; 3 generations, average length 98/3 = 33 years; 3 rulers, average length of reign, 98/3 = 33 years.

Commentary
The Median kingship originated as a tribal chieftainship, whose chiefs assumed the leadership of a group of tribes in the face of repeated Assyrian assaults. An earlier king, Deioices, who is mentioned by Herodotos, may be part of the dynasty, as may an Ukatas and a Khshathrita, but these kings are not reliably attested, and to insert them as part of the dynasty goes beyond the evidence; nor is it attested that these men were ever more than local chiefs. It has to be said that the dynasty is not well-recorded, and that the dates of all the kings, except the last, are unreliable and in dispute. On the other hand Cyaxares was the king who destroyed the Assyrian capital at Nineveh in 612 BC, and Astyages faced and was defeated by Cyrus the Great; they are thus reliably attested.

References
JM Cook, *The Persian Empire* (London, 1983).
IM Diakonoff, 'Media', *Cambridge History of Iran*, vol. 2 (Cambridge, 1985).
AT Olmstead, *History of the Persian Empire* (Chicago, 1948).

Mercia, England, AD 626–757

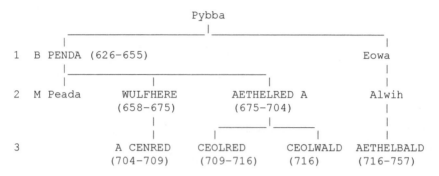

```
                                    Pybba
                                      |
       _____
       |                                                              |
 1   B PENDA (626-655)                                             Eowa
       |                                                              |
       _____                       |
       |                 |                    |                       |
 2   M Peada         WULFHERE           AETHELRED A              Alwih
                     (658-675)            (675-704)                    |
                         |                    |                       |
                         |             _____                   |
                         |             |          |                   |
 3               A  CENRED        CEOLRED     CEOLWALD    AETHELBALD
                   (704-709)      (709-716)    (716)      (716-757)
```

Statistics
Duration: 131 years, reigning for 128; 3 generations, average length $131/3 =$ 44 years; 7 rulers, average length of reign, $128/7 = 18$ years.

Commentary
The Mercians were originally a single tribal group among many in the English Midlands, of which Pybba was probably the hereditary chief. His son Penda welded many similar groups into a single kingdom, which then dominated England all through the seventh and eighth centuries. The progenitor, Pybba, probably began the process of expansion but it was Penda who completed it, above all by defeating both the East Anglian and the Northumbrian kingdoms, and he is to be seen as the first king to rule the historical Mercian kingdom. His defeat and death in battle halted Mercian expansion, and briefly broke up the kingdom, which was reconstituted once more by his son Wulfhere, who abandoned his father's paganism and enlisted the Christian Church as a royal supporter, thus defusing a major element in the opposition to the dynasty.

The Anglian process of inheritance tended to be lateral, from brother to brother, and then through cousins. In Mercia this ended in 716 with the death of Ceolred and Ceolwald (the latter's existence is in fact somewhat doubtful). It was also seriously affected by the habit of abdication (as with Aethelred and Cenred), which was one effect of the Christianization of the dynasty – the kings tended to go off to be monks in their last years.

After Ceolwald – the fourth king in twelve years – the throne passed to his cousin Aethelbald, who may only just be reckoned part of the original dynasty; when he died it passed to Offa, who was four generations from Eowa, and cannot seriously be included in this dynasty.

References
EB Fryde, *Handbook of British Chronology*, 3rd ed. (London, 1986).
DP Kirby, *The Earliest English Kings*, 2nd ed. (London, 2000).
B Yorke, *Kings and Kingdoms of Early Anglo-Saxon England* (London, 1990).

Merovingians, France and neighbouring lands, AD *c.*460–751

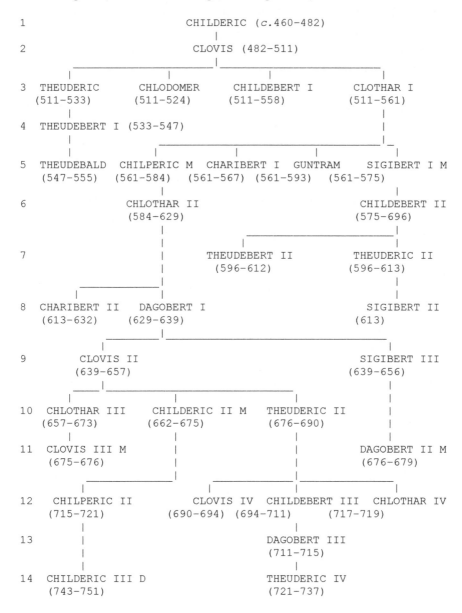

```
1                         CHILDERIC (c.460-482)
                                  |
2                         CLOVIS (482-511)
                                  |
       _____
       |              |           |                    |
3    THEUDERIC    CHLODOMER    CHILDEBERT I         CLOTHAR I
     (511-533)    (511-524)    (511-558)            (511-561)
       |                                               |
4    THEUDEBERT I (533-547)                            |
       |          _____|_
       |          |            |            |          |     |
5    THEUDEBALD CHILPERIC M CHARIBERT I  GUNTRAM    SIGIBERT I M
     (547-555)  (561-584)  (561-567)   (561-593)  (561-575)
                    |                                     |
6               CHLOTHAR II                           CHILDEBERT II
                (584-629)                             (575-696)
                    |                   _____|
                    |            |            |            |
7                   |       THEUDEBERT II  THEUDERIC II
                    |       (596-612)      (596-613)
       _____|                                     |
       |            |                                     |
8    CHARIBERT II DAGOBERT I                          SIGIBERT II
     (613-632)    (629-639)                           (613)
          _____|_____
          |                                                |
9     CLOVIS II                                       SIGIBERT III
      (639-657)                                       (639-656)
      ____|_____                |
      |            |            |          |               |
10  CHLOTHAR III CHILDERIC II M THEUDERIC II              |
    (657-673)    (662-675)     (676-690)                  |
      |            |            |                          |
11  CLOVIS III M  |            |                       DAGOBERT II M
    (675-676)     |            |                       (676-679)
      _____|     _____|_____
      |           |     |            |             |
12  CHILPERIC II  CLOVIS IV   CHILDEBERT III   CHLOTHAR IV
    (715-721)     (690-694)   (694-711)        (717-719)
      |                            |
13    |                       DAGOBERT III
      |                       (711-715)
      |                            |
14  CHILDERIC III D            THEUDERIC IV
    (743-751)                  (721-737)
```

Statistics

Duration: 291 years, 14 generations, average length, 291/14 = 21 years;
33 rulers, average length of reign, 291/33 = 9 years.

420   Ancient Dynasties

Commentary

The Frankish kingdom was the most stable of those that were founded in the ruins of the Western Roman Empire, though this was scarcely true of, or due to, the ruling dynasty. The first king of a sizeable state was Childeric I, whose accession was in the mid fifth century, but who was descended from a line of earlier tribal kings, here omitted. The conquests of Clovis provided the Franks with a large kingdom, but the practice of joint succession forced the usual choices: either a collective kingship or the division of the state; the four sons of Clovis chose to split up the kingdom into separate parts, but they were still regarded as Frankish kings, and the kingdom was seen as a single entity. The various parts were redistributed at each generation.

The dynasty was, in effect, seen as distinct from the kingdom, and the latter was maintained intact, even if the dynastic divisions seemed to break it up. So none of the kings established a breakaway dynasty, and the areas they ruled were not usually inherited by their children, though some segments were ruled by successive kings. The reason for this failure to disintegrate was partly the separation of state and dynasty, partly that the kings were generally short-lived, tending to die young, and partly the institution of Mayors of the Palace, men who governed in the kings' names, and whose interest was to maintain the kingdom's overall unity. The kings themselves came to be regarded as a semi-sacred group.

Many of the kings died either without issue or when their children were young, so there were many minorities. This would seem to have been in part a genetic matter, for the incidence of violent death amongst the kings was fairly low – only four or five out of thirty-three – though the habit of their Mayors of pushing kings into monastic retirement when they showed signs of any political initiative or ambition certainly reduced reign lengths and reproductivity. The family was certainly prolific enough to have gone on ruling longer, however, though Childeric III, the last king, was also the last living member of the family when he was deposed by his Mayor of the Palace.

References

E James, *The Origins of France, from Clovis to the Capetians, 500–1000* (London, 1982).
JM Wallace-Hadrill, *The Long-Haired Kings* (Toronto, 1982).
H Wolfram, *The Roman Empire and its Germanic Peoples* (Berkeley and Los Angeles, 1997).
I Wood, *The Merovingian Kingdoms, 450–751* (London, 1994).

Munster, Eoganacht Dynasty, Ireland, AD 490–820

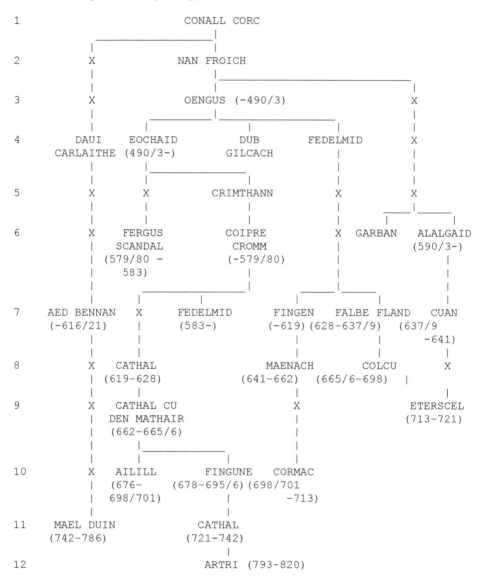

```
1                              CONALL CORC
                          _____|
          |                            |
2         X                       NAN FROICH
          |                            |
          |                            |_____
3         X                       OENGUS (-490/3)                      |
          |          _____|_____                |
          |         |            |                    |               |
4       DAUI     EOCHAID        DUB              FEDELMID              X
      CARLAITHE (490/3-)      GILCACH               |                  |
          |         |_____                   |                  |
          |         |           |                   |                  |
5         X         X       CRIMTHANN               X                  X
          |         |           |                   |            ____|____
          |         |           |                   |           |        |
6         X      FERGUS       COIPRE                 X       GARBAN   ALALGAID
          |     SCANDAL       CROMM                  |                (590/3-)
          |    (579/80 -    (-579/80)                |                    |
          |       583)          |                    |                    |
          |      _____|___                ___|___                  |
          |     |            |        |         |        |                |
7    AED BENNAN X       FEDELMID   FINGEN    FALBE   FLAND   CUAN
      (-616/21)  |       (583-)   (-619) (628-637/9) (637/9
          |      |                   |              |      -641)
          |      |                   |              |        |
8         X    CATHAL             MAENACH       COLCU        X
          |  (619-628)          (641-662)    (665/6-698)     |
          |      |                   |                        |
9         X   CATHAL CU              X                   ETERSCEL
          |  DEN MATHAIR            |                   (713-721)
          |  (662-665/6)            |
          |      |_____        |
          |      |         |        |
10        X    AILILL   FINGUNE  CORMAC
          |   (676-   (678-695/6)(698/701
          |   698/701)    |        -713)
          |               |
11   MAEL DUIN          CATHAL
     (742-786)        (721-742)
                         |
12                    ARTRI (793-820)
```

Statistics

Duration: 330 years, reigning for 234 years; 12 generations, average length $330/12 = 28$ years; 25 rulers, average length of reign, $234/25 = 10$ years.

(For a commentary on all the Irish dynasties, see the entry on Ireland: High Kings.)

Nabataeans, North Arabia, *c.*175 BC–AD 106

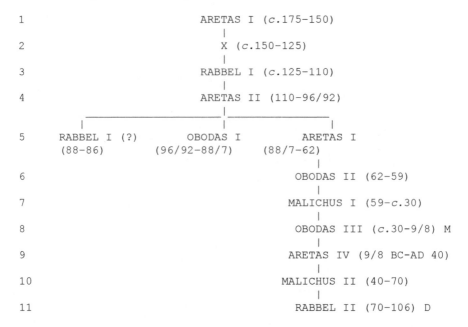

```
1                                    ARETAS I (c.175-150)
                                         |
2                                    X (c.150-125)
                                         |
3                                    RABBEL I (c.125-110)
                                         |
4                                    ARETAS II (110-96/92)
            _____|_____
           |                         |                    |
5    RABBEL I (?)              OBODAS I              ARETAS I
      (88-86)                (96/92-88/7)            (88/7-62)
                                                         |
6                                               OBODAS II (62-59)
                                                         |
7                                               MALICHUS I (59-c.30)
                                                         |
8                                               OBODAS III (c.30-9/8) M
                                                         |
9                                               ARETAS IV (9/8 BC-AD 40)
                                                         |
10                                              MALICHUS II (40-70)
                                                         |
11                                              RABBEL II (70-106) D
```

Statistics

Duration: 281 years 11 generations, average length, 281/11 = 26 years;
13 rulers, average length of reign 281/13 = 22 years.

Commentary

The first Nabataean ruler who is known by name, Aretas I, is referred to in
168 as a 'tyrant', which does suggest a certain local power and independence;
it is a term generally used to indicate a man whose claim to rule was based
on force rather than inheritance, and he may be seen as the originator of the
kingdom and the dynasty. He may well be the current member of an older
dynasty of chiefs, whose earlier names are unknown. His successors steadily
expanded their territory until blocked by the Hasmoneans in Judaea, and by
the Romans. The Nabataeans' remoteness on the eastern side of the Jordan
River, with a kingdom stretching south well into Arabia, ensured the relatively
long survival of both the kingdom and the dynasty, but it has also restricted
the sources of information about them, and even the names of the kings are
in some cases unknown or uncertain. Few of the dates in the table are at all
secure, and the dates of the earliest kings are only approximations. Neither
are the relationships of the kings to one another always attested; in particular
the five kings from Obodas I to Malichus I might have different relationships

than those shown here, particularly in view of the generally long-lived nature of the men before and after that period.

The last king may or may not have been deposed by the Roman conquest: he may or may not have died violently. The incidence of violent death in the dynasty is commendably low – so far as we know. This continuing uncertainty is all too typical of the dynasty as a whole. At the same time, it is unlikely that any kings are missing (though one king's name is not known), and the end of the dynasty's rule in AD 106 is certain; the beginning of the reign of Aretas I is certainly before 168 BC, so, assuming a start at 175 is a guess, but one likely to be close to correct.

References

N Glueck, *Deities and Dolphins, the story of the Nabataeans* (London, 1966).

PC Hammond, *The Nabataeans, their History, Culture and Archaeology* (Gothenburg, 1973).

KA Kitchen, *Documentation for Ancient Arabia*, I (Liverpool, 1994).

A Negev, 'The Nabataeans and the Provincial Arabia', *Aufstieg und Niedergang des Romischen Welt*, II, 8 (1977) pp. 520–66.

Nashan, South Arabia, 535–480 BC

```
1                        LAB'AN (535-520)
                                |
2                   SUMHU'YAFA YASRAN (520-500)
                                |
3                   YADI'AB AMIR (500-480)
```

Statistics

Duration: 55 years; 3 generations, average length $55/3 = 18$ years; 3 rulers, average length of reign, $55/3 = 18$ years.

Commentary

Nashan was a small kingdom in south Arabia. Only four kings are known by name, three of whom form the family tabulated here, and their dating is extremely vague. The information comes from a single inscription.

References

KA Kitchen, *Documentation for Ancient Arabia*, I (Liverpool, 1994).

Northumbria, England, AD 547–788

A. *First Dynasty*, AD 547-729.

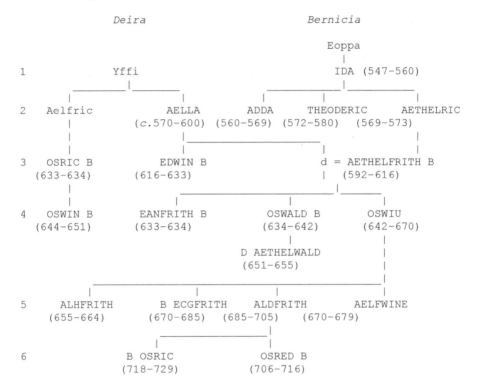

```
                Deira                              Bernicia

                                                   Eoppa
                                                     |
1                    Yffi                          IDA (547-560)
            _____|_____              _____|_____
           |                  |            |          |          |
2     Aelfric              AELLA        ADDA      THEODERIC    AETHELRIC
           |            (c.570-600)  (560-569)   (572-580)    (569-573)
           |                  |_____|          |
           |                  |                        |          |
3     OSRIC B             EDWIN B                    d = AETHELFRITH B
     (633-634)           (616-633)                   |   (592-616)
           |                                         |___|_____
           |              _____|      |
           |             |                        |              |
4     OSWIN B       EANFRITH B                OSWALD B         OSWIU
     (644-651)      (633-634)                (634-642)       (642-670)
                                                 |               |
                                            D AETHELWALD         |
                                             (651-655)           |
          _____|
         |                  |                 |                 |
5     ALHFRITH         B ECGFRITH         ALDFRITH           AELFWINE
     (655-664)        (670-685)        (685-705)           (670-679)
                                                 |
                           _____|
                          |                      |
6                     B OSRIC                OSRED B
                     (718-729)              (706-716)
```

Statistics
Duration: 192 years, reigning for 180; 6 generations, average length, 192/6 = 32 years; 19 rulers, average length of reign, 180/19 = 9 years.

Commentary
Technically this table includes two dynasties, of Deira, modern Yorkshire, and Bernicia, which stretched north from the River Tees as far as the Firth of Forth. Since the two dynasties joined together fairly early, and the united family ruled all Northumbria, they can be treated as one. The two families were rivals for both kingdoms from the start, and Aethelfrith ruled both kingdoms only after disposing of other kings in both kingdoms. The two kingdoms separated again after the death of Edwin in 633, but were reunited by Oswald and then by Oswiu permanently.

There was clearly both a mutual attraction and a mutual repulsion affecting the whole area, but in the 650s the two parts were united once more and remained united until the Danish invasion over two centuries later. The rivalry of division was then replaced by intensive dynastic conflict. The invasion of the Mercians in the 640s did much to persuade the two kingdoms to join together; earlier they had both faced enmity from several 'British' kings from the Scots of Argyll to the Welsh of Gwynedd.

The earliest kings cannot be accurately dated, and the precise relationships of the early Bernician kings is unclear. The first to have reliable dates attached are Aethelfrith and Edwin. The eventual union of the two kingdoms was jeopardized in later times when sub-kings were appointed – hence the overlapping reigns of the sons of Oswiu.

At the same time there were elements of the Anglian – and Germanic – custom of inheritance by the eldest male of the family involved here. Partly this was accommodated as can be seen, by the successive deaths of kings in battle, but it was also in part deliberate. Yet these violent deaths were also in part the result of disputes over the inheritance, and the lack of an accepted system of succession was clearly a major weakness. This first dynasty in effect came to an end in 729 because of this erratic non-system.

B.   *Second Dynasty*, AD 716–788.

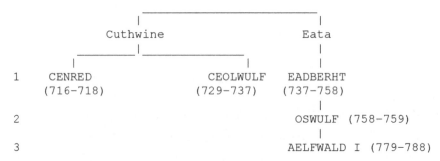

Statistics
Duration: 72 years, reigning for 41; 3 generations, average length, 72/3 = 24 years; 5 rulers, average length of reign, 41/5 = 8 years.

Commentary
Disputes over the kingship were constant in eighth century Northumbria, resulting in the extinction of the original royal family (in Table A), though later claimants and kings usually insisted that they were descended from Ida of Bernicia. Two more dynasties following that in Table B can be discerned in the long and depressing catalogue of murders and betrayals. (There were eighteen kings after the extinction of the old dynasty in 130 years.) The second

dynasty was extinguished with the murder of Aelfwald in 788 and of his two sons by another king in 791. Five different families then provided kings to the kingdom in the eighth century.

References
M Adams, *The King in the North, the Life and Times of Oswald of Northumbria* (London, 2013).
EB Fryde, *Handbook of British Chronology*, 3rd ed. (London, 1986).
DP Kirby, *The Earliest English Kings*, 2nd ed. (London, 2000).
B Yorke, *Kings and Kingdoms of Early Anglo-Saxon England* (London, 1990).

Nubia, Sudan, 468–405 BC

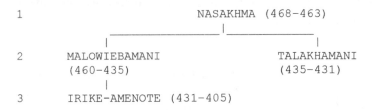

```
1                          NASAKHMA  (468-463)
          _____|_____
          |                                  |
2     MALOWIEBAMANI                      TALAKHAMANI
      (460-435)                          (435-431)
          |
3     IRIKE-AMENOTE  (431-405)
```

Statistics
Duration: 63 years; 3 generations, average length 63/3 = 21 years; 4 rulers, average length of reign, 63/4 = 16 years.

Commentary
Of all the many kings who followed the Nubian dynasty that ruled in Egypt as the 'XXV' dynasty, only this group of four kings can be seen to be related as a dynasty, though in all probability others will be recognized as part of it eventually. The kingdom itself was long-standing, surviving into the fifth century AD at least, and this rather suggests a long domestic stability. It is likely that continuing research will find more dynastic links among the many kings who are known by name.

References
DA Welsby, *The Kingdom of Kush, the Napatan and Meroitic Empires* (London, 1996).
S Wenig, *Africa in Antiquity* (New York, 1979).

Numidia, North Africa, 204 BC–AD 40

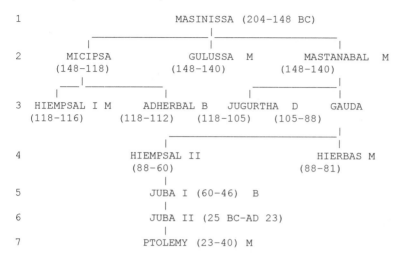

```
1                              MASINISSA (204-148 BC)
          _____|_____
         |                        |                    |
2     MICIPSA                  GULUSSA  M          MASTANABAL  M
      (148-118)                (148-140)           (148-140)
      ___|_____                    _____|
     |                  |          |        |               |
3  HIEMPSAL I M     ADHERBAL B  JUGURTHA  D       GAUDA
   (118-116)        (118-112)   (118-105)   (105-88)
                                                           |
                                     _____|
                                    |                       |
4                            HIEMPSAL II              HIERBAS M
                             (88-60)                  (88-81)
                                 |
5                          JUBA I (60-46)   B
                                 |
6                          JUBA II (25 BC-AD 23)
                                 |
7                          PTOLEMY (23-40) M
```

Statistics

Duration: 244 years, reigning for 223; 7 generations, average length 244/7 = 35 years; 13 rulers, average length of reign, 221/13 = 17 years.

Commentary

Masinissa emerged during the latter stages of the Second Punic War as a major Roman ally, first in Spain and later in his native North Africa. His reward was kingship in Numidia, and it is to his longevity and ability that the kingdom owed its existence. By the time he died his one local enemy, Carthage, was under final attack by Rome, and his kingdom was firmly established and extensive. The Numidian inheritance custom was joint inheritance by all the sons of the previous king, which led to periodic bouts of mutual assassination and civil war, with the survivor becoming sole king of all until his own death; the civil war was thus repeated in each generation – in the 140s, after 118, in the 80s. Jugurtha and Juba I also got involved in Roman internal conflicts, which were fatal to both of them, as did Hierbas, who was executed by Sulla. After Juba I the kingship was suspended until restored by Augustus in 25.

The family tended to long lives, when not cut down early, and this has produced a high average generation length, though the mutual murders severely reduced the average reign length. The last two kings existed only on Roman Imperial sufferance. Juba II was an intellectual, Ptolemy a victim of the suspicious Emperor Caligula, and on his execution at Rome, the kingdom became a Roman province.

References

P Mackendrick, *The North African Stones Speak* (London, 1980).
S Raven, *Rome in Africa* (London, 1993).

Ostrogoths, Italy, AD 493–552

A.   *Amaling Dynasty, AD 493-540.*

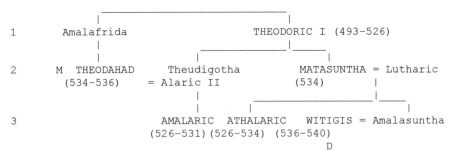

```
       |───────────────────────────────────|
1      Amalafrida                          THEODORIC I (493-526)
       |                         _____|____
       |                        |                     |
2    M  THEODAHAD        Theudigotha           MATASUNTHA = Lutharic
       (534-536)         = Alaric II           (534)         |
                              |            _____|____
                              |           |                      |
                              |           |                      |
3                         AMALARIC   ATHALARIC   WITIGIS = Amalasuntha
                          (526-531) (526-534)  (536-540)
                                                    D
```

Statistics
Duration: 47 years; 3 generations, average length 47/3 = 16 years; 6 rulers, average length of reign, 47/6 = 8 years.

Commentary
The Ostrogoths settled into Italy in the 490s under the leadership of Theodoric I, who had become their leader sometime earlier. He was of a chiefly line in the tribe that claimed descent from the ancestral Amal, probably a mythical figure. This family had produced leaders intermittently before, and their settlement in Italy initially produced a formal kingship imitating Rome, and Theodoric ruled there for three decades. He was followed, however, by a series of short-reigning rulers, who came under attack from the resurgent Roman forces from the east commanded by generals Belisarius and Narses, who were able to appeal to the Roman population in the name of religion, since the Ostrogoths persisted in accepting the Arian version of Christianity. Theodoric's lack of a son made the succession further complicated, and his daughter Matasuntha had the ability to anger almost everyone. (The other daughter Theudigatha had married the Visigothic King Alaric II.) After the deposition of Wittigis, as a result of his defeat by the Romans, a new series of kings who were not members of the old royal family, attempted to rule. Defeat had stripped the Amaling family of its charisma.

B.   *Second Dynasty, AD 531-552.*

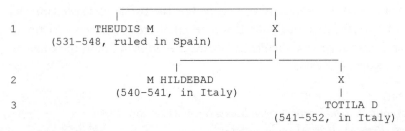

```
             |──────────────────────────|
1               THEUDIS M                X
           (531-548, ruled in Spain)     |
                              |_____|_____
                              |                     |
2                        M HILDEBAD                 X
                       (540-541, in Italy)          |
3                                              TOTILA D
                                            (541-552, in Italy)
```

Statistics
Duration: 21 years; 3 generations, average length, 21/3 = 7 years; 3 rulers, average length of reign, 21/3 = 7 years.

Commentary
The second Ostrogothic dynasty hardly got started. Theudis had been governor of Spain for Theodoric I during the minority of its King Athalaric; when he was killed Theudis was elected king of the Visigoths in his place. His position made his nephew Hildebad important when the Italian Ostrogothic King Wittigis was captured by the Byzantine army and deposed, and this prestige was transferred to Hildebad's nephew Totila when Hildebad was murdered. But Theudis in Spain could not help either man, and anyway was murdered in 548; the Goths of Italy were not numerous enough to survive against the generalship and army of Narses. Totila had been expelled from Italy by 552.

It is only by an indulgent stretch of the definition of the term 'dynasty' that this group can be included here, but it is a good example of the attachment of a people to a dynastic principle even where that is in effect relatively new to them. It was only with Theoderic that a formal kingship came to the Ostrogoths.

References
H Wolfram, *The Roman Empire and its Germanic Peoples* (Berkeley and Los Angeles, 1997).
H Wolfram, *History of the Goths* (Berkeley and Los Angeles, 1988).

Paionia, Greece, pre-358–*c.*227 BC

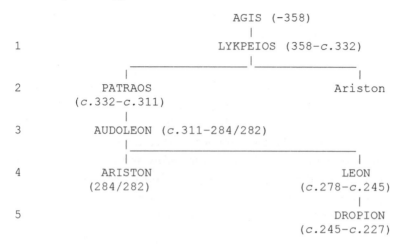

```
                              AGIS  (-358)
                                |
1                       LYKPEIOS  (358-c.332)
        _____|_____
        |                                        |
2     PATRAOS                                  Ariston
     (c.332-c.311)
        |
3     AUDOLEON  (c.311-284/282)
        |_____
        |                                        |
4     ARISTON                                   LEON
     (284/282)                              (c.278-c.245)
                                                 |
5                                             DROPION
                                           (c.245-c.227)
```

Statistics

Duration: 131 years, reigning for 121) 5 generations, average length $131/5 =$ 26 years; 6 rulers, average length of reign $127/6 = 21$ years.

Commentary

The Paionians were a group of tribes who impinge occasionally into wider events, such as the Persian invasions of the sixth and fifth centuries BC (during which a large part of the population was deported to Asia), and tended to be enemies of the Macedonians. Their political organization as a kingdom developed sometime in the late fifth and early fourth century, probably as a result of pressure from its enemies, and Agis, the first king of whom we know, may well actually be the first king of the state. Only the date of his death is known, and he is omitted from the statistical calculations here. The dates of other kings are also to be regarded as approximate, though they are not far wrong.

Ariston, the son of Lykpeios, was a commander of a Paionian contingent in the Macedonian invasion of Asia; the later Ariston was a candidate for the throne, supported, then later expelled, by King Lysimachos. The period between his expulsion and the accession of Leon is marked by the Celtic invasions that caused much damage. The kingdom was finally suppressed by Antigonos III of Macedon in about 227, Dropion being the Paionian king of whom we know most, ironically.

References

IM Merker, 'The Ancient Kingdom of Paionia', *Balkan Studies*, 6 (1965) pp. 35–54.

Palmyra, Syria, AD 260–272

```
                    X
                    |
1          SEPTIMIUS ODAINAT = BATZABBAI/ZENOBIA   M
            (260-267)        |    (267-272)
                             |
2                     WAHBALLAT/ATHENODOROS
                          (267-272)
```

Statistics
Duration: 12 years; 2 generations, average length, $12/2 = 6$ years; 3 rulers, average length of reign, $12/3 = 4$ years.

Commentary
The capture by the Sassanids of the Roman Emperor Valerian in 260 was the lowest point of Roman Imperial history before the final collapse. The eastern provinces of the empire were rescued by a lord of Palmyra, Septimius Odainat, who was recognized by Rome as king as a reward. On his death, his infant son was proclaimed in his place, under the regency of his mother Bathzabbai, whom the Romans called Zenobia. Once the empire had recovered its balance and had disposed of other problems of greater urgency, the Palmyran dynasty was easily suppressed. It had emerged only as a response to a particular crisis. Its control of Palmyra was probably never complete, for it was just one of a group of important political and tribal factions in the city.

References
J Starcky and M Gawlikowski, *Palmyre* (Paris, 1985).
R Stoneman, *Palmyra and its Empire, Zenobia's Revolt against Rome* (Ann Arbor, 1992).
E Will, *Les Palmyreniens, la Venise des sables* (Paris, 1992).

Persis, Iran

A.   *First Dynasty,* 1st century BC–2nd century AD.

```
1                      AUTOPHRADATES II
                              |
2                         DARIUS II
                              |_____
                              |                     |
3                         OXATHRES            NAMOPAT
                              |                     |
4                          PAKUR               KAPAT
```

B.   *Second Dynasty,* 2nd century AD.

```
1                      MANUCITHR I
                              |
2                      MANUCITHR II
                              |
3                      MANUCITHR III
                              |
4                      ARTAXERXES IV
```

Commentary

Persis in southern Iran was the original home of the Akhaimenids and of the Sassanids. It was permitted to develop into a quasi-independence by the Seleukid kings during the third century BC. As the Seleukid power faded that independence became real, but was then threatened by the Parthians who reduced the area to a sub-kingdom. Not all the names of the rulers of this small state are known, but two short dynasties can be reconstructed. No dates can be discerned however, beyond the approximate century for the dynasties, so it is not possible to make any statistical calculations.

It may be pointed out, however, that it was from this relatively small area that the two imperial dynasties emerged, and that many of the royal names in these minor dynasties have imperial echoes. The region had always been difficult for other kingdoms to control, and had often been left autonomous.

References
MAR Colledge, *Parthian Art* (London, 1977).
J Wiesehofer, *Ancient Persia* (London, 1996).

Picts, Scotland, AD 556–845

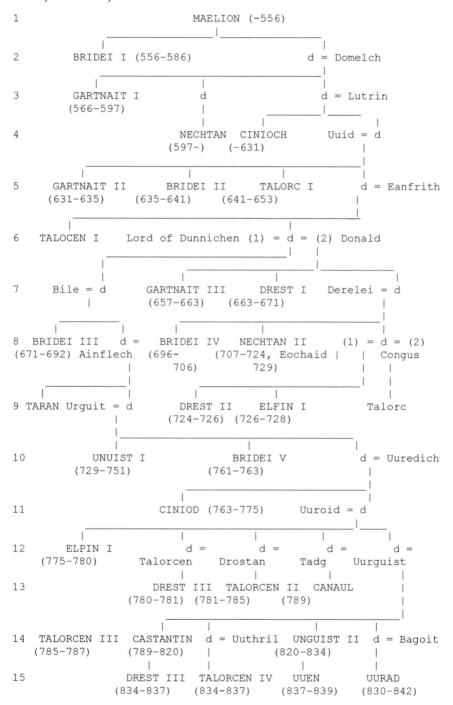

```
1                          MAELION (-556)
                    _____|_____
                    |                      |
2         BRIDEI I (556-586)           d = Domelch
              _____|
              |               |           |
3         GARTNAIT I          d           d = Lutrin
          (566-597)           |        _____|_____
                              |        |           |
4                       NECHTAN  CINIOCH      Uuid = d
                        (597-)   (-631)             |
          _____ |
          |               |             |         |
5     GARTNAIT II     BRIDEI II     TALORC I      d = Eanfrith
      (631-635)       (635-641)    (641-653)       |
      _____|
      |                              |
6  TALOCEN I    Lord of Dunnichen (1) = d = (2) Donald
               _____|  |
               |             _____|_____
               |             |          |         |
7    Bile = d      GARTNAIT III     DREST I   Derelei = d
         |          (657-663)     (663-671)             |
      _____              _____    |
      |       |              |              |       |
8  BRIDEI III   d =    BRIDEI IV    NECHTAN II    (1) = d = (2)
   (671-692) Ainflech  (696-      (707-724, Eochaid |  | Congus
                |       706)         729)            |  |
      _____|             _____    | |
      |          |             |         |       |   | |
9 TARAN Urguit = d        DREST II    ELFIN I      Talorc
             |            (724-726) (726-728)
             |_____
             |              |        |
10      UNUIST I        BRIDEI V        d = Uuredich
        (729-751)       (761-763)            |
                  _____   |
                  |                      |   |
11           CINIOD (763-775)      Uuroid = d
      _____|____
      |            |         |         |        |
12  ELPIN I       d =       d =       d =      d =
    (775-780)   Talorcen  Drostan    Tadg    Uurguist
                    |         |         |        |
13           DREST III  TALORCEN II  CANAUL     |
             (780-781)  (781-785)    (789)      |
             _____   |
             |         |         |         |
14 TALORCEN III CASTANTIN  d = Uuthril  UNGUIST II  d = Bagoit
   (785-787)    (789-820)  |            (820-834)    |
                    |        |            |          |
15           DREST III  TALORCEN IV   UUEN        UURAD
             (834-837)  (834-837)   (837-839)   (830-842)
```

```
                  _____|
          |              |              |              |
16      BRED         KINETH        DRUST IV      d = Foihel
        (842)        (843)        (845-846)           |
                                                      |
17                                                  BRUDE
                                                 (843-845)
```

Statistics

Duration: 289 years; 17 generations, average length 289/17 = 17 years;
35 rulers, average length of reign, 289/35 = 8 years.

Commentary

The kingdom of the Picts occupied the northern and north-eastern part of Scotland, and existed from the Roman period until the ninth century. There is a list of kings that must go back to the fifth century, but it is only from Bridei, who became king *c.*556, that a dynastic succession can be reconstructed. (Maelion is included here on the assumption that he had laid a sound foundation for his son's work.)

The table shown here is that produced, as 'conjectural', by Anderson. Succession in the kingship has been described as 'matrilineal', rather inconsistently, but it does seem that, in the occasional case that is on record, the succession went to men who were the sons of princesses. (A true matrilineal succession would have ruling queens.) Thus Bridei's successor was Gartnait, son of Bridei's sister. All sorts of wild theories have been produced to account for this, including one that ascribes it to the 'pre-Aryan' population. In fact it is more likely to be the result of a combination of the recognition of the existence of a royal family, in which the princesses were included, and practicality. In the ninth century any inheritance in the female line, if it had really existed, began to break down. Thus Drest III was the son of a king but apparently not of a princess; similarly Uuen; and in the next generation all three kings were sons of King Uurad. This was the period of the Viking wars, and most of these kings died in battle. That is, in the emergency, the rules of succession, if that is what they were, were discarded.

The succession system did result in a low reign average, and in the presence in the genealogy of kings from other lands – Eanfrith became king of Northumbria, Bile was a Strathclyde king, as was Uurad (Giud in the Strathclyde table).

References

AO Anderson, *King and Kingship in Early Scotland* (1973).
I Clarkson, *The Picts, a History* (Edinburgh, 2010).
JE Fraser, *From Caledonia to Pictland: Scotland to 795* (Edinburgh, 2007).
AP Smyth, *Warlords and Holy Men, Scotland AD 80–1000* (London, 1984).
A Woolf, *From Pictland to Alba, 789–1070* (Edinburgh, 2008).

Pontos, Asia Minor, 302–63 BC

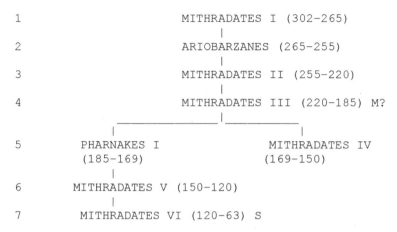

```
1                       MITHRADATES I (302-265)
                               |
2                       ARIOBARZANES (265-255)
                               |
3                       MITHRADATES II (255-220)
                               |
4                       MITHRADATES III (220-185) M?
              _____|_____
              |                               |
5        PHARNAKES I                    MITHRADATES IV
         (185-169)                      (169-150)
              |
6      MITHRADATES V (150-120)
              |
7      MITHRADATES VI (120-63) S
```

Statistics
Duration: 239 years; 7 generations, average length 239/7 = 34 years; 8 rulers, average length of reign, 239/8 = 30 years.

Commentary
The Pontic kings originated with a local lord, Mithradates I, who provided successful leadership against the Macedonian conquest, and so was able to style himself king and expand his power over a fair-sized kingdom along the south coast of the Black Sea. The dynasty proved to be capable and resilient, and the kings long-lived, showing a consistently long reign length as well as a high average generation length. They were assisted also by their remoteness from the great struggles of the period. The final king, Mithradates VI, clashed repeatedly with Rome, often with success, but was finally driven out of his ancestral kingdom. His family continued as kings of the Cimmerian Bosporos for another four centuries, but they are here taken as a separate dynasty.

References
CN Kraay, *The Hellenistic Kingdoms, Portrait Coins and History* (London, 1973).
B McGing, *The Foreign Policy of Mithridates VI Eupator, King of Pontus* (Leiden, 1966).

Ptolemies, Egypt, 323–30 BC

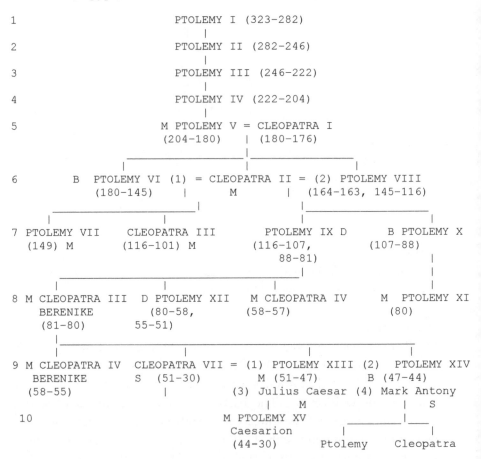

```
1                          PTOLEMY I (323-282)
                               |
2                          PTOLEMY II (282-246)
                               |
3                          PTOLEMY III (246-222)
                               |
4                          PTOLEMY IV (222-204)
                               |
5                     M PTOLEMY V  =  CLEOPATRA I
                        (204-180)  |  (180-176)
              _____|_____
              |                        |              |
6       B  PTOLEMY VI (1) = CLEOPATRA II = (2) PTOLEMY VIII
           (180-145)     |      M       |  (164-163, 145-116)
      _____|              |_____
      |                 |                    |               |
7 PTOLEMY VII    CLEOPATRA III       PTOLEMY IX D      B PTOLEMY X
  (149) M        (116-101) M         (116-107,        (107-88)
                                      88-81)              |
                       _____|            |
      |                 |                    |              |
8 M CLEOPATRA III   D PTOLEMY XII    M CLEOPATRA IV     M  PTOLEMY XI
  BERENIKE            (80-58,         (58-57)              (80)
  (81-80)             55-51)
      |_____
      |                 |                    |              |
9 M CLEOPATRA IV   CLEOPATRA VII = (1) PTOLEMY XIII (2)  PTOLEMY XIV
  BERENIKE         S  (51-30)        M (51-47)      B (47-44)
  (58-55)            |             (3) Julius Caesar (4) Mark Antony
                                      |    M               |  S
     10                          M PTOLEMY XV        _____|___
                                 Caesarion           |            |
                                 (44-30)         Ptolemy      Cleopatra
```

Statistics

Duration: 293 years; 10 generations, average length 293/10 = 29 years;
22 rulers, average length of reign, 293/22 = 13 years.

Commentary

Ptolemy I seized control of Egypt, and later added to it southern Syria,
Cyrenaica, and Cyprus, during the confusion following the death of Alexander
the Great. He maintained that control until his independent rule was
recognized. Technically only a satrap at first, and king only from 305, his rule
in Egypt in fact began in 323, soon after the death of Alexander. He founded a
successful dynasty, whose history divides into two roughly equal halves: until
180, and from 180 to the end. In 180 Ptolemy V was murdered in a palace
coup, and his widow, Kleopatra I, a Seleukid princess, then ruled as regent for

their sons, but those two sons later quarrelled and fought each other. From then on, the dynasty steadily lost power and respect, and its members spent much of their energy in internal fighting.

The first half of the dynasty's history saw a succession by male primogeniture, but the custom developed of sibling marriage, which by the fourth generation saw the king die young and his successor a child. The genetic content of the family was refreshed by the marriage of Ptolemy V with Kleopatra Syra (I), a princess of vigour and ability, but genetic intermarriage was revived in later generations, with the result that the lifespans and abilities of later generations were all erratic. The intervention of female members of the dynasty in the affairs of the kingdom also became increasingly common after Kleopatra Syra. This coincided with the increased prevalence of violent death amongst all the members of the family: ten out of the last thirteen in the table died in battle, were murdered, or committed suicide. The disaster of the Ptolemaic dynasty, long-drawn-out as it was, was also self-inflicted.

References
ER Bevan, *Egypt under the Ptolemies* (London, 1927).
G Holbl, *A History of the Ptolemaic Empire* (London, 2000).
AE Samuel, *Ptolemaic Chronology* (Munich, 1962).
'The Ptolemaic Dynasty', *Wikipedia*, accessed 29 January 2018.

Qataban, South Arabia, 250 BC–AD 160

A. *First Dynasty*, 250-190 BC.

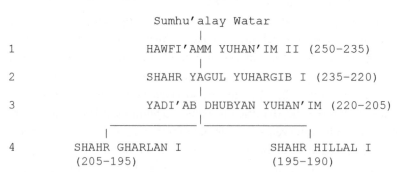

```
                        Sumhu'alay Watar
                              |
1                   HAWFI'AMM YUHAN'IM II (250-235)
                              |
2                   SHAHR YAGUL YUHARGIB I (235-220)
                              |
3                   YADI'AB DHUBYAN YUHAN'IM (220-205)
            _____|_____
            |                               |
4       SHAHR GHARLAN I                  SHAHR HILLAL I
        (205-195)                        (195-190)
```

Statistics

Duration: about 60 years; 4 generations, average length 60/4 = 15 years; 5 reigns, average length of reign 60/5 = 12 years.

B. *Second Dynasty*, 180-107 BC.

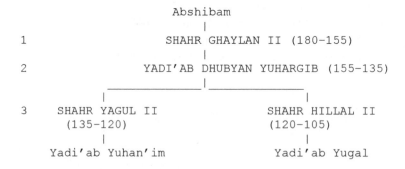

```
                        Abshibam
                           |
1                   SHAHR GHAYLAN II (180-155)
                           |
2               YADI'AB DHUBYAN YUHARGIB (155-135)
            _____|_____
            |                               |
3       SHAHR YAGUL II                   SHAHR HILLAL II
        (135-120)                        (120-105)
            |                               |
        Yadi'ab Yuhan'im                Yadi'ab Yugal
```

Statistics

Duration: 75 years; 3 generations, average length 75/3 = 25 years; 4 rulers, average length of reign, 75/4 = 19 years.

C. *Third Dynasty*, AD 30-80.

```
1                   HAWFI'AMM YUHAN'IM III (30-45)
                              |
2                   SHAHR YUGAL YUHARHIB III (45-65)
                              |
3                     WARAWIL GHAYLAN (65-80)
                              |
                    Fara'karib II Yuhawda
```

Statistics
Duration: about 50 years; 3 generations, average length, 50/3 = 17 years;
3 rulers, average length of reign, 50/3 = 17 years.

```
D.    Fourth Dynasty, AD 120-160.
1                        SHAHR HILLAL IV YUHAQBID (120-135)
                                  |
2                        NABATUM YUHAN'IM (135-150)
                                  |
3                        MARTHADUM (150-160)
```

Statistics
Duration, 40 years; 3 generations, average length 40/3 = 13 years; 3 rulers,
average length of reign, 40/3 = 13 years.

Commentary
Qataban was a long-standing kingdom in south Arabia, of which twenty-
three kings and the rulers are known by name, and eight more are postulated
from various items of evidence. It seems clear that more than one dynasty
was involved but just how many is not known, though the four family groups
listed above can be discerned. Dating is vague, as the repetitive round figures
and multiples of five show, but the kingdom came to an end after AD 160.

References
KA Kitchen, *Documentation for Ancient Arabia*, I (Liverpool, 1994).

Rheged, England/Scotland, AD *c.*570–*c.*630

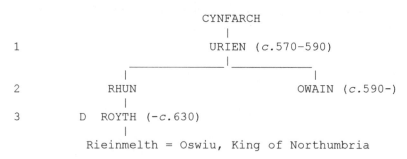

```
                         CYNFARCH
                            |
1                        URIEN (c.570-590)
              _____|_____
             |                       |
2          RHUN                    OWAIN (c.590-)
             |
3      D  ROYTH (-c.630)
             |
       Rieinmelth = Oswiu, King of Northumbria
```

Statistics
Duration of known and datable kings: 60 years; 3 generations, average
length, 60/3 = 20 years; 3 rulers, average length of reign, 60/3 = 20 years.

Commentary
Rheged was a small kingdom possibly centred in northern England or
southern Scotland that emerged in the immediate post-Roman collapse. The
royal family is recorded in several entries in the Welsh genealogies, but who
exactly ruled is not always clear. King Urien is known to have been the ruler in
the late sixth century, which would put Coel Hen, the founder of the dynasty,
as king about a century before, soon after the Roman abandonment in 410;
the genealogies imply at least four kings ruling between Coel Hen and Urien,
though the connection is disputed.

The kingdom was a leading factor in the resistance to Anglian conquest out
of Bernicia and Deira. Urien was killed at the siege of Lindisfarne, about 590;
Owein was host to the exiled Edwin of Northumbria and his daughter. Royth
was, it seems, the last ruling king, being conquered by Oswiu of Northumbria,
who married his daughter. The kingdom probably did not survive the 630s.
The dating of the kings is far too indefinite to permit conclusions to be drawn.

References
I Clarkson, *The Men of the North* (Edinburgh, 2010).
N Higham, *The Northern Counties to AD 1000* (Harlow, 1986).

Rugians, Germany, *c.*456–488

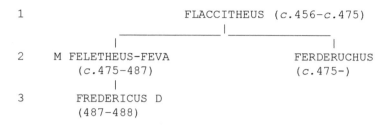

```
1                       FLACCITHEUS (c.456-c.475)
            _____|_____
            |                               |
2    M FELETHEUS-FEVA                  FERDERUCHUS
        (c.475-487)                     (c.475-)
            |
3       FREDERICUS D
        (487-488)
```

Statistics
Duration, 32 years; 3 generations, average length, 32/3 = 11 years; 4 rulers, average length of reign, 32/4 = 8 years.

Commentary
A fragment of the Rugian tribe settled to the north of Italy in the former Roman province of Noricum in the aftermath of the destruction of Hun power at the Battle of Nedao in 455. I have assumed that the dynasty became established at the same time. Flaccitheus was certainly king in 469, and since his father is never named, it seems likely that he was the first of the family to rule, gathering fragments of peoples into a minor kingdom.

The kingdom was never large or important, and we only know of its existence because of the biography of St Severinus, who lived in Noricum at the time. The second king, Feletheus, and his brother, shared power. Feletheus was attacked by the king of Italy, Odoacer, when he made an incautious alliance with the Eastern Roman Empire. The kingdom was destroyed and Feletheus and his queen were taken to Italy and executed. Fredericus survived to attempt a revival next year, but he and his people were then also suppressed once more, and the survivors taken to Italy. The tribe maintained itself within Italy as part of the Ostrogothic kingdom, as a distinct unit, for the next fifty years, but the dynasty had expired.

References
EA Thompson, 'The End of Noricum' in *Romans and Barbarians, the Decline of the Western Empire* (Madison, WI, 1982).

Saba, South Arabia, *c.*790 BC–AD 230

A. *First Dynasty, c.790–725 BC.*

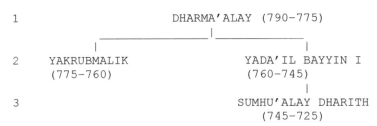

```
1                       DHARMA'ALAY (790-775)
            _____|_____
            |                               |
2      YAKRUBMALIK                  YADA'IL BAYYIN I
       (775-760)                    (760-745)
                                            |
3                                   SUMHU'ALAY DHARITH
                                    (745-725)
```

Statistics
Duration: 65 years; 3 generations, average length 65/3 = 22 years; 4 reigns, average length of reign, 65/4 = 16 years.

B. *Second Dynasty, 527–435 BC.*

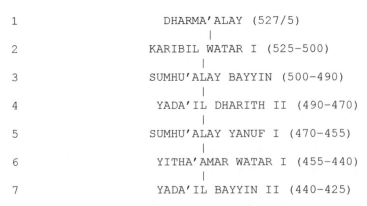

```
1                    DHARMA'ALAY (527/5)
                              |
2                  KARIBIL WATAR I (525-500)
                              |
3                  SUMHU'ALAY BAYYIN (500-490)
                              |
4                   YADA'IL DHARITH II (490-470)
                              |
5                  SUMHU'ALAY YANUF I (470-455)
                              |
6                  YITHA'AMAR WATAR I (455-440)
                              |
7                  YADA'IL BAYYIN II (440-425)
```

Statistics
Duration: 92 years; 7 generations, average length, 92/7 = 12 years; 7 rulers, average length of reign, 92/7 = 12 years.

C. *Third Dynasty, 425–350 BC.*

```
1                    YITHA'AMAR (425-415)
                              |
2                  KARIBIL BAYYIN I (415-400)
                              |
3                  DHARMA'ALAY WATAR (400-380)
                              |
4                   SUMHU'ALAY YANUF II (380-365)
                              |
5                  YITHA'AMAR BAYYIN II (365-350)
```

Statistics
Duration: 75 years; 5 generations, average length 75/5 = 15 years; 5 rulers, average length of reign, 75/5 = 15 years.

```
D.   Fourth Dynasty, 200-140 BC.
1                    KARIBIL WATAR II (200-180)
                          |
2                   YADA'IL BAYYIN V (180-165)
                          |
3                  YAKRUBMALIK WATAR II (165-150)
                          |
4                   DHARMA'ALAY YANUF (150-140)
```

Statistics
Duration: 60 years; 4 generations, average length, 60/4 = 15 years; 4 rulers, average length of reign, 60/4 = 15 years.

```
E.   Fifth Dynasty, 140-15 BC
1                   YITHA'AMAR BAYYIN IV (140-125)
                          |
2                  SUMHU'ALAY DHARIH II (125-105)
                          |
3                   KARIBIL BAYYIN II (105-90)
                          |
4                   YADA'IL DHARIH III (90-80)
                          |
5                  YITHA'AMAR WATAR III (80-60)
                          |
6                  SUMHU'ALAY YUSUF V (60-45)
              _____|_____
              |                              |
7      YADA'IL WATAR I               DHARMA'ALAY BAYYIN I
         (45-30)                          (30-15)
```

Statistics
Duration 125 years; 7 generations, average length 125/7 = 18 years; 8 rulers, average length of reign 125/8 = 16 years.

```
F.   Sixth Dynasty, AD 150-230.
1                   WAHABIL YAHUZ (150-165)
              _____|_____
              |                              |
2       ANMAR YUHAN'IM             KARIBIL WATAR YUHAN'IM II
         (165-170)                        (170-185)
                                              |
3                                     YARIM AYMAN (185-190)
                                              |
4                                    'ALHAN NAHFAN (190-205)
                                              |
5                                     SHA'AR AWTAR (205-230)
                                              |
                                      Hayu'athar Yada'
```

Statistics
Duration: 80 years; 5 generations, average length 80/5 = 16 years; 6 rulers, average length of reign 80/6 = 13 years.

Commentary
Saba was the most ancient of the south Arabian states, originating perhaps as early as the twelfth century BC, and famous enough to provide the story of the Queen of Sheba to the Bible. (But the dating of the Queen depends on the dating of King Solomon, who may not have existed, and the story reflects the wealth of Saba in the sixth century BC, not the tenth.) The names of well over fifty rulers are known, but their dating is extremely hazardous. Six family groups can be sorted out, and the dynasties here labelled C, D and E follow on from each other directly, so either they were new dynasties, or they descended by junior lines. The kingdom was taken over at the end of the first century BC, but an independent kingdom of Saba re-emerged in the mid second century AD, after a period of rule by others, with a new dynasty that is relatively well documented ('F' here), though, as before, the dates are unclear. The dates assigned here to all the kings and dynasties are clearly extremely artificial, based on an average reign length and generation length of only fifteen years, which is extremely unlikely.

References
KA Kitchen, *Documentation for Ancient Arabia*, I (Liverpool, 1994).

Scythians, *c.*675–*c.*390 BC

A. *First Dynasty,* c.675-600 BC.

```
1                         ISHPAKAI (c.675)

2                         BARTATUA ('Protothyes') (c.675-672)
                          |
3                         MADYES (c.650-c.600)
```

Statistics
Duration: 75 years; 3 generations, average length 75/3 = 25 years; 3 rulers,
average length of reign, 75/3 = 25 years.

B. *Second Dynasty,* Seventh/Sixth Centuries BC.

```
1                       SPARGAPEITHES (C7 BC)
                               |
2                         LYCUS (C7-6 BC)
                               |
3                         GNURUS (C6 BC)
                   _____|_____
                  |                         |
4         SAULIUS (mid C6 BC)        Anacharsis
```

C. *Third Dynasty* (c.490-c.390 BC)

```
                       ARAPEITHES (c.490-460)
          _____|_____
         |                     |                     |
      SKYLES              OKTAMASADES             OREIAS
    (460-440)             (440-390)                (C5)
```

Statistics
All dates are approximate and liable to change; it would therefore be fruitless
to attempt any statistical calculations.

Commentary
The source for these kings are Greek writers sometime later (particularly
Herodotos), and accuracy is not guaranteed. Several more kings, who cannot
be genetically connected to those noted here, are also known. The reason
for this interest is partly due to Anacharsis, who provides a single firm date
of 589 BC when he arrived in Athens at the time of Solon's influence. The
existence of Skyles is confirmed by the discovery of a ring engraved with his

name in the tumulus in the Ukraine that was his grave. The graves of others are also identified in the same region, not necessarily correctly.

References

A Yu Alekseyev, 'Scythian Kings and 'Royal' Burial-mounds of the Fifth and Fourth Centuries BC, in David Braund (ed.) *Scythians and Greeks, Cultural Interactions in Scythia, Athens, and the Early Roman Empire (sixth century BC– first century AD)* (Exeter, 2005) pp. 39–55.

Spoleto, Italy, AD 663–742

```
1          TRANSAMUND I (c.663-703)
              |
2           FAROALD II (703-724)
              |
3          TRANSAMUND II (724-739, 740-742)
```

Statistics
Duration: 79 years; 3 generations, average length, 79/3 = 26 years; 3 rulers, average length of reign, 79/3 = 26 years.

Commentary
Spoleto was one of the Lombard duchies that were established early in the conquest of Italy. For most of the Lombard period its duke was under the ultimate or even at times the immediate control of the Lombard kings, but in the period of extreme royal weakness in the seventh and eighth centuries, this dynasty of dukes did emerge, to enjoy a period of near independence, as did their southern neighbour in Benevento. When the royal power revived, however, the dynasty ended, and new dukes were thenceforward appointed by the king.

References
PS Barnwell, *Kings, Courtiers, and Imperium: the Barbarian West 565–725* (London, 1997).
N Christie, *The Lombards: the Ancient Lombards* (Oxford, 1995).
C Wickham, *Early Mediaeval Italy* (London, 1981).

Strathclyde or Alt Clut, Scotland, AD *c.*450–872

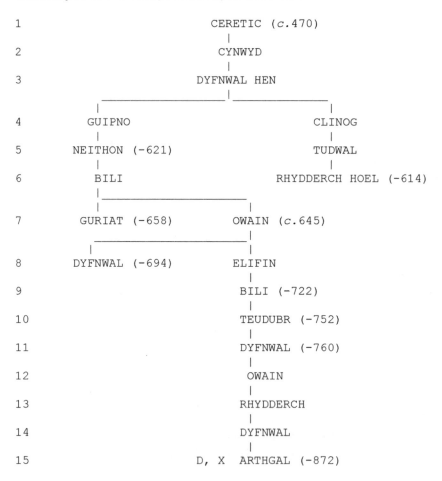

```
1                              CERETIC (c.470)
                                    |
2                                 CYNWYD
                                    |
3                              DYFNWAL HEN
             _____|_____
            |                                        |
4        GUIPNO                                    CLINOG
            |                                        |
5      NEITHON (-621)                             TUDWAL
            |                                        |
6        BILI                          RHYDDERCH HOEL (-614)
            |_____
            |                      |
7      GURIAT (-658)        OWAIN (c.645)
      _____|
     |                            |
8  DYFNWAL (-694)              ELIFIN
                                  |
9                              BILI (-722)
                                  |
10                           TEUDUBR (-752)
                                  |
11                          DYFNWAL (-760)
                                  |
12                             OWAIN
                                  |
13                          RHYDDERCH
                                  |
14                           DYFNWAL
                                  |
15                  D, X  ARTHGAL (-872)
```

Statistics
Duration: 422 years; 15 generations, average length 422/15 = 28 years; 22 rulers, average length of reign, 422/22 = 19 years.

Commentary
Strathclyde emerged in the aftermath of the Roman collapse in Britain. It was centred on the great fortress on Dumbarton Rock in the Clyde estuary, which was called at the time Alt Clut, and that is sometimes given as the kingdom's name. The kingdom survived until it was incorporated into the united Scots-Pictish state in the 870s. The line of descent is fairly well established, though the dates of the kings are only intermittently known, for the whole construct depends on references in connection with other states and in teasing out the

references in Welsh sources. But the origin and end of the dynasty are clear. It counted itself as Welsh. A Viking expedition conquered Alt Clut in 870, and abducted King Arthgal, killing him two years later. He was survived by a son, Rhun, who was king a little later, but the kingdom was so extensively damaged that it had to be protected by the Scots-Pictish kings, who provided kings for it for the next two centuries.

References
AO Anderson, *Early Sources of Scottish History*, vol. 1 (Edinburgh, 1922).
I Clarkson, *The Men of the North* (Edinburgh, 2010).
JE Fraser, *From Caledonia to Pictland: Scotland to 795* (Edinburgh, 2007).
AP Smyth, *Warlords and Holy Men, Scotland AD 80–1000* (London, 1984).
A Woolf, *From Pictland to Alba, 789–1070* (Edinburgh, 2008).

Sueves, Spain, AD 410–456

```
1                    HERMERIC (419-438) A
                         |
2                    RECHILA (438-448)
                         |
3                    RECHIARIUS (448-456) M
```

Statistics
Duration: 46 years; 3 generations, average length 46/3 = 15 years: 3 rulers, average length of reign, 46/3 = 15 years.

Commentary
The Sueves were a barbarian German people who arrived in Spain in 409 along with several other tribes. After a preliminary ravaging, the tribes drew lots for the parts of Spain they would each occupy, and the Sueves found themselves stuck in the mountainous north-west, Galicia. This proved to be their salvation for a time, since their fellow allottees were soon destroyed or expelled, while the Sueves survived in their remote and distant mountains. They had the distinction of being the first invaders of the Roman Empire to seize part of the empire and make it into an independent state outside the empire.

The dynasty that ruled them for a time appears first in 419 when Hermeric is named as king at the moment when the tribe had just survived a massive attack. Presumably it was the continued danger of extermination that required the tribe, ultimately, to submit to a king but in 456 the last of the dynasty was killed by his Visigoth enemies. From then until the end of the kingdom in 585 no other dynasty is known to have ruled it. Indeed, even the kingship seems to have been only intermittent. At the same time it may be emphasized that, for the last century of its life, the sources of the kingdom's history are somewhere between meagre and non-existent.

References
EA Thompson, 'The Suevic kingdom of Galicia', in his *Romans and Barbarians* (Wisconsin, 1982).

Syracuse, Sicily, 491–212 BC

A. *Deinomenid Dynasty*, 491–465 BC.

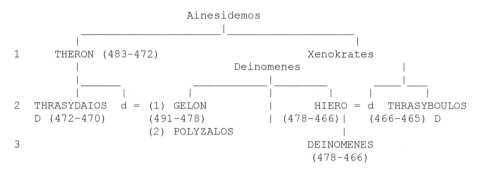

```
                            Ainesidemos
        _____|_____
       |                                               |
1   THERON (483-472)                            Xenokrates
       |                         Deinomenes             |
       |_____                 _____|_____      ___|___
       |     |               |         |       |    |       |
2   THRASYDAIOS  d = (1) GELON          |      HIERO = d  THRASYBOULOS
    D (472-470)      (491-478)          |    (478-466)|   (466-465) D
                     (2) POLYZALOS      |             |
3                                          DEINOMENES
                                           (478-466)
```

Statistics

Duration: 26 years; 3 generations, average length 26/3 = 9 years; 7 rulers, average length of reign, 26/7 = 4 years.

Commentary

Monarchy was an intermittent habit of the Greek cities of Sicily, based always on control of the main city of Syracuse, but the habit was interrupted by unstable periods of aristocratic or democratic rule in the city, during which the other cities in the island shifted into independence. The first dynasty, in fact, was a collective Sicily-wide affair of tyrants, with the different cities being ruled by various members of two intermingled families. The main members were Gelon and Hiero, tyrants respectively of Gela and Syracuse, and Theron, tyrant of Akragas. This arrangement scarcely survived Hiero's death, and gave way to aristocratic regimes in the various component cities.

B. *Dionysiads*, 405-344 BC.

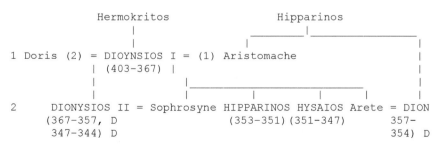

```
             Hermokritos                  Hipparinos
                 |                      _____|_____
                 |                     |                         |
1  Doris (2) = DIOYNSIOS I = (1) Aristomache                      |
             |  (403-367)  |                                      |
             |             |_____             |
             |             |         |         |       |          |
2     DIONYSIOS II = Sophrosyne HIPPARINOS HYSAIOS Arete = DION
      (367-357, D              (353-351)(351-347)      357-
      347-344) D                                       354) D
```

Statistics
Duration 61 years; 2 generations, average length $61/2 = 31$ years; 5 rulers, average length of reign, $61/5 = 12$ years.

Commentary
The tyranny of Dionysios I came into existence when Syracuse came under attack, first from Athens in 413, and then from Carthage in 405. Dionysios' dynasty was similar in construction to that of Theron and Gelon, though it was more a monarchy and less of a collective system. There was much intermarriage within the family, and the dynasty expired in the second generation also similarly, being replaced by democratic regimes in the several cities. The dynasty crumbled away after the death of the founder into a succession of short reigns. Dionysios' monarchy covered much of Sicily and a good deal of southern Italy, and this empire was broken up in the ruin of the dynasty; it was largely reconstructed after a generation by a new tyrant, Agathokles, who seized power during a new bout of warfare with Carthage. It broke up again after Agathokles' death in 289; his attempt to found a dynasty failed.

```
C.  Hieronids, 270-214 BC.

1                         HIERO (270-215)
                             |
2                         Gelon
                             |
3                    HIERONYMOS (215-214)   M
```

Statistics
Duration: 56 years; 3 generations, average length $56/3 = 19$ years; 2 rulers, average length of reign $56/2 = 28$ years.

Commentary
One more reconstitution of the Syracusan tyranny, by Hiero, was largely confined to the city of Syracuse and its immediate neighbourhood, amounting to about a quarter of the island; it lasted half a century before Hiero's grandson chose the wrong side in the Second Punic War, at which the city was besieged and sacked, and its independence was snuffed out by Rome and with it the last Sicilian dynasty. Hieronymos had in fact been murdered in the process of a democratic revolution in the city, but this did not save the city from the Roman attack and sack.

The brief existence of these dynasties (and Agathokles' monarchy was also brief; three decades: 317–289), indicates that it was the deep-rooted political instability of Greek Sicily which was the problem, not the dynasties, which were a symptom of that problem – though their unpleasantness, brutality, and internecine conduct certainly helped to bring them and Greek Sicily down.

There is, in dynastic terms, a clear progression from the obvious collectivity of the Deinomenids, where the several members were assigned a city each, to the family of Dionysios, where two families linked but were dominated by Dionysios I and II, to the clearly one-man monarchies of Agathokles and Hiero (who called themselves kings); these men ruled very much on their own; this progression is also reflected in the increasing length of the average reigns.

References

B Caven, *Dionysius I, Warlord of Sicily* (New Haven, CT, 1990).

TJ Dunbabin, 'The Western Greeks: the History of Sicily and South Italy from the Foundation of the Greek Colonies to 480 B.C.', *The American Historical Review*, (Oxford, 1948).

RJ Evans, *Syracuse in Antiquity, History and Topography* (Pretoria, 2009).

MI Finley, *Ancient Sicily to the Arab Conquest* (London, 1968).

HJW Tillyard, *Agathokles* (Cambridge, 1908).

Tabal 'Proper', Asia Minor, pre-837–713 BC

```
1                TUWATI I (-837)
                    |
2                 KIKKI (836-)

3                TUWATI II (mid C8)
                    |
4               WASUSARMA (740-730) D

5               HULLI (730-726)
                    |
6               AMBARIS (c.721-713)  D
```

Statistics
Duration: more than 124 years; uncertainty on dynasties, dates, and reigns makes further calculations impossible.

Commentary
Tabal was a region of central Anatolia that was, by the mid ninth century BC, divided between five or six kingdoms. That of Tabal 'Proper' – the term is Assyrian – or northern Tabal, was probably the most important, and was perhaps the original state from the others that had broken away. It was certainly the only one where a sequence of kings is known, though they may or may not have formed a dynasty. The first two groups ('A' and 'B') have the repeated name Tuwati, but at least one king, perhaps more, is to be expected between Kikki and to Tuwati II. The third pair ('C'), is expressly stated to have been imposed by Assyria, after Wasusarma was removed. The kingdom was extended in Ambaris' reign, but, like Wasusarma, he displeased the Assyrian king and was deposed.

References
T Bryce, *The World of the Neo-Hittite Kingdoms* (Oxford, 2012).

Tarkondimotids, Cilicia, 64 BC–AD 17
Statistics

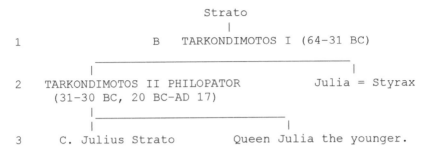

```
                            Strato
                              |
1                    B     TARKONDIMOTOS I (64-31 BC)
         _____
         |                                      |
2   TARKONDIMOTOS II PHILOPATOR           Julia = Styrax
    (31-30 BC, 20 BC-AD 17)
         |_____
         |                               |
3   C. Julius Strato            Queen Julia the younger.
```

Duration: 81 years, reigning for 71; 2 generations, average length, 81/2 = 40 years; 2 rulers, average length of reign, 71/2 = 36 years.

Commentary

Tarkondimotos I was selected by Pompey the Great to rule an area of mountainous Cilicia based around the future city of Hierapolis Castabala. His father Strato had been, it seems, a local chieftain in the area. Tarkondimotos successfully navigated the problems of loyalty to the various Roman commanders who ruled in the east during his reign – backing Pompey against Caesar, Cassius against Octavian and Antony, and Antony against Octavian, but he was finally killed in the Battle of Actium in 31 BC. His son succeeded him briefly, was deposed by Octavian because of his loyalty, but was then reinstated by the same man ten years later. So far as can be seen he continued to rule until AD 17. A queen called Julia the Younger is referred to in an inscription, and Styrax is called father of kings (in the plural) elsewhere. Styrax's description suggests that there was at least one other ruler of the family, and it may be Queen Julia, who may well have been married to the ruler of another principality, at Olba, also in the mountains. The dynasty effectively needled in AD 17.

References

G Dagron and D Fiessel, *Inscriptions de Cilicie* (Paris, 1987).

AHM Jones, *The Cities of the Eastern Roman Provinces* (Oxford, 1937).

TB Mitford, 'Rough Cilicia', *ANRW*, II, 7.

Jennifer Tobin, 'The Tarkondimotid Dynasty in Smooth Cilicia', in A Jean, AM Dincol and S Dourgoud (eds.), *La Cilicie: Espaces et Pouvoirs Locaux*, (Paris, 2001).

Thessaly, Greece, *c.*404–352 BC

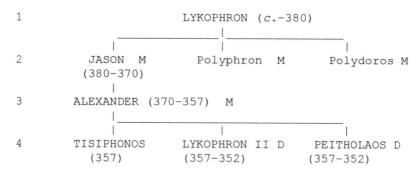

```
1                          LYKOPHRON (c.-380)
        ┌──────────────────────┼──────────────────────┐
        │                      │                       │
2     JASON   M         Polyphron   M          Polydoros M
      (380-370)
        │
3    ALEXANDER (370-357)   M
        │
        ┌──────────────────────┬───────────────────────┐
        │                      │                       │
4    TISIPHONOS        LYKOPHRON II  D         PEITHOLAOS  D
      (357)            (357-352)               (357-352)
```

Statistics

Duration: 52 years; 4 generations, average length, 52/4 = 13 years; 5 rulers, average length of reign, 525 = 10 years.

Commentary

The family of Jason was centred on the Thessalian city of Pherai, but their ambition encompassed all of that country. Jason is the best known of this family of tyrants. He was either the son or son-in-law of Lykophron, who made himself tyrant of Pherai about the end of the Peloponnesian War. A war with Larissa, which was supported by the king of Macedon for a time, helped him to consolidate his power at home, but the enmity of other Thessalian tyrants kept him pinned down to Pherai.

His successor, Jason, in power from about 380, was more successful, and by 370 he was the ruler of most of Thessaly, with the title of Tagos. He could expand because Sparta, hitherto the predominant power in Greece, was weakening, and was interested in controlling matters closer to home. Jason intervened in Boiotia, and allied with Athens and Epeiros, but in 370, while about to embark on a new adventure, he was murdered. Then one of his brothers, Polyphron, was murdered by another, Polydoros, who was in turn murdered by Alexander, who was probably Jason's son.

By this time the family's power was once more restricted to Pherai, though its ambition remained to unify Thessaly. This brought sturdy opposition from other Thessalians, and repeated interventions by Thebes and Macedon, for neither relished the prospect of a powerful and united Thessaly on their borders. The net result for Alexander was submission to Thebes as a means of keeping his power.

Alexander's regime was very brutal, and his unpleasantness extended to his own family; he was murdered by a conspiracy led by his wife and her brothers.

Tisiphonos ruled briefly for a while, then Lykophron and Peitholaos, who were expelled in 352 by Philip of Macedon. These survivors took refuge in Athens and made several attempts to return to Pherai, where they had a substantial body of supporters, but their success was never more than momentary. The rule of the family effectively ended in 352.

References
J Boardman, *Cambridge Ancient History*, vol. IV (Cambridge).

Thrace, *c.*480 BC–AD 46

A. *The Odrysai Dynasty, c.480–c.340 BC.*

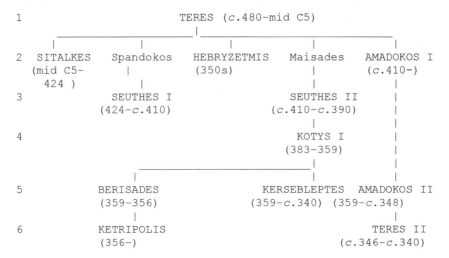

```
1                           TERES (c.480-mid C5)
       _____|_____
       |          |          |          |           |
2  SITALKES   Spandokos  HEBRYZETMIS  Maisades   AMADOKOS I
   (mid C5-       |       (350s)         |        (c.410-)
    424 )         |                      |           |
3            SEUTHES I               SEUTHES II       |
            (424-c.410)             (c.410-c.390)     |
                                         |            |
4                                     KOTYS I         |
                                     (383-359)        |
                     _____|            |
       |                          |              |    |
5  BERISADES               KERSEBLEPTES    AMADOKOS II
   (359-356)              (359-c.340)    (359-c.348)
       |                                      |
6  KETRIPOLIS                            TERES II
   (356-)                             (c.346-c.340)
```

Statistics
Duration: 140 years; 6 generations, average length, 140/6 = 23 years;
12 rulers, average length of reign, 140/12 = 12 years.

B. *The Seuthids, c.240-c.140.*

```
1                    SEUTHES (c.240)
                          |
2                    KOTYS (c.170)
                          |
3                    BITHYS (c.140)
```

Statistics
Duration: about 100 years; 3 generations, average length 100/3 = 33 years;
3 rulers, average length of reign, 100/3 = 33 years.

C. The Sapaean Dynasty, 100 BC-AD 46.

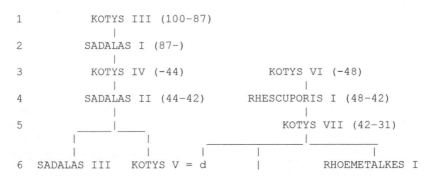

```
1          KOTYS III (100-87)
                  |
2        SADALAS I (87-)
                  |
3          KOTYS IV (-44)              KOTYS VI (-48)
                  |                          |
4        SADALAS II (44-42)        RHESCUPORIS I (48-42)
                  |                          |
5        _____|____                 KOTYS VII (42-31)
         |          |            _____|_____
         |          |        |        |              |
6  SADALAS III  KOTYS V = d       |         RHOEMETALKES I
```

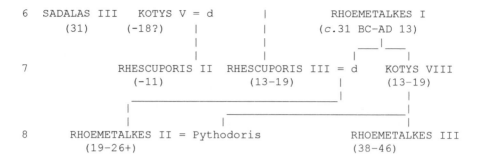

```
6   SADALAS III    KOTYS V = d            |          RHOEMETALKES  I
      (31)        (-18?)     |            |         (c.31 BC-AD 13)
                             |            |                 ___|___
                             |            |           |            |
7                  RHESCUPORIS II  RHESCUPORIS III = d    KOTYS VIII
                       (-11)           (13-19)     |        (13-19)
                        _____|          |
                       |                   _____|
                       |                  |                          |
8       RHOEMETALKES II = Pythodoris                  RHOEMETALKES III
           (19-26+)                                      (38-46)
```

Statistics

Duration: 146 years; 8 generations, average length, 146/8 = 18 years;
15 rulers, average length of reign 146/15 = 10 years.

Commentary

The royal families of Thrace, of which I have distinguished three here, are
probably all related, though the connections between them are no longer
visible. The first dynasty developed out of the tribal chieftains of the Odrysai,
one of the main Thracian peoples, and becomes visible in our sources from
the time of the Persian Wars. The disturbance caused by the passage of the
Akhaimenid armies through Thrace on their way to Greece in 481–480,
seems to have provoked and allowed Teres to expand his authority over much
of the country.

Inheritance was not always to a single ruler, and it was a common practice
for cadet males of the dynasty to be given an appanage to rule, which, of
course, they then endeavoured to render independent and hereditary. The
result is a multiplicity of kings and great difficulty in detecting the precise
extent of their powers and the dates of their times in office. It may be that
there were other kings besides those in the table. The relationships are about
right, however, and the dates of the start and the end of the dynasty are fixed;
the end came with the conquest of Thrace by Philip II of Macedon in about
340, and there follows a gap in the sequence of kings.

A second dynasty surfaced a century later, after the decline of Macedonian
power, and after the power of an invading band of Galatians had also begun
to fade. The repetition of the names of the former dynasty suggests that this
may be a revival of a branch of that family, but it is very poorly attested. The
dates used are only approximations.

The third dynasty – again largely using some of the same set of names,
which may be due to inheritance, or may be the use of recognized royal
names by those not connected – emerged in two parts of Thrace during

the turbulence of the Roman conquest of the east. The two lines merged with some difficulty, and despite several of its members falling foul of the various Roman warlords during their civil wars, the dynasty survived for almost another century, becoming a part of the intricate web of relationships among the many royal families who ruled on behalf of Rome from Numidia to the Cimmerian Bosporos and Judaea. The kingdom and the dynasty were eventually suppressed by the Emperor Claudius. The partible inheritance practices had continued to the end, and it seems clear that several kings were in office at any one time.

References
Z Archibold, *The Odrysian Kingdom of Thrace* (London, 1998).
R Sullivan, 'Thrace in the Eastern Dynastic Network', *ANRW*, II, 77.1.

Ulster, Ireland, AD 553–857

A. *Northern Ui Neill*, AD 566-734.

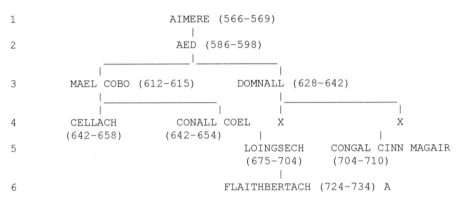

```
1                          AIMERE (566-569)
                                |
2                          AED (586-598)
           _____|_____
          |                                 |
3    MAEL COBO (612-615)           DOMNALL (628-642)
          |_____            |_____
          |                |           |                |
4     CELLACH       CONALL COEL        X                X
     (642-658)      (642-654)          |                |
5                                  LOINGSECH      CONGAL CINN MAGAIR
                                   (675-704)        (704-710)
                                       |
6                             FLAITHBERTACH (724-734) A
```

Statistics

Duration: 168 years, reigning for 93; 6 generations, average length 168/6 = 28 years; 9 rulers, average length of reign, 93/9 = 10 years.

B. *Dal Fiatach*, AD 553-857.

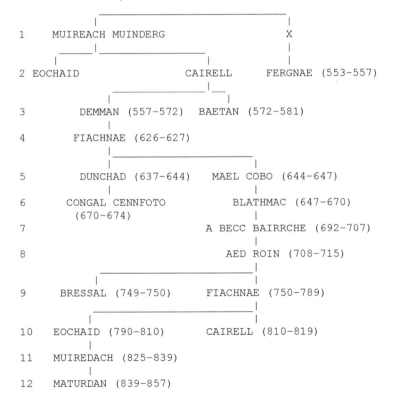

```
          _____
         |                               |
1     MUIREACH MUINDERG                   X
       _____|_____           |
      |                        |          |
2 EOCHAID                  CAIRELL    FERGNAE (553-557)
              _____|__
             |                  |
3       DEMMAN (557-572)  BAETAN (572-581)
             |
4       FIACHNAE (626-627)
             |
             |_____
             |                        |
5       DUNCHAD (637-644)    MAEL COBO (644-647)
             |                        |
6     CONGAL CENNFOTO         BLATHMAC (647-670)
        (670-674)                     |
7                         A BECC BAIRRCHE (692-707)
                                      |
8                            AED ROIN (708-715)
          _____|
         |                             |
9   BRESSAL (749-750)         FIACHNAE (750-789)
          _____|
         |                            |
10  EOCHAID (790-810)        CAIRELL (810-819)
         |
11  MUIREDACH (825-839)
         |
12  MATURDAN (839-857)
```

C. *Dal nAraidi* (i.e. Dalriada), AD 553-749.

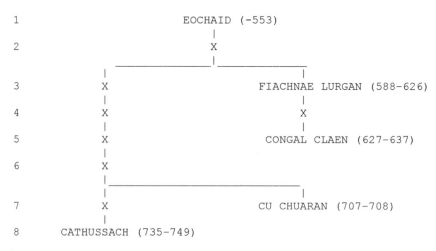

```
1                              EOCHAID (-553)
                                    |
2                                   X
          _____|_____
         |                                                  |
3        X                               FIACHNAE LURGAN (588-626)
         |                                                  |
4        X                                                  X
         |                                                  |
5        X                               CONGAL CLAEN (627-637)
         |
6        X
         |_____
         |                                            |
7        X                               CU CHUARAN (707-708)
         |
8  CATHUSSACH (735-749)
```

Statistics
Duration: 304 years, reigning for 189; 12 generations, average length,
304/12 = 25 years; 22 rulers, average length of reign, 189/22 = 9 years.

Statistics
Duration: 196 years, reigning for 63; 8 generations, average length 196/8 =
24 years; 6 rulers, average length of reign, 63/6 = 11 years.

   (For a commentary on all the Irish dynasties, see the entry on Ireland: High
Kings.)

Urartu, Asia Minor, 844–625 BC

A. *Sardurid Dynasty*, 844-660 BC.

	Latipri	'Secure' Dates.
1	SARDURI I (844-828)	831
2	ISHPUINI (828-810)	818
3	MINUA (810-785)	
4	ARGISHTI I (785-760)	
5	SARDURI II (760-730)	743
6	RUSA I (730-714)	714
7	ARGISHTI II (714-685)	689
8	RUSA II (685-660)	673

Statistics
Duration: 184 years, 8 generations, average length, 184/8 = 23 years; 8 rulers, average length of reign, 184/8 = 23 years.

B. *Rusid Dynasty*, 660-625 BC.

	Erimina	
1	RUSA III (660-)	655
2	SARDURI III	
3	SARDURI IV (-625)	

Statistics
Duration: 35 years; 3 generations, average length, 35/3 = 12 years; 3 rulers, average length of reign, 35/3 = 12 years.

Commentary
The kingdom of Urartu, which is claimed by Armenians as the first Armenian state, was a powerful enemy of Assyria for two centuries. Its defeat was the factor that permitted the Assyrian conquest of Syria to go ahead.

The ruling dynasty's origin is unclear, but it is probable that Sarduri I seized the throne from his predecessor. An earlier king called Arame is known in the 850s, and he appears to have made substantial progress towards uniting the several small Urartian states; meanwhile Latipri, Sarduri's father, is not recorded as a king. It is assumed that Sarduri I took over Arame's kingdom and extended it. The descent from Sarduri is clear until Rusa II, though the dates of the reigns are largely assumption. The 'secure dates', which are provided by the Assyrian records, are noted; it will be seen that in most cases only one datable reference for any one king is available. It follows that the dates for the reigns provided here are largely hypothetical.

After Rusa II, whose kingdom had been much reduced by Assyrian victories, there are two hypotheses available. One is that he was succeeded by his son and grandson, Sarduri III and IV; the other is that these two followed another king, Rusa (Rusa III), who was the son of Erimina. In the first hypothesis Rusa III comes after Sarduri IV. Only one Assyrian date is available, for one of the Sarduris, in 639. However, there is also a reference to a Rusa, who may or may not be a king, in 655, and this may be Rusa III rather than Rusa II.

The problem is insoluble with the present evidence. I have assumed that the second hypothesis is correct, and that we have two dynasties. The dating of the second dynasty is, however almost impossible to find. It may have lasted as shown, but all dates are approximate.

References
M Chahin, *The Kingdom of Armenia* (Beckenham, Kent, 1987).
BB Piotrovski, *The Ancient Civilization of Urartu* (London, 1969).
L Vanden Berghe and L de Meyer, *Urartu, een vergeten cultuur uit het bergland Armenie* (Gent, 1983).

Vandals, North Africa, AD 426–534

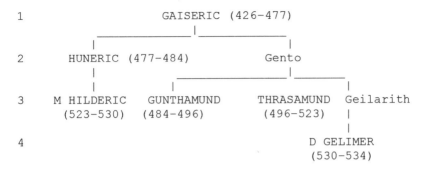

```
1                         GAISERIC (426-477)
                  _____|_____
          |                                      |
2      HUNERIC (477-484)                       Gento
          |                           _____|_____
          |              |                        |         |
3    M HILDERIC     GUNTHAMUND           THRASAMUND    Geilarith
     (523-530)      (484-496)            (496-523)     |
                                                       |
4                                              D GELIMER
                                               (530-534)
```

Statistics
Duration: 108 years; 4 generations, average length $108/4 = 27$ years; 6 rulers, average length of reign, $108/6 = 18$ years.

Commentary
The Vandal kingship existed as a tribal leadership before the people invaded and settled in North Africa under the rule of the able Gaiseric (who actually dated his kingship from 439, when he captured Carthage, though he was ruling the people by 426). Only when the African settlement was established can a clear dynasty be discerned. The rulers were all long-lived – Gaiseric had been born about 390 – but most of them came to power as old men, and so they ruled only briefly. The succession system was for the eldest male to succeed.

Gelimer provided the exception, and the death blow. He usurped the throne from his cousin Hilderic, whom he murdered, and then killed off his other royal relatives to prevent them doing the same to him. This unusual vigour made him dangerous. He was then attacked by the Byzantine army led by Belisarius and gave up the struggle almost at once with scarcely a fight, no doubt in part as a result of the failure of his people to support him – the Vandals already had no support from the Catholic Roman population, since they persisted in cleaving to Arianism, and Gelmer's pusillanimity and cowardice lost him the support of his own Vandals. The whole nasty episode is a compressed example of the self-immolation of many ancient dynasties.

References
C Courtois, *Les Vandales et l'Afrique* (Paris, 1955).

H Wolfram, *The Roman Empire and its Germanic Peoples* (Berkeley and Los Angeles, 1997).

Visigoths, Aquitaine and Spain, AD 395–714

A. *The First Dynasty, AD 395–531.*

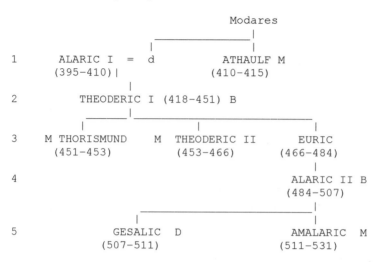

```
                                    Modares
                            _____|
                           |                |
1           ALARIC I  =  d            ATHAULF M
            (395-410)|                (410-415)
                     |
                     |
2              THEODERIC I (418-451) B
               _____|_____
              |               |                        |
3      M THORISMUND    M   THEODERIC II            EURIC
       (451-453)           (453-466)             (466-484)
                                                      |
4                                              ALARIC II B
                                               (484-507)
                                   _____|
                                  |                   |
5               GESALIC  D                   AMALARIC  M
                (507-511)                    (511-531)
```

Statistics
Duration: 136 years; 5 generations, average length, $136/5 = 27$ years; 9 rulers, average length of reign, $133/9 = 15$ years.

B. *The Second Dynasty, AD 567–603.*

```
              |_____
1           LIUVA                            LEOVIGILD
            (567-572)                        (568-586)
                                                 |
2                                           RECCARED I
                                            (586-601)
                                                 |
3                                           LIUVA II    D
                                            (601-603)
```

Statistics
Duration: 36 years; 3 generations, average length $36/3 = 12$ years; 4 rulers, average length of reign, $36/4 = 8$ years.

C. *The Third Dynasty, AD 680-714.*

```
1                    ERVIG (680-687)
                            |
2                    d = EGICA (687-702)
                            |
3                    WITTIGIS ((702-710)
                            |
4                    AGILA II (711-714)
```

Statistics
Duration: 34 years; 4 generations, average length, 34/4 = 9 years; 4 rulers, average length of reign, 34/4 = 9 years.

Commentary
The first barbarian king to establish a kingdom within the Roman Empire was Alaric I of the Visigoths. The kingdom at first was moveable, and Alaric at one point found himself besieging and capturing Rome itself, but from 418 the kingdom was settled at Toulouse in southern Gaul, where it remained for nearly a century; from that base they conquered Spain. In 507 a serious defeat by the Franks pushed the kingdom out of Toulouse and most of Gaul. Spain remained the Visigothic state territory for two more centuries.

Alaric's dynasty expired long before the kingdom. With one king killed in the decisive battle in 507, another soon deposed, and his brother, a nasty piece of work, murdered, the dynasty ended in 531. From then on, the Visigothic kingdom became in a way elective, though any man chosen as king immediately developed ambitions to establish a new dynasty.

Only two of them succeeded in achieving this aim, and then only briefly. Too many of the nobles of the kingdom had similar ambitions to allow the establishment of a new royal dynasty for very long. The result was a series of elected kings, often of considerable ability, but also an unstable polity in which each king tended, because he acceded when mature or even old, to have only a short reign. The tension between elective and dynastic poles tended to produce political situations very liable to slide into civil conflict, but the attachment of the Visigoths to the elective idea was too strong to be removed. The state succumbed all too easily to an attack by Muslims from North Africa that in origin was little more than a raid. The attempt by the third dynasty to establish its authority had so divided the kingdom that resistance proved quite unavailing. The kingship of Agila II existed only in Narbonensis in southern France and in the north-east of Spain at the time of the Muslim conquest; he may or may not be the son of Wittigis.

References
R Collins, *Early Mediaeval Spain* (London, 1983).
EA Thompson, *The Goths in Spain* (Oxford, 1969).
H Wolfram, *The Roman Empire and its Germanic Peoples* (Berkeley and Los Angeles, 1997).

West Saxons, (Cerdingas), England, AD 538–685

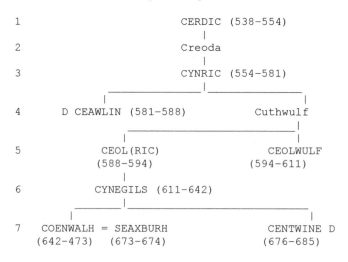

```
1                          CERDIC (538-554)
                             |
2                          Creoda
                             |
3                          CYNRIC (554-581)
             _____|_____
            |                                 |
4    D CEAWLIN (581-588)                   Cuthwulf
          _____            |
         |                        |           |
5      CEOL(RIC)                CEOLWULF
       (588-594)                (594-611)
         |
6      CYNEGILS (611-642)
       _____|_____
      |                                                   |
7  COENWALH = SEAXBURH                            CENTWINE D
   (642-473)   (673-674)                          (676-685)
```

Statistics
Duration: 147 years, reigning for 145; 7 generations, average length, 147/7 = 21 years: 9 rulers, average length of reign, 145/9 = 16 years.

Commentary
Cerdic is usually accepted as the founder of the West Saxon kingdom and dynasty, despite his Celtic name. Recent studies have led to a revision of the old dating of the dynasty, with Cerdic's 'landing', if that is what happened, now put at about 532, and the inauguration of his kingship six years later (none of these dates are certain, of course). His son is named in most Anglo-Saxon sources as Cynric, the second king, but this may mean omitting Creoda, whose name is recorded elsewhere. I have assumed Creoda existed, but that he was not actually king.

The succession moved about among the men of the family, omitting sons in favour of brothers – Ceawlin, for example, had three sons. This led in the end to increasingly distant cousins inheriting when the direct line expired with Centwine's deposition. His predecessor Aescwine, was five generations from Cynric, and his successor, Caedwalla, was equally distant, descended from Ceawlin. In other words, by the late seventh century, the hereditary principle had been accepted only in the most indirect sense, but the West Saxons had dispensed with direct succession. In the eighth century even the hereditary principle was abandoned, and most kings were not related to one another.

References
EB Fryde, *Handbook of British Chronology*, 3rd ed. (London, 1986).
DP Kirby, *The Earliest English Kings*, 2nd ed. (London, 2000).
B Yorke, *Kings and Kingdoms of Early Anglo-Saxon England* (London, 1990).

Section IV

Imperial Dynasties

Assyrian Empire, 1191–612 BC

A. *First Dynasty*, 1191-722 BC.

```
1                          NINURTA-APIL-EKUR (1191-1179)
                                     |
2                           ASHUR-DAN I (1178-1133)
                  _____|_____
                 |                               |
3   NINURTA-TUKULTI-ASHUR            MUTAKKIL-NUSKU
         (1133)                           (1133)
                                            |
4                               ASHUR-RESH-ISHI I (1132-1115)
                                            |
5                               TIGLATH-PILESER I (1114-1075)
              _____|_____
             |                      |                |
6  ASHARED-APEL-EKUR     ASHUR-BEL-KALA       SHAMSHI-ADAD IV
    (1075-1074)           (1073-1056)          (1053-1050)
                                |                    |
7                          ERIBA-ADAD I   ASHUR-NASIR-PAL I
                           (1055-1054)      (1049-1031)
                   _____|
                  |                                 |
8         SHALMANESER II                    ASHUR-RABI II
           (1030-1019)                       (1012-972)
                  |                                 |
9         ASHUR-NIRARI IV                  ASHUR-RESH-ISHI II
           (1018-1013)                       (971-967)
                                                    |
10                              TIGLATH-PILESER II (966-935)
                                                    |
11                                ASHUR-DAN II (934-911)
                                                    |
12                                ADAD-NIRARI II (911-891)
                                                    |
13                              TUKULTI-NINURTA II (890-884)
                                                    |
14                                ASHUR-NASIR-PAL II (883-859)
                                                    |
15                                SHALMANESER III (858-824)
                                                    |
16                         SAMMURAMAT = SHAMSHI-ADAD V
                            (811-806)  |  (823-811)
                                       |
17                             ADAD-NIRARI III (810-783)
         _____|_____
        |                 |            |                        |
18 SHALMANESER IV   ASHUR-DAN III ASHUR-NIRARI V   TIGLATH-PILESER III
    (782-773)        (772-755)     (754-745) M        (744-727)
                                                          |
19                                                SHALMANESER V M
                                                    (727-722)
```

Statistics
Duration: 469 years; 19 generations, average length, 469/19 = 24 years; 29 rulers, average length of reign: 469/29 = 17 years.

Commentary
This is one of the few dynasties that can be certainly followed without a break from the late Bronze Age through well into the Iron Age. The first king on this table, Ninurta-apil-Ekur, could in fact trace his royal ancestry back much further, but his immediate predecessors were not his own forebears, the line having become broken in the thirteenth century BC. Assyria had been only a minor kingdom in the Bronze Age; in the Iron Age, from the reign of Adad-Nirari II, it began for the first time to grow seriously powerful, and in size became, for a time, the greatest power on earth.

The succession *after* Ashur-Rabi II is direct from father to son for ten generations, and many of these kings showed frightening military and political abilities. The eighteenth generation, however, showed the limitations of a hereditary succession system. Of the four brothers who successively inherited the throne, only the youngest, Tiglath-Pileser III, showed the family abilities, but in a particularly violent and brutal form – and to bring him to the throne his predecessor had been murdered, another innovation in the dynasty. His son, Shalmaneser V, seems to have been very much a cipher; he was deposed and probably murdered by Sargon, whose family connection with his predecessor is not known, and was probably non-existent; he was thus the founder of a new (the 'second') dynasty.

The dating of these reigns, and of the second Assyrian dynasty that follows, is derived from the record of the city officials of Ashur, the earliest centre of Assyrian power. Hence the curious historiographical custom of starting the dates of a new reign the year after the death of the previous ruler. This in fact means that the calculations are probably a little wrong overall – for some of the dates are certainly wrong – but not greatly enough to seriously affect the results.

B.   *Second Dynasty*, (Sargonid) 721-612 BC.

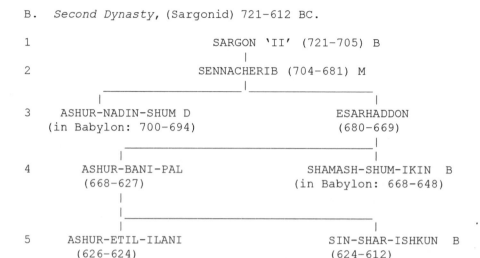

```
1                          SARGON 'II' (721-705) B
                                    |
2                          SENNACHERIB (704-681) M
        _____|_____
        |                                               |
3   ASHUR-NADIN-SHUM D                            ESARHADDON
    (in Babylon: 700-694)                         (680-669)
                 _____|
                 |                                      |
4       ASHUR-BANI-PAL                        SHAMASH-SHUM-IKIN  B
        (668-627)                             (in Babylon: 668-648)
            |
            |
            |_____
            |                                       |
5     ASHUR-ETIL-ILANI                        SIN-SHAR-ISHKUN  B
      (626-624)                               (624-612)
```

Statistics

Duration: 109 years; 5 generations, average length 109/5 = 22 years; 8 rulers, average length of reign: 109/8 = 14 years.

Commentary

The second Assyrian dynasty was even more wedded to organized violence and conquest than its predecessor, and it is thus somehow fitting that four out of the seven of the kings died violent deaths, three of them in battle. The control of the enlarged empire by one man proved to be impossibly difficult, and the outlying provinces, particularly Babylon, repeatedly rebelled. One attempted solution to the problem was a joint kingship of Esarhaddon and his brother, Ashur-Nadin-Shum, and of Ashur-bani-Pal and his brother, Shamash-Shum-Ikin, both pairs sharing the rule of Babylon and Assyria between them – though in both cases the experiment failed when the Babylonian king 'rebelled'. The Assyrian king always was the more powerful and controlled the imperial army.

An Assyrian king in Babylon was still an Assyrian, and he was trapped between his brother, who controlled the dynasty's armed force, and his inimical Babylonian subjects: Shamash-Shum-Ikin was killed in yet another Babylonian rebellion. The circumstances of the dynasty's seizure of power – in a *coup d'état* by Sargon when Shalmaneser V was murdered – cannot have encouraged a peaceable method of rule, and it certainly encouraged disaffection. After Ashur-bani-Pal's death in 627 his two successors showed little ability, and the last kings, following Sin-Shar-Ishkun, and ruling a small region for a few years, were apparently not of the royal family.

References

JA Brinkman, 'Mesopotamian Chronology of the Historical Period', in AI Oppenheim, *Ancient Mesopotamia* (Chicago, 1977).

Cambridge Ancient History, vol. 3.

RA Kitchen, *Documentation for Ancient Arabia*, I (Liverpool, 1994).

JE Mawby, *Dynasties of the World* (Oxford, 2002).

G Roux, *Ancient Iraq* (Harmondsworth, 1966).

'Neo-Babylonian' Empire, 627–539 BC

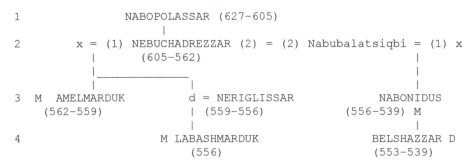

```
1                       NABOPOLASSAR (627-605)
                              |
2         x = (1) NEBUCHADREZZAR (2) = (2) Nabubalatsiqbi = (1) x
              |          (605-562)                         |
              |_____                           |
              |                |                          |
3   M  AMELMARDUK        d = NERIGLISSAR             NABONIDUS
       (562-559)         |   (559-556)             (556-539) M
                         |                               |
4                  M LABASHMARDUK                  BELSHAZZAR D
                      (556)                         (553-539)
```

Statistics

Duration: 88 years; 4 generations, average length 88/4 = 22 years; 7 rulers, average length of reign: 88/7 = 13 years.

Commentary

A rebellion against the Assyrian domination of Babylon finally succeeded in the 620s, and their leader, a chieftain out of the southern marshes called Nabopolassar, became king in the city, and then proceeded to replace the collapsing Assyrian Empire throughout the Fertile Crescent with a Babylonian one, which for its subjects was similarly violent and burdensome. His son, Nebuchadrezzar, also copied Assyrian methods of conquest, and made the Babylonian name just as detested as the Assyrian.

Nebuchadrezzar's successors all failed after a short or medium length reign. Two kings were murdered, and the other, Neriglissar, was already old when he acceded, and his son was rapidly murdered. Nabonidus, a stepson of Nebuchadrezzar, was hoisted to power by a popular revolt, not a good basis for success. Nabonidus shared power with his son, who finally lost the kingdom to Persian conquest. The dating of the dynasty is quite firm as are the relationships.

References.

Brinkman, *Political History of the Post-Kassite Babylonia* (Rome, 1968).

KA Kitchen, *Documentation for Ancient Arabia*, I (Liverpool, 1994) pp. 254–256.

JG McLean, *Babylon* (London, 1964). G Roux, *Ancient Iraq* (Harmondsworth, 1966).

Akhaimenid Empire, 635–330 BC

A. *First Dynasty, c.635–522 BC.*

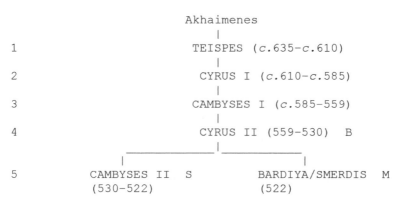

```
                         Akhaimenes
                             |
1                    TEISPES  (c.635-c.610)
                             |
2                    CYRUS I  (c.610-c.585)
                             |
3                   CAMBYSES I  (c.585-559)
                             |
4                    CYRUS II  (559-530)   B
              _____|_____
             |                               |
5      CAMBYSES II   S            BARDIYA/SMERDIS   M
       (530-522)                     (522)
```

Statistics

Duration: 113 years; 5 generations, average length, $113/5 = 23$ years; 6 rulers, average length of reigns: $113/6 = 19$ years.

Commentary

The royal family of the first Persian Empire claimed descent from Akhaimenes, but Akhaimenes himself seems to have been no more than a local chieftain. It was his son Teispes who first bore the titles 'Great King, King of Anshan', no doubt after conquering Anshan, a city in south-eastern Iran, which was their capital until Cyrus II (the Great). Cyrus expanded the small kingdom he inherited into a huge empire, successively conquering the Medes in northern Iran, the Neo-Babylonian Empire, and the Lydian kingdom, in each case with surprising ease, and by targeting the dynasty while conciliating, in advance, their subjects. Cambyses conquered Egypt, but the dynasty broke down in the civil war of 522–521, and was replaced by the second Akhaimenid dynasty, which descended in a parallel family but also ultimately from Akhaimenes.

The dating of the earliest kings of the family is problematic. Teispes is often dated in the early seventh century, half a century earlier than shown here. If so, two other kings will have to be inserted between Cyrus I and Cambyses I, another Teispes (II) and another Cyrus (II). There is indeed some evidence for this, but here I have accepted a later dating, so taking the shorter of the two possible genealogies, as being the less unlikely.

B.   *Second Dynasty, 522–330 BC.*

```
1                              DARIUS I (522–486)
                                      |
2                              XERXES I (486–465)
                                      |
3                           ARTAXERXES I (465–424)     M
              _____|_____
             |                    |                    |
4       XERXES II   M        SOGDIANUS   M        DARIUS II
         (424)                (424–423)           (423–405)
                                                       |
              _____     |
             |                                    |
5       ARTAXERXES II (404–359)              Ostanes
             |                                    |
6       ARTAXERXES III (359–338) M           Arsames
             |                                    |
7       ARSES IV (338–336) M        DARIUS III (336–330) M
```

Statistics

Duration: 192 years; 7 generations, average length, 192/7 = 27 years; 10 rulers, average length of reigns 192/10 = 19 years.

Commentary

The second Akhaimenid dynasty is better attested than the first, for, after all, it was an imperial dynasty whose lives, deeds, and deaths were very public. The three earliest kings, Darius I to Artaxerxes I, had good long reigns, covering a full century between them, but a succession squabble between brothers in 424–423, which included the murders of two kings, was ominous. Eighty years later the repeated massacres of siblings on behalf of Artaxerxes III and IV, when these men acceded, and the murder of these two kings by their vizir Bagoas, eliminated the direct dynastic line. Darius III, three generations away from a kingly ancestor, would have started a new dynasty had he not been defeated by Alexander the Great, and then murdered by his own followers. The incidence of violent death in this dynasty is also noteworthy, but it is perhaps not atypical of an imperial dynasty.

References
JM Cook, *The Persian Empire* (London, 1983).
W Culican, *The Medes and Persians* (London, 1965).
IM Diakonoff, 'Media', *Cambridge History of Iran*, vol. 2 (Cambridge, 1985).
AT Olmstead, *History of the Persian Empire* (Chicago, 1948).
J Wiesehofer, *Ancient Persia* (London, 1996).

Seleukids, 312–64 BC

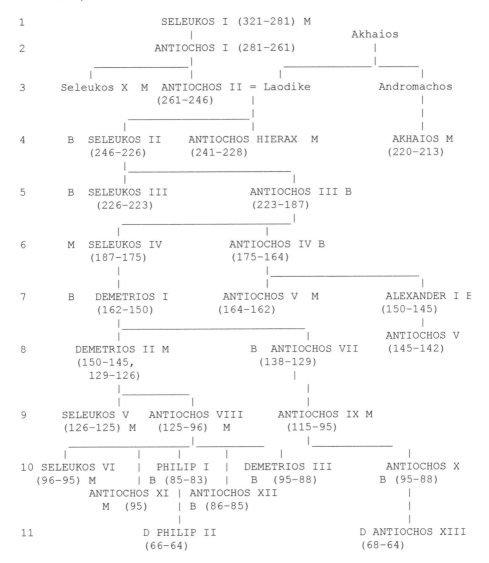

```
1                    SELEUKOS I (321-281) M
                            |                      Akhaios
2                    ANTIOCHOS I (281-261)            |
            _____|              _____|_____
            |               |              |                     |
3     Seleukos X   M  ANTIOCHOS II = Laodike          Andromachos
                       (261-246)    |                     |
            _____|                  |
            |                     |                        |
4     B  SELEUKOS II     ANTIOCHOS HIERAX  M          AKHAIOS M
         (246-226)       (241-228)                   (220-213)
                |
                |_____
                |                                 |
5     B  SELEUKOS III               ANTIOCHOS III B
         (226-223)                  (223-187)
                                          |
                _____|
                |                     |
6     M  SELEUKOS IV            ANTIOCHOS IV B
         (187-175)              (175-164)
                |                     |
                |                     |_____
                |                     |                   |
7     B    DEMETRIOS I      ANTIOCHOS V  M         ALEXANDER I E
           (162-150)        (164-162)              (150-145)
                |                                        |
                |_____   ANTIOCHOS V
                |                                |   (145-142)
8        DEMETRIOS II M              B  ANTIOCHOS VII
         (150-145,                     (138-129)
          129-126)                         |
                |                          |
                |_____               |
                |          |               |
9     SELEUKOS V   ANTIOCHOS VIII    ANTIOCHOS IX M
      (126-125) M  (125-96)   M      (115-95)
      _____|_____        |_____
      |          |      |          |        |                   |
10 SELEUKOS VI   |   PHILIP I   |  DEMETRIOS III        ANTIOCHOS X
   (96-95) M     |   B (85-83)  |   B  (95-88)          B (95-88)
           ANTIOCHOS XI |  ANTIOCHOS XII                    |
             M    (95)  |  B (86-85)                         |
                        |                                    |
11                 D PHILIP II                        D ANTIOCHOS XIII
                   (66-64)                            (68-64)
```

Statistics

Duration 248 years, reigning for 229; 11 generations, average length 248/11 = 23 years; 25 rulers, average length of reign, 229/25 = 9 years.

Commentary

Seleukos I was the most successful and the most durable of Alexander the Great's commanders. By adding carefully and slowly to his original territory in Babylonia he put together an empire stretching from the Hellespont to

India, but then he was murdered as he set out to take control of Macedon after yet another victory. His son Antiochos I put most of the empire back together again, having abandoned any efforts to secure Macedon; but in the process he found it necessary to execute his eldest son.

Antiochos I died in bed, the only king of the family to do so. The casualty rate in the family, from battle and murder, is quite astonishing. In the circumstances it is remarkable that the family lasted so long, and in fact in 223 it was reduced to a single life, the teenaged and unmarried Antiochos III, who was facing two rebellions, a court plot, and defeat in a foreign war, all at the same time. He survived and prospered, and may be reckoned as the second founder of the dynasty. But the violent deaths continued, from now on mainly as a result of internal conflict. In 162, when Demetrios I had his cousin Antiochos V murdered, the dynasty was again reduced to a single life.

The first usurper, Akhaios in 220, was in fact a member of the family, but later usurpers in the 140s and 150s were a symptom of the earlier Seleukid dynasty's failure, and family murders in the 170s and 160s. (Alexander I is counted as a member of the dynasty here, as the son of a concubine of Antiochos IV, though his membership is doubtful.) The internal quarrels graduated from murder to civil war, with the result that the family failed to hold on to their lands, partly by conquest by enemies, partly by fragments breaking off to form new kingdoms. But the later generations of the family were also prolific – the five sons of Antiochos VIII all became kings, though this was scarcely a source of strength. Even so, there were still two competing Seleukid kings when the Romans reached Syria in the 60s, and another of the family still had ambitions ten years later.

The contrast between the average generation length of twenty-three years and that of the reigns, nine years, is the result of this long sequence of violent deaths.

References

A Bouché-Leclerq, *Histoire des Seleucides*, 2 vols. (Paris, 1913).
ER Bevan, *The House of Seleucus*, 2 vols. (London, 1902).
JD Grainger, *A Seleukid Prosopography and Gazetteer* (Leiden, 1999).

Parthia, 246 BC–AD 228

A. *First Dynasty*, 246 BC–AD 50.

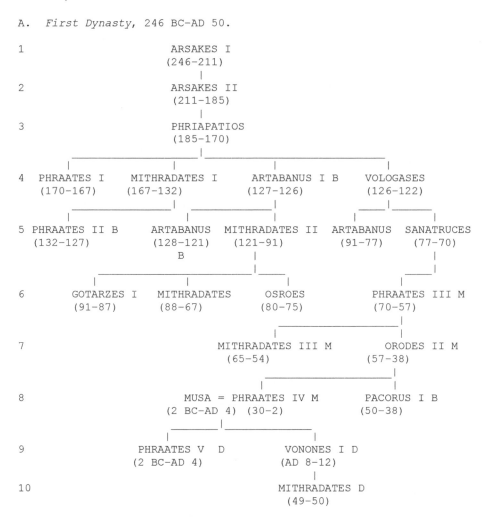

Statistics

Duration: 296 years, reigning for 255; 10 generations, average length 296/10 = 30 years; 24 reigns, average length of reign 255/24 = 10 years.

B.   *Second Dynasty*, AD 12–228.

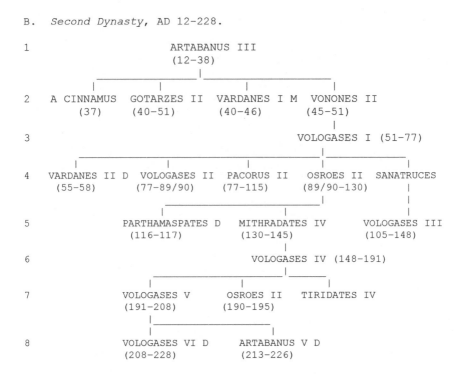

```
1                           ARTABANUS III
                               (12-38)
              _____|_____
         |          |              |              |
2    A CINNAMUS  GOTARZES II  VARDANES I M  VONONES II
         (37)      (40-51)      (40-46)      (45-51)
                                                |
3                                          VOLOGASES I  (51-77)
              _____|_____
         |              |              |              |          |
4    VARDANES II D  VOLOGASES II  PACORUS II    OSROES II  SANATRUCES
        (55-58)      (77-89/90)   (77-115)    (89/90-130)     |
                            _____|___          |
                        |                    |              |
5              PARTHAMASPATES D     MITHRADATES IV      VOLOGASES III
                  (116-117)          (130-145)          (105-148)
                                         |
6                             VOLOGASES IV  (148-191)
                        _____|_____
                    |                 |              |
7              VOLOGASES V       OSROES II    TIRIDATES IV
                (191-208)        (190-195)
                    |_____
                    |                  |
8              VOLOGASES VI D     ARTABANUS V D
                (208-228)          (213-226)
```

Statistics
Duration: 216 years; 8 generations, average length $216/8 = 27$ years;
20 reigns, average length of reign, $216/20 = 11$ years.

Commentary
The First Parthian king, Arsakes I, gave his name to the whole dynasty, but his
name was also taken as the throne name for almost all of his successors, with
the result that the sequence of names and dates of the successors is often very
uncertain – the names used by historians, as here, are thus the personal names
the kings bore before coming to the throne. It is not too much to say that this
is one of the most difficult dynasties of the ancient world to tabulate. The
uncertainty begins with 'Arsakes II' who may in fact be two kings: Tiridates I
and Artabanus I. The succession is, however, reasonably certain until the first
century BC, though then for a century it becomes very confused. There are
several other men who appear to have been kings but who cannot be inserted
into the genealogy; they may actually be another dynasty, or rebels, or possibly
sub-kings.

This confusion ends with a new dynasty, beginning with Artabanus III; this
may well have a connection back to the original dynasty, but after the confusion

of the previous century it seems best to reckon it as a new royal family. It will be noticed all along that at times several kings ruled simultaneously, particularly brothers, and it is evident that the inheritance custom of the dynasty tended towards a collective monarchy, together with sending younger brothers off to govern provinces – Arsakid dynasties ruled in Armenia and the Caucasus. The end came with conquest by the Sassanids, originally rebels.

References
MAR Colledge, *The Parthians* (London, 1967).
MAR Colledge, *Parthian Art* (London, 1977).
KW Dobbins, The Succession of Mithradates of Parthia', *Numismatic Chronicle*, (1975) pp. 19–45.
M Kareas-Klapproth, *Prosopographische Studieng zu Geschichte des Partherreiches* (Bonn, 1988).
AM Simonetta, 'Some Remarks on the Arsakid Coinage', *Numismatic Chronicle*, (1966) pp. 15–40.
'List of Parthian Kings', *Wikipedia*, accessed 26 Jan 2018.

Roman Empire, 48 BC–AD 472

Emperors in CAPITALS.

A.   *Julio-Claudians*, 48 BC–AD 68.

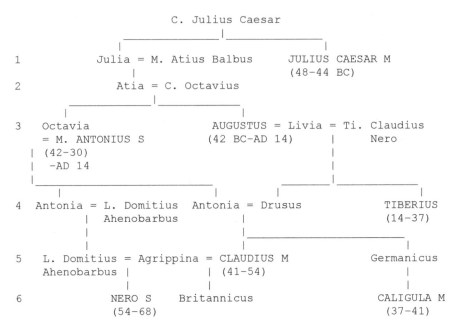

```
                          C. Julius Caesar
              _____|_____
             |                                 |
1        Julia = M. Atius Balbus        JULIUS CAESAR M
             |                            (48-44 BC)
2          Atia = C. Octavius
        _____|_____
       |                 |
3  Octavia          AUGUSTUS = Livia = Ti. Claudius
   = M. ANTONIUS S   (42 BC-AD 14)   |     Nero
   | (42-30)                         |
   |  -AD 14                         |
   |_____     ___|___
       |              |      |   |       |
4  Antonia = L. Domitius  Antonia = Drusus      TIBERIUS
       |   Ahenobarbus       |                   (14-37)
       |                     |_____
       |                     |                         |
5  L. Domitius = Agrippina = CLAUDIUS M          Germanicus
   Ahenobarbus  |            |  (41-54)               |
               |            |                        |
6         NERO S     Britannicus               CALIGULA M
          (54-68)                               (37-41)
```

Statistics

Duration: 116 years, reigning for 114; 6 generations, average length 116/6 = 19 years; 7 rulers, average length of reign 114/7 = 17 years.

Commentary

The first Roman Imperial dynasty is a genealogically messy affair, in which it set a pattern for all future Roman dynasties, but whose curious arrangement seems to be inherited from the republican dynasties from which it came, and even from the long-distant royal monarchy. Even simplified to the essentials, as here, it is extremely strange. It is also difficult to know just where to start, though its end is clear enough with Nero's suicide/murder. Technically Julius Caesar was a dictator, not an emperor, and Augustus' sole rule began only in 30 BC, when he defeated his brother-in-law M. Antonius in battle. In detailing the power of the ruling dynasty, however, Julius Caesar is an essential inclusion, being the first of the family to hold such a commanding position; and a man who ruled the whole Roman Empire for several years, no matter what his title, was in effect, an emperor; given his inclusion, both Octavian/Augustus and

M. Antonius must also be included from the time of their reaching shared supreme power in 42 BC.

It is stretching the definition of a 'dynasty' somewhat to include all the emperors from Caesar to Nero in a single family, but genealogical connections did exist connecting all the emperors – the crucial member being Livia, whose marriages provided the link between the two parts. The universal attitude has always been to see the whole group as a dynastic unit. On the other hand, the name of the dynasty – Julio-Claudian – is a recognition of unease over this, and indicates quite clearly that the dynasty is a composite, or perhaps a coalition of families; in fact, it was made up of four republican dynasties – Antonii, Julii, Claudii, and Domitii. The Julians were replaced by the Claudians with the accession of Tiberius, and Nero was in fact a Domitius, though a quadruple name for the dynasty would clearly be even clumsier than the double; Antony was the ancestor of three emperors, Augustus of none, an ironical outcome of the civil war.

With this complex genealogy it is still somewhat surprising to note that Nero and Caligula were in fact of the same generation, even though their reigns were separated by that of Claudius, their uncle and stepfather respectively. There are also two others who might be included as rulers. Britannicus, Claudius' son, was only a child when his father died, and could be considered a joint emperor with the young Nero; he only survived for a year before being murdered; Agrippina, his mother, was partly responsible for his death, and acted as regent for her other son Nero for some years (before he had her murdered in turn). But neither Britannicus nor his mother actually had any independent power, and I have decided not to include them as rulers.

The complications of the dynasty are compelling, but perhaps less surprising when compared with other Roman dynasties. The Antonines, the Septimians, the House of Constantine, the Theodosian-Valentinian House, and on into the Byzantine period dynasties, all exhibit similarly complicated lines of descent – and all mirror also the relatively brief duration of the Julio-Claudians and the prevalence of violent death that brought the dynasty to its early end.

B. *Flavians*, AD 69–96.

Statistics

Duration: 27 years, 2 generations, average length 27/2 = 14 years; 3 rulers, average length of reign, 27/3 = 9 years.

Commentary

A brief but surprisingly effective dynasty, founded by the victor of a nasty civil war. Vespasian succeeded in restoring and strengthening the old system of government that had been founded by Augustus, and Domitian administered it vigorously and with considerable effect. But the emotions of the civil war – neither that which brought Augustus to power, nor that won by Vespasian – did not go away, and Domitian fell to an assassin from his own household, who had been encouraged by senatorial ambition and acquiescence. This dynasty is one of the few of the Roman Empire that is reasonably straightforward, but note that Titus had no sons, and Domitian had had to adopt two teenage cousins as his heirs (who, of course, in the event did not succeed). Had the dynasty lasted another generation it would have presented a very much more complicated picture.

C.   *The Antonines, 98–192.*

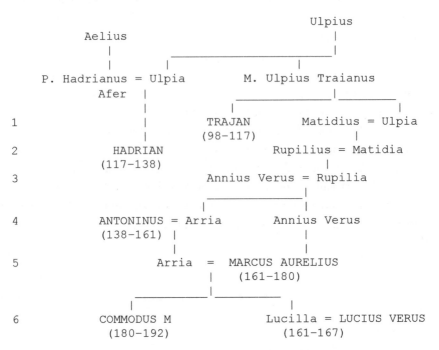

```
                                                   Ulpius
                  Aelius                              |
                    |              _____|
                    |             |                    |
        P. Hadrianus = Ulpia         M. Ulpius Traianus
               Afer   |                  _____|_____
                      |                 |                         |
   1                  |               TRAJAN       Matidius = Ulpia
                      |               (98-117)                |
   2               HADRIAN                      Rupilius = Matidia
                  (117-138)                                |
   3                               Annius Verus = Rupilia
                                          _____|
                                         |              |
   4          ANTONINUS = Arria       Annius Verus
             (138-161)  |                     |
                        |                     |
   5              Arria   =   MARCUS AURELIUS
                          |    (161-180)
                   _____|_____
                  |                     |
   6        COMMODUS M           Lucilla = LUCIUS VERUS
           (180-192)                      (161-167)
```

Statistics
Duration: 94 years; 6 generations, average length 94/6 = 16 years; 6 rulers, average length of reign, 94/6 = 16 years.

Commentary
It is only by accepting the conventional designation of this group of Roman emperors as a dynasty that I can so include them, and the clearly invented name is a sign of its artificiality. In reality they are two separate and brief dynasties: Trajan and his cousin Hadrian might be considered one dynasty (which might be called 'Ulpio-Aelian'), and Antoninus, his son-in-law Marcus Aurelius, and Marcus' son and son-in-law, are another ('Antonino-Aurelian'). There was no blood relationship between Hadrian and Antoninus, and the connection between Marcus and Trajan was remote. (Marcus was Trajan's great-great-grand-nephew.) In reality there are four families involved: Ulpii, Aelii, Antonini, and Aurelii; in this complication it very much resembles the Julio-Claudians.

Nevertheless, by treating this group as a dynasty, several points may be made. The Romans themselves seem to have thought of them as a group, and the emperors made use of the time-honoured Roman practice of adoption to reinforce these claims. In fact Trajan had been adopted as his son by his predecessor Nerva, but there was no other relationship; I could not bring Nerva into the dynasty. Adoption was thus the technical method of designating a chosen successor, but this was a dangerous post, and several of Hadrian's choices died or were killed before Antoninus emerged and succeeded him, perhaps he might be considered the last man standing when Hadrian finally died; Hadrian also organized the eventual succession of Marcus before he died.

Despite this apparent care, flexibility, and careful selection, the 'dynasty' lasted less than a century. Once a brutal and incompetent emperor took power, in the person of Commodus – only the second direct father-to-son succession in two centuries – the usual Roman political mechanism took over: Commodus was murdered in a plot involving a group of senators. The lack of real legitimacy was thus once again emphasized, for this man had the best hereditary claim of all these emperors. This lack was something that clearly existed all along; the failure of all emperors but Marcus to father any sons who survived them was largely accidental (and sexual preference) and made the dynasty dependent on Roman aristocratic goodwill and tolerance. Commodus' behaviour forfeited that tolerance. The Roman Imperial dynastic instability was thus endemic, even institutional. Each succession, even when organized, arranged in advance, enforced by imperial power, and apparently accepted, was accompanied by violence, with the exception of that of Marcus and Lucius, and Marcus had been a subordinate emperor for fourteen years already by the time that Antoninus died.

D.   *Severans, 193–235.*

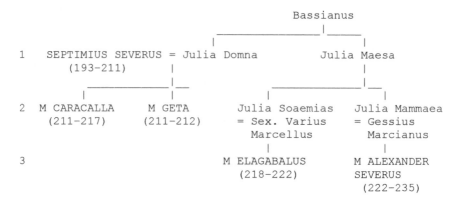

```
                                          Bassianus
                               _____|_____
                              |                      |
1     SEPTIMIUS SEVERUS = Julia Domna          Julia Maesa
         (193-211)       |                          |
              _____|__              _____|__
             |           |               |            |
2    M CARACALLA     M GETA         Julia Soaemias   Julia Mammaea
       (211-217)     (211-212)      = Sex. Varius    = Gessius
                                      Marcellus        Marcianus
                                         |               |
3                                   M ELAGABALUS     M ALEXANDER
                                     (218-222)        SEVERUS
                                                      (222-235)
```

Statistics
Duration: 42 years, reigning for 41; 3 generations, average length 42/3 = 14 years; 5 rulers, average length of reign 41/5 = 8 years.

Commentary
The progenitor, L. Septimius Severus, was a Roman general who seized power in a military rebellion during the confusion following Commodus' murder, and held it against more than one rival rebellion. His two sons inherited shared power, but quickly quarrelled and both were eventually murdered. After a brief interruption two other family members (distantly so) were enthroned, but both fell to murderers also. These latter two may in fact also be descendants of the old Emesan dynasty of Samsigeramus.

As a dynasty this family clearly falls into two parts (like the Antonines, and in fact also like the Julio-Claudians), and could be so divided, but the application of this term 'dynasty' clearly has to be elastic in the Roman Empire, where dynasties were always unusual constructs. The Severans were thus not atypical among Roman dynasties, though they were perhaps briefer in power and more disastrous in their results than most.

E. *Gordians, 238-244.*

```
1                        GORDIAN I  (238)  S
                          |
                          |_____
                          |                        |
2                        GORDIAN II (238)  B       d = Antonius
                                                      |
3                                         M GORDIAN III (238-244)
```

Statistics
Duration: 6 years; 3 generations, average length 6/3 = 2 years; 3 rulers, average length of reign, 6/3 = 2 years.

Commentary
I include the dynasties of the third century AD with reluctance. None of them lasted more than two or three generations, or more than a few years. Yet the duration of some of them falls within the parameters I have set out, and their construction is often very like that of the Flavians, so they have to be included.

The elder Gordians, I and II (M. Antonius Gordianus), were joint emperors for only three weeks, and only in the province of Africa, of which the elder was governor, and they were acknowledged only there and briefly at Rome before Gordian II died in the first battle, against a loyalist governor from the neighbouring province, and his father as a result committed suicide. The third of the family was elevated as an adolescent out of some sentimental attachment to the elders, and because he was young enough to be pliable to his supporters. He did not last long: that he reigned for six years is a measure

F. *Messians, 249-251.*

```
1                        B DECIUS (249-251)
                  _____|_____
                  |                        |
2      B HERRENIUS ESTRUSCUS        HOSTILIANUS
              (251)                    (251)
```

of his pliability.
Statistics
Duration: 2 years; 2 generations, average length 2/2 = 1 year; 3 rulers, average length of reign 3/2 = 1 year.

Commentary

Decius (C. Messius Traianus Decius) became emperor by grace of the soldiers, and killed the previous emperor, Philip the Arab, and his son in battle. Decius himself was soon also killed in battle, as was his elder son Herrenius, whom he had already proclaimed emperor. His second son, similarly proclaimed,

```
G.  Licinians, 253-268.

1                         D VALERIAN  (253-260)
                                  |
2                         M GALLIENUS  (253-268)
                                  |
3                         M SALONINUS  (260)
```

died soon after, possibly naturally. Decius was widely admired, except by Christians, whom he persecuted.

Statistics

Duration: 15 years; 3 generations, average length 15/3 = 5 years; 3 rulers, average length of reign 15/3 = 5 years.

Commentary

Valerian (P. Licinius Valerianus) was made emperor by his troops, and then defeated and killed his predecessor. Leaving his son in charge in Rome and Italy, he then went off to fight on the frontiers. This scheme worked, since father and son, for once, trusted each other, until Valerian was defeated and captured by the Sassanids, and Gallienus' son Saloninus was murdered by a rebel general in Cologne – which events took place all in the same year. Gallienus survived to rule for eight more years, but large parts of the empire had seceded from his rule by the time he died.

   This dynasty bade fair to permanence for a time, until the senior, Valerian, suffered his disaster in the eastern war, and the grandson was murdered. Gallienus faced numerous rebellions, and without heirs he was in a hopeless

```
H.  Aurelians, 282-285.

1                         CARUS  (282-283)
                    _____|_____
                    |                        |
2          M NUMERIAN                   M CARINUS
           (283-284)                    (283-285)
```

position. He fell, as did so many in this century, to an army coup.

Statistics

Duration: 3 years; 2 generations, average length, 3/2 = 2 years; 3 rulers, average length of reign, 3/3 = 1 year

Commentary

The accession of Carus (M. Aurelius Carus) was the result of the murder of his predecessor. He set off to war in the east, but died on campaign in Babylonia. His two sons succeeded peacefully, Numerian in the east, and Carinus in the west, but Numerian was murdered, to be succeeded in the east by Diocletian, who then fought Carinus; Carinus was murdered in the end by one of his own officers.

One of the basic causes of this sorry story, from the time of the Severans until that of Diocletian, is clearly the failure of the imperial system to constitute an acceptable system for choosing an emperor; or rather the failure to choose which system to operate. It is clear that the hereditary principle was widely accepted, but the aristocracy was unhappy that a single family should thus monopolize the imperial power. The tension between these two was aggravated by the demands of the army, of which emperors were

I. *Tetrarchs, 284-363.*

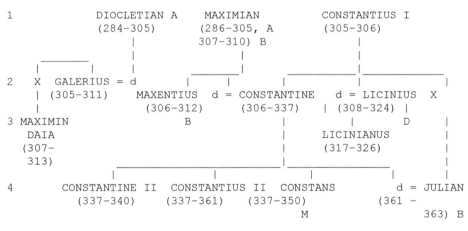

commanders-in-chief. The result was the frequent slaughter of emperors – and of their children, an ironic recognition of the power of the hereditary idea.

Statistics

Duration: 79 years; 4 generations, average length, 79/4 = 20 years; 13 rulers, average length of reign, 79/13 = 6 years.

Commentary

The collapse of the Roman Empire in the mid third century, which is signalled in this study by the series of brief dynasties 'E', 'F', 'G', 'H' (there were also many more emperors without dynastic connections), brought as a political response a series of measures (militarization and bureaucratization, particularly), which were designed to grip the empire more firmly in the hands of the rulers. The man who finally brought these measures together into some sort of a system was Diocletian, raised to the purple by his soldiers in yet another military coup. His imperial scheme included appointing co-emperors, of whom Maximin was the first, the adoption of junior emperors, and the regular retirement of the seniors in favour of those junior colleagues. Each emperor, senior and junior, had a part of the empire to administer, and a section of the frontier to defend. A series of marriages between the several rulers was supposed to knit them into a single family, of whom Constantine became the second head, and who added Christianization to the collection of new policies.

The resulting dynasty that Diocletian constructed bears a strong resemblance to all the previous (and later) Roman Imperial dynasties, notably the Julio-Claudian and the Antonines, in being an amalgam of several families, and having a complex system of succession; the earlier ones were perhaps less formalized, which may be Diocletian's personal construction to Roman dynastic construction, but his dynastic and political scheme was no more successful than any other; the 'dynasty' fell into the internal bickering, civil warfare, and incompetence that had characterized all the others. Its duration was only in the average range for a Roman dynasty, though the number of rulers in it was well above the average. Its genealogical complexity, though having a novel origin, is normal for a Roman dynasty, and its casualties by violent death are well up to the usual proportion. Diocletian's policies, though apparently new, were thus, in dynastic terms, in fact very similar in their results to those of other Roman rulers.

J. *Valentinian-Theodosian Dynasty*, AD 364–472.

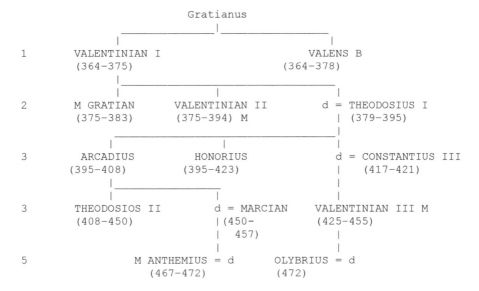

```
                         Gratianus
                  _____|_____
                 |                                 |
   1     VALENTINIAN I                        VALENS B
         (364-375)                            (364-378)
             |
    _____|_____
   |                    |                          |
   2    M GRATIAN       VALENTINIAN II      d = THEODOSIUS I
        (375-383)       (375-394) M         |   (379-395)
                                            |
                 _____|
                |             |             |
   3     ARCADIUS        HONORIUS       d = CONSTANTIUS III
         (395-408)       (395-423)      |   (417-421)
             |                          |
     _____|_____          |
    |                 |                 |
   3    THEODOSIOS II      d = MARCIAN   VALENTINIAN III M
        (408-450)          |(450-        (425-455)
                           |   457)             |
                           |                    |
   5          M ANTHEMIUS = d        OLYBRIUS = d
                (467-472)            (472)
```

Statistics
Duration: 108 years, reigning for 98; 5 generations, average length $108/5 =$ 22 years; 13 rulers, average length of reign, $98/13 = 8$ years.

Commentary
The attraction of being emperor of Rome, despite an extremely high casualty rate by violence, was such that men could be relatively easily brought into power by marrying the daughters of the rulers. Here is a family where this happened several times. Valentinian I and Valens brought order to the empire after the upheaval of Julian's reign, and the extinction of the family of Constantine. When the sons of Valentinian I looked to be unable to cope after the death of Valens, Theodosius I was brought into the family. Similarly Constantius III was brought in as a means of boosting the military reaction to the barbarian invasions. Marcian similarly proved a useful and competent successor to Theodosius II.

Along with Theodosius II, this exhausts the capable members of the extended family, for the rest tended to be powerless or to be children, and Anthemius and Olybrius only married into the family after it had lost serious power – and Valentinian III was an ineffective emperor. They were, in fact, emperors only in the west, and made so by the warlords who controlled the western half of the empire. By the time they became emperors much of the western empire had been more or less lost. The effective end of the dynasty was really 457.

References
B Baldwin, *The Roman Emperors* (Québec, 1980).
F Millar, *The Emperor in the Roman World* (London, 1977).

Sassanids, AD 224-651

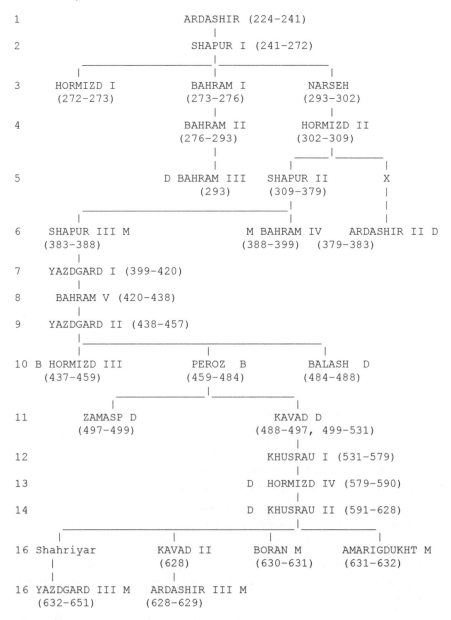

```
1                              ARDASHIR (224-241)
                                      |
2                              SHAPUR I (241-272)
                                      |
          _____|_____
          |                          |                   |
3     HORMIZD I                   BAHRAM I            NARSEH
      (272-273)                   (273-276)           (293-302)
                                      |                   |
4                                 BAHRAM II           HORMIZD II
                                  (276-293)           (302-309)
                                      |                   |
                                      |          _____|_____
                                      |          |                |
5                              D BAHRAM III   SHAPUR II            X
                                  (293)       (309-379)            |
                      _____|               |
          _____|           |
          |                                       |               |
6     SHAPUR III M                           M BAHRAM IV    ARDASHIR II D
      (383-388)                              (388-399)      (379-383)
          |
7     YAZDGARD I (399-420)
          |
8     BAHRAM V (420-438)
          |
9     YAZDGARD II (438-457)
          |_____
          |                       |                       |
10 B HORMIZD III              PEROZ   B              BALASH   D
      (437-459)               (459-484)              (484-488)
                      _____|_____
          |                                             |
11      ZAMASP D                              KAVAD D
        (497-499)                             (488-497, 499-531)
                                                    |
12                                            KHUSRAU I (531-579)
                                                    |
13                                    D   HORMIZD IV (579-590)
                                                    |
14                                    D   KHUSRAU II (591-628)
       _____|_____
       |                   |                   |                 |
16 Shahriyar         KAVAD II           BORAN M          AMARIGDUKHT M
       |               (628)            (630-631)          (631-632)
       |                   |
16 YAZDGARD III M    ARDASHIR III M
      (632-651)        (628-629)
```

Statistics

Duration: 427 years; 16 generations, average length 427/16 = 27 years;
28 rulers, average length of reign, 427/28 = 15 years.

Commentary

The Persian Sassanid dynasty was one of the most successful of the ancient world, wielding authority at imperial level for over four centuries, and only losing power to the Muslim conquest. Further, Ardashir I, the first *shahanshah* of the family, was descended from a local dynasty in Fars that claimed to have held local power for ten generations already, possibly even truthfully, though their dynastic name comes only from the grandfather of Ardashir I. Few dynasties could claim to have lasted so long and no imperial ones.

Not that 'success' means an uninterrupted rule. Primogeniture was the normal rule in the family, but internal disputes were not thereby excluded, as the deposition of Bahram III in favour of his grand-uncle, Narseh, showed while the successors of the enormously long-lived Shapur II scarcely ruled undisturbed. A second period of dynastic upheaval came in the 480s, with several depositions taking place before a certain calm was restored by Kavad and Khusrau I who between them ruled for ninety years.

The dynasty was thus an intermittently turbulent family. The Muslim attack in the seventh century came at another of these times of internal dynastic disturbance. In the period following the deposition of Khusrau II in 628, there were six rulers before Yazdgard III established himself only four years later; two of these usurpers, almost unprecedented, two of them women, wholly unprecedented, and three of them were murdered. Under normal circumstances one would predict that the dynasty was about to be removed from power after inflicting such a sequence of humiliations upon itself. And so it was, but by the unexpected Muslim invasion rather than by its replacement by a new dynasty – though the two non-Sassanid usurpers did rule briefly. But when the Muslim attack came it did so just as Yazdgard III was mastering the internal problem, and given a few more years he would surely have recovered full authority. The attack thus clearly came at a moment of extreme dynastic vulnerability – and presumably not by accident. But this dynasty had recovered from its two previous periods of near collapse, and it is noticeable that the last king, Yazdgard III, survived under the Muslim attack for nearly two decades. Without the Muslim invasion, it is likely that the dynasty would have recovered once more.

References

T Noldeke, *Geschichte der Perser und Araber zur Zeit der Sassaniden aus des Arabische Khronik des Tabari* (Leiden, 1879).

E Porada, *Ancient Iran* (London, 1965).

J Wiesehofer, *Ancient Persia* (London, 1996).

Huns in Europe, AD 420–474

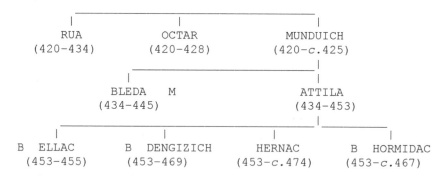

```
         |                    |                            |
        RUA                 OCTAR                      MUNDUICH
     (420-434)            (420-428)                   (420-c.425)
                                                          |
                _____                  |
                |                                          |
            BLEDA    M                                  ATTILA
           (434-445)                                   (434-453)
                                                          |
     _____        _____
     |                    |                 |     |             |
  B  ELLAC          B  DENGIZICH       HERNAC      B  HORMIDAC
   (453-455)         (453-469)        (453-c.474)   (453-c.467)
```

Statistics

Duration: 54 years; 3 generations, average length, $53/3 = 18$ years; 9 rulers, average length of reign, $54/9 = 6$ years.

Commentary

The Huns who reached Europe in the late fourth century seem to have had only occasional, ad hoc, leaders who gathered disparate groups of warriors together to raid their neighbours, and whose period of authority lasted only until their first defeat. Faced by the concentrated continental power of the Roman Empire, however, a family of 'kings' emerged briefly. Rua, Octar, and Munduich were joint war leaders, and Rua, who survived his brothers, passed on his power to his nephews, of whom the greatest was Attila. On his death, his sons inherited, again jointly. But this time, instead of ruling (and raiding) as a collective, each man took one of the subjugated peoples to rule, a system that lasted no longer than it took these peoples to organize a revolt. Ellac died in the final battle at the River Nedao that freed most of the German peoples. At least three of his brothers, all identified as 'sons of Attila' maintained a small kingdom between the Danube and the Theiss Rivers on the Hungarian steppe, and occasionally raided into the Eastern Roman Empire without much success, and – too late – ruling in the Hun fashion collectively. The last of them seems to have been Hernac, who apparently regularly argued that they should refrain from raiding. The date of 474 is the last notice we have of any of them. The kingdom cannot have lasted much longer.

References

EA Thompson, *A History of Attila and the Huns* (Oxford, 1948).

Byzantine Empire, AD 457–802

A. *Leonid Dynasty*, AD 457–518.

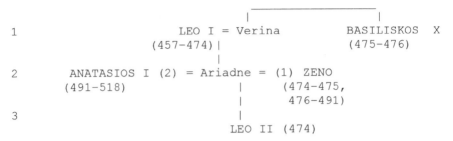

```
                              |                      |
1                         LEO I = Verina         BASILISKOS  X
                        (457-474) |              (475-476)
                                  |
2          ANATASIOS I (2) = Ariadne = (1) ZENO
           (491-518)             |        (474-475,
                                 |         476-491)
3                                |
                             LEO II (474)
```

Statistics

Duration: 61 years; 3 generations, average length, $61/3 = 20$ years; 5 rulers, average length of reign, $61/5 = 12$ years.

Commentary

Leo I was made emperor by Aspar, a barbarian general in Roman service, when Marcian, the last member of the attenuated Theodosian dynasty, died in 457. Aspar clearly intended to continue to be the real power in the empire, and persuaded Leo to give his son the rank of Caesar, and to promise the boy his daughter in marriage: clearly, he was aiming for the boy to be the next emperor. But Leo struck first, having Aspar and his supporters murdered.

Having only daughters, Leo made his grandson Leo II his heir, but the child was only six years old when the old man died. His father Zeno became his regent, then joint emperor, and so he achieved sole power when the child died after only a few months, probably naturally. Within a year Zeno had been expelled by the rebellion of Basiliskos, the brother of Verina, Leo I's widow, but he returned in triumph a year and a half later. He had to survive other rebellions and was understandably constantly suspicious, and arbitrary in his pre-emptive strikes at perceived enemies.

On Zeno's death his widow Ariadne was able to choose his successor more or less freely, and she selected Anastasios, an experienced and well-known official. Like Zeno, Anastasios was troubled by rebellions, and like Zeno, he made no provision for his successor. This was presumably deliberate, since when he died after a long reign he was eighty years old, so he had plenty of time to consider the problem and to make a choice. As a dynasty, that of Leo is thus of very strange construction, but it is perhaps no more so than many of the others of Rome and Byzantium.

B. *Justinianic Dynasty*, AD 518-582.

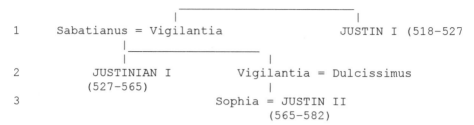

```
1      Sabatianus = Vigilantia                    JUSTIN I (518-527
              |
              |_____
              |                        |
2         JUSTINIAN I          Vigilantia = Dulcissimus
          (527-565)                     |
3                               Sophia = JUSTIN II
                                         (565-582)
```

Statistics

Duration: 64 years; 3 generations, average length, 64/3 = 21 years; 3 rulers, average length of reign, 64/3 = 21 years.

Commentary

Despite containing one of the most renowned Romano-Byzantine emperors, the Justinianic dynasty was relatively brief, even by Roman standards. It did, however, conform to the peculiar Roman pattern of indirect inheritance. The family is said to have originated amongst the Balkan peasantry, from which Justin I emerged to pursue a successful career in the army. His competence as a ruler was sufficient to provide a firm political platform for the inheritance of his nephew Justinian, whose ambition to revive the full might and extent of the old Roman Empire was only partly successful, and what he achieved came at the cost of a substantial strain imposed on the imperial strength. But there had been no such extensive imperial conquests since the reign of Augustus. Only by his own standards can Justinian be considered unsuccessful. The financial and material cost was aggravated by a devastating attack of plague during his reign, in which perhaps a third of the population died.

The last member of the dynasty, Justin II, is often regarded as 'weak-minded', whatever that means, and does seem to have gone insane in his last years. Having to follow Justinian I would be strain enough for any ruler, particularly as some of the latter's conquests, principally those in Italy, were being lost during his reign. He eventually died after five years of intermittent insanity, during which his wife Sophia acted as regent for him, assisted by Tiberius, a general and administrator, whom Justin made his heir in a brief lucid moment. After Justin's death, Tiberius II rapidly removed Sophia and was then followed by a succession of other military men, who, like him, ruled only briefly, and also failed to found dynasties.

C. *Herakleid Dynasty*, AD 600-711.

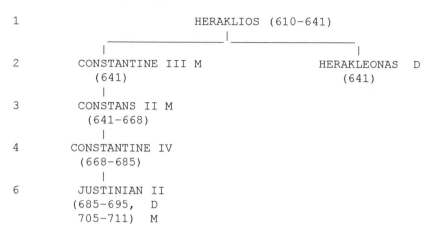

1   HERAKLIOS (610-641)

2   CONSTANTINE III M   HERAKLEONAS D
            (641)   (641)

3   CONSTANS II M
            (641-668)

4   CONSTANTINE IV
            (668-685)

6   JUSTINIAN II
            (685-695, D
            705-711) M

Statistics

Duration: 101 years, reigning for 91 years; 5 generations, average length $101/5 = 20$ years; 6 rulers, average length of reign, $91/6 = 15$ years.

Commentary

Heraklios was governor of Africa when he led a rebellion aimed at displacing the previous Byzantine emperor, a ferocious, insecure, and hated soldier, Phokas. In Africa he had been spared the direct effects of the devastating Persian invasions that had conquered Syria and Egypt from the Byzantines between 610 and 620, and had also subjected Asia Minor to extensive ravaging. Posing as the saviour of the state, he first recovered Egypt, then took Constantinople, to much popular acclaim. There then followed a long war of recovery and revenge against the Sassanids, which was then almost immediately followed by the invasions of the newly united Muslims from Arabia, in which the same lands that Heraklios had just recovered, Syria and Egypt, were once again lost.

Despite this erratic history, the dynasty survived. Heraklios' first two successors were quickly removed, and his grandson, Constans II, then ruled for almost three decades. He was murdered when he seemed to be planning to remove the imperial capital to Sicily. The final emperor, Justinian II, was thoroughly insecure, and was deposed and mutilated. This meant he was technically ineligible to rule, but it did not prevent his return as emperor ten years later, though he did so in such a savage temper that he was eventually murdered. The violent ends of many of the rulers mirrored in a sense the violent beginnings of the dynasty.

D.   *Isaurian Dynasty*, AD 717–802.

```
           LEO III (717-741)
                 |
         CONSTANTINE V (741-775)
                 |
             LEO IV = IRENE
         (775-780) | (780-802) D
                 |
         CONSTANTINE VI (780-797)
```

Statistics

Duration: 85 years; 4 generations, average length, 85/4 = 21 years; 5 rulers, average length of reign, 85/5 = 17 years.

Commentary

Leo III had much military experience as a result of commanding against the Muslims on the Syrian border; he became emperor by popular acclaim when it had become clear that a great Muslim invasion was imminent. He commanded in the successful defence of Constantinople in 717–718, and his family thereby secured a strong grip on the throne. Leo IV died suddenly, and his widow Irene became regent for their son, but when Constantine VI was of age to take up the rulership for himself, she arranged his murder, then, to considerable surprise, ruled alone for nearly six years. She became involved in negotiations with Charlemagne, whose coronation as a new Roman emperor in Rome in 800 was portrayed as an insult to Constantinople, and was only possible because there was no emperor in the city. Irene was arrested and deposed by a well-executed *coup d'état*.

References

JB Bury, *The Later Roman Empire* (London, 1923).

P Grierson, 'The Tombs and Obits of the Byzantine Emperors (337–1042)', *Dumbarton Oaks Papers*, 16 (1962) pp. 1–63.

J Herrin, *Women in Purple* (London, 2000).

AHM Jones, *The Later Roman Empire, 284–602*, 2 vols. (Oxford, 1964).

JM Hussey et al., *The Cambridge Mediaeval History, Vol. IV. The Byzantine Empire* (Cambridge, 1996–1967).

The First Muslim Caliphs, AD 622–661

```
     (                                    ABU BAKR      OMAR M
1    (                                    (632-634)  (634-644
     (                                        |           |
     (    Khadija (1)  =  MUHAMMAD   =  (2) Aisha  (3)  Hafsah
                       | (622-632)
                       |
                       |_____
                       |                 |                      |
2         ALI = Fatima        Ruqaypah = UTHMAN = Umm Kulthum
          (656-661)                      (644-656)
```

Statistics
Duration: 39 years; two generations, average length 39/2 = 20 years; 5 rulers, average length of reign 39/5 = 8 years.

Commentary
To describe this group of caliphs as a dynasty is stretching the meaning of the term to breaking point. None of the four men who served as caliphs had any blood relationship to any of the others, or to Muhammad, and the only connections between them were by marriage. But it is included partly because of the obvious historical importance of this group of men, and partly to suggest the confused beginning of the Islamic polity; a confusion that has largely continued ever since. Muhammad has been included as one of the rulers and the origin of his reign arbitrarily placed at 622, the year of the *Hegira*.

References
B Rogerson, *The Heirs of the Prophet Muhammad and the Roots of the Sunni-Shia Schism* (London, 2006).

Umayyads, AD 661–750

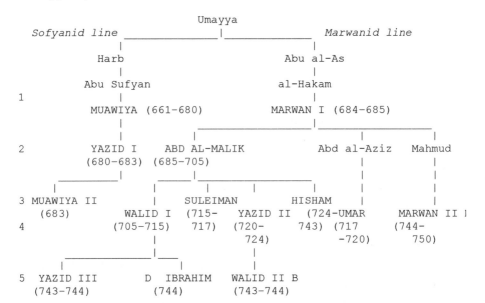

```
                                Umayya
        Sofyanid line _____|_____ Marwanid line
                |                                    |
              Harb                              Abu al-As
                |                                    |
          Abu Sufyan                            al-Hakam
1               |                                    |
          MUAWIYA (661-680)                     MARWAN I (684-685)
                |                     _____|_____
                |           |                           |              |
2             YAZID I    ABD AL-MALIK              Abd al-Aziz      Mahmud
            (680-683)   (685-705)                      |              |
        _____|        _____|_____      |              |
        |                  |       |          |        |              |
3 MUAWIYA II               |    SULEIMAN    HISHAM      |              |
    (683)            WALID I  (715-   YAZID II  (724-UMAR      MARWAN II ]
4                  (705-715)   717)   (720-    743) (717       (744-
                       |              724)            -720)      750)
             _____|___
        |                  |        |            |
5   YAZID III          D  IBRAHIM  WALID II B
    (743-744)             (744)    (743-744)
```

Statistics
Duration: 89 years; 5 generations, average length, $89/5 = 18$ years; 14 rulers, average length of reign, $89/14 = 6$ years.

Commentary
The first Umayyad caliph, Muawiya, had been governor of Syria for twenty years before he seized the caliphal throne. His immediate successors failed within four years of his death, but the family continued to rule, as the Umayyad dynasty, by the succession of Marwan I, a cousin of Muawiya's generation, even though he only ruled for a year. The real second founder was Abd al-Malik (the fifth caliph in five years), who ruled for twenty years, but his sons and grandsons then squandered their inheritance. The sudden rash of murders and depositions in the 740s heralded the end, which came with the Abbasid rebellion led by disenchanted Khorasanis, who spoke for all the enemies whom the Umayyads had alienated during their rule. The multiplicity of rulers and the brevity of their tenure was clearly the main cause of the dynasty's failure, but the sibling and cousin inheritance system was another clear source of weakness by producing so many brief reigns.

References
GR Hawting, *The First Dynasty of Islam*, 2nd ed. (London, 2000).
PK Hitti, *History of the Arabs* (London, 1961).

Index

Individual members of dynasties are not indexed unless they appear in the studies; all dynasties are listed.

Papirii, 30, 273–4
Parthia, 8–11, 16–23, 29, 50, 56, 66, 82,
    102, 110, 129, 143, 481–3
    see also Arsakid dynasty
Parysades III, Crimean king, 100
Parysades IV, Crimean king, 100
Patin, Syria, 171
Patrick, Saint, 33
Pausanias, traveller, 39, 68
Peisistratos, tyrant of Athens, 27–8, 85
Pelayo, Spanish ruler, 134
Perdikkas I, Macedonian king, 70
Pergamon, Asia Minor, 83
Perperna, 276
Persian Empire, 10, 25, 55
    see also Akhaimenid Empire
Persis, Iran, 23, 31, 434
Pharnabazid dynasty, Iberia, 378
Pharnakes, King of Pontos, 18, 58, 100
Pheretime, Battiad Queen, 99
Philip II, King of Macedon, 46
Philip II, King of Spain, 34
Phokas, Emperor, 25–6
Phraortes, Median king, 24
Picts, 33, 61, 134, 435–6
Piankhy, Pharaoh, 119
Plautii, 277–8
Plotina, 99
Poetilii, 279
Pompeii, 78, 280
Pompeius Magnus Cn., 30
Pomponii, 281
Pontos, 9, 18, 22, 24, 50, 56, 60, 63, 72, 74,
    95, 113, 437
Popilii, 145, 282
Porcii, 283
Postumii, 30, 284–5
Potidaia, Greece, 86
Prytanis, Crimean Queen, 100
Ptolemaic dynasty, Egypt, 25, 46, 48, 50,
    77, 80–2, 96–9, 102, 112–13, 135, 438–9
Ptolemy I, king of Egypt, 22, 84, 96, 128
Ptolemy II, king of Egypt, 46, 84–5, 96–7
Ptolemy III, king of Egypt, 97
Ptolemy IV, king of Egypt, 97
Ptolemy V, king of Egypt, 65, 77, 97, 122
Ptolemy VI, king of Egypt, 97–8, 102, 122
Ptolemy VIII, king of Egypt, 98–9, 122

Ptolemy IX, king of Egypt, 122
Ptolemy X, king of Egypt, 122
Ptolemy Keraunos, 84–5, 96
Publilii, 286
Pybba, Mercian dynastic ancestor, 13, 15,
    45
Pyrrhos, King of Epeiros, 31, 47
Pythodoris, Galatian Queen, 101

Qataban, Arabia, 440–1
Quinctii, 287

Republics, 4
    Republican dynasties, 4
Red Sea, 42
Regni, Britannia, 126
Rehoboam, king of Judah, 43
Rezon, king of Damascus, 27
Rezonid dynasty, Damascus, 160
Rheged, England, 442
Rhoemetalces I, Thracian king, 106
Rochester, Kent, 15
Roman Empire, 5, 7, 11, 16, 18, 20–2, 28,
    50, 55, 74–5, 91–4, 108, 121, 131, 136,
    142–6, 484–93
Roman kings, 10–11, 41, 44, 89–90, 108,
    172–3
Rome, 4, 65, 105, 130–1, 141–6
    republican dynasties, 8–10, 22, 30, 53,
    59, 61–2, 77–8, 89–91, 93, 115–16,
    134, 141–2
Romulus, Roman ancestor, 108
Romulus Augustulus, Emperor, 113
Rugians, Noricum, 21, 61, 105, 131, 443
Rusid dynasty, Urartu, 466
Russia, 3, 143, 147
Rutilii, 289

Saba, Arabia, 444–6
Sais, Egypt, 32
Saite dynasty, Egypt, 362
Salamis, Cyprus, 27
Salome Alexandra, 11, 99
Samal, Syria, 17, 43, 128, 131, 177
Samara Albania, 40
Samaria, Palestine, 24
Samos, Greece, 63, 83, 178
Samsigeramos, Emesan king, 35